1. *An irreverent view of the Burmese army.* (London Graphic, *October 4, 1879, pp. 336-337*).

KING THEBAW
AND
THE ECOLOGICAL RAPE
OF BURMA

The Political and Commercial Struggle Between British
India and French Indo-China in Burma
1878-1886

by
CHARLES LEE KEETON 3rd

Foreword by
JOHN F. CADY

MANOHAR BOOK SERVICE
1974

First edition

Published by
Ramesh C. Jain for
Manohar Book Service
2, Darya Ganj, Ansari Road,
Panna Bhawan,
Delhi-110006

Printed by
Prem Printing Press,
257-Golaganj,
Lucknow-1

FOREWORD

This monograph contributes substantially to the understanding of one of the most controversial periods of Anglo-Indian relations with Burma, the reign of King Thebaw from 1878 to 1885. It is part of a larger research effort going back to 1852, but was submitted in this form as a doctoral dissertation at the University of Delhi.

The author has explored an enormous mass of primary sources currently available in the India Office Library, the British Museum and the Record Office of London, plus the Indian National Archives at Delhi. He has also covered a wealth of published material relevant to the period. Like others who have attempted to gain research access to the private records of the Bombay Burmah Trading Corporation prior to 1885, he was denied such privilege. But the breadth and depth of his study provides a basis for a fairly definitive assessment of the merits of the controversial fine levied on the BBTC by the Burma Government in 1885.

More importantly, the study places the problem of Burma-British relations in the context of the morass of intrigue which characterized the Mandalay Court throughout Thebaw's rule. It also demonstrates the wide divergence of opinion which prevailed within British-India governmental circles during the same period. The author's very extensive bibliography includes published Parliamentary Papers and Burma Gazetteers, plus the private papers of Dufferin, Lytton, Northbrook, and Ripon found mainly in the India Office Library. Also examined are numerous volumes of Burma and India Proceedings, both Political and Secret, plus Record Office documents relating to French relations, Admiralty Records, and General Prendergast's Field Operations reports from 1885-1886, the latter two drawn from the British Museum.

Under the well-intentioned but weak King Thebaw, the Mandalay Court was torn by factional rivalry. The domineering Queen Supayalat was desperately determined to exercise control, especially following the death of her infant son from smallpox in 1879. Her other children were all girls. The most nefarious Court faction was led by the disreputable Yanaung, who gained favour with

Thebaw by providing him with an alternative candidate for Chief Queenship, and who controlled lucrative trade monopolies. He was eventually clubbed to death by Supayalat's agents.

At the near opposite pole from Yanaung was the reform-minded Kinwun Mingyi (Prince), who was not above customary bribe-taking, but was generally straight forward and concerned to maintain good relations with the Indian Government. In between was the unprincipled but politically astute Taingda Mingyi, who developed a semi-bandit following and demonstrated an amazing capacity for intrigue. Rival Court factions would doubtless have been far more numerous if four-score princely relatives had not been eliminated in the royal massacre of February 1879. Reflecting the near anarchy at court, insurrections gradually spread from Shan and Kachin country to the vicinity of the capital. Thus the Mandalay Court itself constituted a major liability for the survival of Burma as an independent state.

Probably the only hope for Burma's survival was to strengthen the influence of the Kinwun Mingyi. Unfortunately, his rule was prejudiced by the abrupt withdrawal of the British Resident from Mandalay in the fall of 1879, a step taken by reason of Calcutta's confused concern at the time that the massacre of the British mission in Kabul, Afghanistan, might be repeated at Mandalay. The Kinwun's subsequent treaty negotiation efforts of 1879-1882 were hampered by official British intransigence at Rangoon, but were finally sabotaged by unresolved Court rivalries raging in Mandalay. The absence of the British Resident from Mandalay after 1879 left the field open to the machinations of a coterie of disreputable Europeans resident at the capital. They numbered nearly a hundred, including double-agent spies, elite prostitutes, and other agents profiting from intrigue. The French consul, Frederic Haas, looked highly respectable in such company.

Friction between Burman and Indian authorities was cumulative after 1880. British insistence on wearing shoes in the royal presence, and on the size of the Residency guard based on considerations of face, were countered after 1882 by persistent efforts on the part of the Mandalay government to develop diplomatic relations in Western Europe and to obtain arms denied them by the British. The principal grievance of the Burma Court against the British authorities was the latter's insistence that Mandalay deal externally only via the Government of India. The moderating influence of Gladstone's liberal Government from 1880 to June of 1885 was reflected in curbing aggressive tendencies at Rangoon and Calcutta, but no Secretary of State for India advocated acknowledging full independent status for Burma.

British spokesmen differed sharply from time to time over the desirability of achieving unimpeded commercial contact with Yunnan, and on the basic problem of whether Thebaw should be replaced by a more satisfactory princely-puppet or the Burma kingdom be annexed out-right. Unfortunately, the supply of acceptable princely candidates ran out. It was the eventual spectre of a developing French threat on India's northeastern border similar to the Russian threat to the northwest frontier that apparently inspired the final decision to conquer Burma in late 1885. The move took place when Gladstone was temporarily out of power. The Conservative Secretary of State for India, Randolph Churchill, hoped that the timely capture of Mandalay would aid the Tory Party's prospects in the elections of November 1885.

Keeton's account reveals that the teak extraction program of the BBTC was extravagantly conducted. The Corporation was prepared to pay bribes when required, and to take advantage of all possible loopholes in the carelessly enforced lease agreements of 1880-1885. It managed to avoid paying duties on many of the logs obtained on the Burma side after 1880 by cutting much of the timber just short of the 18 feet minimum dutiable length. In 1885, BBTC agents had girdled (killed) an estimated half million trees in Upper Burma for prospective export. The timber glut became embarrassing in Rangoon when the teak prices in Europe fell by one-half in 1885. The Burmese ministers, on their part, negotiated two new BBTC lease-agreements in order to realize the substantial advance-payment of over five additional lakhs of rupees with even more in prospect for the future. They then proceeded to dicker with the French consul Haas for railway, bank, and teak concessions. The Taingda prompted phony private contractors to instigate suits against the Corporation for alleged frauds as a method of extracting further blackmail from the BBTC. There was abundant evidence of avarice on all sides.

When the final decision was made to serve an unacceptable ultimatum on Mandalay in late October 1885, the Bombay Burmah fine and the machinations of Haas provided welcome excuses, although at the time both questions appeared capable of peaceful settlement. The most reputable of the British actors in the situation were the Resident Shaw (who had died in June, 1879); Gladstone's Commissioner Bernard at Rangoon; General Prendergast, Commander of the invading forces in 1885; and Colonel Sladen, the long-time friend of the Kinwun. Several of them later suffered careerwise for their conciliatory approach. The British business community at Rangoon was, for the most part, perennially belligerent.

Valuable items presented in the author's appendices include the full texts of successive treaty agreements between Mandalay and the Indian Government from 1862, and between France and Burma from 1873 and 1885. They also contain a description of the administrative reform proposals made by the Kinwun Mingyi. Not every reader will come to the same conclusions regarding responsibilities for specific developments, but all serious students of South and Southeast Asian History and of the imperialist era generally will welcome a look at the evidence here provided. The author's industry, his clarity of presentation, and attempted objectivity deserve high commendation.

Ohio University.   John F. Cady

PREFACE

KING THEBAW AND THE ECOLOGICAL RAPE OF
BURMA is the first full study ever made of the reign of Burma's
King Thebaw (1878-1885), and in particular of his wife, Queen
Supayalat. The book describes the ecological and diplomatic
occurrences that convulsed the Burmese kingdom of Mandalay
during its last years of independence, and the events that led up
to the Third Burmese War in 1885 and the annexation of Upper
Burma to the Indian Empire in 1886.

The book has utilized all relevant primary and secondary
sources to be found at the National Archives of India, New Delhi;
the Commonwealth Office Library and Records, London ; the
Maritime Museum, Greenwich ; the National Library of India,
Calcutta; and elsewhere. The book also uses all the pertinent
newspapers, periodicals, and books of the period. Such accounts
were often more sympathetic in their views of the Burmese
Government than the later historical studies made by British
officials or scholars. The newspapers, periodicals, and books of
the period were also often more accurate than the present-day
accounts written from the Burmese nationalist point-of-view.

The book describes the relationship between ecological processes and the rise and fall of human societies; in this case the
effects of the race between French and British commercial interests
—and with the eager cooperation of the Mandalay officials—to
deforest Upper Burma. This process of Deforestation set-off a
number of other ecological disturbances in Upper Burma, culminating in the partially man-made 'drought' of 1883-1885. This in
turn disrupted much of Upper Burma's social and political life,
thus making the country an even more inviting area for further
French expansion westward from French Indo-China.

The British in India could not allow this extension as India's
eastern frontier would be directly under threat from the French ;
and the potential new British trade in Yunnan and Southern China
would be blocked by the intrusion of France into Upper Burma.
Ultimately, this threat resulted in the Third Burmese War in 1885,
and in the eventual annexation of Upper Burma in 1886.

This book is the first of two studies concerning Burma's attempts after the Second Burmese War, 1852-1853, to modernize itself on its own terms in the face of the Western 'threat' from without. The second study to follow is on the subject of King Mindon and modernization the Burmese way, 1852-1878. Also to follow is a somewhat similar study on the efforts of King Mongkut to modernize Siam from 1851-1868.

The author wishes to thank the many persons who have helped him with the book. In particular, he wishes to express his gratitude to Dr. Amba Prasad, professor and former head of the Department of History, Delhi University, for his tact and patience. Without Professor Prasad's gentle encouragement and many wise and helpful suggestions, the following study would surely never have been completed.

The author also wishes to thank Shri S. Ray, the former assistant director of the National Archives of India, for the many helpful suggestions regarding documents and other material on Burma. The author also wishes to thank the Hattie M. Strong Foundation, Washington D.C., U.S.A., whose generous loan enabled the author to study for more than four years in India, and to complete the research for this and other studies. Lastly, the author wishes to thank his friend, Shri Raghunath Singh Dhariwal, assistant cashier of Delhi University, who typed the manuscript.

CONTENTS

		Page
INTRODUCTION:	An Ecological Interpretation of Burmese History	.. 1

Chapter
1. The End of the Old Arrangements .. 17
2. The Burmese Reaction .. 62
3. Mandalay Refuses a New Treaty .. 87
4. Mandalay Gains Concessions from France .. 119
5. The Ecological Devolution of Upper Burma .. 143
6. The 'French Threat' to British Interests .. 163
7. The Deforestation of Upper Burma, 1862-1885: The BBTC Teak Case .. 199
8. The Ultimatum .. 233
9. The Removal of Thebaw .. 274
10. 'Dacoity' and Annexation: the Vicious Circle .. 297

CONCLUSION: Some Relationships Between Ecology and Empires .. 327

APPENDICES .. 338
BIBLIOGRAPHY .. 403
INDEX .. 419

ABBREVIATIONS

(BM)   British Museum.
(IOL)   India Office Library, India Office Records, CRO.
(IpRO) Ipswich and East Suffolk Record Office.
(NAI)   National Archives of India.
(NMM) National Maritime Museum.
(PRO)   Public Record Office.
(ULTC) Un. of London-Tottenham Court Library Annex.
(JBRS) *Journal of the Burma Research Society.*

"For some of our mountains at present will only (scarcely) support trees, but not so very long ago trees fit for the roofs of vast buildings were felled there and the rafters are still in existence. There were also many other lofty cultivated trees which provided unlimited fodder for beasts. Besides, the soil got the benefit of the yearly 'water from Zeus,' which was not lost, as it is today, by running off a barren ground to the sea."

> Plato (427-347 B. C.) on the deforestation of ancient Greece.

"To these things [Man and his domesticated animals] is owing the bare and stripped appearance of the mountain, and when people now see it they think it was never finely wooded. But is this the nature of the mountain?"

> Mencius (372-289 B. C.) on the deforestation of northern China. The resulting erosion provided the silt which gave the 'Yellow' River and the 'Yellow' Sea their names.

"The overcrowded island of Java is in danger of becoming a desert if a current forestation plan fails, according to Indonesian public works minister, Dr. Sutami......According to agriculture officials, 23 per cent of Java was covered by forest in 1962, but this has now dropped to less than 15 per cent."

> "Java May Become a Desert,"
> (San Francisco) *Chronicle*,
> March 23, 1972, p. 9.

"That Man is......a member of a biotic team is shown by an ecological interpretation of history. Many historical events, hitherto explained solely in terms of human enterprise, were actually biotic interactions between people and land."

> Aldo Leopold, "The Land Ethic," in Paul Shepard and Daniel McKinley, eds., *The Subversive Science*, Boston, 1969, p. 403.

Introduction
An Ecological Interpretation of Burmese History

The Burman Drive Towards the Surpluses of the Delta

The Pyus, and the Burmans who ultimately absorbed the Pyus, began to move down into Burma from southern China about 2,000 years ago. The Burmans settled in Burma's Dry Zone, which lay north of a string of Mon port-states in the Delta.[1] The Mons had built the original irrigation-systems in the 'parched lands' (as the Mons called them) at Kyaukse near Mandalay. The Burmans seized these facilities from the Mons during the ninth century A. D.[2] The Burmans improved the irrigation-systems, changed the name of the area to the 'Ledwin' (the rice country), and raised irrigated rice, jowar, sesamum, millet, maize, peas, sugar-cane, cotton, and other crops.[3]

It appears that the Dry Zone had more forests in about 900 A.D. than at the present time. It also appears that an enormous amount of timber was burned to make "countless millions" of fired-bricks that composed the thousands of pagodas and other edifices at Pagan and elsewhere.[4] A process of partial Deforestation appears to have occurred whereby many areas were partially denuded of trees and other ground-cover. The rain-water—formerly *stored* by trees and other ground-cover in a 'sponge effect'—was allowed to rush-off into the streams or to evaporate.[5]

The loss of such moisture had a disastrous effect upon the Dry Zone, a marginal, semi-desert area of only twenty to forty inches of annual rainfall. The slightest cyclical-dip of only an inch or two in the annual rainfall could easily cause a local drought crop-failures, and even hunger. As a consequence, the '*dominant*', recurring-'pattern' in Burmese history has been the desire of the Dry Zone Burmans—with few surpluses—to move towards the Mons and the surpluses of the Delta.[6]

The Delta including Arakan and Tenasserim received 100-200 inches of annual rainfall. The Mons of the Delta were able to generate enough surpluses in rice, teak, cotton, aloes, velvetstuffs, ivory, rhinocerous horn, gold, silver, precious stones and yak-hair for fly-flaps, that they could be exported in quantity.[7]

The surpluses attracted Persian and Arab ships by the ninth century. It also attracted textile-traders from Gujerat, Malabar, Tamilnad, Orissa, and Bengal. They called at Mon ports such as Thaton and Pegu, the latter having been founded as Ussa (Orissa) in 825 A. D.[8] The Bengalis, in particular, did a good business in Buddhist images, although Buddhism had virtually died out in Bengal and in India.[9]

Mon teak-ships were sea-worthy for a century and more, and found a ready sale in Island S. E. Asia—especially among the Javanese—perhaps as early as the first or second century B. C. Java had been short of wood from very early times, and the Javanese needed Mon ships to take Moluccan spices to Malayan and Sumatran ports. From there the spices were taken by Indian and Arab ships to ports in western India. From there the Arabs, Persians, and others took the spices to Egypt and other points near the Red Sea and the Persian Gulf where Europeans and other traders bought them for resale all over Europe and the 'middle East'.[10]

The Mons developed an annual trade-pattern over the centuries. In about 1500 A. D., sixteen to twenty cargo-ships a year left the Delta ports in February or March bound for Malacca in Malaya, and for Pedir and Pasai in Sumatra. The ships carried rice, vegetables, sugar, lac, and Martaban's famous black jars, which were prized by sailors as rice and water containers. The Mons also brought rubies, benzoin, and musk from the Dry Zone, for which they had traded the Burmans commodities, such as rice, salt, *ngape* (dried fish), and fish oil.[11]

The Mon ships returned to the Delta during the following monsoon carrying Sumatran pepper; Chinese silks and porcelain; Malayan tin, gold, and iron; copper; Borneo camphor; and Javan-Moluccan spices. The Mons received cloth directly from Gujerat, and also from Nagore and Pulicat on the Bengal-Orissa coast.[12] During this time, the Mon King's chief government revenues came from exports of lac, sandal-wood, brazil-wood, cotton, silk, and Dry Zone rubies.[13]

The Struggle For the Surpluses of the Delta, 1000-1600

The surpluses of the Delta were a rich temptation for a would-be Burman imperialist. The Burmans and the Mons were first united during the reign of King Anawrahta (1044-1077). The Indianized Mons at first provided the trading facilities, the religious rites and nomenclature, the arts and architectural forms, and kept the state records and official inscriptions. The Burmans always provided the political and military power, and during the following two centuries the Pagan Empire ruled over much of what is today modern Burma.[14]

The Pagan Empire collapsed in 1287 during the Mongol invasions. They had been caused by the execution in 1272 of a mission from Kublai Khan, which had allegedly refused to take-off their shoes when in the presence of the Burmese King.[15] This "Shoe Question" was still an issue 600 years later, and was as important a reason as any for the British invasion and annexation of Burma in 1885-1886.

For the next 250 years (to 1554) the Burmans of the Dry Zone were often ruled by Shan (Tai) invaders with their capital at or near Ava.[16] Tabinshwetti (1531-1550) of a local Burman dynasty at Toungoo reconquered the Delta and the Mons by 1546, and was crowned at Pegu with both Burman and Mon rites.[17] After Tabinshwetti was assassinated in 1550, Bayinnaung (1551-1581), his brother-in-law, completed the destruction of the Shan power in the Dry Zone. He conquered the Shan States, and constantly invaded Manipur, Chiengmai, Laos, and Ayuthia (Siam). He used the profits from the Delta's export-import trade, and the population and food surpluses, to fight his many wars.[18]

By Bayinnaung's death in 1581, he had exhausted the food and population surpluses of the Delta.[19] At some date immediately after 1569, the usual Mon exports of rice and other food-stuffs to Malacca and Sumatra were largely cut-off, because of the almost annual ravaging of the Delta by rival armies, Siamese and Burmese.[20] Finally in 1599-1600, the armies of Arakan, Ayuthia, and Toungoo destroyed Pegu. The Delta was now a 'depopulated desert' around Pegu, Bassein, Syriam, and Martaban.[21]

By comparison, the Dry Zone now had more rice and population surpluses than did the Delta. The Burman Kings usually forbade the exports of rice and other foodstuffs after 1600, and the Delta soon became a commercial backwater.[22] In 1634, King Thalun (1629-1648) abandoned Pegu, which was no longer a sea-port as its harbour was silted up, and moved his capital back to Ava.

He was crowned with solely Burman rites, and the idea of a national Kingship of both Dry Zone and Delta peoples was largely forgotten.[23]

The Burmans Hoard the Surpluses of the Delta, 1600-1852

During the 1600's, several efforts were made by the Portugese, the Dutch and the English East India Companies, and the French *Compaigne Royale des Indes Orientales* to establish trading-'factories' at Syriam and elsewhere in the Delta. However, the Burman Kings usually monopolized the export trade in precious stones and metals, benzoin, lac, teak, Martaban jars, and other goods. Ganza and saltpetre were usually not allowed to be exported.[24] In short, the Burman Kings, after fighting from 1287 to 1546 to recapture the surpluses of the Delta, were not about to allow these surpluses to leave the country—except at an exorbitant profit to themselves.

Eventually, the English Company at Madras found it more profitable to license petty 'country' traders on the Madras-Syriam trade route to obtain those Burma goods needed by the Company. The Company bought what it needed from these 'country' traders, and saved the cost of an unprofitable permanent 'factory' in Burma.[25]

After about 1680, both the French and English Companies needed a Burmese harbour in order to build and to repair ships. In the early 1700's both Companies established repair yards at Syriam.[26] However, the English Company found that teak ships could be made more cheaply and with better workmanship at Indian ports.[27] Both the French and English shipyards were closed down by 1743 during the 1740-1758 Mon Revolt, which temporarily in 1752 enabled the Mon King, Binnya Dala, to conquer most of the Dry Zone.

The Mons were finally crushed by King Alaungpaya (1752-1760).[28] In the meantime, the French and the English Companies in India had been fighting since 1740 for control over much of India. The naval advantages of Syriam again became obvious. Both Companies sent cannons and muskets to both sides in order to curry favour with the eventual winner. Alaungpaya returned the 'impartiality' by burning the French representative to death over a fire, and massacring the English settlement on Negrais Island on

October 6, 1759. Alaungpaya did, however, realize the value of foreign trade, and built a new harbour at Rangoon.[29]

French commercial and political power was virtually ousted from India under the 1763 Treaty ending the Seven Years War. The Company had little to fear from French 'meddling' in Burma, and so allowed diplomatic relations with Burma to lapse for over thirty years.[30] When the Company renewed relations with the Burmese King in the 1790's, it was primarily in response to the renewed threat that the French would use Rangoon as a naval base.[31] Relations between the English and the Burmese now developed along basically political lines[32] and culminated in three wars during the ninteenth century. These were the First Burmese War (1824-1826), the Second Burmese War (1852-1853), and the Third Burmese War (1885).

The First Burmese War was fought basically because the Burmese had received the unfortunate impression that the Company was weak, because it had not been able to control the Arakanese refugees in Bengal.[33] These refugees raided constantly into Arakan, which had been conquered in 1784 by the Burmese King Bodawpaya (1782-1819). The Burmese did not realize that the British were fully occupied in Europe with Napoleon until 1815; in North America against the United States in the 1812-1815 War; and, in India with the Marathas, Pindaris, and Gurkhas until 1818. In 1819, the Burmese conquered most of Assam, and made a series of aggressive raids into Bengal, which the British could now afford to resent. They declared war in 1824, and defeated the Burmese within two years.[34]

By the terms of the 1826 Yandabo Treaty, the Burmese had to pay a Rs. 10,000,000 indemnity (£1,000,000).[35] The British took possession of Assam, Manipur and Arakan to protect Bengal, and Tenasserim to support Penang and Singapore. Tenasserim did not pay its administrative costs for two generations. In 1833, Gov. Gen. William Bentinck thought of giving Tenasserim back to Burma. But he gave up the idea when reminded of the mass-genocide that Burmese troops had inflicted upon the Mons, Karens and other rebels, including the 'pro-British' Governors of Prome, Henzada, and Podaung after the British had evacuated the Delta in 1826.[36] In 1840, the Indian Government withdrew its envoy (Resident) from Burma after several attempts by both countries to establish more cordial relations.[37]

The British developed the rice-production of Arakan, until it soon exceeded that of Arakan's golden years in the 1600's. Akyab was for a time around 1852 the rice-exporting capital of the world—until superseded by the phenomenal increase of rice-exports from Rangoon following the Second Burmese War. Moulmein port in Tenasserim was developed as a teak exporting outlet for the Karenni forests, and as a rice-exporting and ship-building centre.[38]

The Delta, however, retained the function that it had had since about 1546, *i.e.* to produce men, rice, *ngape* (dried-fish), fish oil, salt, and other basics.[39] These were taken for the Burman King's service, and to supplement the Dry Zone's periodic food shortages.[40] It was only after the British conquest of the Delta in the 1852-1853 Second Burmese War that the Delta once more became the area of great surpluses that it had been prior to 1569-1600.[41] The right to export these surpluses for profit was the key reason why enormous surpluses were quickly created by the Delta's rice farmers.[42] The regular deliveries possible with the sail-boat, steam-boat, and railroad made the Delta and Arakan the rice-exporting area of the world.[43]

However, it was not rice or commercial advantage that prompted the Indian Government to fight the Second Burmese War (1852-1853). In July 1851, the Rangoon Governor fined two British ships Rs. 1,000 for alleged violation of the port regulations. Gov. Gen. Dalhousie rejected the exaggerated claims of 'injury' on the part of the ship captains, but decided that an issue would have to be made of the fines. The political prestige of the Indian Government was at stake, because it appeared as though it could not protect its subjects from unfair oppression. Dalhousie sent Commodore Lambert to Rangoon aboard H. M. S. *Fox* along with two Company ships to demand that the Governor be sacked, and that the fines be redressed.[44]

The Governor was sacked, but his replacement allegedly told Lambert's representatives that there would be no adjustment or even discussion of the fines. Lambert in turn blockaded the Rangoon harbour, and seized a ship belonging to King Pagan. On January 10, 1852, the Burmese shore batteries fired a few return shots to save 'face', but were silenced by a broadside from the *Fox*. After destroying every Burmese warboat in the harbour, "the combustible Commodore" (as Dalhousie called him) sailed back to Calcutta.[45]

Both sides soon declared war, and the Indian Government speedily annexed the Delta (Pegu), including the rich Toungoo teak-forest up to 19½ degree latitude. However, the richest teak-areas from 19½ to 20¼ degree latitude in the Ningyan Forest still remained in Burmese hands.[46] In 1885, the Ningyan Forest would be the scene of the famous BBTC Teak Case, which was the "convenient pretext" for a Third Burmese War. Finally, on February 18, 1853, Crown Prince Mindon of the peace party overthrew his brother, King Pagan, and the war ended.[47]

Mindon Introduces Industry—and Fosters Trade with Lower Burma—in an Attempt to Overcome Dry Zone Shortages

As the Burman state centered upon the Dry Zone could no longer draw upon the Delta as a colony to make-up the Dry Zone's periodic shortages, King Mindon (b. 1816) tried to generate sur-pluses within the Dry Zone itself. He endeavoured to do this in two ways, (1) by establishing industrial factories at Mandalay, and (2) by encouraging trade with southern China, the Shan States, Lower Burma, India, and with European countries such as Britain, France and Italy.[48]

As a consequence, Mindon signed two commercial treaties with the Indian Government in 1862 and in 1867. They established a British Political Agent at Mandalay after 1862; and abolished all Burmese monopolies after 1867, except in precious stones, timber, and earth oil.[49] Mindon, however, never totally abolished his Royal monopolies.[50] This remained a sore point with Burmese, Chinese, European, and Indian merchants at Rangoon, although they reluctantly admired Mindon's abilities as a broker.

Mindon's people could usually raise and export almost any-thing they liked. However, if Mindon wished to export a crop, such as gram or teel-seed, he usually bought it at the Upper Burma free-market price. He then resold it at a higher price to Lower Burma merchants. Mindon's export-monopolies often included palm and cane sugar, cotton, wheat, sesamum, pickled-tea; and his three legal monopolies of earth-oil, precious stones, teak, cutch, and other timber.[51]

Mindon was also frequently the largest importer of piece-goods and rice into Upper Burma. He often sent agents to Rangoon to buy cotton and silk piece-goods in bulk from the large

European export-import houses. If they did not give sufficient credit and low prices, Mindon's agents often ordered directly from Calcutta. In order to overcome the shortages of food in Upper Burma, Mindon bought an average of 68,000 tons of rice annually from the Delta cultivators.[52]

Mindon frequently used his profits to set up foundries and factories at Mandalay, Sagaing and elsewhere. They processed lac, indigo, cutch, sugar, sulphur, salt, lead, iron, and other raw-materials ; and manufactured such items as glassware, crockery, and piece-goods.[53] He developed a fleet of twelve river-steamers, ten steam-launches, and five gun-boats to carry Burmese exports and imports and to keep order on the Irrawaddy.[54] He built a telegraph-line from the Lower Burma frontier to Bhamo via Mandalay; a line from Mandalay to Mong Nai in the Shan States via the Natteik Pass; and, a line from Minhla to Taungdwingyi. He did everything possible to revive the Bhamo to Yunnan caravan-trade in cotton, salt and other goods, which had been largely disrupted by the Panthay War in Yunnan from 1855-1873.[55]

By making a profit in his commercial dealings, Mindon was able to reduce his people's taxes, and to make Upper Burma less economically and politically dependent upon the British. However, several of his factories, especially the firearms factory, remained expensive showpieces because of the prohibitive cost of machinery, which had to be imported from Europe.[56]

After 1868, the Lower Burma customs at Rangoon would usually not allow gun-making machinery or firearms to pass through into Upper Burma. The passage of such items had been guaranteed in the 'Fytche Annexe' portion of the 1867 treaty ; but was later ignored, much as Mindon had ignored the ban on Royal monopolies.[57]

In 1871, Mindon signed a commercial treaty with Italy, and Giovanni Andreino, an Italian merchant at Mandalay, became the Italian Consul. However, a treaty with France negotiated in Paris in 1873 by the Kinwun Mingyi, the Burmese foreign minister, was not ratified. The French Government had become apprehensive of British protests concerning Mindon's demands for firearms and an Offensive-Defensive Alliance. When the French refused to include these two items in the commercial treaty, Mindon then rejected the entire treaty.[58]

Meanwhile, the province of Pegu (*i.e.* the Delta) had paid its administrative costs soon after annexation in 1852.[59]   However, it was not until after the opening of the Suez Canal in 1869 that a majority of the European export-import houses were opened in Rangoon to sell British textiles and other imports to Upper Burma.[60]   These goods and passengers were transported to Upper Burma after 1867 aboard the steamers of the Irrawaddy Flotilla Co. (IFC).   Mindon had allowed the steamer-firm into the country under the terms of the 1867 Treaty.[61]

By doing so, he had gained a second steamer service for all of Upper Burma, including Bhamo the entrepot of the Burma-Yunnan caravan-trains about 800 miles north of Rangoon.[62]   He had also gained a new source of employment and foreign exchange, because over 100,000 Upper Burmese males now rode the IFC steamers to Lower Burma to work the yearly rice harvest.   Mindon kept their families behind, which was a guarantee that the men would return with their earnings to be spent in Upper Burma.[63]

The harvesters' families also had more money than before with which to buy the popular British imports, such as silk and cotton piece-goods, glass lamps, safety matches, crockery, and tinned foods.[64]   As Prof. Furnivall noted : "It would seem that, as formerly after the occupation of the maritime provinces [of Arakan and Tenasserim], the extension of British dominion over Pegu was profitable to Burmans still living under native rule."[65] One should add that it was also profitable for Rangoon's importers and exporters, both non-European and European.

Unfortunately, Mindon's relations with the Indian Government deteriorated towards the end of his reign.   Sir Douglas Forsyth, envoy to Mandalay in 1875, had begged Gov. Gen. Lord Northbrook to state the Indian Government's view on the 'Shoe Question'.   Northbrook avoided answering.

At Mandalay, Forsyth threatened to break-off the Karenni negotiations if Mindon did not agree to receive him wearing his shoes.   However, Mindon smiled, reached in his royal sleeve, and pulled out a telegram addressed to Forsyth *in English!* Someone at the Indian Foreign Office had forgotten to use the secret cipher. Mindon chuckled : "Yes—we know all about that.   You have been told not to press that question too far.   So we tell you that we won't even discuss it."   Northbrook then further bungled the affair by yielding to public outcry in India, and ruled that future Residents would not doff their shoes before the King.[66]

King Mindon, who had been extremely fair to the Indian Government during his reign, was forced to refuse the Indian Government's demand. His royal 'face' or official dignity was at stake. During the last three years of his reign, Mindon had no direct contact with the Resident, Colonel Duncan, a great admirer of Mindon's policies ; or with Duncan's successor, Robert Shaw, the noted Turki scholar and diplomat.[67]

After personal contact between Mindon and the Resident had ceased, the French and Italians in Mindon's service never missed an opportunity to poison his mind against the English. During Thebaw's reign (1878-1885), the foreign females (*kalamas*) at Mandalay, including the French Catholic nuns, were organized into an advisory body to Queen Supayalat. One of these *kalamas*, Mattie Calogreedy Antram, a British subject of Burmese-Greek descent, was influential in the events leading to the loss of Mandalay's independence.

The advice gained from the French, Italian, and *kalama* groups, and from the Armenian, Burmese, Chinese, European and Mogul-Surati merchants at Mandalay, was influential in the Burmese Government's decision to reject the 1882 commercial treaty, and the October 22, 1885 British ultimatum. These two decisions were important contributing factors in the loss of Burmese independence. In short, the 'information' gained from the above foreigners was a poor substitute for the information about British motives that would have come from a British Resident able to talk personally with the Burmese King.[68]

The Strategic-Political Model to be Tested in This Study

In summary, the Dry Zone portion of central Burma had always been a marginal area of between twenty to forty inches of annual rainfall. The early Burmans had partially deforested the Dry Zone and had turned it into a desert around Pagan and in many other areas. Therefore, the Burmans had to make-up their shortages of food and other surpluses by controlling the peoples and surpluses of the rainy Delta of coastal Burma.

This *key* 'pattern' of Burmese history, namely that the scarcity-ridden Burmans of the Dry Zone tended to move towards the surplus-rich peoples of the Delta, was interrupted in 1852-1853 when the British annexed Lower Burma.[69] King Mindon (1852-1878)

attempted to overcome the loss of the Delta colony and its surpluses in two ways, (1) by establishing industrial factories and
(2) by encouraging trade with the surrounding countries and with
European countries such as Britain, France and Italy.

In summarizing the relationship between the Burmese and the
British, one would have to state that the dominant recurring
'pattern' in their relations from about 1600 to 1878 was a *strategic-
political* 'pattern'. This 'pattern' arose from the British desire to
prevent or to minimize the growth of any political or commercial
'threat', especially from the Dutch and French, on India's east.
By keeping the eastern-flank essentially free of any major power,
the British were able to concentrate their major energies on the
more important and continuous 'threat' from the west in India
itself.

It was almost always the western flank that was most 'threat-
ened' by Indian rulers and the rival European trading-concerns.
This predominant 'threat' from the west existed before the English
East India Company became a political power in India in 1757,
and it still existed in 1878 with the 'Russian Threat' to British
India's northwest.

Therefore, it is understandable why the British strove to prevent or minimize the growth of any political or commercial 'threat'
on India's eastern flank in Burma. The degree of 'threat' on the
east was the basic determinant of the Company's political and
commercial advances and withdrawals in Burma before 1824.
There was relatively little commercial profit to be made by British
subjects in Burma, because the Burman Kings usually monopolized
the surpluses of the Delta. Therefore, Burma remained a peri-
pheral area of minor interest as long as another power did not
arise in Burma that would 'threaten' British interests in India.

The two Burmese Wars of 1824-1826 and 1852-1853 were
fought when the British were temporarily not involved in a greater
'threat' on India's western flank and elsewhere in the world. Once
the wars were over the British essentially withdrew their interest
from Burma in order to concentrate once again on the more important 'threat' from the west. In 1878—as was the case earlier in
the 1830's—the 'threat' from the west took the form of the 'Russian
Threat' poised to move down through Afghanistan into India's
northwest.[70]

To summarize, the dominant recurring-'pattern' in British-

Burmese relations from about 1600 to 1878 was the strategic-political 'pattern' described immediately above.   A secondary recurring-'pattern', which complemented the strategic-political 'pattern', was the British desire for commercial profit in Burma. However, there was relatively little profit until the Indian Government annexed portions of Burma following the First and Second Burmese Wars.

In conclusion, this study will indicate some of the relationships between tropical ecology and empires; in this case the effects of the commercial race to deforest Upper Burma after 1862.[71] This process of 'modern' Deforestation set-off a number of ecological disturbances, culminating in the partially man-made 'drought' of 1883-1885.

This in turn disrupted much of Upper Burma's social and political life, and caused a decline in the volume of trade between Upper and Lower Burma.   The depression prompted a number of mercantile and other groups to demand the annexation of Upper Burma.   This study will investigate whether British economic-interests were *more important* than British strategic-political interests (which included the 'Russian Threat' to India's northwest frontier and its eastern counter-part the 'French Threat') in determining British India's relations with Mandalay from 1878 to the annexation of Upper Burma in 1886.

FOOTNOTES

[1] G. Coedes, (trans.   Susan Brown Cowing), *The Indianized States of Southeast Asia,* Honolulu, 1968, pp. 62-63, 76-77, 86-87, 95-96.   The term 'Burman' is used to refer to the majority ethnic group of Burma, while the term 'Burmese' is used to refer to indigenous inhabitants of Burma generally, including minority ethnic groups.   The language of the Burmans and Burma is 'Burmese'.

[2] D. G. E. Hall, *Burma,* London, 1950, pp. 12-13.   *Also:*   John F. Cady, *Southeast Asia : Its Historical Development,* New York, 1964, p. 114.

[3] G. H. Luce, "Economic Life of the Early Burman," (Rangoon) *JBRS,* Vol. XXX, Part 1, April 1940, pp. 283-335.   *See* Appendix A which indicates the several rain-zones in the Dry Zone and in the Delta.

[4] G. E. Harvey, *History of Burma,* London, 1967, pp. 15-16.

[5-6] *See* Appendix B, Deforestation Causes the Collapse of Trade and Order in Upper Burma, 1883-1885.   *See also* Chapters V and VII.   *Lastly:* Robert L. Carneiro, "A Theory of the Origin of the State," (Washington) *Science*, Vol. 169, August 21, 1970, pp. 733-738.

[7] G. E. Harvey, *History of Burma*, pp. 10-11.

[8] G. Coedes, (trans. H. M. Wright), *The Making of South East Asia*, Berkeley, 1966, p. 111.

[9] G. E. Harvey, *An Outline of Burmese History*, London, 1947, p. 9.

[10-12] The Javanese were not allowed to sell their spices, or to buy Mon ships, at Malacca after the Portugese conquered it in 1511. A Javanese and Palambang (Sumatra) trading combine sent 100 ships to blockade Malacca in 1513, but the Portugese guns destroyed all but seven or eight. The Portugese then proceeded to monopolize the Moluccan spice-trade, which had been a Javanese preserve for over 1,500 years. Without Mon ships, the Javanese were in the end unable to resist the sea-going Portugese and Dutch. John F. Cady, *Southeast Asia*, pp. 165-166, 178-180, 209-210. *Also:* D. G. E. Hall, *Europe and Burma*, London, 1945, pp. 13-14, 16-20.

[13] D. G. E. Hall, *Burma*, pp. 36-37.

[14] John F. Cady, *Southeast Asia*, pp. 111, 117-118, 123-125, 128-130. *Also:* D. G. E. Hall, *A History of South-East Asia*, New York, 1964, pp. 137-147.

[15] G. E. Harvey, *History of Burma*, pp. 64, 336.

[16] D. G. E. Hall, *A History of South-East Asia*, pp. 147-157. (*Also:* D. G. E. Hall, *Burma*, pp. 28-41).

[17] *Ibid.* (*Also:* G. E. Harvey, *History of Burma*, pp. 152-162).

[18] *Ibid.*, pp. 238-249. Between 1569-1599, the Delta trade was 'wrecked', and never really recovered until after the British conquest in 1852. However, in 1569, Bassein still received Indian ships with yarn, cotton cloth, and opium. Syriam was visited by Arab ships bringing scarlet and velvet fabrics, woollen cloth, and opium. Martaban received ships from Malacca with Chinese porcelains, sandalwood, Borneo camphor, and Sumatran (Achin) pepper. Pegu in 1569 still exported at least some rice, gold, silver, rubies, saphires, spinelles, benzoin, long pepper, lead, lac, rice-wine, and some sugar. *See:* John F. Cady, *Southeast Asia*, pp. 178-180, 183. *Also:* D. G. E. Hall, *Europe and Burma*, pp. 13-14, 16-20.

[19] D. G. E. Hall, *Burma*, pp. 45-46.

[20] John F. Cady, *Southeast Asia*, pp. 178-180, 183. *Also:* D. G. E. Hall, *Europe and Burma*, pp. 13-14, 16-20.

[21] G. E. Harvey, *History of Burma*, pp. 179-184. *Also:* D. G. E. Hall, *A History of South-East Asia*, pp. 249-254.

[22] John F. Cady, *A History of Modern Burma*, Ithaca, 1958, pp. 46-49.

[23] D. G. E. Hall, *A History of South-East Asia*, pp. 353-365. *Also:* G. E. Harvey, *History of Burma*, pp. 193-205.

[24] D. G. E. Hall, *Early English Intercourse With Burma, 1587-1743*, London, 1968, pp. 9-12, 87-101, 142-144, 153, 221-242, 353, *etc.*

[25] *Ibid.* (*See also:* D. G. E. Hall, *Europe and Burma*, p. 52).

[26] *Ibid*, pp. 10-11, 129-138, 145-146, 190-191, 224-227. (*Also:* G. E. Harvey, *History of Burma*, p. 353.)

[27] *Ibid*, p. 227.

[28] G. E. Harvey, *History of Burma*, pp. 211, 224-236, 345-346.

[29] *Ibid. Also:* D. G. E. Hall, *Early English..*, pp. 337-344. *Also:* D. G. E. Hall, *A History of South-East Asia*, pp. 381-389.

[30] D. G. E. Hall, *Early English..*, p. 353. *Also:* D. G. E. Hall, *Michael Symes,* London, 1955, pp. xxiv-xxv. *Lastly:* D. G. E. Hall, *Europe and Burma,* pp. 74-85. A general description of trade conditions in Burma after 1760.

[31] D. G. E. Hall, *Michael Symes,* pp. xxv—lxxxix. *Also:* D. G. E. Hall, *Burma,* pp. 100-105. *Lastly:* D. G. E. Hall, *Europe and Burma,* pp. 96-120.

[32] D. G. E. Hall, *Early English..*, pp. 241-242.

[33] John F. Cady, *A History of Modern Burma,* pp. 68-75. *Also:* D. G. E. Hall, *Europe and Burma,* pp. 96-120. *Lastly:* D. G. E. Hall, *Burma,* pp. 100-105.

[34] *Ibid.*

[35] A. C. Banerjee, *The Annexation of Burma,* Calcutta, 1944, pp. 17-40. *Also:* D. G. E. Hall, *A History of South-East Asia,* pp. 571-587.

[36] G. E. Harvey, *British Rule in Burma, 1826-1842,* London, 1946, p. 64. *Also:* Walter S. Desai, *History of the British Residency in Burma, 1826-1840,* Rangoon, 1939, pp. 60, 130-141, 213.

[37] Walter S. Desai, *History of the British Residency..*, pp. 452-461.

[38] John F. Cady, *A History of Modern Burma,* pp. 80-86.

[39] *Ibid*, pp. 46-49, 75. *Also:* John F. Cady, *Southeast Asia,* pp. 293-294, 299. *Also:* D. G. E. Hall, *Europe and Burma,* pp. 98-99.

[40] Saw Sick Hwa, *The Rice Industry of Burma, 1852-1940,* Ph. D. Thesis, Un. of London, 1963, pp. 329-331.

[41-43] *Ibid.*

[44] A. C. Banerjee, *The Annexation..*, pp. 57-73. (*Also :* D. G. E. Hall, *Europe and Burma,* pp. 138-147. *Lastly:* D. G. E. Hall, *The Dalhousie-Phayre Correspondence, 1852-1856,* London, 1932, introductory section.)

[45] *Ibid.* (*Also :* John F. Cady, *A History of Modern Burma,* pp. 86-89).

[46] *Ibid*, pp. 148-149. *Also :* John Nisbet, *Burma Under British Rule—And Before, Vol. II,* Westminister, 1901, p. 47.

[47] D. G. E. Hall, *A History of South-East Asia,* pp. 571-599.

[48] *Ibid.* (*Also :* Paul J. Bennett, *Conference Under the Tamarind Tree,* New Haven, 1971, pp. 57-70, 106-109, 115-117.)

[49] *Ibid.*

[50] A. C. Banerjee, *The Annexation........*, pp. 229-232.

[51] J. S. Furnivall, *Colonial Policy and Practice,* Cambridge, 1948, pp. 65-68. (*Also see :* the detailed discussion of Mindon's monopolies and other commercial endeavours in Foreign, Secret, September 1878, Nos. 65-134 (NAI).

[52] *Ibid.* (*Also :* Saw Sick Hwa, *The Rice Industry........*, pp. 295-296, 364.)

[53-54] *Ibid.* (*See also :* No. 32, Memorandum on the shipping and fortifications of Upper Burma ; in Foreign, Secret, August 1881, Nos. 31-36 (NAI). *Lastly :* For an estimate of the troop strength of Mindon's forces and their weapons *see* : Nos. 85-87 ; in Nos. 65-134.)

[55-56] *Ibid.*

[57] Foreign, Secret, September 1878, Nos. 65-145 (NAI).

[58] A. C. Banerjee, *The Annexation........*, pp. 235-244.

[59] G. E. Harvey, *British Rule........*, p. 64.

[60] *Ibid.*

[61] Maung Shein, *Burma's Transport and Foreign Trade, 1885-1914,* Rangoon, 1964, p. 30.

[62] *Ibid.* The IFC steamer service to Mandalay was established on a regular basis after 1868, and the service to Bhamo in 1871. By 1878-1886, the IFC service to Mandalay was twice a week, and the service from Mandalay to Bhamo at least once a month.

[63] "In Lower Burma the abundant harvests could not be got in without the high wages paid........[Upper Burmese] come down the Irrawady in their own boats, which they sell at a profit, returning with their savings on the decks of the steamers. Wages in Lower Burma are much higher than in India. In Upper Burma men will not work for less than twelve or fifteen rupees a month, and few care to hire themselves out to work for another, even for that high payment......in Lower Burma [they]........insist upon getting a rupee a day, and more for harvesting......" Grattan Geary, *Burma After the Conquest,* Bombay and London, 1886, pp. 302-303, 320-321.

[64] J. S. Furnivall, *Colonial Policy......,* pp. 65-68.

[65] *Ibid.* Lower Burma's population doubled from about 1,000,000 in 1852 to over 2,000,000 in 1861. After 1870 the rate of population growth was even greater. Many immigrants came from Upper Burma, thereby easing the population pressure on the always-limited food surpluses of the Dry Zone. These immigrants sent considerable funds and goods back to their Upper Burma relatives. This was a further contribution to Upper Burma's relative prosperity during Mindon's and Thebaw's reigns.

[66] A. C. Banerjee, *The Annexation......,* pp. 232-234. *Also :* Bernard to Durand, August 11, 1885; in Mss. Eur. D 727/3 (Book No. 1), Conf. Demi-Off. Letters to H. M. Durand, July 1885-July 1886 (IOL). *Lastly:* 'Shoe Question Editorial', (Calcutta) *Statesman,* June 13, 1885, p. 275.

[67] *Ibid.* The succeeding Viceroys of India, Lords Lytton (1876-1880) and Ripon (1880-1884) disapproved of "Northbrook's mistake" (as Lytton called it). Lord Dufferin (1884-1888) was annoyed with the impasse that Northbrook's ruling had caused.

[68] The European advisers and the various Mandalay merchants had assumed much of the traditional role formerly held by the Armenians in Burma. The Armenians and a small number of Europeans had usually functioned since the 16th century as a middle-man between the Burmese Court and the *kalas.* Now that there was no more direct contact between the Burmese King and the Resident, these disparate opportunists assumed much of the prominence that they had held a century before. *See :* D. G. E. Hall, *Michael Symes,* pp. xviii, xxiv-xxv, xxxix, xli, lxvii, 125.

[69] 'Pattern' as the author uses it in this study is not a predetermined pattern in the Marxist or other determinist sense. One might say that the periodic 'droughts', and the general low rainfall of the Dry Zone, are impersonal historical forces. In other words, a predetermined historical pattern. The *responses* of the Burmans to overcome this pattern—which *they had in fact helped to create* by their partial Deforestation of the Dry Zone—form an essentially human-directed pattern. This is the 'pattern' that the author has in mind.

[70] For a lucid account of the British in India and their preoccupation with the 'threat' from the west, in particular the 'Russian Threat', from about 1790

to 1842, *see*: J. A. Norris, *The First Afghan War, 1838-1842*, Cambridge, 1967.

[71] For a social, political, and commercial description of the Ningyan Forest (Toungoo) area where the greatest amount of Deforestation went on from 1862-1885 *see:* A. C. Pointon, *The Bombay Burma Trading Corporation, Limited, 1863-1963*, Southampton, 1963, pp. 1-25.   *Also see:* R. R. Langham-Carter, "Burmese Rule on the Toungoo Frontier," (Rangoon) *JBRS*, Vol. XXVII, Part 1, 1937, pp. 16-31.

1

The End of the Old Arrangements

The Death of King Mindon

In September 1878, King Mindon was dying of dysentery at Mandalay. The bazaar 'gup' had it that the King was also being fed opium poisoning in his food.[1] Mindon had been afraid to appoint a successor after Mindon's son, the Myngun Prince (b. 1844), had nearly assassinated him and had killed Mindon's brother, the Heir Designate, on August 2, 1866. Except for one abortive attempt to appoint the Mekhara Prince (b. 1847) as his heir in 1875, King Mindon had always refused to appoint a successor, because he said that it would be like signing the man's death warrant as though he were a criminal.[2]

Now a decision would have to be made on the succession, or anarchy would result. Robert B. Shaw, the British Resident at Mandalay, attempted to remain aloof from the scramble for position that was going on at the Palace. Shaw was a former Indian tea-planter, who had become a world authority on Turkestan (present-day Sinkiang) and the Turki language. He had been envoy-designate to Yakub Beg's Court at Kashgar before the Chinese armies reconquered it in December 1877.[3]

Shaw and Sir Douglas Forsyth had made several previous trips to Turkestan to establish friendly relations. The Indian Government was hopeful that the area would form a 'buffer' against the 'Russian Threat' to Persia, Afghanistan, and India's

northwest frontier.   With the reoccupation of Kashgar, China was
now pitted against Russia in Turkestan.⁴   Therefore, Shaw was no
longer needed in that area as an envoy, but the important Resi-
dentship at Mandalay was open.   Shaw was sent to maintain
relations with the 'buffer' that protected India's eastern frontier
from the French advance in Indo-China.

On September 4, Shaw reported to A. C. Lyall, the Indian
foreign secretary, that he had received two separate communications concerning two Burmese princes, the Nyaungyan (b. 1845)
and his younger brother, the Nyaungoke (b. 1849).   The messages
had asked whether the two princes and their families might take
refuge in the Residency in case of danger to themselves arising out
of the death of the King.⁵   Shaw replied that he would accept
Burmese refugees if they would agree to carry on no intrigues from
the virtually defenceless and unguarded Residency.⁶

Meanwhile, at the Palace, a black note-book of dried palm-
leaf was handed to the three sets of officials comprising the
Hlutdaw, the Royal Council, and the upper echelons of the Burmese
Government.   The first set of officials were the *wungyis*, the four
'great burden bearers' of the Kingdom.   These were the Yenangyaung, the war minister; the Kampat, the president of the *Hlutdaw*
and home and justice minister; the Kinwun (b. 1822), the foreign
minister; and, the Shwepyi (Yaw) Atwinwun, one of the greatest
reformers in nineteenth-century Burma, who was officiating as the
industrial development and public works minister in place of the
invalid Luangshe Mingyi.⁷

The second and third sets of officials were the *atwinwuns*,
the personal attendants to the King, who were often *Hlutdaw*
ministers as well; and the *wundauks*, the junior or subministers who
assisted the four *wungyis*.   The note-book, *parabaik*, circulated
among the three sets of officials was a voting-ballot containing the
names of King Mindon's twenty-four sons.⁸

The Kinwun and the Shwepyi, who was soon to assume the
title of Magwe Mingyi, wanted to form a modern ministerial
government under a titular constitutional monarchy.   The King
would act as the presiding 'President of the *Hlutdaw*'; all government orders would carry the phrase 'Order of the King in
Council'; and, all government officials would swear loyalty to the
ministers as well as to the King.⁹

The Kinwun's dreams for the future progress of his country

prompted him to support Prince Thebaw as the next King. Thebaw was a mere lad of nineteen, a monk in a monastery, and was greatly under the influence of a older monk named Yanaung. Yanaung, who had predicted some months previously that Thebaw would some day become the King, was the son of the Myaukdwe Bo, one of the key military figures in the Thebaw faction. Thebaw's only visible accomplishment had been his successful recitation of the 'Three Baskets' of the Buddhist Law during his three years in the monastery from 1875-1878.[10]

The Thebaw faction included the Kinwun as foreign minister and trusted confident of the dying King; the Kinwun's followers such as the Shwepyi and the Pangyet ministers who made up the 'reform' party in the *Hlutdaw*; and, the ambitious Chief Queen, who wanted one of her three daughters to marry Thebaw.[11] Both the Kinwun's 'reformers' and the more crass, office-seeking persons at Court, such as the Chief Queen and the Kampat Mingyi, thought that Prince Thebaw would be mere political 'putty' in their hands. In this monumental miscalculation they had reckoned without Yanaung and Supayalat, the Chief Queen's young daughter (b. 1859) that Thebaw was soon to marry.

In Mandalay, itself, the popular choice of the people and officials was undoubtedly the Nyaungyan Prince, 34, who was also extremely popular with foreigners. However, the Thongze (b. 1843), the Mekhara, and other princes also had their supporters in the *Hlutdaw* meeting held to elect the next King. The Yenangyaung minister, for example, had lobbied vigorously for the election of the Pyinmana Prince, his own grandson. At almost eighty years of age, the Yenangyaung was the senior *wungyi*, the war minister, the operator of Upper Burma's oil wells, and could easily have split the meeting and the country into warring factions.[12]

However, it appears that at some point before the actual meeting, the Kinwun went to the tough old warrior, who had fought the British several times during the Second Burmese War, and made a plea for national unity. Apparently, the Kinwun described the fate in store for their beloved country, *i.e.* annexation to the British Empire, should they now divide themselves into warring factions over the succession.

The Yenangyaung had no fear of the British. He delighted in playing the host to his many European friends, in showing off his youngest wife who was in her early twenties, and in having his guests feel the bullet still lodged in his back from the 1866 Rebellion.   Apparently, it was for the sake of national unity that the Yenangyaung did not push the election of his grandson during the meeting, but instead merely stated that the Prince was available in the hall.[13]

The Kinwun as foreign minister and *thanatwun* (master of infantry) had about 12,000 infantry soldiers at Mandalay under his command, and so he now dominated the situation.   He listened to a long procession of speeches on the moral qualities required in a King.   Finally, the Kinwun gave the cut-off sign, and went outside the building under a tamarind tree with the rest of the Thebaw faction, and they all marked Thebaw's name on the *parabaik* that served as the voting ballot.   The rest of the officials with some reluctance went along with the 'majority will'.[14]

The *parabaik* was taken to Mindon, who looked at it and laid the ballot down by his bed without a sign or word.   The Chief Queen and the Kinwun announced that Mindon's silence meant that he had approved of Thebaw as his heir.   To be certain that Mindon remained silent, troops were brought in from units loyal to the Kinwun to surround the King's bed room, and the other queens, princesses, and relatives of the other princes were kept away.[15]

On September 12, a Royal Order was proclaimed in Mandalay that the twenty-four sons of King Mindon, and the several dozen lesser princes, would report to the bedside of their father.   However, upon entering the Palace the princes were arrested by the Kinwun's troops and jailed.[16]   The order was a forgery, and with their rivals now behind bars, the Thebaw faction drafted the proclamation of Thebaw's accession to the throne on September 15 ; invested him with the insignia of Crown Prince on September 17 ; and, proclaimed the appointment throughout the city on September 19.[17]

On the same day, the relatives of the other princes finally reached King Mindon, and he ordered the princes freed.   Mindon called the Mekhara Prince to his bedroom and divided up the Kingdom into three parts: the Taungdwingyi area southeast of Mandalay to the Mekhara ; the Chindwin River Valley north of Mandalay to the Thongze; and the Irrawaddy River area south of Mandalay to the Nyaungyan.   Mindon did not question the *Hlutdaw's* decision to nominate Thebaw, nor did Mindon give Mandalay to any of the three older princes.[18]

He did, however, give each of them a steamer, and told the

Mekhara to tell his fellow princes, and their followers among the minor princes, to leave Mandalay immediately for their respective areas. It seems that Mindon wanted to get the princes and their families away from the capital, so that there wouldn't be the usual massacre of the surplus princes that had occurred at the start of almost every reign. Apparently, Mindon hoped that most of his twenty-four sons, their families, and their followings among the minor princes would crowd on board the three steamers and flee to British Burma.[19]

The Mekhara Prince went to the North Palace Garden to tell the assembled princes and their families of the news, and to assure them that none of them would be killed. However, the Kinwun was violently opposed to the division of the country among the three hostile brothers, because their constant brawling would surely disrupt the Irrawaddy River trade and give the British a bully excuse to annex the country. The Kinwun hurried to the Chief Queen. They decided to ignore Mindon's orders, and the Kinwun ordered the Inner Palace-Guard to rearrest the princes.

As the Mekhara spoke, the troopers burst into the garden. The Mekhara was cut over the head, the Thongze hurt himself trying to climb the garden wall, and the rest of the princes were beaten up and tossed into prison. To allay suspicion, Thebaw was arrested and shackled in prison with the others. However, the Chief Queen soon announced that Mindon had ordered Thebaw's immediate release so that he might give the King his medicine.[20]

Unfortunately for the plotters, Mindon's condition continued to improve ever so slightly for two or three days. The ministers panicked, and only after much persuasion was the Chief Queen able to stop them from releasing the prisoners and allowing them to leave Mandalay as Mindon had ordered. This time no one from any faction opposed to Thebaw was allowed near the dying King, and he never knew that his orders had been disregarded. As the Burmese Chronicles put it:

There was therefore no one to tell the King........and he believed that the Princes were set free and said..... "Now they have got to the steamers. Now they have started. Now they are going full of joy and gratitude to assume their new duties." But the Princes lay loaded with chains in their crowded cell.[21]

The Escape of the Two Princes

Only the Nyaungyan and the Nyaungoke along with about a dozen members of their families escaped the first mass arrests on September 12. Mons. d' Avera, a Frenchman of many years service to King Mindon, and the Rev. James A. Colbeck, an SPG missionary, slipped them into Shaw's Residency.[22] Shaw told the Burmese Government that he was neutral and that it was up to the princes as to whether they would return to the Palace.[23]

Shaw remained neutral after Mindon's death on October 1,[24] and resigned himself to reassuring the Nyaungyan during his almost "daily fits of alarm."[25] The two princes were further alarmed by the news on October 31 that 200 ruffians under orders from the Governor of Myingyan had kidnapped thirty Burmese passengers off the *Yankeentoung* IFC steamer.[26]

Upon a protest from Shaw, the Mandalay Government investigated and sacked the Myingyan Governor. On November 5 several other judgments were announced. The officials responsible for the placing in the stocks of two Indian dhobis were given ten lashes apiece. The Gateway Guard Commander responsible for placing IFC Captain Doyle in the stocks was sacked and jailed. Notices were placed in the bazaars that no ill treatment of European subjects would be allowed as they were the subjects of friendly governments.[27]

On November 9, the Kinwun and the Magwe ministers came to see Shaw. They confided that they wanted the two princes to go into exile in India, as did the princes themselves. However, to say this officially would be embarrassing, and would be a retraction of the earlier order that the princes should return to the Palace.[28]

Shaw replied that unless he was asked by the Mandalay Government to assist in the exiling of the princes, he was perfectly content to allow them to remain in the Residency. The prospect of the two princes continuing to defy the Royal Order was an embarrassing one for the two ministers. Finally, the Magwe spoke up. He had devised the Burmese telegraphic code,[29] and was a public advocate of beer-drinking.[30] He suggested that "we might write to you and say, as the Princes have requested to be allowed to go to British territory, be pleased to assist them in attaining their desire."[31]

Shaw readily agreed. On November 11, a letter came from

the Kinwun, which recognized that the proposal for the princes' departure had not come from the Resident or the Indian Government. The princes were free to go whenever they wished, and the Mandalay Government would send a steamer with soldiers behind the princes' steamer as far as the frontier.[32]

The princes and their families left on November 15. The Rev. Colbeck recorded that "One or two of them were nearly inclined to cry at parting from us."[33] The Nyaungyan Prince made Colbeck promise to give him his photo, and promised his own and that of his wife and children in return. It was a relieved Shaw who heard from his assistant resident, Mr. Davis, that he had escorted the two princely families down to Thayetmyo in British territory.

The Era of Good Feeling

A temporary 'era of good feeling' existed between Shaw and many of the ministers between October 1, 1878 and February 15, 1879. It existed because both sides were anxious for a settlement of at least some of the key issues between them.

The first and most important issue was the Resident's lack of access to the King. This was due to Viceroy Lord Northbrook's rule preventing the Resident from doffing his shoes in the King's presence.[34] This "Shoe Question" had arisen from the 'Meru-centric' tradition which envisioned the Burmese King as the counterpart of Lord Indra, King of the Gods atop Mt. Meru. Obviously, if the parallel was to be exact all human beings would have to doff their shoes before the earthly Lord Indra.[35]

The Indian Government had listed an end to the "Shoe Question", a new riverside Residency, and an increased Residency Guard, as three key concessions that should be gained from the new King.[36] The Indian Foreign Dept. stated in an October 17, 1878 letter to Lord Cranbrook, secretary of state for India, that these three concessions, and a revision of the 1862 and 1867 Treaties, were necessary in order to protect the lives, property, and trading rights of British subjects in Upper Burma.[37]

Shaw had already been working for a relaxation of the "Shoe Question". He was encouraged by the fact that he and Giovanni Andreino, the Italian consul, had been allowed to attend Mindon's funeral held *out-of-doors*. They had been seated in chairs in a special pavilion while wearing full Consul's uniform, sword, and shoes. The other *kalas* (foreigners) had to doff their shoes. The protocol innovation, which was near-revolutionary, had not extended to unofficial foreigners.[38]

On October 14, Shaw broached the idea of a relaxation *indoors*, but the Kinwun's response was not encouraging. Shaw felt confident with such an enlightened minister in power that matters would be arranged more in accordance with the customs of great states.[39] The Kinwun's only reply was that some customs were difficult to change.[40]

Along with the "Shoe Question", Shaw pressed for an enlargement of the Residency Guard to thirty men. The Residency was virtually defenceless within its flimsy walls. Shaw insisted that the Residency Guard, which had been set at fifty men in the 1826 Yandabo Treaty, was not a matter of popular custom which was hard to change. Instead, it was a Governmental arrangement, a single act.[41]

Shaw finally agreed that when the guard of thirty men arrived, he would show that it had been sent-up in a friendly spirit.[42] The ministers hoped that the matter would be reconsidered.[43] However, the Kinwun retreated gracefully before the *fait accompli* in a January 24 note to Shaw.

The note did not admit the existence of the 1826 Yandabo Treaty, which had permitted a Residency Guard of fifty men. The Kinwun, as if he were bestowing a token of His Majesty's kindliness upon the *kalas*,[44] stated that the 1862 and 1867 'Royal Friendship Treaties' had not mentioned anything about an armed guard of thirty men. Nevertheless, Royal permission had been granted "in order to make manifest tokens of......genuine Royal friendship."[45]

On February 7, Shaw enthused over "a marked step taken in ......cordial social intercourse."[46] On the evening of February 6, the Kinwun had invited the Residency officials to a dinner party at his rambling country villa. They were properly met, and the conversation was animated and cordial. A special dinner-entertainment where the host and other high Burmese officials had dined with their visitors had not been given previously.[47]

Shaw and other Residency members were even introduced to some of the ministers' wives, although Shaw remarked that the ladies did not dine with them but ate afterwards. This was proper Burmese etiquette and was the basis for a popular joke at the

Palace; namely that Queen Supayalat had already become so dominant over her husband that she even ate her meals first.

An almost euphoric Shaw, confident that relations would become even more cordial, interviewed Maung Paw Tun, the new Burmese Consul to Calcutta, on February 14. Shaw commented that he could not be certain that Viceroy Lord Lytton would greet the Consul, since the King of Burma did not receive the British Resident. The Myotha Wundauk, the assistant foreign minister who had come with the Consul, said that of course Shaw could see the King at any time. The Burmese Consul would in turn conform completely to British etiquette, *i.e.* keep his shoes on and sit in a chair in Lord Lytton's presence.[48]

Shaw's answer was probably the best defence ever presented of the British view on the "Shoe Question". He pointed out that the Indian Government had never insisted on agents of foreign states adopting customs contrary to those of their own countries.[49] The English had the custom of showing respect by removing their hats, because they wore a light and easily removable head-dress. The 'Mussulmans' on the other hand usually shaved their heads and wore an elaborate turban. It was inconvenient and even unseemly for them to remove their head-dress, therefore, such had never been asked of them.[50]

On the other hand, Shaw claimed that many Oriental races as a rule wore light and easily removable coverings for the feet and were in the habit of removing them indoors.[51] By contrast, the British wore boots or shoes difficult to take off, and they found it hard to walk bare-footed without such protection for their feet. Shaw concluded that the Mandalay Government had ignored such inconveniences, and without looking beyond their own local customs, had insisted upon the removal of shoes as a condition of foreign envoys visiting the King.[52]

Perhaps some advance might have been made, which would have allowed Shaw to retain his shoes, and to meet the King in an informal series of *outside* garden interviews. There had been a similar "Shoe Question" with the Chinese Emperor, and a meeting in an outside garden or building had been the temporary solution. Unfortunately, the more 'traditional' groups were gathering strength at the Mandalay Palace.

The Decline of the 'Reform' Party

The decline of the 'reform' party at Court headed by the Magwe and the Kinwun Mingyis was the result of several factors. During December 1878, Supayalat, the younger of the two brides of Thebaw, had used her exquisite sensual-charms (her eyes were her best feature according to all reports) and her superior will-power to shove aside Supayagyi, Thebaw's other Queen and Supayalat's older sister.[53]

Their mother, the former Chief Queen, complained to Supayalat about her behaviour towards her older sister. Supayalat rebelled against her mother's dominance, and temporarily pushed her into the background with the full cooperation of many of the ministers who had grown weary of the old Queen's constant meddling in state affairs. Supayalat then sent her older sister back to their mother's apartment where she remained for the next seven years. Supayalat was now the sole Queen and wife of the King, although there was always the potential danger that her mother might try to marry her third and youngest daughter to Thebaw.[54]

The ministers having unwisely allowed Supayalat's mother to be thrust into the background, now found themselves and the Royal party to be the only two powers at the Palace. The Royal Couple and their personal attendants, the *atwinwuns*, resented the idea of ministerial control over the treasury; and particularly the concept that the Royal Couple would have to allow the *Hlutdaw* to vote them an annual privy purse to be limited at the ministers' pleasure.[55]

In an effort to secure a wider power-base against the Royal onslaught, the 'reformers' broadened the membership of the *Hlutdaw* to a prototype parliament of between twenty-five and thirty government officials. But, ironically, instead of uniting the officials and the people behind the concept of ministerial control over the King, the enlarged *Hlutdaw* caused intense dissatisfaction.[56]

The enlarged membership of the *Hlutdaw* caused the execution of public business to come to a near halt. Formerly, anyone with a problem had been required to give a present to one of the officials, who in turn introduced him to the King. The King also required a present, but afterwards could usually dispose of the petitioner's problem in a few minutes.[57]

However, under the enlarged *Hlutdaw*, the petitioner had to give a present to all thirty of the *Hlutdaw* members. It was a 'democratic' body, and therefore any one member could veto the petitioner's plea if he had overlooked a present to the member or had been too niggardly the first time. The delays, the endless debates, and the increased cost of doing business with the Palace caused intense dissatisfaction among mercantile and other groups, and greatly strengthened the *atwinwuns* and the other supporters of the old supreme Royal authority.[58]

The Magwe Mingyi sharply attacked the increasing extravagances of the Royal Couple, and their continued refusal to recognize that the *Hlutdaw* retained the right to limit the royal expenditures to an annual Privy Purse. He stated that the Royal Couple "should remember that the [tax] money was not obtained for nothing, but was wrung out of hard working cultivators and [should] not be squandered as if it were sand or pebbles."[59]

On January 20, the Magwe and the Yenangyaung Mingyi, the old minister who now advocated replacing Thebaw with the Mekhara Prince, were sacked from their posts, charged with corruption and malfeasance while in office, and tossed into prison.[60] However, they were both soon released and bundled into an ignominious retirement.

The *atwinwuns*, such as the Taingda Atwinwun, and the other supporters of the supremacy of the King were soon appointed to a majority of the *Hlutdaw* and ministerial posts. For the next seven years, the Royal or 'traditional' party led by the Yanaung, and later the Taingda Atwinwun, generally ruled supreme over the ministerial or 'reform' party led by the Kinwun. Thebaw although King remained an amiable cipher. The old Chief Queen, Supayalat's mother, was safely tucked away where she could do little more than annoy her daughter with her constant advice. Supayalat was in fact the real ruler of Upper Burma.

The February 15-17, 1879 Massacre

But there were still other rivals for both Thebaw's throne and his amourous interests. There were several hundred members of the Royal Family, including twenty-four queens, twenty-four princes, and thirty-five princesses who had either been married to or were off-spring of the late King Mindon.[61] The Armenian,

French, and Italian employees of the Court told Supayalat that the British would never interfere in a massacre of the Royal relatives, unless British subjects' profits were threatened.

The European Royal employees also told her that British military power was collapsing.   Great Britain was involved in the Second Afghan War in Afghanistan in an effort to keep Russia out of that country, and away from India's northwest frontier. The British were also fighting a second major war in South Africa against the Zulu's Chief Cetewayo, who had given the British a savage beating at Isandhlwana.[62] The South African Boers also seemed about to fight.   The last thing that the British wanted at such a time was a third major war.

Reassured, Supayalat resolved to do away with more than eighty Royal relatives leaving only herself to rule—with Thebaw of course.[63]   The Kinwun agreed to the upcoming massacres. He believed, as did his main rival, the Taingda Atwinwun, that such a 'liquidation' would make for greater stability, and fewer princely revolts in the countryside. Apparently, the Kinwun still hoped that reforms could be continued.   With the two greatest reformers, besides himself, in prison after January 20, the Kinwun must have suddenly realized that he was becoming isolated.[64]

Shaw was also rather isolated in his Residency, and the news of the Massacre was a great shock to him.   However, the affair could not have been much of a shock to many Mandalay residents, who had probably been anticipating the slaughter for the previous two months.   One obvious sign of such a massacre to come had been the phenomenally large order of red velvet that had been given out by the Palace in December to the French weaver Mons. Denigre and his daughter, Maria.[65]

The order was apparently initiated by Supayalat, her mother, and a group about them including the six officials who actually officiated over the murders.   There were also reports of Palace ladies cutting and sewing the red velvet into large sacks, which was a certain sign that a Royal massacre was imminent.   Red velvet sacks were used to enclose the condemned of high or Royal rank. They were then killed with seven or eight blows of a thick sandalwood club at the front or back of the neck.[66]

The red-velvet sacks hid the wounds and blood.   It was a sacrilage to touch the person of a man or woman of Royal blood, to say nothing of harming or killing them.   Also, a Buddhist was not supposed to kill any living thing. Of course all concerned in the massacre were Buddhists. The red-velvet sacks, and the belief that it had been the *karma* (fate) of the condemned to die in the massacre, were the subterfuges by which the secular and religious proprieties were maintained. Shaw's February 19 diary entry was a terse description of the horror that had followed :

....on Saturday night [February 15]....Some were killed.... and the rest on the two succeeding nights. A large hole had been dug in the jail precincts. Into this their bodies were thrown....the women pleaded for their lives....Their out-cries were stifled by the hands of the executioners grasping their necks till they were strangled. Others were killed with bludgeons, which in the hands of half-drunken men [were] often required to be used repeatedly before the victims were put out of their pain. The executioners were some of the worst ruffians released for the purpose from the jail.... Of the Princes the eldest, Thongze [b. 1843], alone showed courage. He is said to have laughed and said to his brothers "see, I told you we should have no release but death." On Sunday night (the 16th) eight cart-loads of the bodies of Princes.... are said to have been conveyed out of the city by the western (or funeral) gate, and thrown into the river according to the custom. The other ladies were all thrown into the hole already dug in the jail.[67]

Shaw added further grisly details in his February 20 entry:
....infants were taken from their mothers' arms and their brains were dashed out against the wall. Others were struck on the head and thrown only half-dead on to the heap of bodies in the pit. The Queens and Princesses were stripped.. to search their clothes for secreted jewels. Some....were dishonoured before being killed, though this is perhaps untrue. All was effected under the superintendence of the personal followers of the King [atwinwuns]. No official of the Hlut or Minister's Court was present. The remaining Ministers [wungyis and wundauks]... are said to be in fear of their lives and to have no power left, although they still attend the King as usual.[68]

Shaw commented that apparently some ministers had tried to stop the upcoming massacres. Therefore, Thebaw, *i.e.* Supayalat and her mother acting in his name, had removed the Magwe and

Yenangyaung ministers on January 20 to forestall their opposition. With their removal, the power of the ministers opposed to the Massacre had been much weakened. The King's mother was said to have urged the King to massacre his relatives.[69] Such was doubtful, however. Thebaw was apparently *not* told of the Massacre made in his name until after it was over on February 18.[70]

Shaw also stated that the Taingda was the chief mover in the Massacre.[71] However, the Taingda, the ex-General of the South and recently promoted by Thebaw and Supayalat to *atwinwun*, personal attendant to the King, was no more responsible for the Massacre than the Kinwun or any other minister or *atwinwun*.[72] Nevertheless, it was the Taingda; the Hlaythin, admiral of the war boats; the Yanaung, Thebaw's great favourite; and two other key officials who actually oversaw the killings.[73] Yanaung's brother, the Pintha, was apparently also involved.

Shaw was also incorrect in his estimate that the Salen Princess was almost the only one of Mindon's descendants left alive.[74] The Massacre had occurred primarily in the families of the Mekhara and the Thongze Princes; and also in the family of the late Heir Designate, who had been assassinated on August 2, 1866 by Prince Myngun. These three families were the key remaining rivals to Supayalat's power. In order to retain a hold on the exiled Nyaungyan Prince, Supayalat kept his mother in prison. The more distant Royal relatives were murdered for more capricious reasons, and some were even freed from prison and restored to Royal favour.

The average Burmese, commoner or official, felt an overwhelming sense of relief that the Massacre had taken place. Apparently, almost the only Burmese horrified by the bloodshed were those persons actually murdered, and their relatives and close associates. In fact, the average Burmese applauded the Massacre at the most effective way to begin the new King's reign.[75]

What else could have been done with several dozen princes, all with as good or a better claim to the throne than Thebaw? The princes would have revolted, as Burmese princes had always revolted throughout Burmese history. In their struggles over the throne, the common man in the villages would have suffered—as he had always suffered—from the resulting disorder and 'dacoity'.[76]

Then, in the background and always a threat were the exiled Nyaungyan and Nyaungoke Princes. But a greater threat than these two was the Myngun Prince, who had nearly murdered his father, King Mindon, in 1866 and seized the throne. Myngun was exiled at Banares, and a country divided among many warring princes would have been an open invitation for him to escape. Or, the Indian Government might have helped him or the Nyaungyan or Nyaungoke Princes to become the new King. An Upper Burma divided among several warring princes would not have remained independent for long. As an old Burmese official said years later:

I would do it again. We had no alternative. At the annexation [of Upper Burma by the Indian Government in 1886] it took you English five years to curb dacoits led by a few sham princes. How long would it have taken you if they had been led by seventy real princes? By taking those seventy [*sic*] lives we saved seventy thousand.[77]

London Rejects War

The Massacre abruptly broke-off the 'Era of Good Feeling'. The outside world first heard of the Massacre via Shaw's telegrams; and C. U. Aitchison, chief commissioner of Lower Burma, added his own comments.[78]

Aitchison had been the Indian foreign secretary under both Viceroys Lord Mayo (1869-1872) and Lord Northbrook (1872-1876), but was now in temporary 'exile' having been replaced as foreign secretary by his jealous rival, Alfred Lyall. Aitchison had disagreed with the 'forward policy' of Viceroy Lord Lytton (1876-1880), which since Nov. 21, 1878 had involved the Indian Government in the unpopular Second Afghan War.

Yet, on February 19, 1879, Aitchison proposed what was surely a 'forward policy' for India's eastern frontier and Upper Burma.[79] He suggested that a stern remonstrance ought to be made to Mandalay over the Massacre. Consideration should also be given for the breaking-off of relations between India and Upper Burma, and for an immediate withdrawal of the Resident.[80]

Lord Cranbrook, the secretary of state for India, replied on February 21. He accepted Aitchison's proposal that the Indian Government should protest the Massacre. However, Cranbrook refused the proposal for a withdrawal of the Resident. A withdrawal would only give Thebaw more freedom to commit additional 'barbarities'.[81]   Shaw had already protested the Massacre. On February 20, the Kinwun replied pleading the right of any sovereign state to protect itself from internal and external enemies.[82] This remained the Kinwun's able defence in the months ahead.

On February 23, Shaw telegraphed that the armed guard of thirty men for the Residency had arrived, and that the Residency was somewhat less vulnerable.[83]   The killings had temporarily stopped due to his protests, coupled with those of Giovanni Andreino, the Italian consul, and Dr. Clement Williams, the former British agent from 1861-1865. Cranbrook again telegraphed on February 23 that "A remonstrance is all that can be done...."[84]

But Lytton and his Council felt that something more than a strong protest was in order. Lytton, apparently, did *not* much care whether Upper Burma was annexed by India,[85] or if Lower Burma was given back to an independent Upper Burma.[86]   Either proposal would probably have quieted the eastern frontier. Lytton could have returned his attention to the main problem, namely the northwest frontier, the Second Afghan War, and the 'Russian Threat'.

Lytton attempted to persuade Cranbrook to modify his February 20 and 23 telegrams. On February 28, Lytton wrote to Cranbrook stating that if Shaw were removed from Mandalay, Thebaw's power would collapse. Consequently, Burmese overtures would soon be received for the re-establishment of relations "on a more satisfactory footing."[87]

Lytton of course meant relations on a footing that would allow his government to again concentrate on the Afghan War and the 'Russian Threat' thought to be poised for a strike down through the northwest frontier into the heartland of India.[88]   On March 7, Lytton's Council filed an additional plea of fourteen lengthy paragraphs.

It listed as major political and commercial complaints (1) the "Shoe Question"; (2) the resultant lack of access to the King; (3) the repeated violent attacks on British subjects and their property while in Upper Burma; (4) the repeated injustices shown to British subjects as a result of the Burmese 'sabotage' of the Mixed Court; and (5) the recent intrusions of Burmese frontier outposts into Lower Burmese territory.[89]

The conclusion amounted to an ultimatum to Mandalay. The

Council proposed that a note be sent to Thebaw informing him that satisfaction was expected on the above and other complaints. The note was also to demand a full revision of all previous treaty relations between the two countries.[90]

The possibility of a new war on India's eastern frontier was not lost upon Cranbrook in London. Disraeli's Conservative Government was faced with not only the Second Afghan War, but also with the Zulu War in South Africa. The British public was violently opposed to both wars; and the next Election would probably be held sometime in 1880. Cranbrook was not in any haste to do anything that might cause a third major war. The fear that such a war might break out prompted him to send four despatches after March 10 warning against involvement in Upper Burma.[91]

Therefore, the Indian Government's March 7 'ultimatum' proposal had an instant effect upon Cranbrook when it reached his desk at the end of March. His April 1 telegram ordered Lytton that "Of course you will not send anything like ultimatum to King."[92] Lytton telegraphed back in suave retreat that of course he did not contemplate an ultimatum or even a protest to Thebaw at any time without previous reference to London.[93]

Cranbrook followed up his telegram with an April 3 letter that emphatically overruled the March 7 'ultimatum' despatch. He noted that Thebaw's government had not committed any actions calculated to aggravate the long-standing tensions between the two states. Cranbrook concluded that an ultimatum based upon old grievances would appear more as a hostile act than as a plea for more friendly relations.[94]

After April 1, 1879, Lytton lost all hope of ending the eastern frontier 'problem' with either a withdrawal of the Resident, or by the sending of an ultimatum. Aitchison also knew that Cranbrook had adhered to his February 20 and 23 telegrams that the Resident was *not* to be withdrawn, and that a protest was all that could be done. Cranbrook's April 1 and 3 despatches had also *ended* any hope of an ultimatum to Mandalay. Yet, Aitchison continued after April 1 to agitate for the above two 'solutions' to the now subsiding 'crisis' in Upper Burma. Aitchison became a great source of embarrassment to Lytton, who felt constrained on several occasions to explain to London that Aitchison was mentally unstable.[95]

In summary, Aitchison was afraid that the 'panics' in Upper

Burma, and the Burmese troop build-up on the frontier, endangered the Residency and British subjects' interests.[96] Aitchison wanted to demand 'explanations' (*i.e.* an ultimatum) and to withdraw the Residency in order to force the Mandalay Government to settle the issues between the two countries. Hopefully, Thebaw's Government would fall, and the Nyaungyan Prince and the Kinwun would seize power.

However, the Indian Government after April 1 had *explicit* orders from London not to get involved in a Burma war. A demand for 'explanations' (ultimatum) would probably have been refused by Mandalay. The consequent withdrawal of the Resident and British subjects from Mandalay would probably have resulted in a rupture. As Lyall, Indian foreign secretary, put it :

....war is the natural....sequence to an open rupture of relations between contiguous States. More especially is this the case when....one [state] is civilized, the other barbarous, and demands deliberately put forward by the former have been decisively rejected by the latter....[97]

It is interesting to note that in late-1885 and early-1886, Aitchison was lieutenant governor of the Punjab, and Lyall was lieutenant governor of the N.W. Provinces and Oudh. Both officials, especially Aitchison, were most outspoken and articulate in their *opposition* to the impending annexation of Upper Burma. In short, the 1879 controversy between these two men was a clash between two jealous rivals as much as it was an irreconcilable difference of views concerning Burma and India's eastern frontier.

The Kinwun and Shaw Restore Relations

Meanwhile, Shaw kept his superiors informed with a stream of telegrams, letters and diary entries written in a relaxed tone. To have done otherwise would not have contributed much towards a restoration of cordial relations. The Mandalay Government had become thoroughly frightened that the protests concerning the Massacre would be used as an excuse for an invasion of Upper Burma.

Mandalay rushed troops to the frontier above Thayetmyo by the end of February 1879, and the Indian Government in turn poised Indian regiments at Thayetmyo. But even these troops could not have saved Mr. Shaw and the Residency members from the rumoured massacre that was supposed to take place on the night of March 12.[98]

The result of the exchange of telegrams between Rangoon and Calcutta was that the Indian Government had no solution. They shifted the responsibility back to Shaw.[99] Lyall telegraphed to Shaw on March 8, and stated that Shaw had full discretion to withdraw from Mandalay with the Residency personnel and records.[100]

Fortunately, no attack occurred on the virtually defenceless Residency, and the excitement subsided.[101] Shaw returned his attention to some of the permanent points of disagreement between the two Governments. These included : (1) the "Shoe Question"; (2) the lack of access to the King; (3) the physical attacks on British subjects; (4) a rejuvenation of the Mixed Court to assure a fair trial for British subjects ; and, lastly, (5) a river-side site for the proposed new Residency. The Burmese had offered inland sites, which offered little chance for the Residency members to escape to the river if attacked.

On March 25, the Kinwun enquired the reason for the IFC steamers' change of procedure. Formerly when docked at Mandalay, they had let their fires go out and their steam-pressure go down. However, recently, the steamers had only banked their fires, and their steam-gauges were still at a high reading.[102] The Burmese Government considered this change in procedure to be most suspicious. On March 28, Shaw informed the Myotha Wundauk, the Kinwun's assistant in foreign affairs and the Burmese judge of the Mixed Court, that the IFC was afraid of an attack.[103]

The Myotha countered that his Government was not to be reassured so easily. It had read the reports carried in the Rangoon newspapers concerning a British envoy said to be on his way to Mandalay with an 'ultimatum'. The newspapers had even listed the contents of the document. The seemingly suspicious behaviour of the four IFC steamers then at Mandalay in not letting their fires go out, as formerly, only seemed to confirm the Rangoon press reports.[104]

Shaw replied in a March 29 letter to the Kinwun that the IFC owners had read Rangoon newspaper reports of disorders in Upper Burma. The IFC was afraid that 'dacoits' would rob their crews and steamers.[105] Shaw stated that he had already telegraphed to Rangoon to say that the Rangoon newspapers should not be believed. They had made false statements about the Indian Government sending an envoy with an 'ultimatum' to Mandalay, and had, likewise, frightened the IFC owners with equally false reports of anarchy in Upper Burma.[106]

Shaw concluded by asking the Kinwun to write a letter stating that precautions were not necessary. The Kinwun wrote the letter, and Shaw presented it to the steamer officials. They, however, refused to take a chance. Shaw considered this to be "only wasting their fuel," and "an irritating show of mistrust."[107]

On April 4, just as the Rangoon press was at a discount, reports came that the Nyaungyan Prince had landed in Rangoon to start a revolution to overthrow Thebaw. Even as Shaw was summoning the Myotha to the Residency, reports of the Nyaungyan's arrival were being telegraphed up from mercantile-agents in Rangoon. Rumours were afloat everywhere in the Mandalay bazaar.[108] Shaw's quick thinking spared the Mandalay Government the official humiliation of having to ask Shaw if the bazaar 'gup' was true.

The Myotha expressed great satisfaction that the information was so freely given and that Rangoon had deported the Nyaungyan back to Calcutta.[109] Shaw reassured the Myotha that the Government of India had known nothing of the Prince's flight, and that the Nyaungyan had been taken back after staying only one night in Rangoon.[110]

However, Shaw was wrong. The escape of the Nyaungyan was a personal project of Lord Lytton and his crony, Sir Ashley Eden, former chief commissioner of Lower Burma and now lieutenant governor of Bengal. Lytton had noted in a March 19 letter to Cranbrook, secretary of state for India, that one way out of the impasse over Burma would be if the Nyaungyan escaped and overthrew Thebaw. However, Lytton thought that such was unlikely, and said he would see to it that Nyaungyan did not 'intrigue' while on Indian soil.[111] Then, Lytton and his friend, Eden, released Nyaungyan. Eden, without Lytton's knowledge, gave the Prince a letter of introduction to Col. Horace A. Browne, commissioner of Pegu.[112]

Browne was initially tempted to help the Prince when he appeared with a letter from Eden. The letter asked Browne to smuggle the Prince into Upper Burma where his supporters were organizing a revolution.[113] Browne was in favour of Thebaw's overthrow, but then Browne concluded that the scheme was another example of Viceroy Lytton's 'preoccupation' with the north-west while 'endangering' the Mandalay Resident.

Browne claimed to be confused that Eden had written directly to him, instead of conveying the request through the Viceroy, the chief commissioner, and then to Browne as was the usual procedure. Browne reported the letter and the presence of the Nyaungyan to Aitchison, "who characterizes the affair as 'a very dirty trick'."[114] Browne expressed surprise that Lytton through his friend Eden would release the Nyaungyan to start a revolution in Upper Burma, and yet refuse to allow the Resident to withdraw. Such, in Browne's view, was like "throwing a torch into a powder magazine."[115]

However, since the Nyaungyan had been sent back, Browne surmised that Thebaw would hear of it, and believe that the Rangoon Government was not intending to overthrow him. Browne concluded that "this little escapade will probably do more good than harm...."[116] In general, Browne was correct. Relations at Mandalay became distinctly warmer, while relations between Rangoon and Calcutta-Simla became decidedly *colder*.[117]

On April 24, it was Shaw's turn to enquire if a rumour was correct, namely that Thebaw had publicly declared in the *Hlutdaw* that he would neither hear nor speak of further accommodation with the British.[118] The Kinwun denied the rumour, and said that his Government desired closer relations with the Indian Government. Similar 'Grand Friendships' were desired with other countries in Europe and elsewhere.[119]

Shaw considered this to be a very conciliatory reply.[120] The Kinwun and the 'reformers' had regained much of their old influence with the King and Queen, because their policy of reconciliation had proved to be correct. Thebaw had realized that the Taingda Atwinwun and others had been mistaken in their advice to make a troop build-up on the Lower Burma frontier. This had become obvious, because the Indian Government had not invaded, had not sent an 'ultimatum', had sent reassuring statements, and, lastly, had returned Prince Nyaungyan to Calcutta.[121]

By desiring 'Grand Friendships' with other foreign nations, the Burmese Government wished to avoid an exclusive, sole relationship with the Indian Government, which "would imply or lead to....dependence...."[122] The Burmese wished to ignore any special influence that the Indian Government had as a consequence of the common frontier between the two countries, and the possession by India of the Irrawaddy, Mandalay's life-line to the Bay. Instead, the Burmese wished to have the same relationship with India that Burma would have had with a distant European state that had no common frontier with Burma.[123]

In addition to a policy of keeping the Indian and London Governments at arms-length, the Mandalay authorities were also seeking ways to show friendship.[124]   Shaw had previously told the ministers that they should show 'friendship' if they wished the Indian troops on the frontier between the two Burmas to be withdrawn.[125]   Consequently, Shaw's relations with the Myotha, who was also the Burmese judge of the Mixed Court, had become cordial.[126]

However, there were limits to such 'friendship'. Shaw had noticed whenever the officials' prerogatives were challenged by the terms of the 1862 and 1867 Treaties that the Kinwun and the 'reformers' allied themselves with their 'rivals', the Taingda and his group.   Unfortunately, it was such prerogatives that British subjects in Upper Burma trade found most galling. On the other hand, in cases of possible political rupture between Upper Burma and India, the 'reformers' would check the Court hotheads.[127]

Shaw attributed most variations in Burmese foreign policy to the day-to-day relationship between the Kinwun's group and the Taingda's group.   As 'reformers' the Kinwun's group did not, usually, threaten the traditional economic and social prerogatives of the more 'traditional' groups.   In fact, the Kinwun in his role as foreign minister was very useful to them whenever their privileges, such as sales of Royal monopolies in 1881, were threatened by *kala* demands that monopolies be halted. This usefulness of the Kinwun explained how the Kinwun and his supporters were able to retain considerable power for so long.[128]

The Kinwun's group, therefore, was best able to tell Shaw that the Mandalay Government had shown 'friendship' towards British subjects in Upper Burma.   As there was no longer any threat to British subjects' lives, property, or to their right to trade in Upper Burma, it was now time for the Indian Government to withdraw their troops from the frontier.[129]

Shaw agreed that some of the troops might be withdrawn. British subjects trading or working in Upper Burma were about as safe, or unsafe, as they had been during Mindon's time. Shaw

noted in his May 22 despatch to Lyall that the Burmese demand
for the withdrawal of Indian troops from the frontier had probably
been initiated by the most parochial of the ministers.[130]   However,
the demand could only have been drafted by the Kinwun and his
group.   Shaw commented that :

> Their recent demands... against us are.. . an attempt to take
> advantage of the feeling against war that has been expressed
> at home...Their care to keep within legal lines, and to imitate
> civilized nations in their remonstrances, seems.. . .to indicate
> that these are partly meant for English or European consump-
> tion and to set up a counter-irritant against our demands.[131]

The Death of Shaw

Shaw died unexpectedly of rheumatic fever on June 15, 1879.
The Burmese seemed to realize that they had lost a true friend.
They staged an elaborate parallel funeral to the Christian one
conducted by the Rev. Colbeck, with elephants, outriders, bands,
and retainers.   Thebaw contributed Rs. 1,000 towards the ceremony,
which was "significant as neglect or discourtesy could have been so
safely and easily shown."[132]

The Myotha, with whom Shaw had spent many an hour of
hard bargaining, came in his capacity as judge of the Mixed Court.
He exclaimed over the outpouring of officials of both nations that
"This is good.   All the people will know how the two governments
love one another.   It.. .should be known everywhere and printed
in all the foreign papers."[133]

It would have been impossible for the Burmese Government
to fully appreciate how great a friend the patient Shaw had been.
Apparently, they also did not fully understand the segment of
opinion in Lower Burma and in India that would no longer be
opposed by Shaw's despatches.   This opinion was expressed perfectly in the Allahabad *Pioneer Mail*, the so-called 'unofficial voice
of the Indian Foreign Department' :

> The Nyoung Yan Prince's advent to Rangoon was inopportune,
> but it will have to be repeated, and I think Sir Ashley Eden
> will have his way.   In the present circumstances of our world-
> wide embroglios I think the policy of annexation pure and
> simple, would be extremely injudicious.   I am confident that
> annexation would be a mistake *now*.[134]

Colonel Browne Becomes the Temporary Resident

As long as Shaw remained at Mandalay, his patience and his personal influence with the Indian Government would have prevented a withdrawal of the Mandalay Resident. His death, however, revived the debate of what to do with the now vacant post. His temporary replacement was Col. Horace Browne, an 'old Burma hand' who was impatient with the 'problem' at Mandalay. Browne's views were fairly close to those of Aitchison. Both men advocated (1) a demand for 'explanations' (ultimatum) from the Mandalay Government, and (2) the withdrawal of the Resident in the hope that Thebaw's Government would collapse.

Aitchison wrote to Lyall on June 19 that Browne would remain temporarily at Mandalay, until the question of withdrawing the Resident was settled. Aitchison suggested that no permanent Resident be appointed, until there was a satisfactory revision of relations with Mandalay.[135] On July 3, Aitchison suggested to Lyall that the Resident be withdrawn. The withdrawal would probably cause Thebaw's Government to collapse. Thebaw's successor would settle the issues between the two Governments, and relations would soon be on a more satisfactory basis.[136]

Aitchison stated that nothing could be worse than the continued series of 'panics' in Upper Burma, which seriously harmed British subjects' administrative, commercial, and political interests. Implied, but not stated, was Aitchison's great worry since February 19, namely that the 'panics' endangered the Residency.[137]

Meanwhile, Browne had arrived in Mandalay on June 22, 1879. He was courteously greeted by the Myotha Wundauk and other high officials,[138] including the reticent Taingda on the following day.[139] It is important to note that Browne *never* received the slightest rudeness or discourtesy from any Burmese official or commoner.[140] His relations with the ministers were *always* correct and proper.

The Kinwun wrote to Browne on June 24 in response to a query by the late Mr. Shaw concerning the health of Prince Nyaungyan's mother and sister. The two ladies were double-chained in a filthy prison-cell, which registered up to 105 degrees F. during the day. The Kinwun claimed that the ladies had been released along with other prisoners during Thebaw's recent Royal Coronation.[141]

However, Browne's information sources refuted the claim.[142] In fact, the Nyaungyan's relatives and five other former queens were let out only once between early-1879 and November 28, 1885.[143] Supayalat held their liven is her hands in order to check the Nyaungyan's ambitions to gain her husband's throne.[144]

In his July 4 report to Aitchison, Browne commented upon the question of withdrawing the Resident. His comments showed that he was rather more pragmatic in his analysis than was Aitchison, whose views on the Resident had not changed since February 19, 1879. Browne wrote that "my departure would have great effect, if junior officer remained....... If whole Residency were withdrawn crisis would be precipitated and withdrawal might be difficult."[145]

Browne complained in a July 10 letter to Lyall that British subjects' interests had been hurt rather than helped by his arrival. The Resident and the Myotha Wundauk, the Burmese judge, composed the Mixed Court, which was to hear cases involving Burmese and British subjects. Unfortunately, the Mixed Court had not met since Browne's arrival, because the Myotha had been temporarily jailed for being 'too friendly' with the late Mr. Shaw.[146] Business was almost at a standstill, and British subjects with a grievance refused to come to Browne, because they knew that by doing so they would only reduce their chances of obtaining redress.[147]

Browne commented again upon the question of withdrawing the Resident. A withdrawal would be the best policy if by doing so a domestic crisis would occur at Mandalay that would result in a settlement of differences between the two countries. In other words the Nyaungyan Prince would probably take power, and accept the Indian Government's views on outstanding issues between the two countries. However, Brown cautioned that Thebaw's Government might well survive the withdrawal. If so, the Indian Government would be "merely......playing into their hands by withdrawing......insignificant as such a position is."[148]

Browne warned that a withdrawal should not take place without a cause strong enough to warrant still stronger measures.[149] The Resident should not be withdrawn as an isolated act in itself, although the post had degenerated into a mere news-collector's job. Browne suggested that to retain a Resident at Browne's salary was a waste of money, as the work could be entrusted to a very junior officer.[150] In a later July 17 letter to Lyall, Browne reiterated the above position.[151]

Aitchison agreed with Browne in a July 24 letter to Lyall. It would not be wise to withdraw the Resident as an isolated act in itself. If on the other hand, the Resident's withdrawal was part of an overall plan to obtain a 'general settlement' of the differences with Burma, it was advisable.[152]

Aitchison had some second thoughts, reverted back to his old positions, and two days later on July 26 wrote another letter to Lyall. Aitchison suggested that no permanent successor to Mr. Shaw be appointed until "we receive....satisfactory assurances of a change of attitude on their part and......a revision of our general relations with them."[153] If a permanent Resident was appointed without such assurances, the rabid Court element would only be encouraged in their anti-*kala* stand.[154]

Browne's views were accepted.[155] Both of Aitchison's proposals were refused, in particular his July 26 proposal that no permanent Resident be appointed without 'satisfactory assurances' from Mandalay. This proposal was essentially Aitchison's *persistent* stand since February 19, 1879 for (1) 'explanations' (ultimatum) from Mandalay and (2) withdrawal of the Resident.[156] These views had been refused repeatedly since February 21, 1879 by Cranbrook, and also by the Indian Government after April 1, 1879.[157]

Browne's plea for a 'news-collector', instead of a Resident, was accepted.[158] Browne returned from Mandalay on August 29 leaving the Residency in the capable hands of H. L. St. Barbe, the former commercial agent at Bhamo.[159] The Indian Government did not admit it, but they had in essence established St. Barbe as the commercial agent at Mandalay.

The Indian Government had temporarily de-emphasized the political paramountcy that the term 'Resident' had usually implied, and which had so worried the Burmese Government since 1826. The Indian Government was able to do this, because the French in Tongkin were as yet no real 'threat' to India's eastern frontier or to British subjects' interests in Upper Burma, which were mostly commercial.

Lytton could now return his attention to the main issue in India's foreign relations. This was the 'Russian Threat' to India's northwest frontier, which had been somewhat reduced by the Indian occupation of Afghanistan. The Treaty of Gandamak ending the Second Afghan War had been signed on May 26, 1879; and in July Sir Louis Cavagnari was installed as the new British Resident at Kabul.

Browne's Report and the Kabul Massacre

On September 5, after talking with Aitchison, Browne filed his report. It was a routine summary of previous views despatched during his two months as temporary Resident. The letter, like several previous ones, warned that the Residency was in danger ; and that the members were subjected to a series of petty 'harassments' as was Shaw before him.

First of all, Browne wrote that several plots for the burning of the Residency and murder of the inhabitants had been advanced during Shaw's time, and once while Browne was at Mandalay. The Kinwun's group was said to have halted such plots from execution.[160] The Myotha Wundauk, the Burmese judge of the Mixed Court, had stated that no wall could be built around the proposed new Residency. Browne wrote that "they intend that the new Residency shall be as defenceless as the present one."[161]

Browne also commented that there were many rumours afloat of conspiracies to put the Nyaungyan Prince on the throne. Browne requested that the Nyaungyan not be allowed to leave Calcutta until the Resident had left Mandalay.[162] The Nyaungyan's second arrival in Lower Burma "would certainly cause King Thebaw to 'clear away' the British Residency."[163]

Browne made one other statement in his September 5 report that could have been considered 'alarmist'. He stated that if Thebaw was not overthrown in the crisis that might follow the downgrading of the Residency to a 'news-collectorship', still worse events would happen. The Lower Burma trade to Upper Burma would be gradually strangled by disorders and blatant Burmese disregard of the 1862 and 1867 Treaties.[164]

The strangulation of the export trade to Upper Burma would cause a drop in the customs revenue of Lower Burma. More Indian troops would have to be posted on the frontier between the two Burmas to protect British subjects' rights, lives, and property in Upper Burma. The end result would be "the certainty of our being ultimately compelled to adopt those measures which, if adopted now, might avert all this loss."[165]

There was nothing in Browne's September 5 despatch that had not been said or implied by either he or Aitchison since February 19. However, on September 3, Sir Louis Cavagnari, the British Resident at Kabul, and his staff were murdered by an Afghan mob. This caused the resumption of the Second Afghan War. The news reached Rangoon by telegraph on September 7.[166]

On September 8, the Indian Government telegraphed to Aitchison that he had full discretion to withdraw St. Barbe at any time. St. Barbe was immediately notified that he could withdraw from Mandalay at any time for any reason.[167] Such was a complete about-face from Lyall's August 12 telegram to Browne accepting his 'news-collector' proposal. Browne's reaction to the about-face was a comment in his Diary that "This is the outcome of the Kabul scare, which has done for us in a day what we have been vainly trying to get done for the best part of a year."[168]

On September 19, Lytton received Browne's routine demi-official report of September 5. The Viceroy found it "perfectly inexplicable."[169] He made a number of angry accusations against Browne in a September 21 letter to Cranbrook. Lytton claimed that Browne had suddenly discovered on September 5 that the Residency was in grave danger of attack. Yet, Browne's previous letters had claimed that the Residency, although indefensible, was not in any immediate danger, and that it would be safe in the hands of St. Barbe, a junior officer.[170]

Browne's letters had never made such statements. For example, Browne's June 30 letter to Lyall admitted that he did not know if the Residency was in danger. He hoped that it was not, however, it was almost impossible to get accurate information about the activities of the various groups at Court, or of their day-to-day feelings towards the Residency. However, "Should there be any successful intrigue against....[the Kinwun], the Residency would be in great danger."[171]

Browne's July 7 letter to Aitchison warned that if a *coup* took away the Kinwun's control of the army, "we should have to retreat to our ships....the difficulty would be to reach the ship. There is no doubt, however, that we should have to attempt it, for here we are like so many rats in a trap."[172]

Among later letters, Browne's August 16 letter to Lyall was most explicit. Browne compared the Court to a bunch of beasts in a menagerie. One never knew which beast would attack—or when.

If the Kinwun lost his office, "the occupants of the British Residency would be in a very considerable danger."[173] Browne went on in even more detail :

the situation appears to be getting gradually more precarious in consequence of the increasing intemperance of the King, which renders him even more capricious than before........ If anything is done, it will be done suddenly and without any warning either to ourselves or to the older ministers, who would oppose anything of the kind.[174]

The behaviour of the Burmans in the capital all more or less intimately connected with the Palace, is not a bad index of the temper of the ruling powers; and recently, *although I myself have never experienced any rudeness,* Mr. St. Barbe and others complain that they cannot go outside the Residency, although well attended, without being grossly insulted....[175]

In summary, most of Browne's letters had warned or implied that the Residency was in some danger ; and that the members were subjected to a series of petty 'harassments' as was Shaw before him.[176] Browne had also stated that the Resident's task could be performed by a 'news collector', *i.e.* a junior officer. Browne had written in the context of administrative efficiency, and not in the context which Lytton tried to place upon it. In short, Lytton was wrong when he claimed that Browne had not given any warnings prior to September 5 that the Residency and is wanger.[177]

Lytton proceeded in his September 21 complaint to Cranbrook that it had been upon Browne's own advice that he had been allowed to leave Mandalay. Once safe at Rangoon Browne wrote his September 5 demi-official letter, which required fifteen days to reach its destination. Lytton questioned the propriety of Browne's conduct as he had only then warned that the lives of the officers left behind in Mandalay were in grave danger. They were dependent upon the precarious influence of one minister, the Kinwun, whose fall would probably be the signal for a murderous assault upon the Residency.[178] Lytton wondered why Browne had left when his colleagues were in danger, and then reported the danger by the slowest form of official correspondence.

Many official letters of the period were despatched in demi-official form. Lyall's reprimand to Browne was demi-official in form, and was forwarded through Aitchison. The reprimand did not reach Browne until October 18. Lytton was certainly more excited on September 19 to receive Browne's report than Browne had been when he mailed it on September 5. Therefore, one wonders why Lyall's reprimand to Browne was not sent in the form of a telegram?

Furthermore, Browne never stated in his September 5 letter that the Kinwun's influence was all that was keeping a mob from assaulting the Residency. Browne's June 30, July 7, and August 16 letters cited above did make such a statement. Browne's August 16 despatch was received on September 4 within hours of the receipt of the first news of the Kabul Massacre. It is obvious that Lytton confused Browne's August 16 and September 5 despatches in the excitement, or else Lytton deliberately confused the despatches so as to better protect his government from charges of 'negligence' at Mandalay.[179]

Lytton made further accusations in his September 21 complaint to Cranbrook concerning Browne's conduct.[180] Browne had claimed in his September 5 letter that it was unfair and even dangerous to place the responsibility upon the Resident to determine whether he would withdraw from Mandalay. Browne had stated that no man with any spirit would have left the Residency until it was actually under attack for fear of being branded a coward throughout his official career.[181]

Lytton refuted this. He claimed that the power to withdraw the Resident was held by Aitchison as senior officer in Lower Burma.[182] However, Lytton was somewhat misleading. Aitchison, like most Indian officials, usually acted according to the advice of the official closest to the scene. So, despite Lytton's wordage, the Resident still had to decide whether he would advise his own removal.

Lytton proceeded to denigrate Aitchison for several sentences, and claimed that "the conduct of the Chief Commissioner is extremely aggravating."[183] Then, Lytton linked Aitchison and Browne together:

My own impression is that neither [official]. . . has any good ground for . . . serious alarm .... But . . . panic-struck by the news from Kabul, and the gossip at Rangoon, they have failed to realise the . . . disloyal character of the communication made . . . with the object of forcing the hand of a Government, whose instructions Mr. Aitchison appears to have persistently misunderstood and resented. But, . . . I have (after what happened at Kabul) felt bound to lose no time in authorising the immediate withdrawal of . . . our Residency. . . Notwithstanding *the* [September 5] *report, which appears to have been simultaneously received by the editor of the Calcutta Daily News,*. . . I do not. . . apprehend any. . . injury to. . . [Residency] members [other than from possible] clumsiness. . . in the steps taken by Mr. Aitchison for their immediate withdrawal. . .[184]

Lytton knew, of course, that no news about the September 3 Kabul Massacre could have reached Rangoon before Browne despatched his report on September 5. In fact, the news about Kabul reached Rangoon on September 7. So, when Lytton claimed that Browne and Aitchison were overcome with the news from Kabul, he was apparently describing his own mental condition. Lytton referred to their actions as 'disloyal', because the editor of the Calcutta *Daily News* had apparently also received a copy of Browne's September 5 letter. The fear haunted Lytton that certain persons at Rangoon, who disagreed with his and Lyall's policies, might try again to place official and most embarrassing correspondence into the public prints. He wrote:

Although but for that letter, I should not have withdrawn the Residency so soon, still I have always contemplated its withdrawal, a few months hence, as a measure which might be inevitable ; and would, in any case, be expedient. And, *although I cannot but resent the manner in which I think Mr. Aitchison has been trying to force my hand. . .* I do not think we shall have any cause to regret the result, if the withdrawal of the Residency is safely effected. . .[185]

A search through Lytton's correspondence during 1879 does not reveal any such projected withdrawal of the Residency in a few months time. So one can conclude that Lytton hastily withdrew the Mandalay Residency when he was faced with the threat of Browne's September 5 letter becoming public, and before a 'Mandalay Massacre' occurred to further embarrass the Conservatives.[186]

In historical perspective, it was Lytton and not Aitchison or Browne who was correct. Lytton knew that he could ignore the eastern frontier problem only so long as there was an agent at Mandalay to negotiate all grievances. Lytton knew that to withdraw the agent was a mistake, despite the disagreement of both

Browne and Aitchison. However, Lytton was out-maneuvered, and he never had a chance after October 6, 1879 to ignore the eastern frontier problem in his own particular and workable fashion.[187]

The Withdrawal of St. Barbe

St. Barbe had an uneventful tenure as agent at Mandalay before leaving under orders on October 6, 1879. He was not in favour of withdrawing the Residency, although he did want to get the other Residency members out of 'danger'. St. Barbe was not much concerned about himself, because he suffered from haemorrhoids, lumbago, and frequent infections of the eyes.[188]

However, there was another gentleman who did set great value on his life. When Browne had left Mandalay, he sent the Kinwun a notification in advance. However, Browne neglected to give a date for his departure.[189] Lytton quoted from a note allegedly written by St. Barbe that:

Colonel Horace Browne, on quitting Mandalay, solemnly took leave of us all, with an air as tragic as if we were standing on the hangman's drop. He was himself afraid of being assassinated before he got away, and he slipped out of Mandalay, like an escaping prisoner, without letting any one know the day, or hour, of his departure.[190]

Lytton quoted St. Barbe as believing that the Residency would probably not be attacked "if it does not invite attack...."[191] Lytton wrote that he had gained great comfort from St. Barbe's alleged note, and that it had removed every doubt from Lytton's mind concerning his order to withdraw the Residency.[192]

Considering that Lytton was the man who did not want to remove the Residency, and had had his hand forced by Aitchison, Browne, and the news from Kabul, such was a most supple use of 'reverse-English'. But Lytton was a poet, and proficiency with words was his forte.

St. Barbe, meanwhile, was the careful diplomat and appeared to have much more in common with his former mentor, Mr. Shaw, than with Lytton, Aitchison or Browne. St. Barbe reported that along with the latest Palace executions,[193] there was also a coalition between Supayalat, her mother, and Thebaw's mother. This coalition acted to restrain the Court from extreme acts that might have caused the Indian Government to invade.[194]   St. Barbe's theory was strengthened at 3 a.m., September 9, when Supayalat gave birth to a boy.[195]

Supayalat's position as Chief Queen was now secure with a son as Heir to the throne, and with most of her rivals dead.   It was logical that in the future she would become more cautious and more conciliatory.   However, on September 11 the news of the Kabul Massacre reached Mandalay.   Thebaw enquired about the number of Europeans killed.   One thousand was the figure stated to him, and he gave orders that a census should be taken of the approximately 100 *kalas* living in Mandalay.[196]

St. Barbe telegraphed Aitchison that he did not expect any trouble so long as the Indian Government maintained its present attitude of 'reserve'.[197]   One company that St. Barbe thought was not showing 'reserve' was the IFC.   The firm had continued since March 1879 to keep their steamer-fires banked while at Mandalay.[198]   In the final analysis, St. Barbe thought that the safety of the Residency would depend greatly upon the Rangoon press, whose sensational reports in April 1879 had "very nearly proved fatal to the Residency party."[199]

But the Rangoon papers and the Kabul Massacre were ignored amidst the celebrations over the birth of the new Heir.   They coincided with the end of 'Buddhist Lent', and the opening of still *another* lottery office in Mandalay.[200]   On the same day (September 11) that the news of the Kabul Massacre reached Mandalay, St. Barbe was told by Burmese officials that orders had been issued to prevent any further attacks upon Residency personnel.   One recent attack had been that upon Dr. Ferris, the Residency surgeon, as he was returning from saving a Burmese woman's life.[201]

The 'thaw' in relations seemed to continue over the next few weeks, even in two cases where, apparently, the Burmese had a right to arrest without consulting any Indian Government authority.[202]   The Kinwun requested that a former Burmese official charged with swindling, and who had absconded on board the *Talifu* IFC steamer, be delivered up to Burmese authorities.   St. Barbe considered the request to be quite an unusual act of courtesy.   The Burmese Government certainly had the right to arrest its own subjects within Burmese territory upon presenting a proper warrant to the steamer authorities.[203]

Again, on October 3, just three days before St. Barbe left

Mandalay, the Kinwun again wrote and stated that a former King's page was attempting to escape on board the *Yunnan*. The page and his family were delivered up, and he was executed.[204]   After October 6 and the withdrawal of the Residency from Mandalay,[205] it became much harder for both Governments to show similar little signs of courtesy and friendship to each other.

The Consequences of the Withdrawal : a Systems Model

The withdrawal of the Resident caused the Kinwun to lose some of his usefulness and influence with the more 'traditional' groups.   Their prerogatives were not now so obviously threatened by the presence in Mandalay of the *kala* Resident.   In the absence of the Resident there was a pronounced 'rivalry' between the Kinwun and the Taingda.   However, this 'rivalry' was mostly for local power and prerogatives.   Virtually all groups at Mandalay closed ranks against the foreigners when a threat came from that quarter.

The Kinwun was not 'pro-British', and the Taingda was never 'pro-French'.   The views of both ministers as concerned the British, the French, and foreign policy were largely determined by which power or policy was thought to be of more help in gaining and retaining local power.

The Kinwun almost always advocated a conciliatory policy towards the Indian Government.   He was more aware than the others of the enormous power of the British having been to England and Europe twice as roving Ambassador in the early 1870's. Also, he was the frequent recipient of 'gifts' from various British subjects seeking commercial privileges at Mandalay.

The Taingda and the others in order to get their share of 'gifts', and to resist the Kinwun's influence at Court, would usually advocate resistance to the *kala* demands.   One way of showing resistance was to advocate closer ties with the French with their expanding empire to the east in Tongkin, Annam, Cochin China and Cambodia.

Such resistance to the *kala* demands had enormous nuisance value.   It assured the Taingda's group of large 'gifts' from British subjects in business, who were anxious to placate the two great ministers at Mandalay.   Likewise, the Kinwun had a similar nuisance value *vis-a-vis* French subjects in business, which assured him of additional 'gifts' from that quarter.

Even if the Taingda temporarily gained the upper-hand, he had to call upon the Kinwun to help him to maintain his privileges whenever there was a challenge from the *kalas*. If the Resident had remained after October 6, 1879, or if the Indian Government had made steady demands, it would probably have gained most of them. But the Indian Government made only sporadic demands after October 1879, and the threat to the 'traditional' groups was not so great or so persistent as it had been with a Resident at Mandalay.

With the removal of the steady Indian Government pressure against Mandalay, many of the reforms proposed by the Kinwun and the 'reformers' were ignored or abandoned. Consequently, the Kinwun and his group had less power than they would have had, had the Indian Government been steady in its demands. Without such British pressure, which the Kinwun could claim was a 'greater menace' to Mandalay than could be counter-balanced by the French, the Kinwun was unable to stop the Taingda and his late-1885 drive for total local power.

The Indian Government invaded Upper Burma in November 1885, in order to counteract the supposed influx of French influence under Taingda. This assertion of total power would probably never have been necessary had the British retained the Resident at Mandalay to exert day-to-day steady demands, and also explanations.

To summarize, the withdrawal of the Resident caused the Kinwun and his 'reformers' to lose some of their usefulness and influence with the more 'traditional' groups. Their prerogatives were not now so obviously threatened. Many of the reformers' proposals for change were abandoned as not being necessary in the absence of the Resident. Therefore, many grievances between the two countries remained unsettled, such as the "Shoe Question", alleged Burmese violations of the 1862 and 1867 Treaties, and the 'French Threat' to Upper Burma and to India's eastern frontier. A Third Burmese War was made almost inevitable by the unnecessary withdrawal of the Resident.

FOOTNOTES

[1] Grattan Geary, *Burma After the Conquest,* p. 125.

[2] In 1875 Mindon secretly appointed the Mekhara Prince as his heir; however, the secret document soon became public knowledge. There was such a scream of protest from the mothers and wives of the princes who had been passed over that Mindon hastily withdrew the nomination. "It is said that he made a vow at the time that nothing would ever induce him to take such a step again...." *See*: K. W. No. 1, Rivers Thompson to A. C. Lyall, September 5, 1878; in Foreign, Secret, October 1878, Nos. 449-489, pp. 3-6 (NAI).

[3] Bisheshwar Prasad, *The Foundations of India's Foreign Policy, 1860-1882,* Delhi, 1967, pp. 65-82. *Also*: Bisheshwar Prasad, *Our Foreign Policy Legacy,* New Delhi, 1965, pp. 17-18, 20, 22, 81-82.

[4] *Ibid.*

[5] No. 463, Shaw to Lyall, September 4, 1878; in Nos. 449-489.

[6] *Ibid.*

[7] J. George Scott and J. P. Hardiman, *Gazetteer of Upper Burma and the Shan States,* Vol. 1, Part 1, Rangoon, 1900, pp. 29, 78-84.

[8] *Ibid. See* also: W. K. Baretto, *King Mindon,* Rangoon, 1935, pp. 105-114.

[0] *Ibid.* The proposed reforms of the Magwe, the Kinwun, and their collaborator, Dr. Clement Williams, the former British Political agent at Mandalay from 1861-1865, are discussed in Appendix G.

[10] *Ibid.*

[11] On July 24, 1878, Shaw wrote: "The King has no son by his Chief Queen, only daughters......there are many sons by other wives, [but]....only one is of royal blood on both sides, his mother being a [Shan] princess of the royal [Alaungpaya] family. This is the Thibo Mengtha.... It was proposed to marry him to one of the daughters of the present Chief Queen (to his half sister therefore). This custom prevails in the royal family, where the eldest daughter of a King is generally kept unmarried in order to marry the future king, whoever he may be. The proposal [in July 1878]....to provide a wife for the Thibo Prince led to the belief that it was intended to proclaim him heir-apparent (as it probably was). Many warning placards, whose authors could not be traced, were hung up about the palace, protesting against the measure; and the marriage was....held in abeyance." No. 449, Shaw to Lyall, July 24, 1878; in Nos. 449-489.

[12] Paul J. Bennett, *Conference Under........*pp. 72-74.

[13] *Ibid.* Bennett's excellent study does not imply some sort of a tacit agreement between the two *wungyis* for the sake of national unity. I assume such an agreement because of their friendship going back to the Kinwun's rapid rise to the highest posts in the Kingdom after the 1866 Rebellion.

[14] *Ibid.*

[15] J. George Scott and J. P. Hardiman, *Gazetteer....,* pp. 78-84.

[16] *Ibid. (See also:* No. 471, Mandalay Confidential Diary, September 11-13, 1878, in Nos. 449-489.)

[17] *Ibid. See also :* Nos. 63, 68, 74, MCD, September 14-October 2, 1878; in Foreign, Secret, March 1879, Nos. 60-111 (NAI).

[18-19] *Ibid.* (*See also:* Paul J. Bennett, *Conference Under....*pp. 74-76.)

[20] *Ibid.* (*Also see:* E. C. V. Foucar, *They Reigned at Mandalay,* London, 1946, pp. 58-64. Shway Yoe (J. G. Scott), *The Burman; His Life and Notions,* London, 1896, pp. 447-449. Philippe Preschez, "Les Relations Franco-Burmese aux XVIII et XIX Siecles," (Paris) *France-Asie*, Vol. XXI, No. 3 (189-190), 1967, pp. 340-343.)

[21] *Ibid.*

[22] James Alfred Colbeck, *Letters From Mandalay,* Knaresborough, 1892, pp. 4-7.

[23] Nos. 63, 74, September 14-18, September 22-October 2, 1878 ; in Nos. 60-111.

[24] *Ibid.*

[25] No. 78, Shaw to Lyall, October 5, 1878 ; in Nos. 60-111.

[26] Enclosure 1 in No. 5, Telegram from Shaw to Lyall, November 5, 1878; in C. 4614, Corr. Since the Accession of King Thebaw, p. 5 (NAI).

[27] Enclosure 1 in No. 4, Telegram from Shaw to Lyall, November 5, 1878 ; in C. 4614, p. 5.

[28] No. 170, MCD, November 9, 1878; in Foreign, Secret, March 1879, Nos. 158-187 (NAI).

[29] Ma Kyan, "King Mindon's Councillors," *JBRS*, Vol. XLIV, June 1961, Part 1, pp. 58-59. The Magwe Mingyi was known as the Shwepyi Atwinwun before his brief promotion to *mingyi (wungyi)* from November 1878-January 1879.

[30] *Ibid.* "The King [Mindon]... heard that the Atwinwun used to say publicly that he saw no harm in drinking beer as it was nothing... When asked by the King, he repeated the statement which made the King so angry that he was dismissed from office... for a long time."

[31] No. 170, MCD, November 9, 1878 ; in Nos. 158-187.

[32] No. 178, MCD, November 11, 1878; in Nos. 158-187.

[33] James Alfred Colbeck, *Letters From Mandalay,* pp. 24-25.

[34] No. 3, Indian Foreign Dept. to Cranbrook, October 17, 1878; in C. 4614, pp. 3-4.

[35] *See :* Appendix H entitled The "Shoe Question" and the 'Meru-centric' Tradition.

[36] No. 3; in C. 4614, pp. 3-4.

[37] *Ibid.*

[38] No. 81, MCD, October 7, 1878; in Nos. 60-111.

[39] No. 159, MCD, October 14, 1878; in Nos. 158-187.

[40] *Ibid.*

[41] No. 285, MCD, January 13, 1879; in Foreign, Secret, July 1879, Nos. 248-471 (NAI).

[42-43] *Ibid.*

[44] A comment on the term *Kala* (or *Kula*). According to A. Anandeswaran, it "literally means 'one who has come from [India] across the sea.' Innocuous enough : but the overtones of derision and ridicule concentrated in the epithet must be felt to be believed." A. Anandeswaran, "Mere Talk of Indian Unity Will Not Help," (Delhi) *The Sunday Standard*, March 2, 1969, p. 6.

[45] No. 290, Kinwun to Shaw, January 24, 1879; in Nos. 248-471.

[46] No. 298, MCD, February 7, 1879; in Nos, 248-471.

[47] *Ibid.*

[48] No. 295, MCD, February 14, 1879; in Nos. 248-471.

[49-50] *Ibid.*

[51-52] *Ibid.* In 1831, one of the Burmese ministers made an interesting comparison between Burmese and English customs. The minister exclaimed to Major Henry Burney, the British Resident, that: "Your and our customs are so completely opposite in so many points. You write on white, we on black paper. You stand up, we sit down; you uncover your head, we our feet in token of respect." Walter S. Desai, *The British Residency........,* p. 129.

[53] No. 273, MCD, December 24-29, 1878; in Nos. 248-471. (*See also :* J. George Scott and J. P. Hardiman, *Gazetteer........,* pp. 86-87.)

[54] *Ibid.*

[55-58] *Ibid.* For a discussion of the proposed reforms of the 'reform' party, *see* Appendix G.

[59] *Ibid. Also see:* Ma Kyan, "King Mindon's Councillors," pp 58-59.

[60] *Ibid See also:* Nos. 287, 289, MCD, January 17-26, 1879; in Nos. 248-471. *Lastly:* J. George Scott and J. P. Hardiman, *Gazetteer........,* p. 84.

[61] No. 352, Browne to Lyall, August 5, 1879 ; in Foreign, Secret, September 1879, Nos. 351-356 (NAI). The most accurate and thorough list of the Royal Family of Upper Burma.

[62] The news of the Isandhlwana disaster reached London on February 11-12, 1879. *See:* Gen Horace A. Browne, *Reminiscences of the Court of Mandalay*, Woking, 1907, pp. 152-153. Browne wrote in his diary that his friend, Dr. Clement Williams, the former British agent at Mandalay from 1861-1865, believed "that the immediate cause of the massacres last month was our recent disaster in South Africa. This is a queer concatenation of events; but no one is better informed than Dr. Williams. The news of our defeat encouraged Thibaw in his bellicose designs against us, but before putting them into execution, he judged it prudent to clear his own house of all potential enemies. Hence the slaughter."

[63] H Fielding-Hall. *Thibaw's Queen*, London, 1899, pp. 48, 54-58. *Also see:* Grattan Geary, *Burma After the Conquest*, pp. 209-211.

[64] It becomes easier to understand why the Kinwun had the popular nickname of *Tamat Yay-poolah Sha Hlweh-de-lu*, which meant "The man who swerves his tongue to one side when the hot congi water flows into his mouth." F. T. Jesse, *The Lacquer Lady*, New York, 1930, p. 197.

[65] F. T Jesse, *The Story of Burma*, London, 1946, pp. 57-58. *Also:* F. T. Jesse, *The Lacquer Lady*, pp. 175-190. These volumes are of historical value, because they are in part based upon Jesse's conversations with Mattie Calogreedy Antram, who had been the confidant of Queen Supayalat from 1878-1885.

[66] *Ibid.*

[67] No. 339, MCD, February 19, 1879; in Nos. 248-471. When the rotting bodies bloated and swelled with gas, the level of the ground rose. Ele-

phants were brought in to trample the ground flat again.

68 Enclosure 7 in No. 12, MCD, February 20, 1879; in C. 4614, pp. 21-22. Please *also see* J. G. Scott and J. P. Hardiman, *Gazetteer of Upper Burma...*, p. 85; *also*, F. T. Jesse, *The Lacquer Lady*, p. 184; and, Shway Yoe, *The Burman....*, pp. 449-453.

69 No. 339, MCD, February 19, 1879; in Nos. 248-471.

70 Grattan Geary, *Burma After the Conquest*, pp. 209-211.

71 No. 339, MCD, February 19, 1879; in Nos. 248-471.

72 Grattan Geary, *Burma After the Conquest*, pp. 209-211.

73 No. 339, MCD, February 22, 1879; in Nos. 248-471. *Also see:* E. C. V. Foucar, *They Reigned At Mandalay*, pp. 74-78.

74 No. 339, MCD, February 19, 1879; in Nos. 248-471.

75 Shway Yoe, *The Burman...*, pp. 449-453. *Also see:* Grattan Geary, *Burma After the Conquest*, pp. 209-211, 326.

76 *Ibid.* Since 1760, there had been killings or revolts at the start of every reign, and much the same had occurred at the start of every reign throughout Burmese history. Prof. G. E. Harvey stated that the 1879 Massacre "probably differed from its forerunners neither in extent nor horror but only in taking place in the full light of modern publicity." G. E. Harvey, *History of Burma*, p. 338. Harvey lists other massacres of the kinsmen on pp. 75, 80, 117, 120, 145, 201, and 265.

77 G. E. Harvey, *Outline of Burmese History*, p. 181. About eighty males and females were murdered. *See also:* Foreign, Secret, September 1879, Nos. 351-356 (NAI). Col. Horace A. Browne, temporary Resident at Mandalay from June-August 1879, stated that one queen, fourteen sons, and four daughters of the late King Mindon were murdered in the Massacre. "The numerous other victims consisted of the sons' wives and families, of the descendants of the late Crown Prince [assassinated in 1866 by the Myngun Prince], and of other more remote connections of the Royal Family."

78 No. 187, Telegram from Aitchison to Lyall, February 19, 1879; in Foreign, Political-A, March 1879, Nos. 194-225 (NAI).

79-80 *Ibid.* For the September 1878 beginnings of the quarrel between Aitchison and Lyall concerning Burma *see:* K. W's. 1-10; in Nos. 449-489.

81 No. 207, Telegram from Cranbrook to Lytton, February 21, 1879; in Nos. 194-225.

82 Enclosure 8 in No. 12, Kinwun to Shaw, February 20, 1879; in C. 4614, p. 22.

83 No. 215, Telegram from Shaw to Lyall, February 23, 1879; in Nos. 194-225.

84 No. 14, Cranbrook to Lytton, February 23, 1879; in Mss. Eur. 218, Lytton Papers, 516/4, pp. 72-73 (IOL).

85 Lytton to Marquis of Salisbury, October 25, 1876; in Lytton Papers, 518/1, p. 563. Lytton stated "It is a great pity we did not annex it [Upper Burma] before annexation became unpopular." Lytton stated in a March 8, 1879 letter to Aitchison that "few things would better please me than a really good pretext... for annexing a large slice of Upper Burma." Lytton's reasons were that annexation would put an end to the constant border disturbances, and of course improve trade and revenue. The eastern frontier

of India would again become quiet. Lytton to Aitchison, March 8, 1879; in Lytton Papers, 518/4, pp. 176-177.

[86] Lytton to Sir James Stephen, January 28, 1878; in Lytton Papers, 518/3, pp. 76-77. Lytton stated that by giving Lower Burma back to an independent Upper Burma "we shall do penance for one act of spoliation...." Also, such a cession would reaffirm the "sacred principle of nationalities," and would show that Great Britain recognized its obligations to restore independence and territories "as soon as we have civilized it...." The precedent for such a cession was Great Britain's ceding of the Ionian Islands to Greece. Most important, the Indian Government would be rid of "a very troublesome addition to our frontier questions."

[87] Lytton to Cranbrook, February 28, 1879; in Lytton Papers, 518/4, pp. 154-158.

[88] Adrian William Preston, *British Military Policy and the Defense of India... During the Russian Crisis, 1876-1880*, Ph.D. thesis, Un. of London, 1966. A good study of the military steps taken to keep the 'Russian Threat' away from India's northwest.

[89-90] No. 11, Lytton to Cranbrook, March 7, 1879; in C. 4614, p. 16. The Mixed Court was composed of the British Resident and the Burmese Judge appointed by the Mandalay Government. Cases concerning Burmese and British subjects were tried by this Court. *See* the Mixed Court Rules in Appendix C.

[91] (1) No. 20, Cranbrook to Lytton, March 10, 1879; in Lytton Papers, 516/4, p. 95. (2) No. 22, Cranbrook to Lytton, March 16, 1879; in Lytton Papers, 516/4, p. 105. (3) No. 24, Cranbrook to Lytton, March 24, 1879; in Lytton Papers, 516/4, p. 110b. *Lastly :* (4) No. 26, Cranbrook to Lytton, March 31, 1879; in Lytton Papers, 516/4, pp. 115-115b.

[92] No. 5 (A), Telegram from Cranbrook to Lytton, April 1, 1879; in Foreign, Secret, August 1879, Nos. 5(A) to 5(L) (NAI).

[93] No. 5(B), Telegram from Lytton to Cranbrook, April 2, 1879; in Nos. 5(A) to 5(L).

[94] No. 13, Cranbrook to Lytton, April 3, 1879; in C. 4614, p. 23.

[95] *For example:* on March 26 Lytton wrote, "I am afraid that Aitchison is going off his head. Mr. Shaw's telegrams do not seem....to justify [Aitchison's]....panic....Nothing....leads me to suppose that the King.. will....pick a quarrel with us." (Lytton to Cranbrook, March 26, 1879 ; in Lytton Papers, 518/4, p. 214). On March 28, Lytton wrote to Sir Alexander Arbuthnot, president of the India Council, that "Aitchison continues to write very alarmist letters...." (Lytton to Arbuthnot, March 28, 1879 ; in Lytton Papers, 518/4, pp. 224-225).
On April 3 Lytton wrote to Cranbrook that "The Chief Commissioner's letter appears to me very wild, but....the Resident keeps his head cool." (Lytton to Cranbrook, April 3, 1879 ; in Lytton Papers, 518/4, pp. 232-233). On April 21, Lytton wrote to E. Stanhope that Shaw was the "only one.... who seems to be keeping his head cool." (Lytton to Stanhope, April 21, 1879 ; in Lytton Papers, 518/4, pp. 309-310). On the same day, April 21, Lytton wrote to Cranbrook and stated that there was "no cause for serious

alarm if only Mr. Aitchison will keep quiet, and cease to fidget either his sword or his bible." (Lytton to Cranbrook, April 21, 1879 ; in HA 43/T501, Cranbrook Papers/51 (IpRO).

Upon Shaw's death on June 15, Lytton wrote to Cranbrook that Shaw was "a great loss to us at this moment for both King Thibaw and Aitchison seem to be losing their heads." (Lytton to Cranbrook, June 16, 1879; in Lytton Papers, 518/4, p. 476). In a final parting shot in 1880 at Aitchison's head, which Lytton seemed particularly concerned about, he wrote that Aitchison's "head is too wooden...." (Lytton to Ripon, June 8, 1880; in Lytton Papers, 518/6, pp. 364-365).

96 *For example, see* : Enclosure 17 in No. 17, Aitchison's Secretary to Lyall, May 22, 1879; in C. 4614, pp. 33-34. *Also:* Aitchison to Lyall, July 3, 1879; in Mss. Eur. F. 132, Sir Alfred Comyn Lyall Papers/20 (IOL).

97 Enclosure 6 in No. 17, Lyall to Aitchison, July 14, 1879; in C. 4614, pp. 37-40. Among similar despatches *see :* Lyall to Aitchison, April 14, 1879; in Lyall Papers/19. *Also :* Lyall to Aitchison, April 26, 1879; in Lyall Papers/19.

98 No. 316, Telegram from Aitchison to Lyall, March 7, 1879; in Nos. 248-471.

99 No. 317, Telegram from Lyall to Aitchison, March 7, 1879; in Nos. 248-471.

100 No. 320, Telegram from Lyall to Shaw, March 8, 1879; in Nos. 248-471.

101 Lyall's March 8 reply aroused the ire of Col. Horace A. Browne, who succeeded Shaw at Mandalay from June-August 1879. Browne wrote in his Diary for March 8, 1879 that "The Viceroy has at last been slightly moved ....'he leaves it to Shaw's discretion to withdraw if....necessary for his personal safety.' ....It throws all the responsibility on Shaw's shoulders ....and he will probably think it his duty to stick to his post until some overt.... hostility occurs, when it may be too late.

The Viceroy persists....'on political grounds, the withdrawal of the Resident is not desirable.' ....these 'political grounds'....may be connected either with Afghanistan or with home politics; most probably the latter. So the safety of the Resident is to be jeopardized for the sake of a few votes in Parliament." Gen. Horace A. Browne, *Reminiscences of..Mandalay,* p. 151.

102 No. 406, Kinwun to Shaw, March 25, 1879; in Nos. 248-471.

103 No. 409, MCD, March 28, 1879; in Nos. 248-471.

104 *Ibid.*

105 No. 410, Shaw to Kinwun, March 29, 1879; in Nos. 248-471.

106 *Ibid.*

107 No. 417, MCD, April 2, 1879; in 248-471.

108 No. 417, MCD, April 4, 1879; in No. 248-471.

109-110 *Ibid.*

111 Lytton to Cranbrook, March 19, 1879; in Cranbrook Papers/78.

112 Lytton to Eden, April 5, 1879; in Lytton Papers, 518/4. *See also:* Eden to Lytton, April 9, 1879; in Lytton Papers, 519/10.

113-16 Gen. Horace A. Browne, *Reminiscences of....Mandalay,* pp. 153-154.

117 Aitchison to Lyall, April 6, 1879; in Lyall Papers/19 (IOL). *Also:* Lyall to

Aitchison, April 14, 1879; in Lyall Papers/19.

[118] No. 435, Shaw to Kinwun, April 24, 1879; in Nos. 248-471.

[119] No. 436, Kinwun to Shaw, April 26, 1879; in Nos. 248-471.

[120] No. 434, MCD, April 26, 1879; in Nos. 248-471.

[121] K. W. No. 2, Shaw to Lyall, April 27, 1879; in Foreign, Secret, August 1879, Nos. 53-63A, p. 1 (NAI).

[122] K. W. No. 2, Shaw to Lyall, May 22, 1879; in Nos. 53-63A, pp. 6-7.

[123] *Ibid.*

[124] K. W. No. 2, Shaw to Lyall, April 27, 1879; in Nos. 53-63A, p. 1.

[125] K. W. No. 2, Shaw to Lyall, May 22, 1879; in Nos. 53-63A, pp. 6-7.

[126-28] *Ibid.* (*See also :* Browne to Lyall, June 30, 1879; in Nos. 53-63A, pp. 11-14.).

[129-31] *Ibid.*

[132] St. Barbe to Lyall, June 18, 1879, pp. 4-5; in Mss. Eur. F. 132/20, Burma: Trouble in Mandalay—No. 2, June 1879-November 1879 (IOL).

[133] *Ibid.*

[134] "Occasional Notes" (Allahabad) *Pioneer Mail*, May 10, 1879, p. 2. The italics are in the original.

[135] Aitchison to Lyall, June 19, 1879; in Lytton Papers, 519/11. *Also see:* Gen. Horace A. Browne, *Reminiscences of....Mandalay*, pp. 155-156.

[136] Aitchison to Lyall, July 3, 1879; in Lyall Papers/20.

[137] *Ibid.*

[138] No. 40, MCD, June 22, 1879; in Foreign, Secret, August 1879, Nos. 39-43 (NAI).

[130] No. 40, MCD, June 23, 1879; in Nos. 39-42.

[140] Browne to Aitchison, July 7, 1879; in Nos. 53-63A, pp. 17-18. "I have not met with the slightest incivility yet.. ." *See also:* K. W. No. 1, Browne to Lyall, August 16, 1879; in Nos. 24-33, p. 7. "...although I myself have never experienced any rudeness,... others complain that they cannot go outside the Residency, although well attended, without being grossly insulted..."

[141] No. 41, Kinwun to Browne, June 24, 1879; in Nos. 39-42.

[142] No. 44, MCD, June 27, 1879; in Foreign, Secret, August 1879, Nos. 43-52 (NAI).

[143] Grattan Geary, *Burma After the Conquest*, pp. 160-161. *See also:* F. T. Jesse, *The Lacquer Lady*, p. 151. *Also:* Gen. Horace A. Browne, *Reminiscences of ... Mandalay*, p. 163. *Lastly:* No. 44, MCD, July 1, 1879; in Nos. 43-52.

[144] "Burma," (Calcutta) *Englishman*, July 17, 1879, p. 3.

[145] No. 58, Browne to Aitchison, July 4, 1879 ; in Nos. 53-63A.

[146-147] No. 54, Browne to Lyall, July 10, 1879 ; in Nos. 53-63A. The Myotha was jailed on July 9, but was released a few days later.

[148-50] *Ibid.*

[151] No. 55, Browne to Lyall, July 17, 1879 ; in Nos. 53-63A.

[152] No. 60, Aitchison to Lyall, July 24, 1879 ; in Nos. 53-63A.

[153] No. 56, Aitchison to Lyall, July 26, 1879 ; in Nos. 53-63A.

[154] *Ibid.*

[155] No. 62, Government of India to Cranbrook, August 11, 1879 ; in Nos.

53-63A.

[156] No. 187, Telegram from Aitchison to Lyall, February 19, 1879 ; in Nos. 194-225.

[157] *For example :* Enclosure 6 in No. 17, Lyall to Aitchison, July 14, 1879 ; in C. 4614, pp. 37-40. *See also :* Lyall to Aitchison, July 15, 1879 ; in Lyall Papers/20.

[158] Lyall to Browne, August 12, 1879 ; in Foreign, Secret, November 1879, Nos. 24-33, pp. 5-6 (NAI).

[159] No. 848, Telegram from Aitchison to Lyall, August 31, 1879 ; in Foreign, Political A, September 1879, Nos. 848-850 (NAI). *Also :* No. 8, Browne to Kinwun, August 27, 1879 ; in Foreign, Secret, November, 1879, Nos. 1-14 (NAI).

[160] Enclosure 3 in No. 23, Browne to Lyall, September 5, 1879 ; in C. 4614, pp. 51-54. Such plots, however, had not greatly excited Calcutta previously. *For example:* Shaw's telegram of March 7, 1879 that warned of the rumoured assault on the Residency on March 12.

[161-162] *Ibid.*

[163] *Ibid.* (Browne had stated this warning in a previous August 11, despatch to Lyall. "......the great majority of the people—armed forces included— are in favour of the Nyoungyan, who would only have to show himself at the frontier to ensure success. ......I sincerely trust he won't be allowed to do anything of the kind until I and the other members of the Residency are out of Mandalay." Browne to Lyall, August 11, 1879 ; in Nos. 24-33, pp. 4-5.)

[164-165] *Ibid.*

[166] Gen. Horace A. Browne, *Reminiscences of......Mandalay*, pp. 188-189.

[167] Enclosure 2 in No. 23, Telegram from Aitchison to St. Barbe, September 8, 1879 ; in C. 4614, p. 51.

[168] Gen. Horace A. Browne, *Reminiscences of......Mandalay*, pp. 189.

[169] Lytton to Cranbrook, September 21, 1879 ; in Lytton Papers, 518/4, pp. 777-780.

[170] *Ibid.*

[171] Browne to Lyall, June 30, 1879 ; in Nos. 53-63A, pp. 11-14.

[172] Browne to Aitchison, July 7, 1879 ; in Nos. 53-63A, pp. 17-18.

[173] K. W. No. 1, Browne to Lyall, August 16, 1879 ; in Nos. 24-33, p. 7.

[174] *Ibid.*

[175] *Ibid.* Italics added.

[176] *For example:* the demonstration in front of the Residency on August 1, 1879. H. L. St. Barbe had been attacked by a vicious dog, which he stuck with his walking-stick. A large crowd of Burmese soldiers and civilians tried to enter the Residency compound, and beat the *kala* who had struck the dog. Three Burmese were taken prisoner by Residency personnel, and the crowd then dispersed. Enclosure 1 in No. 22, MCD, July 31-August 2, 1879 ; in C. 4614, pp. 48-49.

[177] Lytton to Cranbrook, September 21, 1879 ; in Lytton Papers, 518/4 pp. 777-780. Browne wrote in his diary that "If there is one point......that my predecessor, I myself, and Mr. Aitchison have been dinning *ad nauseam*

into the ears of a deaf Government for months past, it is the unsafe position of the Residency." Gen. Horace A. Browne, *Reminiscences of......Mandalay*, p. 191.

[178] *Ibid.*

[179] Browne commented on his reprimand : "the Secretary's letter partly contradicts itself for he admits that he received from me, on September 4, a serious warning (written August 16), and then accuses me of having given no such warning before September 5 (received September 19). The remark that 'the news of the Kabul disaster came almost simultaneously' throws a significant light on the origin of all this fuss. The Viceroy is suffering from a severe attack of 'Kabulities.' Clearly no particular attention had been paid to my previous communications. The nerve-shattering shock from Kabul alone made them open their eyes as to the state of affairs at Mandalay." Gen. Horace A. Browne, *Reminiscences of........Mandalay*, pp. 192-194.

[180] Lytton to Cranbrook, September 21, 1879; in Lytton Papers, 518/4, pp. 777-780.

[181-83] *Ibid.*

[184-85] *Ibid.* Italics not in the original.

[186] Browne's final reaction was a saucy comment in his diary. "The real, though unavowed, cause of the rebuke administered to me is that I encouraged thereto by Aitchison, ventured to make remarks on the Viceroy's policy which were eminently distasteful, and which, if publicly known, might be inconvenient; this I cannot deny, so I let the Viceroy have the last word...." Gen. Horace A. Browne, *Reminiscences of... Mandalay*, p. 194.

[187] *See also*: Ernest Chew, "The Withdrawal of the Last British Residency from Upper Burma in 1879," (Singapore) *Journal of Southeast Asian History*, Vol. X, No. 2, September 1969, pp. 253-278. A lucid study.

[188] Lytton to Cranbrook, October 1, 1879; in Lytton Papers, 518/4, pp. 825-827. When St. Barbe struck a vicious dog on August 1, which resulted in a mob attacking the Residency, he had just regained his eyesight after two months of semi-blindness.

[189] Browne to Kinwun, August 27, 1879; in Nos. 1-14.

[190-92] Lytton to Cranbrook, October 1, 1879; in Lytton Papers, 518/4, pp. 825-827. Lytton did not state whether St. Barbe had written privately to him, or to another person.

[193] No. 13, MCD, September 5, 1879; in Nos. 1-14.

[194] No. 13, MCD, September 5, 6, and 9, 1879; in Nos. 1-14.

[195] No. 13, MCD, September 9, 1879; in Nos. 1-14.

[196] No. 56, MCD, September 15, 1879; in Foreign, Secret, November 1879, Nos. 55-62 (NAI).

[197] No. 13, MCD, September 9, 1879; in Nos. 1-14.

[198] No. 56, MCD, September 15, 1879; in Nos. 55-62.

[199] No. 13, MCD, September 9, 1879; in Nos. 1-14.

[200] No. 60, MCD, September 25, 1879; in Nos. 55-62. This particular office was closed as inauspicious when the first draw was won by a leper; who, incidentally, was murdered by 'dacoits' three days later. One of the City

Magistrates, who ran a lottery office, advertised that "he would present a woman to every winner of the first prize in his lottery. He has since had to withdraw this tempting announcement." No. 13, MCD, September 8, 1879; in Nos. 1-14.

[201] No. 13, MCD, September 11, 1879; in Nos. 1-14. *See also:* No. 10, MCD, September 1, 1879: in Nos. 1-14.

[202] No. 114, MCD, September 29, 1879; in Foreign, Secret, November 1879, Nos. 113-115 (NAI).

[203] No. 60, MCD, September 24, 1879; in Nos. 55-62.

[204] No. 114, MCD, October 3, 1879; in Nos. 113-115.

[205] Enclosure 1 in No. 25, St. Barbe to Aitchison, October 11, 1879; in C. 4614, pp. 56-57. *Also see:* "Burma," (Calcutta) *Englishman*, October 27, 1879, p. 3.

2

The Burmese Reaction

The Myaungla Wundauk's Treaty Mission

The initial Burmese reaction to the withdrawal of the Resident was to send a mission headed by the Myaungla Wundauk, which arrived at Thayetmyo in Lower Burma on October 27, 1879. Lytton considered the mission "rather curious,"[1] but it was not curious to the Kinwun. The abrupt withdrawal of the Residency had shocked the Court, for such could only mean that the British were going to invade. Thus, the speedy announcement by October 21 of the mission. The Kinwun wanted to show that his Government had no intentions of harming the Residency, and that the withdrawal had been strictly the hasty decision of the Indian Government.

The Myaungla Wundauk, a genial diplomat known in Lower Burma as 'Pio Nono' from his physical resemblance to the Pope, met Col. H. D. Davies, assistant commissioner at Thayetmyo. The Myaungla, who had headed the 1876-1877 Burmese mission to Italy, Portugal and Spain, said he had no powers beyond the expressions of good-will in the official letter that he carried for the Viceroy. The Myaungla also had no power to enter into a new treaty, nor authority to express a desire for the return of the Resident. The purpose of the Mission was solely to allay the fears that had arisen from the abrupt withdrawal of the Resident.[2] Such fears had already caused a decline in trade and customs receipts.

Aitchison's reaction to Lyall on November 1 was that no advantage could come from any discussions with such a Mission. It was not authorized to explain or to give satisfaction for the long course of "unfriendly conduct."[3] Lyall generally concurred on November 18. He cautioned Aitchison not to send the Mission back to Mandalay, and also not to receive it.[4]

While allowing the Mission to remain temporarily at Thayetmyo, no recital of demands and grievances would be made. This was to avoid giving the Myaungla the false idea that the Indian Government wanted to bargain for the return of the Resident to Mandalay. Instead, the Myaungla should be requested to gain more explicit instructions from Mandalay, or otherwise his Mission could not be received.[5]

Four months of waiting followed with the Calcutta Government doing nothing, and the ambassadors at Thayetmyo rather enjoying themselves as guests of the Lower Burma Government. The envoys, in particular, enjoyed Davies' brandy and beef-steaks, two luxuries *verboten* in Buddhist Mandalay.[6] Finally, in early February 1880, the ambassadors received further instructions from Mandalay, which included a model treaty that they wished adopted.

Col. Davies, who had been the contact-officer since October 27, 1879, stated that the new instructions gave the Mission no real power. All points outside the terms of the model treaty had to be referred to Mandalay. Davies claimed that not only were the ambassadors mere go-betweens, but they were of a lower rank than would have been sent to Peking, or even to neighbouring Siam, a country that was inferior by Burmese diplomatic standards.[7] Davies was wrong on this point.

Davies conceded that the Kinwun and the other ministers had shown great tact in sending the mission, and thereby "drawing our teeth by professions of friendliness which they undoubtedly do not feel...."[8] Despite profuse expressions of "Great Royal Friendship," which the late Mr. Shaw had said was the basis upon which treaties were made in Europe, Davies thought that the proposed treaty was not acceptable.

For example, there was no provision for a new river-side Residency at Mandalay. When the treaty mentioned 'suitable' residencies for the two Governments it meant at Calcutta and Simla. These were two places where no permanent Burmese political-agents had yet been placed,[9] although the Burmese Government had had the right to do so since the 1826 Yandabo Treaty. The Myaungla's proposed treaty also implied that a Burmese political-agent would be posted at London. The Mandalay Government had long desired to establish direct relations with London, instead of having to go through Rangoon and Calcutta-Simla in a chain of command.[10]

Concerning the clause on extradition of *political* as distinct from criminal prisoners, Davies told the Burmese that they did not give a trial by jury. The Myaungla and his colleagues agreed.[11] As concerned the clauses for steamer-wharfs at Mandalay, such clauses might easily be interpreted in Mandalay's favour and against the steamers of British subjects.[12]

The remaining Royal monopolies of timber, precious stones, and earth oil had been largely suspended at the start of Thebaw's reign. The Myaungla's proposed treaty would have restored them.[13] The arms clause allowed even cannon to be imported into Upper Burma.[14] The 'most favoured nation' clause was also a 'trap' in Davies' opinion. It meant that the privileges received by India in any treaty with a foreign power would also be received by Upper Burma. Davies asked how such a clause could apply to an inland-country like Upper Burma where a foreign government held its outlet to the sea.[15]

The Burmese would probably interpret the clause to mean that Thebaw could send his war-boats down to Rangoon, and that French, Italian, and other foreign warships could sail up the Irrawaddy to Mandalay.[16] Finally, there was no apology for the 'disrespect' which the Mandalay Government was considered to have shown to the former Residents.[17] Davies concluded that the Mission should not be allowed to go further, and that the proposed Treaty was of little value.[18]

Aitchison generally agreed with Davies' assessment of the proposed treaty. Aitchison recommended that if Mandalay would agree in advance to receive a shod and seated Resident—and also agree to a new well-guarded Residency on the river-bank—that any further problems between the two states could easily be solved.[19] If the Mandalay Government was not willing to give such an advance agreement, the Myaungla Mission should return to Upper Burma.[20]

Mandalay promptly sent back 'full powers' to the Mission to

negotiate.[21] The Myaungla was asked if such powers enabled him to propose a relaxed position on the "Shoe Question"; a stockaded river-side Residency; and, a revitalized Mixed Court. The Myaungla replied that he had no such powers or proposals.[22]

Aitchison's response was that "there was no use in any [further] discussion at all, whither personal or by letter...."[23] After several additional requests of the Mission that they present some preliminary proposals agreeable to both sides, the Myaungla decided to submit one last letter and return to Upper Burma. Aitchison refused the letter, and returned it on June 1, 1880. Unfortunately, no copy of the letter is in existence. However, Aitchison stated that its contents were "incorrect."[24]

Aitchison stated that he and the Indian Government had been willing to meet with the Mission once the ambassadors had presented definite proposals likely to be acceptable to both sides. The failure of the Mission to do this was the reason for Aitchison not allowing the Mission to proceed any further than Thayetmyo.[25] On June 4, 1880, the Myaungla Mission left Thayetmyo to return to Mandalay.[26] After arriving at Mandalay, the Myaungla died after a couple of weeks, apparently from the violent smallpox epidemic which had killed Supayalat's baby son and hundreds of other Mandalay residents.

In summarizing the reasons for the failure of the Myaungla Mission, one can conclude that neither side really wanted to negotiate. The Burmese Government had negotiated a number of treaties since 1826, and had sent at least fifteen missions to India, China and elsewhere during King Mindon's reign. The Kinwun, for example, had headed the 1872-1873 mission to England, France and Italy, and had also headed the 1874-1875 mission to France. The Pangyet Wundauk had been his key assistant during the 1872-1873 mission, while the Myaungla had been secretary to the 1872-1873 mission and had been the Kinwun's assistant in 1874-1875. In 1876-1877, the Myaungla had headed the mission to Italy, Portugal and Spain; and, had spent the Easter holiday in 1877 with his son who was attending a school in Turin, Italy. In 1878-1879, the Pangyet had again gone to France where he had once been a student for ten years, and also to Italy.

In short, the Burmese Government was aware of what was meant by the term 'full powers'. The Myaungla could have agreed to a prior agenda for discussion. The fact was that the Myaungla

Mission had come almost solely to excuse Mandalay from any part in the October 6, 1879 withdrawal of the Residency. The Mission felt that having once done this the Indian Government would not attack or seek to reestablish the Resident by force.

Lord Hartington, the new Liberal secretary of state for India, refused at first to approve the Indian Government's stand towards the Myaungla Mission.[27] Eventually, on September 17, 1880, Hartington did give his approval. However, he pointed out that the Myaungla had been given "general powers sufficiently wide to justify continuance of negotiations," although not authorized to make the prior concessions desired by the Indian Government.[28] Hartington thought that the personal discussion, which the Myaungla had desired with Aitchison and Lytton, might possibly have led to a satisfactory result.[29]

It would have been better if the Myaungla and his party had been invited down to Rangoon after receiving 'full powers' in Thebaw's Royal Order of March 29, 1880. A Rangoon official could have met with the Mission daily until they either proposed something of value, or broke off the talks. On the other hand, Aitchison could hardly be blamed for realizing the essentially non-serious intent of the Mission, and refusing to meet them until mutually acceptable proposals were brought forth.

Without such proposals, Aitchison was not in favour of restoring the Resident, particularly since trade moved along as well without a Resident as it had previously with a Resident. Also, Aitchison had established a 'news-collector' at Mandalay after October 1879 in the person of A. E. Rawlings, the new foreigners' postmaster. Rawlings had his post office on a mail-steamer in the Irrawaddy at Mandalay, and took over the task which had been previously performed by Andreino, the Italian Consul. Until 1884, when Andreino also became an Indian Government 'news-collector', Rawlings was the only regular source of news concerning Mandalay affairs.

Aitchison had one other reason for not wishing to meet with the Mission. He was leaving Rangoon in June 1880 to assume his new duties as a member of Viceroy Lord Ripon's Council. The last thing that Aitchison wanted were negotiations extending beyond his tenure in Burma that might in any way reflect on his part in the withdrawal of the Residency at Mandalay. Until the Mission proposed solutions that would reflect favourably on Aitchison as the negotiator, he refused to meet it. His successor, Charles Bernard, former officiating home secretary to the Indian Government and nephew of the late Gov. Gen. Sir John Lawrence (1864-1869), could do as he liked.

Thebaw Protects British Subjects' Interests

While the above negotiations were going on, both Mandalay and Rangoon felt the need for the sort of contact formerly performed by the Resident. Lyall informed Aitchison on October 28, 1879 that letters concerning British interests in Upper Burma should be addressed directly to the Kinwun. Such letters should be limited to local and commercial affairs, and should not establish a precedent whereby the Kinwun or Mandalay could ever say that such temporary correspondence had reduced the need for reinstating the Resident.[30]

The Kinwun began writing to various Burmese, Chinese, European, and Indian merchants in Lower Burma to assure them that the Mandalay Government had only their best interests in mind. He wrote to Aitchison, and received his assurances that the IFC steamers would continue to run in Upper Burma.[31] The Kinwun also met with a number of Lower Burma mercantile delegations. He assured them of his Government's determination to maintain order along the Irrawaddy, and to encourage trade in every possible way.[32]

Thebaw himself joined the campaign to restore the confidence of the Rangoon mercantile community. By the end of 1879, the campaign was gaining good notices in the Rangoon and Indian newspapers, along with reports of Thebaw's drunkenness. A typical such news-story was the account describing the thirty-minute interview of the IFC manager with King Thebaw:

They found Theebaw in an uncommonly complaisant mood. He expressed a hope that they had met with civility and proper treatment everywhere as he had desired. Theebaw seemed to be getting stout, and although only 21 years of age his face a good deal puffed out and his eyes deep sunk, or having the appearance of being so, probably on account of the bloated condition of the rest of his face. He was very simply dressed with a yellow silk putsoe ['sarong'] white linen jacket, and a spray of diamonds on his top knot, a very large sapphire ring being also noticeable on one of his fingers. The party had the satisfaction of seeing that if his Majesty insisted on their taking off their boots before him he did so himself before sitting down. [The]... party left, declaring that Theebaw, notwithstanding many little drawbacks, was "a very good fler," and retired to the [Italian] Consul's house where they drank his health in champagne.[33]

Other Lower Burma merchants went to Mandalay, and made arrangements so that their trade would go on as before. The only difference was that Burmese officials were responsible, whereas before the merchants who were British subjects had depended upon the Resident. Perhaps a few more bribes had to be paid in comparison to the time when the Resident was at Mandalay, but no doubt many merchants did not mind the extra investment so long as Mandalay kept its word.

In particular, there were three steamer assaults that helped greatly to convince most Rangoon merchants that Mandalay was serious about protecting the rights of British subjects. The first steamer assault was against the *Shwe Myo* (Golden City) on November 13, 1879. Captain Vince had ordered a Surati, Mahomed Ismael, to get off the forward deck which had been freshly painted.[34]

An argument flared. Mahomed Ismael summoned twenty local coolies loitering on shore, and they rushed on board the steamer and a brawl ensued. Eventually, two or three coolies were flogged by Burmese authorities. Many persons knew that Mahomed Ismael was in business with Mulla Ibrahim, the greatest purchaser of Royal monopolies in Upper Burma, and thought that the attack had been deliberate.[35]

The second steamer assault was against the *Yunnan* steamer carrying British subjects' mail. At 10 a.m., May 26, 1880, the steamer answered a cargo-flag hoisted on shore at Salaymyo. However, when the steamer touched shore, the jaggery (raw sugar) baskets were found to be empty. The local Governor claimed that war had been declared between Mandalay and Rangoon, and he refused to let the *Yunnan* proceed until 8 p.m., May 27.[36] The Governor was eventually replaced. Orders were given to all river-town Governors and military commanders that they were to assist the steamers, and were not to place any armed troops on board them.[37]

The third steamer assault occurred against the *Thambyadin* at 7:45 a.m. on October 10, 1880. Steamer officers had argued for an hour with Ko Law Ko, a Chinese who insisted on placing his cookstove on the wooden deck where it would have caused a fire. After Ko turned violent and was delivered over to Burmese authorities at 7:30 a.m., a mob of 100 Chinese swarmed on board.

Captain Beckman fired two shots into the legs of two toughs, and E. R. Wells, the mate, wounded another in the arm, and the mob fled.[38] The local Chinese headman was jailed by Mandalay, until he agreed to give security for his people's future good-behaviour. The headman's money was to be confiscated by Government if there was any further trouble.[39] The mob's ringleaders were also jailed.[40]

These three incidents showed that Mandalay was determined to prove that law and order did prevail in Upper Burma, and that British subjects could work and trade with no fear of harm to ther lives or property. The Kinwun forbade attacks on the IFC's sixteen steamers and thirty-one flats, because he knew that 13,600 Indian troops and 11,200 tons of war-material could leave Rangoon on these same IFC steamers and flats. If unhindered, they could dock at Mandalay—within three miles of the Palace—in eight to ten days.[41]

In addition, law and order usually prevailed on the Irrawaddy, because there were extensive profits to be made by both Government and merchants. Such profits were *not* going to be threatened by local Governors, or groups, who sought their profit by intercepting on one pretext or another the various IFC steamers. The ensuing good order along the Irrawaddy River from late-1879 through 1881 gave a great boost to trade.

London Rejects Proposals to Withdraw from Treaties

But some Rangoon merchants and officials thought that business would only reach its maximum if Mandalay was made a 'protected' state, or even annexed outright.[42] Aitchison opposed the idea of annexation, although it was a popular issue at Rangoon. Aitchison much preferred the idea of a 'protected' state, and wrote to Lyall on November 15, 1879 that "Our interests......are commercial rather than political; and all we really want is a......

respectable administration in Upper Burma."[43]

Aitchison envisioned the Nyaungyan Prince as the best candidate to replace Thebaw on the throne. Six guarantees would have to be gained from the Nyaungyan's 'protected' Government.[44] These guarantees were: (1) a strong Indian Army cantonment at Mandalay and elsewhere; (2) the routing of Burma's foreign relations through the Indian foreign secretary; (3) an Indian Government say in the Royal Succession; (4) new arrangements for settling disputes between Burmese and British subjects; (5) an equalization of customs duties; and, lastly, (6) the King would act upon the Resident's advice.[45]

Cranbrook's reply on December 29 accepted Aitchison's proposal of a 'protected' Upper Burmese state ruled by the Nyaungyan Prince—if it came about as a result of Burmese aggression.[46] Cranbrook was not in favour of the Indian Government committing the first blow against Upper Burma. He added that he was pleased with Aitchison's opposition to the annexationists, the "Violent Party at Rangoon."[47] Cranbrook concluded that "There is hardly a Colony or port all over the world where there are not Englishmen who would drag their country into war to sell an extra bale of goods, or make an opening for their speculations."[48]

Cranbrook's reply did not satisfy the more 'active' members of the Viceroy's Council. On January 14, 1880 the Council submitted a request to Cranbrook that the Indian Government be allowed to withdraw unilaterally from the 1862 and 1867 Commercial Treaties with Upper Burma. Withdrawal was urged in part as a protest against the *Shwe Myo* steamer affair, which the Mandalay Government had not as yet 'explained' to the Indian Government's satisfaction.[49]

The despatch concluded by asking that the Indian Government be allowed to withdraw from the 1862 and 1867 Treaties, if Mandalay did not make proper apologies and punish those responsible for the *Shwe Myo* steamer riot.[50] However, London cautioned that no rash moves should be made until after the Burmese Government had had a chance to reply concerning their action, or lack of it, in the *Shwe Myo* incident.

The April 1880 British elections gave Gladstone and his Liberals a large majority in the House of Commons. Lord Ripon was appointed the new Liberal Viceroy and Governor General of India. He took up his new post on June 8, 1880. If the outgoing Lytton Council was to do anything further about the Burma situation, they would have to move quickly. The May 26, 1880 seizure of the *Yunnan* mail-steamer made a perfect occasion. On June 1, a second request was made for withdrawal from the Treaties, not so much on the grounds of the latest *Yunnan* outrage but rather on the grounds of the earlier *Shwe Myo* incident.[51]

Lord Hartington, the new Liberal secretary of state for India, had just taken office. His attention was focussed almost entirely on ending the Second Afghan War, and upon the 'Russian Threat' to India's northwest frontier. The Liberals were as uninterested in India's eastern frontier, and in Upper Burma, as were the outgoing Conservatives. Consequently, no decision was taken on the June 1, 1880 despatch.

Aitchison left Rangoon in June 1880. His successor Charles Bernard immediately polled all the Rangoon merchants.[52] The importers of British-manufactures were mostly Europeans. Non-Europeans held the lion's-share of the export-trade of British imports to Upper Burma, and of exports coming from Upper Burma into Lower Burma.[53] Mr. Darlington, the Rangoon customs collector, summed up the general opinion as well as any:

......My general impression is, that the Rangoon merchants desire to be let alone [with no renunciation of the 1862 and 1867 Treaties]; unless......the British Government are prepared to replace their Resident at Mandalay, and to secure for him a stronger position and more potential voice with the Ava Court than he has hitherto enjoyed. They think the Irrawaddy trade is doing very well now, and will continue...... under the King's protection, unless panic is caused by some action......of the British Government, or of the King. They firmly believe that the King is anxious to avoid a rupture......although he probably bears us no good will.[54]

They believe also that the King desires to foster trade, and to show that traffic with Upper Burma is quite as secure without a Resident, as with a Resident......[55]

On the whole, the merchants do not lean much on......the protective clauses of the treaties, now that there is no Resident at Mandalay. But they feel that the existence of these protective clauses does......make their position safer......[56]

Bernard continued his policy reassessment on August 11, 1880.

He stated that the political stalemate could be broken, if the Indian Government defined the preliminary issues to be agreed upon by both countries before negotiations began.[57]   Bernard proposed that a commercial Consul be placed at Mandalay in preference to the political Resident, since "our principal anxiety is for our trade on the Irrawaddy and to Bhamo......"[58]   But regardless of whether the agent was called a commercial Consul, or a political Resident, he would have to exercise full jurisdiction over all cases involving British subjects.[59]

Bernard did not emphasize the necessity of a stockaded Residency as had Aitchison.[60]   However, Bernard did desire the following concessions from Mandalay.   The Resident or Consul would have access to the King and ministers without 'degrading ceremonial' ; the Resident would receive a new river-side Residency ; and lastly, all Royal captives would be released in return for the Indian Government's promise to prevent the exiled-princes from escaping to Upper Burma.[61]

Bernard summed up his long August 11 report with six conclusions.   (1) The Indian Government could not make the first overtures for restoration of the Resident.   (2) The Mandalay Government was also not likely to make such an overture at that time.   (3) Trade moved along smartly even without the Resident. Therefore, there were no reasons for an immediate restoration of the Resident.[62]

(4) However, the eventual restoration of the Resident was desirable "in the interest of trade to and beyond Upper Burma [to Southern China]."[63]   (5) Therefore, the Indian Government might decide upon the preliminary concessions that they would demand, and announce them.   Lastly, (6) the chief commissioner should encourage any overtures concerning the restoration of the Resident that might come from Mandalay.[64]

Mortimer Durand's reply of October 18, 1880 as officiating foreign secretary mirrored the much tougher line towards Burma that was prevalent on the Viceroy's Council.   Durand stated that the Burmese were well aware of what were the British demands regarding the diplomatic privileges of the Resident, his proper accommodation at Mandalay, and his reception by the King.[65]

Furthermore, Mandalay knew that any chief commissioner could negotiate, just as soon as Mandalay presented preliminary proposals mutually acceptable to both sides.[66]   Durand stated that

Ripon and the Council did not think that a commercial agent or Consul would suffice at Mandalay.[67] Once Mandalay discovered that a commercial agent or Consul was of lower rank than a political Resident, it would give the Court a pretext for permanently lowering the footing upon which the agent could claim to be treated. This was a change exactly opposite to that desired by the Indian Government.[68]

There were persons on the Viceroy's Council of an even stronger mind towards Burma than Mortimer Durand. C. U. Aitchison, W. Stokes and Sir John Strachey had never been satisfied with the Burmese explanations for the incidents on the *Shwe Myo* (November 13, 1879), and on the *Yunnan* (May 26, 1880). The assault on the *Thambyadin* on October 10, 1880 seemed a good opportunity to petition London for a third time to withdraw from the 1862 and 1867 Treaties.[69]

Ripon, however, disagreed.[70] His dissent along with those opposing comments of four of his colleagues on the Council[71] were forwarded to London on November 9, 1880. Ripon stood by his earlier comments that "it is with great hesitation that I find myself inclined to doubt the propriety of the step......"[72]

Ripon thought that if Mandalay suffered from the lapse of the Treaties, Lower Burma trade would also suffer. If, on the other hand, Mandalay survived the end of the Treaties, which they might according to Aitchison,[73] then voiding of the Treaties was totally unwarranted. The point of voiding the Treaties was to put pressure upon Mandalay until it restored the Resident upon British terms, allowed a river-side Residency, established the Mixed Court upon a fairer basis, and permanently abolished all Royal monopolies. If Mandalay could survive such pressure tactics, would British subjects be *better* treated in Upper Burma?[74]

While the Indian Government awaited Hartington's reply, Bernard at Rangoon submitted a January 3, 1881 compromise proposal. He suggested that if Thebaw would occasionally receive a shod and seated Resident, the Resident would doff his shoes the rest of the time.[75]

A. C. Lyall, again the Indian foreign secretary, refused Bernard's compromise on February 7, 1881. Lyall stated that "our Resident, whenever he goes to the [inside of the] Palace, shall......appear in his proper political dress, and be shod and seated after the fashion of his civilized country......"[76] Lyall made a counter-proposal concerning a possible meeting between the King and the Resident *outside* the Palace.   This was based on the Chinese system whereby the Emperor met shoe-wearing Europeans in a building or garden away from the inner throne-room with its cosmological and sacred formalities.[77]   Such an outside meeting would be acceptable at Mandalay.   However, the Indian Government could not initiate such a concept, but would have to wait for any suggestion to be first proposed by Mandalay.[78]

Lyall's suggestion for an *outside* garden or building interview was never mentioned again.   Yet, it was bold, inspired, and would most likely have contributed to a rapid solution of most of the issues between the two countries, and thusly have prevented the Third Burmese War.   Meanwhile, Hartington had rejected the Indian Government's letters of January 14, 1880, June 1, 1880, and November 9, 1880 urging withdrawal from the 1862 and 1867 Treaties with Upper Burma.[79]

Hartington concurred with the established positions, such as those outlined by Aitchison in his February 20, 1880 despatch to Lyall, and Bernard's August 11, 1880 letter to Mortimer Durand. These established positions included a seated and shod Resident with access to Thebaw, and a riverside Residency with increased guard.[80]   However, Hartington refused to accept another sugges-tion that Mandalay be asked to swear that they would commit no further massacres as an initial condition for the restoration of relations.   Such a demand could not be enforced, and the issue was primarily a domestic concern of the Burmese King.[81]

Hartington emphasized that the several steamer incidents were simply not of the gravity to warrant a reaction that "would destroy all prospect of improved relations with Burma, whether political or commercial."[82]   Hartington concluded that a with-drawal from the Treaties, and the resultant suspension of com-mercial relations with Upper Burma, was "at present, neither necessary nor advisable...."[83]

Hartington's rejection put an end to much speculation.   The Indian Government was not going to invade Upper Burma, or withdraw from the Treaties, or force a new Resident upon Mandalay.   By 'ignoring' Upper Burma, the British were able to advance the commercial interests of Lower Burma.   Hartington's decision also forced the Indian Government to return to the main political issue, *i.e.* to secure stability in Afghanistan, and to protect India's northwest frontier from the 'Russian Threat'.

Within a few months, Mandalay officials grew 'over-confident' due to the comparative lack of pressure from the Indian Government. Thebaw's favourites, such as the Yanaung Mintha, began selling Royal monopolies, and squeezing British subjects out of the Upper Burma trade.[84]

Mandalay Tries to Monopolize Trade

All Royal monopolies except in earth oil, timber, and precious stones had been abolished under the provisions of the 1867 Treaty. However, King Mindon had never totally abolished his monopolies. Instead, he often employed ostensibly 'private' agents to purchase and sell a large portion of the exportable surpluses of Upper Burma. Such a procedure was not literally against the wording of the 1867 Treaty.[85]

As a consequence, Mindon had never bothered with a formal restoration of the pre-1867 Royal monopolies. He had the legal right to do so, however, because the Treaty ban on Royal monopolies had been for *only* ten years. In March 1878, Mindon *refused* to extend the ban on monopolies for another ten years; because the Indian Government still refused to recognize the 'Fytche Annexe' in the 1867 Treaty, which had allowed for the unlimited import of arms into Upper Burma.[86]

After Thebaw's accession on October 1, 1878, most of the so-called 'private' agents were retired. A comparatively free market remained in force for the first two years of Thebaw's reign.[87] However, the Yanaung Mintha and other favourites began selling Royal monopolies after late 1880, and especially after July 1881. These monopolies effected (1) the imports from and the exports to Lower Burma; (2) the imports from and the exports to Yunnan and Southern China; and, (3) Upper Burma forest products.

Thebaw's monopolies were different from the old monopolies, which Mindon had usually personally administered, and which he had almost never given to favourites. The new monopoly buyers were haunted by the fear of British intervention. The buyers were anxious to get as much money as they could before Thebaw's rule collapsed, or before they lost their monopoly to another favourite.[88]

Thusly, they paid the growers the lowest possible prices, which

was something that Mindon's agents had almost never made the
mistake of doing.   Many growers finding their labour in vain,
gave up farming or working in the forests.   The consequence was
a decline in trade with Lower Burma, and an inability on the part
of many Upper Burmese to pay the 1882 House Tax of about ten
rupees.[89]

Thebaw probably would not have revived the monopolies,
except that their substitute had become corrupted by maladminis-
tration.   According to the 1867 Treaty, there was a customs duty
limited to five per cent. on most imported and exported goods,
except on the three legal Royal monopolies of timber, earth-oil,
and precious stones.   Rice and food were imported free of duties;
and wine, whiskey, opium and other imported drugs were charged
at least ten per cent. duty.

The three duty collectorates at Mandalay had become so
corrupt that they kept most of the customs receipts for themselves,
while the Royal Treasury was nearly bankrupt.   The *Englishman*
stated that:

[All]......goods reaching Mandalay....from China, or produced from the forest in Burmah, pay a 5 per cent. duty to
either the *Daywoon* [China imports] or *Thittaw* [forests]
collectorate, and then pay another 5 per cent [to the
Yaydanabhon] to export it to British Burma, thus evading the
terms of the 1867 treaty and paying a levy of 10 instead of
only 5 per cent.[90]

By July 25, 1879, the Yanaung, Thebaw's great favourite, had
taken over most of the *Yaydanabhon* collectorate.[91]   Col. Horace
Browne, Resident at Mandalay from June to August 1879, wrote
that he had met the Yanaung on July 25 at the Mandalay Customs
shed.   The Yanaung had taken over the imports duty-collection
and nearly all of the exports, except for the earth-oil duties, from
Mulla Ibrahim.[92]

Browne discussed this with the Myotha Wundauk, the
Burmese judge of the Mixed Court, on the following day.   Under
the category of timber, which was charged ten per cent. duty, were
such items as buffalo hides, bullock hides, soapstone, cutch, lac,
horns, lead, wax, pots, pans, and other items.   Browne reminded
the Myotha that under the 1867 Treaty only earth-oil, timber, and
precious stones could be Royal export monopolies, and therefore
liable to more than a five per cent. duty.   Browne neglected to

mention that the ban on Royal monopolies had *expired* in 1877. The Myotha laughed, and agreed that the above named items were mostly not timber. But, such had been done for years as 'Burmese custom', and Rangoon had *never* complained before.[93]

Browne admitted that the Myotha was correct, but insisted that the 1867 Treaty had to be observed. Browne asked why garlic and onions had been sold as Royal monopolies contrary to the Treaty.[94] Two men had also bought the pickled-tea import business from the Shan States at Rs. 55,000 per month. The Myotha said that the pickled-tea monopoly had been cancelled. Browne remained unconvinced that Mandalay would abolish anything so profitable without a strong protest from Rangoon.[95]

Rumours continued throughout 1879 and 1880 of proposed new Royal monopolies, but there was little evidence that such were actually being sold. In 1880 the Mandalay Government ruled that all imports brought into Upper Burma should be carried in Upper Burmese steamers, whenever they were working and space was available. Upper Burmese traders were also ordered to export their goods to Lower Burma in Thebaw's steamers.

When Ko Set Kyee, a wealthy Upper Burma Chinese, purchased the jaggery monopoly in early January 1881, he was also required to export his monopoly to Lower Burma on Thebaw's steamers. The IFC was rather unhappy about this, but the *Englishman* commented that "the arrangement....is perfectly fair......as it gives the Burmese the same advantages in British territory as we have in the Burmese possessions."[96] In reply to a February 23, 1881 protest from Bernard about the jaggery monopoly, the Kinwun replied on April 26 that the 1867 Treaty had not been violated. Nor had anything been done to cause a decline in trade between the two Burmas.[97]

Ko Set Kyee's jaggery monopoly was against the 1867 Treaty, except that the ban on Royal monopolies had expired in 1877. Then, a most *embarrassing* British-violation of the 1867 Treaty came to light. It was discovered that Article 4 required an annual-exchange of pricelists of articles of export-and-import; and, that all customs duties were to be computed from such lists.[98] Bernard conceded that although Mandalay had faithfully sent the valuable lists year after year, Rangoon had probably never since 1867 sent the required counter-lists.[99]

Without the price-lists from Rangoon, the Mandalay Government had charged whatever duties the market would bear. The merchant, of course, would claim a very low value for his export or import goods. The customs officials would counter by offering to buy the goods for that amount. The merchant would find this completely unacceptable as it did not reflect his 'transportation' or 'handling' costs. The haggling would reach a crescendo with the merchant storming that he would rather throw his goods into the river than allow leeches to suck his blood. The officials would then become placating and reassure the merchant that they were, like himself, only poor men who sought to fill their rice bowls by performing some wretchedly paid but honest work. After more haggling, a higher value would be mutually agreed upon, and the five (or more) per cent. duty paid on that valuation. Actually, the daily bargaining between oily-merchants and 'grease'-seeking officials more accurately reflected the current value of goods than did an annual price-list.

Bernard wrote that the price-lists should be sent *immediately* to Mandalay. This would show that the Indian Government wished to meet all conceivable obligations, according to the Treaties, "excepting the exportation of arms and munitions of war into Upper Burmah."[100] The importation of arms, munitions, and gun-making machinery into Upper Burma had been permitted under the 1867 Treaty, but had never been observed. Simla gave its approval to Bernard's proposal to send the price-lists, and they were despatched to Mandalay.[101]

The price-lists were of little interest to the Yanaung Mintha, who was Thebaw's great favourite; or to the Pintha, Yanaung's brother; or to the Taingda Atwinwun. These three and others in the Yanaung's Party at Mandalay began a general sale of export-monopolies in July 1881. The Kinwun *officially* opposed the sales, but kept an unofficial interest in the Yanaung's Party by encouraging a rich relative to bid on the lucrative cotton monopoly. On July 3, 1881, Giovanni Andreino, who was the BBTC and IFC agent at Mandalay as well as the Italian Consul, reported that Ko Set Kyee, the jaggery monopolist, had also bid for cotton, hides, and cutch.[102] Not so incidentally, Ko's wife was a good friend of Queen Supayalat.

Finally, on July 20, the cotton monopoly was sold to the Kinwun's relative, the Shway Laung Peh-hnin, for Rs. 120,000 annually; and cutch went to Mulla Ismail for about Rs. 85,000

annually. The hides monopoly went to Ko Set Kyee for an unknown amount, and he then bid for the salt monopoly.[103] The
other monopolies of grains, tobacco, and cigar leaves and sticks
for making Burmese cheroots were also said to be up for sale.

Raids were made on steamers carrying monopolised goods,
and all such goods not procured from the monopolists were taken
off and expropriated.[104] Chinese cotton dealers were forced to
disgorge the contents of their Upper Burma warehouses at one-
third of their actual value.[105] There were numerous other incidents,
and eighty non-European merchants at Rangoon joined with the
IFC manager to send a joint-letter to Bernard on July 29.[106]

The IFC manager stated that the IFC had established its
Upper Burma runs after 1867 on the assurances of the 1867
Treaty. It had provided for free trade, except in the three legal
Royal monopolies of earth-oil, timber, and precious stones.
Trusting that such assurances would last, the IFC had invested
£500,000 in equipment. The new monopolies threatened not only
the IFC's investment, but also all merchants and traders, European
and non-European alike.[107]

Bernard made a recommendation to Simla after receiving
the IFC manager's letter, a letter from the Rangoon Chamber of
Commerce,[108] and appeals from numerous commercial delegations.
Bernard's August 15 letter rejected three of the solutions that were
being pressed upon him.

First, a diplomatic mission to Mandalay was not likely to be
well received so long as Thebaw was in power. Secondly, a uni-
lateral withdrawal from the 1862 and 1867 Treaties would be of
little value, because it would invite reprisals from Mandalay, and
would paralyze trade on the Irrawaddy. Still another result might
be an absolute rupture and war.[109] Thirdly, unless an Indian
Army force was poised at Thayetmyo in preparation for an invasion of Upper Burma, a threat to intervene in Upper Burma would
not be advisable. The monopolies were not likely to be abolished
by mere threats from Rangoon. Also, Bernard did not feel that the
Burmese 'violations' of the Treaties warranted such intervention.[110]

Bernard could see only one path of action, namely the sending of a strong protest to Mandalay. It would strengthen the
many persons at Mandalay who opposed the monopolies, such as
the Kinwun and the Chinese merchants.[111] The Indian Government concurred.[112] On September 28, 1881, Bernard despatched a

strong protest against the sale of export monopolies in jaggery, cutch, cotton, pickled-tea, and hides. He expressed strongly the concern of the Rangoon merchants that similar monopolies would soon be granted in salt, gram, *ngape*, and other items.[113]

The Kinwun's reply of October 30, 1881, repeated his previous April 26, 1881 letter that the monopolies had not violated the 1862 and 1867 Treaties. Article 1 of the 1867 Treaty had lapsed in 1877, and there were no hindrances on Upper Burma's right to create both export and import monopolies.[114]

The Kinwun was discrete and did not remind Bernard that the Rangoon Government *also* had its government-owned monopolies, namely (1) the rail-road monopoly; (2) the forest monopoly; (3) the sale of opium and the making of spirits and beer; (4) the erection of bazaars; (5) the contract for carrying the public mails, which was always awarded to the British India Steam Navigation Co., no other private firm being allowed to bid; and lastly, (6) the salt monopoly. The Kinwun also discretely refrained from reminding Bernard that the BBTC had recently purchased the Upper Burma cutch monopoly, and that there were also other Lower Burma merchants bidding for portions of various Royal monopolies.

Viceroy Lord Ripon visited Rangoon while on tour during Christmas 1881, and discussed the monopolies issue with Bernard. Immediately after Ripon's departure, U Kyi, a Burmese envoy from the Kinwun, arrived on December 28. U Kyi expressed Mandalay's willingness to discuss all outstanding issues.[115] Such an expression from Mandalay had been the Indian Government's criteria for the opening of serious talks between the two Governments.

It appeared that the despatch of the envoy had been a private diplomatic venture by the Kinwun, who had always opposed the monopolies and their chief benefactors, the Yanaung Mintha and his party. Bernard considered the proposal to negotiate all outstanding issues, and also Ripon's order that a third protest concerning the monopolies be sent to Mandalay.

On January 4, 1882, Bernard despatched a strongly-worded protest to the Kinwun.[116] Bernard quoted Viceroy Lord Ripon that if the monopolies continued, the Indian Government would believe that Mandalay did not care about having good relations. In conclusion, Bernard emphasized that if the monopolies continued, or if trade continued to decline because of the monopolies, Thebaw would be held personally responsible.[117] When the ominously worded despatch reached Mandalay, it immensely strengthened the Kinwun and Queen Supayalat in their struggle against the Yanaung's group, which had benefited most from the sales of monopolies.

FOOTNOTES

[1] Lytton to Cranbrook, October 23, 1879; in Lytton Papers, 518/4, p. 939.

[2] Enclosure 2 in No. 26, Davies to Aitchison's Secretary, October 27, 1879; in C. 4614, pp. 60-61.

[3] Enclosure 2 in No. 26, Aitchison's Secretary to Lyall, November 1, 1879; in C. 4616, p. 59.

[4] Enclosure 3 in No. 26, Lyall to Aitchison, November 18, 1879; in C. 4614, pp. 63-64.

[5] *Ibid.*

[6] No. 73, Summary of Upper Burma Affairs, November 15, 1879; in Foreign, Secret, December 1879; Nos. 72-73 (NAI). *Also see:* "Rangoon," (Calcutta) *Englishman,* December 30, 1879, pp. 2-3. *Also:* "Rangoon," (Calcutta) *Englishman,* February 18, 1880, p. 3. *Finally:* No. 82, Aitchison's Secretary to Lyall, January 9, 1880; in Foreign, Secret, January 1880, Nos. 82-84 (NAI).

[7] Enclosure with K. W. No. 1, Davies to Aitchison's Secretary, February 11, 1880; in Foreign, Secret, March 1880, Nos. 117-133 (NAI).

[8-10] *Ibid.* Burmese commercial Consuls were already located at Calcutta and Rangoon.

[11-18] *Ibid.* The Burmese always claimed that the 'Fytche Annexe' to the 1867 Treaty allowed Mandalay to import cannon, breech-loading rifles, and any other arms that they wished in peace-time. The author agrees. *See* Appendix C for the 1867 Treaty, and the 'Fytche Annexe'.

[19] K. W. No. 1, Aitchison to Lyall, February 17, 1880; in Nos. 117-133.

[20] Enclosure 1 in No. 33, Aitchison's Secretary to Lyall, February 20, 1880; in C. 4614, p. 76.

[21] Enclosure 3 in No. 35, Royal Order of King Thebaw, March 29, 1880; in C. 4614, p. 84. *Also:* Enclosure 3 in No. 35, Kinwun to Aitchison, March 28, 1880; in C. 4614, pp. 84-85.

[22-23] *Ibid.*

[24] Enclosure 2 in No. 38, Aitchison's Secretary to Davies, June, 1, 1880; in C. 4614, pp. 94-95.

[25] *Ibid.* Aitchison did oblige the Ambassadors' request for four guns, ten rounds of powder, forty rounds of small shot, and five boxes of caps.

[26] No. 147, Telegram from Aitchison to Lyall, June 5, 1880; in Foreign, Secret, June 1880, Nos. 145-151 (NAI).

[27] No. 42, Hartington to G.G. in Council, September 17, 1880; in C. 4614, p. 97.

[28-29] *Ibid.*

[30] Lyall to Aitchison, October 28, 1879; in Foreign, Secret, November, 1879, Nos. 146-147 (NAI).

[31] "Rangoon," (Calcutta) *Englishman*, November 3, 1879, p. 3.

[32] "Rangoon," (Calcutta) *Englishman*, November 10, 1879, p. 3. The article also described the customs inspection on the frontier. "British steamers are stopped immediately [as] they pass the frontier and boarded by the Burmese authorities, who take care to inform the passengers that they have come to search the steamer. They "loaf" about for... a quarter of an hour, chewing betelnut, and conversing affiably enough with any one who will talk to them....One of the officials was asked what he was looking for? He replied, I do not know, but I am told to search."

[33] "An Interview With King Theebaw," (Calcutta) *Englishman,* December 24, 1879, p. 3. Andreino was the Italian Consul and the IFC's agent at Mandalay. He also was the BBTC's Mandalay agent.

[34] Enclosure 2 in No. 31, Davies to Aitchison's Secretary, November 20, 1879; in C. 4614, pp. 70-71.

[35] *Ibid. See also:* Enclosure 2 in No. 36, Aitchison's Secretary to Kinwun, Jan 5, 1880; in C. 4614, pp. 89-90. *Also:* No. 83, Mandalay Affairs ending January 9, 1880; in Foreign, Secret, January 1880, Nos. 82-84 (NAI). *Also:* Enclosure 5 in No. 36, Burgess to Lyall, April 30, 1880; in C. 4614, p. 91.

[36] Enclosure 4 in No. 37, Aitchison's Secretary to Kinwun, May 31, 1880; in C. 4614, p. 93.

[37] Enclosure 1 in No. 44, Kinwun to Aitchison, July 24, 1880; in C. 4614, p. 101. *Also:* Enclosure 2 in No. 44, Aitchison's Secretary to Kinwun, August 13, 1880; in C. 4614, p. 102.

[38] No. 188, Extract from *Thambyadine's* log; October 10, 1880; in Foreign, Political-A, December 1880, Nos. 186-193 (NAI).

[39] No. 190, Telegram from Rawlings, Steamer Postmaster (and Indian Government 'spy') at Mandalay to Bernard's Secretary, October 11, 1880; in Nos. 186-193.

[40] No. 192, Telegram from Rawlings to Bernard, October 18, 1880; in Nos. 186-193.

[41] "Burma," (Calcutta) *Englishman*, May 16, 1879, p. 3. According to Dr. Maung Shein, the IFC in April 1882 had twenty-nine steamers, seven steam-launches, and forty-five flats. Maung Shein, *Burma's Transport and Foreign Trade, 1885-1914*, pp. 30-31.

[42] Aitchison to Lyall, November 15, 1879; in Foreign, Political-A, January 1880, Nos. 215-230 (NAI).

[43-45] *Ibid.*

[46] No. 103, Cranbrook to Lytton, December 29, 1879; in Lytton Papers, 516/4, pp. 417b-418.

[47-48] *Ibid.*

[49] No. 31, Indian Foreign Dept. to Cranbrook, January 14, 1880; in C. 4614, pp. 67-69.

[50] *Ibid.*

[51] No. 36, Government of India Foreign Dept. to Hartington, June 1, 1880; in C. 4614, pp. 88-89.

[52] K. W. No. 1, Bernard to Lyall, July 8, 1880; in Foreign, Secret, November 1880, Nos. 107-111 (NAI).

[53-55] *Ibid.* Bernard polled all groups of merchants, Burmese, Chinese, European, and Mogul-Suratti, with non-European merchants having the greater number in business at Rangoon. The importers of the British-manufactures were mostly Europeans. Non-Europeans held the lion's-share of the export-trade of British imports to Upper Burma, and of exports coming from Upper Burma into Lower Burma.

[56] *Ibid.*

[57] No. 103, Bernard to Lyall, August 11, 1880; in Foreign, Secret, November 1880, Nos. 103-106 (NAI).

[58-59] *Ibid.*

[60] Enclosure 1 in No. 33, Aitchison's Secretary to Lyall, February 20, 1880; in C. 4614.

[61] No. 104, Bernard to Lyall, August 11, 1880; in Nos. 103-106.

[62-64] *Ibid.* This probably meant some sort of unofficial or official exchange of views with Mandalay, which would have led to a mutual acceptance of certain preliminary points.

[65] No. 105, Durand to Bernard, October 18, 1880; in Nos. 103-106.

[66] *Ibid.* Durand was typical among the Council members with a strong line towards Upper Burma. In a notation with the papers concerning Bernard's July 8, 1880 report of mercantile opinion at Rangoon, Durand wrote: "The Government of India is distinctly committed......that withdrawal from the Treaties would be advantageous, and it is questionable whether this letter of Mr. Bernard's supplies any strong argument against that view....." K. W. No. 1, Durand's Comments on Bernard's July 8, 1880 despatch, September 8, 1880; in Nos. 107-111.

[67-68] *Ibid.*

[69] No. 44, G. G. in Council to Hartington, November 9, 1880; in C. 4614, p. 103.

[70] Ripon's dissent, August 27, 1880; in Ripon Papers, Br. Mus. Add. Mss. 43,574, Vol. LXXXLV, p. 230 (BM).

[71] Four Council members' comments on Ripon's August 27, 1880 dissent, September 4, 1880 and September 6, 1880; in Ripon Papers, Vol. LXXXLV, p. 232.

[72] Ripon's dissent, August 27, 1880; in Ripon Papers, Vol. LXXXLV, p. 230.

[73] Enclosure 5 in No. 31, Aitchison's Secretary to Lyall, December 6, 1879; in C. 4614, pp. 71-72.

[74] Ripon's dissent, August 27, 1880; in Ripon Papers, Vol. LXXXLV, p. 230.

[75] Bernard to Lyall, January 3, 1881; in Foreign, Secret, February 1881, Nos. 136-137, pp. 2-3 (NAI).

[76] Lyall to Bernard, February 7, 1881; in Nos. 136-137, pp. 3-4.

[77-78] *Ibid. See also:* Lyall's comment on Bernard's January 3, 1881 letter, January 18, 1881; in Nos. 136-137, p. 6.

[79] No. 45, Hartington to G. G. in Council, January 13, 1881; in C. 4614, pp. 103-104.

[80] *Ibid.*

[81-83] *Ibid.*

[84] British subjects included Armenians, Burmese, Chinese, Mogul-Surattis, and others. Such merchants far out-numbered European or British merchants at Rangoon. These non-British and non-Europeans had the lion's share of the export trade to Upper Burma, and most of the imports from Upper Burma. As British subjects they received the same rights as the British owners of the large export-import houses and rice-mills at Rangoon.

[85] A. C. Banerjee, *The Annexation....*, pp. 229-232.

[86] *Ibid. See also:* the detailed discussion of Mindon's monopolies and the efforts to revise the 1867 Treaty in Foreign, Secret, September 1878, Nos. 65-134 (NAI).

[87] Shway Yoe, *The Burman....*, pp. 523-524. *Also:* J. S. Furnivall, *Colonial Policy....*, pp. 65-69.

[88-89] *Ibid.*

[90] "Burma", (Calcutta) *Englishman*, April 15, 1879, p. 3. The writer thought that the *Daywoon* (Chinese imports) Collector should be placed at Bhamo in the north, which was the entrepot for the Yunnan caravan trade. The *Thittaw* (forest) Collector should be placed at the mouths of the creeks where the logs were floated out of the forests. The *Yaydanabhon* (imports from and exports to Lower Burma) Collector should remain at Mandalay. By doing such, each producer or importer-exporter of goods would pay the legal five per cent., and no more.

[91] No. 266, MCD, July 26, 1879; in Foreign, Secret, September 1879, Nos 265-267 (NAI).

[92] *Ibid.* (The 1879 Mandalay tariff schedule of thirteen printed pages listed five per cent. British-import items as diverse as wash hand-basins, empty bottles, pills, frying pans, onions, edible birds' nests and puff boxes. Mandalay exports liable to five per cent duty charges included walnuts, human hair, cheese, preaching benches, dolls, and brass rings with mock jewels. Imported Chinese items into Upper Burma travelling through on their way to Lower Burma, included Yunnan ivory, rhinoceros horns, camphor, silver, tigers' skin, tigers' milk, dried shrimps, peacocks' tails, gold dust, and Shan ponies. The *Pioneer Mail* writer hoped that the last item was a mistake, because the tariff schedule stated that China imports were "brought in by Shans on their shoulders." "Occasional Notes," (Allahabad) *Pioneer Mail*, August 6, 1879, p. 4).

[93-95] *Ibid.* Browne claimed that the two pickled-tea monopolists bought the tea at Rs. 40 to 45 per 100 viss (equal to 2.5 kilograms). They sold it in Lower Burma at Rs. 115 per 100 viss, compared to the old free-market price of Rs. 65-70. "Formerly some 8,000 to 10,000 bullock-loads used to come in monthly......this has decreased to some 4,000 or 5,000 a month."

[96] "Rangoon," (Calcutta) *Englishman*, January 23, 1881, p. 2. *Also:* "Rangoon," (Calcutta) *Englishman*, February 3, 1881, p. 2. A description of how Mulla Ibrahim's duty-collectors checked for smuggled items by

plunging iron-rods into cutch boxes, bundles, and other goods "on the pretense that it contains raw sugar." A gratuity, of course, paid to the duty-collectors prevented such destruction of one's goods. The jaggery (sugar) monopoly especially angered Lower Burmese, who had always had the trade before. It annoyed them that their 'own King' at Mandalay would sell the jaggery to a Chinese, Ko Set Kyee.

[97] Enclosure 4 in No. 3, Kinwun to Bernard, April 26, 1881; in C. 3501, Burmah (1883), p. 17 (NAI). The Lower Burma Government also operated several monopolies: (1) the railroads, (2) the sale of opium and making of spirits and beer, (3) the erection of bazaars, and (4) the contract for carrying the public mails which was always awarded to the British India Steam Navigation Co. No other private firm was allowed to bid. "British Burma," (Allahabad) *Pioneer Mail*, April 5, 1881, pp. 298-299.

A later newspaper writer pointed out that the Lower Burma Government forests sold teak by the ton to the private teak-dealers regardless of soundness. "When the King of Burmah started cutch as a monopoly (taken up, I hear, by the Bombay-Burmah Trading Corporation) the British Forest Department at once advanced the selling rates of cutch trees in this province, thus taking advantage of the natural rise in values which the Upper Burmah monopoly would cause." Burma column, (Calcutta) *Statesman*, September 26, 1881, p. 1023.

Furthermore, the *Ananda Bazar Patrika* noted that the Indian Government was angry at Thebaw because of his proposed salt monopoly. But did not the Indian Government have a salt monopoly, "which enables it to raise a large revenue ? Why then blame Burmah for granting monopolies ?" *Ananda Bazar Patrika*, January 30, 1882; in *Report on Native Newspapers (Bengal), January-December, 1882,* pp. 43-44 (NAI).

[98] No. 265, Burgess to Lyall, May 18, 1881; in Foreign, Political-A, June 1881, Nos. 265-266 (NAI).

[99-100] *Ibid.*

[101] No. 266, Foreign Dept. to Bernard, June 18, 1881; in Nos. 265-266.

[102] Enclosure 8 in No. 1, Andreino to IFC Rangoon Manager, July 3, 1881; in C. 3501, p. 9.

[103] Enclosure 8 in No. 1, Andreino to IFC Rangoon Manager, July 20, 1881; in C. 3501, p. 9. Actually, the fee on the cotton monopoly was only one lakh (Rs. 100,000) as the extra 20,000 went in bribes. Mulla Ismael got his cutch for Rs. 75,000 with 10,000 extra in bribes and Mulla promptly turned about and sold it to the BBTC !

[104] Enclosure 8 in No. 1, IFC Myingyan Agent to IFC Rangoon Manager, July 19, 1881; in C. 3501, p. 10.

[105] Enclosure 10 in No. 1, Diary entry of *Ashley Eden* Preventive Officer, July 22-24, 1881; in C. 3501, pp. 10-11.

[106] Enclosure 8 in No. 1, IFC Rangoon Manager to Bernard's Secretary, July 29, 1881; in C. 3501, pp. 7-8.

[107] *Ibid.*

[108] Enclosure 9 in No. 1, Rangoon C. of C. Secretary to Bernard's Secretary, July 28, 1881; in C. 3501, p. 10.

[109] Enclosure 5 in No. 1, Bernard's Secretary to Foreign, Dept., August 15, 1881; in C. 3501, pp. 4-6.

[110] *Ibid.* Two weeks later Bernard rejected a fourth 'solution', which advocated starving Upper Burma into submission. Upper Burma received about 20-40 inches of rainfall annually. The halting of shipments of *ngape* (pickled fish and oil), betel nut, salt, rice, and paddy to Upper Burma would have caused mass hunger. However, Bernard pointed out that a £3,000,000 annual trade would also be ruined. The Burmese would retaliate, and a crescendo of such retaliations could only lead to rupture, and war. Enclosure 11 in No. 1, Bernard's Secretary to Foreign Dept., August 29, 1881; in C. 3501, pp. 11-12.

[111] *Ibid.*

[112] Enclosure 15 in No. 1, Grant to Bernard, September 10, 1881; in C. 3501, p. 13.

[113] Enclosure 2 in No. 3, Bernard to Kinwun, September 28, 1881; in C. 3501, pp. 15-16.

[114] Enclosure 5 in No. 3, Kinwun to Bernard, October 30, 1881; in C. 3501, p. 17.

[115] K. W. No. 1, Maung Pho's Report to Bernard, January 4, 1882; in Foreign, Secret-E, January 1883, Nos. 524-629. p. 4 (NAI). *See also:* Enclosure 8 in No. 3, Talk with the Burmese Envoy, December 30, 1881; in C. 3501, pp. 18-19. *Also:* Enclosure 9 in No. 3, Further Talk With Burmese Envoy, January 3, 1882; in C. 3501, pp. 19-21.

[116] Enclosure 7 in No. 3, Bernard to Kinwun, January 4, 1882; in C. 3501, pp. 17-18.

[117] *Ibid.*

3

Mandalay Refuses a New Treaty

Introduction

In order to understand why Bernard's January 4, 1882 protest made an impact, while his two protests in 1881 had been curtly dismissed by the Kinwun, it is necessary to study the Mandalay Court factions from 1880 to March 1882. During these years the Kinwun had been reduced to a titular Prime Minister, and Bernard's January 4, 1882 remonstrance was a weapon which the Kinwun used to effect his return to power.

Bernard had demanded that the monopolies be abolished. Since the Yanaung's group had gained the most from the monopolies, an abolition of the monopolies would probably also mean an end to Yanaung's power. The following sections describe the Kinwun's downfall after July 26, 1880, the rise of Yanaung, and how his overthrow resulted in the despatch of a treaty mission to Simla.

The Kinwun Loses Influence

Even before the failure of the Myaungla's Mission on June 4, 1880, the Mandalay Government had come to believe that the Indian Government would not invade Upper Burma, but would restrict its displeasure to written protests. Therefore, the Yanaung, the Taingda, the Hlaythin, and the other 'traditional' groups at Mandalay had less need of the Kinwun's abilities in foreign affairs.

In addition to this *first* key factor, there were three other factors which led to the Kinwun's downfall by July 26, 1880.

The death of the six-months-old Crown Prince from smallpox on about March 26, 1880 was the *second* factor. Thebaw was also reputed to be suffering from a non-fatal case of smallpox, or from some 'loathsome disease'.[1] It was thought that the city's guardian-spirits had lost their power to reisst the smallpox-spirits, which had caused the mass epidemic.

The officials, therefore, arrested perhaps 100 persons, and killed an unknown number on the theory that the deceased would act as guardian-spirits of the city, and drive away the evil small-pox. "In the dark nights of terror, when no one ventured about Mandalay streets, people were buried under each of the posts at the twelve gates, as a compromise between the fear of the spirits and the fear that the English troops would cross the frontier."[2]

The death of the Crown Prince removed a key factor for caution in Mandalay's foreign policies. The security that Supaya-lat had felt with a son was gone. The succeeding annual procession of daughters did not give the long-range stability that a male heir to the throne would have given.

A *third* factor responsible for the Kinwun's downfall was Thebaw's *petite mal* epilepsy that had left him much weakened. Unfortunately, Yanaung aggravated Thebaw's condition by plying him with drugs and drink so as to control him. Consequently, Thebaw was often unwilling and indeed physically incapable of considering the Kinwun's advice.[3]

It was the *fourth* factor, the escape of the Nyaungoke Prince, which was the immediate cause of the Kinwun's downfall. The Nyaungoke escaped from Calcutta in May 1880, one year after his older brother, the Nyaungyan, had been secretly released. The Nyaungoke's escape was apparently without Indian Government assistance, although Mandalay officials suspected otherwise. The Prince was defeated by the Hlaythin, and driven back into Lower Burma where he was captured and shipped back to Calcutta.[4]

Many Upper Burmese remembered the 'escape' of the rebel Myngun Prince from Rangoon in 1867. It was widely believed that the Rangoon authorities had secretly released him. King Mindon was rumoured to have signed the 1867 Treaty in turn for the British re-capturing the Myngun, and shipping him to India where he had remained ever since.[5]

The parallel between 1867 and 1880 was obvious. Both 'escapes' had occurred just as diplomatic negotiations had ended in failure, and both appeared to be British interference in Upper Burmese affairs. The Kinwun received the blame for being so 'naive' as to negotiate. The Kinwun and others were also blamed for not warning Thebaw of the impending escape of the Nyaunggoke, and for not having prevented the Prince's invasion. Thebaw was reported to have thought that the Kinwun and others had been negligent, or had not wanted to warn him.[6]

By July 26, 1880, the Kinwun had lost his Foreign Affairs 'portfolio' to the Kampat Mingyi of the Yanaung Party, which dominated the new *Hlutdaw*.[7] The Kinwun also lost his command over a portion of the army, which was given to the Taingda, his other great rival. The Taingda now commanded the artillery, cavalry, and *elephanterie*. The infantry was commanded by Yanaung, while the Hlaythin continued to command the war-boats. The Kinwun was appointed as a titular, almost powerless 'Prime Minister and President of the *Hlutdaw*'.[8] One of his few remaining powers was to sign all letters to the Indian Government.

The Yanaung Takes Almost Total Power

Yanaung became even more influential in August 1880, when he allegedly intercepted a monk, U Keikti, carrying a long knife near the Royal Apartments. Yanaung's enemies claimed that he had deliberately planted the *dah* and layman's clothing upon the unfortunate monk, who was then immediately hustled outside, tortured until he confessed to having plotted to murder Thebaw, and then executed that night. Supayalat gave birth to her first daughter a few days later, and she of course greatly appreciated Yanaung's strength and loyalty to her husband at such a time.

Nevertheless, Supayalat was persuaded by her crony, Mattie Calogreedy Antram, and the French Catholic nuns at Mandalay, to state that she disapproved of Yanaung's harem, which had electric buzzers attached to each girl's room. Whenever Yanaung desired a particular girl, he punched the buzzer for her room and she would come; and when he wanted them all (which was frequent) he punched all the buzzers, and all the girls would come running. Despite his lewd reputation, there is evidence to indicate that Supayalat greatly admired Yanaung. She only turned against him later when he threatened her control over Thebaw by bringing in other women.[9]

Yanaung did this not only for the erotic control that they gave over Thebaw, but also because Yanaung was an astute observer. He knew that the Shan States were in revolt partially because Thebaw had refused to accept the Tsawbwas' daughters as his queens. For centuries the Tsawbwas had sent their daughters, but Supayalat had stopped all this. She was determined to be the only wife that the King would possess—other than her older sister who was Thebaw's first wife.[10]

The Yanaung knew that additional Queens would dilute Supayalat's influence, and of course strengthen his own. Additional wives accepted from insurgent Tsawbwas, and other formerly loyal officials, would go far towards restoring their loyalty. Supayalat, on the other hand, was determined to retain her influence over her husband. Her influence had been noticeably reduced after the death of her baby son in March 1880. Yanaung suggested that Thebaw should take another wife in order to assure a male heir. Supayalat resented this.

The most lovely of the girls that Yanaung found for Thebaw was Mi Hkin-gyi, 17, who was the daughter of the Kanne Atwinwun, minister of mineral products and public works. She was also the grand-daughter of the Kampat Mingyi, the foreign minister; and niece of the Pagan Atwinwun. Thebaw, however, feared Supayalat's wrath, and the secret affair became a Court joke.[11]

A plot was formed to overthrow Supayalat, and replace her with Mi Hkin-gyi. The plotters included Yanaung, and Mi Hkin-gyi's relatives. Other plotters included the Pintha, Yanaung's brother; the Taungtaman-Lesa; the Ekkahabat Myingwun; and considering the Kinwun's ability at keeping an interest in all factions, perhaps the Shway Laung Peh-hnin, the Kinwun's relative and co-owner of the cotton monopoly with Yanaung. There were others, such as the Taingda, who had gained considerable offices from the Yanaung clique which dominated the *Hlutdaw* The Taingda stood aside from both the plotting and any support to Supayalat, while the Hlaythin supported her.

Supayalat was quite advanced in her third pregnancy in April 1881. She readily agreed to Thebaw's desire to receive a *betthet*, a blessing with consecrated water from the Brahmin *punas*. She also agreed that it would be necessary for Thebaw to keep a solitary fast for seven days in preparation for the ceremony.[12]

Supayalat thought that she too would keep a fast to be worthy of receiving the *betthet* with her husband. Two small wooden palaces were built in the South Garden for them to remain isolated from each other for the seven days. No courtiers came to see her by custom during the solitary fast, and no servant dared to tell her the truth. The entire Court laughed at the spectacle of Supayalat being made a fool of, for once.[13]

Thebaw was not in the other temporary Palace in the garden. He was celebrating his honeymoon with Mi Hkin-gyi, and his favourites, including Yanaung, the Pintha, the Taungtaman-Lesa, the Ekkahabat Myingwun, and others. Supayalat remained unaware of the trick that had been played upon her, and shortly afterwards in July 1881 gave birth to a second girl. Thebaw at that inappropriate moment decided to tell Supayalat about his *new* wife. He said that he wanted her to be his Chief Queen, instead of Supayalat, in order to get a son.[14]

Supayalat became hysterical. At one point Thebaw, encouraged by Yanaung's expostulations to be a man, chased Supayalat through the Palace with a spear. He would have stabbed her, except that she managed to reach her mother's apartment and bolted the door.[15] It was then that Supayalat began to listen once more to her mother, who was very friendly with the Kinwun.

The Royal quarrel was becoming famous. The Indian newspapers carried stories of the epic disagreements between the two.[16] These included a story in the Calcutta *Statesman* of November 7, 1881 that Supayalat had demanded a divorce. Thebaw was said to be considering the quiet of a monastery.[17] A week later, the *Statesman* reported that the Royal Couple had become reconciled.[18]

At this point in late-1881, Thebaw had another attack of *petit mal* epilepsy. It was made worse by the drink and drugs with which Yanaung controlled him.[19] Consequently, the Kinwun's advice had even less influence than usual. When he heard of the approaching visit of Viceroy Lord Ripon to Rangoon in December 1881, the Kinwun sent a secret envoy. The envoy was instructed to time his arrival at Rangoon a day or so after Ripon's departure.[20]

This was done in order to avoid any embarrassment or rumour should Ripon refuse to see the envoy. The envoy, U Kyi, expressed surprise to Bernard that he had missed Ripon, but said that the Mandalay government wished negotiations to take place on all outstanding issues.[21]   Bernard immediately despatched his January 4, 1882 letter remonstrating strongly against the monopolies.

The Overthrow of Yanaung

When Bernard's protest arrived at Mandalay, it aroused considerable anxiety among many court officials.   The Kinwun told Supayalat and her mother that the monopolies should be abolished, and a treaty mission despatched to Simla to negotiate all issues between the two countries.[22]   He explained that if such was not done, the alternative would be a British invasion.

When the Taingda heard that the Kinwun and Supayalat had joined forces, Taingda quietly changed sides,[23] although he had benefited handsomely from his ties with the Yanaung's group, Taingda had unobtrusively supported Yanaung's view that Thebaw should marry the customary four queens, and had also favoured Thebaw's marriage to Mi Hkin-gyi. However, it had become apparent to Taingda that his power was no longer safe with Thebaw so completely dominated by Yananug.   Also, Taingda's power was not safe because the real strength of character at Court was held by Supayalat.

Supayalat assumed the role of the loyal wife, and warned her husband that Yanaung was plotting to dethrone him.   But Thebaw would not listen to her.[24]   A few days later in mid-Janaury 1882, Thebaw left the Palace and went out into Mandalay.[25]   Thebaw left the Palace only two or three time during his reign, because he was afraid that it would be seized by a rival in his absence.   Such a seizure had almost occurred on August 2, 1866 when King Mindon left the Palace *i.e.* 'Mt. Meru', and was nearly murdered by his son, the Myngun Prince.[26]

Thebaw's January 1882 foray into Mandalay was the occasion for the placing of petition boxes at key points in the city.   Anyone was allowed to drop in complaints or petitions for Thebaw to read.   One petition among a number against the Yanaung :
was a very long document and most cleverly written.   It told the King of the stoppage of trade which the monopolies had caused, of the wide-spread ruin and misery brought about by the lotteries, of the manner in which the Yanoung Mentha

oppressed the poor, of the powerlessness of the Ministers, etc. This petition, some say, emanated from the Kinwoon Mingyee, and its effect on the King was soon perceptible.[27]

The shock to Thebaw's trust in Yanaung was traumatic. The erst-while favourite told Andreino, the Italian consul, that the King's mind had been so poisoned by the petition that Yanaung feared he would soon lose some of his offices.[28] A few days later Yanaung was removed from the post of *thanatwun*, master of the approximately 12,000 infantry soldiers at Mandalay, and the Kinwun was put in his place.[29] This was said to be a most popular move among the people, and supposedly prevented a revolt.[30]

On February 9, Rawlings, the 'news-collector' at Mandalay, wrote to Bernard's secretary that the proposed mission to India would probably start in March. Supayalat wished the mission to proceed not so much for friendship's sake, but because she thought that she and those ministers opposed to Yanaung would be safer with a Resident at Mandalay.[31]

On February 20, Bernard telegraphed that Thebaw's Rangoon agent had informed him that all monopolies had been stopped as of February 16. The reply to Bernard's January 4 remonstrance would be brought by the mission, which was standing by at Mandalay awaiting Viceroy Lord Ripon's willingness to receive them.[32] Despite the mercantile celebrations—the BBTC excepted as it had owned the cutch monopoly—no one missed the semantic difference between the words 'abolished' and 'stopped'. The monopolies had been only 'stopped'. There were four reasons for this.

(1) If the Kinwun had been strong enough in mid-February to abolish the monopolies outright, he would have done so. However, as soon as the monopolies ceased, Thebaw lost a good source of income. By March 12, he was apparently considering a partial restoration of the monopolies, as he had run short of funds.[33]

(2) The Court had become preoccupied with preparations for the March 7 circumnabulation about the city on the moats.[34] This was the last portion of Thebaw's June 1879 Coronation, and symbolized Lord Indra taking possession of the universe. This was an act that the earthly Lord Indra had not dared to perform before March 1882, because he had been afraid of a revolt during his absence from the Palace.

(3) Most of the courtiers wanted to stop the monopolies, which were extensively influenced by the Yanaung, only to seize them for themselves. Such persons included Supayalat, who wanted to give the right to levy duty on all the imports to Ko Set Kyee. Ko was the original buyer of the jaggery export-monopoly, which presumably he would not lose as his wife was one of Supayalat's best friends.[35]

(4) But there was still another reason why the monopolies were not abolished outright. The Yanaung still retained some influence over Thebaw. During the first two weeks of March, it appeared that the balance was slipping back to Yanaung away from the Kinwun. The chances for an immediate despatch of the proposed mission had lessened.[36]

The Kinwun's group decided to imprison Yanaung, because of his continued interference in governmental affairs.[37] Yanaung realized that he would have to act, or he would probably die. He arranged for a group of men to attack the Royal Barge during the March 7 circumnabulation about the city moats, and to assassinate the King and Queen. Yanaung would then seize 'Mt. Meru' and proclaim himself 'Lord Indra'.

Somehow, the Kinwun discovered the plot. Or, perhaps the entire plot was a creation of his or Supayalat's fertile mind. At any rate Thebaw was informed. He asked Yanaung to ride with the Royal Couple in the Royal Barge, and to dismiss his own men and barge and send them home. Yanaung could not allow the plot to proceed when he would also be in the line of attack. Also, he could hardly refuse such a signal honour. The *coup* failed.[38]

Petition boxes were placed about the city as had been done earlier during Thebaw's January sojourn outside the Palace grounds. There were over 2,500 petitions, and they took Thebaw over one week to read.[39] Many were unsigned, but there were at least eight-seven petitions complaining against the Yanaung, and one petition in particular with thirty-six signatures.

The petition accused the Yanaung of keeping bands of 'dacoits' in the countryside near Mandalay and of sharing their loot ; of plotting to dethrone Thebaw ; of illegally using Thebaw's Royal Peacock Seal (a capital offense) ; of appointing officials without Thebaw's knowledge ; of forcibly taking away wives and killing their husbands ; and, lastly, of lying to Thebaw concerning the true crisis in the country.[40]

On March 16, Thebaw sent for Yanaung and accused him of disloyalty. Yanaung crouched down apparently hurt that his 'brother' suspected him of treason. Instead of his servility placating Thebaw, it made him hysterical. He thought that Yanaung was too guilt-stricken to speak. Finally, Yanaung murmured that "if you want to kill me, kill !"[41] Only the interference of the Hlaythin Atwinwun, admiral of the war boats, prevented Thebaw from stabbing Yanaung.[42] Rawlings described the Yanaung's final humiliation:

> The Prince was carried out of the palace by the north gate, a
> sure sign....that he will be put to death; and....a mob
> collected....some abusing him and dancing around him, over-
> joyed at his downfall. On his arrival in the prison, the Yan-
> oung sat on a little cot, but the Shwelun Bo knocked him off
> and beat him severely with his slippers [the worst Burmese
> insult], telling the Prince he was only a slave, and then wren-
> ched the nahdoungs from the Prince's ears, hurting him greatly
> as his ears were torn open.[43]

The Pintha, Yanaung's brother, was seized at Madeya, a village twelve miles from Mandalay where he was attending a *poay*, play. Also arrested were the Kampat Mingyi, the foreign minister; the Kanne Atwinwun, his son and minister of mineral produce and public works; and the Kanne Atwinwun's wife, the mother of the unfortunate Mi Hkin-gyi. Her uncle the Pagan Atwinwun, the Taungtaman-Lesa, the Ekkahabat Myingwun, the Kaunghan wun, the Ngwekun wun, a royal princess, the head maid of honour, and a number of other officials were also arrested. By 5 p.m. on March 16 all were in jail,[44] and by the next morning all monopolies were abolished.[45]

Over 500 fire-arms and 1,000 *dahs*, swords, were found at the residences of the Yanaung and his brother. Many were buried under the ground and between the roof and ceiling of their houses. Over 800,000 rupees were allegedly found, besides gold and diamonds of great value. Supayalat was said to have exclaimed : "Why he has more than I do !"[46] Creditors of the two brothers were ordered to submit lists of debts.

Supayalat chided the Roman Catholic nuns for not telling her fully of Yanaung's doings. She said that of all her *kalamas*, foreign women favourites, only Mattie Calogreedy Antram had kept her informed. Mattie was assigned to write a 'true account' of what had happened and send it to the *Rangoon Gazette*.[47]

Confessions were obtained of a 'plot' to depose Thebaw and to place the Yanaung on the throne with Mi Hkin-gyi as his Chief Queen. But Thebaw was weakening, and beginning to doubt whether Yanaung was as bad as portrayed.[48] In order to forestall Yanaung's release, Supayalat had him clubbed to death on March 20. The late 'brother' of Thebaw was rolled up in a cheap straw mat, and carried to the burial ground at night by four drunken ruffians.[49] The Kinwun was again appointed Foreign Minister, and the Mission, which was the Kinwun's ultimate reward, left on April 2, 1882.[50]

The Mission Leaves for Simla

Meanwhile, the India Office in London defined the British position for the upcoming negotiations with Mandalay. The two chief British aims were as always to guarantee the tranquillity of India's eastern frontier, and to assure the lives and rights of British subjects in Upper Burma.

On January 26, 1882, Lord Hartington, the secretary of state for India, despatched a confidential memorandum on Burma, which had been drafted by Col. Sir Owen T. Burne, head of the India Office political and secret department.[51] Sir Burne suggested that a compromise should be reached whereby the Resident might see the Burmese King. In Burne's opinion, Viceroy Lord Northbrook had been wrong in 1875-1876. Northbrook had refused to allow Colonel Duncan, the Resident at Mandalay, to doff his shoes when interviewing King Mindon inside the Palace.[52]

The Indian Government had also been unfair to Burma on the Arms Question.[53] The Indian Government had always refused to recognize the arms provision of the 1867 Treaty, especially the 'Fytche Annexe'. This refusal had been caused by King Mindon's requests in 1868-1870 for 100 rifled cannon, 10,000 breechloading Snider rifles, and other precision-weapons not considered to be strictly 'arms and ammunition'.

In Burne's opinion, the question was not that the arms provision was poorly worded, or that Chief Commissioner Albert Fytche had been foolish in offering the 'Fytche Annexe'. The point was that with the 'Fytche Annexe' the Indian Government had gained the 1867 Treaty.[54] Since then the Indian Government had not kept its word. Burne advocated giving "the King so many arms and indeed guns also, as would appease his vanity and maintain [Upper Burma's] internal tranquillity.[55]

Meanwhile at Mandalay, Rawlings reported on March 16, the day of Yanaung's arrest, that the object of the upcoming mission was to restore affairs to what they had been in Mindon's time.[56] A prospective new treaty had been drafted by the officials who had been to Europe. There were perhaps three or four issues that the Burmese Mission would consider to be of special importance.

(1) The Mission was prepared to surrender the "Shoe Question" provided the Indian Government insisted upon the matter.[57] This was solely a maneuver to gain the very best terms for Mandalay. (2) The Mission would resist any enlargement of the Residency Guard to more than the fifty men allowed under the Yandabo Treaty of 1826. (3) As concerned arms, the Mission would fight very hard to have the prohibition lifted on free import of arms. Lastly, (4) the Manipur boundary dispute, which was a minor irritant to both sides, ought to be resolved.[58]

The Mission left Mandalay on April 2, a day designated by the Court astrologers as being particularly auspicious. The Mission arrived at Calcutta on April 15, and at Simla on April 30. The scholarly R. Hope Pilcher, on leave from his post at the Thayetmyo assistant commissioner's office, acted as the interpreter and escort. Leader of the Mission was the Pangyet minister, son-in-law of the Taingda Atwinwun. The Pangyet was a graduate of French schools, and had lived ten years in France and Europe. He spoke fluent French and capable English.[59] He was the Kinwun's chief assistant in foreign affairs with the title of Kyauk Maung Atwinwun.[60]

The second man in the Mission was the Tangyet Wundauk. He was a graduate of a Woolwich, England school, and spoke excellent English and French. The third man was the Wetmasut Wundauk, who had never been out of Upper Burma but was a loyal Kinwun supporter.[61] The fourth member was Maung Paw Tun, who had been the Burmese Consul at Calcutta in 1879-1881. The fifth man was U Mya, and like Maung Paw Tun, was a secretary. U Mya had never been out of Upper Burma. The sixth and final member of the Mission was the Bo (Colonel) of the South 150 of the Palace Guard. He had no actual powers, but had been sent along as a sop to remnants of the Yanaung faction.[62]

Pilcher recorded some of the process used to put the Mission members into the 'proper mood' for negotiations. One should remember that the Bo was bigoted against foreigners, and had been a Yanaung follower. Under the guise of perfect courtesy, the Pangyet was acquainting the Bo with the military and political realities. Pilcher wrote that :

The "Bo"...is somewhat of a favourite...and the Ambassador [Pangyet minister] is anxious that he should be treated with consideration...and...that he...get a just idea of our strength and carry back a report to the King....On the way up [to Calcutta] Captain Darvall was good enough to show us how quickly the 4½ ton guns could be fired....at night....I did not see the "Bo's" face when the two blank rounds were fired from each gun, but it must have been a sight....

....Unluckily, the Ambassador in going back to bed got too far into his cot and tumbled out the opposite side. So..he was the only man wounded in the action! He was not much hurt, but was a little frightened.

Then coming up the river we dropped a barrel into the water and practised at it with a gatling from the "maintop" at about 1,000 yards. As we landed, the *Ranger* saluted the Ambassador very effectively with a little 7-pounder [the average large Burmese cannon], which made terrific re-echoing explosions, to the infinite delight of my friends. And as we stepped ashore, ...[a 15-gun] salute was fired at the fort. So I think...all that was possible has been done to create a due impression in the mind of the "Bo".[63]

On April 30, the Mission arrived in Simla. There they were met by the Indian Government's negotiating team, which consisted of Charles Grant, officiating secretary of the Indian Foreign Dept.; D. Fitzpatrick, secretary of the Legislative Dept.; and Pilcher as the interpreter and liaison.[64]

The Negotiations

The Pangyet and his fellow ambassadors promptly submitted a proposed treaty. The Indian Government found the treaty as objectionable as the similar 1880 treaty proposed by the Myaungla Mission.[65] To begin with, the Introduction to the 1882 proposed treaty, and Articles 1 and 2, were drawn not between the Mandalay and Calcutta Governments, but between the King of Upper Burma and the Queen-Empress of England.[66]

Articles 3 and 4 would have allowed the Burmese Ambassador a permanent embassy at London, and with direct access to the Queen-Empress. Article 3 contained a 'most favoured nation' phrase. It would have entitled the Burmese Ambassador to every privilege that a 'big power' ambassador would have enjoyed by reason of his country's importance. In summary, the Indian Government objected to the proposed loss of its 'middle-man' role between Upper Burma and Great Britain. The first four articles of the Burmese treaty would have established a direct diplomatic relationship between Mandalay and London.[67]

In Articles 3 and 4 nothing was said about the "Shoe Question", the most important political issue so far as the Indian Government was concerned. Nor was anything mentioned about a 'proper' Residency Guard, although fifty men had been allowed under the terms of the 1826 Yandabo Treaty.[68]

Article 9 prohibited ships of British subjects from carrying arms into Upper Burma. All arms, including privately-owned pistols, were to be surrendered at the first Burmese customs station. Upon the return down-stream, they could be re-claimed. Grant and the Indian negotiators claimed that British subjects would have been placed at the mercy of 'dacoits' if Article 9 had been accepted.[69]

Articles 10 through 15 detailed an elaborate system of customs-inspections and reports, which were considered by the Indian negotiators to be restrictive.[70] Article 16 established two new Royal monopolies on jaggery and pickled tea. Article 17 raised the import duty on liquors, opium, ganja, and other intoxicants and drugs to thirty per cent. Most other goods imported into Upper Burma were to be charged ten per cent. duty, or double the current rate. As with the current treaties, there was no import duty charged on rice and other foodstuffs.[71]

Grant argued that if Mandalay raised its duties to ten per cent., which was allowed under the 1867 Treaty, then the Indian Government had the right, also under the 1867 Treaty, to reimpose the 1862 frontier-duties. Grant suggested that it was not to the interest of either Government to start a tariff war.[72]

Article 18 established a tonnage dues on all merchant ships and barges entering Upper Burma. One rupee per ton was to be paid if the vessel weighed over 150 tons, and one-half rupee per ton if it weighed less than 150 tons. Grant noted that such tonnage dues "would have effectually crippled the river-traffic."[73] Articles 19 through 22 set down a series of complex customs, duty collections, and declaration procedures to be made on the value of goods. These articles along with Articles 10-15 and 23 to 26 made provisions "for subjecting British subjects...to a most vexatious, and unprecedented system of restrictions...."[74]

Articles 23 and 25 required that all British subjects in Upper Burma would have to be registered under more complex procedures than the current registration. Grant commented that such restrictions would be of great inconvenience to British subjects working in the Upper Burmese forests and in other industries.[75]

Article 24 stated that British subjects residing permanently in Upper Burma would pay taxes and duties "just like Burmese subjects." However, they would not have to pay any war levies. Grant thought that such articles might be used to harass Burmese on the Lower Burma side of the frontier.[76] Article 26 took away freedom of speech and contract from British subjects while in Upper Burma.[77]

Articles 27 through 31 re-established the Mixed Court, which had been in abeyance since the withdrawal of the British Resident on October 6, 1879. However, Grant stated that in general the articles were a further weakening of the legal protections of British subjects in Upper Burma.[78] Articles 32 through 36 provided for the extradition of not merely criminal offenders, but also political offenders. Grant stated that such a provision was against the legal customs of all European nations with any pretensions to a free society. Such articles were "specially repugnant to English opinion and traditions."[79]

Articles 37 through 39 provided for the unlimited importation of arms of all types, including gun-boats and Armstrong field guns. The unlimited importation of machinery to manufacture the above and other arms was also allowed. The Indian Government's reaction was to cite these articles "as a fresh instance of the impracticable nature of the terms which they offered us."[80]

After six weeks of sharp probing it became obvious that the Burmese would accept many, if not all, of the Indian Government's objections. In return, the Indian Government would have to (1) allow a treaty giving Mandalay the right to deal directly with the

Queen-Empress in London ; (2) cooperate with Upper Burma in collecting duties and in preventing revolts against Thebaw's authority; and (3) allow the import of arms into Upper Burma.[81]

Therefore, the reception of a Burmese ambassador by Queen Victoria, and the corresponding reception of a British resident by King Thebaw, was discussed. The Pangyet pointed to Siam, a state he considered to be of inferior rank to Burma, which nevertheless had direct relations with London.[82] Grant replied that in the 1820's Siam had ended the archaic Court ritual that had caused the "Shoe Question" in Upper Burma.

The Indian Government rejected the plea for direct Burmese representation at London, because (1) it would have placed Upper Burma on a par with Great Britain; and (2) would have by-passed the Indian Government entirely. The Indian Government was not willing to allow such freedom to a 'buffer state', which ran contiguously with India's eastern frontier.

Finally in late-June 1882, the Pangyet indicated interest in two separate treaties. The first was to be a commercial treaty between the Upper Burmese and Indian Governments. The second treaty was to be a direct friendship treaty between the King of Upper Burma and the Queen-Empress.[83]

Unfortunately, the earlier 'maltreatment' of a British subject at Mandalay had by then become widely publicized. The 'cruelties' at Mandalay now became the crucial issue at the Simla Conference. The issue threatened to make a dead letter of all proposals for a new treaty between the two countries.

Mandalay 'Mistreats' British Subject

Rawlings, the 'news-collector' at Mandalay, wrote on April 24, 1882 that Mattie Calogreedy Antram, a British subject, and a number of Armenian ladies had been arrested at Mandalay and probably beaten.[84] This report and others, including a May 15 news-communication from the Nyaungyan Prince,[85] aroused great concern at Simla.

The May 11, 1882 Calcutta *Daily News* commented that the Armenians had been plotting to put Mi Hkin-gyi, Thebaw's mistress, on the throne as Chief Queen. This was the reason given for her execution in late April. The *Daily News* stated that Mi Hkin-gyi "was beaten to death in the presence of the Queen, and that she underwent this dreadful punishment when far advanced in *pregnancy*...."[86]

The Burmese official account had first claimed that the Armenians were plotting to restore the Nyaungyan Prince, and that they had been writing to him towards this end.[87]   However, by May 23, the official account had changed the name of the prince involved to the late Yanaung Mintha.[88]   The change had been made because Yanaung was both unpopular and dead.

The excitement soon subsided.   J. A. Bryce, who was negotiating the BBTC's 1882 'Shorts' Contract at Mandalay, wrote to Bernard on May 17.   Bernard in turn repeated the gist of Bryce's remarks in a May 25 letter to Grant.   Bernard stated that "Mrs. Antram never got into trouble, but is in favour at Court."[89]   The J. S. Manook family—whose late-father had been *kala wun* (sub-minister in charge of foreigners) under Mindon—was banished to Shwebo.   The family included the mother, two daughters, and two other Armenian relatives, Mrs. George and Mrs. M. C. Vertanez.[90]

Mandalay officials stated that the Armenians would have been punished even more severely in other countries.[91]   On the other hand, Rangoon friends of the Armenians claimed that the ladies had been exiled as the result of mere spiteful accusations.[92]   The May 27 Calcutta *Statesman* summed up the entire affair by stating that the Mandalay Government had played "into the hands of their detractors and enemies."[93]

London's Reaction

The *Statesman* was correct.   The lurid reports seemed to remind the Simla and London Governments of the February 15-17, 1879 Mandalay Massacre.   Lord Ripon's June 24 telegram to Lord Hartington had proposed two separate treaties with Burma.   One treaty was to be a commercial treaty between Upper Burma and India, and the second treaty was to be a direct friendship treaty between King Thebaw and Queen Victoria.[94]   Hartington had telegraphed his approval on June 27, provided that both Treaties stated that diplomatic relations would be conducted as always through the Indian Foreign Dept.[95]

But Hartington changed his mind as additional reports of the 'brutalities' at Mandalay reached London.   On July 8 he telegraphed to Ripon that Queen Victoria had at first refused to agree to a direct friendship treaty, unless an 'anti-massacre' clause was placed among its provisions. Hartington had finally gained the Queen's consent for the treaty provided an unwritten understanding was reached with the envoys that no future massacres were to take place.[96]

Ripon telegraphed back on July 9 that "I think I shall be able to do what you suggest......."[97] Consequently, on July 10, Pilcher approached the Pangyet, but was met with a cool reception. The Pangyet:

objected most to the proposed guarantees against further atrocities. He said that the Armenian women were criminals, and they had a perfect right to punish them, and that interference on our part would amount to an attempt to usurp their criminal jurisdiction; in fact we might as well ask them to change their King at once.[98]

Ripon advised Hartington in a July 12 telegram that an 'anti-massacre' clause would be unenforceable. Ripon recommended that the envoys should be informed again of the great concern felt by the Queen-Empress over such massacres. Similar sentiments should be stated in a letter to Thebaw. These two actions would accomplish about as much as could be done.[99] Hartington wired back his approval on July 15.[100]

The Pangyet then accepted the idea of two treaties. The first treaty was to be a commercial treaty between Upper Burma and India, and the second treaty was to be a direct friendship treaty between King Thebaw and Queen Victoria with no reference to massacres. The Pangyet also seemed to accept a provision for the British Resident to operate under European etiquette at Mandalay. The Pangyet seemed to object to only one remaining item. This was the provision for a Residency Guard at Mandalay with no specific limit on the number of men.[101]

Nevertheless, on July 18 the Pangyet asked for a pause in the negotiations.[102] Grant and the negotiating team presented a formal draft of the two treaties to the Pangyet on July 28. This was an effort to present the scattered articles in one coherent whole, and to hurry the Mandalay Government along towards a decision. On the same day, Grant sent a report to Ripon.

Grant stated that "If they break at all, it will probably be on the armed guard."[103] He reminded Ripon that when the ambassadors had arrived they had presented a long list of demands. However, it had also been known that the ambassadors' real demands were only three. These were (1) direct relations with Queen Victoria; (2) guarantees that the Indian Government would assist in duty collection and would prevent the 'escape' of the exiled princes; and (3) the importation of arms into Upper Burma. Once having gained these three demands, the ambassadors were prepared to concede anything, except an enlargement of the Residency guard to more than the fifty men allowed under the 1826 Yandabo Treaty.[104]

Grant thought that the ambassadors should be reminded once more that they had gained a *direct friendship treaty* with Queen Victoria. In Grant's opinion, the only counterbalancing concessions that the Indian Government had received were the 'shoe' concession in Article 2 of the commercial treaty, and the continuation of duties at five per cent in Article 11.[105] The latter, however, was actually no concession as the Indian Government had the right to reinstate the old 1862 frontier duties should the Burmese Government raise their duties above five per cent.

Grant stated that the Burmese had obtained their *second* demand without giving any equivalent in return.[106] Article 16 of the proposed commercial treaty stated that the Indian Government would help Mandalay to enforce all duty provisions in Articles 10-15, and elsewhere. Articles 22-23 stated that the Indian Government would work with Mandalay to keep off rebel incursions.[107] This was a guarantee against any more 'escapes' of India-exiled princes, such as the 1867 'escape' of the Myngun Prince, and the 1879 'escape' of the Nyaungyan Prince. Grant stated that such guarantees "may not seem very much to us, but the Burmese attach great importance to them."[108]

Equally important, the Burmese had received their *third* demand, namely the importation of arms.[109] Article 21 provided for 5,000 breech-loading rifles, and 500,000 rounds of ammunition, to be supplied immediately after ratification of the commercial treaty. Grant stated that the 'Fytche Annexe' of the 1867 Treaty had obligated the Indian Government to allow the import of arms to Upper Burma.

The obligation existed even though "the Fytche Annexe was made without our authority and even without our knowledge, and was never formally ratified......"[110] Grant must have known that he was skirting dangerously close to an official lie at this point. He did so, apparently, to save the 'face' of the Indian Government.[111]

Grant almost certainly knew that Parliament had approved the 'Annexe' as part of the 1867 Treaty. The 'Fytche Annexe' was published along with the other relevant treaty provisions and correspondence as Parliamentary Paper-House of Commons 251, June 8, 1869. The 'Fytche Annexe' was placed on page 38 under the letter A. immediately below the regular treaty provisions. Consequently, it was approved by every official who had any business with the 1867 Treaty. Such officials included the Viceroy, the Secretary of State for India, Parliament, Queen Victoria, the Mandalay *Hlutdaw*, and King Mindon.[112]

In concluding his July 28 report to Ripon, Grant thought that overall the Burmese had the best of the treaty. Therefore, if the Pangyet finally insisted on British subjects being charged duty at Bhamo, which was prohibited under the current Treaties, then the ambassadors should offer some concession in return.[113]

In summary, one must conclude that the Pangyet was a shrewd diplomat. He was able to disregard the many demands that his Government had loaded him with in order to secure the three demands that would assure his country's survival. These were (1) a direct friendship treaty; (2) duty assistance and guarantees against Royal 'escapes'; and (3) arms. The Pangyet had shrewdly secured the weapons that would assure both internal order, and consequent foreign respect. Unfortunately, for the outcome of the Conference, and indeed for the future independence of Upper Burma, there were persons at Mandalay who would have been hurt by a treaty 'normalizing' the relations between the two countries.

The Ambassadors Return to Mandalay

On August 15, Pilcher wrote to Grant that despite frequent requests the Pangyet had not yet received approval from Mandalay. The Pangyet's father-in-law, the Taingda, was said to be ill and governmental business at Mandalay had come to a near-halt because of the hot weather.[114] Ripon told Grant to wait a few more days, and thanked Grant for the Burmese ambassadors' photograph.[115]

Finally on August 22, the Pangyet stated that his Government had called him home for further consultations. Grant told him that only the draft commercial treaty could be offered, if the Pangyet wanted this further postponement. The lack of eagerness on the part of Mandalay had convinced the Indian Government that the offer of a direct friendship treaty should be withdrawn.[116] The Pangyet presented an explanation for the ending of the conference during an August 29 farewell reception held by Viceroy Ripon :

The main points on which His Majesty has declined to accept the Treaty are not......trade or commerce. [But]......in the Treaty presented to the Embassy......the custom and etiquette of the Burmese Government is altered; and, in addition, there are one or two other articles of a similar character......For myself, I could concede a great deal, but....my Government has to look not only to the opinion of the individual Ministers......but......public opinion has also to be regarded.[117]

One can only suggest that the 5,000 breech-loading rifles and 500,000 rounds to be supplied upon ratification of the treaty would have moulded 'public opinion' for both the treaty and for the continuance of Thebaw's rule. At any rate, on September 19, Bernard had a long chat with the Pangyet as his party was passing through Rangoon on the way home.

Bernard found the Pangyet much more relaxed and confiding than he had been on the way up to Simla. Bernard seemed rather charmed by the Pangyet's voracious interests. "The Envoy seems a reforming sort......He took away a number of books and Acts; and was much interested in the Rangoon water-works scheme."[118]

Bernard reported that the local Burmese, Chinese, European, and Indian merchants, who traded with Mandalay, were most unhappy over the collapse of the negotiations.[119] The merchants thought that the Pangyet and the 'enlightened' ministers at Mandalay had genuinely desired to conclude a treaty.

The chances for approval of the Treaty appeared brighter when Thebaw gave a cordial welcome to the Pangyet and his party on September 30.[120] Thebaw expressed his appreciation for the Viceregal gifts of two sets of telephones, an electro-motor railway, and other technological devices.[121] Unfortunately, two key factors among many, namely (1) the clique of Italians and *kalamas* at

Mandalay, and (2) the 1882 Egyptian War, had already virtually negated the Pangyet's brilliant diplomacy.

The Groups Against the Treaty

There were persons and companies, such as the BBTC, in both Upper and Lower Burma, who had owned interests in the former Mandalay monopolies outlawed under the proposed 1882 Commercial Treaty. However, the increased stability and trade that the Treaty held-out to all merchants probably offered a way for the former monopolists to recoup their losses.

Also, the monopolies had been abolished by the Mandalay Government before the despatch of the Pangyet's Mission. Therefore, most merchants in both Burmas, whether former monopoly-owners or not, probably realized that their best move was to support the Treaty and to work for its approval.[122]

However, there were two groups among others at Mandalay, the Italian weapons-makers and the *kalamas*, who were not benefited by the proposed Treaty. Their activities must be placed against the background of Britain's early defeats at the hands of Ibn Arabi, the anti-British Egyptian general, in the Egyptian War during the summer of 1882.

The Italian Weapons-Makers

The Italian weapons-makers at Mandalay would not have benefited from the Treaty, which allowed the free importation of arms into Upper Burma, and a British Resident with access to Thebaw. Bernard heard about the weapons-makers from an unnamed British informant, who spoke fluent Italian.[123] The informant claimed that "affairs in Egypt had attracted much attention in the Palace ; ......the troops were undergoing a lot more drill than usual."[124]

The informant said that the Palace courtiers were outdoing each other with claims of what they would do if the British were defeated by Ibn Arabi in Egypt. One minister proposed an immediate massacre of all British in Upper Burma. This worried the other Europeans at Mandalay, who thought that they might also be massacred. Such a fear did not seem to bother the Italian weapons-makers, because they encouraged such talk among their

Palace acquaintances.[125]

The Italian group had come to Mandalay from Italy ten months previously with machinery and a government contract to make 30,000 Martini breech-loading rifles.[126] However, some of the necessary machinery had not yet arrived. Bernard's informant claimed that it was cheaper and quicker for the Italians to smuggle the rifles up to Mandalay,[127] and then "palm them off on the Government as [being] of local manufacture."[128] He claimed that during July 1882, 500 revolvers and rifles had been smuggled up in an oil shipment, possibly with the shipment on an IFC steamer piloted by Captain Patterson.[129]

The Italian contractors could not properly complete the lock-action on Martini rifles manufactured at Mandalay. The contractors' greatest fear was that some jealous European in Thebaw's service would point out the defect.[130] Tavarozzi Angelo, a discharged Italian mechanic, had told Bernard's informant that an Italian General in Thebaw's service was determined to point out the defect in the looks, and to recommend that the entire lot be rejected.[131]

Therefore, the contractors magnified the British defeats in Egypt during the summer of 1882. The Italians advised the Court that it would be foolish to sign a treaty with the Indian Government. Better terms could be gained by waiting a few months, until after the British were decisively beaten in Egypt. The weapons-makers must have secretly dreaded such a possibility. 'Better terms' would have allowed more fire-arms into Upper Burma, which would have made the contractors' defective rifles even more worthless.

The Kalamas

There was a second group of Europeans, Armenians, and Eurasians at Mandalay, who were unhappy over the prospect of a new Treaty. These were the *kalamas*, foreign females, who provided information to Supayalat in return for gifts and the vicarious thrill of being near the seat of power. Supayalat in order to be certain of their loyalty had made them swear an oath of obedience to her.[132]

The October 3, 1882 Rangoon *Times* described the distorted picture of the Egyptian war that the *kalamas* and other Europeans had given to Supayalat. Great Britain was supposed to have 40,000 troops tied down in Egypt, with nearly the same amount engaged in rebellious Ireland. Great Britain was supposed to be almost prostrate with the French, Italians, and all of Europe ready to attack.[133] The Italians at Mandalay, in trade, in weapons-making, and in posts in Thebaw's Government, were said to be especially adept in their elaborations on this theme of imminent British collapse.[134]

The *Times* explained that it was easy for the *kalamas* and the other Europeans to mislead Supayalat, because she trusted them to be her advisers on foreign affairs. Indeed, they had to tell her what she wanted to hear in order to retain her favour. The leading *kalamas* consisted of Mattie Calogreedy Antram, a British subject and the young widow of IFC Capt. Antram; Mrs. Calogreedy, Mattie's mother and Supayalat's former nurse; and, Sister Therese and Sister Sophia, two of the several French Roman Catholic nuns at Mandalay.

In the absence of the British Resident, persons seeking favours of a commercial or political nature at Mandalay usually routed their requests through the *kalamas*.[135] For example, the BBTC had received favourable treatment in their recent 1882 Chindwin Forest negotiations by paying a widowed *kalama* Rs. 8,000 to intercede for them.[136] This widow was probably Mattie Calogreedy Antram. The *Times* claimed that she had "already received several offers of marriage from people anxious to avail themselves....of the influence she is believed to possess."[137]

The *kalamas* knew that their role as 'middlemen' would lose most of its importance on the day that the British Resident returned to Mandalay with direct access to the Royal Couple.[138] The *kalamas*' chief strength, ironically, lay in Supayalat's antipathy towards *kalas*.[139] Therefore, the *kalamas* recommended that Mandalay should postpone approval of the Treaty for a few months, until after the British were defeated in Egypt. Many additional concessions could then be wrung from the hated foreigners.

In summary, the arrival of a new British Resident would have reduced the political and commercial influence of most Europeans at Mandalay to the lower level that it had been prior to the withdrawal of the Resident on October 6, 1879. The selfish interests of the weapons-makers, the *kalamas*, and of most Europeans in trade at Mandalay, or in Thebaw's service, were best served by not having a new Treaty. Therefore, they all in their own way advised against the Treaty, and subverted it as best as they could.

Mandalay's Rejection of the Treaty

Thebaw and his Court gave a cordial welcome to the returning Pangyet Mission on September 30. The October 3, 1882 *Statesman* stated that the news of recent British victories in Egypt had not had time to reach Upper Burma. The *Statesman* thought that had the victories occurred "when the Burmese embassy was at Simla, the ambassador would not have been so suddenly recalled by his government."[140]

When the news of the Pangyet's cordial welcome reached Calcutta, the *Statesman* commented that "Perhaps the success of Sir Garnet Wolseley in Egypt has already had its effect on King Thebaw and his advisers."[141]   One can probably agree. The sudden turn in British fortunes had probably convinced many Mandalay officials that the proposed Treaty should receive swift approval.

However, the Taingda and others cited the various Mandalay Europeans as authorities on the British. The Kinwun and the Pangyet defended the Commercial Treaty as the best that could be gained at that time. They argued that the Indian Government would not accept any new treaty proposals. Such proposals would only cause the Mandalay Government to lose the considerable gains represented by the current Treaty.

Their protests, however, were discounted as a sign of their 'weakness' in dealing with a power, which most Mandalay Europeans agreed was in sad disrepair. The majority of the Court and the Royal Couple were persuaded to reject the Treaty, and to submit two new treaties to the Indian Government by the December 31, 1882 deadline. The Kinwun was called upon to draft the new treaties.

Suddenly, on December 4, the Myngun Prince escaped from Banares where he had been living under casual surveillance for about a dozen years.[142]   He reappeared in Chandernagore, the French enclave in Bengal, and proclaimed his intention of seizing Thebaw's throne. Burmese officials suspected that the Indian Government had again allowed the Myngun to 'escape' in order to compel Mandalay to approve a treaty. He had allegedly been allowed to 'escape' once before from Rangoon on February 6, 1867 after the collapse of the initial negotiations for the 1867 Treaty.[143] The escape of the Nyaungoke Prince in May 1880— after the failure of the Myaungla's Mission—was thought to be a similar example of Indian Government 'interference'.

There was no evidence that the Indian Government had arranged an escape of the Myngun Prince similar to his reputed 'escape' in 1867. Nevertheless, the Mandalay Government did not wish to run any risks. The Kinwun completed the new treaties, which included among their provisions a slightly altered version of Articles 9-12 of the Burmese draft treaty presented at Simla. On December 13, the Kinwun wrote to Grant and suggested that the two treaties be accepted in lieu of the August 29 Commercial Treaty.[144]

On January 4, 1883, Viceroy Ripon telegraphed Lord Kimberley, the new secretary of state for India, that he had received the Kinwun's December 13, 1882 letter and two draft treaties.[145] The first treaty was drawn-up between the King of Upper Burma and the Queen-Empress, and concerned only non-Indian British subjects. The treaty provided for an exchange of Residents at Calcutta and Mandalay. It conceded the "Shoe Question" to non-Indian British subjects, but made no mention of a Residency Guard at Mandalay.[146]

The second treaty was drawn-up between the King of Upper Burma and the Viceroy of India, and limited the Indian Government's jurisdiction to Indian British subjects. The treaty provided for the mutual exchange of Residents, but did not mention a Residency Guard. Also, the "Shoe Question" was not waived in the case of Indian British subjects. The treaty established a new monopoly on tea, and allowed the future establishment of other monopolies. The treaty also required the extradition of political offenders as well as criminal offenders, and "is open to other objections."[147]

Ripon particularly objected to the Burmese attempt to distinguish between Indian and non-Indian British subjects, and to limit the Indian Government's jurisdiction to only the former.[148] Ripon asked permission to reject the proposed treaties, and Kimberley wired his approval on January 10.[149] A later bid by the Kinwun to reopen negotiations was rejected on July 9, 1883, and the Simla Conference was finally over.[150]

Without breech-loading rifles, it was only a matter of time before Thebaw would have faced widespread revolts. The Indian Government might have felt it necessary to invade in order to protect the lives and rights of British subjects in Upper Burma. To forestall both possibilities, the Mandalay Government attempted to get arms and other concessions from the French during 1883-1885.

FOOTNOTES

[1] K. W. No. 2, Aitchison to Durand, April 9, 1880; in Foreign, Secret, April 1880, Nos. 93-99 (NAI). *See also:* No. 468, Telegram from Aitchison to Durand, March 20, 1880; in Foreign, Political-A, March 1880, Nos. 468-469 (NAI); *See also:* "Rangoon," (Calcutta) *Englishman*, April 2, 1880, p. 2; "The Terror at Mandalay," (Calcutta) *Statesman*, April 21, 1880, p. 350; and, *lastly:* "Rangoon," (Calcutta) *Statesman*, May 5, 1880, p. 396.

[2] Shway Yoe, *The Burman* . . . . . . , pp. 477-479.

[3] Bryce to Bernard, May 29, 1882; in Foreign, Secret-E, July 1883, Nos. 125-146 (NAI). J. A. Bryce was the younger brother of Lord Bryce, member of Parliament for Tower Hamlets and author of *The Holy Roman Empire.* 'Young Bryce' wrote in part that: "Dr. Barbieri [the Italian doctor at Mandalay] . . . . . . says that from what he saw before he thinks there is a disposition to epilepsy, which in the serious attack at the end of last year [1881] was aggravated by the drugs and drink with which the Yanoung had plied him . . . . . ." Bryce was the BBTC's chief timber-contract negotiator in Burma, and lived much of the time at Mandalay.

[4] K. W. No. 2, Aitchison to Lyall, May 28, 1880; in Foreign, Secret, June 1880, Nos. 152-173, pp. 3-4 (NAI). *Also see:* K. W. No. 4, Kisch to Cockerell, May 28, 1880; in Nos. 152-173, pp. 4-5. *Also:* No. 18. Col. Davies to Bernard's Secretary, June 7, 1880; in Foreign, Secret, July 1880, Nos. 17-23 (NAI). *Also:* No. 112, Col. Davies to Bernard's Secretary, June 28, 1880; in Foreign, Secret, September 1880, Nos. 96-121 (NAI). *Lastly:* No. 110, Bernard's Secretary to Kinwun, July 2, 1880; in Nos. 96-121.

[5] Occasional Notes," (Allahabad) *Pioneer Mail*, January 24, 1883, p. 69.

[6] "A Coming King," (Calcutta) *Statesman*, July 28, 1880, p. 698.

[7] No. 144, Rawlings to Bernard's Secretary, July 26, 1880; in Foreign, Political-A, September 1880, Nos. 143-149 (NAI). *See also:* No. 14, Telegram from Bernard to Durand, July 30, 1880 ; in Foreign, Political-A, August 1880, Nos. 14-15 (NAI).

[8] *Ibid.*

[9] No. 215, Bernard to Foreign Dept., January 15, 1882; in Foreign, Political-A, January 1882, Nos. 208-216 (NAI). *See also:* K. W. No. 2, M. Hla

2. *Supayalat and Thebaw.*

2a. *Supayagyi, Supayalat's older sister and Thebaw's first wife, with the Dowager Queen, the mother of Supayagyi and Supayalat. The Dowager Queen had put Thebaw upon the throne in September 1878. (London Graphic, February 27, 1886, p. 236).*

Oung to E. R. Henry, April 16, 1882; in Foreign, Secret-E, May 1883, Nos. 40-79, pp. 5-6 (NAI).

[10] H. Fielding-Hall, *Thibaw's Queen*, pp. 82, 100-111.

[11] E. C. V. Foucar, *The Reigned At Mandalay*, p. 94.

[12] J. G. Scott, and J. P. Hardiman, *Gazetteer of Upper Burma and the Shan States,* Vol. 1. Part 1, pp. 87-88.

[13] *Ibid.*

[14] *Ibid.* (*Also:* E. C. V. Foucar, *They Reigned At Mandalay*, p. 96).

[15] *Ibid,* pp. 88-89.

[16] Burma column, (Calcutta) *Statesman*, October 10, 1880, p. 1077.

[17] Burma column, (Calcutta) *Statesman*, November 7, 1881, pp. 1199-1200.

[18] Burma column, (Calcutta) *Statesman*, November 14, 1881, p. 1225.

[19] Bryce to Bernard, May 29, 1882; in Nos. 125-146.

[20] K. W. No. 1, Maung Pho's Report to Bernard, January 4, 1882; in Nos. 524-629. *See also:* Enclosure 8 in No. 3, Talk With the Burmese Envoy, December 30, 1881; in C. 3501, pp. 18-19. *Lastly:* Enclosure 9 in No. 3, Further Talk With Burmese Envoy, January 3, 1882; in C. 3501, pp. 19-21.

[21] *Ibid.*

[22] Rawlings (?) to Bernard's Secretary, March 19, 1882; in Nos. 125-146, pp. 7-8. Rawlings' name was often deleted from his reports when they were printed. This was done to avoid trouble should printed copies of Rawlings' reports fall into Burmese hands.

[23] E. C. V. Foucar, *They Reigned At Mandalay*, p. 96.

[24] No. 215, Bernard to Foreign Dept., Janauary 15, 1882 ; in Nos. 208-216.

[25] Rawlings (?) to Bernard's Secretary, March 19, 1882; in Nos. 125-146.

[26] For a description of the Myngun's revolt *see :* Thaung Blackmore, "Dilemma of the British Representative to the Burmese Court After the Outbreak of a Palace Revolution in 1866," (Singapore) *Journal of Southeast Asian History,* Vol. X, No. 2, September 1969, pp. 236-251. A good study.

[27] Rawlings (?) to Bernard's Secretary, March 19, 1882 ; in Nos. 125-146.

[28-30] *Ibid.*

[31] K. W. No. 2, Rawlings (?) to Bernard's Secretary, February 9, 1882 ; in Foreign, A-Political-E, November 1882, Nos. 1-50, p. 5 (NAI).

[32] No. 414, Telegram from Bernard to Grant, February 20, 1882 ; in Foreign, Political-A, February 1882, Nos. 411-416 (NAI). *See also :* No. 412, Telegram from Bernard to Grant, February 18, 1882 ; in Nos. 411-416.

[33] No. 1, Telegram from Bernard to Grant, March 12, 1882 ; in Nos. 1-50.

[34] Rawlings (?) to Bernard's Secretary, March 2, 1882 ; in Nos. 1-50, pp. 8-9.

[35] K. W. No. 2, Rawlings to Bernard's Secretary, February 9, 1882 ; in Nos. 1-50.

[36] No. 1, Telegram from Bernard to Grant, March 12, 1882 ; in Nos. 1-50.

[37] Rawlings (?) to Bernard's Secretary, March 19, 1882 ; in Nos. 125-146.

[38] *Ibid.*

[39-40] *Ibid. Also :* Rawlings (?) to Bernard's Secretary, March 20, 1882 ; in Nos. 125-146, pp. 6-7. *See also :* H. Fielding-Hall, *Thibaw's Queen,* pp. 101-102.

[41] H. Fielding-Hall, *Thibaw's Queen*, pp. 116-118.

[42] Rawlings (?) to Bernard's Secretary, March 19, 1882 ; in Nos. 125-146. *Also* : Rawlings (?) to Bernard's Secretary, March 20, 1882 ; in Nos. 125-146.

[43-44] *Ibid.* A Bo is a Colonel.

[45] Royal Edict Abolishing Monopolies, March 17, 1882 ; in Nos. 1-50, p. 10.

[46] Rawlings (?) to Bernard's Secretary, March 19, 1882 ; in Nos. 125-146. *Also :* Rawlings (?) to Bernard's Secretary, March 20, 1882 ; in Nos. 125-146.

[47] *Ibid.*

[48] H. Fielding-Hall, *Thibaw's Queen*, pp. 118-122. *Also :* J. G. Scott and J. P. Hardiman, *Gazetteer of Upper Burma and the Shan States,* Vol. 1, Part 1, p. 90.

[49] Telegram from Rawlings (?) to Bernard's Secretary, March 23, 1882 ; in Nos. 125-146.

[50] "Rangoon Correspondent," (Calcutta) *Statesman,* August 19, 1882, p. 1180. The Kampat (ex-Foreign Minister) was freed in late July, 1882. The Pintha and others were supposed to be freed later. The Pagan Atwinwun, who was Mi Hkin-gyi's uncle, and the Ekkhabat Myingwun were killed in late March. The Taungtaman-Lesa was later secretly assassinated on orders from Supayalat while the official was being exiled to Mogaung. Mi Hkin-gyi was killed by Supayalat's order in late April, 1882.

[51] Burne Memorandum on Burma in Hartington to Ripon, January 26, 1882; in Ripon Papers, Br. Mus. Add. Mss. 43568, Vol. LXXVIII (BM).

[52-55] *Ibid.*

[56] Rawlings (?) to Bernard's Secretary, March 16, 1882; in Nos. 125-146, pp. 5-6.

[57-58] *Ibid.* (Manipur had been a persistent irritant since the First Burmese War of 1824-1826. *See :* Enclosure 1 in No. 65, Bernard's Secretary to Indian Foreign Dept., June 2, 1884; in C. 4614, pp. 112-114. A summary of the Manipur problem during the period 1878-1884. *Also :* Foreign, Political-A, January 1882, Nos. 48-55 (NAI). *Lastly:* "Relations Between Upper Burma and Manipur," (Allahabad) *Pioneer Mail*, January 24, 1882, pp. 68-69).

[59-62] *Ibid.* The Pangyet, the Tangyet, and the Wetmasut were the Kinwun's three major assistants in foreign affairs. The Pangyet and the Wetmasut had the sad task on November 26, 1885 of coming down to Ava, and surrendering the country to the invading British. The Tangyet, in the meantime, was the Burmese ambassador to Paris. The Bo was killed in early-January, 1884 when a large Burmese force was defeated by the rebel Shan Tsawbwa of Mong Nai. *See :* "Burma...," (Allahabad) *Pioneer Mail,* February 6, 1884, p. 146.

[63] K. W. No. 1, Pilcher to Grant, April 18, 1882; in Foreign, A-Political-E, November 1882, Nos. 1-50 (NAI).

[64] Pilcher was an authority and so designated by the Indian Government in the Shan language and culture.

[65] No. 8, Indian Foreign Dept. to Hartington, September 15, 1882; in C. 3501, pp. 22-27. *See also:* Enclosure 11 in No. 8, The Burmese Draft Treaty; in C. 3501, pp. 36-45. *Also see :* Foreign, Secret-E, January 1883, Nos. 524-629 (NAI).

[66]-[69] *Ibid.*

[70]-[71] *Ibid.*

[72] Enclosure 17 in No. 8, Grant to Pangyet, August 30, 1882; in C. 3501, pp. 49-52.

[73]-[74] *Ibid.*

[75]-[77] *Ibid.*

[78] No. 8, Indian Foreign Dept. to Hartington, September 15, 1882; in C. 3501, pp. 22-27.

[79] Enclosure 17 in No. 8, Grant to Pangyet, August 30, 1882; in C. 3501, pp. 49-52.

[80] No. 8, Indian Foreign Dept. to Hartington, September 15, 1882; in C. 3501, pp. 22-27.

[81]-[82] *Ibid.* In the 1820's, John Crawfurd and Major Henry Burney, Indian envoys to Siam, were both allowed to retain their shoes while interviewing King Rama III. Although Siam had the same 'Meru-centric' tradition and divine kingship as did Burma, there was no corresponding "Shoe Question".

[83] No. 1026, Telegram from Ripon to Hartington, June 24, 1882; in Ripon Papers, I. S. 290/6, pp. 239-240 (BM).

[84] No. 60, Rawlings to Bernard's Secretary, April 24, 1882; in Foreign, Secret-E, November 1882, No. 47-87 (NAI). *Also see:* No. 74, Note on Mrs. Antram, May 11, 1882; in Nos. 47-87. This note indicated that Mattie Calogreedy Antram had always had considerable influence at Court, and that her parents were always registered as British subjects. When she married Capt. Antram of the IFC in 1873, she acquired British nationality if she had not already possessed it from her parents.

There was some humour, perhaps unintentional, in the report when the writer noted that: "At first she used to go up and down the river with her husband; but as he ran his steamer on a sandbank where it had to remain the whole season, the......Company objected to the presence of his wife on board ship, and thereafter Mrs. Antram lived at Mandalay."

[85] Nyaungyan to Grant, May 15, 1882; in Nos. 125-146, pp. 8-9.

[86] No. 74, Extract from Calcutta *Indian Daily News*, May 11, 1882; in Nos. 47-87. *See* another account of Mi Hkin-gyi's execution in: Burma Column, (Calcutta) *Statesman*, May 2, 1882, p. 610.

[87] Burma Column, (Calcutta) *Statesman*, May 16, 1882, p. 681.

[88] Rangoon Column, (Calcutta) *Statesman*, May 23, 1882, p. 718.

[89] No. 75, Bernard to Grant, May 25, 1882; in Nos. 47-87.

[90] *Ibid.*

[91] Rangoon Column, (Calcutta) *Statesman*, May 23, 1882, p. 718.

[92] *Ibid.*

[93] Rangoon Column, (Calcutta) *Statesman*, May 27, 1882, p. 755.

[94] No. 1026, Telegram from Ripon to Hartington, June 24, 1882; in Ripon Papers, I. S. 290/6, pp. 239-240.

[95] No. 1031, Telegram from Hartington to Ripon, June 27, 1882; in Ripon Papers, I. S. 290/6, p. 241.

[96] No. 1054, Telegram from Hartington to Ripon, July 8, 1882; in Ripon Papers, I. S. 290/6, pp. 239-240.

[97] No. 1055, Telegram from Ripon to Hartington, July 9, 1882; in Ripon Papers, I. S. 290/6, p. 247.

[98] No. 34, Grant to Ripon, July 10, 1882; in Ripon Papers, I. S. 290/8, pp. 30-31.

[99] No. 1068, Telegram from Ripon to Hartington, July 12, 1882; in Ripon Papers, I. S. 290/6, p. 250.

[100] No. 1075, Telegram from Hartington to Ripon, July 15, 1882; in Ripon Papers, I. S. 290/6, p. 251.

[101] No. 8, India Foreign Dept. to Hartington, September 15, 1882; in C. 3501, pp. 22-27.

[102] No. 62, Grant to Ripon, July 18, 1882; in Ripon Papers, I. S. 290/8, p. 54.

[103] No. 98, Grant to Ripon, July 28, 1882; in Ripon Papers, I. S. 290/8, p. 90. (*Also see:* Direct Draft Treaty, July 28, 1882; in C. 3501, pp. 45-46. *Also:* Commercial Draft Treaty, July 28, 1882; in C. 3501, pp. 42-45. *Lastly:* Commercial Treaty, August 29, 1882; in C. 3501, pp. 52-55.)

[104-08] *Ibid.* The Guard Question might have been solved. Article 25 of the July 28, 1882 proposed commercial treaty reinacted Articles III and IV of the 1826 Yandabo Treaty. Article VII, which provided for a fifty-man guard, might also have been reinacted. The fifty soldiers could have had one or two 'servants' apiece, who were also soldiers. Such an arrangement might have saved the 'face' of the Mandalay Government, because there would have been no mention of a Residency Guard in the 1882 treaty.

[109-10] *Ibid.* The August 29, 1882 commercial treaty presented to the Burmese envoys was almost word for word that of the July 28 draft treaty. The article numbers used above are those in the August 29, 1882 treaty.

[111] It is interesting to note that when the papers in C. 3501 were being readied in early 1883, references to the 'Fytche Annexe', and an expression of Ripon's concerning the "long-pending difficulty," were deleted. *See* telegrams: No. 1478, Ripon to Kimberley, February 16, 1883; No. 1479, Kimberley to Ripon, February 18, 1883; No. 1498, Ripon to Kimberly, February 23, 1883; and No. 1499, Kimberley to Ripon, February 23, 1883: in Ripon Papers, I. S. 290/6, pp. 342, 347.

[112] *See* the 1867 Treaty and the 'Fytche Annexe' in Appendix C. Since the Burmese could not import arms legally, they smuggled them illegally. *See* Appendix I entitled Mandalay Arms Smuggling.

[113] No. 98, Grant to Ripon, July 28, 1882; in Ripon Papers, I. S. 290/8, p. 90.

[114] Pilcher to Grant, August 15, 1882, pp. 2-3; a hand-written, loose letter (one of three items) within L/P & S/20, Pol. and Sec. Dept. of India Office, D. 180 Burma Embassy File, 1882-1883 (IOL).

[115] No. 123, Ripon to Grant, August 15, 1882; in Ripon Papers, I. S. 290/8, p. 87.

[116] Enclosure 19 in No. 8, Farewell Reception to Ambassadors, August 29, 1882; in C. 3501, pp. 56-57.

[117] *Ibid.*

[118] Bernard to Grant, September 19, 1882; in Nos. 125-146, pp. 10-11.

[119] *Ibid. See also:* "Burma," (Calcutta) *Englishman*, September 18, 1882, p. 3.

[120] "The News From Burmah," (Calcutta) *Statesman*, October 17, 1882, pp. 1455-1456.

[121] Foreign, Secret-E, November 1882, Nos. 1-3 (NAI).

[122] "Burma, (Calcutta) *Englishman*, September 18, 1882, p. 3.

[123] K. W. No. 5, Memo dated August 2, 1882 with Bernard to Grant, August 15, 1882; in Nos. 524-629, p. 3.

[124-25] *Ibid.*

[126] *Ibid.* This was only the latest contract for such rifles and other fire-arms. Such manufactures had been attempted many times during Mindon's reign.

[127] K. W. No. 5, Memo dated August 3, 1882 with Bernard to Grant, August 15, 1882; in Nos. 524-629, p. 3.

[128] K. W. No. 5, Memo dated August 2, 1882; in Nos. 524-629.

[129] *Ibid.*

[130] K. W. No. 5, Memo dated August 3, 1882; in Nos. 524-629.

[131] *Ibid.*

[132] No. 83, Rawlings to Bernard's Secretary, May 29, 1882; in Nos. 47-87.

[133] K. W. No. 5. Extract from Rangoon *Times*, October 3, 1882; in Nos. 524-629, pp. 6-8.

[134] *Ibid.*

[135-39] *Ibid.* The *Times* said that the *kalamas* had been especially keen on spying-out Thebaw's affair with Mi Hkin-gyi, because "if a new Queen got into favour, they would lose their work, and the chance of costly presents...."

[140] Burma Column, (Calcutta) *Statesman*, October 3, 1882, p. 1395.

[141] "The News From Burmah," (Calcutta) *Statesman*, October 17, 1882, pp. 1455-1456.

[142] No. 285, Telegram from Banares Agent of Gov. Gen. to Foreign Dept., December 4, 1882; in Foreign, Secret-E, April 1883, Nos. 285-349 (NAI).

[143] "Occasional Notes," (Allahabad) *Pioneer Mail*, January 24, 1883, p. 69. The Myngun had nearly killed his father, King Mindon, on August 2, 1866, and had assassinated his uncle, the Heir-Designate. The rebel princes held the Irrawaddy River from Myingyan down to the Lower Burma frontier, until King Mindon appealed to Chief Commissioner Sir Arthur Phayre to drive them out.

Phayre agreed since a new treaty was being negotiated, and more concessions might therefore be gained from King Mindon. Two of Mindon's steamers then at Rangoon were armed, and sent up-river with "a lot of riffraff on board...." As some of these wore red coats, the rebel princes thought that they were British troops. The princes ran the gauntlet through them to Thayetmyo in Lower Burma territory on October 6, 1866.

After Phayre was unsuccessful in obtaining a new treaty, the Myngun was allowed to 'escape' on February 6, 1867. In late 1867, Gen. Albert Fytche, the new chief commissioner of Lower Burma, visited Mandalay in another attempt to make a treaty. "Very early in the negotiations, the King remarked that his "Akaung-gale," or "little beast of a son," was giving him a lot of trouble on the frontier, and once more the....runaway had to shift his quarters." Mindon in return for this, and some other concessions such as the import of arms, signed the 1867 Treaty.

[144] Enclosure 3 in No. 12, Kinwun to Grant, December 13, 1882; in C. 3501, pp. 63-66.

[145] No. 10, Telegram from Ripon to Kimberley, January 4, 1883; in C. 3501, p. 59.

[146] *Ibid.   See also:* Enclosure 4 in No. 12, The Proposed Treaty Applying Only to Non-Indian British Subjects, December 13, 1882; in C. 3501, pp, 67-70.

[147-48] *Ibid.   See also:* Enclosure 5 in No. 12, The Proposed Treaty Applying Only to Indian British subjects, December 13, 1882; in C. 3501, pp. 70-75.

[149] No. 11, Telegram from Kimberley to Ripon, January 10, 1883; in C. 3501, p. 59.   *See also:* Enclosure 8 in No. 12, Grant to Kinwun, January 26, 1883; In C. 3501, pp. 76-77.   *Lastly:* No. 13, Kimberley to Gov. Gen. in Council, March 16, 1883; in C. 3501, p. 77.

[150] No. 58, Bernard's Secretary to Kinwun, July 9, 1883; in Foreign, Secret-E, August 1883, Nos. 57-58 (NAI).

4

Mandalay Gains Concessions from France

The Paris Mission, 1883-1884

C. H. T. Crosthwaite was the new chief commissioner of Lower Burma as Charles Bernard had taken health-leave. Crosthwaite received an April 26, 1883 note from the Kinwun announcing the departure to Europe of a Burmese scientific and industrial mission.[1] The leader, the Myothit Atwinwun, impressed Crosthwaite as "a nice looking gentlemanly Burman, who [has] never left Upper Burma before."[2] The Myothit was an amiable member of the Taingda's group, and was friendly with most Court factions.

The No. 2 man was the Tangyet Wundauk, a Kinwun supporter, who had also been the No. 2 man in the 1882 Simla Mission under the Pangyet. The Tangyet was fluent in both French and English, and it was he who performed most of the actual negotiations for the next two years at Paris. The No. 3 man was U Paw Tun, No. 4 man in the 1882 Simla Mission, who had also been the Burmese Consul at Calcutta in 1879-1881. U Paw Tun's rank was *sayaygyi* or secretary.[3]

One of the other members of the Mission was the Comte de Trevelec, a French cavalry adviser for the previous eight years at Mandalay. The Comte was a rather seedy representative of the French nobility, and it was said that he carried his lands in his fingernails. Much of his income came from the sales of fruit juices and syrups to the passengers and crews of IFC steamers. Pilcher, assistant commissioner at Thayetmyo, described de Trevelec as an 'eccentric gentleman' who was going home with the mission.[4]

The Mission arrived in Paris in early August, 1883. British Ambassador Plunkett wrote to Earl Granville, British foreign secretary, that the Mission would stay for only one month.[5] Instead, it stayed for nearly two years, and became a source of increasing annoyance to the London and Indian Governments. Ambassador Plunkett stated that the Mission had probably come to gain ratification of the 1873 Burmese-French Treaty.[6] The Treaty had never been ratified by the French, because Mindon had wanted a supplementary treaty giving him arms and an Offensive-Defensive Alliance. Also, the French representative at Mandalay in 1873 had exceeded his instructions.

On August 21, Plunkett reported that three British merchants had interviewed the Burmese ambassadors, who were rather reluctant to discuss business.[7] The three merchants were unhappy, because it was rumoured that French businessmen were submitting bids for concessions in Upper Burma.

Almost nothing was heard of the Mission from late August, 1883 to December 26, 1883. Enquiries were made by Lord Lyons, the new British ambassador, to Challemel-Lacour, outgoing French foreign minister, on November 7, 1883;[8] to Jules Ferry, the new foreign minister, on November 14, 1883;[9] and, again to Jules Ferry on December 13, 1883.[10] The enquiries brought the reply that the minister had not heard much of the Burmese. Ferry said that he did not know exactly what they were trying to accomplish.[11] Lyons replied that Britain and France stood in very different positions as concerned Burma. France could have only a very secondary interest in Upper Burma, but the country was of "the utmost concern to England."[12]

Lyons' concern was consistent with the British Government's long-time concern over India's eastern frontier and concern for British subjects' interests in Upper Burma. While India's eastern frontier was never the cause of as much concern as was the northwest frontier and the 'Russian Threat', it had been a policy of the British in India since the early 1600's either to neutralize the French (and other Europeans) in Burma, or to keep them out of the area entirely.

On December 26, 1883, Ferry finally said that the Mission was in contact with the Quai d'Orsay concerning commercial matters. However, they did not have the proper powers, which were requested before serious talks could begin. Ferry added that he did not know of any new Burmese envoy with adequate powers having been despatched from Mandalay. As of that date there was no one qualified to represent the Burmese.[13] Nothing further was heard publicly of the Mission for four months.

On April 5, 1884, Ferry received the Ambassadors. They signed the Treaty of 1873, which was to go into force on June 1, 1884.[14] On April 10, Lyons interviewed Ferry, who was also president of the council (Premier). Ferry told him that negotiations had started on a Supplementary Commercial Treaty. Ferry stated that the Burmese would not be given any rights to import arms through Tongkin. Lyons asked him to carefully search any commercial agreement, or "otherwise stipulations having grave political consequences might slip in."[15]

Ferry conceded on May 21 that the Burmese were pressuring him to include the free passage of arms through Tongkin. This he would not do. Such arms might also be used against the 17,000-man French force fighting the Chinese in Tongkin. Lyons repeated his stand that India's contiguous frontier with Upper Burma gave Great Britain special interests in Burma which no other country could have.[16]

The 1873 Treaty went into effect on June 1, 1884. The India Office, London, protested to the British Foreign Office that Article 3 allowed a reciprocal appointment of diplomatic agents between the two nations. The India Office maintained that any French diplomatic agent appointed to Mandalay should be of a commercial nature alone.[17] Lyons proposed this on July 11, but Ferry said that it was *hard* to draw a line between commercial and political functions. The French agent who would be stationed at Mandalay would be in charge of *all* French interests. Then Ferry remarked that France was about to become Burma's *neighbour*.[18]

Lyons retorted that France could not possibly be a political neighbour to Burma in the sense that Burma was a neighbour to British India.[19] Ferry asked if there were any special treaties between India and Upper Burma that precluded the Burmese from entering into treaties with other countries. Lyons avoided admitting that there were none by stating that there were "very special political relations....which rendered it......[most] objectionable that....[Upper Burma] should enter into....alliance with another Power."[20]

Ferry then belittled the current Supplementary Treaty negotiations as most unpromising. The Burmese had refused to allow French citizens in Upper Burma to be placed under the exclusive jurisdiction of the proposed French agent at Mandalay. Also, there was the "Shoe Question". It involved the doffing of shoes before the King, and also before officials of lesser rank.

The Burmese seemed to desire arms more than any other concession. But Ferry reiterated that the French Government would not supply arms, because of the Chinese-French War near Upper Burma. Lyons again asked Ferry for a promise that France would appoint only a commercial agent to Mandalay. Ferry reiterated that any agent would have to handle all French interests.[21]

A week later, on July 16, Ferry stated that France did not contemplate making any special political alliance with Burma.[22] However, Ferry reiterated that it would be impossible to draw an exact line between the political and commercial functions that the French agent might perform. "For instance," Ferry offered as an example, "there might be questions of *neighbourhood*."[23]

Lyons confessed that he could not understand how there could be such a political question between Burma and France. Ferry replied that between Tongkin and Upper Burma, and on the left bank of the Mekong River, were several small states, the *pannas*. Burma claimed suzerainty over these states, but she did not exercise it in reality.[24]

The ceding of the *pannas* to France seemed to be implied in Ferry's remarks. Ferry did reassure Lyons that the French Government would not accept an Offensive-Defensive Alliance, although the Burmese desired to "throw themselves into the arms of France."[25] All France wanted was to establish friendly relations, and to secure orderly commercial intercourse. Ferry added that there would be no secret political negotiations, and that the French Government would keep the British Government informed of the Supplementary Treaty negotiations.[26]

An article in the London *Standard* on the following day, July 17, 1884, contradicted almost every word that Ferry had uttered.

The *Standard* reported that a Mons. Deloncle of the French Foreign Office had negotiated a secret Offensive-Defensive Alliance with Mandalay. In return, Burma had ceded the *pannas* east of the Mekong River to France. The article surmised that Deloncle had probably exceeded his instructions, and that the French Government would reject the Offensive-Defensive Alliance.[27]

The article interested Lyons. He asked Ferry on July 29 if there was any truth to the rumoured secret political agreement. Ferry said that France would not make any special political alliance with Mandalay. The Supplementary Treaty—if there ever was one—would be of a commercial nature. However, Ferry repeated his stand that the French agent would have to handle all French interests in Upper Burma.[28]

The Deloncle Mission

Brian L. Lewis wrote that the French between 1858-1885 were often silent in their expansion east of Burma. This meant that "by the time the various acts of expansion were fully accomplished, the French Foreign Minister was usually denying any such actions to the British Government."[29] The Deloncle Mission appeared to be a classic example of the above French technique, although eventually disowned by the Quai d'Orsay.

Charles Bernard was once again chief commissioner after his health-leave. He first became aware of Deloncle's visit on June 3, 1884, and informed the Indian Foreign Dept.[30] Andreino, the Italian consul, reported on June 10, via Kennedy, the Rangoon IFC Manager, that Deloncle's doings at Mandalay were rather mysterious. No clerks and servants were allowed at an all-night meeting at the Kinwun's house between Deloncle and top Government officials.[31] Rawlings, the 'news-collector' at Mandalay, reported on June 11 that Deloncle had denied any connection with the Quai d'Orsay. Nevertheless, letters were posted to him after his departure addressed in care of the French Ministry of Foreign Affairs.[32]

Deloncle had arrived at Mandalay on May 12, 1884, and was received by the Kinwun, the Pangyet, and the Taingda.[33] P. H. Bonvillain, the common-law husband of Mattie Calogreedy Antram, Supayalat's great favourite, acted as the interpreter. Also attending the meetings were the Ministers for Finance and Public Instruction.[34]

Deloncle said that his visit was a private endeavour to speed-up the Paris negotiations. On May 21, he presented a declaration drawn-up in the name of the Kinwun. Deloncle was to carry the Kinwun's Declaration and an 'Article 10' to the Burmese ambassadors in Paris. The two items were to be a confidential guide concerning the latest desires of the Mandalay Government.[35]

At this point Bonvillain became most important. Thebaw owed Bonvillain Rs. 118,000 for some supplies.[36] Bonvillain had also lost his house, and over Rs. 20,000 worth of cutch in the April 2 and 5, 1884 fires at Mandalay.[37] In order to make certain that the Mandalay Government would continue to exist, and that he would recoup his losses, Bonvillain asked Deloncle to insert Articles 1 and 2 providing for an Offensive-Defensive Alliance into the Kinwun's Declaration.[38]

The Kinwun protested that he did not want an Offensive-Defensive Alliance as outlined in the two articles. Deloncle wrote in his report to the Quai d'Orsay that he was personally unconcerned about the precise wording. He had inserted Articles 1 and 2 in order to help a fellow countryman in distress.[39] Deloncle suggested that a regularly-accredited French envoy to Mandalay could easily settle the two articles—which would have plunged France into future Burmese quarrels with India. Burma would likewise have been involved with French imbroglios in Indo China.[40]

Article 3 of the Kinwun's Declaration promised that the French would assist Mandalay in building roads between Burma and Tongkin.[41] Article 4 would allow Mandalay to import medicines and other essentials, *i.e.* arms, though Tongkin.[42] Article 5 ceded the *pannas* east of the left bank of the Mekong to French Tongkin.[43]

The Kinwun also sent an 'Article 10' that he wished included in the Supplementary Commercial Treaty. The article would have established French jurisdiction over all French subjects accused of crimes in Upper Burma. Accused French subjects were to be turned over to the proposed French agent at Mandalay.[44]

The Kinwun's Declaration concluded by stating that 'Article 10' would become effective only when France accepted a clause in the Supplementary Treaty that both nations would exchange envoys. These envoys would observe the official etiquette of the country concerned. In other words, the French agent would doff his shoes in the King's presence.[45]

Voisson, the French consul at Rangoon, immediately appealed to the Quai d'Orsay that he be allowed to void the Offensive-Defensive Alliance.[46] Also, Article 5 of the Kinwun's Declaration was *unnecessary*. The French Tongkin frontier had *already* been pushed westward to the left bank of the Mekong, according to the Tientsin Treaty with China in May 1884.[47]

However, Voisson did advise acceptance of the formal Burmese cession of the *pannas* formerly under their rule east of the Mekong's left bank. Such *pannas* would make an ideal natural frontier between the two countries and, as a result, smoother relations.[48] Voisson also advised the acceptance of the remaining articles.

Voisson's appeal had some influence on Ferry's July 16 and 29 conversations with Lord Lyons. Ferry rejected any suggestions that France would sign an Offensive-Defensive Alliance with Burma. However, Ferry reserved France's right to the commercial and territorial concessions gained from the Deloncle Mission, while denying that such secret negotiations had ever taken place.

The Kinwun's Declaration did not have much influence on the eventual January 15, 1885 Supplementary Commercial Treaty. After the conquest of Upper Burma, Viceroy Lord Dufferin telegraphed Lord Randolph Churchill, the secretary of state for India, that: "There is....nothing to show that French Government knew or approved [of] Deloncle's proceedings."[49] In summary, Paris knew of the agreement, but it was a 'dead letter'.

The January 15, 1885 Treaty

On November 26, 1884, Voisson telegraphed to Ferry that he had heard of an "English intrigue [at] Xieng Tong-Zimme [Chiengmai]. Urgent sign [Supplementary Commercial Treaty] immediately."[50] This message placed a sense of urgency about the treaty negotiations, which Ferry had not desired. He had wanted to sign the Supplementary Treaty only after Thebaw had approved it. Ferry was not desirous of repeating 1873 all over again.[51]

However, Ferry's voting majority in the Chamber of Deputies was declining under the attacks of Clemenceau and others. They opposed France's renewed involvement in the Chinese-French War in Tongkin and Southern China, which had initially been settled in France's favour by the May 1884 Tientsin Treaty. The Chinese had agreed to withdraw their troops from Tongkin, and had conceded France's claim to a protectorate over both Annam and Tongkin. However, French forces had been ambushed at Bac-Le, and Ferry had become involved in a second and most unpopular war with China.[52]

With the arrival of Voisson's November 26, 1884 telegram, Ferry resolved to sign the Supplementary Treaty as quickly as possible. There were three reasons for Ferry's 'haste'. The first reason was that the British might steal away with the territories east of the left bank of the Mekong. Ferry was certainly not willing to see the *pannas* fall under British influence or actual domination.[53]

The second reason for Ferry's 'haste' was that his Government was threatened with an adverse vote in the Chamber of Deputies and the Senate before the Burma Treaty could be presented to the two bodies for ratification. As indicated above, Ferry's voting majority in the Chamber of Deputies was declining under the attacks of his critics, such as Clemenceau. They reflected the growing public resentment of 'Ferry's War' in Tongkin, and also of 'Ferry's Folly', his entire Indo-Chinese colonial 'adventure'.[54]

The third reason for Ferry's 'quick' acceptance of the Burma Treaty was that he wanted to get it out of the way before overtures came from China for a new treaty. Indeed, on January 17, 1885—just two days after the signing of the Burma Treaty—initial overtures came from James Duncan Campbell, the Paris agent of Sir Robert Hart, the inspector general of the Chinese customs.[55]

Ferry knew that a second treaty with China would retain the concessions gained in the May 1884 Tientsin Treaty, and would halt the unpopular war. French public opinion would then probably be aroused in favour of Ferry's Indo-Chinese Empire, which his critics had threatened to dismantle the moment they could get Ferry out of office. With a second successful China Treaty in hand, the ratification of the Burma Treaty—a further extension of French political and commercial influence in Indo-China—would be a matter of course.[56]

On January 16, 1885, Ferry told Lyons that the Burma Treaty had been signed on the previous day. A Consul, who would handle all French commercial and political affairs, would soon be despatched to Mandalay. Lyons was assured that there were no military or political articles, such as an Offensive-Defensive Alliance, in the new Treaty.[57]

However, unknown to Lyons there was a separate and secret note signed by Ferry and given to the ambassadors. The note stated that when it was convenient, France would allow arms to be brought from Tongkin through the Lao and Shan States to Mandalay.[58] This note was no more than an expressed intention at some future unspecified date. It was a sop to the Burmese desire for arms, which they had wanted more than anything else.[59]

In late July 1885, Ferry's Secret Letter and the full contents of the Supplementary Commercial Treaty were smuggled into the hands of the Indian Government. Until July 1885, nothing was known about the Supplementary Treaty, except for the publicly-released text. Rumours, however, were rampant about secret clauses and the like.

Meanwhile, the Burmese Mission signed a commercial treaty with Germany on April 4, 1885, which provided for the most-favoured-nation status.[60] In this case, London did not show any suspicions towards the German Government's official explanation. Germany had no possessions bordering Upper Burma as did France, which could have threatened India's eastern frontier and British subjects' interests in Upper Burma.

In the same week, the Burmese ambassadors entered into negotiations with the Italian Government. The ambassadors wished to insert the most favoured-nation clause into the 1871 Burma-Italy Treaty. The Tangyet accepted the Italian offer of a permanent clause. But he was overruled by the Myothit, his superior, who wanted only a one year trial-period.[61]

The Italian negotiators refused the proposal as it would have defeated the whole purpose of such a clause, namely to bring about the equality of treatment between nations.[62] The Italians made a counter-demand that the Italian subjects in Thebaw's service be paid their wages in arrears. Such was impossible, however, because the Mandalay Government was nearly bankrupt. The Mission would probably have been stranded in Europe had the Mandalay Government not borrowed almost three lakhs from the BBTC on March 24, 1885. The negotiations with Italy collapsed, and in mid-April the Mission left for Rangoon via the Suez Canal.

Bernard's Analysis of the January 15, 1885 Treaty

Was the January 15, 1885 Treaty a 'threat' to British subjects' interests ? Charles Bernard stated in a May 13, 1885 letter to Mortimer Durand, Indian foreign secretary, that the Treaty might be a potential 'threat'. However, only one new monopoly in *letpet* (pickled-tea) had been established, according to the publicly released text of the Treaty.[63]

The Treaty provided official Burmese Government assistance to Frenchmen seeking to collect debts owed them by Burmese subjects. Bernard did not explain how such a provision would have enabled Bonvillain to collect the Rs. 118,000 debt owed to him by Thebaw. Or, how such a provision would have enabled the French employees of Thebaw to collect their wages in arrears.

The French Consul at Mandalay was supposed to render reciprocal assistance to Burmese, who were owed money by French subjects. French ships and French subjects in Upper Burma could carry as many arms as were necessary for their own protection, but no more without notifying the Mandalay Government.[64] French ships and subjects would be given the most-favoured-nation treatment, while in Upper Burmese waters. Burmese subjects would, of course, be given similar treatment while in France.[65]

The extradition of criminal offenders, as distinct from political offenders which the French had refused, was provided for in the Treaty. One of the crimes listed as a 'criminal offense' was arson.[66] This was a great diplomatic *coup* for the wily Burmese ambassadors. Revolutionaries against the Burmese throne, *i.e.* 'political offenders', almost always burned down sections of Mandalay in order to distract the authorities before making their attack on the Palace (Mt. Meru).[67]

Bernard stated in his letter to Durand that the Treaty was entirely commercial. However, the numerous most-favoured-nation clauses in the Treaty were not to be found in the 1862 or 1867 British treaties with Upper Burma. Such clauses might eventually give the French privileges which British subjects could not claim.[68]

Bernard stated that such French 'privileges' posed no immediate 'threat' to British subjects' commercial interests. At present, almost no French trade reached Mandalay, except through Rangoon and Lower Burma. Between 1878-1884, the total imports of Lower Burma had averaged Rs. 37,200,000 annually with French imports totalling only about Rs. 30,000 annually.[69]

Bernard stated that the annual trade between the two Burmas was then rising close to £3,500,000 a year. Burmese exports to Lower Burma—as compared with exports to China or French Tongkin—composed probably ninety per cent of Mandalay's entire exports. The Burmese exports through Lower Burma were carried mostly on IFC steamers.[70]

Bernard could not verify or deny the numerous rumours concerning French mining, banking, and railroad concessions in Upper Burma.[71] He thought that the French might eventually have sufficient political influence at Mandalay to enable French speculators to gain the above and other concessions. With French political influence secured, such speculators would find it easy to eliminate British subjects from trade in Upper Burma.[72]

Although Bernard did not say so, this was the French technique in Southeast Asia of first securing political influence in order to introduce French commerce.[73] This was the opposite of the British whose subjects introduced commerce, which was then usually protected by the extension of British political influence.[74]

Bernard concluded his May 13, 1885 letter to Durand by stating that British political influence—sufficient to protect British subjects' interests—would be lacking at Mandalay until the Resident was reinstated. In the absence of the Resident, the French might even "try to get....the teak forests and the teak trade of Burma, to the exclusion of the...Bombay Burma Trading Corporation... and British subjects now trading in teak with Upper Burma."[75]

'Unofficial' Relations With the Myngun, 1883-1884

The Indian Goverment made several unofficial contacts in 1883-1884 with Queen Supayalat, and also with her chief opponents, the Myngun, the Nyaungyan, and the Nyaungoke Princes. These contacts were the Indian Government's chief effort in 1883-1884 to settle affairs at Mandalay before the French 'intruded' into the area under the terms of the January 15, 1885 Treaty.

The Indian Government's contacts with the Myngun Prince were perhaps most important. The Prince appeared to be an excellent replacement for Thebaw should it be necessary. Therefore, the Indian Government had kept Myngun out of Burma, and also out of the clutches of the French.   Myngun, however, escaped from Banares on December 4, 1882, and took refuge at Chandernagore, the tiny French enclave in Bengal.

Under the 1879 British-French Treaty, the British could not ask for the extradition of political prisoners.   Myngun waited at Chandernagore from December 1882 to June 1884.   He sent petition after petition to the Indian Government asking them to help him become King.[76]   The Foreign Secretary's reply was always the same.   If the Myngun would leave French territory, and surrender to Indian Government officials, his request would be considered.[77]

Myngun never accepted such terms.   He had hoped that his request for an interview with Lord Ripon would be granted, and that the Indian Government would guarantee that he would not be arrested should the interview be unsatisfactory.   Without such a guarantee, Myngun refused to leave Chandernagore.[78]   As his hopes for an early interview faded, Myngun considered becoming a French 'protege', and going to Paris to plead his case.[79]

However, the Quai d'Orsay was not overjoyed with the idea, because there was already a Mission from King Thebaw negotiating a new treaty between the two countries.   The Quai d'Orsay appreciated having the Myngun in reserve, but for the present he would have to remain at Chandernagore.[80]   Finally, the Myngun resolved to escape to the Shan States where his supporters were already building him a temporary Palace.[81]

A large box was made and Myngun practised lying in it until he could stay there for hours.   Judge Lhermitte of Chandernagore joined the plot, and the box was placed with the departing Judge's other baggage.   It went through customs in Calcutta and was loaded on the *Tibre* on June 16, 1884 bound for Colombo.[82]   As the ship steamed away, Myngun crawled out of his box, which he later denied using, and was well on his way to freedom when the monsoon storms made him foully sea-sick.   In order to get more comfortable quarters, he announced his identity.[83]   At Colombo, the British authorities could not touch him under the terms of the 1879 British-French Treaty.

However, the French under pressure from the British arrested him and took him to Pondicherry, the French enclave on the southeast coast of India.   Myngun remained there until February 1886 when he made another spectacular escape on board the same *Tibre* steamer. His escape, apparently, was influential in Viceroy Lord Dufferin's decision to annex Upper Burma. However, the Myngun again became seasick, and surrendered himself at Pondicherry.[84]

The French eventually took him to Saigon where he made other spectacular escapes, one as late as the mid-1890's. He was recaptured, and lived on in Saigon until his death in 1921. In the final analysis, the Myngun's thirty-year struggle to become King was foiled not by British gunboats, nor by wily French diplomacy, but by what is known in medical circles as 'a sloshing of the inner ear'.

But such was in the future. In 1883-1885, Myngun loomed up over Burma much like a monsoon-cloud. As the great 'drought' of these years caused men to go hungry and to turn to 'dacoity', it was Myngun who seemed to promise relief. Thebaw had usually been afraid to leave the Palace-grounds for fear of a revolt in his absence. As a result, he had never performed the 'Meru-centric' Plowing Ceremony, which signified Lord Indra blessing the crops and calling down the rains. Therefore, the peasants *blamed* Thebaw for the 1883-1885 'drought'. Many Upper Burmese began to look about for a more suitable King, who would live by the 'Meru-centric' tradition.[85]

Thebaw, himself, was at first willing to resign in favour of Myngun. Thebaw believed that he was fated to be King for only five years. Supayalat, however, cordially detested the Myngun, and regarded Thebaw's idea as crazy. She resolved that she would retain the Mandalay throne despite her husband.[86]

More 'Unofficial' Relations

Supayalat remained alert, because there were intrigues everywhere. Her own mother was plotting against her. The Dowager Queen had conceived the idea of marrying her youngest daughter, Supayalat's younger sister, to Myngun. One could say that Supayalat's mother was remaining 'flexible'. On March 23, 1884, she sent a maid of honour to Rangoon on the way to see Myngun in Chandernagore. A box of diamonds and Rs. 50,000 in cash accompanied the maid. However, the scheme was discovered.[87]

Thebaw's only son had died in March 1880 of smallpox. Two

of his daughters born since had also died of smallpox, and it appeared that he would never get another son.   As a consequence, he was hysterically angry when he heard of his mother-in-law's 'flexibility'.   He told her that she would eat the arsenic-laced food before her, or the troops behind the thin curtain would chop her into pieces.[88]   As an alternative, her youngest daughter would marry Thebaw the same day.   He ignored Supayalat's anger that her younger sister would be made a queen equal with herself and her older sister.   Thebaw persisted, the old lady surrendered her daughter, and Thebaw married her a few hours later.[89]

Meanwhile, the Indian Government was unofficially dealing with not only the Myngun, but the Nyaungyan and the Nyaungoke Princes as well.   In March 1884, Government agents entered into an understanding with Prince Nyaungyan.   If he could not gain the throne on his own efforts, the Indian Government would help him.   In return, the Nyaungyan would end the archaic Court ritual that had caused the "Shoe Question".   He would receive the reinstated British Resident in the European fashion, *i.e.* shod and seated in a chair.   The Nyaungyan would also not recognize either the 1873 Burma-France Treaty, or any other Supplementary Treaty then being negotiated at Paris.[90]

After Myngun's June 16, 1884 escape, the *convention secrete primitivement* between agents of Viceroy Lord Ripon and Prince Nyaungyan was amended.[91]   If Myngun left Pondicherry with or without the approval of the French Government, Nyaungyan would also be allowed to leave Calcutta.   He would receive unofficial financial and military assistance.   Upon becoming King, he would accept the Resident as one of the *Hlutdaw* members.   The Resident would also have a Residency Guard of 300 men.[92]

It appeared that the Kinwun, Pangyet, and others at Mandalay knew of this secret agreement and supported it.   R. Hope Pilcher, the assistant commissioner at Thayetmyo, kept the group informed of the Indian Government's dealings.[93]   Meanwhile, the Taingda was intriguing with the Taungwin Mingyi to place the Myngun upon the throne.

In mid-August 1884, Bernard realized that the Nyaungyan was not nearly so popular as Myngun.   Bernard recommended that the Indian Foreign Dept. send a messenger to Myngun to ask him what written proposals he wished to make of the Indian Government.[94]   Pilcher apparently informed   the various ministers at

Mandalay of the change from Nyaungyan to Myngun.[95]

However, Myngun replied that the Indian Government surely knew by then where he stood, and of his general willingness to go along with their wishes.[96] He in turn requested that the Indian Government should state what proposals and demands they wished him to clarify.[97] So, in September 1884, some more unofficial talks were held with the Nyaungyan. He promised that he would not ratify the upcoming Supplementary Treaty, and would not favour French businesses in Upper Burma.[98]

It must have been obvious to the three exiled Princes that they would be used—or ignored—to the degree that they would further the aims of the Indian Government in Upper Burma. These aims were as always to protect India's eastern frontier, and to protect the interests, mostly commercial, of British subjects in Upper Burma. In short, the Indian Government was also 'flexible'. One final example of such 'flexibility' involved the several letters from the Rev. Kerr, Viceroy Ripon's chaplain, to Sister Therese, one of Supayalat's French *kalamas*.

Sister Therese had initially written Rev. Kerr to see if the differences between the two countries might be eased.[99] Viceroy Ripon had always opposed Viceroy Lytton's 'forward policy' against the 'Russian Threat' to India's northwest, a policy which had resulted in the Second Afghan War, 1878-81. Nevertheless, in September 1884, Ripon made the following Burma proposals through Rev. Kerr.[100]

If Supayalat would decide quickly, Thebaw could easily call back the Burmese ambassadors then in Paris. Mandalay could enter into an alliance of friendship with Ripon's Government, and turn away from further French 'entanglements'. The Indian Government would guarantee the continued existence of the Burmese monarchy, *and* the integrity of the territories of Upper Burma, including the *pannas* on the left bank of the Mekong which were rumoured to have been ceded to France.[101]

This last proposal of territorial integrity was a remarkable one, and would have placed British India across French Tongkin's advance towards the Mekong River. France had two treaties, the Kinwun's Declaration and the May 1884 Tientsin Treaty, that stated that the *pannas* east of the Mekong belonged to France. Perhaps Ripon did not realize the ramifications of his proposal, which was a *forward policy for India's eastern frontier*.

Rev. Kerr emphasized that a prompt answer would have to be given. Apparently, a serious discussion took place at the Palace. But by the time Sister Therese went to Rangoon in late-October to discuss the proposals with Bernard, the idea was in abeyance. By then, the public announcement of a treaty with Mandalay would have set-off cries of horror that the Indian Government would treat with such a 'barbaric power'.[102]

The Mandalay 'Jailbreak'

The September 21-22, 1884 Mandalay 'Jailbreak' resulted in the massacre of more than 300 prisoners and bystanders, and negated all of Sister Therese's diplomatic labours. The 'Jailbreak' also negated much of Charles Bernard's defence of the Mandalay Government.

Immediately before the massacre, the September 16 *Englishman* reported that great excitement prevailed at Mandalay because of certain portents. A comet had appeared foretelling a new King and a *tayinthi* fruit pickled in salt for months at the Myngun's house had sprouted. This had "convinced the Burmese that the Mengoon is the coming man."[103] There was a new rumour every day that the Myngun had escaped, and was on his way to the Shan States to 'liberate' his people.[104]

There was a sense of anticipation among both the commoners and the courtiers. The Kinwun, the Taingda, and the Taungwin Mingyis were all secretly writing to—or supporting—one of the three exiled Princes. The Pangyet, the son-in-law of Taingda and the Kinwun's chief assistant in foreign affairs, had also been in contact with R. Hope Pilcher concerning the Indian Government's choice of a new King.

The supporters of Myngun, such as the Taingda and the Taungwin, had gone the furthest in their support. They had expected that the Prince would soon arrive in the Shan States to take charge of the growing movement in his behalf. But the Myngun was still in Pondicherry. His supporters had committed themselves so far that their lives were now in extreme danger.[105]

Supayalat had discovered their plotting. Messengers sent by the Taingda and the Taungwin to Myngun were captured as they returned to Mandalay, and were tortured to make them reveal the identity of their masters.[106] Taingda, Taungwin, and other ministers sent assassins in the night, but the assassins were also caught and tortured.[107] A triumphant Supayalat thought that she was about to discover which ministers had sent messengers to the three exiled Princes.[108]

The Taingda and the treasury minister were also secretly protecting several large 'dacoit' gangs around Mandalay, and were taking a fat percentage of their robberies as protection money. Some of the 'dacoits' had been captured, however, and were now in the Mandalay Jail along with the messengers that the Taingda and other ministers had sent to the three exiled Princes.[109]

Most of these ministers were also bitter rivals. Each rival had recently jailed a number of his rivals' supporters in order to obtain confessions that would involve his rivals in 'dacoity', rebellion, and support for the three exiled Princes. The ministerial rivals now recognized the danger that threatened them all, and they decided to liquidate their mutual problem with a 'Jailbreak' Massacre.[110]

One can see with this ruse how far Mandalay had come since February 15-17, 1879 towards an understanding of the *kala* mind. 'Diplomacy' had to be exercised in order to avoid a remonstrance or worse from the Indian Government, and to avoid any interruption in the treaty negotiations at Paris.[111]

The ministers hurried to Thebaw. They told him that Yanmin, Upper Burma's most famous 'dacoit', was about to break out of Mandalay Jail and start a revolution in favour of Myngun.[112] The accusation was enough to doom Yanmin. The ministers then went to the head jailer, and asked him to tell Yanmin confidentially that Thebaw was going to execute them all by an early date. The head jailer did so after being persuaded to accept a gratuity.

The Times of India seemed to enjoy the ironic justice that the first man killed in the massive 'Jailbreak' was the jailer. He "was conveniently mistaken for an escaped prisoner, cut down and thrown into the flames. In this way the plotters avoided any indiscreet...disclosures on the part of their accomplice and made the entire massacre appear to fit the official Burmese explanation."[113]

Yanmin and thirty other desperadoes were said to have seized the swords and *unloaded* muskets of the guards, while they were eating lunch. The prisoners broke for the eastern gate of the city. Yanmin was wounded, took refuge in a house, was thrown out of it, and staggered to the road near the bazaar where he fell down. Yanmin's head was chopped off, and carried away in triumph.[114] Seven of the other runaways were killed, but the rest twenty or more got away.[115] Strangely enough, the 'Jailbreak' went on for three or four hours before anyone bothered to close the main city gates.

As prisoners were not fed or clothed by the jailers, the rest of the prisoners were eating lunch which was being brought by friends and relatives. Taingda, Taungwin, and others in on the ministers' plot brought up a troop of drunken musketeers and surrounded the jail.[116] Andreino, the Italian Consul, wrote that:

...an indiscriminate slaughter began, specially directed by the Tinedah Mingyee, against the harmless people who were begging for mercy. Finding themselves fired upon from all sides, they tried to break the fence and get out. At this...the Tinedah gave orders to set fire to the jail at the east corner, and from the Toung-win Mingyee's house the musketry fire was kept up. The flames drove the poor creatures to the gate, where they were hacked to pieces one after another.[117]

Rawlings, the foreigners' postmaster at Mandalay, wrote that over 300 prisoners and bystanders were slaughtered, among them eleven women, three Chinese, two Burmese princes, and one Buddhist monk.[118] A civil prisoner who had been jailed for a debt of Rs. 15 was murdered, as well as some fifteen of the jail-beggars who were allowed to beg their daily food outside the jail.[119] There were apparently only eleven genuine 'dacoits' among the dead. Rawlings wrote that although the 'Jailbreak' had occurred at the main jail, there were two other Mandalay jails and a general slaughter had occurred there also.[120]

In some of the most descriptive lines ever penned in the English language, Rawlings wrote of the aftermath:

Some of the heads of the victims were stuck up on bamboos in the cemetery, and others were carried through the streets...
....there were the mutilated bodies lying in ghastly and festering heaps, some of them not only riddled with shot, but hacked to pieces with *dahs* past all recognition, whilst a number of fiends in human shapes were actually chopping off arms and legs to save the manacles and shackles! Not only that, but the dead and dying had been carted off together, and in some cases the quivering of a limb told that the death

agony was not yet over. ....the carcasses were being huddl-
ed, four and five together, into shallow graves, with no more
than a foot of earth to cover them. The pigs and pariahs
had already been feasting on the slain, and their banquet will
be continued after the sextons have withdrawn. In horrible
contrast..I saw little children playing about, all unconscious
of their dreadful surroundings.[121]

Rawlings concluded by noting the festivities being held to
mark the 'victory of the nation over the nation's foes':

Poays [plays] are being held nightly, and the Parsee Theatrical
Company have just arrived in good time to make sport in the
palace. Ministers are swaggering about on elephants, and
the wretched passers-by dare hardly to lift their heads from
the dust while in their presence ; boats with bands of music on
board are numerous on the river; a king's steamer gaily deco-
rated was sent down to Sagine, and excursionists invited to
take free passage; and the King has rewarded all those who
took part in the slaughter :

Oh ! if the Mengoon Prince, or, better still, a British
gunboat were only here![122]

The Mandalay 'Jailbreak' marked the virtual end of attempts
by the Indian Government to reach an amiable agreement
with Mandalay, or with any of the three exiled Princes. After
September 22, 1884, there were increasing demands from Rangoon
merchants and others that Upper Burma be forced to accept a new
King under the 'protection' of the Indian Government, or else
be fully annexed.

Such drastic action was said to be necessary in order to
prevent further massacres, and to prevent the French from endangering British subjects' lives and interests in Upper Burma. India's
eastern frontier would also be saved from the 'French Threat',
which was conceived by many to be the eastern equivalent of the
'Russian Threat' in the northwest. It was amidst the hysteria
following the 'Jailbreak' that Bernard made some of his last and
best defences of the regime at Mandalay.[123]

FOOTNOTES

[1] No. 82, Kinwun to Crosthwaite, April 26, 1883; in Foreign, A-Political-E,
June, 1883, Nos. 79-84 (NAI). *See also:* No. 145, Telegram from Crosth-

waite to Foreign Dept., May 9, 1883; in Foreign, A-Political-E, May 1883, Nos. 145-147 (NAI).

² Crosthwaite to Indian Foreign Secretary, May 17, 1883; in Nos. 79-84, pp. 1-2. *Also see:* Pilcher to Crosthwaite's Secretary, May 10, 1883; in Nos. 79-84.

³ Crosthwaite to Indian Foreign Secretary, May 17, 1883; in Nos. 79-84, pp. 1-2.

⁴ Pilcher to Crosthwaite's Secretary, May 10, 1883; in Nos. 79-84.

⁵ No. 48, Plunkett, H. M.'s Ambassador to Paris, to Granville, August 13, 1883; in C. 4614, p. 106.

⁶ *Ibid.*

⁷ No. 24, Plunkett to Granville, August 21, 1883; in Foreign, A-Political-E, December 1883, Nos. 22-28 (NAI).

⁸ No. 51, Lyons to Granville, November 7, 1883; in C. 4614, p. 107.

⁹ No. 53, Lyons to Granville, November 14, 1883; in C. 4614, p. 107.

¹⁰ No. 56, Lyons to Granviile, December 13, 1883; in C. 4614, p. 108.

¹¹⁻¹² *Ibid.*

¹³ No. 59, Lyons to Granville, December 26, 1883; in C. 4614, p. 109.

¹⁴ No. 61, Lyons to Granville, April 6, 1884; in C. 4614, p. 110. *See* the 1873 Treaty in Appendix D.

¹⁵ No. 62, Lyons to Granville, April 10, 1884; in C. 4614, p. 110.

¹⁶ No. 64, Lyons to Granville, May 21, 1884; in C. 4614, p. 110.

¹⁷ No. 66, Godley, India Office, to Pauncefote, Foreign Office, June 28, 1884; in C. 4614, p. 116.

¹⁸ Enclosure 1 in No. 68, Lyons to Granville, July 11, 1884; in C. 4614, pp. 117-118.

¹⁹⁻²¹ *Ibid.*

²² Enclosure in No. 69, Lyons to Granville, July 16, 1884; in C. 4614, p. 119.

²³⁻²⁶ *Ibid.*

²⁷ No. 470, "Burmese Politics," (London) *Standard,* July 17, 1884; in Foreign, External-A, October 1884, Nos. 453-472 (NAI). Deloncle was ostensibly an agent of Ferdinand d'Lesseps, the builder of the Suez Canal. Deloncle came to Mandalay on his way back from surveying a possible Canal Route across the Kraw Isthmus of southern Siam. This was the route that J. G. Scott in *France and Tongkin* described as appealing *only* to canal contractors in their offices.

²⁸ No. 472, Lyons to Granville, July 29, 1884; in Nos. 453-472. (*Also see:* K. W. No. 1, Burne's Report on 1873 Franco-Burmese Treaty, July 18, 1884; in Nos. 453-472, pp. 1-2).

²⁹ Brian L. Lewis, *The Attitudes and Policies of Great Britain and China Towards French Expansion in Cochin China, Cambodia, Annam and Tongking, 1858-1883*, Ph.D. Thesis, Un. of London, 1961, p. 472.

³⁰ K. W. No. 2, Bernard to Foreign Dept., June 3, 1884; in Foreign, Secret-E, June 1884, Nos. 479-480, p. 2 (NAI).

³¹ Kennedy to Bernard, June 10, 1884; in Nos. 479-480, p. 2.

³² Rawlings to Bernard's Secretary, June 11 ,1884; in Nos. 479-480, p. 3.

³³ Philippe Preschez, "Les Relations...," pp. 351-352.

[34] *Ibid.*

[35] *Ibid*, pp. 352-353. (*See also:* No. 470, "Burmese Politics," (London) *Standard*, July 17, 1884; in Nos. 453-472).

[36] *Ibid.*, p. 354.

[37] "The Fires in Mandalay," (Calcutta) *Englishman*, April 22, 1884, p. 5.

[38] Philippe Preschez, "Les Relations...." p. 354.

[39-40] *Ibid.*

[41-42] *Ibid*, p. 352. (*See also :* No. 470, "Burmese Politics," (London) *Standard*, July 17, 1884; in Nos. 453-472).

[43] *Ibid*, pp. 353, 380-386.

[44-45] *Ibid.* (*See also:* No. 470, "Burmese Politics," (London) *Standard,* July 17, 1884; in Nos. 453-472. The article claimed that Thebaw was overjoyed at having put France and England at each other's throat. When Deloncle left, Thebaw deputized the Kinwun to salute him in the Continental fashion, *i.e.* to kiss him).

[46-48] *Ibid.* p. 354.

[49] No. 730, Telegram from Dufferin to Churchill, January 25, 1886; in Foreign, Secret-E, January 1886, Nos. 727-730 (NAI).

[50] Philippe Preschez, "Les Relations....," p. 384 (trans. excerpt from *Correspondence politique*, Rangoon, folio 121, 26 nov. 1884).

[51] *Ibid.* *Also see:* Thomas F. Powers, *Jules Ferry and the Renaissance of French Imperialism*, New York, 1944, pp. 180-186.

[52-54] *Ibid.*

[55-56] *Ibid.*

[57] No. 77, Lyons to Granville, January 16, 1885; in C. 4614, pp. 123-124. (*Also see:* Enclosure in No. 75, Lyons to Granville, January 5, 1885; in C. 4614, p. 122.)

[58] *See* Appendix D for the January 15, 1885 Treaty and Ferry's Secret Letter.

[FV] *Ibid.*

[60] No. 85, Scott, H. M.'s Ambassador at Berlin, to Granville, April 8, 1885; in C. 4614, p. 157.

[61] No. 21, Lumley, H. M.'s Ambassador at Rome, to Granville, April 10, 1885; in Foreign, Secret-E, August 1885, Nos. 1-33 (NAI).

[62] *Ibid.*

[63] No. 88, Bernard's Secretary to Durand, May 13, 1885; in Foreign, Secret-E, October 1885, Nos. 88-90 (NAI).

[64] *Ibid.*

[65-66] *Ibid.*

[67] Shway Yoe, *The Burman..*, p. 540.

[68] No. 88, Bernard's Secretary to Durand, May 13, 1885; in Nos. 88-90.

[69-72] *Ibid.*.

[73] Brian L. Lewis, *The Attitudes..*, p. 472. Lewis wrote that, 'The British were most sensitive to the French in Burma, particularly, Upper Burma. Britain sought political control as the result of the presence of British commercial interests, as opposed to the French, who were attempting to establish commercial interests through the imposition of political control."

[74] *Ibid.* *See also:* John L. Christian, *Modern Burma*, Berkeley, 1942, p. 61.

75 No. 88, Bernard's Secretary to Durand, May 13, 1885; in Nos. 88-90.

76 No. 328, Leslie to Grant, February 14, 1883 ; in Foreign, Secret-E, April 1883, Nos. 285-349 (NAI). Leslie was Myngun's Calcutta lawyer. *Also see :* Foreign, Secret-E, September 1883, Nos. 195-221 (NAI). *Also :* Foreign, Secret-E, January 1884, Nos. 248-253 (NAI). *Also :* Foreign Secret-E, May 1884, Nos. 259-260 (NAI). *Lastly:* Foreign, Secret-E, September 1884, Nos. 23-37 (NAI).

77 No. 329, Martindale to Leslie, March 6, 1883; in Nos. 285-349.

78 No. 337, Note on Myngun Prince, Wilkins to Peacock, March 10, 1883; in Nos. 285-349. This is a detailed note on the the Myngun's supporters in Upper and Lower Burma. They included the Taingda and Taungwin Mingyis at Mandalay, and the Tsabwas of Mong Nai, Kengtung, and the leaders of one-half of the Shan States who had been in revolt against Thebaw's rule since 1879-1880. Lower Burma supporters included several prominent Rangoon Burmese lawyers, and most of the timber, *putsoe* ('sarong'), pickled-tea, and grain dealers of Rangoon and Tharawaddy.

79 *Ibid.*

80 Philippe Preschez, "Les Relations....," pp. 366-367.

81 *Ibid,* p. 369.

82 No. 36, Moh. Isqu to Green, July 2, 1884; in Nos. 23-37. The plotters were said to have received Rs. 10,000 apiece. *See also*: "Burma," (Allahabad) *Pioneer Mail*, June 29, 1884, p. 643. The article claimed that a local French resident at Mandalay assisted in the plot.

83 Grattan Geary, *Burma After the Conquest,* pp. 196-197. (*See also:* "British Burmah," (Bombay) *The Times of India,* July 9, 1884, p. 2. *Also:* "Rangoon," (Allahabad) *Pioneer Mail,* July 20, 1884, p. 63. *The Times of India* thought that the people of Upper Burma would have risen in Myngun's favour had he been able to reach Karenni as planned. The *Pioneer Mail* doubted that the Burmese would have supported Myngun. If the Burmese were discontented with Thebaw's rule, they usually fled south into Lower Burma.)

84 *Ibid*, pp. 199-200.

85 A number of European and non-European firms at Rangoon were also interested in placing Myngun upon the throne. The agent of a large European firm told Bernard that the teak firm of Darwood and MacGregor, certain Chinese dealers, and the agent's own firm, wanted to furnish the Myngun with a steamer, and take him from Pondicherry to Bangkok. Bernard did not know what the Indian Government's reaction would be, but he doubted that they would be able to detain the Myngun in Bangkok as they had in Colombo. The agent replied that the Myngun would then have little trouble in getting to the Shan States, and seizing the Burmese throne. The agent left for Pondicherry to discuss the scheme with the Myngun; however, the attempt was never made. *See:* Bernard to Grant, October 19, 1884; in Foreign, Secret-E, November 1884, Nos. 161-171 (NAI). *Also see*: K. W. No. 2, Bernard to Grant, October 31, 1885; in Foreign, Secret-E, April 1885, Nos. 25-47, p. 1 (NAI).

86 "Rangoon," (Allahabad) *Pioneer Mail*, January 9, 1883, pp. 62-63.

87 Philippe Preschez, "Les Relations....," p. 367.

[88] "British Burma," (Bombay) *The Times of India*, July 4, 1884, p. 4. This marriage to Supayalat's younger sister did give Thebaw his long-awaited son—in November 1885.

[89] *Ibid.*

[90] Philippe Preschez, "Les Relations....," p. 369.

[91-92] *Ibid.*

[93-95] *Ibid.*, pp. 369-370.

[96] *For example see :* No. 203, Myngun to Ripon, May 1883 (no exact date); in Nos. 195-221. "Should I be put in power, I hope by a conciliatory tone to preserve peace between the two Governments, as I feel what the fate of Burma will be, in the event of there being another war with England." *See also:* No. 211, Myngun's Statement of Views, June, 29, 1883: in Nos. 195-221. Myngun accepted the Indian Government's view on the "Shoe Question" and on most issues. He balked on the issue of an enlarged Residency Guard to more than the fifty men allowed under the 1826 Yandabo Treaty. "I would prefer a Resident with as few followers as possible, and I will be responsible to the British Government for his safety." *Lastly see :* "Occasional Notes," (Allahabad) *Pioneer Mail,* April 25, 1883, p. 419. A lengthy interview during which the Myngun said that he would have only one wife, be easy of access to his people, and would allow every one to visit him "in the English fashion." He stated that his country's interests lay in friendship with England. He would have only the three Royal monopolies of timber, earth-oil, and precious stones; and he would have a civil list, *i.e.* an income budgeted by the *Hlutdaw.* The interviewer was impressed with the Myngun, but concluded that it was up to the Burmese people. The Indian Government had no reason to interfere in Burmese affairs.

[97-98] Philippe Preschez, "Les Relations...," pp. 369-370.

[99] *Ibid.*, pp. 370-371.

[100] *Ibid.*, p. 371.

[101] *Ibid.*

[102] *Ibid.*, pp. 371-372.

[103] "France and Burmah," (Calcutta) *Englishman*, September 16, 1884, p. 4.

[104] "The Mengoon Prince," (Calcutta) *Englishman*, September 3, 1884, p. 4. A typical example of the Myngun "escape" story to be found in many papers.

[105] "The Mandalay Massacre," (Bombay) *The Times of India*, October 18, 1884, p. 3.

[106] *Ibid.*

[107] "Philippe Preschez, "Les Relations....p. 371.

[108] "The Mandalay Massacre," (Bombay) *The Times of India,* November 1, 1884, p. 4.

[109-113] *Ibid.*

[114] Andreino to Kennedy, September 24, 1884; in Foreign, Secret-E, November 1884, Nos. 161-171, pp. 11-12 (NAI).

[115] *Ibid.*

[116] F. T. Jesse, *The Story of Burma*, p. 7.

[117] Andreino to Kennedy, September 24, 1884; in Nos. 161-171, pp. 11-12.

[118] Rawlings (?) to Bernard's Secretary, September 24, 1884 (?), enclosed with Enclosure 2 in No. 83, Bernard's Secretary to Foreign Dept. Sec., October 3, 1884; in C. 4614, pp. 128-129.

[119-20] *Ibid.*

[121-22] *Ibid.*

[123] For a slightly different version of the 'Jailbreak' *see:* Account of Agent of Messrs. Finley, Fleming & Co., (no date); in Nos. 161-171, p. 12.

5

The Ecological Devolution of Upper Burma

Introduction

The 'Jailbreak' Massacre set-off a heated debate between Bernard and many of the Burmese, Chinese, European, and Mogul-Surati merchants at Rangoon. The merchants claimed that Thebaw's 'misrule' had caused a 'drought' and crop failures in the southern provinces of Upper Burma during 1883-1885.[1]

In 1884, more than 250,000 Upper Burmese from the provinces south of Mandalay—out of a total Upper Burmese population of about 3,000,000—had fled to Lower Burma to escape the food-shortages and 'dacoity'.[2] By mid-1884, about 26,000 Burmese were migrating every month on the steamers to Lower Burma, and with the tacit permission of the Burmese Government. The near-bankruptcy of the Burmese treasury, and a decline in trade via the Irrawaddy, had followed. In the merchants' opinion, these aspects of Thebaw's 'misrule' could be removed only by British annexation of Upper Burma.

The 1883-1885 'drought' and the other calamities attributed to Thebaw's 'misrule' were, in the main, caused by 'modern' Deforestation. King Mindon had first leased extensive portions of his forests to the BBTC in 1862. Within twenty years many cutch, teak, and other timber areas in the provinces south of Mandalay and elsewhere were largely denuded of trees and other ground cover. The deforested soil had lost its 'sponge ability' to *hold* back rain-water.

As a result, the rains tended to evaporate at a much higher rate, or to rush-off into the streams. The silt washed into the streams *clogged* many of the irrigation-canals and water-storage areas behind tanks and dams near Mandalay and elsewhere, and some of these irrigation systems were being abandoned even before 1883. When a slight cyclical-dip in the annual rainfall occurred, the result was the 1883-1885 'drought' in the southern provinces of Upper Burma, and many of the other calamities attributed to Thebaw's 'misrule'.[3]

Bernard Defends Mandalay

Bernard's October 3 response to the 'Jailbreak' Massacre was cautious.[4] He reported that the Tsawbwas of Mong Nai, Kengtung, and almost one-half of the Shan States, had been in revolt for more than three years.[5] At Mogaung north of Bhamo there had been a Kachin revolt earlier in 1884.[6]

Several pretenders to Thebaw's throne were active, including the three exiled Princes. They, however, were not allowed to use Lower Burma as a staging area for the invasion of Upper Burma. By such a refusal, the Indian Government was assisting Thebaw to retain his throne. Therefore, the Indian Government should send Thebaw a firm protest concerning the 'Jailbreak' Massacre.[7]

Bernard's main report was filed on October 16 as a result of the Rangoon 'Indignation Meeting' held on October 11 by certain annexationists and merchants. The result of the meeting was a resolution of four parts. The first part stated that Thebaw's 'misrule' had caused 'drought' and anarchy in Upper Burma, which had in turn depressed the trade between the two Burmas.

The second part stated that 'dacoity' in Upper Burma had overflowed into Lower Burma. The third part stated that the Indian Government should interfere in Upper Burma to end such anarchy. The fourth and last part advised either annexation or the establishment of a new King under a 'protected state'.[8]

Bernard refuted the first charge in the resolution that Thebaw's 'misrule' had caused a depression of trade between the two Burmas. The average yearly river trade between the two Burmas during 1880-1884 was larger than the average during the last four years of Mindon's reign.[9] The trade figures from 1874-1878 showed an average yearly total of £3,061,174; with exports to Upper Burma averaging £1,514,069, and imports from Upper Burma averaging £1,547,105. The 1880-1884 average yearly total was £3,224,814 ; with exports to Upper Burma averaging £1,651,345, and imports from Upper Burma averaging £1,573,469.[10]

The average from 1880 to 1884 had risen slightly even though trade had suffered in 1881-1882 from the Royal monopolies, which had especially effected imports from Lower Burma. During late-1884 Bernard conceded that trade, except for rice and food-stuffs, had been almost at a standstill.[11] He said that this was due to the fear of an invasion by Prince Myngun.

Bernard could not agree to the Resolution's second premise that 'dacoity' in Upper Burma had overflowed into Lower Burma. There had been a steep rise in violent crime in Lower Burma. But Bernard pointed out that the *worst* districts, namely Hanthawaddy, Pegu, Henzada, and Tharrawaddy, were far removed from the frontier.[12] (*See* footnote 30, p. 159).

The Resolution's third point was that the Indian Government should interfere in Upper Burma to restore law and order, and to protect British subjects' lives and trade.[13] Bernard demurred by stating that the two countries were in a friendly alliance, according to the 1862 and 1867 Treaties. Except for the 'Jailbreak' Massacre, the Indian Government had no occasion under international law to interfere in the internal affairs of Upper Burma. In practical terms, the relations between the two states were fairly cordial, and had been so for the previous five years.[14]

Such relations were reflected in the large trade figures between the two countries. Trade across the Lower Burma frontier with Upper Burma equalled 62 per cent. of all trade across the whole frontier of India from Quetta on the west to Tenasserim on the east. Bernard cited the 1881-1882 Hamilton Report, which stated that the value of the total trade across India's frontier was £5,145,000. Between the two Burmas the trade had averaged £3,224,814 annually during Thebaw's reign.[15]

Bernard commented on the fourth and last recommendation of the Resolution, namely that Mandalay should be annexed or that a new King should be placed on the throne of a 'protected state'. Despite some possible trade benefits, Bernard did not think that this was sufficient justification for a 'protected state' or annexation. He concluded that "If King Theebaw's Government transgressed British frontiers, invaded British allies, maltreated British subjects, broke treaties, continued to commit massacres, rejected British protests, and refused redress, matters would be different."[16]

Bernard received a second missile from the Rangoon annexationists when J. Stuart, secretary of the Chamber of Commerce, wrote to complain of the adverse trade conditions. He claimed that European importers at Rangoon were selling only one-fifth of the goods that they had eighteen to twenty-four months previously. Most of their former sales had been to non-European Rangoon merchants, who exported the goods to Upper Burma.[17]

Most of the imports of British and European manufactures were controlled by British traders and other Europeans at Rangoon. However, the export of these manufactures to Upper Burma was almost entirely in the hands of Rangoon Burmese, Chinese, and Indian traders. The non-European traders also controlled the rice-exporting trade to Upper Burma, and competed with European firms in exporting rice and other products to Europe.

In particular, the Rangoon Chinese controlled the salt exports to Upper Burma, while the Burmese controlled the jaggery exports. The three groups of non-European traders also held timber contracts in Upper Burma, although no one operator was as large as the BBTC. With such a varied group of non-European merchants handling the export trade to Upper Burma, and the lucrative return-trade from Mandalay to Rangoon, it could not be said that only Europeans were hurt by the decline of Upper Burmese purchases of British and European imports.

Stuart claimed that the decrease in trade was due to the 'dacoity' and anarchy beyond the frontier, and that annexation would best protect British subjects' lives and trade.[18] However, if such was not possible, then a 'protected state' with the Nyaung-yan as King would be acceptable. Stuart was particularly unhappy, because the immediate and unexpected result of the October 11 'Indignation Meeting' had been a further drop in business confidence—and in business volume.[19]

The Rangoon customs figures seemed to cast doubt upon Stuart's claim that European importers at Rangoon were selling only one-fifth of the goods that they had eighteen to twenty-four months previously. In fact, the 1883-1884 imports of British-goods were at an all-time high of £7,313,451. The official Rangoon customs figures of imports from England since 1876 were (1876-1877),

£4,709,404; (1877-1878), £4,644,116; (1878-1879), £5,922,123; (1879-1880), £5,970,002; (1880-1881), £7,040,640; (1881-1882), £6,384,893; (1882-1883), £6,789,635; and lastly, (1883-1884), £7,313,451.[20]

Bernard stated in an October 18 letter to Grant that the customs figures refuted Stuart's claim. However, Bernard did concede that the imports at Rangoon from April 1 to September 30, 1884 had dropped fifteen lakhs below the corresponding 1883 figure.[21] The amount of British imports exported to Mandalay had also declined drastically during the last months of 1884.

On the other hand, the failure of the 1884 rice-crop had caused the rice-exports to Upper Burma to increase in value by nearly 300 per cent. The rice-export figure for April-September 1884 was Rs. 4,280,047 as compared to Rs. 1,346,074 for the first half of 1883-1884, and Rs. 1,122,433 for the first half of 1882-1883. Bernard thought that the thirty extra lakhs spent on rice from April-September 1884 would have been available for the purchase of British imports, except for the Upper Burma 'drought'.[22]

Bernard stated that the October 11 'Indignation Meeting' had "frightened the Rangoon Native dealers, in whose hands is all the trade from British Burma to Ava."[23] Bernard asked the Indian Government to make a quick decision on his plea for a strong remonstrance about the 'Jailbreak' Massacre. Bernard concluded that the panic and paralysis of trade would continue until the Indian Government stated that it would not favor annexation, or any immediate interference in Upper Burmese affairs.[24]

The Bernard-Kennedy Letters

On November 19, 1884, a complaint came from F. C. Kennedy, Rangoon IFC manager. His steamer crews were afraid for their safety, while in Upper Burma, due to the increasing 'dacoit' raids.[25] He stated that various river-town Governors had asked IFC captains to anchor their steamers in mid-stream at night—and under steam—instead of tying-up at shore.

At Mimu in the vicinity of Mandalay, 700 'dacoits' had sent a challenge to 1,000 King's troops to come out and fight.[26] Apparently, Thebaw's troops had not responded. Kennedy noted that such disturbances would hurt trade as well as possibly hurt or kill British subjects in Upper Burma. Consequently, he requested that a strong remonstrance be sent to Mandalay.[27]

Bernard requested further evidence of 'dacoit' activity, and instances where they had threatened British subjects. Kennedy replied on December 30 that the Salaymyo Governor had asked all IFC captains to keep their steamers in the middle of the stream at night. The Governor had been attacked in his court in broad daylight by 'dacoits', and had narrowly escaped with his life.[28]

Kennedy added that Magwe was another river district where 'dacoits' had murdered a *myothugyi,* township headman. In Kennedy's view, the 'dacoit' problem would become worse, because of the December 7, 1884 capture of Bhamo. It had caused a drastic shift of Burmese troops. They had been sent northwards to Bhamo to recapture it from Chinese and Kachin bandits under the adventurer King Kueh Yee.[29]

The area between Mandalay and the Lower Burma frontier would soon be denuded of Burmese troops, and would become a preserve for 'dacoits' to prey upon British subjects. Kennedy again requested Bernard to send a strong remonstrance that would help to protect the lives and property of British subjects north of the frontier. By way of contrast, the *Times of India* thought that there were *more* 'dacoities' in Lower Burma.[30]

Aftermath of the Fall of Bhamo

In September 1884, the Burmese garrison at Bhamo fired cannon shots through the locked doors of a local Chinese temple. The act of desecration was an attempt to dislodge King Kueh Yee, 35, a dissident Chinese trader and mercenary with his 135 followers.[31] The group was allowed to leave the city. But at 2 a.m., December 7, 1884, King re-entered Bhamo with 200 Chinese and 100 Kachin troops, and chased the 350 Burmese soldiers down-river. King looted and held Bhamo until February 19, 1885 against all Burmese attempts to recapture it.[32] Bernard telegraphed the news of the fall of Bhamo to Durand on December 28, 1884.[33]

The disturbance at Bhamo was extremely damaging to the winter trade in both Burmas. Bhamo was the chief commercial city in northern Burma, and was composed of 2,000 houses within a stockade forty miles south of the Chinese frontier. The city was the chief entry-point for Chinese imports, such as wool, cotton, and silk goods, which were being brought down in the winter caravans.[34] The capture of Bhamo by an obscure adventurer caused a panic in Lower Burma. On January 9, Bernard's secretary wrote to the Kinwun requesting that British subjects' lives and property be protected.[35]

The Chinese exporters at Rangoon had suffered heavy losses in the sack of Bhamo where most of the trade was in Chinese hands. However, several European firms had also sold large salt orders on credit to Bhamo merchants. On January 10, 1885, J. Stuart, secretary of the Rangoon Chamber of Commerce, wrote to Bernard to enquire when he intended replying to Stuart's October 14, 1884 letter.[36]

Stuart repeated the common rumor that the Taingda and another minister were taking a percentage from several of the 'dacoit' bands about Mandalay, one of which totalled 1,500 men. Stuart claimed that other bands in the Sagaing, Salaymyo, Magwe, and frontier districts would soon attack the steamers. When the steamers ceased running into Upper Burma, the remaining trans-frontier trade would be ended. With it would go all hope that a merchant might have had concerning the collection of debts owed to him by Upper Burmese.[37]

Stuart brought up the spectre of a Chinese conquest of Upper Burma. King Kueh Yee claimed to be the agent of the Chinese Governor of Yunnan, which the Governor later denied. Stuart claimed to believe that Chinese armies would advance upon Mandalay and capture it. This new 'Chinese Threat' could be met only by prompt British interference. All other efforts to protect British subjects' interests and India's eastern frontier had proved insufficient.[38]

Stuart's letter was passed on to the Indian Foreign Dept. along with Bernard's comments. Among other points, Bernard did not think that the anarchy at Bhamo 800 miles up-river from Rangoon would stop the running of the steamers to Mandalay, about 550 miles up-river from Rangoon. However, he did concede that steamers could not go up to Bhamo, because there was little trade. The increasing anarchy in Upper Burma had caused a considerable decline in commerce between Rangoon and Mandalay during the previous three months.[39]

Bernard proposed four contingencies. The first was that King Kueh Yee would continue to hold-out at Bhamo.[40] The second was that King's raiders would carry reprisals down the Irrawaddy. The third was that the rumored attack on the Shan State of Thebaw by Shan rebels would be successful, and that the Shan and Chinese raiders would then invade the Dry Zone in force, and perhaps even attack Mandalay. The fourth contingency was that the local 'dacoits' around Mandalay would continue their rampages.

A combination of most or all four contingencies would probably result in a revolution, and Thebaw would lose his throne. Only then would the Indian Government be entitled to intervene to protect British subjects' lives and property, and to put the Nyaungyan or some other prince on the throne.[41] However, if Thebaw was able to retain his throne, but without being able to stop the four contingencies above, the Indian Government would have no right of interference. Bernard advised against the use of force merely because trade had been allegedly hurt by Thebaw's 'misrule'.[42]

No definite word had yet come from the Indian Foreign Dept. concerning the several commercial petitions and Bernard's rebuttals. Stuart, the Chamber secretary, again wrote to Bernard on February 4 to complain about the lack of action. Stuart ran through the usual complaints, namely that the anarchy in Upper Burma was a threat to British subjects' lives and property; Rangoon businessmen were failing because of the lack of trade; the decline in Lower Burma revenue was now certainly obvious; and, lastly, the new Burmese-French Treaty was a typical example of the "aggressive spirit which animates modern French policy in the East."[43]

Bernard's February 6 rebutal claimed that the 'dacoits' and disorder in Upper Burma had not caused the failures of several European rice-firms exporting to Europe. However, there had been several failures in the two previous months among non-European firms, which exported British imports to Upper Burma. The failures had come because of the firms' inability to collect money owed to them by Upper Burmese traders.[44]

The Chinese dealers at Rangoon had lost heaviest in the sack of Bhamo where most of the trade was in Chinese hands. Consequently, failures among the Chinese and other non-European export houses were bound to affect European firms, who sold British imports on long or short credit in the Rangoon bazaar.[45]

Bernard said that the gross value of trade to Upper Burma had increased during the last half of 1884 to Rs. 15,352,940. This compared favorably with the 1883 figure of Rs. 12,596,673. The increase had been mainly due to the increase in the exports of rice and foodstuffs, which had filled "the deficit caused by failure of the food crop in 1883-84."[46]

There was little money available with which to buy British imports, although the unexpected rise in the sales of British silk to Upper Burma had more than compensated for the drop in cotton twist and piece-goods. Bernard concluded that the exports of British goods to Upper Burma in early-1885 would fall below the corresponding figures for previous years.[47]

One day later on February 7, the official *British Burma Gazette* published a February 4, 1885 statistical report of the Irrawaddy River trade. It compared the trade to and from Upper Burma for the last half of 1883, and the last half of 1884. The report stated that trade with Upper Burma had increased during 1884. The study was analyzed in the February 13, 1885 *Rangoon Times* by a writer who used the name 'A Merchant'. He stated that the rise in trade was mainly due to the increased exports of rice to Upper Burma, and that this was *not* a sign of general 'prosperity'.[48]

'A Merchant' debunked the theory that the increase in the number of trips made by the IFC steamers was another sign of prosperity. 'A Merchant' said that the extra trips in 1884 took place because thousands of Upper Burmese had taken refuge in Lower Burma "from the poverty and starvation, which confronted them in their own homes."[49] The rise in trips had also been caused in part by the rise in 'dacoities', which had made it dangerous to ship goods overland between the two Burmas.

Likewise, the increased shipments of cow and buffalo hides from Upper Burma was not a sign of reviving trade. It meant that more cattle than usual had died from disease, or had been killed for their hides and meat.[50] The increased volume of Upper Burmese teak shipped down the Irrawaddy and Sittang Rivers was also no indication of increased business 'prosperity', because most of the teak shipments were owned by one firm, the BBTC.[51]

The sharp increase in the sales of imported British silk to the Mandalay Palace was—once again—not a sign of general 'prosperity'. The orders had filled the vacuum caused by the virtual stoppage of silk-weaving in Upper Burma. The brisk sales of imported British silk did not effect the Rangoon merchants to the degree as did their unsold bales of wool-yarns and cotton piece-goods. As a result, there had been a sharp drop in the amount of piece-goods and yarns imported into Rangoon during the last four months of 1884—as compared to the corresponding months in 1883.[52]

'A Merchant' concluded that the merchants were in a serious financial bind, because they could not collect the debts owed to them by Upper Burmese. He predicted more losses among European importers, and more failures among non-Europeans exporting British goods to Upper Burma.[53]

The Influence of Business Petitions
Upon the Indian and British Governments

In summary, business was better than ever for Rangoon's Chinese and other rice traders exporting to Upper Burma. Except for some periods when they glutted the Upper Burmese rice market, and had to sell at a loss, the Rangoon food-exporters made good profits during 1883-1885. This was in contrast to many of their commercial brethren, who were going bankrupt exporting rice to Europe.

Business was also better than ever for Rangoon silk-dealers exporting British-silk to Upper Burma, and for British silk-weaving centers such as Macclesfield. Bernard had noted that the increased sales of British-silk to Upper Burma had more than compensated for the decline in cotton twist and piece-goods. Naturally, this was no comfort for European importers at Rangoon in those other items besides silk, and also no comfort for non-Europeans who had formerly exported large quantities of British imports—other than silk—to Mandalay.

On April 18, 1885, the 'silk-centric' Macclesfield Chamber of Commerce wrote to Lord Kimberley, secretary of state for India. They asked him to re-establish the Resident and the Mixed Court at Mandalay.[54] On April 20, the Glasgow Chamber of Commerce made a similar request to Kimberley.[55] In direct contrast, the Rangoon, Calcutta, London, and other Chambers advised that Upper Burma should be either annexed or made into a 'protected state'. The various Chambers remained divided in their recommendations, and in the intensity of their appeals, for several months.

For example, it was usually those Chambers in 'depressed' cities, such as Manchester and Birmingham, who were most shrill in their cries for annexation. They claimed that the untapped markets of Yunnan and Southern China would be thrown open to British commerce—if Britain annexed the approaches to Yunnan. The new trade with Yunnan would re-employ the thousands of British workingmen, who had lost their jobs because of the brisk commercial competition from Germany, France, the United States, and other newly industrialized nations.

The business groups in silk-weaving towns such as Macclesfield, and Glasgow which exported more goods to Burma than any other city, were less strident in their appeals, and indeed preferred the *status quo* in Burma in order to profit themselves. In fact, they wished to go back to the time when the Mixed Court still functioned and there was a British Resident at Mandalay.

After France 'intruded' into Upper Burma during the summer of 1885, the Chambers of Lower Burma, India, and Great Britain became united in their appeals to Government. They stated that Upper Burma should be either annexed or made into a 'protected state'. If prompt action was not taken, the French would gain commercial and political influence in Upper Burma. They would also control the approaches to Yunnan and the lush, untapped markets of Southern China.

In the British Government's view, the securing of new British markets in Yunnan, and the retention of current markets in Upper Burma, were issues that were *not* as important as the political considerations. While never forgetting the important commercial aspects, the British Government was more concerned with the imminent political crisis that would erupt when French Indo-China ran contiguously with India's eastern frontier. In the final analysis, the Chamber petitions had only a *minor* influence on the decisions and events involving Upper Burma in 1885-1886.[56]

Lord Dufferin's Reaction

Meanwhile Viceroy Lord Dufferin was preparing a decision on the mercantile complaints enclosed with Bernard's rebuttals that had accumulated since October 3, 1884. Dufferin accepted all of Bernard's views, except the proposed protest of the 'Jailbreak' Massacre.[57] On February 10, 1885, Dufferin presented a systems interpretation of events in his letter to Lord Kimberley, the secretary of state for India:

As the Rangoon merchants were pressing Bernard......I authorized him to inform them that the Government...... had no intention of annexing Burmah. Nor do I believe is their present.......position occasioned by the troubles in Mandalay and Bhamo. The real causes of their ruin are the speculative trade generated by the high prices of rice [in Europe] in 1882 and 1883 and the present low prices of food-grains in Europe. During the last year there has been a loss of £1 per ton on 635,000 tons of rice exported abroad [to rice-glutted Europe]. On the other hand, the failure of the rice crop in Upper Burmah, and the short rice crop of 1884 in British Burmah, has reduced the demand for foreign [British] goods, to which result the disturbances in the Upper Valley of the Irrawaddy have also contributed.

Then again the teak trade has gone to pieces, teak averaging only £29 a ton last January [in Europe], as compared with £60 a ton the year before. Nor can the price of teak be expected to rise until ship-building becomes more active in Europe and railways are pressed on in India. Under these circumstances, no change of Government at Ava would very materially benefit either the rice trade or the timber trade [to Europe].[58]

Dufferin had previously requested an analysis of the Burma situation. On February 19, G. S. Forbes of the Indian Foreign Dept. presented a memorandum concerning the relations between Burma and France.[59] Forbes stated that the January 15, 1885 Treaty was the latest move in France's Burma strategy, which had been set into operation as far back as 1873. In that year, the Bill Committee had recommended the confirmation of the 1873 Burma-France Treaty on the grounds that Upper Burma's closeness to French Indo-China made Upper Burma a valuable area for future French commerce.[60]

At the present time, the French were expanding northwards from Cambodia into the Lao States held by Siam. From the east, the French were extending their influence westwards from Tongkin into the *pannas* and independent Lao States lying between Tongkin and Upper Burma. When the new French Consul arrived at Mandalay, the French would occupy still another post from which to extend their power over the lands lying between India and French Indo-China.[61]

The Forbes Memorandum discussed the Indian Government's

response to the rising French influence in Upper Burma. To begin with, "Burma has not shown active hostility against us nor caused material injury or danger."[62] The Indian Government had refused the pleas of some merchants and other annexationists to interfere actively in Upper Burma. The Government had concurred with Bernard's views that both annexation and a 'protected state' were unjustified. Therefore, Forbes concluded that the Indian Government's only possible response to the rising French influence was to re-establish the British Resident at Mandalay.[63]

Dufferin indicated four drawbacks to the re-establishment of the Resident in a March 24 despatch to Kimberley. The first drawback was that Mandalay had been informed that overtures for the re-establishment of the Resident, or for revision of relations between the two countries, would have to be initiated by Mandalay.[64] Such had been followed by the Kinwun in December 1881 when he had sent his secret envoy. The result had been the 1882 Simla Conference. Such a Burmese initiative was not likely to happen again.[65]

A second and different drawback was involved if the Indian Government initiated the overtures. It appeared that Mandalay would not graciously accept them, except under pressure from the Indian Army. The present time was not opportune for a military action against Mandalay.[66]

A third drawback was that a Resident could not re-establish British influence where there were already treaties or agreements between Burma and France that might run counter to British subjects' interests.[67] A fourth and last drawback would occur if the Mandalay Government did finally accept a new Resident which was likely. This would be an embarrassing sign of Burmese friendship in case the Indian Government decided to invade on the grounds of Mandalay's 'continued unfriendly conduct'.[68]

Therefore, Lord Dufferin's Government could not recommend any specific course of action concerning the re-establishment of the Resident.[69] Lord Kimberley replied on May 1, 1885, and authorized the Indian Government to re-establish the Resident whenever they thought it best.[70] Unfortunately, this was never done, and another opportunity to ease the tensions between the two countries went abegging.

An Ecosystems Model of the Consequences of Deforestation

The change in the Dry Zone after 1882 was sudden and shock-ing. The change was so abrupt that most observers concluded that the problem was one of political misrule that would be solved only with British annexation, or with another King in place of Thebaw. One exceptional observer was Grattan Geary, editor of the *Bombay Gazette*, who travelled over Upper Burma immediately after the Third Burmese War. Geary stated that:

the tendency to drought, which has caused so much alarm for some years past, is due to the destruction of timber and the denudation of the hills.[71]

The 1883-1885 'drought' in the Dry Zone had been caused in the main by the excessive Deforestation of cutch, teak, and other ground-cover in the provinces south of Mandalay and elsewhere during the two decades after 1862. The effects of this long-term Deforestation process were apparently exaggerated by a slight cyclical-dip in the annual rainfall from 1883-1885.[72]

The 1883-1885 'drought' caused considerable crop failures, a shortage of food, and a significant drop in the tax receipts extract-ed from the provinces south of Mandalay. Hungry peasants from these provinces fled to Lower Burma or became so-called 'dacoits', and were preyed upon in turn by other hungry 'dacoits'. Thebaw had to withdraw many of his troops from the Chinese, Kachin, and Shan rebels in the north and east, and use the troops to keep order between Mandalay and the Lower Burma frontier.

The move, necessary as it was, only increased Thebaw's diffi-culties in asserting his hegemony over the outlying portions of his empire. The Kachins, Shans, and other hill-tribes were already raiding further down into Upper Burma than they had in years. Some roving bands of Shans had even come down the mountainous ridges to within seven miles of Mandalay.

Meanwhile, in the Shan States proper, the Tsawbwas of Mong Nai, Kengtung, and their allies had been in revolt against The-baw's rule since 1879-1880. During Mindon's reign, the Shan States had paid an annual tribute of about twenty lakhs a year, or about twenty to twenty-five per cent of the Burmese Government's annual income of about 100 lakhs. During Thebaw's reign, the tribute had declined to about half of what it had been in 1878-1879.[73]

Since Thebaw's Government lacked a regular supply of modern

breech-loading rifles, there was no way that he could force the Shans to once again pay the customary tribute.[74] In order to get enough money for daily operating expenses, Thebaw's Government had to sell more and more timber leases to the BBTC, and to other Burmese, Chinese, European, and Mogul-Surati timber cutters. The consequent Deforestation and 'drought' forced Thebaw to concentrate still more of his remaining troops around Mandalay to put down the 'dacoits'.

Therefore, disorders sprang up everywhere, around Mandalay, at Mogaung and Bhamo, and in the Shan States. The ecological cycle went round and round. It was accelerated by the rapid disappearance of the forests and other ground cover, which had to be sold to get enough money to import Lower Burma rice to avoid hunger and possible revolution. The Mandalay treasury was almost empty. Consequently, there was little money left over for British imports.[75]

Rangoon observers suggested that it was Thebaw's 'misrule' that was to blame, and that a change of Kings or perhaps annexation was in order. Mandalay observers also blamed Thebaw for the poor crops, the lack of rain, and the continued lack of a male heir to the throne. Thebaw had usually been afraid to leave the Palace, and had never performed the annual Plowing Ceremony. This ceremony was supposed to represent Lord Indra, King of the Gods, blessing the crops and calling down the rains. Since Thebaw as the earthly manifestation of Lord Indra had not performed the ceremony, it meant that he had *caused* the 'drought'. As the popular bazaar-joke put it: the *only* seed Thebaw had ever sowed was that in Supayalat, which resulted in girl after girl.

In summary, the Rangoon and Mandalay explanations appeared to be incomplete. Thebaw's rule in 1883 to 1885 was very much the same as his rule in 1880, which both the Rangoon merchants and, apparently, his own people had applauded. So, the explanation for the 1883-1885 'drought', and the consequent deterioration of order and trade, would have to be found in some *other* more basic explanation. Deforestation—in combination with a slight cyclical-dip in the annual rainfall from 1883-1885—appears to be that explanation. It ought to be kept in mind while reading the remaining chapters, especially Chapter VII entitled The Deforestation of Upper Burma, 1862-1885 : The BBTC Teak Case; and, Appendix B, Deforestation Causes the Collapse of Trade and Order in Upper Burma, 1883-1885.

158   *King Thebaw and the Ecological Rape of Burma*

FOOTNOTES

[1] G. E. Harvey, *Outline of Burmese History*, London and Calcutta, 1947, p. 181. *See also* : "Rangoon," (Allahabad) *Pioneer Mail*, June 1, 1884, p. 547. *Lastly:* J. G. Scott and J. P. Hardiman, *Gazetteer ...*, Part One, Vol. II, p. 341.

[2] *Ibid.*

[3] *See* : Appendix B entitled Deforestation Causes the Collapse of Order and Trade in Upper Burma, 1883-1885.

[4] Enclosure 2 in No. 83, Bernard's Secretary to Grant, October 3, 1884 ; in C. 4614, pp. 126-127. (Some other excellent descriptions of conditions in Upper Burma are : K. W. No. 3, Bernard to Grant, October 2, 1884 ; in Foreign, Secret-E, November, 1884, Nos. 161-171, pp. 10-11 (NAI). *Also see :* Bernard to Grant, October 19, 1884 ; in Nos. 161-171, pp. 13-14.)

[5] *Ibid.* (*Also see* : Sao Saimong Mangrai, *The Shan States and the British Annexation,* Ithaca, 1965, pp. 101-112.)

[6] *Ibid.* (*See also :* Enclosure No. 2 from Andreino to Bernard's Secretary and enclosed with K. W. No. 2, Bernard to Durand, March 5, 1884 ; in Foreign, A-Political-E, March 1884, Nos. 272-273 (NAI). *Also :* "Rangoon," (Allahabad) *Pioneer Mail*, March 26, 1884, p. 321. *Lastly :* "British Burma," (Bombay) *The Times of India*, July 9, 1884, p. 2.)

[7] *Ibid.*

[8] Enclosure 3 in No. 83, Bernard's Secretary to Grant, October 16, 1884 ; in C. 4614, pp. 130-135.

[9] *Ibid.*

[10-11] *Ibid.* All figures used in this chapter that speak of the trade between the two Burmas refer to the river-trade.

[12] *Ibid.* (In 1878-1879, the number of crimes reported in Lower Burma was 27,564. By 1884-1885, the number of crimes reported in Lower Burma had risen to 43,406. *See :* Burma portion, *1878-1879 Moral and Progress Report of India,* Calcutta, p. 11, (NAI). *Also :* Burma portion, *1884-1885 Moral and Progress Report of India,* Calcutta, p. 10 (NAI).

[13-15] *Ibid.* (*See also :* footnote 30, p. 159.)

[16] *Ibid.*

[17] Enclosure A in No. 83, Stuart to Bernard's Secretary, October 14, 1884 ; in C. 4614, pp. 139-140.

[18] *Ibid.*

[19] *Ibid.*

[20] Enclosure 4 in No. 83, Bernard's Secretary to Grant, October 18, 1884 ; in C. 4614, pp. 137-139.

[21] *Ibid.* A lakh is 100,000 Indian rupees, or £6,666 at 1885 valuation. A lakh is written as 1,00,000.

[22-24] *Ibid.* About 87,100 tons of rice went up to Mandalay in 1884, and 96,400 tons in 1885. This compared with 58,300 tons in 1878 during the last year of Mindon's reign; 41,800 tons in 1879; 5,700 tons in 1880; 5,200

tons in 1881; 39,800 tons in 1882; 37,800 tons in 1883; and lastly, 87,100 tons in 1884.

From 1865-1885, it was estimated that "In a normal year about 68,000 tons were usually bought by Upper Burma." Saw Sick Hwa, *The Rice Industry of Burma, 1852-1940,* pp. 295-296, 364. In other words, much of Thebaw's high purchases of rice in 1884 and 1885 came from his 'under normal' purchases in 1878 to 1883, and from having lived several years on Mindon's stored backlog.

[25] Enclosure 6 in No. 83, Kennedy to Bernard's Secretary, November 19, 1884; in C. 4614, p. 143.

[26-27] *Ibid.*

[28] Enclosure 8 in No. 83, Kennedy to Bernard's Secretary, December 30, 1884; in C. 4614, p. 144.

[29-30] *Ibid. The Times of India* correspondent tried to put 'dacoity' in both Burmas into perspective. An acquaintance with twenty-seven years of trading in Upper Burma claimed that 'dacoit' bands about Mandalay were most unusual.

> ....for one dacoity in Upper Burmah in ordinary times there are a score on this side of the frontier.... My friend went on to say that he was never once robbed in Upper Burma, though travelling....with large sums of money....and in the most out-of-the-way places. In this British province, however, he has been repeatedly looted. If he had lost any property across the frontier, the village in which he was lodged would have been compelled to refund the full value. An acquaintance....was relieved on one occasion of Rs. 700 in cash. In a few days the loser was handed over the entire sum...., the money having been raised by the villagers under whose protection he was at the time." "British Burma," (Bombay) *The Times of India,* July 17, 1884, p. 4.

The August 30, 1884 *The Times of India* reported that "scarcely a day passes without the report of some brutal murder having been committed" in Lower Burma. Dacoities in Upper Burma "If not so numerous as in British Burma, are conducted on a much more ambitious scale. The dacoits go about here not in gangs of four to a dozen men, but in bodies of 50 to 100 men." "British Burma," (Bombay) *The Times of India,* August 30, 1884, p. 5.

[31] "British Burma," (Bombay) *The Times of India,* September 12, 1884, p. 4.

[32] "The Capture of Bhamo," (Allahabad) *Pioneer Mail,* December 31, 1884, pp. 669-670; *also:* "General Summary," (Bombay) *The Times of India,* January 2, 1885, p. 1; and "General Summary," (Bombay) *The Times of India,* January 16, 1885, p. 2; and, *lastly:* No. 214, Telegram from Bernard to Durand, February 27, 1885; in Foreign, External-A, March 1885, Nos. 205-214 (NAI).

[33] No. 207, Telegram from Bernard to Durand, December 28, 1884; in Nos. 205-214.

[34] "General Summary," (Bombay) *The Times of India,* January 2, 1885, p. 1.

[35] Bernard's Secretary to Kinwun, January 9, 1885; in C. 4614, pp. 144-145.

[36] Enclosure 11 in No. 83, Stuart to Bernard's Secretary, January 10, 1885; in C. 4614, pp. 146-147.

[37] *Ibid.*

[38] *Ibid.*

[39] Enclosure 10 in No. 83, Bernard's Secretary to Durand, January 15, 1885; in C. 4614, pp. 145-146.

[40] King Kueh Yee was killed in the February 19, 1885 recapture of Bhamo. His marauders fled into Yunnan where they were captured by Chinese troops. K. W. No. 2, Telegram from Kinwun to Bernard, April 8, 1885; in Foreign, External-A, April 1885, Nos. 255-256, p. 3 (NAI).

[41] Enclosure 10 in No. 83, Bernard's Secretary to Durand, January 15, 1885 ; in C. 4614, pp. 145-146.

[42] *Ibid.*

[43] Enclosure 17 in No. 83, Stuart to Bernard's Secretary, February 4, 1885; in C. 4614, pp. 153-154.

[44] Enclosure 13, in No. 83, Bernard's Secretary to Durand, February 6, 1885; in C. 4614, pp. 147-148.

[45] *Ibid.* (Some of the largest importers-exporters, who complained the most about 'dacoits' and 'misrule' in Upper Burma, had partly caused the above collapse of several firms. They refused further credit, and dealt only on a cash basis. It apparently did not occur to them that the cutting-off of credit contributed to the downward spiral of trade. "Burma," (Bombay) *The Times of India,* September 15, 1885, p. 15. A pertinent comment on Lower Burma business since September 1884.)

[46-47] *Ibid.*

[48] Enclosure 18 in No. 83, Letter in *Rangoon Times,* February 13, 1885; in C. 4614, pp. 154-155. (The February 4, 1885 River Trade Report adjoins these pages. *Note:* The rise in trade via the Irrawaddy during 1884 was also caused in part by the rise in 'dacoity', which made it 'risky' to ship goods overland between the two Burmas. *See:* "Rangoon," (Allahabad) *Pioneer Mail,* August 24, 1884, p. 174.)

[49-52] *Ibid.*

[53] *Ibid.*

[54] No. 88, Macclesfield C. of C. to Kimberley, April 18, 1885; in C. 4614, p. 160.

[55] No. 89, Glasgow C. of C. to Kimberley, April 20, 1885; in C. 4614, p. 160. The Glasgow C. of C. later revised its view to call for the annexation of Upper Burma or at least a 'protected state'.

[56] A glance at Lower Burma trade figures from 1858-1885 will help to substantiate this statement. In 1858-1859, Rs. 39.8 lakhs worth of goods were exported to Upper Burma; and Rs. 31.9 lakhs were imported from Upper Burma. In 1865-1866 before the IFC came to Upper Burma in 1868, Rs. 83.4 lakhs were exported; and Rs. 72.5 lakhs were imported. In 1877-

1878, Rs. 177.6 lakhs were exported; and Rs. 200.1 lakhs were imported. In 1881-1882, the total of exports and imports over the border between Lower and Upper Burma amounted to 62 per cent. of all the trade that passed over India's land borders from beyond Quetta on the west to Tenasserim on the east. In the very bad trade year of 1884-1885, and with a famine raging in much of the Dry Zone, Rs. 200.1 lakhs were exported; and Rs. 196.0 lakhs were imported. J. S. Furnivall, *Colonial Policy......*, pp. 65-68.

In short, trade with Upper Burma and Yunnan could hardly have been better even if Upper Burma was part of the Indian Empire. Also, the gain in trade since 1858 had been accomplished *without* the expensive administrative costs that annexation of Upper Burma would have involved. The Indian Government kept this fact foremost in mind when confronted with cries for full annexation from mercantile groups.

[57] No. 10, Dufferin to Kimberley, February 10, 1885; in Dufferin Papers, Reel 517/18, p. 35.

[58] *Ibid.*

[59] No. 45A, Forbes' Memorandum on Burmese-British Relations, February 19, 1885; in Foreign, Secret-E, April 1885, Nos. 25-47 (NAI).

[60-63] *Ibid.* The Bill Committee's exact phrase concerning Upper Burma was: "The wealth and the position of this country very near our possessions in Cochin-China, can make these new commercial and friendly relations become very important for us."

[64] No. 46, Dufferin to Kimberley, March 24, 1885; in Nos. 25-47. Forbes' February 19, 1885 memorandum was enclosed with this letter.

[65-69] *Ibid.*

[70] Kimberley to Dufferin, May 1, 1885; in L/P & S/7, Political and Secret Letters and Enclosures to India, Vol. II, pp. 18-22 (IOL). *See also:* Kimberley to Dufferin, March 26, 1885; in Dufferin Papers, Reel 517/18, p. 39.

[71] Grattan Geary, *Burma After the Conquest,* pp. 312-313.

[72] *See* Appendix B entitled Deforestation Causes the Collapse of Order and Trade in Upper Burma, 1883-1885.

[73] Even with the drop in Shan tribute, Thebaw's Government still took in about 100-103 lakhs annually. The figures were as follows: capitation tax, 40; customs, 15; royal lands, 10; Shan tribute, 10; petty cesses and levies, 9; precious stones monopoly, 8; pickled-tea monopoly, 8; and lastly, earth oil monopoly, 3. Total: 103 lakhs. This figure did not include the revenue from the timber monopoly. No. 2, Dufferin to Churchill, January 12, 1886 ; in Dufferin Papers, Reel 517/18, p. 5.

In 1885, due to the 'drought' the Government's income declined to eighty-five lakhs. No. 34, Moylan to Bernard's Secretary, February 5, 1886; in Foreign, Secret-E, November 1886, Nos. 1-65 (NAI). The public debt of Upper Burma, including the private debts of Thebaw and Supayalat, totalled only Rs. 13-15 lakhs. When the public debt was measured against the annual revenue, Upper Burma had probably the lowest debt in the entire world! Unfortunately, much of the country's revenues were wasted on extravagances. *See* Appendix L on Thebaw's annual budget.

74 There were over 1,000 Martini-type breech-loading rifles in the Mandalay Armory. However, most of Thebaw's 30,000 troops and police involved in the Shan fighting were armed with muzzle-loaders. "Rangoon" (Allahabad) *Pioneer Mail*, November 28, 1883, p. 553. The Shans were armed with equivalent weapons, and were said to be better shots. If Thebaw had been able to import 5,000 or 10,000 breech-loading rifles, his troops could probably have crushed the Shan rebellion in a few months.

75 Thebaw, however, had forced down the price of rice by encouraging large imports from Lower Burma. In late-1883, the price per basket had been Rs. 4 and 4.50, but by January 1884 the price had dropped to Rs. 2.50. "Large quantities......stored along the banks of the river......are being retailed at prices unremunerative to the sellers. The Chinese merchants are the principal sufferers; for in their avidity to make money they overstocked the market....and are now obliged to sell at a dead loss." Rangoon," (Calcutta) *Englishman*, January 23, 1884, p. 5.

The 'French Threat' to British Interests

Fall of the Ferry Ministry

The Jules Ferry ministry at Paris fell on March 30, 1885, and ironically at the moment of Ferry's greatest triumph. He had received a draft treaty from the Chinese that gave Ferry virtually everything that he had asked, except an indemnity for the Bac-Le ambush. Only minor details remained to be settled when reports came on March 25 and 28 of a French defeat in Tongkin. A drunken Colonel Herbinger had "unecessarily ordered a precipitous abandonment of Langson."[1]

Ferry's enemies at Paris, including Clemenceau and Rochefort, treated the minor skirmish as a great national catastrophe to be compared with Waterloo or Sedan. On March 31, another rumour reached Paris, which claimed that Langson had been a victory. The report came a few hours too late to save Ferry's government; it had gone down to defeat by a vote of 306-149.[2]

Ferry had a draft of the new China treaty, but he was afraid to fluant it before the Chamber of Deputies for fear that its premature announcement might disrupt the negotiations. Bismarck helped Ferry by urging the Chinese to make an immediate announcement of the Treaty, before the French Government would feel obliged to avenge the Langson incident.[3]

An announcement of the draft treaty by either Ferry or the Chinese on March 30 might well have saved Ferry's Government.

As it was, the vote was not against Ferry's colonial policies in Tongkin or his expansion into other areas of Indo-China, but rather against his domestic policies. Such was the view of most observers, including Lord Lyons, the British ambassador to Paris.[4]

De Freycinet, the foreign affairs minister in the succeeding Boisson Government, did not abandon Tongkin, or any other French interests in the East. On the contrary, a June 9, 1885 treaty was signed between China and France at Tientsin, whereby China recognized the provisions of the May 1884 Tientsin Treaty, and gave up all claims to Annam and Tongkin. France was allowed to trade with China along the Tongkin border, and to enjoy *lower* tariffs along this route than were prevalent in the Chinese treaty ports. France was to withdraw her troops from Chinese soil within one month.[5]

French demands for an indemnity for the Bac-Le ambush, which had sparked-off the renewed fighting after the first Tientsin Treaty of May 1884, were given-up. France, however, had secured Annam and Tongkin at the cost of several hundred men killed and after expenditures of over Frs. 100,000,000.[6]

The collapse of the Ferry Government, and the ceding of Tongkin and Annam to France, did nothing to relieve British anxieties. It appeared that France was about to assume important commercial influence in Yunnan and Upper Burma, because France had—via the Red River Valley of Tongkin—the *only* natural railroad-route to Southern China. The French had also gained commercial *access* to Yunnan under the terms of the June 9, 1885 Tientsin Treaty, and with a four per cent. customs limitation. Also, the Chinese had ceded the *pannas* between Tongkin and Burma—in short French Indo-China now ran *contiguously* with Burma's eastern frontier.

The British were worried that France would soon gain important political-influence at Mandalay due to its 'commercial Consul', who was to handle *all* French affairs. The ending of the Chinese-French War over Tongkin and Annam meant that France's energies could now be devoted to new 'adventures' in Indo-China and Upper Burma.[7]

The Concession Hunters

During 1883-1885, several French and Italian speculators negotiated almost identical contracts for Upper Burma's coal, iron, and ruby mines, as well as for the teak forests, and for the right to build a Toungoo-Mandalay Railroad and a Mandalay Royal Bank. The Burmese welcomed the bribes that each speculator presented, and stated that there would be no contractual conflicts, because the Mandalay Government would ultimately recognize only one contract for each concession.

Each of the contracts had a clause requiring the approval of the King before the contract could take effect. It is a fact that Thebaw never approved any of the contracts with any of the concessionaires mentioned in this chapter.[8] However, this detail was not known until after the Third Burmese War.

The first concessionaire was Mons. Hecquard, who signed a contract for the Mogok Ruby Mines with the Burmese ambassadors to Paris on October 15, 1883. Hecquard's interests were to pay an advance payment of Frs. 100,000, and three lakhs annually for twenty years. Hecquard's group was to make a survey in Upper Burma for iron and coal deposits. If the survey proved unpromising, Hecquard's advance payment of Frs. 100,000 was to be refunded.[9]

The deal fall through. J. A. Bryce, the BBTC's contract negotiator at Mandalay, wrote that "I told Andreino [the BBTC's Mandalay agent] to 'drop a stone' on the project."[10] But there were other applicants for the Ruby Mines, and also for the various teak-leases in Upper Burma.

Alexandre Izambert, a French engineer representing large French interests, visited Mandalay within a month after the collapse of the Hecquard deal. Izambert offered three lakhs annually for the Ruby Mines, although the Mandalay Palace records showed that the Mines returned only Rs. 1,000 annually.[11] Izambert requested the right to build a road from Mandalay to the Mines, which were located about ninety miles northeast of Mandalay. The firm was to have land rights of 750 metres on each side of the road.[12] Izambert also requested that the firm be allowed to cut and ship the teak from the surrounding forests.[13]

The deal was all but signed, when Andreino heard of the scheme. He protested to the Pangyet, who made a formal opposition to the contract at the very last minute. Izambert had to return to Paris empty-handed. Voisson, French consul at Rangoon, thought that the Burmese ambassadors at Paris should be told that either the Izambert deal went through, or the entire Treaty would be threatened.[14]

An amusing bit of Gallic worldliness was attached by a Quai d'Orsay official to Voisson's report advocating diplomatic black-mail. The note read: "Nous l'avons fait a plusieurs reprises."[15] ("Why not, we have done it many times.") However, the final January 15, 1885 Treaty contained no reference to the Izambert contract for the Ruby Mines, and further negotiations continued with other petitioners.

P. H. Bonvillain, the French engineer and royal supplier at Mandalay who had inserted the Defensive-Offensive Alliance into the June 1884 Kinwun's Declaration, was in Paris at this time. He and a French group were also negotiating for the Ruby Mines. He claimed to have an 'inside track' at the Mandalay Palace due to his common-law wife, Mattie Calogreedy Antram. Mattie as Maid of Honour had perhaps more influence over Queen Supayalat than anyone.

By February 4, 1885, it was reported that Bonvillain had gained the contract to work the Ruby Mines for twenty years at three lakhs annually.[16] He was supposed to make an advance down-payment of eleven lakhs within a fortnight. He was to have the right to keep 200 to 300 French guards at the mines.[17] Also, arms and ammunition were to be supplied to the Mandalay Govern-ment, apparently from the French Government in Tongkin.

The 'crisis', if it was one, passed over quickly. Bonvillain and his interests in Paris did not—or could not—pay the eleven lakhs in advance by February 19, 1885. According to Bonvillain's petition to Thebaw, Bonvillain would have had to pay a total of thirteen lakhs within twenty days after a final signing.[18] Another nine lakhs were due a month after this, or in essence, over seven years of payments in advance. With such terms, it was under-standable why the deal was in abeyance.

More Deals

There were other concession hunters seeking other concessions besides the Ruby Mines and the various teak-leases. There were also potential iron and coal mines to be sold, along with the right to build a Toungoo-Mandalay Railroad, and the right to found a Mandalay Royal Bank. The Burmese ambassadors at Paris encouraged speculators by signing almost identical contracts with several parties. This practice had already been followed in the case of the Ruby Mines.

On April 10, 1884, the ambassadors signed an iron and coal mines contract with Signor Prato of Milan, who represented a large Italian syndicate.[19] This contract, however, was identical with the April 13, 1885 iron and coal mines contract signed with the Comte A. Mahe de la Bourdonnais, a French engineer who had travelled extensively in Burma and Siam.[20]

De la Bourdonnais had also signed for a Royal Bank at Mandalay to be capitalized at Frs. 25,000,000. The firm was to be sponsored by the French Government. This was probably a clause inserted by de la Bourdonnais to ensure that he would not lose his money. It appears that the French Government did not have any official connection with the proposed Bank,[21] although the Quai d'Orsay undoubtedly supported the venture on an *unofficial* basis. The key Article 13 of de la Bourdonnais' Royal Bank Contract stated that:

> Sums which may be borrowed by the King [at ten per cent. per annum from the Bank] shall always be warranted either by the revenues of the custom house or all other Royal incomes [teak forests ; pickled-tea ; earth oil ; iron mines ; coal mines ; ruby mines ; railroads ; telegraph lines ; proceeds from the navigation on the Irrawaddy, Salween and other rivers; proceeds from toll and other roads, canals, bridges, etc.]....[22]

Many of the 'Royal incomes' included in Article 13 were being bid for by speculators. Some 'Royal incomes', such as the coal and iron mines, had already been sold to both Signor Prato and de la Bourdonnais. Regardless of who owned a particular 'Royal income', all of the owners of 'Royal incomes' were liable to a Royal levy to pay Bourdonnais' Bank. The Bank had pre-emptive rights on all such 'Royal incomes' to the amount of the loan and interest that Thebaw had borrowed from the Bank.[23]

De la Bourdonnais would have been liable for a good share of such financial legerdemain. He had also contracted to build the Toungoo-Mandalay Railroad, and additional telegraph lines.[24] These 'Royal incomes' would have of course been liable to a Royal levy to reimburse de la Bourdonnais' Bank.

But there was a more important ramification to Article 13. The French Government was named in the contract as the sponsor of the Royal Mandalay Bank.   Consequently, this meant that Article 13 gave the French Government eventual control over all 'Royal incomes' in Upper Burma.[25]   The main reason for this was the Mandalay Court itself.   The Royal Couple had become famous for their gay parties and fabulous gifts to favourites.   They presided over a Court eager to wear the latest French perfumes and jewels. Even Supayalat's serving-maids were said to discard their silken clothes after one wearing.

The Mandalay Government had become almost bankrupt in early-1885 as a result of such extravagance, and also from the process of Deforestation outlined in the last chapter.   The 1883-1885 Mission to Paris would probably not have been able to come home, except for an emergency loan of almost three lakhs from the BBTC in March 1885.   In fact, the BBTC Teak Case was largely brought about by Mandalay's need to find a quick ten or twenty lakhs.   It would not have required many years before the French Government (via de la Bourdonnais' Bank) would have taken one-third, one-half or even more of the 'Royal incomes'.   French political control of Upper Burma would have inevitably followed.

It now becomes somewhat easier to understand why the proposed Bank Contract, and the Toungoo-Mandalay Railroad Contract, caused so much excitement in Lower Burma, India, and in Great Britain.   It appeared from these Contracts that France had the political control of Upper Burma, and the potential markets of Southern China, almost within its grasp.   It is understandable why British officials found it most *difficult* to believe that the Quai d'Orsay was apparently not the official sponsor of the Bank and other Contracts.

De la Bourdonnais' Bank Contract was rejected at Mandalay, "on account of some objection which the Kinwun Mingyi had to it."[26]   One would surmise that the Kinwun had objected to Article 13.   However, when the Tangyet returned to France in August 1885, he held an identical Bank Contract (plus a Railroad Contract) drawn-up in the name of the Comte de Trevelec.[27]   This was the French cavalry officer at Mandalay, who had accompanied the 1883-1885 Burmese Mission to Paris.   This was the man whom R. Hope Pilcher, assistant commissioner at Thayetmyo, had considered in 1883 to be eccentric!

There was a delicious irony to the entire, complex affair.   The August-October 1885 confrontation between Britain and France over de Trevelec's contracts, which appeared to have the French Government's official sponsorship, finally revealed the real promoter of the contracts—an *Englishman*.

Haas Arrives at Mandalay

The above reports of French commercial dealings with Upper Burma had made the Rangoon, Calcutta, and London Governments distinctly uneasy. The additional rumours of the impending arrival of Mons. Frederic Haas, the new French consul to Mandalay, caused further anxiety. Viceroy Dufferin reported to Kimberley on February 19, 1885 that Haas was expected to arrive at any moment on a French warship. If the ship would attempt to steam up the Irrawaddy to Mandalay, Rangoon authorities would have to interdict it. Fortunately, the question did not arise because the Irrawaddy was then only five feet in depth.[28]

Mons. Haas, "a very courageous and honourable man,"[29] arrived on commercial transportation in late-April 1885. Haas, the former chief secretary to the French Governor-General of Pondicherry, met Bernard. Haas said nothing about his new assignment, and left for Mandalay on April 29.[30] He lodged temporarily at Mulla Ismael's house. The noted tax 'farmer' and others urged Haas to meet the Kinwun immediately. This Haas refused to do, unless he could keep his shoes on his feet.

The Kinwun refused. Haas doffed his shoes on May 17, and told the Kinwun that Thebaw's position was extremely critical. French friendship was most valuable to Thebaw, because the French could supply him with any amount of guns and ammunition from the Tongkin side.[31] Furthermore, Haas reminded the Kinwun that by releasing the Myngun from Pondicherry, the French could harm Thebaw far more than could the British.[32]

Haas confided the above to Andreino as well as his annoyance at having to doff his shoes. Haas asked Andreino if the British Resident had visited the Kinwun with his shoes on his feet. The answer was yes, and Haas became angry.[33] Haas did not know it, but the incident was to be the first of a whole series of rebuffs by the Kinwun, who even refused to answer over fifteen of Haas' letters. Nevertheless, the particular incident of the shoes was only a momentary setback to French pride. Andreino wrote that with Haas' arrival at .Mandalay "the French community both male and female have been swelling themselves like the frog in the fable; there is no absurdity that they don't do or say."[34]

There were two other reasons for French pride. Several agents representing French commercial interests had arrived in Mandalay on the steamer preceding Haas'.[35] On May 12, after nearly two years in Paris and Europe, the Myothit and the Tangyet ambassadors left Rangoon to return up-river to Mandalay.[36] In summary, it is understandable why the French community at Mandalay was filled with pride. During May 1885, three separate groups of people had arrived, and they all seemed to be symbols of the new French influence at Mandalay.

Haas became more friendly with Andreino, and the wily Italian passed on their conversations to the Indian Government. Haas had apparently come to Mandalay expecting that there would be a Court party strong enough to support him in his proposals for radical changes. If Thebaw refused such changes, then Haas had thought to replace him with the Myngun. A French-Burmese company much like the old British East India Company would then be formed for the development of Upper Burma's resources.[37]

The Company would exercise the ultimate civil and criminal authority.[38] The puppet-King, whether Thebaw or Myngun, would closely resemble Mir Jafer, the puppet-Nawab that Robert Clive had placed upon the throne of Bengal in 1757. Perhaps, in his roseate dreams Haas imagined himself to be Clive.[39]

However, Haas confided that for the present the French had no intention of crossing the Mekong. They would be satisfied if they were able to turn the commerce of Yunnan, the Shan States, and Upper Burma in the direction of French Tongkin. Eventually, a powerful French steamer company would challenge the the IFC's control of the Irrawaddy, and "time may see many changes."[40]

On June 14, Haas decided that his refusal to doff his shoes for the King was not logical, considering that he had already done so for a mere Foreign Minister.[41] Haas confided to the Kinwun and Taingda that he wished to speak to the King in private with an interpreter so as to tell him the true state of the country. The Ministers objected on various grounds. They claimed that the French-speaking ministers did not desire to interpret disagreeable things to His Majesty.[42]

Haas told the ministers that Mandalay should immediately

invite the Indian Government to send up a new Resident. Haas warned that if Mandalay did not do so, a British ultimatum would contain much stiffer requirements.[43] By restoring the Resident, the Burmese Government would draw the teeth of those annexationists and others, who desired an end to Burmese independence. It would prove conclusively that Mandalay wished to keep on friendly terms with all nations.[44]

The ministers did not appear to understand Haas' remarks. Haas presented a written version of his suggestions; however it was in French as he still had no interpreter.[45] Andreino doubted that such letters were ever translated.[46] Andreino should have known. The translator in the Burmese Foreign Dept., who was assigned to Haas' letters, was in Andreino's pay.

The ministers did not seem to have such difficulty in understanding other French proposals, where a more immediate and pecuniary gain was involved. The several French businessmen, who had come on the steamer before Haas' to survey the mining potential, were said to have already made several contracts. Mons. Lambay, for example, had secured the salt mines. Mons. Geranger contracted for a tramway in Mandalay, which British interests had desired. Haas told Andreino that he expected that the Indian Government would honour such contracts held by French subjects even if Mandalay were annexed.[47]

Similar contracts held by British subjects were apparently not on such firm ground. The Pouk Myine Atwinwun, a friend of Taingda, had become the Finance Minister. He told Andreino that if the Taingda's group were able to cancel the BBTC's teak leases, they would then cancel all contracts of British subjects.[48] The Pouk Myine's remarks referred to the serious charges laid against the BBTC concerning the BBTC's alleged timber-thefts in the Ningyan Forest. The case was becoming extremely serious, and Bernard expressed concern in a June 16 letter to Durand.[49]

The suspicions of many at Rangoon now turned towards Haas. What would happen if Haas interfered to offer French timber-firms in place of the BBTC? Haas could make such an offer. If he would, his usefulness to the Court would make them forget his *gaucherie* over the "Shoe Question". Bernard expressed the general concern in his June 16 letter: "If those leases were to be cancelled and the forests were to be leased to Frenchmen, we should have some difficult and unpleasant work."[50]

Haas Attempts to Minimize the 'French Threat'

Haas repeatedly used Andreino to broadcast his desire that Mandalay should reinstate the British Resident, and establish diplomatic and commercial relations with other European nations. When Haas outlined his commercial plans for Upper Burma, they were a challenge to British subjects to compete peacefully in the mercantile arena. If such competition led to annexation, Haas informed the Indian Government through Andreino that French subjects should be allowed to retain their contracts.

While advancing French subjects' interests in Upper Burma, Haas skillfully used Andreino to notify the Indian Government that French interests were solely of a commercial nature. Haas stated that the French had no intention at present of making political advances beyond the Mekong River. They only wanted to turn the pattern of trade in that direction, and towards French Tongkin.

Haas, in his own fashion, assured the Indian Government that its political predominance in Upper Burma was not in question. The only thing in question was the commercial predominance of British subjects. The French commercial challenge would be mounted by private French companies, such as the proposed French steamer-firm. The French commercial challenge in Upper Burma would not be mounted by the usual French method in Southeast Asia, which first established French political control in order to create French commercial interests.

In summary, Haas and the Kinwun were more similar than one might think. Both men attempted, in their own way, to reassure the Indian Government that there was no political 'French Threat' to British subjects' interests in Upper Burma or to India's eastern frontier.

Mattie Calogreedy Antram's Revenge

The Nyaungyan Prince, who was the only Indian Government alternative to Thebaw and the 'pro-French' Myngun, died of protracted fever on June 26, 1885.[51] The Indian Government did not keep the Prince's death a secret. The July 19, 1885 *Pioneer Mail*,[52] and the August 11, 1885 *Times of India*[53] reported that the Palace had received the news of Nyaungyan's death with great rejoicing and celebrations.

The Nyaungyan's death was a savage blow against Andreino's interests, and against those interests of the BBTC and IFC which he represented at Mandalay. Andreino had climbed high in twenty-seven years at Mandalay, becoming Italian Consul and agent for the two biggest British firms in Burma. His income other than his Consul's salary was Rs. 2,500 a month. This was considerable for a man who had begun life—in the tart words of the late Mr. Shaw—"as an illiterate organ-grinder, who could hardly write his name."

It appeared that Andreino's work of twenty-seven years was about to be swept away in the Taingda's investigation of alleged BBTC timber-thefts in the Ningyan Forest. The death of the Nyaungyan Prince had removed all major opponents of Thebaw's Government, except for the Myngun. As a consequence, the Burmese authorities would feel free to seize the BBTC's Upper Burma teak leases, and sell them to French concession-hunters. It was at this moment that *salvation* came to Andreino from the most pro-French woman in Mandalay, although a British subject.

As indicated several times during this study, Mattie Calogreedy Antram was the confidant and favourite of Queen Supayalat. It was Mattie's great influence at the Palace that had at first attracted Bonvillain, the French military adviser and royal supplier. Later, of course, their relationship had assumed a sensual side. By Burmese custom their common-law marriage was a legitimate marriage, and Mattie had always regarded it as such.

Bonvillain had spent much of 1884 and early 1885 in Paris obtaining financial backing in order to bid on the contracts for the Ruby Mines and other concessions. Mattie had remained behind in Mandalay, retaining her contacts and influence at the Palace, and dreaming of the day when Bonvillain would return.[54]

However, Bonvillain married a French girl in Paris,[55] and brought her with him when he returned to Mandalay with the Burmese ambassadors in May 1885. When Bonvillain did not return to their house, Mattie went to Bonvillain's house.[56] He explained that he was married. He expressed a hope that Mattie would understand as she was a reasonable person.[57]

According to F. T. Jesse, "Mattie was nearly out of her mind with grief and rage."[58] After a few days, her hysteria turned to thoughts of revenge. She remembered that one of the Kinwun's secretaries had always admired her, and had made frequent proposals. She also remembered that the Burmese ambassadors had brought back copies of the Treaties signed in Europe, as well as contracts and other business papers.[59]

Mattie went to the Kinwun's secretary, who was apparently not the translator that Andreino had in his secret employ.[60] The Kinwun's secretary received several times what he had always wanted from Mattie. She eventually received copies of all the important treaties and papers. With them she would have her revenge on not only Bonvillain, but also on the new woman and on the entire French nation.[61]

Mattie met Andreino in a private cabin on Rawlings' mail-steamer anchored in the middle of the Irrawaddy at Mandalay. At first, Andreino behaved in a patronizing manner. It did not occur to him that she might be useful in other ways besides the sensual. Then, she said that she had documents which proved the French had promised to ship breech-loading rifles into Upper Burma via Tongkin.[62]

Andreino's smugness disappeared. A long conversation followed with Andreino attempting with oily charm to persuade the little Burmese-Greek girl to give up the papers. Such papers would bring the British Government into the picture, and his jobs would be saved.[63]

Andreino gained the papers, and promised to give Mattie due credit when he passed them to the Indian Government. The pain on Mattie's face can be imagined—she said that she wanted no 'credit'.[64] Andreino quickly agreed to take sole credit "as the mysterious and trustworthy....source of news to the powers that were to be."[65]

Andreino Passes the Documents

Andreino divided his cache of documents into two groups. Those of a political nature, he immediately sent down-river to Bernard. He held back until July 19 those papers of a commercial nature, *i.e.* contracts for a Royal Bank and a Railroad seemingly sponsored by the French Government.[66] Andreino certainly had motive enough for his 'campaign'. He and his superiors realized that only the active interference of the Indian Government would save the BBTC from a ruinous—and not totally undeserved—fine in connection with its alleged teak-thefts in the Ningyan Forest.

On July 6, 1885, Bernard's secretary forwarded a sheaf of translated Burmese documents "from a source which renders it probable that they are of an authentic character."[67] The documents included copies of (1) the 1873 Burmese-French Treaty with the June 1, 1884 Declaration activating it; (2) the January 15, 1885 Burmese-French Treaty; (3) the April 2, 1885 Burmese-German Treaty; and, (4) a comparison of the three treaties with the versions already released by the French and German Governments.[68]

But it was item (5) which aroused British suspicions. This was a letter given by Ferry on January 15, 1885 to the Burmese ambassadors, and sealed in a separate envelope with the French Foreign Office seal.[69] This separate letter was perhaps a faint echo of the Kinwun's Secret Declaration of June 1884.

There were three provisions in the letter. The Myngun and other political refugees would not be allowed to escape from Pondicherry or other French possessions. The French Government also promised to "render what help they may be able" when Mandalay began construction on the proposed road from Mandalay to Tongkin.[70] But it was the third provision in Ferry's Secret Letter that was most interesting. It read:

With respect to the transport through the province of Tongkin to Burma of arms of various kinds, ammunition, and military stores, generally, amicable arrangements will be come to with the Burmese Government for the passage of the same, when peace and order prevails in Tongkin and the officers stationed there are satisfied that it is proper and that there is no danger.[71]

This passage did not excite either Bernard or the Indian Government, until Bernard reported on July 27 the apparent French Government sponsorship of a bank and a railroad in Upper Burma. Then, this 'arms through Tongkin' passage became 'extremely important'. Actually, it was a most convenient club with which to prod the French Government into conceding Britain's superior political and commercial interests in Upper Burma.[72]

On July 8, 1885, Andreino took the next step in his 'campaign'. He reminded Bernard of remarks that Andreino had made in a previous letter that France intended to establish a bank, railroad, and mines in Upper Burma.[73] The reminder was Andreino's way of arousing the Indian Government's interest before passing the commercial documents, which he was to do on July 19.

But Bernard's interest was already aroused. On July 4 he reported a current rumour to Durand.[74] The rumour claimed that Frs. 25,000,000 were to be subscribed under French Government auspices in order to establish (1) a Royal Bank; (2) a French steamer line; (3) a road from Tongkin to Mandalay; and, lastly (4) to exploit the Mogok Ruby Mines.[75]

However, Bernard added that probably "more than half of this is talk, and....the other half....will not come to pass at present."[76] It was Andreino's aim—at the proper time—to alter this 'complacent' view. His July 8 letter stated that Haas had made little headway with the ministers. Consequently, Haas was dealing mostly with the *Thathanabaing*, the Buddhist archbishop of Upper Burma, who had promised to get Haas an audience with King Thebaw.[77]

Haas received his interview with Thebaw.[78] But it was only ten minutes in length. It was shorter than those interviews often given to tourists, who were willing to pay several hundred rupees for the honour of having an interview with the 'mad monarch of Mandalay'.[79] Haas had also received a six-strand *tsalive*, a sash of six gold-strands or cords.

This was the standard rank given to Andreino, the Italian Consul; to European businessmen, such as Jones of the BBTC and Kennedy of the IFC; and to wealthy tourists.[80] When one recalled that Thebaw's *tsalive* was twenty-four strands, that King Mindon had given Gladstone one of sixteen strands, and that the Kinwun's was twelve, it was obvious that Haas had been given the polite minimum.

Haas presented two petitions. One was the usual compliments and list of presents. The other explained the benefits that Burma would receive through her alliance with France. Haas offered to assist the ministers in organising the administration and finances of the country.[81]

Haas reiterated the essence of Ferry's January 15, 1885 Secret Letter. Haas said that as soon as peace and order was restored in Tongkin, the Burmese could have passage through Tongkin of whatever they required.[82] It was at this point that Thebaw got up, and interrupted Haas' speech by saying that he should see the ministers for such things. Thebaw left, and Haas was annoyed that his well-meant advice had been ignored.[83]

4. *Supayalat's younger sister, Supayalat and Thebaw in mid-1885.*
(London Graphic, January 16, 1886, p. 60).

On July 14, Haas made several further proposals to the Tangyet Wundauk, who was about to leave again for France to formalize the January 15, 1885 Treaty.[84] Unfortunately, the ministers did not seem to understand Haas' proposals. They still seemed concerned over his initial refusal to doff his shoes before King Thebaw.

The Tangyet had apparently informed Haas that the Mandalay Government intended to start a war with Lower Burma as soon as the British would "get their hands filled elsewhere with troubles."[85] Haas replied that it would not be a good idea, until Mandalay had strengthened itself by treaties with other European powers.[86]

Haas reminded the ministers that the British Government had made many warnings concerning India's special relationship with Upper Burma. The presence of British subjects in trade in Upper Burma, and the propinquity of Mandalay with India's eastern frontier, gave India a relationship with Upper Burma that no other country could have. Later, Haas told acquaintances that he had repeatedly reminded the ministers of their special relationship with India.[87]

This was a clever way for Haas to inform the Indian Government that he was aware of Britain's claims to special influence in Upper Burma. At the same time, Haas did not surrender any of France's ambitions. He said that he was pressing the ministers very hard to have proper treaties made with France, Germany, and Italy. Each of these countries should declare Upper Burma to be a 'neutral' country.[88] Although not stated, this implied in the context of 1885 that the Irrawaddy River would be an international waterway for all ships of all nations as was the Danube. The concept of 'neutral' also implied that all nations would have equal commercial and political rights in Upper Burma.

Haas thought that such proclamations of 'neutrality' could be gained from the three European nations in about four months' time. Haas was pressing the Court very hard on the point, and urged them to take advantage of the apathy of the British Government.[89] Haas urged the Tangyet to propose the concept of 'neutrality' when he negotiated with France, Germany, and Italy.[90]

Haas' proposals were passed on to the Indian Government in a July 15 letter. It concluded that if Burma was "declared neutral by these three powerful nations, England would....feel helpless."[91] Four days after this ominous warning had been despatched to

Rangoon, Andreino delivered his *coup de main*. He wrote that the rumours were true concerning a Royal Bank and Railroad to be sponsored by the French Government. He claimed that the contracts were already signed at Mandalay. The Tangyet, who was returning to Europe shortly, would take them with him for final negotiations. Andreino enclosed detailed 'resumes' of the contracts with his letter.[92]

But more important was the fact that on some date *prior* to July 19, Andreino had sent other 'resumes' of the contracts to S. G. Jones, Rangoon BBTC manager. The main points of these contracts were telegraphed to the London office to young J. A. Bryce, who had negotiated the BBTC's 1880 and 1882 teak-leases with Mandalay. It is this telegraphing of the contracts to London *before* July 19 that most clearly establishes the prior understanding between these three men to involve the British Government in the BBTC's dispute at Mandalay.

The Indian Government's Reaction

The Rangoon Government received 'resumes' of the contracts on July 25. A telegram *from London* enquiring about such contracts arrived at Simla on the same day, July 25. This could only mean that Andreino had mailed other copies of the contracts to his superiors at Rangoon before his July 19 mailing to Bernard. In turn Bryce had been notified in London, and a prompt 'enquiry' had been made of Lord Randolph Churchill, the new secretary of state for India in the new Conservative Government. Churchill's July 25 telegram to Dufferin ran as follows:

Secret. Burma. Following from Bombay-Burmah Trading Corporation, Rangoon, to its London Correspondent has been communicated privately to me :—*Begins*. French Government has arranged with Burma for construction of railway from Mandalay to frontier, France providing two millions sterling and completing in seven years; interest seven and half per cent; also for Bank at Mandalay with capital twenty-five million rupees, Burma getting requirements at twelve and half per cent, and giving ruby mines and revenues of Letpet [pickled-tea] for security. Earth oil, share of profits, and Irrawaddy duties, jointly collected, pledged as guarantee for interest. Embassy proceeds immediately to France to ratify. *Ends*. Have you any confirmation of this, and what are your views as to course which should be followed ?[93]

Dufferin replied on July 26 that there had been rumours of contracts sponsored by the French Government. However, Bernard in his July 4 letter had been unconcerned about them. Haas, the French Consul, had seemed anxious to avoid anything that might cause a collision between Mandalay and Britain.[94] This last statement of Dufferin's indicated the success that Haas had had in projecting his views through Andreino to the Indian Government. But then Andreino's July 19 letter enclosing the contract 'resumes' arrived at Rangoon on July 25.

In a July 27 telegram,[95] and in a despatch later in the same day,[96] Bernard commented that he had with reluctance brought up the question of annexing Upper Burma. However, it was impossible for him to agree to a French domination of the Upper Irrawaddy Valley, or to a French colony positioned between Lower Burma and Southern China.[97]

In another despatch on the following day, July 28, Bernard listed the areas of Upper Burma's national life that would be held by the French if such contracts were actually ratified. The French Government would directly, or through a syndicate, control (1) the main sources of revenue, (2) most of the Irrawaddy boat and steamer trade, (3) the Toungoo-Mandalay Railroad, and (4) the only route from Lower Burma to the potential new markets of Yunnan and Southern China.[98]

Bernard believed that such French concessions would make France dominant, "and would in the end extrude British trade from ......the valley of the Upper Irrawaddy."[99] France would hide her domination by persuading other European nations to declare Upper Burma to be a 'neutral' zone between British India on the west and French Indo-China on the east. France would also attempt to open the Irrawaddy River to ships of all nations on a footing similar to that enjoyed by an international waterway, such as the Danube.[100]

Bernard proposed that a letter of warning be sent to the Kinwun. The letter would list the concessions that the Indian Government would not like to see leased to Frenchmen. If Mandalay insisted on giving them to Frenchmen, the Indian Government would consider such acts to be 'unfriendly', as well as breaches of the 1862 and 1867 Treaties.[101]

The 'unfriendly' concessions were the Toungoo-Mandalay Railroad, the customs duties on the Irrawaddy River, and the pickled-tea monopoly. The conclusion of the letter would state that no concessions were to be given to the French, if such concessions restricted trade between the two Burmas contrary to the 1862 and 1867 Treaties.[102]

Bernard stated that such a letter would have little value, unless the Indian Government was willing to support it with force, and if necessary, willing to annex Upper Burma.[103] Bernard emphasized that he had always opposed intervention of any kind, to say nothing of annexation. But if Mandalay "threw themselves into the arms of any foreign power," then the Indian Government would have to abandon non-intervention.[104]

The annexation would have to be complete with European administration at the higher levels. The possible alternative of setting up another Burmese King in place of Thebaw was not a feasible idea. The French would only make another attempt to gain influence. They might even release the Myngun Prince, who would have a good chance of overthrowing any British sponsored King.[105] In conclusion, if such a letter was approved, this would mean that troops would have to be gathered at Thayetmyo on the frontier. Complete invasion preparations would have to be made along with the drafting of the letter, and its despatch to Mandalay.[106]

On the same day, July 28, Mortimer Durand, the Indian foreign secretary, attached a comment to Bernard's July 27 telegram. Durand did not know on what grounds the Indian Government could object to the proposed concession as "contrary to treaty." He added that the Indian Government apparently had the right to object to the complete establishment of any foreign influence at Mandalay.[107]

On July 30, the Tangyet Wundauk and three other ambassadors arrived at Rangoon on their way to Paris with the January 15, 1885 Treaty for final ratification.[108] The presence of three wives in the ambassadorial party was a radical innovation, as no previous Burmese mission had taken their wives. It seemed to imply that the ambassadors were *permanently* assigned to Paris and the Continent.[109]

A dinner party in the Mission's honour was given on August 4, just before the ambassadors sailed. The Tangyet told Bernard's secretary that the two commercial contracts for a Mandalay Bank and a Toungoo-Mandalay Railroad had been proposed in Paris in August 1884. They were in no way officially sponsored by the French Government.[110]

The proposals had originally come from the Comte de Trevelec, the French cavalry instructor at Mandalay, who had accompanied the 1883-1885 Burmese Mission to Paris. De Trevelec had a British connection in Paris, a businessman "whose name is something like Farmer."[111] The Tangyet further confided that it had been proposed that the railroad builders, a joint British-French firm, be given land alongside both sides of the track after the system followed in America.[112]

The railroad builders were to advance the money, and build the road, which would become the property of the Burmese Government after ninety-nine years. Mandalay was to pay an annual interest of seven and one-half per cent. on the money advanced for construction of the road.[113] The interest charge was a low one, and compared rather favourably with the fifteen and more per cent. interest that King Mindon had often paid for loans.

The hitch in the negotiations was the proposal that part of the security for the railroad loans would be the duties of the Irrawaddy River traffic. This Mandalay had refused. However, the Tangyet was going to negotiate further on the matter in Paris, as it was the chief remaining difficulty before signing the two contracts.[114]

On August 2, Dufferin's Council at Simla concluded unanimously that dominant or extensive French political or commercial influence at Mandalay would constitute a *threat* to India's eastern frontier and to British subjects' interests in Upper Burma. Such French influence would have to be stopped even at the risk of war with Mandalay.[115] The Council recommended that Mandalay be asked to place its foreign affairs under the direction of the Indian Government. Mandalay should also be asked to immediately restore the Resident.[116]

If Mandalay refused the above demands, then an invasion and conquest of Upper Burma should occur. However, before such a step was taken, correct information had to be gained as to the actual extent of French influence.[117] The Council suggested that the authorities in London should notify all European nations that the Indian and British Governments could not accept the dominant influence of any other power at Mandalay. The Council suggested that the notification be done quickly before the French became further involved in Upper Burma.[118]

The Council concluded most emphatically that "we should consider it a misfortune, on many accounts, to be forced to adopt coercive measures of this description."[119]   The time was most inopportune, "we are opposed on principle, to annexationist policy, and the acquisition of Upper Burmah would entail upon us considerable responsibilities."[120]   Lastly, in reference to Bernard's July 27 and 28 recommendations, "we do not see how the alleged concession to French subjects can be objected to as contrary to treaties."[121]

Churchill Demands Explanations from Paris

Lord Randolph Churchill, the new secretary of state for India, telegraphed the next day, August 3.   He asked that all such proposals be postponed until the new Conservative Government of Lord Salisbury could obtain explanations from Paris of their policy towards Mandalay.

On August 7, Churchill wrote to Dufferin and agreed that "we should avoid to our utmost any policy entailing annexation of Burmah."[122]   Churchill said that he had urged Lord Salisbury to determine first if France was actually involved in the reputed dealings with Mandalay.   If so, it would be more acceptable to the British public if London demanded explantations from Paris and let Thebaw strictly alone.[123]

Churchill added that Viceroy Lytton's Government in 1876 should have left Amir Shere Ali alone in an analogous situation involving Russian interference at Kabul, Afghanistan.   Instead of demanding explanations of Shere Ali, Lytton should have demanded explanations from St. Petersburg concerning the Russian Mission (or Consul) to Kabul.[124]   The Conservatives would then have avoided great unpopularity, the Second Afghan war, and a disastrous defeat in the April 1880 Elections.[125]

Left unstated in Churchill's letter was the fact that the Conservatives had narrowly regained the Government on June 25, 1885. There was to be an Election in late-November and early-December 1885 as soon as the new voter-lists could be drawn-up.   Churchill thought that a campaign promising the expansion of British markets overseas would have a great appeal among British industrial-workers ; in particular among those in Birmingham,

Manchester, and the other depressed industrial-cities of the Midlands and northern England. Many of these workers blamed the Liberals for the 1885 depression of trade, which had thrown thousands of British workers out of work.[126]

Churchill, himself, was running at Birmingham for a Commons seat against John Bright, Britain's most famous 'radical'. Bright detested colonial and overseas commercial 'adventures', because they took away British taxes and capital from needed social-improvements at home. Churchill refuted this by stating that the Conservatives would put the British workingman back to work by pushing the expansion of British businesses and markets overseas. This would help to counter the rising commercial competition from Germany, America, France, and other newly-industrialized nations, which since 1870 had eaten into England's overseas markets.[127]

Therefore, Churchill was anxious in his August 7 letter to Dufferin to avoid those mistakes that had earlier in the case of Afghanistan led to the Second Afghan War, and to the Conservatives' defeat in April 1880. Thebaw would therefore be left strictly alone, while explanations would be demanded from Paris. The British markets in Upper Burma as well as the potential new markets in Yunnan were to be saved—and British jobs multiplied—by forcing the French out of Upper Burma before they had time to be fully established.[128]

Churchill stated that his stand would have to be changed if the French Government was not officially involved in the Bank and Railroad Contracts.[129] He would further alter his view if such contracts were being promoted by private French interests, or if the French Government evaded responsibility for the actions of its Mandalay agents, such as Haas.[130]

As it turned out, the French Government was not officially involved in such contracts, which were of a private nature. The French Government also evaded responsibility for Haas' actions; and claimed that if Haas had actually promoted such contracts, he had exceeded his instructions. By mid-October 1885, Churchill had changed his view to one of demanding explanations from Mandalay, instead of from Paris. By November, he defended the Indian Government's invasion of Upper Burma as being absolutely necessary to protect India's eastern frontier, and British jobs and British markets.[131]

Paris Denies All Knowledge of the Contracts

On the same day, August 7, that Churchill wrote to Dufferin, the French Chamber of Deputies approved the January 15, 1885 Burmese-French Treaty. The Chamber passed the Treaty on to the French Senate for their eventual approval.[132] It was also on August 7 that Lord Salisbury, British prime minister and foreign secretary, saw Waddington, the French ambassador to London, at the British Foreign Office.

Salisbury told Waddington that the presence of French concessionaires controlling the post office, railways, steam navigation, and several branches of the Upper Burma revenues, could not be allowed. In particular, such concessions could not be allowed, because it appeared that the French Government had officially sponsored them.[133]

Salisbury said that his government could no more admit French contracts in Upper Burma, than could the French Government admit British contracts in Tunis.[134] If the concessionaires insisted on proceeding, then Thebaw would have to be reduced in his powers and liberty to approve such enterprises.

Waddington claimed to know nothing of such arrangements. He said that he had always personally frowned on such things when he had been Minister for Foreign Affairs in a previous French Government. When he had received a similar offer from a concession-hunter, he had refused the fellow by the expediency of not even answering.[135]

Waddington promised at this meeting, and at later ones with Salisbury, to request full information from his Government.[136] Also, he would enquire about the second reason for Salisbury's enquiries, namely Ferry's Secret Letter concerning arms imports through Tongkin. Salisbury confided that Ferry's Secret Letter had greatly excited the Rangoon and Simla Governments, to say nothing of Lord Randolph Churchill. Waddington once again pleaded that he knew nothing whatsoever of such a 'secret letter' which sounded to him like a rumour fresh from the bazaars of Rangoon.[137]

Waddington made enquiries of de Freycinet, the French minister for foreign affairs. On August 13, de Freycinet responded that:

It is obvious that by the communication addressed to the Burmese Ambassadors at the time of the signing of the complementary commercial treaty, the Government of the Republic has reserved the faculty to allow, in agreement with the Burmese Government, the import of arms and ammunition of war into Burma, when it will decide that the import of arms to Tongking is compatible with our own security.   You can easily understand the real aim of this enunciation and the practical value that the present troubled situation of Annam and Cambodia obviously assigns to it.[138]

The essence of the above was communicated to Lord Salisbury, and the issue receded into the background having served its purpose as an excuse for London to make its views known.   Salisbury continued to press very hard for clarification of the French Government's reputed sponsorship thru Hass of a Mandalay Bank and Railroad.   Waddington could only repeat his claim to know nothing of such contracts, and that enquiries were under way at Paris.

The news had reached London that Haas had made an August 3 offer to provide French teak-firms in place of the BBTC should Mandalay desire it.   On August 12, the *Hlutdaw* had fined the BBTC ten lakhs for alleged teak-thefts from the firm's Ningyan Forest leases.   On August 25, J. A. Bryce of the BBTC's London office sent a letter of enquiry to de Freycinet about Haas' offer.

Bryce also enquired about the Bank and Railroad Contracts said to be officially sponsored by the French Government.   Bryce enclosed detailed 'resumes' of the two contracts, which he had received from his Rangoon office.[139]   Then, the news reached London that the *Hlutdaw* had on August 23 raised the fine against the BBTC to Rs. 23,59,066 (£153,333).

On August 31, Bryce forwarded another set of the 'resumes' to Lord Randolph Churchill in an intensive effort to involve the British Government on the BBTC's behalf against Haas and the looming 'French Threat' at Mandalay.[140]   However, Churchill had already on August 28 urged Salisbury to once again request explanations from Paris concerning Haas' actions and the Bank and Railroad Contracts.[141]

On September 9, Salisbury ordered Walsham, the acting British ambassador at Paris, to demand explanations concerning the alleged French Government sponsorship through Haas of the Bank and Railroad Contracts.[142]   De Freycinet, the foreign affairs minister, promised Walsham on September 16 that he would obtain full information.

Meanwhile, the Paris newspapers were filled with reports that the contracts formed part of a 'secret treaty' between Burma and France. On September 23, the official *Agence Havas* denied that the French Government was involved in any way with the rumoured contracts, or that they formed part of a 'secret treaty'. The denial ("Ces informations sont purement imaginaires.") was inserted in the *Agence Havas* under the heading 'Informations'. Such a heading almost always indicated an official French Government statement.[143]

De Freycinet asked Walsham to reiterate the French Government's denial to Lord Salisbury; particularly as the Paris newspapers had picked-up the 'secret treaty' story from *The Times* which had carried it several days previously.[144] The Foreign Affairs Minister said that Ambassador Waddington in London had also been instructed to deny the story.[145]

Waddington reiterated his Government's denial on September 28, and proposed to Salisbury that 'spheres of interest' be set up in Indo-China between the two countries. Waddington said that although de Freycinet did not have time to study the proposal right then, he had authorized Waddington to propose the idea of 'spheres of interest' on behalf of the French Government.[146]

Salisbury was agreeable to the idea, and suggested that perhaps Siam would be the dividing line (as it already was informally). To this Waddington said nothing, and the proposal was dropped temporarily.[147] One would surmise that Waddington did *not* have Siam in mind as the 'neutral' area. One surmises that he envisioned Upper Burma as the dividing area between the British 'sphere of interest' to the west, and the French 'sphere of interest' to the east.

With Upper Burma 'neutral', France would have a free hand to get whatever political or commercial influence that she could. Indeed, Haas' entire maneuvering at Mandalay was directed towards turning Upper Burma into a 'neutral', and Bernard had also stated that this was France's aim in Burma.[148]

Nothing was done about Salisbury's 'spheres of interest' proposal centered upon Siam, instead of Upper Burma. France was not likely to accept it, instead of a 'neutral' Upper Burma, because France would have had to abandon her attempts at political and commercial influence at Mandalay. France would have had to behave towards Upper Burma as Britain had behaved earlier towards Annam and Tongkin.   Lewis stated that :

throughout the period 1858-83 the British did not counter French intrigues at Hue or Hanoi, although had they signed a commercial treaty with Annam (approval for which they won by their protest of 1874-75) they could have embarrassed the French in the extreme.[149]

Churchill Remains Unsatisfied

On October 5, Churchill's office wrote to the Foreign Office. The letter stated that Sir John Walsham, acting British ambassador at Paris, had never claimed on September 16 that the French Government had incorporated the Bank and Railroad Contracts as part of a 'secret treaty' with Mandalay.[150]   Instead, Walsham had said that Haas and a French capitalist had persuaded King Thebaw to agree to several commercial contracts such as the Bank and Railroad Contracts.   Walsham had stated that the British Government could not allow these contracts to go into effect.[151]

Churchill concluded that it was up to Lord Salisbury to determine whether the Government should make further enquiries on the subject to the French Government.[152]   In any case, Churchill stated that Walsham should carefully watch the Tangyet Wundauk.[153]   The Burmese Ambassador and his Mission had just arrived in Paris.   The Tangyet had publicly stated that he had come solely to formalize the Jannary 15, 1885 Treaty after the French Senate had voted its approval.[154]

It was at this tense moment of increasing British suspicions concerning the real motives of the Quai d'Orsay that a Mr. Farman, a London *Standard* correspondent, appeared at Walsham's Paris office.   Farman admitted that *he* was the mysterious British capitalist, whom the Tangyet had said was named "something like Farmer."[155]

Farman explained that about a year before he had approached the Tangyet, and the other members of the 1883-85 Mission to Paris, with a proposal to build a Toungoo-Mandalay Railroad. Farman emphasized that the French Government had nothing to do with the purely commercial transaction.   He added that he was associated with the Comte de Trevelec, a Frenchman attached to the 1883-85 Burmese Mission and at present in Mandalay.[156]

Farman stated that before the Burmese Mission had returned to Mandalay in April 1885, draft proposals had been drawn-up by the two senior Burmese ambassadors in consultation with de Trevelec and himself.[157]   The Mandalay Government had not given its final approval to the terms,[158] and the Tangyet had come to Paris to negotiate the remaining differences.

Farman did not indicate whether he was also associated with de Trevelec in the Mandalay Bank scheme, although probably he was.   A key rival to the Farman-de Trevelec group was the Comte A. Mahe de la Bourdonnais. He claimed later that he had finalized *his* version of the Royal Bank Contract with the Tangyet on October 15, 1885.   As the Comte's contracts were no more binding —or worthless—than the duplicates signed by other parties, it appears that Farman thought that he could save the Railroad and Bank Contracts for his group by confiding in—and involving—the British Government.

In a second meeting with Farman on October 11, Walsham stated that it would be impossible for the British Government to approve of the entrance into Upper Burma of any French 'interference'.   This ruled out a joint Anglo-French Railroad from Toungoo to Mandalay.[159] Farman said that he understood completely. He cheerfully remarked about his French partner that "there would be no difficulty...in getting rid of him."[160]

Farman said he could speak definitively on this point. In recent talks with the Tangyet, the Ambassador had indicated that Mandalay would be happy to have a British firm build the line.[161] Farman asked Walsham if he would be permitted to continue negotiations for a contract to make a British line from Toungoo to Mandalay. Walsham said he would enquire of his superiors about the matter.[162]

Farman also confided that the Tangyet's party had not received any secret instructions for negotiations with the Quai d'Orsay. However, they had received instructions to sound out the British Government about the re-establishment of the Resident at Mandalay. If London showed interest, Mandalay would immediately send a special Mission to London to finalize the restoration on the old basis.[163]

The Tangyet had not mentioned the "Shoe Question", which had always been the foremost political question between the Burmese and Indian Governments.   Nor was there any indication that a larger Residency Guard would be allowed. The Tangyet had insisted that a Burmese representative be stationed in London in return for the re-establishment of the Resident at Mandalay. The Tangyet told Farman that he envied the Bangkok Government as it was represented in London, while his was not. It was at this point that Walsham broke off the interview with Farman.[164]

Lord Lyons, again H. M.'s ambassador to Paris, had a long talk with de Freycinet on the afternoon of October 12. The Minister for Foreign Affairs said that he had authorized Waddington in London to make three related statements. These were that the French Government had (1) no knowledge of any banking and railroad concessions in Upper Burma for French firms; nor, (2) had it given authority to anyone to obtain such concessions; nor, (3) had the French Government any knowledge that any Frenchmen had obtained such concessions.[165]

De Freycinet added that if there was any truth to the allegations that Haas had promoted the Bank, Railroad, and other concessions, then the Consul had acted without authority from Paris. At any rate, the issue was now closed, because Haas had fallen sick and had requested permission to leave Burma. His request for sick leave had been granted.[166]

De Freycinet stated that the Tangyet Wundauk had come to finalize the January 15, 1885 Treaty, and would probably not stay longer than one month. Lord Lyons concluded the conversation by stating that he hoped the Tangyet would be careful not to give encouragement to concession-hunters. Such concessions "could never be brought…into effect, but…might be productive of very serious inconveniences to his Government and himself."[167]

The warning was also directed at de Freycinet. Apparently, the warning registered with the Foreign Affairs Minister. The next day, October 13, the Tangyet presented his letters of credence to the French President.[168] On the same morning a short article appeared in the official newspaper *Journal des Debats*. Lyons immediately reported its contents to Salisbury.[169]

The *Journal* claimed that courteous talks had been going on between France and Britain. Such talks had proceeded in spite of the provocative articles in *The Times* and other British newspapers, which demanded the annexation of Upper Burma in order to forestall French 'designs' on that country.[170]

The *Journal* stated that the French Government desired the

"maintenance of the natural influence which her situation in the extreme East gives her in Burmah."[171]   However, the French Government could not think of adopting any policy, "which would harm British interests."[172]   Such a French policy would only *increase* the difficulties that France had already encountered in establishing her authority in Annam and Tongking.[173]

In summary, the article was a French admission of the British predominance in Upper Burma, and yet it yielded no essential or future French interests.   It was the *future* political and commercial ambitions of France in Upper Burma that worried Churchill. He and many others were not reassured by the mid-October translation of the Lanessan Report.

France's Long-Range Ambitions in Upper Burma

Some indications of France's future plans for Upper Burma were revealed in the Lanessan Report issued by the French Senate committee appointed to study the January 15, 1885 Treaty.   The Report recommended that the French Senate should approve the Treaty, and also made several comments about French policy in Southeast Asia.   These comments, as with the entire Lanessan Report, added considerably to British suspicions.[174]

Lower Burma, for example, was described as subject to the "protectorate of England" when the province was an integral part of the Indian Empire.[175]   Upper Burma and Siam were described as not being "regularly organized kingdoms."[176]   They were classed with the Lao States, such as Bassac and Luang Prabang, as being ideal areas where the imposition of French political influence would lead to the introduction of French commerce.[177]   The Lanessan Report also commented on the commercial possibilities of Upper Burma:

> The commerce of the Burmese provinces of which England took possession hardly thirty years ago, has risen to the value of 400 million francs, whilst the trade entering and leaving the port of Rangoon alone, through which pass the imports and exports of Upper Burma, reaches 300 millions. ....our interests require the presence of an intelligent and experienced agent [at Mandalay], not only with regard to political questions, but specially also with regard to commercial questions, for Upper Burmah cannot fail to play an important

part in the future relations of European commerce with Southern China.[178]

Col. Sir Henry Yule had attached concluding remarks to the official British translation of the Lanessan Report. Yule could look back on more than thirty years of diplomatic negotiations with Upper Burma beginning after the Second Burmese War, 1852-1853. Therefore, his views were important. He claimed that "the day is probably still distant when the neighbourhood of France on the eastern frontier of Burma can be so effective as to render communication free, and the introduction of arms by that door extensive."[179]

However, Yule emphasized that the political vacuum at Mandalay caused by the absence of the British Resident would continue to be filled by French 'intriguers'. Such persons had been "rife in Burma ever since 1854-55, and will not cease....to find high backing when opportunity offers, whilst our influence there remains so inactive as it has been in recent years."[180]

Yule seemed to be recommending the return of the Resident to Mandalay. A similar suggestion had been made by G. S. Forbes in his February 19, 1885 Indian Foreign Department memorandum. At different times Charles Bernard and Lord Kimberley, former secretary of state for India, had made similar proposals. However, as Dufferin had indicated in a March 24, 1885 letter, the 'French Threat' to India's eastern frontier and to British subjects' interests in Upper Burma would not be stopped by the mere restoration of the Resident.

Churchill had indicated in an August 7 letter to Dufferin that Thebaw should be left strictly alone, and that demands for explanations concerning the rumoured French concessions would be addressed to Paris. However, the French Government had denied all knowledge or sponsorship of such concessions. It claimed that if Consul Haas had promoted such concessions, he had exceeded his instructions.

Therefore, the following two chapters will bring the narrative back to Mandalay in order to describe the 1885 BBTC Teak Case, and the events that led up to the Third Burmese War. The Indian and London Governments were now to demand explanations from Mandalay concerning the continued spread of the 'French Threat' to British subjects' interests in Upper Burma, and to India's eastern frontier.

FOOTNOTES

[1] Thomas F. Powers, *Jules Ferry* . . . . . ., pp. 188-190.

[2] *Ibid.*

[3]-[6] *Ibid.*

[7] Brian L. Lewis, *The Attitudes* . . . . . ., pp. 460, 469-470, 472-473.

[8] No. 237, Burne Memo, January 22, 1886; in Foreign, Secret-E, April 1886, Nos. 221-239 (NAI).

[9] *Ibid. Also:* No. 37, 37A, BBTC-London to BBTC-Rangoon, November 8, 1883; in Foreign, Secret-E, February 1884, Nos. 35-40 (NAI).

[10] K. W. No. 2, Bryce to Crosthwaite, January 16, 1884; in Foreign, Secret-E, February 1884, No. 70 (NAI).

[11] Philippe Preschez, "Les Relations . . . . . .," pp. 359-360. (This figure is debateable. The October 3, 1882 Calcutta *Statesman* claimed that the daily income from the Ruby Mines was Rs. 5,000, out of a total daily Burmese Government revenue of Rs. 21,000. *See:* "Rangoon Correspondent," (Calcutta) *Statesman*, October 3, 1882, p. 1395.)

[12]-[14] *Ibid.*

[15] *Ibid*, p. 360.

[16] Messrs. Finlay, Fleming & Co. to Durand, February 4, 1885; in Foreign, Secret-E, April 1885, Nos. 279-293, p. 9 (NAI).

[17] *Ibid.*

[18] No. 292, Bonvillain's Petition to Work the Ruby Mines, n. d.; in Nos. 279-293.

[19] No. 391, Bernard's Secretary to Bernard, March 23, 1886; in Foreign, Secret-E, July 1886, Nos. 390-397 (NAI),

[20] *Ibid.*

[21] Philippe Preschez, "Les Relations . . . . . .," p. 360. After the annexation of Upper Burma in 1886, the representatives of the Comtesse de Moissant stated that she too had signed a Mandalay Royal Bank Contract. Her appeal for compensation to the Indian Government was refused as were all such claims by concession-hunters.

[22] No. 184, de la Bourdonnais' Bank Contract, March 2, 1885; forwarded by No. 183, Bryce to de Freycinet, August 25, 1885; in Foreign, Secret-E. October 1885, Nos. 164-186 (NAI). *See also:* 185, Further Terms of the Bank Contract, no date; in Nos. 164-186. No. 184 was signed by de la Bourdonnais with the Burmese Government. No. 185 stated that it was officially sponsored by the Burmese and French Governments; the contract appears to complement No. 184. De la Bourdonnais appeared to have the French Government's official sponsorship.

[23] *Ibid.*

[24] Philippe Preschez, "Les Relations . . . . . .," p. 360. *See also:* No. 186, The Toungoo-Mandalay Railroad Contract, April 13, 1885; in Nos. 164-186. The contract stated that it was officially sponsored by the Burmese and French Governments.

[25] No. 184; in Nos. 164-186. *See also:* No. 185; in Nos. 164-186.

[26] Andreino to Jones, September 30, 1885; in Foreign, Secret-E, January 1886, Nos. 37-63, p. 8 (NAI).

[27] No. 185, de Trevelec's Bank Contract, and No. 186, de Trevelec's Railroad Contract; in Nos. 164-186. These Contracts stated that they were officially sponsored by the Burmese and French Governments.

[28] No. 659, Telegram from Dufferin to Kimberley, February 19, 1885; in Foreign, Secret-E, March 1885, Nos. 659-661 (NAI).

[29] Major E. C. Browne, *The Coming of the Great Queen*, London, 1888, p. 104.

[30] No. 404, Bernard's Secretary to Durand, April 30, 1885; in Foreign, External-A, May 1885, No. 404 (NAI). French sources say that Haas arrived at Mandalay on June 1, 1885. This may be the first duty day for the new French Consul, or perhaps it was the date of his first official despatch.

[31] No. 276, News from Mandalay thru Messrs. Finlay Fleming & Co., May 17, 1885; in Foreign, Secret-E, June 1885, Nos. 275-278 (NAI).

[32-33] *Ibid.*

[34] No. 277, News From Mandalay thru Andreino, May 16, 1885; in Nos. 275-278.

[35] *Ibid.*

[36] No. 86, Bernard's Secretary to Durand, May 15, 1885; in Foreign, External-A, June 1885, No. 86 (NAI). The Tangyet had also visited Glasgow where he had negotiated for the purchase of a steamer.

[37] No. 230, Andreino to Bernard's Secretary, June 14, 1885; in Foreign, Secret-E, July 1885, Nos. 229-230 (NAI).

[38-39] *Ibid.* (The comparison with the East India Company was Andreino's. But according to Lewis : "One cannot overestimate the feelings of inferiority which haunted the French in the East at this time. The ghost of Dupleix was often exercised in despatches." Brian L. Lewis., *The Attitudes* ....p. 477).

[40] *Ibid.*

[41] "The French at Mandalay," (Bombay) *Times of India*, June 23, 1885, p. 12. Haas' doffing his shoes for the Kinwun was considered to be a great innovation, "and is likely to be regarded by...the Burmese as a sign of national submission." When Andreino heard of Haas' humiliation, the gleeful Italian wired his Government that Italy's great defeat at the hands of France on November 3, 1867 was now avenged ! "Mentana is avenged," chortled Andreino. *See also:* Comment on Haas' refusal to doff shoes, (Calcutta) *Statesman*, June 13, 1885, p. 275.

[42] No 230, Andreino to Bernard's Secretary, June 14, 1885; in Nos. 229-230.

[43-47] *Ibid.*

[48] *Ibid.*

[49] No. 191, Bernard to Durand, June 16, 1885; in Foreign, Secret-E, July 1885, No. 191 (NAI).

50 *Ibid.* The Teak Case is studied in great detail in Chapter VII.

51 No. 47, Nyaungoke Prince to Durand, June 26, 1885; in Foreign, External-B, September 1885, Nos. 47-50, p. 10 (NAI).

52 "Burma," (Allahabad) *Pioneer Mail,* July 19, 1885, p. 58.

53 "General Summary," (Bombay) *Times of India*, August 11, 1885, p. 3.

54 F. T. Jesse, *The Story of Burma*, London, 1946, p. 73. Jesse knew Mattie Calogreedy Antram as an old woman, who ran a tourist knick-knack shop in Mandalay until her death in 1930. Jesse had read most of the official papers in the Government files at Rangoon, and had interviewed many elderly survivors of the Mandalay Court.

55 *Ibid.* See also : Maung Htin Aung, *The Stricken Peacock*, The Hague, 1965, pp. 82-83.

56 F. T. Jesse, *The Lacquer Lady*, New York, 1930, pp. 310-315. (This was a slightly fictionalized 'novel' about Mattie Calogreedy Antram, which was published right after her death. According to John L. Christian, the book was of considerable historical value. *See*: John L. Christian, *Modern Burma*, p. 48.)

57 *Ibid.*

58 F. T. Jesse, *The Story of Burma*, p. 73.

59 F. T. Jesse, *The Lacquer Lady*, pp. 315-316.

60-62 *Ibid.*

63-65 *Ibid.*

66 *See*: No. 764, Bernard's Secretary to Durand, January 12, 1886; in Foreign, Secret-E, January, 1886, Nos. 764-767 (NAI). This despatch, like the others in the folder, described Andreino's services. *See also :* Foreign, Secret-E, July, 1886, Nos. 398-403 (NAI). This group of papers concerned the award of £5,000 to Andreino in 1886 for his services. *See* especially the notation by G. S. Forbes, June 15, 1886, p. 5. It stated that "There is little doubt that the copies [of the treaties and contracts] were obtained through Andreino." *See also* p. 7 concerning Andreino's award as announced in the June 8, 1886, Calcutta *Englishman*.

67 No. 40, Bernard's Secretary to Durand, July 6, 1885; in Foreign, Secret-E, August 1885, Nos. 40-49 (NAI).

68 *Ibid.*

69 No. 46, Letter from Ferry to Ambassadors, January 15, 1885; in Nos. 40-49.

70-71 *Ibid.*

72 Philippe Preschez, "Les Relations....," pp. 357-358.

73 No. 154, Andreino to Bernard, July 8, 1885; in Foreign, Secret-E, August 1885, Nos. 150-175 (NAI).

74 Enclosure 1 in No. 109, Bernard to Durand, July 4, 1885; in C. 4614, pp. 170-171.

75-76 *Ibid.*

[77] No. 154, Andreino to Bernard, July 8, 1885; in Nos. 150-175.

[78] *Ibid.*

[79] "General Summary," (Bombay) *Times of India,* August 4, 1885, p. 2. *See also:* "Burma," (Allahabad) *Pioneer Mail,* July 19, 1885, p. 58.

[80] *Ibid.*

[81] No. 154, Andreino to Bernard, July 8, 1885; in Nos. 150-175.

[82] *Ibid.*

[83] E. M. Pascal's Report on Foreigners in Mandalay, Sept. 12, 1885; in Foreign, Secret-E, October 1885, Nos. 198-200 (NAI).

[84] No. 165, 'Moung Looglay' to 'Mr. Rumble', July 15, 1885; in Nos. 150-175. The author is not absolutely certain that this letter was from Andreino. If not, it was either from a friend of Andreino's, or from another news-source of Bernard's at Mandalay. 'Moung Looglay' claimed that 'his sister' had extracted the above information from Haas during a conversation at dinner on July 14.

[85-86] *Ibid.*

[87-90] *Ibid.*

[91] *Ibid,*

[92] No. 164, Note from the News-writer at Mandalay, July 19, 1885 ; in Nos. 150-175.

[93] No. 155, Telegram from Churchill to Dufferin, July 25, 1885 ; in Nos. 150-175. It is interesting to note that reference to the BBTC as the originator of the body of the above telegram was deleted from the C. 4614 version (p. 168). The C. 4614 version begins "Following has been communicated privately to me."

[94] No. 99, Telegram from Dufferin to Churchill, July 26, 1885 ; in C. 4614, p. 168.

[95] No. 158, Telegram from Bernard to Durand, July 27, 1885 ; in Nos. 150-175.

[96] No. 163, Bernard to Durand, July 27, 1885 ; in Nos. 150-175.

[97] *Ibid.*

[98] Enclosure 3 in No. 109, Bernard's Secretary to Durand, July 28, 1885 ; in C. 4614, pp. 173-174.

[99] *Ibid.*

[100-04] *Ibid.* A 'letter of warning' is an 'ultimatum'.

[105-06] *Ibid.*

[107] Durand's Comment on Bernard's July 27, 1885 Telegram, July 28, 1885 ; in Nos. 150-175, pp. 2-3.

[108] No. 172, Burgess' Note on Talk with Tangyet Wundauk, August 4, 1885 ; in Nos. 150-175.

[109] "Another Burmese Embassy," (Allahabad) *Pioneer Mail,* August 9, 1885, p. 124.

[110] No. 172 ; in Nos. 150-175.

[111-113] *Ibid.*

196 *King Thebaw and the Ecological Rape of Burma*

Ibid.

No. 185, Telegram from Dufferin to Churchill, August 2, 1885; in Dufferin Papers, Reel 519/25, p. 66.

Ibid. (The Burmese view on foreign affairs was given by the Tangyet in an interview with the Bombay *Gazette* before sailing for Europe. The Tangyet avoided comment on the contracts, but said that the "Shoe Question" was no longer a problem. Also, Mandalay was willing to abide by Calcutta's decision as to how many arms Upper Burma could have for defence.

The only remaining problems were (1) the right of Mandalay to have a London-based representative (which Siam already had); and (2) the size of the Residency Guard that the re-established British Resident at Mandalay would bring with him.

The Tangyet claimed that the reports of anarchy in Upper Burma were rather over-blown. Actually Bernard's Government was pleased with the cooperation shown by Mandalay officials in the mutual extradition of 'dacoits', who were no longer allowed to get free from Lower Burma into Upper Burma (or vice versa).

The Tangyet emphasized that the Treaty of January 15, 1885, and Haas' presence at Mandalay, were strictly of a commercial nature. In addition, the Tangyet doubted that Mandalay would ever lease the Ruby Mines to any foreign concessionaire. "The Burmese Embassy," (Bombay) *Gazette*, September 6, 1885, pp. 233-236.)

117-21 *Ibid.* Two interesting notations were attached to Bernard's July 6, 1885 letter enclosing the several Treaties and Ferry's Secret Note. On July 31, G. S. Forbes, a top Indian foreign official, wrote : "There is nothing particularly cordial in M. Ferry's communication." On August 3, Dufferin and Durand jointly initialed a statement that read in part : "the realization of their [Burma's] wishes [for arms] seems distant." K. W. ; in Nos. 40-49.

No. 63, Churchill to Dufferin, August 7, 1885 ; in Dufferin Papers, Reel 517/18, pp. 124-125.

123-25 *Ibid.*

126-28 *Ibid. (See also :* Briton Martin Jnr., "The Viceroyalty of Lord Dufferin, Part One," (London) *History Today*, December 1960, pp. 824-830. *Also :* Briton Martin Jr., *New India, 1885*, Berkeley, 1969, pp. 134-138, 141-143, 154-155.)

129-130 *Ibid.*.

In particular, two of Churchill's speeches reported in *The Times* of October 24, 1885 and November 21, 1885.

No. 54, Pauncefote to Under-Secretary, India Office, August 7, 1885 ; in Foreign, Secret-E, October 1885, Nos. 53-57 (NAI).

No. 106, Salisbury to Walsham, August 7, 1885 ; in Foreign, Secret-E, September 1885; Nos. 98-106 (NAI).

134-36 *Ibid.*

Ibid.

Philippe Preschez, "Les Relations....", p. 358. [trans. excerpt from *Correspondance politique* Angleterre, Vol. 812, folio 59-60 (13 aout 1885)].

[139] No. 183, Bryce to de Freycinet, August 25, 1885; in Nos. 164-186. Bryce enclosed No. 184, de la Bourdonnais' Bank Contract; No. 185, de Trevelec's Bank Contract; and No. 186, de Trevelec's Railroad Contract.

[140] No. 170, Bryce to Churchill's Secretary, August 31, 1885; in No. 164-186.

[141] No. 144, Walpole to Pauncefote, August 28, 1885; in C. 4614, pp. 176-177.

[142] No. 335, Salisbury to Walsham, September 9, 1885; in Foreign, Secret, January 1886, Nos. 333-341 (NAI).

[143] Enclosure 1 (and 2) in No. 126, Walsham to Salisbury, September 24, 1885; in C. 4614, pp. 220-221.

[144-45] *Ibid.*

[146] Salisbury to Walsham, September 28, 1885; in Home Correspondence, Vol. 80, 1885 (IOL).

[147] *Ibid.*

[148] Enclosure 3 in No. 109, Bernard's Secretary to Durand, July 28, 1885; in C. 4614, pp. 173-174.

[149] Brian L. Lewis, *The Attitudes...*, pp. 473-474.

[150] No. 123, Godley to Pauncefote, October 5, 1885; in C. 4614, pp. 210-211.

[151-52] *Ibid.*

[153-54] *Ibid.*

[155] No. 254, Walsham to Salisbury, October 6, 1885; in Foreign, Secret-E, December 1885, Nos. 252-264 (NAI).

[156-57] *Ibid.*

[158] *Ibid.*

[159] No. 261D, Walsham to Lord Lyons (who had once again assumed the Paris Ambassadorship), October 12, 1885; in Nos. 252-264.

[160] *Ibid.*

[161-63] *Ibid.*

[164] *Ibid. See also:* No. 261B, Godley to Foreign Office Under-Secretary, November 5, 1885; in Nos. 252-264. *See* Chapter VIII for the details of British-French relations from October 13, 1885 to November 17, 1885.

[165] Enclosure 1 in No. 129, Lyons to Salisbury, October 12, 1885; in C. 4614, p. 222.

[166-67] *Ibid.*

[168] No. 260, Lyons to Salisbury, October 14, 1885; in Nos. 252-264.

[169] Enclosure 2 in No. 129, Lyons to Salisbury, October 13, 1885; in C. 4614, p. 222.

[170-73] *Ibid.*

[174] "The Report of the Commission on the Franco-Burmese Commercial Treaty," (London) *The Times*, November 6, 1885, p. 13. *The Times* commented: "Although Lord Salisbury had obtained from M. de Freycinet a disclaimer of any intention....to pursue an anti-English policy in Indo-China, there is no doubt that the action of French agents in Burmah has had a great deal to do with precipitating events in the valley of the Irra-

waddy. This impression will be strengthened by a perusal of M. Lanessan's report." *See also:* "Burmah, Siam and Indo-China, Translation of a Report....by M. de Lanessan, Deputy;" in L/P & S/20, Burma Memoranda, 1878-1885, Political and Secret Department, India Office, December 1, 1885 (IOL).

175-78 *Ibid. See also:* "The Relations of Burmah With France," (Allahabad) *Pioneer Mail*, November 27, 1885, pp. 14-15. The article joked that it was doubtful that Haas had lived up to the Lanessan Report's requirement for "an intelligent and experienced agent" at Mandalay. However, the Report "indicates the designs of the French Government upon the independence and integrity of the various States in the Indo-Chinese Peninsula." *See also:* Grattan Geary, *Burma After the Conquest,* pp. 155-157.

179 Note by Col. Sir Henry Yule, October 17, 1885; in L/P & S/20, "Burmah, Siam, and Indo-China...." pp. 75-82.

180 *Ibid.*

7

The Deforestation
of Upper Burma, 1862-1885:
The BBTC Teak Case

Introduction

In October 1885, the British Government decided to cease
demanding explanations from Paris concerning French expansion in
Upper Burma. Instead, an October 22 Ultimatum was sent to
Mandalay. The "convenient pretext" for the Ultimatum was
Mandalay's refusal to accept arbitration of the BBTC Teak Case.[1]

The Case had been initiated in April 1885 by about a dozen
self-styled 'foresters' in the employ of the Taingda. They claimed
that the BBTC owed them money for huge amounts of timber
extracted for which the BBTC had not paid royalty to Mandalay.
The *Hlutdaw* passed an *ex parte* Judgment against the company on
August 12, 1885, and a fine order of Rs. 23,59,066 on August 23,
1885.[2]

The Judgment was particularly unjust in that the real complainants in the Case, the *Hlutdaw*, were also the prosecutors, the
judges, the jury, and the sentencing agency all combined. The
Hlutdaw actually had no right to 'try' the Case, according to the
1867 Burmese-British Treaty. It had stated in the context of cases
involving Burmese and British subjects that they should be tried
by the Mixed Court at Mandalay composed of a Burmese judge
and the British Resident.[3]

After St. Barbe withdrew the Residency on October 6, 1879,
the Mixed Court was allowed to die by both Governments without

a further session. If this had not been done, or if either Government had proposed a revived Court in 1885, the Teak Case would probably have been tried there.[4]

Instead, Bernard was instructed to send an August 28 request for arbitration, which the Mandalay Government refused on October 3. This refusal was made the "convenient pretext" for an October 22 Ultimatum to the Mandalay Government. The Ultimatum, although ostensibly an effort to negotiate the Teak Case, was in reality designed to oust all French influence from Upper Burma.

The 1880 and 1882 Teak Contracts

William Wallace of the BBTC gained the first BBTC teak-leases from King Mindon in November 1862. After 1864, the BBTC contracted with the *myothugyis* of Ela and Lewe, and with other independent Burmese and European teak-firms, to work their Upper Burma teak-leases. The outside contractors worked the BBTC's leases until 1880, especially in the BBTC's leases in the Ningyan Forest above Toungoo.[5]

In 1871, the *Hlutdaw* sent U Gaung to be *akunwun*, revenue officer, of the Ningyan area. U Gaung, who was later known as the Kinwun Mingyi, held the position for only a year, but increased the revenue and improved the administration.[6] There is little doubt that the Kinwun received a number of 'gifts' from the BBTC through the years, but so did almost every other minister. In return, the BBTC received very 'reasonable' terms in the several teak contracts.[7]

In January 1875, the BBTC's Mr. Goldenberg paid King Mindon Rs. 2,00,000 for a further six-year lease of the Ningyan Forest.[8] In 1875, only a few persons realized that the extensive Deforestation of an area would most likely cause a Dry Zone or desert. However, Capt. G. A. Strover, the British resident at Mandalay, had noticed that the evaporation-rate of water at Mandalay—an area which had been largely denuded of trees for perhaps 1,000 years—was half-an-inch per day.[9] Strover had also noticed that a rapid Deforestation was occurring in the still relatively 'wet' Ningyan Forest:

The teak forest at Burmese Toungoo....will be worked steadily for another six or seven years, by which time it will be probably completely exhausted. Some four or five lacs of logs have already been extracted...., and 26,000 logs are now ready for removal and export. With no system of conservation, this forest must be exhausted before long.[10]

In 1880 the BBTC eliminated all outside contractors from its Ningyan and other Upper Burma forest leases. The BBTC began advancing money to its own covenanted employees to harvest its forest leases. After 1880, the BBTC regarded "their old contractors as fierce rivals for the concessions."[11]

In 1880, J. A. Bryce and H. Maxwell resided one year in Mandalay and signed the 1880 Variable Duty Contract. The contract was gained only after "hard bargaining......and severe competition."[12] It gave the BBTC new leases in the Chindwin, Moo, Yaw, and Pyaungshu Forests. According to the BBTC's official historian, the Contract established the BBTC in the heart of the teak-bearing areas of Upper Burma, and enabled the BBTC to control "a significant part of Burma's supplies."[13]

The 1880 Variable Duty Contract provided for a duty per log to be paid to local Burmese forest officials.[14] The duty schedule established duties to be paid on all possible sizes and qualities of logs. However, teak logs 4'6" or more in girth, but under 18' in length, were *not* listed. They, therefore, were allowed to go out free of duty.[15]

This omission whether by accident or by design was a most profitable one for the BBTC.[16] Some of the largest and most valuable pieces of teak that reached Moulmein and Rangoon measured less than 18' in length.[17] This was because trees of large girth could not be dragged by elephants, unless the log was cut into short lengths.[18]

It was probable that the BBTC took logs 4'6" or more in girth, and 18' or more in length, and paid no duty on them. This was done by cutting them into chunks of less than 18'.[19] In 1882, Mr. Walker of Goldenberg, Darwood and Walker reported this to the Mandalay Government, and offered to buy the lease on all logs under 18' in length.[20] Andreino, the BBTC agent at Mandalay, quoted Walker as saying that there had been a large number of logs at Ningyan in 1881-1882 that could not be brought out under the 1880 Variable Duty Contract.[21] The question comes to mind: why not?

No genuine 'short' under 4'6" in girth, under 18' in length, was prohibited.[22]　Nor was any Burmese official likely to quibble over such a worthless thing.　The logs that the BBTC could not ship in 1881-1882 were probably logs 4'6" or more in girth, which had been cut to less than 18' in order to avoid payment of duty. The Burmese officials had apparently caught many of these, and knew that they had missed others.　As a result, they were receptive to Walker's proposed 'shorts' contract.

The BBTC was forced to agree to a 'Shorts' Contract that was to go into effect from October 1882 for five years, and would cost the BBTC one lakh a year in advance.[23]　The BBTC's official position on the 'Shorts' Contract was that it violated the principles of good conservation:

> The Corporation have never desired to fell under-sized timber, and their own forest rules especially forbid it.... The Corporation were forced......into the "shorts contract" owing to....another timber merchant, who offered to pay....a large sum for the right of felling and removing under-sized timber in the forests leased by the Corporation. Up to that period [October 1882] the Corporation had never consented to any small timber being felled in their forests.[24]

Therefore, the logs at Ningyan in 1881-1882, which the BBTC was not allowed to ship, were probably not true 'shorts'.　It is not likely that Mr. Walker would have offered the original 'shorts' contract to remove genuine 'shorts'.　Therefore, one is forced to conclude that the BBTC took advantage of the 1880 Variable Duty contract, which made no provision for duty on logs 4'6" or more in girth, and less than 18' in length.　Was the desire to continue this arrangement the BBTC's real motive for opposing the 1882 'Shorts' Contract?　One does think so.[25]

The 'Shorts' Contract gave the BBTC "the right to take possession of all the timber rejected under the present [1880 Variable Duty] lease."[26]　The 'Shorts' Contract also gave the BBTC the right "to work all timber under three cubits [4'6"] in girth, *and timber not full 12 cubits* [18'] *in length.*[27]

A few comments are in order.　First of all, there was no such provision in the 1880 Variable Duty Contract that allowed the BBTC to reject non-Royal timber.[28]　Also, the timber that the BBTC was allowed to take possession of could not have been genuine 'shorts'.　The BBTC had stated above that it had *not* harvested 'shorts' until after October 1882, when it was forced to accept the 1882 'Shorts' Contract.

The provision allowing the BBTC to take possession of timber rejected under the 1880 Contract was a mere 'face'-saving device.[29] The provision actually meant that the timber, which had been held back by Burmese foresters as being full-sized timber that had been cut to less than 18', could now be brought out after payment of one lakh a year. But not so simple to explain was the phrase in the 'Shorts' Contract that allowed the BBTC "to work all timber under three cubits [4'6''] in girth, *and timber not full 12 cubits* [18'] *in length.*"[30]

The BBTC said that the phrase meant all 'short' timber under 4'6" in girth, and under 18' in length. The Indian Government shared this interpretation. A typical example was Bernard's letter of August 31, 1885 when he stated that: "The contract of 1882 [is]....for....unsound timber and timber under 4½ feet in girth and 18 feet in length......which they [BBTC] were entitled to reject under the lease of 1880.''[31] However, to the working 'teak-wallah' in the deep woods, the above phrase in the 'Shorts' Contract had an entirely different meaning.

An article in *The Indian Forester* said that the 'Shorts' Contract was for "logs under 3 cubits [4'6"] in girth......and short logs *under 12 cubits* [18'] *in length........without stipulation to girth.*"[32] A later *Indian Forester* article indicated that the 'Shorts' Contract provided for the unlimited removal of logs *"under 18 feet in length (any girth),* or........under 4½ feet in girth (any length).*"[33]

The writer added that the BBTC had no right under the 1880 Variable Duty Contract to reject any logs on the grounds that they were 'shorts' under 4'6" in girth, and under 18' in length. The writer commented that there was "an unexplained mystery" about the 'Shorts' Contract.[34]

The writer may have had a point. He added that many logs of great girth were cut into short chunks in order that the elephants might drag them to the streams. The writer thought that there was a great temptation present under the 'Shorts' Contract to shave a few inches off a full-sized log, and pass it through as a 'short'.[35] The BBTC probably did yield to temptation, and logs were shaved to less than 18', and taken out under the 'Shorts' Contract. Apparently, the BBTC benefited as much from the 1882 'Shorts' Contract as they had from the 1880 Variable Duty Contract.

The 1884 'Lump Sum' and Renewal Contracts

Berthold Ribbentrop, head Indian forester, wrote that if the BBTC had stolen logs or avoided paying duty at Ningyan "it would have necessitated the connivance of local [Ningyan] officials."[36] It was apparently this tendency that made the Mandalay Court decide in April 1883 to thwart both the BBTC and the Royal foresters.

A new 'Lump Sum' Contract was signed authorizing the BBTC to harvest whatever logs it could regardless of size or condition.[37] The BBTC was no longer to pay a duty on each log to the local forest officials. Instead, the BBTC paid a 'Lump Sum' in advance to the Mandalay Finance Minister. The initial 'Lump Sum' paid in October 1884 totalled Rs. 5,28,000, and was scheduled to rise to about Rs. 7,72,000 by October 1887.[38]

An interesting examination follows of the 'Lump Sum' Contract, which went into effect on October 19, 1884. It superseded both the 1880 Variable Duty and the 1882 'Shorts' Contracts. Also included below is an examination of the 'Lump Sum' Renewal Contract, which was signed in January 1884 even before the original 'Lump Sum' Contract went into effect on October 19, 1884. The original 'Lump Sum' Contract follows immediately below:

(1) Ningyan Forests leased to 1891: Rs. 4,50,000 [£29,999] per annum.
(2) Chindwin Forests leased to 1891; duty per log to October 1887; lump sum of Rs. 2,50,000 per annum for succeeding years to 1891.
(3) Yaw Forests leased to 1891; Rs. 32,000 per annum.
(4) Taungdwingyi Forests leased to 1890; Rs. 26,000 per annum.
(5) Pyaungshu Forests leased to 1887; Rs. 10,000 per annum.
(6) Malun Forests leased to 1890; Rs. 10,000 per annum.[39]

The total of the original 'Lump Sum' Contract would have been about Rs. 7,72,000 (almost £53,000) after October 1887. The 'Lump Sum' Renewal Contract was signed in January 1884, and extended the original 'Lump Sum' Contract up to 1903 in one of the forests. The 'Lump Sum' Renewal Contract follows below:

(1) Ningyan Forests renewed lease 1891-1896; Rs. 4,50,000 per annum.

(2) Chindwin Forests renewed lease 1891-1899; Rs. 2,50,000 per annum.

(3) Yaw Forests renewed lease 1891-1899; Rs. 32,000 per annum.

(4) Taungdwingyi Forests renewed lease 1890-1898; Rs. 26,000 per annum.

(5) Pyaungshu Forests renewed lease 1887-1903; Rs. 20,000 per annum.[40]

The annual payment in the 'Lump Sum' Renewal Contract totalled about Rs. 7,78,000 up to October 1896. In summary, the Mandalay Government had by January 1884 secured a guaranteed annual income of over seven lakhs up to October 1896; of over three lakhs from 1896-1899; and of Rs. 20,000 from 1899 to 1903. Was the arrangement a profitable one for Mandalay? One would have to answer in the affirmative. However, the arrangement was even more profitable for the BBTC.[41]

Further Details of the Leases

The effect upon the shipments of logs from the Ningyan Forest was immediately evident after the signing of the two 'Lump Sum' Contracts in April 1883 and January 1884. The annual shipment of logs from the Ningyan Forest rose from an average of 33,000, which it had been before 1884, to 44,000 in 1884, and then to 61,000 logs in 1885.[42]

The 'Lump Sum' annual payment for the Ningyan Forest was Rs. 4,50,000. The payment would have been somewhat high for 33,000 logs, which was the average yearly shipment before 1884 from the Ningyan Forest.[43] The 1884 shipment of 44,000 logs at the above payment would have averaged Rs. 10.50 per log, which was the average duty paid per log under the 1880 Contract.[44] But the 1885 shipment of 61,000 logs would have averaged only Rs.7.36 per log.[45]

In 1886, or within a year or two later, the BBTC would have entracted from the Ningyan Forest "not less than 1,20,000 logs per annum and may be much more."[46] At Rs. 10.50 per log this would have represented at least Rs. 12,60,000 per annum under the terms of the 1880 Contract.[47] As noted above, Mandalay had already committed itself with the 'Lump Sum' Renewal Contract to receive only Rs. 4,50,000 per annum from the Ningyan Forest until 1896. In turn, the BBTC was allowed to remove all the timber it desired.

A considerable jump in teak shipments would probably have occurred in all the BBTC's forest leases. Perhaps the rise would not have been as great as the rise in the Ningyan Forest from 33,000 logs before 1884 to an estimated 120,000 logs in 1886 or 1887. A key BBTC employee told Berthold Ribbentrop, head Indian forester, that the BBTC had 'girdled'—*i.e.* killed—500,000 trees in Upper Burma during 1885.[48] These trees were to be cut down within the following two or three years as soon as the timber had dried sufficiently to float down the streams. Ribbentrop estimated that the trees in question totalled 150,000 tons in weight.[49] In conclusion, the extensive Deforestation of the teak, cutch, and other forests after 1862 was the main cause of the Dry Zone 'drought' of 1883-1885, and of the consequent deterioration in order, trade, and revenues in the provinces south of Mandalay.

The Teak Case to June 17, 1885

Many Burmese ministers regretted having sold their forests so cheaply,[50] but it had been necessary in order to compensate for the serious drop in general revenues. Before the 1883-1885 'drought', the annual revenue not including the various teak-lease payments had been about 100-103 lakhs. In 1885, the annual revenue slumped off to only eighty-five lakhs.[51]

The Mandalay Government was virtually bankrupt, but it had probably the smallest public debt in relation to the annual revenue of any country in the world. The debt, including the private debts of the Royal Couple, totalled only about fifteen lakhs.[52] It was obvious that the Government was basically sound, and most of the ministers thought that the country's problems would be rectified with the return of 'normal' Dry Zone rainfall in a year or so.[53]

Until then, it was necessary to find an extra fifteen or twenty-five lakhs with which to run the Government. The Pouk Myine Atwinwun, who was the finance minister ; the Taingda ; and other ministers began to seek a way of either raising the BBTC's payments or of reselling the leases at a higher price to other firms.[54]

The Taingda also hoped that he could make the Kinwun the scapegoat for the disastrous contracts, although all the ministers had approved of the contracts and had been suitably rewarded by the BBTC. The Taingda knew that the Kinwun would oppose any large fines against the BBTC, or any move to void the leases before the expiration of the contracts.

The Kinwun would, no doubt, argue that a harsh punishment of the BBTC would have an important and perhaps dangerous influence upon the relations between the Burmese and Indian Governments. The Taingda schemed to place the Kinwun in the position of 'protecting' the *kala* firm, an unpopular position to say the least. The Taingda had hopes of manipulating the issue until he could reduce the Kinwun's influence, or perhaps even drive him from office.

There would then be no other rival strong enough to stop the Taingda's group from voiding the BBTC's leases, and re-selling them to the highest bidder.[55] Naturally, a good portion of the higher payments would remain with the Taingda's group. In the final analysis, the humiliation of the Kinwun was probably as strong a motive for the Taingda as any of the financial considerations.

There was a February 1885 meeting between Andreino and the three great *mingyis*, Kinwun, Taingda, and Taungwin. Taingda told Andreino in blunt terms that twenty-two lakhs were required by the Mandalay Government. Andreino was told that the BBTC would advance that amount, or the BBTC would not work its teak leases.[56]

Andreino refused stating that the BBTC had already advanced the Burmese Government ten lakhs on the 'Lump Sum' Contract, which had gone into force on October 19, 1884.[57] The BBTC could not give any further advances until the present 'Lump Sum' advance—almost two years of normal payments—had been reduced by a sufficient amount of worked-out timber.[58]

Nevertheless, on about March 24, 1885, Andreino lent the Court Rs. 2,68,143. Of this, the BBTC paid Rs. 73,881 directly to the Burmese Mission in Europe in order that the Mission might have sufficient funds to return home.[59] It is rather ironic that the BBTC's loan assisted in the establishment of Burmese-French relations, and in the posting of Haas to Mandalay where he offered French firms to take-over the BBTC's leases. It is still more ironic that at the moment the Taingda was despatching forged royal orders to the Ningyan Forest for 'foresters' to file suit against the BBTC, Andreino was claiming that the BBTC would not have to make any further advances until April 1886.[60]

On April 20, Bernard received an initial complaint from S. G. Jones, Rangoon BBTC manager and former engineer in King Mindon's service, about some difficulty in the Ningyan Forest.[61] It was not the first time that charges of theft had been brought against the various timber firms. For example, in early-1880, John Darwood of Goldenberg, Darwood and Walker had been put into a sort of 'honourable confinement', while he considered the Burmese Government's demand for an additional fifteen lakhs.[62] A settlement was eventually made, and the Indian Government was of course not involved.

Bernard despatched an enquiry about the BBTC's problem on April 22,[63] and the Kinwun replied on May 17. His reply was brought down to Rangoon by several Burmese forest officials. The Kinwun stated that certain BBTC foresters claimed to have worked out over 80,000 logs from April 15, 1883 (start of Burmese year 1245 B. E.) to April 13, 1885 (end of 1246 B. E.).[64] However, they said that they had been paid for only about 32,000 logs.[65]

It was alleged that the BBTC also owed duty on thousands of logs shipped prior to the expiration of the 1880 and 1882 Contracts on October 19, 1884. After that date, the 'Lump Sum' Contract had come into effect. The alleged thievery of logs prior to October 19, 1884 had been accomplished by bribing the Ningyan Governor and forest officials.[66]

The Kinwun asked Bernard to allow the bearers of the letter to examine the books at the Lower Burma Forest Offices at Toungoo and Shwegyin on the Sittang River.[67] The Burmese forest officials were to note the number and kinds of Ningyan Forest logs that had floated past the two Forest Offices from April 15, 1882 (start of 1244 B.E.) to April 13, 1885 (end of 1246 B. E.).[68]

The Kinwun's proposal was accepted, and was much admired in Rangoon's boardrooms as the latest example of the Kinwun's cool-headed diplomacy. The Burmese forest officials were given every cooperation at the two Forest Offices, and the BBTC presented evidence on its behalf to Bernard.[69]

Finally, on June 17, Bernard replied to the Kinwun's May 17 letter. Bernard stated that the two Forest Offices did not make a distinction between logs harvested in the Ningyan Forest in one year, but floated down the next.[70] The total number of logs harvested in the Ningyan Forest in one year would *not* necessarily agree with the total of logs reaching—or leaving—Toungoo Forest Office in that same year. This was an extremely important point.[71]

The record also took *no* account of the quality of the logs, or of their girth. Instead, it recorded two inaccurate sizings by length, namely the 'dugyi' and the 'hlwaza.'[72] These sizings had no more meaning than, say, 'large' and 'small' or 'long' and 'short'. The sizings were so broad that 'yathits' and so-called 'stumps' were included in them. The 'yathit' was a 'short' log under 4'6" in girth, and of any length, while the so-called 'stump' was a log *of any girth, and under eighteen feet in length.*[73]

The record also did not differentiate between logs harvested under the three different contracts of 1880, 1882, and 1884.[74] It would be impossible for the record to do so, because logs harvested in the Ningyan Forest often did not reach Toungoo until a year or two later. The Toungoo Forest Office recorded *only* the date when an individual log left the Office, and its approximate length.[75]

Bernard did not emphasize the fact in his letter, but the dozen 'foresters', who had filed the original petitions against the BBTC, were apparently not legitimate. Apparently, 342 genuine BBTC foresters signed a petition stating that most of the original complainants against the BBTC had never been BBTC foresters.[76]

A few of the complainants had once been BBTC foresters, but had been discharged long before because of dishonesty and slovenly work-habits.[77] Lastly, several of the complainants were still BBTC foresters, but said that they knew nothing of such petitions, and had not given their names to be used for such purposes.[78]

Bernard concluded his June 17 letter to the Kinwun by stating that Maung Po Zan, an associate of Taingda, had been circulating a royal order about Rangoon. The royal order, which bore Thebaw's Royal Peacock Seal, stated that the BBTC's leases had been cancelled, and that new bidders would be welcomed. Bernard hoped that the document was not genuine, and that the BBTC would be allowed to continue working their leases "to the benefit of the two countries."[79]

The Effects of Bernard's Letter

Andreino was unhappy that Bernard's letter had not mentioned the forged royal orders, which Taingda had sent to the foresters in order to get them to file suits against the BBTC. Some of these so-called 'royal' orders were in Taingda's name. Andreino had hoped that Bernard would protest the forged orders, because this would have given the Kinwun a strong weapon in his power-struggle with the Taingda.[80]

However, the Kinwun's cunning had apparently saved the BBTC's leases even without a protest from Bernard. It appeared that U Kyi, King Thebaw's commercial-agent at Rangoon, was in reality a nominee of Andreino's;[81] and, was also the Kinwun's trusted agent who had initiated 'feelers' for the 1882 Simla Conference. The Kinwun's May 17 letter had been written at the suggestion of U Kyi and Andreino. It had been the idea of these two along with the Kinwun to send the Kinwun's letter to Rangoon with 'reliable' forest officials, who would then check the Forest Office records. The Kinwun and Andreino had even told U Kyi what to say when presenting the letter and the forest officials to Bernard. In short, the BBTC had friends at Mandalay.[82]

Andreino wrote to Jones on July 8 that Bernard's June 17 letter had caused the *Hlutdaw* ministers to accuse each other of starting the case.[83] The Taingda found himself saddled with the blame, because it was he who had sent the forged royal orders summoning the foresters to Mandalay to file suit against the BBTC.[84] It was rather *difficult* for the Taingda to deny his involvement, because some of the *hmazas* bore his name.[85]

The ministers seemed amused that Maung Po Zan, an associate of Taingda, was in Rangoon with still another forged 'royal' order. According to Bernard's June 17 letter, the document bore the Royal Peacock Seal of King Thebaw, and cancelled the BBTC's leases and invited new bidders. The Taingda doubted the existence of such a document. If it did exist, he denied having any connection with it, or with having illegally used the King's Seal—a capital offence.[86]

But the Myothit Atwinwun, the head of the 1883-1885 Paris Mission, stated that he had seen and read the document when returning home through Rangoon in early May. "The Taingda felt rather stumped when he was so flatly made out a liar in the presence of the Ministers."[87]

Andreino concluded his July 8 letter to Jones by stating that the *Hlutdaw* would not make a prompt reply to Bernard's June 17 letter. They would wait until after the Burmese forest officials checked the records at the Forest Offices, and returned to Mandalay to make their report. Until then, there was no great crisis,[88] particularly since Andreino had already begun to pass the stolen French treaties and contracts to Bernard. This was an act which Andreino and his BBTC superiors hoped would involve the British Government in the BBTC's quarrel with the 'pro-French' Taingda group at Mandalay.

Haas' Recommendations Ignored

Meanwhile, the French Consul Frederic Haas had employed two staff members. The first was Mons. Du Pina de St. Didier, who was employed as chancellor or assistant. The second employee, a secretary, was Mons. Bentabole, a Mandalay fire-brigade commander, and a bugler in Thebaw's service. Du Pina was a reputable enough gentleman. However, Bentabole was a fool right out of a Rabelaisian comedy, and was considered to be of no stature whatsoever at Mandalay.

Haas then commenced a series of recommendations to his Government. These should be studied before mentioning Haas' August 3 offer to provide French teak-firms in case the *Hlutdaw* voided the BBTC's leases. One realizes that Haas was isolated when one studies the reception that Haas' despatches received at the Quai d'Orsay. In short, the Quai d'Orsay was apathetic.

On July 7 Haas recommended that French capital be officially encouraged to invest in Upper Burma. His suggestion received the following notation at the Quai d'Orsay: "What nonsense. How is French capital to be found to be sent to Burma when they could not find any for the New Herbrides."[89]

Haas followed this despatch with another on July 15. He advised that French subjects accused of crimes in Upper Burma should be tried by French authorities. Until Mandalay accepted the provision, France should not ratify the January 15, 1885 Treaty. France should also receive preference in mining and railroad concessions.[90]

On August 3, Haas made an offer to the *Hlutdaw* on behalf of

French capital to take-over the BBTC's leases. He told the Kinwun that if the teak-forests and other Upper Burmese enterprises were leased to French capital, it would weaken the ability of Great Britain to interfere in Upper Burmese affairs. Haas advised the Quai d'Orsay that it would be most desirable if the Mandalay Government would authorise the Burmese Mission to lease the teak-forests to French firms.[91]

On August 12, Haas wrote that it would be easy to enquire as to the progress of his August 3 proposal to take-over the BBTC's leases. It would also be easy to begin arrangements with French capital should the Mandalay Government actually void the leases. Haas conceded, however, that the Kinwun had not yet replied to his August 3 offer; and in fact had not replied to any of his previous letters.[92] Haas did not mention how many of his letters had gone without a reply, but at this time the total was about fifteen.

The above missile was not accorded a very gracious reception at the Quai d'Orsay. Three notations were attached to it. The first read: "It is always the same incomprehensible jargon." The second notation asked: "Why this intervention in an affair that seems to be exclusively the concern of the British and the Burmese Government?" The third notation stated that: "All this indicates attempts at interference which ought to be deplored, for they are at the same time binding and yet in vain."[93]

An August 18 telegram to Haas from the Quai d'Orsay advised "the greatest reserve" in any commercial concessions or dealings that might conceivably involve the British Government.[94] According to Preschez, Haas did not fully inform his superiors of his further proposals to the Kinwun and other officials. British documents record at least one further dealing on September 5, and Preschez claimed that Haas made another advance to the Kinwun in October.[95]

On October 17, Haas made a further proposal to the Quai d'Orsay. He thought that it was his duty to repeat his previous offers to the Kinwun to supply French capital in case Mandalay voided the BBTC's teak leases. The Burmese Government could easily send a telegram to the Burmese Mission at Paris. They would have no difficulty in finding French capital to work the Upper Burma teak forests.[96]

An interesting notation was attached to Haas' letter by a Quai

d'Orsay official. He wrote that Haas' letter confirmed the allegations in the British press of French 'interference' at Mandalay.[97]
Haas had been placed on his "absolute reserve" as of August 18.
Despite the warning, and the severe tensions between England and
France concerning some of his reputed dealings at Mandalay, Haas
had still not hesitated to repeat his August 3 offer to supply French
teak-firms in place of the BBTC.[98]

The most revealing of all Haas' comments came at the end of
his October 17 letter. He complained that "all my letters to the
Kinwun Mingyi were communicated to Mr. Andreino."[99] In fact,
Andreino had almost succeeded in suppressing Haas' August 3
letter, which offered French firms in place of the BBTC.

Haas' Letter 'Ignites' the Judgment

Haas' August 3 letter was not translated and formally presented
to the *Hlutdaw* for several days. The translator, who was
in Andreino's secret employ, knew that he had a letter of great
importance. He carried it about on his person for four days, and
then slipped into Andreino's house on August 7. The translator
was about to hand over the letter, but Haas arrived at that moment
to see Andreino and almost caught them in the act.[100]

The interruption was a great disappointment to Andreino. He
had hoped to suppress the letter entirely, but that was no longer
possible. He asked the translator not to translate the letter, until
after the *Hlutdaw* had made its decision on the BBTC Teak Case.
If the letter could be held back until after the decision was made,
then Haas' offer would be disregarded along with all his other
letters.[101]

But Haas had become suspicious. He sent Bentabole, his
secretary, to the Palace to enquire if the letter had been translated.
Bentabole's enquiries forced the translation of the letter, and its
formal presentation to the *Hlutdaw*.[102] On August 9, Andreino
wrote to Jones that Haas' letter had given the *Hlutdaw* a freedom
of choice that they had never had before. Haas' letter "will
entirely banish the fear of having the forests left on their hands,
should they take them from us."[103]

On August 11, Andreino was summoned to the Palace, and
was confronted with the statistics that the Burmese forest-officers
had brought back from the Toungoo and Shwegyin Forest

Offices.[104] The discussion lasted four hours, and Andreino again returned to the Palace on the following morning.[105] But his explanations were in vain and the *Hlutdaw* passed a Judgment on the same day.[106]

The Judgment stated that there were 114,133 Ningyan Forest logs recorded as having passed through the two Forest Offices from April 15, 1882 (start of 1244 B. E.) to April 13, 1885 (end of 1246 B. E.). John Darwood of Goldenberg and Darwood owned 1,457 of these logs. Therefore, the BBTC owned 112,676 of the 114,133 logs that had passed through the two Forest Offices between the above dates.[107]

The BBTC had submitted receipts signed by Ningyan Burmese officials, which showed that the BBTC had harvested 56,178 logs between April 15, 1882 to April 13, 1885. Of this total, 44,008 logs were dugyis 4'6" or more in girth, and 30' or more in length. The remaining 12,170 logs were hlwazas 4'6" or more in girth, and with a length of 18' or more but under 30'.

The two Forest Offices had recorded a total of 93,791 dugyis, 20,021 hlwazas, and 321 yathits ('shorts') between April 15, 1882 and April 13, 1885. The Judgment deducted John Darwood's 1,457 logs, and the 321 'shorts' from the above totals. The Judgment stated that the BBTC had taken out in excess of its claimed figures, 48,326 dugyi logs and 7,851 hlwaza logs, or a total of 56,177 logs.[108]

Andreino's rebutal to the above portion of the Judgment was the statement of Mr. Poppert, the Pegu Circle conservator of forests. Poppert's statement was attached to the findings of the Burmese forest officials. When reading Poppert's statement below, one should particularly note his conclusion :

the logs worked out [in the Ningyan Forest] during one year do *not* necessarily come into our [Toungoo Forest Office] books during the same year....I can certify that a very large number of logs were neaped [in the Ningyan Forest] at the end of the floating season 1881-82, and only came into our books in 1882-83.

The registers of the logs despatched [from Toungoo] are made out in two classes, viz., doogies and lozars [dugyis and hlwazas].

These classes are *not* accurate; the logs are *never* measured, nor is any notice taken of the quality of the timber.[109]

Poppert's conclusion was extremely important:

The logs [registered at the Shwegyin Forest Office], which in these statements are called "drift", have already appeared in the [Toungoo Forest Office] despatches of some previous year ...the number of the drift must therefore be *deducted* from the total number of logs shown in these statements.[110]

The Shwegyin Forest Office below Toungoo on the Sittang River had the primary function of retrieving logs that had drifted away from the various teak-*gaungs* or rafts. The Burmese forest officials had inspected the 'drift' record, and had been told that it represented logs already recorded at Toungoo.[111]   There were only a few 'drift' logs, and therefore the three categories of dugyis, hlwazas, and 321 yathits ('shorts') were accurate.[112]

However, the ministers did not appear to be overly concerned with accuracy. They ignored the fact that the Toungoo Forest Office record did *not* differentiate between logs harvested under the three different contracts of 1880, 1882, and 1884. It would be impossible for the record to do so, because logs harvested in the Ningyan Forest often did not reach Toungoo until a year or two later. The ministers also ignored the fact that the Toungoo log sizes were *not* accurate.   But they did not ignore the 321 yathits ('shorts') recorded at Shwegyin even though these had *already* been recorded at Toungoo as either a 'dugyi' or as a 'hlwaza'.[113]

The Judgment stated that the 321 'shorts' were all the 'shorts' that the BBTC had removed under the 1882 'Shorts' Contract. Therefore, the Judgment ruled that the gap of 56,177 logs between the total of the Forest Office, and the total of the BBTC, was composed of 48,326 dugyis and 7,851 hlwazas, which the BBTC had taken out without paying any duty.[114]

The Judgment was correct after a fashion—the BBTC had not shipped many genuine 'shorts'.   The BBTC had cut logs of 4'6" or more in girth into lengths of less than 18'.   The BBTC had bribed local Ningyan Forest Officials to let the logs out free of duty.   The BBTC had provided for a 'loophole' to accommodate the above category of log in both the 1880 and 1882 Contracts.   Indeed, the only limit on the BBTC's export of such logs appeared to be the cupidity—and knowledge—of local Ningyan Forest Officials.

Berthold Ribbentrop, head Indian forester, stated that any thievery of logs at Ningyan "would have necessitated the connivance of local officers."[115]   Such connivance was widely suspected, and would have been almost 'normal' behaviour for many of the Ningyan officials. Most of the officials had bought their posts. The charge-sheet ran from Rs. 5,000 for the *myowun*, governor, down to Rs. 500 for the *ywathugyi*, village officer.[116] Therefore, the original charges against the BBTC were probably correct, namely that the firm had bribed the local officials to let-out thousands of logs without the payment of duty.

In early August, Gov. U Gyi was fired from his post for taking bribes from the BBTC.[117] He was placed in the public stocks like a common criminal.[118] He was probably still in them on August 12 when the Judgment was passed. Despite this, the Judgment ignored the involvement of Gov. U Gyi and other officials in the Ningyan teak-thefts.

Instead, the *Hlutdaw* manipulated the Forest Office figures in a dishonest manner. The ministers were afraid to admit the mutual-guilt of Burmese officials, because it would have cost them 'face', *i.e.* official dignity. The end result was a Judgment, which the Kinwun described as "aligah," nonsense.[119]

The August 12 Judgment fined the BBTC ten lakhs, and in a separate decree the Ningyan Forest leases were cancelled. The alleged 'foresters' were ordered to sue for their moneys separately. The Judgment had *not* ruled on their petitions, despite the fact that the 'foresters' were the ostensible plaintiffs of the Case.[120]

The Teak Case to August 27, 1885

When Andreino returned from the *Hlutdaw* meeting on August 12, he wrote to Jones stating that Haas must have had a hand in the Judgment. The *Hlutdaw* would never have done such a thing, except for Haas' August 3 offer.[121] However, Andreino in his excitement had over-looked one omission in the Judgment. It did not contain the finalizing phrase : "The dispute was ended as both parties ate the pickled-tea offered to them."[122] Without both parties to a dispute having drunk the tea to restore harmony between them, no Judgment was final or binding.[123]

The *Hlutdaw*, according to Grattan Geary, had deliberately left the above phrase out of the Judgment. The ministers had assumed that the BBTC would make an appeal to the King for Royal Review, which was the usual procedure when one of the parties in a dispute refused to accept the court's decision. Therefore, the *Hlutdaw* could not understand the protests, which follow-ed the Judgment. The entire *Hlutdaw* felt insulted by the allega-tions of corruption and malpractice.[124]

In normal times, Andreino would probably have noticed the lack of the important formality within the Judgment. The BBTC would have appealed to King Thebaw for a Royal Review of the Case. The BBTC would have eventually paid several lakhs in 'fines'. This was all the money that the ministers had expected to get, despite the Judgment's fine of ten (later twenty-three) lakhs.[125] However, the times were not normal. Andreino's judgment was apparently twisted by fear of the consequences of Haas' offer to take-over the BBTC's leases. The offer, also, had an adverse effect on the *Hlutdaw*, and gave that body a false sense of euphoria and release.[126]

By nightfall on August 12, the *Hlutdaw* had withdrawn its decision—made earlier in the day—to cancel the BBTC's Ningyan leases. King Thebaw had thought that more money could be gained by passing a larger fine. He stated that at least four to five lakhs could eventually be extracted from the BBTC.[127] If the BBTC refused to pay, the Government could then seize the firm's timber to the amount of the fine, or could easily cancel the leases.[128]

The Taingda and his group took their cue from the King, and immediately proposed an increase in the fine. The Kinwun reali-zed that he had two options. The first option was that the BBTC could fight the increase. The fine would probably be reduced through negotiations to perhaps four or five lakhs. The BBTC would then be tempted to forego an appeal to the Indian Govern-ment, and would probably pay the smaller fine in order to end the case. This would give the Taingda a quick and easy victory over both the BBTC and the Kinwun.[129]

The Kinwun's second option involved the raising of the fine to an outrageous amount. The BBTC would then surely appeal to the Indian Government. If the Indian Government reacted with a vigorous protest, Thebaw would probably realize that the extreme fine and the Judgment were unjust. Thebaw would probably put an end to the Taingda's 'meddling' in the BBTC's affairs. This would restore the rough equilibrium between the Kinwun and the Taingda factions, which had been thrown off-balance by Haas' August 3 offer to take over the BBTC's leases.[130]

The Kinwun, therefore, demanded that the *kala* company be fined Rs. 23,59,066, or about £153, 333. The fine was to be paid in four monthly instalments within four months.[131] The Kinwun's party in the *Hlutdaw*, which included the Taungwin Mingyi, the Hlaythin Atwinwun, the Pangyet, the Myothit Atwinwun, and the Wetmasut Wundauk, gave noisy assent to his proposal. The Taingda's group had proposed a comparatively small increase in the fine, and suddenly found themselves in the unfamiliar position of seeming to be the BBTC's *protector*. Despite their suspicions concerning the Kinwun's motives, the Taingda's group had *no* alternative but to fall into line and vote for the enormous fine.[132]

Bernard's August 28, 1885 Arbitration Request

In response to an August 21 enquiry from Durand, Bernard telegraphed on August 22 that he had not previously asked the Mandalay Government to arbitrate the Teak Case. He had been afraid that they would nominate Haas as the arbitrator. But since the BBTC had been saddled with a large fine of ten lakhs, Bernard proposed to ask the Mandalay Government if they would accept an arbitration of the Case with an arbitrator appointed by Viceroy Lord Dufferin.[133]

Durand approved of the idea. In the meantime, S. G. Jones, the BBTC manager at Rangoon, was trying to enlist Bernard's help in resisting the latest fine of twenty-three lakhs. On August 28, Bernard wrote to the Kinwun to ask if the Manadaly Government would (1) temporarily suspend the Judgment; (2) allow an arbitrator appointed by Lord Dufferin to arbitrate the dispute; and (3) would Mandalay accept the arbitrator's decision?[134]   On August 31, Bernard sent a telegram asking the Burmese Government to "suspend pressure" against Andreino and the other BBTC employees, until the Government had received and considered Bernard's request for arbitration.[135]

Bernard's despatches tended to restore some balance between the Taingda and Kinwun factions, which had been thrown off-balance by Haas' August 3 offer to take over the BBTC's leases. Bernard's despatches also strengthened Andreino's bargaining position, and probably kept him from a physical and nervous collapse.[136]

In theory, the two despatches were unnecessary, because the

1867 Burmese-British Treaty had provided for a Mixed Court at Mandalay to try all cases between Burmese and foreigners.[137] However, after the withdrawal of St. Barbe on October 6, 1879, both Governments had let the Court die without a further session. Therefore, the Indian Government took the position that as there was no Mixed Court to handle the BBTC Teak Case, Viceroy Dufferin would appoint an arbitrator.[138]

This was not a statesman-like proposal. One can only suggest that Bernard should have been instructed to propose a revived Mixed Court composed of the re-established British Resident and the Burmese judge. Mandalay would probably have accepted such a proposal, especially after a bit of sabrerattling from Simla. But of course the proposal was not made. The Indian Government took the stand that in the absence of a functioning Mixed Court the Viceroy would appoint the arbitrator.[139] One can only conclude that the Judgment of August 12 had spawned an equally arbitrary response from the Indian Government.

The Reaction at Mandalay

On September 4, Haas despatched a long telegram concerning the BBTC to Paris through the Mandalay telegraph office. The telegram was in cypher, but the BBTC's name was in plain words. Andreino was apparently informed of the transmission by E. Vengeance, who was the Mandalay telegraph-master and a spy for the Indian Government.[140]

On the evening of September 5, Consul Haas went to the Kinwun's house. Shortly afterwards a rumour swept Mandalay. Haas and Bonvillain, the former common-law husband of Mattie Calogreedy Antram, had apparently offered their services to the Burmese Government in arbitrating the BBTC Case. Such assistance was rumoured to have been accepted, and both men were given power-of-attorney.[141]

On September 12, Haas was in a talkative mood at a dinner party held at General de Facieu's house. Haas claimed that the British Government could not interfere in the BBTC Teak Case, or in any other segment of Upper Burmese affairs. There were now other countries vitally interested in Upper Burma. If the British desired to interfere, they would have to make some prior agreement with France.[142]

Haas remarked that he had tried to give the Mandalay Government good advice upon all possible occasions. However, the Kinwun had always vetoed his ideas, while the Taingda and the other ministers were quite willing to listen and to accept his advice. Haas seemed very annoyed with the Kinwun's attitude.[143]

In short, Haas' offer of August 3 to provide French teak firms in place of the BBTC, and his offer of September 5 to assist in arbitrating the Teak Case, had been emphatically refused.[144] The Kinwun had retained sufficient influence at Court to persuade the *Hlutdaw* and the Royal Couple to ignore Haas' proposals. Bernard's August 28 arbitration request had temporarily prevented the Taingda's group from seizing the BBTC's property in the Ningyan forest. On September 15, Bernard summarized the situation in a letter to Durand, the Indian foreign secretary.

Bernard stated that the ministers would probably scale down their demand for twenty-three lakhs. They would probably also decline any arbitrator appointed by the Indian Government, and would also complain that the BBTC had previously failed to make matters clear. Bernard stated that he did not think the Teak Case was over, "but I do not anticipate that it will assume a very acute form for some little time to come."[145]

In the meantime, no embargo on the export of BBTC logs had occurred. No attempt had been made to expropriate BBTC property, or to physically harm the BBTC's agents or foresters. This was a significant restraint on the part of Mandalay, because the BBTC's establishment in Upper Burma was a tempting prize. It employed several thousand non-British subjects, over 2,000 British subjects, and fifteen to twenty Europeans. The firm had 900 elephants, almost 10,000 buffaloes, and 150,000 teak-logs in the various stages of preparation for export to Lower Burma.[146] The total value of the BBTC's investments in Upper Burma was at least fifty to seventy-five lakhs.

In Bernard's view, the lull in the Teak Case did not touch upon the main issue so far as the British Government was concerned. The main issue was the French attempt to gain ascendancy in Upper Burma. The Burmese Government had temporarily ignored Haas' proposals. This was due in part to the Kinwun's advice, and partly due to the Government's preoccupation with the continued 'drought'. The first rice-sowing and other crops were said to have failed in the area extending from sixty miles north of the Lower Burma border to sixty miles north of Mandalay.[147]

However, the 'drought' would not last forever. The French would become extremely active once the proposed Bank and Railroad Contracts were approved along with the January 15, 1885 Treaty. If the Bank and Railroad were actually constructed, Mandalay would become a French dependency in a few years' time.[148]

This was a significant modification of the earlier views which Bernard had expressed in an August 11 letter to Durand. In that letter Bernard stated that once the contracts were granted "within three or four years, Frenchmen and Agents of the French Government would become paramount in Upper Burma.....any resistance on the part of the King would only fasten the French yoke tighter."[149]

Bernard concluded his September 15 letter by stating that such a dire prophecy might not take place. However, even if the British Resident was re-established at Mandalay, he would be in a constant struggle with the French Consul for supremacy, or for some kind of an understanding.[150]

On September 20, Andreino wrote to Jones that it appeared that the Taingda's group had persuaded the *Hlutdaw* to reject Bernard's August 28 request for arbitration. The Royal Couple did not believe that the Indian Government was serious in its request. Most of the ministers thought that a courteous rejection of Bernard's letter would bring out the Indian Government's real demands. Serious negotiations could then take place, and the Indian Government would probably compromise by proposing a foreign arbitrator acceptable to both sides.[151]

The Kinwun asked Supayalat's mother, the Dowager Queen, to persuade the Royal Couple to accept Bernard's request for arbitration, and to show mercy to the BBTC. The Kinwun knew that if the Indian Government took forcible steps, such as an ultimatum, his enemies at Court would blame him for the crisis—because it had been his idea for the twenty-three lakhs fine.[152]

The Dowager Queen's appeal failed. The Kinwun had known that it would, but at least he had cleared himself of any blame should an explosion occur as the result of the rejection.[153] A few hours later on September 21 the *Hlutdaw* rejected Bernard's letter, and the Taingda's group began to seize the BBTC's property in the Ningyan Forest.

The BBTC's first instalment on the twenty-three lakhs fine was due by September 22. The Pouk Myine Atwinwun's fine-order of August 23 had stated that if the BBTC did not keep up to schedule in its four monthly payments, the Burmese Government would confiscate the firm's timber to the amount of the fine still owed. The Pouk Myine Atwinwun and Taingda ordered the troops stationed in the Ningyan Forest to fire on the BBTC's teak-rafts. Several rafts-men were beaten, some were arrested, and a number of teak-rafts were seized.[154]

The new Ningyan Governor had forbade such incidents. But his orders were ignored as the soldiers considered their orders from the Finance and Taingda Ministers to be superior.[155] The incident reflected the power-struggle going on at Mandalay. The new Governor was a Kinwun appointee, and a good friend of the BBTC,[156] while the soldiers—also recently despatched from Mandalay—were loyal to the Taingda's group.

The new Governor sent a strong protest concerning the incident to Mandalay. In the meantime, the BBTC solved the problem nicely by paying "a considerable amount of blackmail" to the Burmese soldiers in order that the teak-rafts might pass down the Sittang River into Lower Burma.[157] The BBTC was allowed to continue its teak operations until early-November.

Then the approach of war prompted the BBTC officials at Ningyan to escape into Lower Burma. H. Fielding-Hall, a BBTC employee, was caught by the Burmese frontier-post, but paid a bribe for himself and his crew, and got *drunk* with the post-commander before resuming his escape down the Sittang River.[158]

S. G. Jones, the Rangoon BBTC manager, wrote in reference to the Ningyan Governor that "we consider him good man."[159] The Governor, Maung Shway Gaung, had once been *akunwun*, treasurer, of Hanthawaddy (Rangoon) District under the British. However, in July 1856 he had loaded about Rs. 1,75,000 of the Rangoon treasury on elephants and escaped to Upper Burma.[160] During the Third Burmese War, the Governor protected BBTC men who fell into his hands.[161]

Mandalay Accepts 'Unofficial' Arbitration

On October 3, the Kinwun despatched the official rejection of Bernard's August 28 request for arbitration of the Teak Case. There is evidence that Taingda had second thoughts about the rejection, which he had inspired. It appears that Taingda, or a spokesman, told the correspondent of *The Times of India* that Taingda was *perfectly willing* to have Bernard as the arbitrator.[162] This news-item was the first of a series of newspaper-reports concerning six or more 'unofficial' efforts by Taingda and other officials to obtain a settlement of the Teak Case.[163]

They were *eager* to settle the Case, but they were not willing to say so officially in the October 3 reply to Bernard. They feared that an official acceptance of arbitration would imply that the *Hlutdaw's* Judgment, and fine order of twenty-three lakhs, had not been entirely proper. They knew that an investigation of the Case would show that the *Hlutdaw* had manipulated the forest reports in a dishonest manner. This had been done in order to avoid admitting the mutual guilt of Burmese officials in the teak thefts; an admission that the *Hlutdaw* feared would cost them 'face' or official dignity.

Then, too, the arbitration request was as unfair as the Judgment that had inspired it. For example, the Indian Government's arbitrator was not mentioned by name. The *Hlutdaw* knew with the exception of Bernard, an "independent person", or a Mixed Court, that they had no real chance of receiving a 'fair' settlement with an Indian Government arbitrator. Perhaps *Andreino* was the arbitrator that the Indian Government had in mind?

The Taingda had one additional motive for pushing the official rejection through the *Hlutdaw*. If he had supported arbitration, or if the *Hlutdaw* had supported it, Taingda would have lost 'face'. He would have been shown to be wrong, and the Kinwun would have been shown to be correct. The Taingda and his group would have received the blame for having started the BBTC Case, and for having been the cause of 'grave misunderstandings' between the Indian and Burmese Governments. His removal from power—or worse—would have been the obvious 'face'-saving device by which relations would have been restored to their former cordiality.

The Kinwun spent about one week drafting the October 3 rejection. He restated the arguments of the August 12 Judgment. He then concluded that there was no reason or occasion for the Indian Government to ask whether his Government would or would not abide by any decision of any arbitrator appointed by Viceroy Dufferin. Therefore, the Mandalay Government wished the Indian Government to know that there would be no suspension or change in any Judgment, fine order, or other action taken against the BBTC.[164]

The Indian Government was aware that the Kinwun's reply was an official 'face'-saving device, and that the Teak Case was virtually settled. The Mandalay Government had ignored Hass' August 3 offer to provide French firms in place of the BBTC, and also his September 5 offer to arbitrate the Case.

On about October 9, the Pouk Myine Atwinwun, the Mandalay finance minister, told Andreino that the BBTC could easily settle the Case within a few days by petitioning King Thebaw for a Royal Review. The firm would have paid—at most—a couple of lakhs in 'fines', and the Case would have been closed. This latest 'unofficial' offer to settle the Case and the six or more 'unofficial' offers made in the Indian and London press were brought to the attention of the Indian Government.[165]

The truth was that the Indian and London Governments would not allow a settlement to take place. The official Burmese refusal of arbitration was a "convenient pretext" so tempting that it could not be ignored.[166] An Ultimatum could now be addressed to Mandalay that would eliminate French influence in Upper Burma, and also eliminate the "Shoe Question" and other problems.

FOOTNOTES

[1] Joseph Dautremer, (trans. by Sir J. G. Scott), *Burma Under British Rule*, London, 1912, p. 73. Dautremer added on p. 71 that: "The idea of the French Consul in Mandalay to make Upper Burma an annexe of French Indo-China was clearly the idea of a patriot, and for this he deserves praise."

[2] That is: Rs. 2,359,066 or about £153,333. A lakh or lac is 100,000.

[3] *See* 1867 Burmese-British Treaty (Article V); and Mixed Court Rules, July 26, 1869 in Appendix C.

[4] K. W. No. 1, Forbes' Remarks Attached to Bernard's October 16, 1885 Memorandum, October 28, 1885; in Foreign, Secret-E, August 1886, Nos. 428-520, p. 1 (NAI).

[5] R. R. Langham-Carter, "Burmese Rule on the Toungoo Frontier," p. 24.

[6] *Ibid.*

[7] "Everyone knows that it was never intended that they [BBTC] were to get the timber so cheap, and that they had to pay large sums in the way of

incidentals." "Upper Burma Affairs," (Roorkee) *The Indian Forester*, Vol. XII, No. 2, February 1886, pp. 83-84.

8 No. 501, Mandalay Diary, January 25, 1875; in Foreign, Political-A, March 1875, Nos. 499-505 (NAI).

9 No. 148, Mandalay Diary, February 26, 1873; in Foreign, Political-A, April 1873, Nos. 140-159 (NAI).

10 No. 47, Mandalay Diary, May 14, 1874; in Foreign, Political-A, July 1874, Nos. 46-50 (NAI). *See:* End of Chapter V and Appendix B.

11 A. C. Pointon, *The Bombay-Burmah Trading Corporation....*, p. 13.

12-13 *Ibid.*

14 R. R. Langham-Carter, "Burmese Rule on the Toungoo Frontier," p. 24.

15 "Upper Burma Forest Leases," (Roorkee) *The Indian Forester,* Vol. XIV, No. 7, July 1888, p. 334. (*See also:* No. 58, 1880 Variable Duty Contract; in Foreign, Secret-E, September 1885, Nos. 27-97 (NAI).)

16-19 *Ibid*, p. 335.

20 No. 43, Andreino to Jones, September 6, 1885 ; in Foreign, Secret-E, January 1886, Nos. 37-63 (NAI).

21 *Ibid.*

22 No. 58, The 1880 Variable Duty Contract; in Nos. 27-97.

23 No. 59, The 1882 'Shorts' Contract; in Nos. 27-97.

24 Jones to Bernard's Secretary, February 8, 1886; in No. 1 of February 1886 Upper Burma Forest Proceedings, p. 7; bound within Vol. 2664A, Military, Forests, Foreign, Finance and Commerce Proceedings for Upper Burma-1886 (IOL).

25 "Upper Burma Forest Leases," p. 335. "The complaint of Mr. Jones that this second contract was forced on them seems to indicate that the........ [BBTC] was obliged to agree to the terms in consequence of some other parties offering to compete with them for the working out of the large-sized short timber omitted from the first lease, and there was a report in Burma that such was really the case."

26 No. 59, The 1882 'Shorts' Contract; in Nos. 27-97.

27 *Ibid.* The italicising was not in the original.

28 The 1880 Contract read in the context of Royal timber: "If the Bombay-Burma Co. do not wish to purchase the said timber it may be disposed of as the authorities may desire." However, virtually all BBTC timber was worked out by their own men and elephants. No such rejection clause was stated in the context of non-Royal timber.

29 *Ibid.*

30 No. 59, The 1882 'Shorts' Contract; in No. 27-97. Italics added.

31 No. 87, Bernard's Secretary to Durand, August 31, 1885; in Nos. 27-97.

32 'Tectona Grandis', "The Teak Monopoly in Burma," (Roorkee) *The Indian Forester*, Vol. XII, No. 2, February 1886, p. 81. Italics not in the original.

[33] "Upper Burma Forest Leases," p. 334. Italicising not in the original.

[33-35] *Ibid.*, pp. 334-335.

[36] K. W. No. 1, Ribbentrop's Comment on Bernard's February 3, 1886 Letter; in Foreign, Secret-E, August, 1886, Nos. 650-703, p. 1 (NAI).

[37] No. 60, The 1884 'Lump Sum' Contract; in Nos 26-97.

[38] *Ibid.* That is: Rs. 528,000 and Rs. 772,000.

[39] No. 702, Govt. of India to Sec. of State, India, June 25, 1886; in Nos. 650-703, p. 2. (The figures in £ are for comparison only, as actual payments were usually made in rupees. Eight lakhs at 1885 valuation was £53,328; one lakh equalled £6,666. John Nisbet, *Burma Under British Rule—And Before*, Vol. 1, p. 78).

[40] *Ibid.*

[41-42] *Ibid.* (The BBTC paid an average of about Rs. 10.50 on each log taken out of Upper Burma under the terms of the 1880 Variable Duty Contract. It cost five or six rupees to ship the log to Rangoon where it could be easily sold for Rs. 30-40 (even an inferior log brought this much!) The BBTC paid a little over Rs. 11 per ton of teak in Upper Burma. The BBTC sold a ton of finished teak lumber delivered in Europe for £60. In contrast, the rival teak-firms in the Red Karen Forest above Moulmein had to pay Rs. 85 for the log in the forest that the BBTC was able to get in Upper Burma for only Rs. 10.50. "Rangoon," (Allahabad) *Pioneer Mail*, October 3, 1883, p. 335. *See also*: "Rangoon Correspondent," (Calcutta) *Statesman*, October 24, 1882, p. 1508. *Also: Ibid*, May 15, 1883, p. 700; and *Ibid*, September 1, 1883, p. 1260.)

[43] *Ibid.*

[44] K. W. No. 3, Ribbentrop's Additional Comments on Bernard's February 3, 1886 Letter ; in Nos. 650-703, p. 21.

[45] No. 702 ; in Nos. 650-703, p. 2.

[46-47] *Ibid.*

[48] K. W. No. 1, MacKenzie to Durand, February 13, 1886 ; in Nos. 650-703, p. 8-9. MacKenzie was Home Secretary to the Indian Government.

[49] *Ibid.* MacKenzie wrote that the BBTC would never have been allowed to ship out so much timber without any payment. The local Burmese officials would have intercepted it, and taken a 'cut' before allowing the timber to float down into Lower Burma.

[50] No. 702, Government of India to Secretary of State-India, June 25, 1886 ; in Nos. 650-703, p. 2.

[51] No. 2, Dufferin to Churchill, January 12, 1886 ; in Dufferin Papers, Reel 517/18, p. 5. (*Also see* : No. 34, Moylan to Bernard's Secretary, February 5, 1886 ; in Foreign, Secret-E, November, 1886, Nos. 1-65 (NAI).)

[52] *Ibid.*

[53] The rains again failed during the first rice-sowing season in late-1885, but returned to 'normal' in time for the second rice-sowing in January 1886. The rains remained 'normal' for five or six years until they began to decline once more in the early 1890's.

[54] No. 702, Government of India to Secretary of State-India, June 25, 1886 ; in Nos. 650-703, p. 2.

[55] No. 67, Andreino to Jones, June 14, 1885 ; in Nos. 27-97. *Also see* : Andrews to Jones, August 27, 1885 ; in Nos. 27-97, pp. 9-10.

[56] No. 62, Report of Andreino's Meeting With Three Mingyis, no date ; in Nos. 27-97.

[57] No. 177, Bryce to Churchill, August 17, 1885 ; in Foreign, Secret-E, October 1885, Nos. 164-186.

[58] No. 63, Jones to Bernard's Secretary, October 21, 1885 ; in Foreign, Secret-E, January 1886, Nos. 37-63 (NAI).

[59] No. 682, Annexure Y, BBTC Loans to Burmese Government, March 24, 1885 ; in Nos. 650-703.

[60] Andreino (Andrews) to Jones, June 23, 1885 ; in Nos. 27-97. Andrews, BBTC liaison, wrote that "Andreino is still of the opinion he expressed some months ago that the Corporation need not make........further payments until April next."

[61] No. 45, Jones to Bernard's Secretary, April 21, 1885 ; in Nos. 27-97.

[62] "Burma", (Calcutta) *Englishman*, January 30, 1880, p. 3. *See also* : R. R. Langham-Carter "Burmese Rule on the Toungoo Frontier," p. 24.

[63] No. 46, Bernard's Secretary to Kinwun, April 22, 1885 ; in Nos. 27-97.

[64] No. 47, Kinwun to Bernard, May 17, 1885 ; in Nos. 27-97.

[65-68] *Ibid.*

[69] No. 48, Jones to Bernard, May 25, 1885 ; in Nos. 27-97.

[70] No. 49, Bernard's Secretary to Kinwun, June 17, 1885 ; in Nos. 27-97.

[71] *Ibid.*

[72] *Ibid.* The true dugyi, which the above was not, was a log 4'6" or more in girth, and 30' or more in length. The true hlwaza, which the above was not, was a log 4'6" or more in girth, and with a length of 18' or more but less than 30'.

[73] *Ibid.* It was the italicized category of 'stump' which was the 'loophole' in both the 1880 and 1882 Contracts. The BBTC extracted large amounts of true dugyis and true hlwazas, sawed them into lengths of less than eighteen feet, and after bribing local Ningyan officials, got the 'stumps' out free of duty.

[74-75] *Ibid.*

[76] No. 70, Petition of 342 BBTC Foresters, no date; in Nos. 27-97.

[77] No. 69, Telegram from BBTC Agent, Ningyan, to Jones, BBTC Rangoon Manager, June 12, 1885; in Nos. 27-97.

[78] No. 70; in Nos. 27-97.

[79] No. 49; in Nos. 27-97.

[80] No. 72, Andreino (Louis Andrews) to Jones, June 23, 1885; in Nos. 27-97. Andrews was the secret BBTC liaison between Mandalay and Rangoon. In order to avoid being discovered should the letter fall into Burmese hands, Andrews wrote it as though it had been despatched by Andreino.

[81] *Ibid.* U Kyi had been the Kinwun's secret envoy, who had arrived 'too late' to see Lord Ripon at Rangoon on December 28, 1881. The 1882 Treaty Conference had followed. U Kyi had been the Rangoon commercial agent since about May 15, 1883.

[82] *Ibid.*

[83] No. 73, Andreino to Jones, July 8, 1885; in Nos. 27-97.

[84] Nos. 52-55, Copies of Royal Orders Summoning Foresters to Mandalay; in Nos. 27-97.

[85] *Ibid.*

[86] No. 73; in Nos. 27-97.

[87-88] *Ibid.*

[89] Philippe Preschez, "Les Relations...," p. 361. [trans. excerpt from *Correspondance politique* Mandalay, folio 38-46 (7 juil 1885).] New Herbrides was a French colony.

[90] *Ibid.*

[91] *Ibid.*

[92] *Ibid.*, p. 362.

[93] *Ibid.*, [trans. excerpts from *Correspondance politique* Mandalay, folio 74-83 (12 aout 1885).]

[94-98] *Ibid.*

[99] *Ibid.* [trans. excerpt from *Correspondance politique* Mandalay, folio 134-138 (17 octobre 1885).]

[100] Andrews to Jones, August 24, 1885; in Nos. 27-97, pp. 11-12.

[101] *Ibid.*

[102] *Ibid.*

[103] No. 76, Andreino to Jones, August 9, 1885; in Nos. 27-97.

[104] No. 78, Andreino to Jones, August 12, 1885; in Nos. 27-97.

[105-06] *Ibid.*

[107] No. 86, Judgment Against the BBTC, August 12, 1885; in Nos. 27-97. *See:* Appendix E.

[108] *Ibid.*

[109] No. 82, Mr. Poppert's Statement, n.d.; in Nos. 27-97. Italics added.

[110] *Ibid.*

[111] No. 84, Andreino to Jones, August 15, 1885; in Nos. 27-97.

[112] No. 81, Jones to Bernard, August 21, 1885; in Nos. 27-97.

[113-14] *Ibid.* The 1882 'Shorts' Contract was ignored in the Judgment, except for the highly convenient 321 'yathits'. The October 19, 1884 'Lump Sum' Contract was completely ignored in the Judgment. The 19,000 logs taken-out under the 'Lump Sum' Contract between October 19, 1884 and April 13, 1885 were all considered to be part of the 1880 Variable Duty Contract. Therefore, according to the Judgment, duty was due on them. *See:* No. 63, Jones to Bernard's Secretary, October 21, 1885; in Nos. 36-37.

[115] K. W. No. 1, Ribbentrop's Comment on Bernard's February 3, 1886 letter; in Nos. 650-703, p. 1.

[116] R. R. Langham-Carter, "Burmese Rule on the Toungoo Frontier," pp. 16-24.

[117] *Ibid.,* p. 21.

[118] "Burma News" (Allahabad) *Pioneer Mail,* August 16, 1885, p. 153.

[119] No. 63, Jones to Bernard's Secretary, October 21, 1885; in Nos. 37-63.

[120] No. 86, Judgment Against the BBTC, August 12, 1885; in Nos. 27-97. Later, the BBTC was ordered to set aside an additional five lakhs (£33,333) for the 'foresters', the amounts due to each 'forester' to be determined by the outcome of their individual suits against the BBTC. The five lakhs fine was in addition to the general fine of ten and later Rs. 23,59,066 (£153,333).

[121] No. 78, Andreino to Jones, August 12, 1885; in Nos. 27-97. *See also:* No. 67, Andreino to Jones, June 14; in Nos. 27-97. The names of other Upper and Lower Burma businessmen, who had been mulcted by the Pouk Myine and the Taingda ministers. These two had become so powerful that they had even victimized the Kinwun's relative, the Shway Laung Peh-hnin, who had once owned the 1882 cotton monopoly with the Yanaung Mintha. In what was really an attack upon the Kinwun, the two ministers had revoked the Shway Laung Peh-hnin's contract to raise rice near Kyaukse, and had thereby caused "his entire ruin." Finally, Maung Mon Saw and other British subjects with Upper Burma teak contracts would lose them if the fine attempt against the BBTC was successful.

[122] Grattan Geary, *Burma After the Conquest,* p. 95.

[123] *Ibid.*

[124] *Ibid.*

[125] *Ibid,* pp. 135-136.

[126] To understand the Burmese psychological make-up at such a moment, one might refer to: Lucien Pye, *Politics, Personality and Nation Building,* pp. 71, 141-142, 149-150, 156-157, 167-170, and 180.

[127] No. 83, Andreino to Jones, August 13, 1885; in Nos. 27-97. *Also see:* No. 84, Andreino to Jones, August 15, 1885; in Nos. 27-97.

[128] *Ibid.*

[129] Andrews to Jones, August 23, 1885; in Nos. 27-97, pp. 10-11.

[130] *Ibid.* The Kinwun's group upon this occasion included the Taungwin Mingyi, one of the three senior ministers at Mandalay and co-organizer with the Taingda of the September 21-22, 1884 'Jailbreak' Massacre. Another member was the Hlaythin Atwinwun, son-in-law of the Taingda and one of the six organizers, including the Taingda, of the February 15-17, 1879 Royal Massacre. Another member was the Pangyet, who was the son-in-law of the Taingda, and the head of the 1882 Mission to Simla. Still another member was the Wetmasut Wundauk, No. 3 man in the 1882 Simla Mission. Another supporter on the BBTC issue was the Myothit Atwinwun, head of the 1883-1885 Mission to Paris.

[131] No. 95, The Pouk Myine Atwinwun's Fine Order, August 23, 1885; in Nos. 27-97.

[132] Andrews to Jones, August 23, 1885; in Nos. 27-97, pp. 10-11. *See also:* Grattan Geary, *Burma After the Conquest*, pp. 135-136.

[133] No. 31, Telegram from Bernard to Durand, August 22, 1885; in Nos. 27-97.

[134] No. 88, Bernard's Secretary to Kinwun, August 28, 1885; in Nos. 27-97.

[135] No. 94, Bernard to Kinwun, August 31, 1885; in Nos. 27-97.

[136] K. W. No. 2, Andrews to Bernard's Secretary, August 29, 1885; in Nos. 27-97, p. 9.

[137] Rules of the Mandalay Mixed Court, July 26, 1869. *See* Appendix C.

[138] No. 88, Bernard's Secretary to Kinwun, August 28, 1885; in Nos. 27-97. (*See also:* K. W. No. 1, Forbes' comment on Bernard's October 16, 1885 Memo, October 28, 1885; in Nos. 428-520.)

[139] *Ibid.*

[140] No. 43, Andreino to Jones, September 6, 1885; in Nos. 37-63. *See also:* Foreign, Secret-E, July 1884, No. 48 (NAI). *Lastly:* Foreign, Secret-E, October 1884. Nos. 264-269 (NAI).)

[141] *Ibid.*

[142] No. 137, Andreino to Jones, September 13, 1885; in Foreign, Secret-E, October 1885, Nos. 134-159 (NAI). De Facieu was a general in Thebaw's army, and had served in the British-Indian Army during the 1857 Mutiny.

[143] *Ibid.* (Unfortunately for Haas, he had an Indian Government spy as a frequent guest at his house from July through early-September. E.M. Pascal, the former Burmese Consul at Calcutta during King Mindon's reign, planted a letter in the August 31, 1885 Rangoon *Gazette* that claimed that the Taingda had called Haas a *quaymatha,* son of a bitch. The Taingda said later that he could not recall having said such a thing. The incident was not true, but it shows how little 'threat' Haas really was to British interests at Mandalay. *See* : No. 147, Andreino to Jones, September 16, 1885; in Nos. 134-159. *Also see:* No. 199, Pascal's Report to Bernard, September 18, 1885; in Foreign, Secret-E, October 1885, Nos. 198-200 (NAI). *Lastly:* No. 56, Jones to Moylan, September 19, 1885; in Foreign, Secret-E, November 1885, Nos. 55-56 (NAI). *See* Appendix J.)

[144] *Ibid.*

[145] No. 41, Bernard to Durand, September 15, 1885; in Nos. 37-63.

[146] *Ibid.* As was shown earlier, the BBTC had 'girdled' 500,000 trees during 1885. It is almost inconceivable that there were not at least 100,000 additional logs which had been felled, or were in the process of being dragged to the streams, or were awaiting shipment. Therefore, one should conclude that instead of 150,000 logs, the BBTC had probably 600,000 logs being prepared for export.

[147] *Ibid.* (Mr. Cabaniss, the asst. director of agriculture in Lower Burma, disagreed. He viewed the 'drought' as a series of districts of local scarcity separated by districts of comparative plenty. Cabaniss claimed after a

brief ten-day trip to Mandalay in September 1885 that there was no shortage of food in the river-towns. He stated that "the cultivators expressed no anxiety, the only persons with gloomy forebodings being the Europeans." He was told by river-town Burmese that the crops along the Irrawaddy had failed; however, the crops inland were said to be better. Cabaniss concluded that even if the rains failed again during the second rice-sowing there would be only "a local scarcity in certain districts." "Scarcity in British Burma," (Calcutta) *Englishman*, October 10, 1885, p. 4.)

[148] *Ibid.*

[149] No. 100, Bernard to Durand, August 11, 1885 ; in Foreign, Secret-E, September 1885, Nos. 98-106 (NAI).

[150] No. 41, Bernard to Durand, September 15, 1885; in Nos. 37-63.

[151] No. 153, Andreino to Jones, September 20, 1885; in Nos. 134-159.

[152-153] *Ibid.*

[154] Enclosure 2 in No. 124, Telegram from Bernard to Durand, September 24, 1885; in C. 4614, p. 212.

[155] *Ibid. See also :* H. Fielding-Hall, *A Nation At School,* London, 1906, pp. 35-44.

[156] H. T. White, *A Civil Servant in Burma,* London, 1914, pp. 112-114.

[157] K. W. No. 3, Winser to BBTC-Rangoon, October 12, 1885; in Foreign, Secret-E, January 1886; in Nos. 216-283, p. 3 (NAI).

[158] H. Fielding-Hall, *A Nation At School,* pp. 35-44.

[159] Enclosure 3 in No. 125, Jones to Bernard's Secretary, September 22, 1885; in C. 4614, p. 217.

[160] H. T. White, *A Civil Servant in Burma,* pp. 112-114.

[161] *Ibid.* The power-struggle between the Kinwun and the Taingda was on virtually all fronts. During September, the Hlaythin Atwinwun, a son-in-law of the Taingda, but a Kinwun supporter, took an army out of Mandalay and arrested 1,000 of the Taingda's 'dacoits'. The 'dacoits' said they should not be punished, because they only worked for Taingda, who got most of the plunder. The Kinwun having made his point agreed with the Taingda's plea that the 'dacoits' be shown mercy. They were released after swearing allegiance to King Thebaw, and after having a dacoit tatoo placed on their forehead. If ever caught robbing again, the mark would be their death-warrant.

Nothing was done about tatooing the forehead of the Head Dacoit. However, King Thebaw once asked a local magistrate about the 'dacoit' problem. The magistrate gave a witty reply, which hinged on the word post, *taing* (da). "Oh, your Majesty, they are hiding behind a large *taing*." See: Taw Sein Ko, *Burmese Sketches*, Rangoon, 1913, p. 46. *Also see:* Grattan Geary, *Burma After the Conquest*, pp. 327-328. *Lastly:* No. 56, Jones to Moylan, September 19, 1885; in Nos. 55-56.

[162] "Burmah," (Bombay) *The Times of India*, October 2, 1885, p. 2.

[163] (i) The Kinwun was willing to have a Mixed Court settle the Teak Case.

"The Burmese Question," (Allahabad) *Pioneer Mail*, October 7, 1885, p. 336.

(ii)   The Pouk Myine Atwinwun, who had instigated the Teak Case with the Taingda, told Andreino to petition the King for Royal Review. This would settle the Case quickly. K. W. No. 3(8), Andreino to Jones, October 11, 1885; in Foreign, Secret-E, January 1886, Nos. 216-283, pp. 11-12 (NAI).

(iii)   On October 12, Edmund Kimber, London lawyer, stated in a letter to *The Times* that he had been consulted by agents of King Thebaw. The Burmese King was very willing to have some "independent person" arbitrate the Teak Case. Kimber's Letter, (London) *The Times*, October 12, 1885, editorial page. The letter was reprinted as: "A Defense of King Thebaw," (Calcutta) *Englishman*, November 13, 1885, p. 7.

(iv)   The fine for twenty-three lakhs was, probably, to be reduced to six. The Mandalay Government was so frightened of the impending invasion that they would do anything to keep it away. "The Situation in Burma," (Bombay) *The Times of India*, October 23, 1885, p. 14.

   (v)   The Kinwun asked the BBTC to "humbly petition" King Thebaw, and he would cancel the August 12, 1885 Judgment and the fine of twenty-three lakhs. The offer was made just before the Mandalay Government *officially* rejected the British Ultimatum. "The Burma Crisis," (Calcutta) *Englishman*, November 12, 1885, p. 4. (More 'unofficial' offers by the Tangyet in Chapter VIII).

[164]   K. W. No. 3, Kinwun to Bernard, October 3, 1885; in Nos. 37-63, pp. 8-10.

[165]   K. W. No. 3 (8), Andreino to Jones, October 11, 1885; in Nos. 216-283, pp, 11-12. *See also :* Grattan Geary, *Burma After the Conquest*, pp. 135-136. The *Hlutdaw* apparently ordered the Pouk Myine Atwinwun to ask Andreino to petition for a Royal Review. *See :* The Tangyet's Paris 'feelers' in Chapter VIII.

[166]   *Ibid.   Also see :* Joseph Dautremer, *Burma Under British Rule*, p. 73.

8

The Ultimatum

Introduction

By October 17, 1885, the British Government had decided to make demands of Mandalay that it halt the advance of French interests in Upper Burma. This decision was in direct contrast to Churchill's August 7 letter to Dufferin. In that letter Churchill had stated that Thebaw was to be left strictly alone, while the British Government demanded explanations of Paris concerning the continued French advance at Mandalay. The evolution in the thinking of both Dufferin and Churchill from August 7 to October 17 will be summarized in the following sections.

The 'French Threat' as an Eastern Counterpart of the 'Russian Threat'

But first it is necessary to make a broad sweep over some of England's other world commitments in 1885. This is necessary because the 'French Threat' to Upper Burma, and the concern that it caused among British officials, can be understood only within the larger context of England's defence problems. The 'French Threat' to Upper Burma and to India's eastern frontier appeared to be the eastern counterpart of the 'Russian Threat' to Persia, Afghanistan, and to India's northwest. In short, the British Government was afraid that India was about to become a 'pipkin' ground between two large pots, one Russian and the other French.[1]

During the late-nineteenth century, the defence of India from a possible attack by Russia was the second greatest military concern of the British Government next to the defence of the British Isles.[2] However, it is only recently that historians have begun to give this fact due weight in their historical presentations.[3]   The truth was that Great Britain was over-extended around the world, and it was estimated that only 36,000 troops could have been spared from Britain, itself, in case of war with Russia.[4]

Afghanistan was one of the few places in the world where the British might have been able to attack Russia with some chance of success.[5]   By the same criteria, Russian armies were thought to be capable of moving virtually unopposed through Afghanistan—and down into India.   Lord Roberts, C. in C. of the Indian Army from 1885-1892, thought that the Indian Army would be hard put to stop them.[6]

In 1884, the Russians annexed Merv, an important city just north of Afghanistan. 'Mervousness' had been a term of derision applied during the 1870's and early-1880's to those who had viewed with alarm the steady Russian-advance across Turkestan towards Merv and India's northwest.   But the British Government, itself, became infected with 'Mervousness' after the fall of Merv.   On March 30, 1885, Russian troops defeated Afghan troops at Penjdeh, an oases even closer to the almost legendary city of Herat, which had been 'the Key to India' for numerous *conquerors* of India.[7]

The Russian victory at Penjdeh greatly excited the London Government, coming as it did immediately after the death of Gen. 'Chinese' Gordon and the fall of Khartoum in January 1885.   Prime Minister Gladstone asked Parliament for a war-grant of £ 11,000,000. This was probably the largest such request in the seventy years since Waterloo.   However, Gladstone was ousted from power in June 1885, and Lord Salisbury formed a Conservative Government until the November-December 1885 Election.[8]

The Afghans, in the meantime, said that their muzzle-loading rifles had been rendered useless by the rains at Penjdeh, while the Russians had been armed with new breech-loaders.[9]   Arms shipments were sent to the Afghan Government under Amir Abdur Rahman. During the summer of 1885, it was thought that the Russians might march upon Herat, 'the Key to India', and that the city was then *indefensible*.[10]   Salisbury sent off several warnings to the

Russians that such a march on or conquest of Herat would mean war between the two countries.[11]

Salisbury threatened war, but he did not think that the Russians would begin one immediately. He thought that they would postpone a war for a couple of years until they had extended their railroads a bit further into Turkestan.[12] Once that was done, the Russian troops and supplies could ride all the way to Afghanistan's northern frontier.

Suddenly, on September 10, 1885, the Russians gave tentative approval to the Afghan-British version of about 300 miles of the Afghan boundary.[13] Eight days later, on September 18, a revolt broke out in Eastern Roumelia in the Balkans against Turkish rule.[14] The Roumelians immediately united with Bulgaria ruled by Prince Alexander of Battenberg, who had strongly resisted both Turkish and Russian influences in his Balkan kingdom.

The revolt in Eastern Roumelia was probably no surprise to the Russian Government.[15] The threat of war between Russia and Great Britain over Herat temporarily subsided, because the Russians were faced with a new 'anti-Russian' power in the Balkans that blocked the Russian thrust towards Constantinople and control of the Dardanelles.[16] Scarcely had the Russian pressure lessened against India's northwest, when French pressure began to build anew *against India's eastern frontier.*

Churchill Wants New Markets in Order to Win the 1885 Elections

In late-September and early-October 1885, the Paris Government had denied all official responsibility for the proposed Bank and Railroad Contracts, and for the actions of its Consul at Mandalay. Despite such denials, French activities at Mandalay appeared to be an eastern counterpart of the 'Russian Threat'. It was (1) the 'French Threat', and (2) the Paris Government's denial of such that caused Churchill to revise his August 7 stand against intervention in Upper Burma.

However, there was a third major factor fused with the above two factors. This factor was Churchill's ambition to see the Conservatives as the victors in the 1885 Elections to be held in late-November and early-December. In Churchill's view, victory could be gained by securing new markets in Asia and in Southern China.[17]

The new markets would revive the depressed industries of Birmingham, Manchester, Sheffield, and other British manufacturing cities, which had been hard hit by the rising commercial competition from newly-industrialized nations, such as Germany, the United States, and France. The new markets of Yunnan and Southern China would re-employ thousands of unemployed British workingmen, and help the Conservatives to win the 1885 and future Elections.[18]

Churchill was also running against John Bright, Britain's most famous 'radical', for a Commons seat from a depressed workingmen's district in Birmingham. It was Churchill's ambitions for himself and his party that prompted him to order Dufferin not to miss any opportunities for opening new markets in Yunnan and in Southern China.[19]

Dufferin had formerly been the No. 2 man in the India Office, Gov. Gen. of Canada, Ambassador to Russia and to The Porte, and British High Commissioner in Egypt in 1882. He was a highly skilled diplomat, and was sensitive to even the slightest nuances of policy emanating from his superiors.[20] Dufferin, therefore, accepted Churchill's desire to throw open new markets in Yunnan and in Southern China. Among the several letters between the two men on the subject, the following are the most important.

On August 14, 1885, Dufferin wrote to Churchill and stated that military plans were available for the invasion of Upper Burma, in case the Yunnan markets could not be gained by peaceful means. The real obstacle to a 'Forward Policy' on India's eastern frontier was the continued controversy between India and Russia over Herat that threatened to explode into war at any moment.[21]

The Indian Government simply could *not* afford to become involved, either militarily or financially, on both the northwest and on the east at the same time. Even if there had not been the confrontation with Russia over Herat, the Indian Government was already experiencing severe financial difficulties. The lack of funds had forced a general cutback and retrenchment in railroad building throughout India.[22]

The lack of funds was also the chief obstacle to the proposed Moulmein to Yunnan Railroad, which its promoters claimed would throw open the markets of Yunnan and Southern China to British subjects' trade.[23] The promoters had suggested that the Railroad should run by way of Chiengmai (Zimme) in northern Siam, which they predicted in glowing terms would soon become the 'Clapham Junction of the East'.[24]

Dufferin stated that he recognized the commercial and political advantages of the proposed Moulmein-Yunnan Railroad. But if a subsidy was required from the Indian Government, Dufferin said that his Council would object violently. The Council would prefer to spend any available funds on famine relief, rather than on an 'adventure' in Burmese and Siamese railroad building.[25]

On August 28, Churchill again wrote to Dufferin that he was most impressed with the statements of Archibald Colquhoun, the co-proponent of the proposed Moulmein-Yunnan Railroad. Churchill asked if it would be possible to arrange a commercial treaty between India and China that would throw open the new markets of Yunnan and Southern China to British subjects' trade.[26]

Churchill further proposed that the commercial treaty could be best arranged if direct negotiations were to take place between Dufferin and Viceroy Li of the Yamen, Chinese foreign office. Churchill thought that a Chinese Embassy to Calcutta might be most advantageous.[27]

Churchill was less optimistic about his efforts to persuade the French to desist from their apparent advance in Upper Burma. The French Government had denied all knowledge of the Contracts, and had refused responsibility for the actions of their Consul, Frederic Haas. Churchill concluded that "The only way to avoid annexation of Theebaw's Kingdom is to compel the French, somehow or another, even at the risk of a rupture, to desist from their designs."[28]

Dufferin had Churchill's August 28 proposals studied. On October 12, Dufferin wrote that he sympathized with Churchill's desire to enlarge Indian and British trade with Yunnan and Southern China. However, he had become convinced after a thorough study that the route of the proposed Moulmein-Yunnan Railroad was "impracticable." Dufferin concluded that the real door into Yunnan and Southern China did not lie with the proposed Moulmein-Yunnan route, but through Mandalay and Bhamo.[29]

Dufferin was apparently not advocating a railroad from

Bhamo to Yunnan. Virtually every authority, including Colquhoun and Hallet, conceded that it would have been nearly impossible to construct a railroad over the 7,000 feet high mountains between Bhamo and Yunnan. Dufferin meant that the Bhamo trade-route was the only approach to the Yunnan markets, because the route of the Moulmein-Yunnan Railroad was impassable and would have run dangerously close to French territory.[30] Dufferin—in his diplomatic fashion—was attempting to discourage Churchill from the idea of a Burma-Yunnan Railroad.[31]

On October 16, only four days later, Dufferin telegraphed to Churchill that an Ultimatum should be sent to Mandalay in order to eliminate French influence from Upper Burma.[32] Dufferin was genuinely concerned about the French advance. He based his concern upon the series of letters from Bernard that warned of a French *take-over* of Upper Burma within a few years' time.

Why Dufferin Proposed an Ultimatum

It was Bernard's sympathy for Mandalay, and for the Burmese people, that had made his series of warnings since late-July so influential upon Dufferin's thinking. As recently as February 1885, Dufferin had accepted Bernard's recommendations that Upper Burma should not be threatened with either a change of Kings under a 'protected state' or with annexation.[33]

In late-July 1885, Andreino passed the treaties and the proposed Bank and Railroad Contracts to the Indian Government. Bernard stated that France could not be allowed to gain such concessions, and to position herself between India and Southern China. Bernard reminded the Indian Government that he had always opposed the idea of intervention in Upper Burmese affairs.[34]

However, if Thebaw insisted upon giving the proposed Bank, Railroad, and other concessions to Frenchmen, he would have to be warned not to do so. Indian troops would have to be poised at Thayetmyo along with the despatch of the letter of warning (ultimatum). If nothing were done to counter the proposed Bank, Railroad, and other concessions, the French would soon establish a colony on India's eastern frontier.[35]

On August 11, Bernard warned that the French would rule Upper Burma in three or four years' time once the proposed Bank

and Railroad Contracts were signed.[36] In his August 22 letter to
Durand, Bernard stated that he had been afraid to suggest an
arbitration of the BBTC Teak Case for fear that the Mandalay
Government would propose the French Consul as the arbitrator.
It had been the intervention of Hass on August 3 that had made
the Teak Case so serious. Therefore, Bernard proposed that the
Indian Government appoint the arbitrator.[37]

As the Indian Government rested upon the principle of—
usually—accepting the recommendations of the officer closest to
the scene, Dufferin and his Council reversed their stand against
intervention in Upper Burma. Bernard's proposal would prevent
the French from any further intervention in the Teak Case;[38] and
would perhaps warn them away from other interventions, such as
the proposed Bank and Railroad Contracts.

By September 15, Bernard had become somewhat less
'alarmist'. He warned that once the proposed Bank and Railroad
were built that France would control Upper Burma in a few years'
time. In the same letter, he stated that the Mandalay Government
had rejected Haas' August 3 offer to provide French teak-firms in
place of the BBTC, and Haas' September 5 offer to arbitrate the
Teak Case. Bernard concluded that the Teak Case was of no
great concern, although not settled as yet.[39]

In addition to Bernard's series of despatches since late-July
warning of a French takeover of Upper Burma, Dufferin had
received several letters from his superior. Churchill had
emphasized that he wished to throw open new markets in Yunnan
and Southern China. It was obvious to Dufferin that his superior
would not appreciate seeing the approaches to these markets, and
the markets themselves, fall into French hands. According to
Bernard's despatches since July, such events would occur within a
few years' time.

Even more important was the fact that France would then
have a colony positioned between India and China, and running
contiguously with India's eastern frontier. India would be ground
between the two European imperialisms of Russia in the northwest
and France on the east. As Dufferin had stated in his August 14
letter to Churchill, India simply could *not* afford to become involved, militarily or financially, on both the northwest and on the
east at the same time.

By October 5, Dufferin had become extremely concerned

about the 'French Threat' on India's eastern frontier. The Indian Government informed Churchill that Upper Burma:

> is rapidly becoming a source of danger to us instead of merely an annoyance......it has degenerated in power and resources, and is unable any longer to........resist the pressure and temptation of French or other [European] influences. The danger......is real and we clearly recognize the expediency of putting an end to it. If, therefore, King Thebaw should give us legitimate provocation, it would probably be for our interest to annex the country or take it under our protection.[40]

The Burmese Government had already provided the required provocation. On October 3, the Kinwun officially rejected Bernard's August 28 request for arbitration of the BBTC Teak Case. The official refusal made a most "convenient pretext" for the ultimatum that Bernard had suggested in late-July might be necessary in order to prevent the French take-over of Upper Burma.

On October 16, Dufferin telegraphed to Churchill, and asked permission to send an Ultimatum to Mandalay that would accomplish the above aim as well as eliminate the "Shoe Question", the BBTC Teak Case, and other issues between the two countries. The five demands of the proposed Ultimatum follow below.[41]

(1) The Teak Case would be negotiated by an Indian Government envoy, who would be received at Mandalay with "free access to King....without....humiliating ceremony." The envoy would retain his shoes, and would be seated in the presence of the King under European diplomatic etiquette.

(2) If any move was made against the BBTC before the envoy arrived, the Indian Government would act as they saw fit without any further communication with the Mandalay Government. This was an open threat of war, and was directed primarily at the Taingda and his group.

(3) The envoy, *i.e.* Resident, would be stationed permanently at Mandalay with a new river-side Residency, a proper guard of honour, and a steamer for his protection.[42] The demand settled remaining protocol problems, in particular the notorious "Shoe Question".

(4) In addition to the above, the Mandalay Government would conduct its foreign affairs with France and other countries in accordance with the wishes of the Indian Government "as is

now done by Amir of Afghanistan."[43]

(5) Proper facilities would also be granted by the Mandalay Government for the establishment of British subjects' trade with Yunnan through Bhamo.[44] Dufferin concluded his telegram by stating that the last two demands might be insisted upon after the envoy had arrived in Mandalay.[45]

Why Churchill Accepted Dufferin's Proposed Ultimatum

Churchill, meanwhile, in London had come to the same con- clusion as had Dufferin, namely that an ultimatum would have to be sent to Mandalay. On October 17, Churchill telegraphed his approval of Dufferin's proposed Ultimatum. The three factors that were most influential in Churchill's decision were the following.

(1) Churchill had tried since August to receive assurances from Paris that they would not continue to extend their influence in Upper Burma. But the French Government had denied official sponsorship of the proposed Railroad and Bank Contracts, and had also denied responsibility for Haas' actions.

(2) If the French were allowed to continue their advance, they would block off the potential new markets of Yunnan and Southern China from British subjects' trade. The French advance would make nonsense of Churchill's political claims of wanting to put the British workingman back to work by expanding British markets overseas.[46]

(3) The most important factor was that a French-influenced Upper Burma would directly threaten India's eastern frontier. Dufferin had stated in his August 14 letter that India could *not* fight both the Russians in the northwest and the French on the east simultaneously. Such a contingency might well come to pass if France was allowed to secure control at Mandalay. Nothing much could be done about the Russians in the immediate future. But if an Ultimatum was sent to Mandalay, the 'French Threat' could be removed from India's eastern frontier, and the 1885 Elections could be won.

The 'French Threat' to India's Eastern Frontier was the Main Cause of the War

Churchill's October 17 telegram reflected many of the ideas

discussed in Bernard's July 28, 1885 letter to Durand.   Churchill told Dufferin that the sending of the Ultimatum to Mandalay should be concurrent with the sending of troops and ships to Thayetmyo. Churchill hoped that an 'armed demonstration' on the frontier between the two Burmas would bring the Burmese Government to submission and avoid bloodshed.[47]

If, on the other hand, the Ultimatum was rejected, the troops and ships should immediately advance upon Mandalay via the Irrawaddy River.   The Mandalay Government was to be informed that any injury to British subjects' persons or property would be swiftly punished.   Churchill stated that money was to be no object in view of "all the circumstances of the case."   A reply by Mandalay should be demanded within a specific time-limit.[48]   In a second telegram on the same day, October 17, Churchill asked whether Dufferin preferred annexation, or the setting-up of another Prince in place of Thebaw.[49]

Dufferin telegraphed his reply the next day, October 18.   He repeated Bernard's contention of July 28 that annexation was preferable to the setting-up of another Prince.   Dufferin stated that "If we are to tap China via Bhamo, we ought to have absolute control of the [Irrawaddy] Valley."   Eight thousand troops were being mustered to assure such control.   Bernard had already been instructed to send the Ultimatum, and to require an answer from Mandalay within four days.[50]

Dufferin wrote a long letter on the next day, October 19.   He said that 10,000 troops would be despatched to wait at Thayetmyo until Mandalay sent its answer to the Ultimatum.   However, Dufferin thought that only the presence of the troops at Mandalay, itself, would convince the King and Court of "the nature of their position."[51]

Dufferin then commented upon Churchill's second October 17 telegram.   It had asked whether Dufferin preferred annexation or a 'protected Prince' as the future form of government for Upper Burma.   Dufferin had some serious reservations about annexation, but he had noticed that both Bernard and Churchill seemed to favour it.   Dufferin, therefore, contented himself with a warning that annexation would cause "difficulties."   He waited until future letters to describe these "difficulties."   Instead, he listed five reasons for favouring annexation.[52]

(1) It was enough to be worried about a buffer-state on the

northwest, *i.e.* Afghanistan between Russia and India, without duplicating it on the east with Upper Burma between French Indo-China and India.[53]   (2) A buffer-state required some resilience, *i.e.* some military power of resistance. "Burmah is so soft and pulpy a substance that she could never be put to such a use."[54]   (3) As Bernard had indicated, if a 'protected Prince' was set-up in place of Thebaw, the French would constantly try to influence him. The French might soon regain what little influence they had lost by Thebaw's abdication.[55]

(4) Lord Ripon's contention that the annexation of Upper Burma would cause tensions between India and China was invalid. A contiguous frontier between the two countries would give a tremendous boost to British trade with Yunnan and Southern China.[56]   Lastly, (5) the French were already attempting to establish better trading relations with Yunnan from their side via the Red River Valley in Tongkin. The only possible British approach to Yunnan was through Mandalay and Bhamo, and annexation would secure this route permanently against French 'intrigues'.[57]

Dufferin concluded his letter by stating that the cost of the military expedition to Upper Burma was a reasonable one. He did, however, doubt that the final cost of the Expedition would be as low as the fifteen lakhs estimated by the Indian Military Department.[58]

In a November 18 reply, Churchill made perhaps the best statement on why the 1885 Third Burmese War had occurred. He had just received the news by telegraph that the Burma Expedition had crossed the border into Upper Burma on November 14. He stated that :

It is French intrigue which has forced us to go to Burmah; but for that element we might have treated Theebaw with severe neglect [the usual British policy since October 6, 1879]... If...you finally and fully add Burma to your dominions before any European rights have had time even to be sown, much less grow up, you undoubtedly prevent forever the assertion of such rights, or attempts to prepare the way for such assertion. ...If, on the other hand, this opportunity of protecting India effectually on the East is allowed to pass, these events may follow a course analogous to what has taken place in the N. W. [with Russia]. The aggressions against you need not necessarily be French; they might be German or Italian, or all three.[59]

The news of the war was favourably received by the British electorate, which had commenced voting in the Election that required over two weeks to run its course. Churchill stated in a November 27 telegram that his 'Tory Democracy' campaign to put the British workingman back to work was succeeding. The Conservatives had already gained the majority in cities such as London, Manchester, Liverpool, Leeds, and Sheffield. Churchill thought if the Conservative-counties went Liberal, while the Liberal-boroughs went Conservative, that it would be *"Le monde renverse."*[60]

Then, Churchill added what was most on his mind, namely that it appeared Gen. Harry Prendergast and the Burma Expedition were moving very slowly. Churchill had expected that the news of the fall of Mandalay would have reached London two or three days before.[61] Unexpressed in Churchill's letter was his worry that the Election would be finished before Mandalay fell. The boost that the victory would bring to Conservative candidates would be lost.

The news of the fall of Mandalay on November 28 came too late to have its maximum impact upon the Election. The December 11 tally showed that the Liberals had won 333 seats in the Commons. The Conservatives had won 255 seats, and their 'allies', the Irish Parnellites, had won eighty-six seats. The Conservatives had over-whelmed the Liberals in many workingmen's districts, while losing to many Liberal candidates in the countryside.

A wistful Churchill stated in a December 5 letter to Dufferin that "I wish the Burmah business could have taken place a month earlier, we should have been much strengthened by it."[62] With a Conservative-Parnellite 'majority' of eight in the Commons, Churchill now had to defend his Burma policy, and secure parliamentary approval for the sending of Indian troops outside of India. If approved, it meant that Indian revenues and the Indian tax-payers would pay for the War.

Bernard Issues the Ultimatum

Meanwhile in late-September, Frederic Haas, the French consul to Mandalay, had fallen ill and had come down to Rangoon expecting to die. When Charles Bernard and his wife heard that Haas was staying in a noisy hotel, they invited him to recuperate at their home.[63]   Haas gratefully accepted the offer, and during his recuperation mentioned that he had requested sick-leave from his Government.[64]

Bernard wrote that Haas was a quiet, scholarly man, and was not the sort to exceed his instructions, or to attempt a "forward meddling policy" on his own account.   Haas appeared to be a very different type from Voisson, the French consul at Rangoon.[65]   In short, Bernard and Haas became rather friendly; but Bentabole, Haas' secretary, seemed to be "a less attractive person."[66]

Bernard tried to gain information from Haas, but the Consul was both too sick and too wary.   At dinner when Bentabole blundered and mentioned the code word of "Le diament," the cypher name of the Myngun Prince, Haas told him to be silent.[67] Rumours were again rife at this time that the Myngun was about to descend upon Burma in disguise.   An all-points lookout had been set up in an attempt to intercept him.

Bernard hoped that the Myngun would not arrive in Mandalay at the same time as Haas, who had decided to return to Mandalay until his replacement arrived.[68]   With this danger in mind, Bernard prepared the Ultimatum to Mandalay as prescribed by Durand in an October 19 telegram.[69]

An advance copy of the Ultimatum was to be given to U Kyi, who had been Thebaw's commercial-agent (Consul) at Rangoon since about May 15, 1883.[70]   U Kyi had been recommended for the post by Andreino.[71]   U Kyi had also been the Kinwun's secret-envoy, who had arrived on December 28, 1881 just 'too late' to see Viceroy Lord Ripon.   U Kyi's mission had eventually resulted in the 1882 Simla Treaty Conference.[72]   In a word, U Kyi was 'reliable'.

U Kyi with a combination of train, steamer, and boat, could get the Ultimatum to Minhla, the first large river-town in Upper Burma, in four days.   From there, the Kinwun would probably have received the Ultimatum within an hour or sovia the Minhla to Mandalay telegraph-line.   The time-lapse of four days was two days *faster* than the six days required to send a telegram over the Rangoon to Mandalay telegraph-line.[73]

The Kinwun received the October 22 Ultimatum by October 26 at the latest, and he probably received it as early as October 23 or 24.   It is highly probable that Bernard gave the terms of the Ultimatum to U Kyi on October 19.   The advance notice was given in order that the Kinwun might have more time in which to organize a movement for acceptance of the Ultimatum and to avoid war.

The October 22 Ultimatum was despatched aboard the *Ashley Eden* on October 23.   The *Ashley Eden* was scheduled to arrive at Mandalay on October 30, and would leave again on the morning of November 6 with or without a reply to the Ultimatum.   If the Mandalay Government did not accept the Ultimatum, or if no reply reached Bernard by the evening of November 10, the Indian Government would take whatever actions that were necessary.[74]

Bernard warned Haas that if the Ultimatum was refused, the foreigners at Mandalay might be in danger.[75]   Haas replied that if this was so, he should be at his Consul's post.   He tried very hard to get on board the *Doowoon*, the fast steamer that left on October 22 to warn the Europeans at Mandalay about the coming of the Ultimatum.   Bernard refused Haas' request, because Bernard did not want the other Europeans at Mandalay to learn their first information about the Ultimatum from Haas.   The French Consul was noticeably disappointed.[76]

Haas left for Mandalay on the next day, October 23, on board the slower *Ashley Eden*, which carried the official copy of the Ultimatum.   A few days later, Bernard had a chat with Mons. de Facieu, who had just resigned his General's rank in Thebaw's army. De Facieu said that Haas' stay with Bernard in Rangoon, and Haas' return to Mandalay with the Ultimatum, would discredit him with the Burmese.   They would, thereafter, believe him to be an Indian Government spy.[77]

De Facieu was correct.   Haas had left Mandalay under circumstances that seemed extremely suspicious to the Burmese.[78] Consequently, he was not exactly welcomed with open arms when he arrived on October 30 with the Ultimatum.   Haas fared no better with the other side.   The October 7 *Pioneer Mail* claimed that Haas' sickness was merely his way of spying about Lower Burma and Rangoon.[79]   After he had returned to Mandalay, the November 6 *Times of India* commented that his return proved that French intrigues at Mandalay were continuing, and that nothing would stop them short of war.[80]

Therefore, Haas had virtually no influence or credibility with either side, or with his own Government.   He played little part in the events of November 1885 until the very end.   He was then summoned to the Palace for the supreme irony of his tenure at Mandalay. He assisted in the drafting of the Burmese surrender document, which surrendered both Upper Burma's independence and France's future ambitions in that area.

The Tangyet's Paris 'Feelers'

Meanwhile in Paris, the Tangyet Wundauk, Burmese ambassador to France, was making several diplomatic 'feelers', both official and unofficial, towards preventing the almost-certain invasion of his country. One such official 'feeler' was the Tangyet's conversation with Lord Lyons, British ambassador to Paris, on October 18.[81]

Lyons told the Tangyet that he "deeply regretted" having to make the Ambassador's acquaintance at such a time of stress between the two countries. However, Lyons emphasized that he had no authority to interfere in the Teak Case, which was strictly an affair between the King of Upper Burma and the Government of India. Such issues could be treated only by the Governments actually involved. Lyons hoped that King Thebaw might settle the dispute quickly and satisfactorily.[82]

The Tangyet left a formal letter in French, which was a repetition of the verbal statements that he had made during the interview. He stated that he had telegraphed Mandalay advising them to accept Bernard's arbitration request. He hoped that direct relations might be established between London and Mandalay, and that a Burmese envoy might be stationed permanently in London. Lastly, the Tangyet assured Lord Lyons that no European subjects at Mandalay would be harmed.[83]

Lyons wrote to Salisbury on October 23. Lyons stated that the Tangyet's proposals for direct relations between Mandalay and London, and for a permanent Burmese envoy at London, would have reduced the power of the Indian Government. Lyons, therefore, thought that his refusal to discuss the proposals had been "the prudent course."[84]

The Tangyet, on his part, attempted in an October 20 press-interview with his friend Mr. Farman, the London *Standard* correspondent and hopeful Toungoo-Mandalay Railroad concessionaire, to arouse British public-opinion in favour of the Mandalay Government. The Tangyet stated that he had urged his Government before leaving Mandalay near the end of July to use every honourable means to avoid complications in the BBTC Teak Case.[85] Upon hearing of Bernard's August 28 arbitration request, the Tangyet said that he had immediately telegraphed to his Government urging it to forestall an Ultimatum by accepting Bernard's request.[86]

In general, Mandalay had the greatest desire to cultivate cordial relations with England. France had no interests in Upper Burma, but Britain did. These interests would continue to be protected. No British or other European subjects at Mandalay would be harmed. The Tangyet stated that he had been instructed to ask London if it would consent to receive an Embassy from Mandalay. It would negotiate for the return of the Resident, and for the establishment of a permanent Burmese Legation in London.[87]

These were the proposals of the 'progress' party to which the Tangyet belonged at Mandalay. He stated that there were two conflicting parties at Mandalay, the 'progress' party with the Kinwun at its head, and the other party which was opposed to the introduction of 'progress' into Upper Burma. If the proposals and advice of the 'progress' party were accepted at Mandalay, all further complications between the two countries would be avoided.[88]

In other words, the Tangyet believed that war could be avoided if London would accept the proposed Burmese Embassy to London to settle all outstanding differences between the two countries. The additional acceptance of a permanent Burmese Legation at London would cause the 'progress' party at Mandalay to triumph over its 'reactionary' foes. London had the power to cause a permanent settlement along the above lines, or London could impose the other solution of invasion and annexation.[89]

The Tangyet's interview with Farman was an astute use of the press in an effort to create a public opinion more favourable to his Government; and to prod the British Government into an acceptance of his October 18 proposals. On October 23, the Tangyet's interview with Farman, and a copy of the Tangyet's October 18 letter to Lyons, were published in the London *Standard*. On October 26, a telegram summarizing the article appeared in the Calcutta *Englishman*.[90]

The Tangyet continued his efforts to stop the impending war, and to secure a permanent Burmese Legation at London. On November 2, Lord Lyons refused to accept a second note from the Tangyet, because he had allowed the October 18 letter to be published by Mr. Farman in the *Standard*.[91] Undaunted, the Tangyet sent Mr. Farman to verbally state the contents of the second note.[92]

Finally, on November 3, the Tangyet's letter was delivered to the British Embassy, and the letter reached Lord Randolph Churchill at the India Office by November 6. On the previous day, November 5, the Mandalay Government had officially rejected the October 22 Ultimatum, a fact not known by either the British Government or the Tangyet.

The Tangyet's November 3 letter *accepted* the Ultimatum. He stated that the Mandalay Government would accept the special-envoy to arbitrate the BBTC Teak Case "with all the honours and ...respect due to the Envoy of so great a Power."[93] The Mandalay Government had "already informed Mr. Bernard...by telegraph, that they are prepared to accept the proposed arbitration of the BBTC Case."[94]

The Ultimatum had also demanded the return of the Resident to Mandalay under European etiquette. The Tangyet reminded the London Government that his October 18 letter had expressed the desire to renew the "ancient relations," which had existed between the two countries.[95] Indeed, Mr. Farman in his November 2 interview with Sir G. Bouham, Lyons' assistant, had stated that such had been the Mandalay Government's stand since late-July when the Tangyet had left Mandalay.[96]

Farman reminded Bouham that he, Farman, had said as much a month previously in his two interviews with Sir John Walsham, then the acting British ambassador. Farman told Bouham that the *only* remaining difficulty lay in the Residency Guard "to which the King objected as a matter of principle."[97]

The Tangyet stated further in his November 3 letter that King Thebaw had long wished to establish direct relations between Mandalay and London, *i.e.* a permanent Burmese Legation in London. The Tangyet concluded his November 3 letter with the following appeal: "I can ask my Government by telegraph...... to grant me special authority to enter into negotiations in London with respect to the......dispute between us, and thereby....avoid bloodshed.[98]

It appears that the Tangyet—and the Kinwun—were acting upon their *own* initiative when the Tangyet accepted the Ultimatum in his November 3 letter. For example, the Tangyet began his letter by stating that he was accepting the demands of the Ultimatum, "which, according to well-known information, runs much as follows."[99]

This was *not* the phraseology of an Ambassador with explicit instructions from his Government. Instead, it appears that the Kinwun had acted in the name of the King and possibly without his permission. The Kinwun had apparently sent a telegram on about October 8 giving the Tangyet *carte blanche* powers, and ordering him to make his series of proposals to Lord Lyons and the London Government.[100]

On about October 8 there had been a *Hlutdaw* meeting to discuss what to do about the BBTC. The company had not paid the first instalment of the fine. The troops of the Taingda, which had initially seized the BBTC's timber, had been bribed by the BBTC's Ningyan agents, and the timber was being floated out as usual. The second fine instalment was due on October 22, and the *Hlutdaw* was faced with a second flouting of its August 23 Fine Order.[101]

The Pouk Myine Atwinwun, the Taingda, and three other ministers, argued for an immediate enforcement of the Order, which under the terms of the Fine Order meant that the BBTC's property and leases could be expropriated. But the rest of the ministers rejected the idea as one that might result in a war with the Indian Government.[102] Instead, it appears that they directed the Pouk Myine Atwinwun to tell Andreino that King Thebaw would welcome the BBTC's petition for a Royal Review of the entire Case. The Pouk Myine Atwinwun did so on about October 9.

As soon as the *Hlutdaw* meeting had ended, the Kinwun sent a 2,000 word telegram in cypher to the Tangyet in Paris, and ordered him to make his series of proposals to Lord Lyons.[103] The Kinwun or an associate made certain that the Kinwun's action—taken in the name of the King—would find its way into the Calcutta *Statesman* and *Englishman;* and thereby come to the attention of the Indian Government. In short, the Kinwun's telegram, and the Tangyet's proposals to Lord Lyons in Paris, appeared to be *further* 'unofficial' attempts by Mandalay officials to accept arbitration of the Teak Case and avoid the impending war.[104]

The London Government did not accept the Tangyet's November 3 letter as an official document. They accepted it as an unofficial expression, until the Mandalay Government would send an official acceptance of the Ultimatum to the Indian Government. Churchill was courteous in declining the Tangyet's offer on November 9.

> Lord Lyons should be instructed to thank the Envoy for his friendly communication......it has been conveyed unofficially.... [It] is not possible......to interfere with the direct control exercised by......India over relations with Burmah......[If], as the Envoy represents, the King of Burmah is willing to satisfy the requirements of......India, it is only necessary......to inform the Viceroy, it not being the desire either of his Excellency [Dufferin] or Her Majesty's Government to press with undue harshness on the King, with whom, on the contrary, they have always endeavoured to maintain relations of peace and amity.[105]

As the above letter was being drafted, Churchill despatched a November 8 telegram to Dufferin. It informed him that unofficial communication was being maintained with the Tangyet in order to show that all possibilities for preserving peace had been exhausted.[106] Churchill added that such communication with the Tangyet would not have any practical effect upon Dufferin's proceeding with the war. The contact with the Tangyet was done solely "to appease an uneasy public conscience which might be excited by designing politicians [*i.e.* John Bright] for their own purposes."[107]

Furthermore, the reply to the Tangyet had to be courteously phrased. The Tangyet had used Mr. Farman of the London *Standard* as a 'go-between' upon several occasions. Farman was "evidently an intriguer, who......might easily occasion embarrassment, if not judiciously managed by [Paris] Embassy."[108]

In other words, Churchill's reply had to be courteous with Farman as a confidant of the Tangyet, who would leak what he could to the *Standard* and other papers. Also, the Election was only a few days off, and Churchill was at that moment locked in a dead heat with John Bright for a Commons seat from Birmingham. The Tangyet had cleverly brought the British Government's dealings with Mandalay out into the open at the only tender moment—right before the Election. By November 9, 1885, *The Times of India* and the *Englishman* had run short news-reports about the Tangyet's November 3 proposals.[109]

When one considers the Tangyet's efforts in combination with the six or more 'unofficial' efforts made by Mandalay officials to settle the Teak Case, one must conclude that the Burmese Government did not want a war. However, because of their fear of losing 'face', they could not indicate their desire for peace in the one official way that would have stayed the hand of the Indian Government.

De Freycinet's French 'Feelers'

Meanwhile, de Freycinet, the French foreign affairs minister, was at that very moment attempting a last-minute salvage operation on what little remained of French interests in Upper Burma. On November 9, he ordered Waddington, the French ambassador to London, to gain an interview with Lord Salisbury.[110]

During your conversation, you will perhaps have an opportunity to explain away the aims that they ascribe to us in Burma, and to which, unfortunately, certain imprudences have given some factuality. You are in a position to reduce these misconceptions to their true value and to demonstrate that there is nothing.... to impel the British Government to this violent absorption of Burma......, and that such absorption would not be without big sacrifices now and without the possible danger of complication in the future.[111]

De Freycinet thought that the British would not have sent an expedition to Burma without having first examined the alternatives. Thebaw was hostile to Europeans, and his bad administration and his extravagance had made him unpopular among his own people. Therefore, de Freycinet thought that it would be easy to provoke a revolt against Thebaw in favour of the Myngun.[112]   De Freycinet asked :

Has the Cabinet in London thought of this possibility? Would it have disregarded such a possibility after having recognized that the only conceivable successor would be the Prince Myngun who lives at Pondicherry? ......it would be easy to make......[any British apprehensions] disappear by formal engagements that we would take beforehand, at the same time the British Government would promise that our essential interests would be looked after.[113]

On the same day, November 9, Lord Lyons in Paris wired Salisbury concerning the impending French offer.[114] On November 12, Waddington informed Salisbury that there was a project afoot for the Myngun to go to Burma. The Pondicherry authorities could not oppose his departure after they had originally agreed to respect his right to come and go as he pleased.[115]

Waddington proposed that if Lower Burmese authorities would treat the Myngun in a friendly fashion, he would have little trouble in overthrowing Thebaw. Both England and France could place the Myngun on the Mandalay throne. Waddington said that French interests in Upper Burma were commercial, and not of a political nature. Therefore, French interests were not hostile to British interests.[116]

Salisbury replied that French commercial interests in Upper Burma had nothing to fear. As concerned the Myngun, Salisbury said that he would have to consult Churchill and the India Office. It was a trifle late to change the instructions given to the Government of India. The Burma Expedition was already at the Burmese frontier at Thayetmyo, and might well have crossed it that very day.[117]

Waddington concluded from the conversation that the Myngun would probably not be acceptable to the British. They considered Myngun to be the 'French candidate', and conceived of Upper Burma as a solely British concern. Waddington suggested that the Quai d' Orsay could only wait for the end of the War. Then, perhaps, some unexpected result might revive the Myngun's chances.[118] On the following day, November 13, Waddington wrote again to de Freycinet that:

If they decide for the Protectorate [instead of annexation] Myngoon could have chances, namely if he doesn't commit blunders from now on. In brief, I can but repeat the advice that I have already given......to give up quietly the question of Burma, where we can only give strokes of the sword in water, and reserve our action for the question of sharing the influence in Indo-China [with Britain via 'spheres of interest'].[119]

During another interview with Lord Salisbury on November 16, Waddington was told that the British Government could not at that time consider the candidature of the Myngun Prince.[120]

The question of replacing Thebaw with another Prince would come up only later. Only at that time would the Myngun be considered along with other Princes and solutions, such as Waddington's 'spheres of interest' proposal.[121] It was obvious to all, especially to de Freycinet, that France no longer had many interests in Upper Burma.[122]

Supayalat Influences the Hlutdaw to Reject the Ultimatum

Meanwhile, back at Mandalay, there was great excitement. It had been caused by the arrival of the *Doowoon* on October 26 with news of the impending Ultimatum. The fast *Doowoon* was four days ahead of the slower *Ashley Eden*, which carried the actual document. The *Doowoon* was joined by other IFC steamers on scheduled-runs to Mandalay. They anchored in the middle of the stream waiting to take on board British subjects, and the small European colony at Mandalay of about eighty persons.[123]

The official copy of the Ultimatum arrived on October 30 at a most inconvenient time during the religious *Wabdwin* fast. The *Ashley Eden* would leave with or without the Mandalay Government's reply on the morning of November 6. Therefore, the Kinwun had no choice other than to submit the document to the *Hlutdaw* on October 31. When Thebaw first heard the text he appeared to be very uneasy, and at first did not speak.[124]

The Kinwun told the *Hlutdaw* that the Ultimatum was completely at odds with the trend of British policy all over the world since 1880, and even before.[125] Most of the ministers concurred, and said that they found it hard to believe that Viceroy Dufferin was actually serious about enforcing the Ultimatum. They pointed out that Lord Kimberley, and several of his predecessors as Secretary of State for India, had publicly declared that Upper Burma was an independent state. The Taingda and others of his group spoke of armed resistance.[126]

Suddenly, Thebaw left the chamber, which was an ominous Royal rejection of everything that had gone on in the meeting. Thebaw summoned the *Thathanabaing*, the Buddhist archbishop of Upper Burma, and the old priest advised submission.[127] Consuls Andreino and Haas agreed with the archbishop's advice.[128] On the following day, November 1, the *Hlutdaw* again met with Thebaw and Supayalat.[129] She took part in the debate, although she was five months pregnant with what the entire Court hoped was the future Crown Prince. (It was another *girl*.)[130]

Even at such a critical time, the *Hlutdaw* tended to divide into two groups. The Kinwun's group wanted a 'soft' answer sent to the Indian Government, which would turn away the *kalas*' wrath as such answers had done so many times before. The second group, the Taingda's group, thought that this time the *kalas*' demands could be resisted only by war.

There were also personal reasons motivating the two groups. The Kinwun's group knew that they had always had a good reputation with the *kalas*. The establishment of a new Resident under the terms of the Ultimatum would strengthen the Kinwun's group. It would enable them to finally enact the proposed Constitution and other reforms. These changes had been set aside as unnecessary after the pressure of the Indian Government—as represented by the Resident—had been withdrawn on October 6, 1879. With the arrival of the new Resident, the Kinwun's 'reformers' would finally triumph, and the Taingda's group and the other 'traditionalists' would be overawed.

The Taingda's group knew that they had a very bad reputation with the *kalas*. The Indian Government would not forgive them for their rejection of Bernard's arbitration request. Nor would the British give them any credit for their 'unofficial' efforts to settle the Teak Case, in particular the Pouk Myine Atwinwun's October 9 meeting with Andreino.[131] Therefore, it was mostly the Taingda's group that was described in a *Times of India* article:

the Ministers dread English intervention mainly as implying loss of power and emolument to themselves. They are consequently inflaming the minds of the minor officials and of the soldiery with similar ideas. Contradictory and misleading advice from all sides is tendered to the King. Refugees from British law are joining in assuring him the English are only demonstrating....Some British Indian subjects are said to be supplying Theebaw with money at 48 per cent. [per annum.][132]

There were other interests and groups, besides the above, who had prerogatives that would be threatened by an acceptance of the Ultimatum. For example, the several dozen French and Italians in Thebaw's service had not received their wages for more than two years. They and Supayalat's *kalamas*, foreign female-spies, thought that they would lose their wages and their positions should a new British Resident be accepted. They, therefore, minimized the seriousness of the Ultimatum. One is reminded that it was these two groups, who had been so influential in destroying the 1882 Simla Treaty.

But there was a motivation more influential than any of the above. This was Supayalat's desire to secure her *own* position as Chief Queen by giving birth to a Crown Prince; and then, to *retain* a Kingdom of Mandalay for the Crown Prince to inherit. Her motivation was extremely important, and she had great influence during the November 1 deliberations on the Ultimatum.

The Taingda spoke first. He advised rejection of the Ultimatum because the BBTC had cheated the King. The Indian Government would never hold a true investigation of the Teak Case. The new British Resident would also be the actual King under the terms of the Ultimatum.[133] Therefore, the Taingda advised war as the British were nothing but animals without faith or honour as all the world knew.[134] Speaking in his capacity as a commander of a portion of the armed services, the Taingda stated that the Royal soldiers were trained like the foreigners with the same weapons and tactics. He shouted that "In this war the King shall be victorious."[135]

Supayalat and many of the ministers cheered the Taingda's remarks, but Thebaw remained silent. He then asked the Kinwun for his views on whether to refuse or to accept the Ultimatum. The Kinwun agreed that the demands were unfair and insulting.[136] But, he pointed out that he had been to Europe twice and had seen the British armies, while the Taingda had never been out of Burma. The Kinwun stated, also, in his capacity as commander of a portion of the armed services, that the Royal soldiers could not resist the Indian Army.[137]

He said that it would be better to yield to the Ultimatum. In a few years the soldiers would be better trained and success might come then, but not at the present time. The Kinwun concluded that a reply should be sent accepting all the demands of the Ultimatum. If it was finally necessary to actually fulfil the demands, "it can be done slowly, and meanwhile preparations can be made."[138]

Supayalat condemned such talk, and several ministers sensing a political tide condemned appeasers who would surrender to the *kalas'* Ultimatum. Among those who condemned the Kinwun was a frequent supporter, the Hlaythin Atwinwun, who had been under severe pressure from his father-in-law, the Taingda, to speak up for a strong position. The Hlaythin pointed out with Supayalat's repeated support that revolts could easily be incited in Lower Burma; 'dacoits' could be sent over the border deep into British territory; and, perhaps the French might even come into the war on the side of Burma.[139]

The Pangyet, who had lived ten years in France and had twice been roving ambassador to Paris, knew better than that. But he did not dare to contradict the Hlaythin or the Taingda too vigorously. Like the Hlaythin, the Pangyet had also been under terrific pressure from his father-in-law, the Taingda, to take a strong stand; but, instead, the Pangyet now attempted to support the Kinwun. Finally, the Pangyet started to cry, and stared for a long moment at his father-in-law and sobbed: "this time you've really done it and the country is lost."[140]

Thebaw still did not join in the discussion, or express a view. He remained silent, and asked the opinions of all those present. Finally, the Kinwun made one last attempt to reason with the *Hlutdaw*. He remarked that the King's ancestors—through exactly such bombast as the Court was then indulging in—had lost Assam, Manipur, Arakan, and Tennaserim in the First Burmese War, and Pegu with the city of Rangoon in the Second Burmese War. Would His Majesty go down in history as the King who lost the *rest* of Burma?[141]

The thought of such a disgrace swayed Thebaw towards the Kinwun's view.[142] It had become obvious that the King had not joined with the talk of war from the Taingda's group. It was then that Supayalat became afraid that if her husband surrendered to the Ultimatum, their future son would never rule over a sovereign Burma.

She interrupted to say that the Kinwun's speech was that of a coward.[143] She taunted him with being an old woman: "grand-father, you should wear a skirt, and own a stone for grinding face-powder."[144] She ridiculed the Kinwun's advice. She ordered her servants behind the throne to "Bring him....a petticoat and a fan that he may dress as becomes his words,....and the world shall know him for what he is."[145] Then, she mustered Woman's ultimate weapon—she cried. As Woman's tears have often done, Supayalat's tears ended all further debate.[146]

Thebaw stated that there appeared to be no other alternative, but that of war. In order that the ancient tradition would be upheld, the *Hlutdaw* was directed to meet separately in the Byedaik Hall and make their official decision.[147] However, once away from Supayalat, the majority of the ministers voted for sending an evasive but friendly reply that would avoid both the Ultimatum and war.[148]

The Kinwun had written such despatches many times, which had turned away the *kalas'* wrath. Surely he could do so again. If the *kalas* rejected an evasive reply and invaded, it would imply only a partial loss of ministerial prerogatives and independence. An outright rejection of the Ultimatum would result in war, and would cost them everything. The Kinwun was weeping with humiliation, and said that he would write whatever they told him to write.[149]

But the ministers were faced with a dilemma. It was an ancient custom for the King to accept the *Hlutdaw's* decision, although he had the right to refuse it. The customary procedure had always been to discuss matters thoroughly before-hand with the King. The King would then make his decision, which nearly always harmonized with the majority of the ministers, who naturally approved it.[150]

The dilemma was that Thebaw had thought that he had ascertained the ministerial will when he had declared reluctantly for war. The ministers had the odious problem of voting their true feelings, which they had been afraid to express before Supayalat, and which directly contradicted Thebaw's royal order.[151]

Supayalat was enraged that the *Hlutdaw* would dare to disobey her husband's order, which was actually her own. Thebaw was embarrassed, and at first said nothing. Supayalat's mother, the Dowager Queen who had placed Thebaw on the throne in 1878, argued that the ministers were only trying to save his throne. Supayalat replied that her mother had so much in common with the Kinwun, and his advice, she ought to marry him and go off to a hermitage.[152]

Thebaw had an agonizing decision to make. If he accepted the ministers' decision, he would retain his throne albeit with considerable loss of 'face'. If he refused the ministers' decision, he would *keep* his 'face', but the resulting war would probably cost him his throne. Fielding-Hall stated that:

It was an unheard-of thing for the ministers thus to oppose an order of the king. ....If he had known before-hand that the majority....were for peace he too, perhaps, would have declared for peace. But now he had ordered war and he could not go back, could not say he was wrong and would change. War he had said and war it must be.[153]

The Taingda was placed in charge of the defence of the nation as the new War Minister. The Kinwun was directed to write a reply to the Ultimatum that would both decline it and avoid the dreaded invasion. The Hlaythin Atwinwun, a frequent Kinwun supporter and the best general in Upper Burma, was sent to Minhla. This was the key river-fort and town about forty miles above the frontier. The Hlaythin took with him 600 men to reinforce the reputed 6,000 soldiers already posted in the area.[154]

Some of these troops were sent down-river to Sinbaungwe and Nyaungbinmaw, two river-forts even closer to the frontier between the two Burmas. Such maneuverings were mere rustles and flourishes designed to keep up the Government's 'face'. The Taingda made few preparations for the war. He apparently thought that the 10,000-men Expedition at Thayetmyo was only an 'armed demonstration', a show to boost the 'face' of the Indian Government. The Taingda did not believe that there would be a war until the Expeditionary Force crossed the frontier on the morning of November 14.[155]

Andreino's 'Treachery' Becomes Known to Mandalay

Meanwhile, five IFC steamers were waiting at Mandalay to receive British subjects, and the eighty Mandalay Europeans. Andreino started to leave, but the Taingda's group stopped him, and demanded two lakhs a quarter to settle the Teak Case.[156] Most of the French, Germans, and Italians at Mandalay did not feel greatly concerned at first, because all three countries had treaties with Mandalay.[157]

The several dozen French and Italians in King Thebaw's service were especially reluctant to leave. They feared that Thebaw would use their departure as an excuse to cancel their back-wages; their other financial claims against the Government; and their Royal employment. The French in particular decided to remain, because they thought that this would embarrass the Indian Government.[158]

The Kinwun told Andreino that if the steamer *Doowoon* left Mandalay with any of the eighty European residents, the Kinwun would not be responsible for what might happen between Mandalay and Sinbaungwe. However, if the *Doowoon* remained at Mandalay, the Kinwun promised to guarantee the safety of those on board.[159]

The Taingda's group, meanwhile, was angry that Andreino had warned the Europeans to flee on board the *Doowoon* before the Ultimatum arrived. The Taingda's group took Andreino's verbal warnings to be a deliberate attempt to humiliate the Mandalay Government, *i.e.* the Taingda's group. Andreino knew that he had had a narrow escape. If he had sent his warning in the form of a letter, his French enemies would have taken it to Taingda. The minister would have had him killed instantly.[160]

Unfortunately for Andreino, his thefts of the Treaties and Contracts were about to become public knowledge. At the end of October, the *Pioneer* correspondent at Rangoon decided to scoop his rivals by telegraphing Rangoon's most open secret. He claimed that Andreino had stolen the Treaties, and the proposed Bank and Railroad Contracts, via 'spies' in the Mandalay Palace.[161] The correspondent boasted that he would never have telegraphed the scoop, except that Andreino and the Europeans at Mandalay were by then safe on board the *Doowoon*. They would, no doubt, be in Lower Burma by the time the scoop was published.[162]

On November 4, Bernard wrote an angry letter to G. Allen, editor of the *Pioneer*. Bernard stated that the correspondent must have known when he filed his story that Andreino had not left Mandalay. The correspondent, while not notifying the *Pioneer* of this fact, boasted throughout his article that he had not risked the lives of Andreino and the other Europeans at Mandalay. Bernard made his point clear: "I recommend....arranging for another correspondent very shortly."[163]

Bernard clamped a censor on all telegrams to Upper Burma. On November 5, he wrote to Durand that no telegrams had been sent to Mandalay relating the *Pioneer* story.[164] Bernard added that the story could have been despatched to Mandalay by other means. Anyone could get a message to Minhla, the first important river-town in Upper Burma, in four days by a combination of steamer, train, and boat.[165]   The message would require about one hour more to reach Mandalay via the Upper Burma telegraph line.

The above method of sending messages from Rangoon to Mandalay was two days faster than a telegram sent directly over the telegraph line from Rangoon to Mandalay.[166]   A Burmese agent in Rangoon did notify Mandalay of Andreino's activities. He barely eluded the Taingda's troops, who ransacked his home. After November 14 and the start of the war, Andreino was nearly lynched twice by angry mobs, and he wisely spent most of his days in hiding.[167]

The other foreigners were also in danger of being massacred. Thebaw, however, gave orders that they and their possessions were not to be harmed.[168]   The persons affected by the Royal order included ninety Indian shopkeepers and traders who were mostly British subjects; twenty-eight French, mostly Royal employees; twenty-five leading Chinese traders; eighteen Italians, mostly Royal employees; fifteen Armenians; eight 'Eurasians'; seven Greeks; six Jews; four British; two Americans; and two Germans.[169]

Despite the Royal promise of protection, the Europeans had barricaded themselves at Dr. Barbieri's house.   The Indians had gathered at Mulla Ismael's house-fortress; and the Chinese went with their 7,000 local countrymen in the Chinese Quarter.[170]   Such precautions were necessary.   Another news-report claimed that certain ministers were planning to arrest all foreigners, especially the French and Italian Consuls.[171]

The last news from Mandalay was dated November 11 when the *Talifu* left with the Kinwun's reluctant permission.   There was great excitement in Mandalay, and soldiers were being mustered in different parts of the city.   The residents had become alarmed at the news that had been sent up by U Kyi, Thebaw's Rangoon agent.   He reported that 10,000 men had been placed on board IFC steamers and flats, and were already arriving at Thayetmyo on the frontier to await the signal to invade.[172]

The Kinwun's Reply to the Ultimatum

Amidst the above excitement, the Kinwun's reply to the Ultimatum came almost as an after-thought.   Bernard received the reply on November 8, and on the following morning telegraphed the contents to Durand.   The reply went as follows.

Demands one and two had stated that Mandalay would accept an envoy to negotiate the Teak Case; and that the Burmese Government would not act against the BBTC before the envoy arrived in Mandalay.   The Kinwun replied that Thebaw would be pleased to accept a BBTC petition for a Royal Review of the Case; and would furthermore "be pleased to look after and assist foreign merchants and traders, *so that they should not suffer any hardship.*"[173]

Demand three had stated that a new Resident would be established at Mandalay under European protocol with full access to the King.   The Kinwun replied that the former British Resident had left on his own accord.   If the Indian Government wished to establish a new Resident, he would "be permitted to reside and come in and go as in former times."[174]   The last phrase seemed to indicate that the protocol would also remain as it had been in "former times."

Demand four had stated that Mandalay would place its foreign affairs under the Indian Foreign Dept.   The Kinwun refused the demand.   He proposed that if a controversy arose between the Burmese and Indian Governments "the Burmese Government can follow the joint decision of the three states, France, Germany, and Italy, who are friends of both Governments."[175]   This meant that Mandalay would submit its future controversies with the British to all the nations that had treaties with both Governments.   In other words, Upper Burma would attempt to be 'neutral' between the big powers.[176]

Demand five had stated that Mandalay would assist in the establishment of British subjects' trade with Yunnan and Southern China.   The Kinwun replied that his Government was always willing to help increase British and other subjects' trade with Southern China.[177]

An analysis of the Kinwun's reply is in order.   *The Times of India* commented that the Kinwun's reply to demands one and two meant that Thebaw would withdraw his demand for twenty-three lakhs "if all parties, the Indian Government included, will join in pretending that the withdrawal is an act of royal grace....to a petti-fogging trader.   This is a thoroughly Burmese way of doing things."[178]

The Kinwun's reply to demands one and two was an attempt to save the 'face' of his Government by making the same proposal that Mandalay had been making 'unofficially' for the previous month. The Indian Government was well aware that the BBTC could have settled the Case by a petition for Royal Review. However, the Teak Case was the "convenient pretext" by which French influence would be ousted from Upper Burma. Therefore, the Indian Government would not accept the Kinwun's conciliatory reply to demands one and two.

His reply to demand three had not stated that the "Shoe Question" would be waived. If the Kinwun had been more powerful, he might have persuaded the Royal Couple to accept some 'face'-saving compromise. The Chinese Emperor, for example, met the shod and seated British envoy in a garden or building separate from the inner throne-room. The refusal to end the "Shoe Question" was cause enough to reject the entire reply. The Kinwun had also not accepted the river-side Residency, the enlarged Residency guard, or the Residency steamer mentioned in demand three.

Demand four was the key demand designed to oust all French and other foreign political and commercial influence from Upper Burma. If the Kinwun's reply to demand four had been accepted, there would have been three European powers 'intervening' in Upper Burma, instead of only the French. Increased European activity on India's eastern frontier was completely unacceptable to the Indian Government.[179]

The Kinwun's reply to demand five was totally honest and correct. There is no question that Kings Mindon and Thebaw had encouraged British subjects' trade with Upper Burma and Southern China in almost every possible way. The Indian Government was aware that the Panthay revolt in Yunnan from 1855-1873 had disrupted much of the Bhamo-Yunnan trade. The trade was reviving in the 1880's under Thebaw's comparatively good management.

It is a moot point whether the Bhamo-Yunnan trade would have developed faster under the Indian Government. The question did not concern the British to the degree as did the political issues. The most important of these was the British fear that India was becoming *trapped* between an expansionist Russia on India's northwest, and an equally expanding France on India's eastern-frontier.

In summary, the Kinwun's reply was an able one, but not one likely to halt the impending invasion. If the Kinwun had been strong enough to propose his real beliefs, his country might have been able to retain all or most of its independence. Two of the Kinwun's proposals would surely have been (1) an end to the "Shoe Question", and (2) a proposal that British capital build the Toungoo-Mandalay Railroad.[180]   As it was, the Kinwun was not strong enough to persuade Supayalat and the *Hlutdaw* of the soundness of his ideas.

On November 13, Durand telegraphed to Bernard that the Kinwun's reply was evasive and unacceptable. Therefore, Maj. Gen. Harry Prendergast, head of the 10,000-men Burma Expeditionary Force, would invade as soon as he was ready.[181]   The Mandalay Government had already declared war in a November 7 Proclamation that was signed by all the important officials, including the Kinwun.[182]   On November 14, Prendergast's troops began a sweep up the Irrawaddy River on board the steamers and flats of the IFC.

FOOTNOTES

[1] The analogy is inspired by the remark of Viceroy Lord Lytton, who described Afghanistan in 1876 as a 'pipkin' about to be ground between two iron pots, one Russian and the other Indian.

[2] D. R. Gillard, "Salisbury and the Indian Defence Problem, 1885-1902"; in K. Bourne and D. C. Watt, *Studies in International History*, London, 1967, p. 238.

[3] J. A. S. Grenville, *Lord Salisbury and Foreign Policy*, London, 1961, p. 296. *Also see* : R. L. Greaves, *Persia and the Defence of India, 1884-1892*, London, 1959, p. 192.

[4] D. R. Gillard, "Salisbury...," p. 239.

[5] R. L. Greaves, *Persia...*, pp. 196-199.

[6] *Ibid.*

[7] Dilip Kumar Ghose, *England and Afghanistan*, Calcutta, 1960, pp. 159-210. *(See also* : R. L. Greaves, *Persia...* pp. 71-72.)

[8] *Ibid*, p. 159. *See also* : R. L. Greaves, *Persia...* , p. 71.

[9] R. S. Rastogi, *Indo-Afghan Relations, 1880-1900*, Lucknow, 1965, p. 75.

[10] R. L. Greaves, *Persia...*, pp. 74-76.   *See also* : Greaves' Appendix 1, concerning correspondence about Herat, pp. 227-237.

[11] *Ibid*, pp. 80-84.

[12-16] *Ibid*, Great Britain supported Bulgaria as London had supported the Turks in order to block the Russians from the Dardanelles, and to keep open the 'Life Line to India' via Suez.

[17] Briton Martin Jnr., "The Viceroyalty of Lord Dufferin, Part One," (London) *History Today*, December 1960, pp. 829-830. A summary of the findings of Martin's Ph. D. dissertation on the viceroyalty of Lord Dufferin. (*See also:* Robert Rhodes James, *Lord Randolph Churchill*, London, 1959, pp. 147, 205-215, 372. *Also :* Robert Rhodes James, "Lord Randolph Churchill," (London) *History Today*, Vol. V., No. 3, March 1955, pp. 145-153. *See also:* Henry Pelling, *Social Geography of British Elections 1885-1910*, London, 1967, pp. 10-17, 180. *Lastly :* Winston Spencer Churchill, *Lord Randolph Churchill, Vol. 1*, London, 1906, pp. 517-525.)

[18] *Ibid.* (*See also :* Briton Martin Jr., *New India 1885*, pp. 17-20, 79-101, 134-156, 173-176, 241-255.)

[19] *Ibid.*

[20] *Ibid*, pp. 824-825, 828-829. Dufferin's "diplomatic experience.......had trained him to conduct his missions in accordance with the express wishes and instructions of the Government." He believed that it "was no longer within the province of a Viceroy even to suggest important fundamental changes in the system he had been appointed to administer, for matters of such gravity naturally fall within the competence of the government at home." The result was that Churchill developed Indian policy on those issues that he thought "would enhance the chances of a Tory victory in the forthcoming General Election. For Churchill, then, Indian policy was a means to a domestic political end."

[21] No. 49, Dufferin to Churchill, August 14, 1885; in Dufferin Papers, Reel 517/18, p. 199.

[22-25] *Ibid.* Clapham Junction is the coverging point in southern London for many of England's railroad lines.

[26] No. 67, Churchill to Dufferin, August 28, 1885; in Dufferin Papers, Reel 517/18, pp. 153-157. The Moulmein-Yunnan Railroad was much discussed in depression-ridden England in 1885. The proposed railroad was probably not feasible for the period; however, the Burma Road in World War Two did show that trade would improve dramatically with better communications between Burma and Yunnan.

(*See*: A. R. Colquhoun and H. S. Hallet, *Report on the Railroad Connexion of Burma and China*, London, 1885, pp. 8-13. *Also :* No. 46, Colquhoun's Burma-China Telegraph Proposal, May 15, 1885; in Foreign, Secret-E, November, 1885, Nos. 45-54 (NAI). *Also:* "Upper Burma, Lord Ripon and Lord Dufferin," (London) *The Times*, October 22, 1885, p. 13. Colquhoun's rebutal to Ripon's October 16, 1885 speech against invasion and annexation. *See also :* "The Burmese Question," (London) *The Times*, November 10, 1885, p. 11. Colquhoun and Hallet's letters advocated the (1) annexation of Upper Burma, because of (2) the vast commercial advantages to be gained from access to Southern China, via (3) the Moulmein-Yunnan Railroad.

In addition *see:* Grattan Geary, *Burma After the Conquest*, pp. 332-339. Geary rejected both the proposed Bhamo-Yunnan and the Moulmein-Yunnan Railroads as probably not feasible. For a counter-argument *see:*

A. R. Colquhoun, *Burma and the Burmans, or the Best Unopened Market in the World*, London, 1885, pp. 40-58. *Lastly:* J. G. Scott, *France and Tongkin*, London, 1885, pp. 368-381.)

[27-28] *Ibid.*

[29] No. 57, Dufferin to Churchill, October 12, 1885; in Dufferin Papers, Reel 517/18, p. 236.

[30] *Ibid.*

[31] All the authorities in footnote 26 agreed that the Bhamo-Yunnan route was not suitable for a railroad. One of the few authorities who thought that it might be possible to construct a Bhamo-Yunnan Railroad was Col. Edward Sladen, leader of the 1868 exploration party to Yunnan. The Indian Government resisted his proposals for increased British trade with Yunnan, and until 1885 opposed the idea of a Burma-Yunnan Railroad.

When Dufferin opposed the idea of a Burma to Yunnan Railroad, he was acting in the traditional vein of Indian Viceroys. Perhaps not commonly known is the fact that Col. Sladen was 'blackballed' by the India Office (in particular by Grant Duff) for his 1868 exploration, and his subsequent advocacy of increased British trade with Yunnan. As late as 1885, Sladen wanted to go along with the force invading Upper Burma in order 'to clear his name'. *See:* Sladen to Bernard, September 28, 1885; in Foreign, Secret-E, January, 1886, Nos. 37-63, p. 11 (NAI). *Also:* No. 162, Sladen to Dufferin, August 12, 1886; in Dufferin Papers, Reel 525/37, p. 181.

[32] No. 127, Telegram from Dufferin to Churchill, October 16, 1885; in C. 4614, p. 221.

[33] *See* Chapter V.

[34] *See* Chapter VI.

[35] *Ibid.*

[36] *See* Chapter VII.

[37-38] *Ibid.*

[39] *Ibid.*

[40] Indian Government to Churchill, October 5, 1885 ; in L/P & S/7, Political and Secret Letters and Enclosures Received from India, Vol. 45, p. 896A (IOL).

[41] No. 127, Telegram from Dufferin to Churchill, October 16, 1885 ; in C. 4614, p. 221. (*Also :* J. A. Farrer, "The Burmese War," (London) *The Gentleman's Magazine,* Vol. CCLX, January-June 1886, pp. 62-74. Farrer was totally opposed to the Utlimatum and the Third Burmese War. However, he did state that "the dispute of the [BBTC] Trading Company was ......a pretext to justify an aggressive policy..........the fear of French influence and intrigue at Mandalay......was the real, though not avowed, reason for the......war." (pp. 70-71).

[42-45] *Ibid.*

[46] Churchill's November 20, 1885 speech at Birmingham best expressed his view of how to put the workingman back to work. "The Tory policy for the relief of the depression of trade and in order to procure........better

times would be directed to this end, that the nation should........protect
British trade interests abroad (cheers)." An example of this policy in
action was the Burma War then in progress. "Would you have allowed a
British trading industry [BBTC]......to be plundered........? (Cries of
"No.") Do you think such a policy would have protected........British
trade, or......cause British trade to revive or to flourish ? ("No.")."
Churchill concluded his speech by stating that if Burma had been
allowed to oppress British subjects, then what would have prevented France
and the other Great Powers from doing the same—and putting British
workers out of work ? "Lord R. Churchill at Birmingham," (London)
The Times, November 21, 1885, p. 10.

[47] No. 57, Telegram from Churchill to Dufferin, October 17, 1885 ; in Foreign, Secret-E, January 1886, Nos. 37-63 (NAI).

[48] *Ibid.*

[49] K. W. No. 2, Telegram from Churchill to Dufferin, October 17, 1885 ; in Nos. 37-63, p. 7.

[50] No. 275, Telegram from Dufferin to Churchill, October 18, 1885 ; in Dufferin Papers, Reel 519/25, p. 96.

[51] No. 58, Dufferin to Churchill, October 19, 1885 ; in Dufferin Papers, Reel 517/18, pp. 241-242.

[52] *Ibid.*

[53-58] *Ibid.*

[59] No. 79, Churchill to Dufferin, November 18, 1885; in Dufferin Papers, Reel 517/18, pp. 207-209.

[60] No. 80, Churchill to Dufferin, November 27, 1885; in Dufferin Papers, Reel 517/18, pp. 212-213.

[61] *Ibid.*

[62] No. 81, Churchill to Dufferin, December 5, 1885; in Dufferin Papers, Reel 517/18, pp. 216-217. Churchill lost to John Bright in one of Britain's most 'radical' districts in depressed Birmingham by only 733 votes. Churchill was then returned from South Paddington with a large majority.

[63] Bernard to Durand, October 7, 1885; in Nos. 37-63, pp. 10-11.

[64] *Ibid. See also:* Enclosure 1 in No. 129, Lyons to Salisbury, October 12, 1885; in C. 4614, p. 222.

[65] K. W. No. 3(4), Bernard to Durand, October 16, 1885; in Foreign, Secret-E, January 1886, Nos. 216-283, pp. 5-6 (NAI).

[66] Bernard to Durand, October 7, 1885; in Nos. 37-63, pp. 10-11. *See also:* Philippe Preschez, "Les Relations...," pp. 362-363.

[67] K. W. No. 3(4), October 16, 1885; in Nos. 216-283, pp. 5-6.

[68] K. W. No. 3(6), Bernard to Durand, October 22, 1885; in Nos. 216-283, pp. 6-8.

[69] Enclosure 2 in No. 158, Telegram from Durand to Bernard, October 19, 1885; in C. 4614, pp. 252-254.

[70] *Ibid.* *See also:* Pilcher to Bernard's Secretary, May 10, 1883; in Foreign, A-Political-E, June 1883, Nos. 79-84, pp. 1-2 (NAI). U Kyi came down with the 1883-1885 Burmese Mission to Paris.

[71] No. 72, Andreino (Louis Andrews) to Jones, June 23, 1885; in Foreign, Secret-E, January 1886, Nos. 589-611, pp. 3-4 (NAI) *See:* Chapter VII.

[72] Pilcher to Bernard's Secretary, May 10, 1883; in Nos. 79-84. *Also see:* Chapters II and III.

[73] No. 224, Telegram from Bernard to Durand, October 30, 1885; in Nos. 216-283. *See also:* K. W., Bernard to Durand, November 4, 1885; in Foreign, Secret-E, January 1886, Nos. 589-611, pp. 3-4 (NAI).

[74] Enclosure 4 in No. 158, Bernard to Kinwun, October 22, 1885; in C. 4614, pp. 252-254.

[75] K. W. No. 3(6), Bernard to Durand, October 22, 1885; in Nos. 216-283, pp. 6-8.

[76] *Ibid.*

[77] No. 14, Bernard to Durand, October 30, 1885; in Nos. 216-283, pp. 21-22.

[78] "The Burma Crisis," (Calcutta) *Englishman,* October 26, 1885, p. 4. *See also:* "The Burma Question," (Allahabad) *Pioneer Mail,* October 28, 1885, p. 420. *Lastly, see:* "Burma," (Bombay) *The Times of India,* October 23, 1885, p. 21. A real spy, Col. Robert Carey, head of Indian artillery during the Third Burmese War, was at Mandalay during September studying the fortifications. When found out, he barely escaped ahead of the police aboard an IFC steamer. Capt. Remond, the IFC captain who had brought Carey to Mandalay, was sentenced to death, but released at the end of the War. Carey had gone to see Haas before leaving Mandalay, but Haas claimed that he was too sick to see him. Then Haas left for Rangoon only a *few* hours later! The Burmese naturally assumed that Carey had ordered Haas to report to his British masters. When Haas went to live at Bernard's house while at Rangoon, Burmese suspicions were 'confirmed'.

[79] "The Burmese Question," (Allahabad) *Pioneer Mail,* October 7, 1885, p. 336.

[80] "The Burmese Question." (Bombay) *The Times of India,* November 6, 1885, p. 4.

[81] No. 131, Lyons to Salisbury, October 22, 1885; in C. 4614, p. 223.

[82] *Ibid.*

[83] No. 131, A Translation of the Tangyet's October 18, 1885 letter to Lyons; in C. 4614, p. 224.

[84] No. 262D, Lyons to Salisbury, October 23, 1885; in Foreign, Secret-E, December 1885, Nos. 252-264 (NAI).

[85] "The Burmese Envoy in Paris," (Calcutta) *Statesman,* November 21, 1885, p. 6. The article was reprinted from Farman's article in the October 23, 1885 London *Standard.*

[86-87] *Ibid.*

[88-89] *Ibid.*

[90] "Proposals of Arbitration," (Calcutta) *Englishman*, October 26, 1885, p. 4.

[91] No. 349, Lyons to Salisbury, November 3, 1885; in Foreign, Secret-E, January 1886, Nos. 342-355 (NAI).

[92] No. 350, Farman's Summary of the Tangyet's Letter, November 2, 1885; in Nos. 342-355.

[93] Enclosure 2 in No. 135, Translation of the Tangyet's November 3, 1885 letter to Lyons; in C. 4614, p. 229.

[94-95] *Ibid.*

[96] No. 350; in Nos. 342-355.

[97] *Ibid.*

[98] Enclosure 2 in No. 135; in C. 4614, p. 229.

[99] *Ibid.*

[100] "Editorial Notes," (Calcutta) *Statesman*, October 24, 1885, p. 3. "King Theebaw......has asked the Burmese Envoy......in Paris, by telegram, to enquire whether the British Government will consent to receive a Burmese Embassy to negotiate for the reestablishment of a British Embassy at Mandalay, and the reception of a Burmese Legation in London." *See also:* "The Burma Crisis," (Calcutta) *Englishman*, October 23, 1885, p. 4. *Lastly:* "Burmah," (London) *The Times*, October 28, 1885, p. 5.

[101-102] *Ibid. The Times*' article said that the *Hlutdaw* meeting took place on October 22. This is wrong. *The Times*' correspondent, E. K. Moylan, was also the BBTC's Burma lawyer. He changed the date, and claimed in the article that Thebaw wanted war with the Indian Government. This is wrong. Andreino's accounts were factual; Moylan's were 'public relations' efforts, and were usually false.

[103-104] *Ibid. See also:* the 'unofficial' offers to settle the BBTC Teak Case, and avoid the impending War, which were listed near the end of Chapter VII.

[105] No. 136, Godley to Pauncefote, November 9, 1885; in C. 4614, p. 229.

[106] No. 384, Telegram from Churchill to Dufferin, November 8, 1885; in Dufferin Papers, Reel 519/25, p. 109.

[107-108] *Ibid.*

[109] "King Theebaw's Attitude," (Calcutta) *Englishman*, November 9, 1885, p. 4. The Tangyet's November 2, 1885 proposals were described in part: "A telegram to the *Times of India* from London says that the Woondouk......has informed Lord Lyons......that Theebaw is willing to accept generally the terms offered by the British Government."

[110] Philippe Preschez, "Les Relations......," p. 373.

[111] *Ibid.*, p. 364. [trans. excerpt from *Correspondance politique* Angleterre, vol. 813, folio 29, 9 nov. 1885].

[112] *Ibid*, pp. 373-374. (Preschez pointed out that the Myngun had telegraphed Waddington on November 12, 1885 that he was leaving for Burma or nearby territories. Myngun had made a similar statement in an October 20, 1885 letter to Waddington).

[113] *Ibid.* [trans. excerpt from *Correspondance politique* Angleterre, vol. 813, folio 29, 9 nov. 1885].

[114] No. 355, Telegram from Lyons to Salisbury, November 9, 1885; in Nos. 342-355.

[115] Philippe Preschez, "Les Relations......," p. 374.

[116] *Ibid.*

[117-118] *Ibid.*

[119] *Ibid*, pp. 374-375 [trans. excerpt from *Correspondance politique* Angleterre, vol. 813, folio 64-65, 13 nov. 1885].

[120] *Ibid.* p. 375.

[121] *Ibid*, p. 365.

[122] "The Burmese War," (London) *The Times*, November 16, 1885, p. 6. A translation of an editorial that had appeared in the November 15, 1885 edition of the *Telegraphe*, de Freycinet's Paris organ. The editorial stated that the British had been preparing to annex Upper Burma for twenty years. "A few of our countrymen who had just discovered Burmah [a slap at Jules Ferry] offered the protectorate of France [*sic*], and, with the thought-lessness characterizing our colonial policy, the Government ratified these proposals without considering the embarrassments which would result." The January 15, 1885 Treaty aroused the concern of England, which "can no more tolerate the interference of a European nation in......the Upper Irrawaddy than we can in Cambodia......Let us hope this lesson so un-pleasant for our dignity, will....cure us for a time of our mania of inter-vening everywhere and without occasion in affairs which we ill under-stand."

[123] "The Europeans at Mandalay," (Calcutta) *Englishman*, November 3, 1885, p. 5.

[124] General News Column, (Calcutta) *Englishman*, November 18, 1885, pp. 4-5.

[125-27] *Ibid.*

[128] "The Burma Crisis" (Calcutta) *Englishman*, November 9, 1885, p. 4.

[129] General News Column, (Calcutta) *Englishman*, November 18, 1885, pp. 4-5.

[130] After the death of her first child, the Crown Prince, in March 1880, Supaya-lat gave birth to an annual procession of daughters. On March 7, 1886, Supayalat gave birth to another daughter.

[131] K. W. No. 3(8), Andreino to Jones, October 11, 1885; in Nos. 216-283, pp. 11-12.

[132] "The Burmah Question," (Bombay) *The Times of India*, November 6, 1885, p. 4.

[133] H. Fielding-Hall, *Thebaw's Queen*, pp. 229-230.

[134] *Ibid.*

[135] *Ibid*, pp. 230-231. (*See also* "The Burmah Crisis," (Calcutta) *Englishman*, November 12, 1885, p. 4. *Also*: "The Burmah Expedition," (Calcutta) *Statesman*, November 14, 1885, p. 5. *Lastly*: Grattan Geary, *Burma After the Conquest*, pp. 211-213.)

¹³⁶⁻⁴⁰ *Ibid.* (*See also:* Paul J. Bennett, *The Conference*...., pp. 123-124.)

¹⁴¹ *Ibid.* pp. 229-230.

¹⁴² *Ibid.*

¹⁴³ *Ibid*, pp. 230-231. (*See also:* "The Burmah Crisis," (Calcutta) *Englishman*, November 12, 1885, p. 4. *Also:* "The Burmah Expedition," (Calcutta) *Statesman*, November 14, 1885, p. 5. *Lastly:* Grattan Geary, *Burma After the Conquest*, pp. 211-213.)

¹⁴⁴ Taw Sein Ko: *Burmese Sketches*, pp. 46-47. *See also:* Walter S. Desai, *The British Residency*....p. 74. *Lastly:* D. G. E. Hall, *The Dalhousie-Phayre Correspondence, 1852-1856*, p. 16. The Kyi Wungyi (1825) and the son of Maha Bandula (1852) had also suffered this humiliating insult.

¹⁴⁵ H. Fielding-Hall, *Thibaw's Queen*, pp. 230-232.

¹⁴⁶ *Ibid.*

¹⁴⁷ *Ibid*, pp. 232-233.

¹⁴⁸ *Ibid*, pp. 238-239.

¹⁴⁹ *Ibid. See also:* the sources listed under footnote 143.

¹⁵⁰ *Ibid.* ("Unfortunately, these learned and capable councillors failed to influence the King in making the much needed innovations in the country." Ma Kyan, "King Mindon's Councillors," (Rangoon) *JBRS*, Vol. XLIV, June 1961, pp. 43-60.)

¹⁵¹ *Ibid.* (*The Times of India* correspondent asked the Pangyet—with his ten years in Europe and grasp of affairs—why he did not tell the King a little "unvarnished truth, and try to bring about some genuine reform. His reply was a very significant movement of his hand across his throat, with a brief but pithy *je n'ose pas le dire* [I don't dare!]." "The War in Upper Burma," (Bombay) *The Times of India*, November 27, 1885, p. 4.)

¹⁵² *Ibid*, pp. 239-241. The Kinwun, a widower, and the Dowager Queen were close friends. It was whispered that they were lovers.

¹⁵³ *Ibid*, p. 239. Fielding-Hall added that "When a weak man makes up his mind....he is far harder to turn than a strong man."

¹⁵⁴ "The Burma Crisis." (Calcutta) *Englishman*, November 9, 1885, p. 4.

¹⁵⁵ *Ibid. See also:* Grattan Geary, *Burma After the Conquest*, p. 213.

¹⁵⁶ No. 234, Telegram from Bernard to Durand, November 8, 1885; in No. 216-283.

¹⁵⁷ "The Burma Crisis," (Calcutta) *Englishman*, November 9, 1885, p. 4.

¹⁵⁸ *Ibid. See also:* No. 766, Andreino to Bernard's Secretary, December 17, 1885; in Foreign, Secret-E, January 1886, Nos. 764-767 (NAI). These are Andreino's reports of his 'spying' activities at Mandalay. They earned him a £5,000 gratuity in 1886 from the Indian Government.

¹⁵⁹ "The Burma Expedition," (Calcutta) *Statesman*, November 14, 1885, p. 5.

¹⁶⁰ No. 766, Andreino to Bernard's Secretary, December 17, 1885; in No. 764-767.

¹⁶¹ An Unofficial British Agent At Mandalay," (Bombay) *The Times of India*,

November 6, 1885, p. 13. This was the *Pioneer* story, which was quickly picked-up by *The Times of India* and other papers. *See also:* "Occasional Notes," (Allahabad) *Pioneer Mail*, November 4, 1885, p. 436. The editor boasted about "our Rangoon correspondent, who, as long as the Italian Consul was in Mandalay, refused to imperil him by a single reference to his doings."

[162] *Ibid.*

[163] K. W. No. 3(18), Bernard to Allen, November 4, 1885; in Nos. 216-283, p. 31.

[164] K. W., Bernard to Durand, November 5, 1885; in Nos. 589-611, pp. 3-4.

[165] *Ibid.*

[166] *Ibid.*

[167] No. 764, Bernard's Secretary to Durand, January 12, 1886; in Nos. 764-767.

[168] "The War In Upper Burmah," (Bombay) *The Times of India*, November 27, 1885, p. 4. The article related events before November 10, 1885.

[169] "Burma," (Bombay) *The Times of India*, November 6, 1885, p. 21.

[170] "The War In Upper Burmah," (Bombay) *The Times of India*, November 27, 1885, p. 4. *Also:* General News Column, (Calcutta) *Englishman*, November 18, 1885, pp. 4-5.

[171] "The Burmah Expedition," (Calcutta) *Englishman*, November 14, 1885, p. 5.

[172] General News Column, (Calcutta) *Englishman*, November 18, 1885, pp. 4-5.

[173] Enclosure 9 in No. 158, Telegram from Bernard to Durand, November 9, 1885; in C. 4614, p. 256. Italicising added.

[174-77] *Ibid.*

[178] "The War in Upper Burmah," (Bombay) *The Times of India*, November 27, 1885, p. 4.

[179] *Ibid.* "The necessity for consulting France, Germany and Italy is an outcome of the scheme which the more astute Burmese politicians have always had in their mind, to secure the independence of Burmah by making it a bone of contention among European powers. ....some of his [Thebaw's] Ministers have lived for many years in Europe, and are really well educated and astute. If they could only have spoken freely....better days for Burma might have dawned without intervention from outside; but to have done so would have involved their loss of office certainly, probably of life also."

[180] The Tangyet in Paris had proposed through Mr. Farman of the London *Standard* that the British should build the Toungoo-Mandalay Railroad. This proposal was apparently part of the Tangyet's instructions from the Kinwun. On January 16, 1879, the Magwe Mingyi had signed a contract with Dr. Clement Williams, the former British agent at Mandalay from 1861-1865, to build such a railroad. However, the Mandalay Government had withdrawn the contract after Dr. Williams had died in Europe in 1879 while raising funds. The Kinwun, the Pangyet who had headed the 1882

Burmese Simla Mission, the Tangyet, and other officials were also known to
favour an end to the "Shoe Question"; or at least some sort of 'face'-saving
formula palatable to both countries.

181 Enclosure 12 in No. 158, Telegram from Durand to Bernard, November 13,
1885; in C 4614, p. 258.

182 No. 437, The Proclamation of War, November 7, 1885; in Foreign, Secret-
E, August 1886, Nos. 428-520 (NAI). *See also:* No. 440, Thebaw's Order
to Move Troops to the Front. November 13, 1885; in Nos. 428-520.

The Removal of Thebaw

The Two Weeks War

The Third Burmese War lasted exactly two weeks, and resulted in the capture of Mandalay with only a few stones thrown at the conquerors as they took Thebaw and Supayalat into exile.[1] Before examining some of the military and political reasons for the quick collapse and defeat of Thebaw's army, a short summary of the two weeks war would be useful.

On November 14, the Burma Expeditionary Force crossed the frontier above Thayetmyo, and took two days to get some twenty-miles up-river to Sinbaungwe and Nyaungbinmaw. Both these forts fell after three or four hours of shelling from Col. Robert Carey's 64-lb. guns, and the landing of troops.[2] On November 17, the forts forty miles above Thayetmyo at Gue Gyoun Kamyo and Minhla were taken after one of the two biggest battles of the war.[3]

A number of smaller river-fortifications fell in succeeding days, and Pagan was occupied on November 23 without any fighting. Myingyan was shelled on November 24. The Hlaythin Atwinwun directed a hot return-fire throughout the day and night before abandoning the forts on the morning of November 25. During the following two days, the forts at Sagaing and Ava, which were only eleven miles down-river below Mandalay, surrendered without a shot. Several thousand Burmese troops were disarmed.[4]

On November 28, Mandalay was occupied without any fighting. On November 29, the deposed 'Lord Indra' and Supayalat were taken to the steamer *Thooreah*. On November 30 in the early morning, the steamer moved down-river with the deposed Royal Couple on their way to over thirty years of exile in India.

Some Military Reasons for the Burmese Collapse

The Burmese army was scattered throughout the country. In the east, one-half of the Shan States led by the Tsawbwas of Mong Nai, Kengtung, and their allies had been in revolt since 1879-1880. The struggle had resulted in a stalemate, although at times 30,000 Burmese troops and police were said to be engaged in the area. In the north at Bhamo and at Mogaung, the local garrisons had been greatly strengthened in order to prevent these two key river-towns from being captured a second time by local Chinese and Kachin 'dacoits'.

The distances from Mandalay were considerable, and the means of transportation limited to the occasional steamer, the forced march, or the Shan pony. There was no way that the far-flung units could have reached Mandalay before the end of November or the first two weeks of December.[5] Also, once the troops had left a particular trouble-spot, it would have passed out of the control of the Burmese Government into the hands of a local 'dacoit'. The Mandalay military authorities realized that the provincial units were best left where they were, and that the war would have to be fought without them.

The army that faced the Expedition were those Burmese troops regularly assigned to the various forts and river-towns along the Irrawaddy from Sinbaungwe to Mandalay. They composed a good eighteenth century army of over 15,000 men armed with barrel-loading muskets and flintlocks, and with 1,000 or more Martini-Henrys, Sniders, and other breech-loading rifles. In 1785, the troops would have done well. But 100 years later they "knew they had no chance against.... breech-loaders [which could be fired 7-8 times per minute.]....They seemed quite settled in their determination not to fight."[6]

In contrast, the Expeditionary Force had 10,000 men armed with the latest breech-loading rifles. The troops were placed on board the steamers and flats of the IFC, which averaged sixty to eighty miles a day up the 400-mile stretch between Thayetmyo and Mandalay. Col. Robert Carey's 64-lb. guns were nicknamed "Mother Carey's Chickens", and were mounted on special barges. (By way of contrast, the Burmese guns averaged between 3-lb. and 8-lb., and were of such poor construction that many of their gun-crews had never fired them for fear that they would explode.)[7]

In addition, the Expedition had "more machine guns than were ever together [in one place] in India before; [and] ....more than all that ever came to India [before]."[8] The sixteen machine-guns were mounted on steam-launches, and sent ahead of the regular force as a probing and offensive-weapon. Prendergast used them in much the same fashion as he would have used cavalry in a land engagement.

The occasion was one of the *first* times in which the machine-gun was used as an offensive as well as a defensive-weapon. The machine-gun was, apparently, not used as an offensive-weapon in a regular land-engagement until the 1898 Spanish-American War. The event—a gunner blundered ahead of his unit and had to attack the Spanish troops in order to stay alive—went virtually un-noticed at the time.[9]

Most military authorities continued to conceive of the machine-gun as primarily a defensive-weapon until the late-1930's. Therefore, one can imagine how startling a concept it was in 1885 when Gen. Prendergast used sixteen machine-guns in an offensive as well as a defensive role during the November 1885 amphibious-war.

Such tactics would have been of little value had Prendergast not invaded *immediately*. If the river had been blocked, the entire Expedition would have been stymied because there were only about 100 horses for 10,000 men. The mounted unit was a last-minute private venture by Maj. E. C. Brown. It was composed of about eighty Burmese and European civilians recruited from busi-ness-offices and mills in Rangoon. The Indian Quartermaster had not thought that it was necessary to provide any horses. Brown joked later that, apparently, the Generals were supposed to *walk*.[10]

On November 14, the crews of the *Kathleen* and the *Irrawaddy*, two steam-launches armed with machine-guns, were on a probe above the frontier. They surprised Comotto and Molinari, two Italian engineers in Thebaw's service, in the act of blocking the Irrawaddy with two large flats. These flats were pierced with rows of 10' teak-spikes, which were being sunk under the surface of the water. They would have ripped out the bottom of the first steamer to pass over them. The steamer would have sunk, and further blocked the channel.[11]

Comotto and Molinari leaped into the river to avoid the machine-gun fire. Comotto's maps of fortifications, and later the two engineers themselves, fell into British hands. If Prendergast had invaded only a *few* hours later, the river would have been blocked by the King's steamer *Irrawaddy* and the two flats.[12] This would have held-up the Expedition's advance for at least several days. The blockage would have given the two Italians and the Hlaythin Atwinwun sufficient time to block the river in several more places, and to arrange a proper defence at Minhla and at other points further up-river.[13]

The Hlaythin Atwinwun was supposed to delay or stop the Force at Myingyan. If the Hlaythin failed there, the fiercest kind of defence of Ava, only eleven miles south of Mandalay, would have occurred. Molinari was supposed to attend to Ava's defence of 100 guns bearing on the river, including a reinforcement of the flanks and rear.[14] But as the two Italians were surprised by Prendergast's machine-gunners on November 14, and later captured, the Avan defenders did not have time to arrange a proper defence.

For example, the 'bar' across the river above Ava was composed of two Burmese steamers, three flats, and at least fourteen large wooden cargo-boats filled with sand and stones. The bar should have been sunk down-river from Ava. This would have kept the forts out of range of "Mother Carey's Chickens".[15]

Instead, the Avan defenders placed the 'bar' above the Avan forts, thereby allowing Carey to come as close to the forts as he liked. The prows of the sunken boats, instead of being just under the water to rip open the bottoms of steamers, were out of the water like buoys marking the channel. This considerable error in tactics contributed to the collapse of the efforts to defend Mandalay.[16]

In summary, the Burmese defence was ineffectual, Gratten Geary was of the opinion that a "Commission of Burmese Ladies" could have put up a better defence against the Expedition.[17] Prendergast, however, had a somewhat different view, which was also valid. He wrote that a modern army drilled, disciplined, instructed in tactics, and practised in the use of modern weapons, could easily make fun of the Burmese who were none of these things.   However :

> how would it be if the weapons [and positions] were changed ?
> Till fighting under such conditions has been tried, are we entitled
> to consider Burmans cowards ? They certainly face death with
> the greatest composure.[18]

Some Political Reasons for the Burmese Collapse

The political rersons for the Burmese defeat would include (1) the pseudo-Prince, which many Burmese thought was their favourite Prince coming to take the throne.   Many soldiers and civilians did not fight, especially when (2) conflicting orders were telegraphed down-river by the Kinwun and the Taingda.   Many persons, such as those living in the Ningyan Forest area, were already apathetic about the war.[19] Eventually, (3) the Kinwun and the Taingda joined forces to deliver the Royal Couple into British hands. It is understandable why there was little military or political resistance to the invasion.

An important reason for the Burmese defeat was the pseudo-Prince on board Prendergast's steamer at Thayetmyo.   The 'prince' appeared to be the spur-of-the-moment idea of some tricksters on Prendergast's staff.   They knew that a rumour of a Prince coming with the Expedition would greatly diminish the fighting spirit of Thebaw's soldiers.[20]

The Kinwun on his own volition, and not in cooperation with the British, spread the rumour that the British had come only to supersede Thebaw with the Nyaungyan or another Prince.   The Kinwun was certainly aware that the Nyaungyan had died on June 26, 1885 ;[21] but perhaps the average Burmese soldier was not aware. The Kinwun sent a number of secret-orders to friendly river-town Governors and fort-commanders that they should surrender imme-diately.[22]

The Kinwun sent his messages because he felt that a total submission, and an unconditional acceptance of the October 22 Ultimatum, might pacify the British to the extent that they would forego a full-annexation of Upper Burma into the Indian Empire. Instead, they might allow Thebaw or another prince to remain as a 'protected prince', and ruling under the advice of the Indian Foreign

Dept. and the Mandalay Resident.

By way of contrast, the Taingda sent messages to friendly Governors and other followers down-river urging a stern resistance. He claimed that only 2,000 *kalas* were coming in only three or four steamers, and that they should be seized.[23]   Taingda and his group knew better, of course.   But by then his life was in jeopardy, because it had been his advice concerning the country's ability to fight a modern war that had been very influential in the decision to reject the Ultimatum.

Many provincial officials were confused with two sets of conflicting orders from the two great *mingyis* at Mandalay.   A junior customs officer from Sinbaungwe, the first fortified town above the frontier, came down to Thayetmyo to learn what he could about the Prince that the Expedition was bringing to supersede Thebaw. The Prince's existence was verified by many.   He had even been seen in full royal regalia surrounded by courtiers on the deck of the *Doowoon*, the headquarters ship.   Nevertheless, the customs officer had some doubt about the accuracy of the Kinwun's secret order not to fight.[24]

A friend of the customs officer had a fourteen-year-old son, who spoke English as he was a student on vacation from the Government School at Rangoon.   The boy heard his father and the junior customs officer talking about the Prince, and decided to have a close look at the next King of Upper Burma.   Amidst the tumult and confusion of 10,000 incoming troopers and their equipment, the boy located the *Doowoon* where the Prince was staying.

Using his English, the boy got on board.   He discovered to his amazement that the Prince in full regalia was *not* a Prince, but a former student at his school, Maung Ba Than, who had graduated and had been posted as a clerk in Chief-Commissioner Bernard's office.[25]   The boy told his father and the junior customs officer. The officer questioned the boy, and satisfied, rushed back to Sinbaungwe and telegraphed the truth to river-towns and forts further up the Irrawaddy.   He tried to organize local resistance, but Sinbaungwe fell on November 16.   The customs officer crossed over to Minhla Fort, and on November 17 died fighting with a sword tied to each hand.[26]

The rumours concerning a Prince continued to flourish, and were embellished by further 'eye-witness' sightings.   The three groups supporting either the Myngun, the Nyaungoke, or the late

Nyaungyan Prince, thought that it was their candidate who was coming with the Expedition. Each of the three groups spread the rumour still further in order to rally support for their man against Thebaw and against the two rival Princes.

The cacophony of conflicting rumours about a new Prince tended to undermine the will to resist. There was not much point in risking one's life if the *kalas* were only coming with a new Prince to supersede Thebaw. The three groups supporting the rival Princes decided in large part to save their energies for the real battle still ahead. Their respective Prince would surely require their help in crushing the defenders of the other two Princes.

The Kinwun may have partially believed the 'eye-witness' reports of a Prince coming with the Expedition.[27] In that case, he would have redoubled his efforts to persuade his followers downstream of the futility of further resistance. The author, however, believes that (1) the Kinwun was aware that there was no Prince, and (2) the Kinwun sent his messages about the coming of a Prince on his own volition, and not in cooperation with the British and the ruse of the pseudo-Prince.

In summary, whether the Kinwun did or did not cooperate with the British, his motives remained the same in either case. He spread the rumour of a Prince coming with the Expedition in order to save his country, the useless slaughter of many of his people, and his own position.

The Taingda And Kinwun Join Forces

Taingda had made virtually no preparations for the war, despite his bravado on November 1 before the *Hlutdaw* and the Royal Couple, especially Supayalat.[28] Taingda apparently realized that nothing much could be done beyond the issuance of 'face'-saving proclamations, such as the Declaration of War on November 7 and the Troop Muster Order on November 13. Until November 14, and the invasion of the Expedition, the Taingda had believed that the Indian Government was only making a show of force.[29] Therefore, he made almost no efforts to equip the soldiers for resistance, or to rally his countrymen against the invaders.

A number of *dahs*, iron swords, with tin sheaths were manufactured, and Molinari and Comotto were despatched down-river with the results already indicated. They were supposed to arrange a defence, but few adequate materials were given to them.   The captain of the Burmese gunboat *Bandoola* went to assume command of the ship, but found that the boilers and pipes were rusted, and the guns stuffed with refuse and birds' nests.[30]

The Taingda managed to hide such military unpreparedness from the Royal Couple until after the war began.   The fall of Minhla was announced in Mandalay as a great Burmese victory resulting in the capture of three IFC steamers.   It became steadily more difficult to hide the truth when the Expedition took only seven days to steam the 300 miles from Minhla to Myingyan. Taingda's position became desperate on November 24 when Supayalat could hear in Mandalay the boom of "Mother Carey's Chickens" pounding Myingyan only thirty-five miles away.[31] Taingda's life was now at stake, because it had been he, and not the Kinwun, who had risked the Kingdom by his advice, and who had lost it by his military unpreparedness.

His guards surrounded the Royal Apartments and prevented the Royal Couple from learning any adverse news.   When the Hlaythin Atwinwun abandoned Myingyan on November 25 he telegraphed that he had won a great victory.   Thebaw knew so little of the true state of affairs that he sent the Atwinwun 270 gold medals for distribution to the army, and a number of gold-cups and bowls.[32]   The Hlaythin's claim was fantastic.   On the same night of November 25, the Expedition anchored off-shore from Yandabo's famous 'peace tree'.   It had been near this tree that the 1826 Yandabo Treaty had been signed ending the First Burmese War.[33]

Taingda kept all persons except those whom he trusted away from the Royal Couple.   But he had not thought to prevent the little maids of honour from going home to their parents.   Supayalat had become suspicious of the Taingda's behaviour.   She asked five of the maids what their parents talked about at night, and so the children told her.[34]   It was from these five little girls that the real ruler of Upper Burma had to learn of her doom.   "There was no one now who dared to tell her the truth, who even cared to tell her."[35]

A worried Taingda hastened to repair his relations with the Kinwun whose influence was growing with every new defeat. Taingda agreed with the Kinwun's argument that the British were coming not to make war, but rather to negotiate a new treaty with

Thebaw. Therefore, Thebaw should not flee as planned. He should remain in Mandalay, and send a request for an armistice to Ava eleven miles down-stream.[36]

The Kinwun wanted to keep Thebaw in Mandalay, because no matter what the British finally did with Upper Burma, they would always remember that it had been the Kinwun who had prevented Thebaw from escaping from Mandalay. This would be a giant point in the Kinwun's favour at the time when offices were being distributed in the Burmese Government, be it a 'protected state' or full Annexation.

The Taingda, on the other hand, knew that he would die if Thebaw and Supayalat left the Palace enclosure. Both of them would learn that he had lied. They would learn that the Expedition had passed almost unopposed through the country while the event was concealed from the Court, and especially from Supayalat.[37]

The Taingda also knew that many British officials and news-papers blamed him for the 'French Threat' to Upper Burma; for the BBTC Teak Case; and for the entire war. He knew that the only way in which he could save his own life and curry favour with the victorious enemy was to deliver the Royal Couple into their hands.[38]

Consequently, both the Taingda and Kinwun again urged the Royal Couple not to escape with the fifty elephants and 200 ponies that were being loaded with baggage and treasure. Both ministers claimed that if Thebaw escaped to fight again, he would probably be beaten, and he would be certain to lose his throne. The *kalas* had come only to get a new treaty. The ministers urged Thebaw to negotiate with Gen. Prendergast and Col. Edward Sladen, the political officer and former political agent at Mandalay from 1865-1869. Upon receiving the Treaty, the *kalas* would return to Rangoon.[39]

The Appeal for an Armistice

Frederic Haas, the French consul, was summoned to the Palace. At midnight on November 25-26, Haas assisted the Kinwun, Taingda, and the Pangyet in the drafting of the request for an armistice.[40] The letter was re-written into Burmese. The Pangyet and the Wetmasut Wundauk took it down to Ava where

Prendergast was preparing to bombard the forts and their 8,000 defenders.

Near Nazu village below Ava at 4 p.m., November 26, the Indian lookouts spotted a large golden war-boat with a flag of truce at the bow—and peacock-flag at the stern—coming down the river. The crew consisted of a helmsman and forty-four paddlers. The two envoys from Thebaw were seated in the bow under enormous umbrellas.[41] A steam launch went to meet the envoys, and the war-boat was brought alongside the *Doowoon*, Prendergast's head-quarters-steamer. The two envoys went on board without their shoes.[42]

According to an official report, "The Envoys looked intelligent men....the principal one [the Pangyet]....having a very determined face."[43] They presented their unsigned armistice letter, which conceded everything demanded in the October 22 Ultimatum. The letter stated that the British should have known that the only reason the Burmese Government did not concede all the demands was because "we were not allowed sufficient time for deliberation."[44] The letter added that it must have been apparent from the tone of the Burmese Government's reply that they were eager to remain on terms of friendship.[45]

The letter claimed that Mandalay had not totally rejected the demands of the Ultimatum. The Mandalay Government was therefore grieved to find that the British Government had immediately invaded after receiving the Burmese Government's reply. "We have simply resisted in order to maintain the reputation of the Kingdom, and the honour of the Burmese people."[46]

The letter said that the British were renowned for their just acts. As Mandalay deserved justice, there was no need for it to be annexed, especially as Queen Victoria had once declared that there was no desire to annex Upper Burma unless good cause was shown. "As no such cause exists the great Powers of Europe should not have it in their power to say that the Royal declaration [of Queen Victoria] has not been faithfully observed."[47]

The letter reiterated that Mandalay had resisted only after being attacked. Mandalay now wished that the hostilities would cease, and that a treaty of friendly intercourse would be resumed. As soon as the translation was given to the meeting, a controversy broke out, because the letter was not signed.[48] The letter was regarded as a hoax. The envoys would probably have been kicked over the ship's side, but for the insistence of Colonel Sladen that it was a genuine document, and meant surrender.[49]

Sladen explained that no Burmese king ever signed an official , Royal document. No minister ever presumed to sign a document made out in the King's name, but instead stamped the document with the Royal Peacock Seal. Sladen said that if the armistice letter had been signed it would have been unofficial and worthless.[50]

Prendergast postponed the order to shell the forts. His officers and men at first *refused* to obey, since all the army was eager for a fight.[51] Prendergast's unpopular decision to delay the bombardment—and to accept the forts' peaceful surrender the next day—were decisions that were to eventually *cost* him his career.

Prendergast's 'Weakness'?

Prendergast was greatly criticized for his 'weakness' at Ava. It was said that by not attacking the Burmese defenders, Prendergast had allowed many of them to slip away with their weapons; thus forming the nucleus of the 'dacoit' gangs that sprang up almost simultaneously. In short, Prendergast's misjudgment at Ava had largely caused the 'dacoit' problem from 1885-1890.[52]

This was not a valid criticism. Major Brown estimated that a day-long bombardment and a fire-fight with the retreating Burmese defenders would have culminated in the capture of only 200-300 weapons belonging to the 200-300 Burmese casualties.[53] The rest of the 8,000 Burmese toops would have fled with their weapons. By allowing these Burmese to surrender peacefully, Prendergast was able to capture nearly one-half of the forts' 8,000 defenders and their weapons.[54]

But more important, a bombardment of the Avan Forts would have frightened the King and Queen at Mandalay, and would have given them time to escape.[55] They would have served as a Royal symbol of unity for the succeeding 'dacoit' disturbances, and would have imposed a national organization upon what was essentially only a number of local groups.

The 'dacoit' problem would then have become a true national war of resistance—which it never in fact was—and the fighting would have been much worse. As it was, the Indian Army lost only sixty-two men killed during the worst eight months of fighting.[56]   On the Burmese side, the 'dacoit' groups lacked cohesion, and expended much of their energies by raids on each other and on nearby villages.

In summary, Prendergast allowed the Burmese to surrender peacefully at Ava, and was, therefore, able to capture the King and Queen.   By this one act, Prendergast virtually eliminated the possibility of a true national-movement of resistance; reduced the severity of the 'dacoit' disturbances that did occur from 1885-1890; and, undoubtedly *saved* many lives.[57]

The Surrender of the Royal Couple

At 6 p.m. on November 26, 1885, the Pangyet and the Wetmasut ministers left Prendergast's steamer.   They returned to Ava to telegraph his reply to Mandalay.   He had stated that he had no power to discuss any proposals that would effect his advance on Mandalay.   Therefore, no armistice could be granted.   However, if Thebaw surrendered himself, his army, his capital, and the European residents of Mandalay were unharmed, "General Prendergast promises to spare the King's life, and to respect his family."[58]

Prendergast also said that he would not take action at Mandalay beyond what it took to capture the city.   All matters between the two countries would thereafter be negotiated on terms dictated by the Indian Government.   If he did not receive a reply by 4 a.m., November 27, he would then proceed to bombard the Avan Forts where over 8,000 troops, the largest concentration of the war, blocked the advance to Mandalay.[59]

There was no reply by the 4 a.m. deadline.   The fleet steamed up to Ava, and were readying to fire at 10 a.m. when the golden war-boat came out from the bank.   The Pangyet presented the telegraphic reply from Mandalay.   It gave the Avan commander an explicit order that he was not to fire upon the Expeditionary Force.   Instead, the telegram informed the Pangyet that "The King concedes unconditionally all the demands made....You are to let the English commander know this as quickly as possible."[60]

However, the Bo Hmu-Ken Atwinwun, the commander at Ava, was senior in rank to both the Pangyet and the Wetmasut ministers. The Bo refused to surrender the forts, and refused to allow his 8,000 troops to lay down their arms.[61]   The Bo stated that he would refuse all orders from Mandalay, because he had received so many conflicting orders from the Kinwun and Taingda ministers.[62] The only order that he would obey would be a direct telegraphed order from his King. So Thebaw's last royal act was to order one of his very last supporters to surrender.

By 9 a.m. the next morning, November 28, the fleet had docked at Mandalay. A large crowd watched the arrival from the bank. They had received orders not to oppose the landing or advance, "and appeared only too pleased to obey."[63] At 11 a.m., Colonel Sladen in his capacity as Political Officer sent a letter to the Kinwun requesting his presence by 12 noon on the *Doowoon*, and with King Thebaw accompanying him.[64]

No answer was received by 12 noon. Troops were landed at 1:30, and marched smartly through the city, bands playing and flags waving. "All along the suburbs the population had turned out and lined the roads, as if intent on some ceremonial festival."[65] At 3 p.m., Sladen arrived at the Palace grounds where he was met by the Kinwun, and the two of them went into the Palace. Sladen did not remove his boots, and the "Shoe Question" was answered forever.

Meanwhile, Supayalat, inspite of her pregnant condition, had climbed the great spiral staircase of the red watch-tower in the Palace Grounds. From there she watched the steamers come up to the ghats, and begin to unload troops.[66] When told of the marching troops coming to the Palace, she screamed hysterically in the dust of the courtyard: "It is I—I alone—I the queen that have brought destruction to the king my husband and my people. It is I—I alone."[67]

But Supayalat would once more obstruct her husband, and once more prevent the saving of the Kingdom. Thebaw had assembled over fifty elephants and 200 ponies laden with baggage and treasure to escape up-country. However, Supayalat was in no condition to travel miles upon an elephant, and Thebaw refused to leave her.[68]

The incident was a final irony. Supayalat had always behaved like a man, or perhaps she had had to, dominating Thebaw in the bargain. Once more she had dominated her husband, ironically this time by being uniquely female. She had prevented him from performing the one act that would have established him as a 'man' in the eyes of his people, *i.e.* escape and resistance. Or, was his refusal to leave her an even greater masculinity ?

His wife's pregnancy was much on Thebaw's mind, as the Royal Couple and the Dowager Queen met Sladen in ordinary audience. Thebaw asked if Supayalat and he could remain in the summer pavilion in the Palace garden for three or four months until after the baby was born.[69] Sladen suggested as tactfully as he could that it would be better for Thebaw to prepare for an immediate departure from his capital and country.[70] However, no troops would enter the Palace that night. They would camp in the grounds to keep out danger, and to prevent persons from escaping.[71]

Thebaw was visibly relieved. He had been in tears at the start of the interview, because he thought that Sladen would not remember him from the time when Sladen had been the British agent at Mandalay from 1865-1869.[72] Thebaw explained that he feared assassination, and had been afraid to leave the Palace to surrender to Prendergast on the *Doowoon* as Sladen had requested in his letter.[73]

When cautioned by Sladen that he should not try to escape during the night, Thebaw asked : "Where can I go to ? I have no wish to go anywhere."[74] Nevertheless, Sladen slept the night in the *Hlutdaw* chambers after receiving a guarantee from the ministers that their lives would be forfeited if Thebaw got away.[75]

During the night Taingda and several friends dressed themselves in servants' clothing, and slipped through the troops stationed in the Palace grounds. But they were caught before they reached the outer gate, and sent back.[76] At dawn, the Taingda decided to begin currying favour with his new masters.

He woke Sladen, and reported that Thebaw was afraid of an attack from his own soldiers, and that his life was in danger.[77] Sladen found the Royal Couple and the Dowager Queen almost unguarded in the Royal apartments. Only about sixteen maids remained out of the more than 300 that had been in attendance twenty-four hours before. The rest had escaped in the amnesty that Sladen had declared for all palace women, who wished to go in and out of the West Gate of the Palace.[78]

But 300 townswomen had taken the maids' places. The women were scratching and shrieking in the outer apartments for bolts of imported French-silk, jewelery, perfumes, and other valuables. Thebaw reasoned that if such trash could enter the Palace at will, then assassins could not be far behind.[79]   Sladen agreed, and Hampshire Regiment soldiers drove the women back into the streets.   The Royal Couple and the Dowager Queen were lodged in the summer pavilion in the garden.   Twenty-five soldiers mounted guard over the treasures that remained, and the Royal Regalia.[80]

In the early afternoon, booted troops marched through the Palace to the summer pavilion in the garden where the Royal Pair and the Dowager Queen were seated.   The ministers prostrated themselves on the ground before the pavilion.   Thebaw asked which of them would leave with him, and only one old official volunteered.   Thebaw "regarded them with a somewhat scornful, incredulous look in his small eyes.   He then shook his head angrily, intimating that he would have nothing to say to any of them."[81]

Thebaw asked Sladen if he would come with him as he was an old friend.   Sladen refused politely, and said that his duties prevented him from leaving Mandalay.   Prendergast urged an end to the parley as a three-mile march was ahead of them before the Royal Family would be safe on board the *Thooreah*.   Thebaw asked how much longer he would be allowed, and Prendergast took out his pocket watch and said ten minutes.[82]

But Thebaw dawdled for another forty-five minutes.[83]   His fear of the unknown terrors to come must have been enormous.   He had been out of the Palace grounds only about three times in the previous seven years, and had never been more than five miles from Mandalay in his life.   It is understandable why he hesitated. Finally, Sladen and two staff officers walked up the several steps of the pavilion.   They stood over Thebaw, who had never in his life had any one stand over him in such a manner.   Thebaw stood up, and they urged him down the steps.[84]

Still more new experiences awaited Thebaw.   He shook hands with the burly Prendergast, who was the first person who had ever shaken hands with a Burmese King.[85]   A procession to the street began.   Thebaw showed dignity and tenderness towards his Queens, which Brigadier George White thought was chivalrous at such a time.[86]   An immense crowd of servants carrying bundles followed behind.

When the party reached the street, the Burmese crowd surged against them,   and probably would have *robbed* them had the

Expedition troops not kept the mob back.[87]   Brigadier White thought that some of the bundles must have contained a fortune. "I saw a servant, the moment she got out of the Palace Gate, dash through the......Sepoys with a bundle on her head and disappear in the crowd."[88]   White thought that she must have gained "a good haul."

There was a shortage of conveyances, and glorified hospital-stretchers called 'doolies' were brought up for Thebaw's party. "This he scorned for himself and Queens, and boldly started on a walk, the longest of his life, I should think, from the way he waddled along."[89]   Such would not do, and eventually the party was taken down in bullock carts, *gharis*.

The procession became lost and went at least two miles out of its way.   It was led by two regiments of Indian infantrymen, a screwgun battery, and then the King and Queen.   There were eight white umbrellas—one less than usual—over the King and Queen, which was a most subtle way of telling the populace that Thebaw was no longer King.   They were flanked by double-rows of fixed-bayonets, regimental colours, the clash of bands, and the Hampshire Regiment followed in the rear.[90]

The *Englishman* correspondent reported that crowds of Burmese assembled along the street with many prostrating themselves, and uttering loud cries of lamentation as the *gharis* passed. "The bands, however, struck up and drowned these sounds."[91]   The *Pioneer* correspondent claimed that the townspeople bowed down and raised their voices in wailing, children even joining in the cry.   "Thebaw's passage through the city was a most extraordinary spectacle; the cries of the women being particularly thrilling."[92]

Major Brown pitied the little servant-girls who walked the entire distance with their heavy bundles.   They chattered constantly with the soldiers, who could only grin as they understood not a word. "The poor girls were really very frightened, and thought that by practising their winning little ways on these great rough-looking men...[they] would be more likely to protect them."[93]

At one point, Supayalat leaned out of the small window of the *ghari* and asked the closest soldier for a match.   "What does she say ?" asked the man.   She held up her cigar to express her desire, and a rush took place to supply the required light.   She honoured someone, smiled, and began puffing away.[94]

When the bank of the river was reached, the crowd of curious onlookers became dense, and the troops had to push a way through for Thebaw's *ghari*. A few stones were thrown at the troops.[95] But most of the crowd was more concerned with gazing upon the King and Queen whom the onlookers had *rarely if ever seen*. Finally, even Supayalat hesitated when she saw the *Thooreah*, the steamer that was to take them into exile. She exclaimed : "I don't want to go !"[96]

Thebaw hesitated twice at the foot of the narrow-gangplank which led to the steamer. Twice they signaled to him to come aboard. Finally, Supayalat went forward and put her hand in that of the King, and led him to the steamer "as a mother leads her child when it is lost and afraid."[97]

An Assessment of the Defeat

The military reasons for the Burmese defeat would include (1) the overwhelming military power of the Indian Army ; and (2) the fantastic speed with which the Expedition advanced up the Irrawaddy. The Mandalay Government did not have time to block the river, and thusly the defences up-river were never properly established.

The political reasons for the defeat would include (1) the pseudo-Prince, which many Burmese thought was their favourite Prince coming to take the throne. Many soldiers and civilians did not fight, especially when (2) conflicting orders were telegraphed by the Kinwun and the Taingda. Many persons, such as those living in the Ningyan Forest area, were already apathetic about the war. Eventually, (3) the Kinwun and the Taingda joined forces to deliver the Royal Couple into British hands. It is understandable why there was little military or political resistance to the invasion.

Thebaw also contributed to the Burmese defeat. The Royal Couple could have escaped from Mandalay except that Supayalat was pregnant and Thebaw refused to leave her. Thebaw also committed one other action, which contributed to the Burmese defeat. In mid-November, Andreino's 'treachery' became known.[98] Thebaw could have ordered a massacre of all the foreigners in Mandalay. This would probably have stiffened the national will to resist, and might ultimately have saved Thebaw's throne.

Chastising the 'Foreigner-Barbarian-Monster' has usually been the chief mechanism by which rulers have saved their positions, and united their societies against the intruders from without.[99] However, Thebaw refused such advice.   He summoned the foreigners, mostly merchants, to the Palace, and told them that they would not be harmed, nor would anyone touch their goods. Thebaw kept his word.[100]

In conclusion, Thebaw and Prendergast were both comparatively 'average' men.   It is therefore all the more remarkable that both refused to massacre the 'foreigners' at, respectively, Mandalay and Ava.   Both men knew that their careers would probably be helped by such a massacre, and would probably be hurt if no massacre occurred.   Yet both of these 'average' men refused their 'opportunity'.

FOOTNOTES

[1] "The Burmese War," (London) *The Times*, December 4, 1885, p. 5.

[2] No. 533, Telegram from Bernard to Durand, November 18, 1885; in Foreign, Secret-E, January 1886, Nos. 503-559 (NAI).

[3] 116/73 (Case. 219), Operations in Burmah and Proceedings of Naval Brigade (1885-1886), Part 3, pp. 13-16 (PRO).   An account of the taking of Minhla. (*See also:* Lt. J. R. Dyas, Diary and Letters of Recollection; in Mss. Eur. F. 108/12, Sir George White Collection, p. 2 (IOL).   *Also:* Gen. George White's Private Diary for 1885-January 1886; in MSS Eur. F. 108/118 (LB/2) (IOL).)

[4] *Ibid*, Part 2, pp. 8-10.   An account from the naval point-of-view from the capture of Minhla to the fall of Mandalay.   *Also see :*   Admiralty 127/17, The Burma War 1885-1887 (PRO).   *Also:* BAR/4 and 5, Journal of the Naval Brigade in the Burma War ; in C. J. Barlow Personal Papers (NMM). *Also :* Military Dept. of India, Field Operations in Upper Burma 1885-1886 (Despatches of Gen. H. Prendergast), Simla, 1886 (BM).   *Also:* Enclosure 1 in No. 46; in C. 4887, Burmah No. 3 (1886), pp. 52-53 (NAI).   *Also:* Telegrams Nos. 145-154, 156, 159, 163, and 165; in C. 4614, pp. 232-233, 246-247, 258-260.   *Lastly:* The Historical Record of No. 4 (Hazara) Mountain Battery, Lahore, 1888 (BM).

[5] Enclosure 2 in No. 10, Sladen to Durand, December 16, 1885; in C. 4887, pp. 4-8.

[6] Major Douglas Macneill, *Report and Gazetteer of Burma, Native and British, Part One,* Simla, 1883, p. 308 (IOL).   Macneill spent two months at Mandalay in 1883 spying out Mandalay's defences and troop strength. He stated that the 'modern' brick and masonry forts, which the European engineers in the King's service had constructed along the Irrawaddy, were usually inferior to the old Burmese teak-forts.   The teak-forts would have

absorbed the heaviest modern shell with little damage.   The 'modern' brick and masonry forts would and did shatter into brittle pieces.

If the engineers had used teak in constructing the superior European-style forts with their flank and rear defences, the Burmese forts would have been some of the best in the world.   Their locations were excellent; however, without heavy artillery to answer the Expedition's fire, the forts and their locations were of little value.   Macneill also stated that the Burmese were excellent in advancing across open terrain via a series of foxholes, and in transporting large units of men via Shan ponies.   Neither Burmese advantage could be used in the 1885 War, but they were used later during the 1885-1890 'dacoit' disturbances.

[7] *Ibid.   Also see:* Foreign, Secret, July 1879, No. 441 (NAI).   *Also:* Foreign, Secret, August 1879, Nos. 79-126 (NAI).   *Also:* Foreign, Secret, November, 1879, No. 58 (NAI).   *Also:* Foreign, Secret, March 1880, Nos. 110-113 (NAI).   *Also:* Foreign, Secret, March 1880, No. 114-116 (NAI).   *Also:* Foreign, Secret, August 1880, Nos. 32-36 (NAI).   *Lastly:* Foreign, Secret, August, 1881, Nos. 31-36 (NAI).

Interesting unofficial views of the Burmese Army include: "The Burmese Army," (London) *The Times*, November 14, 1885, p. 11.   *Also:* Shway Yoe, *The Burman*......, pp. 492-503.   *Lastly:* R. R. Langham-Carter, "The Burmese Army", (Rangoon) *JBRS*, Vol. XXVII, Part 1, 1937. pp. 254-276.

[8] No. 460e, Bernard to Dufferin's Secretary, November 14, 1885; in Dufferin Papers, Reel 528/48, pp. 357-358.

[9] The author would appreciate a correction if he is in error on this point.   The statement was part of a tactics lesson, which the author studied while in the military.   For a general description of the evolution of the machine-gun (and the tank) from a defensive to an offensive-weapon, see any standard account of military tactics in the nineteenth and twentieth centuries.   *For example:* Maj. Gen. D. K. Dalit, *War in the Deterrent Age*, London, 1966, pp. 84-92.

[10] Maj. E. C. Brown, *The Coming of the Great Queen*, pp. 133-134.

[11] Lt. H. E. Stanton, ed., *The Third Burmese War*, Simla, 1888, p. 14.

[12] *Ibid.   Also :* E. C. V. Foucar, *They Reigned at Mandalay*, p. 137.   The soldiers captured the Burmese steamer *Irrawaddy*, kept the peacock flag aloft, and sailed the steamer down to Thayetmyo where the sight of a Burmese gun-boat bristling with eight smooth-bore guns caused hysterical excitement.   The troops stood to their posts, and it appeared that the *Irrawaddy* was about to bombard the town.   "Then the naval jesters aboard hauled down the Peacock and ran up the Union Jack, much to the amusement of the troops lining the river bank."

[13] No. 514a, Prendergast to Dufferin, December 4, 1885; in Dufferin Papers, Reel 528/48, pp. 384d-384e.

[14] *Ibid.*

[15] Gratten Geary, *Burma After the Conquest*, pp. 81-82.   *See also:* Lt. H. E.

Stanton, *The Third Burmese War*, p. 33. Stanton was not so critical of the location as was Geary.

[16-17] *Ibid.*

[18] Gen. Sir H. N. D. Prendergast, "Burman Dacoity and Patriotism and Burman Politics," (Edinburgh) *Blackwood's Edinburgh Magazine*, New Series-Vol. V., January-April 1893, p. 276.

[19] H. Fielding-Hall, *A Nation At School*, pp. 35-44. An account of how the BBTC Ningyan Forest personnel fled at the start of the War. Fielding-Hall wrote : "I do not think any facts could better illustrate the Burman kingdom and the people than our escape....Think what would happen in any other country ? Would any one holding our position have got away ? Would not the government have arrested them at once ; would not the people have risen against them ?" (p. 44).

[20] Maung Htin Aung, *The Stricken Peacock*, The Hague, 1965, pp. 89-91.

[21] "Burma," (Allahabad) *Pioneer Mail*, July 19, 1885, p. 58; and "General Summary," (Bombay) *Times of India*, August 11, 1885, p. 3. These articles described the pleased reaction of the Court at Mandalay upon the death of the Nyaungyan Prince.

[22] Maung Htin Aung, *The Stricken Peacock*, pp. 89-91.

[23] No. 495, Telegram from Prendergast to Durand, November 27, 1885; in Dufferin Papers, Reel 528/48, p. 375.

[24] Maung Htin Aung, *The Stricken Peacock*, pp. 89-91.

[25-26] *Ibid.* Maung Htin Aung added that the fourteen-year-old boy was his father, and one of the customs officer's daughters was his mother. Maung Ba Than's father and older brother were well-known officials in Lower Burma.

[27] *Ibid.*

[28] Grattan Geary, *Burma After the Conquest*, p. 213.

[29] *Ibid.*

[30] H. Fielding Hall, *Thibaw's Queen*, p. 245.

[31] No. 264, Telegram from Bernard to Durand, December 1, 1885; in Foreign, Secret-E, January 1886, Nos. 216-283 (NAI).

[32] Lt. H. E. Stanton, *The Third Burmese War*, p. 30.

[33] *Ibid.*

[34] H. Fielding-Hall, *Thibaw's Queen*, p. 271.

[35] *Ibid.*

[36] Grattan Geary, *Burma After the Conquest*, pp. 214-216.

[37-39] *Ibid.*

[40] Philippe Lehault (Frederic Haas), *La France et l'Angleterre an Asie, Tome 1*, Paris, 1892, p. 217.

[41] Lt. H. E. Stanton, *The Third Burmese War*, p. 31.

[42] *Ibid.*

[43] 116/73 (Case 219), Operations in Burmah and Proceedings of Naval Brigade (1885-1886) Part 1, p. 17.

[44] Enclosure A, in No. 10, Kinwun to Prendergast, November 25, 1885; in C. 4887, pp. 8-9.

[45-47] *Ibid.*

[48] Grattan Geary, *Burma After the Conquest,* p. 217.

[49] *Ibid.*

[50-51] *Ibid.*

[52] Maj. E. C. Brown, *The Coming of the Great Queen,* pp. 155, 171-172.

[53-54] *Ibid. Also see:* Lt. H. E. Stanton, *The Third Burmese War,* pp. 32-33.

[55] *Ibid.* Viceroy Lord Dufferin wrote that had Prendergast surrendered to the clamour of his army to attack at Ava, the attack "might have been made to assume the appearance of a victorious battle instead of a useless butchery. But he stood firm, and, as a result, he entered Mandalay unopposed and captured the King." No. 8, Dufferin to Kimberley, February 26, 1886; in Dufferin Papers, Reel 517/18, pp. 17-18.

[56] G. E. Harvey, *British Rule in Burma.* . . . ., p. 24. The casualties totalled about 1.000 a year. As late as 1888, the Indian Army still had 34,712 troops involved along with over 8,000 local policemen. The total cost of the five-year 'pacification' was about £5,000,000, or more than ten times the original estimate.

[57] The Expedition had less than 100 horses for 10,000 men. A lack of horses crippled Prendergast's force after its bloodless capture of Mandalay. The rising 'dacoit' problem out of range of his foot-soldiers forced Prendergast into retirement after March 31, 1886. A popular soldier, who might have succeeded Gen. Roberts as C. in C. of the Indian Army, ended his career as a Resident at several Indian Princely courts.

Every succeeding general in Upper Burma was unsuccessful against the 'dacoits' until late-1886 when enough horses finally arrived for large numbers of mounted infantry and police. In summary, there have always been 'dacoits' in Burma; before 1885, during the British times, and *since 1948.* Prendergast was therefore fighting a centuries-old phenomenon in Burma, and without the proper equipment or horses. Gen. George S. White, who received the ultimate credit for crushing the 'dacoit' disturbances of 1885-1890, stated that: "the [1885] Force was equipped as a fish to fight a dog."

[58] Enclosure B. in No. 10, Prendergast to Kinwun, November 26, 1885; in C. 4887, p. 9.

[59] *Ibid.*

[60] No. 750, Sladen to Durand, December 16, 1885; in Foreign, Secret-E, January 1886, Nos. 749-754 (NAI).

[61] Lt. H. E. Stanton, *The Third Burmese War,* pp. 32-33.

[62] *Ibid.*

[63] *Ibid.*

[64] Enclosure E in No. 10, Sladen to Kinwun, November 28, 1885; in C. 4887, p. 10.

[65] Enclosure 2 in No. 10, Sladen to Durand, December 16, 1885; in C. 4887, pp. 4-8.

[66] F. T. Jesse, *The Story of Burma,* p, 75.

[67] H. Fielding-Hall, *Thibaw's Queen*, pp. 286-287.

[68] F. T. Jesse, *The Story of Burma*, p. 75. "It is the best thing we have heard of him, so let us remember it."

[69] No. 750, Sladen to Durand, December 16, 1885 ; in Nos. 748-754.

[70-71] *Ibid.*

[72] "The War in Burma," (Calcutta) *Englishman*, December 4, 1885, p. 4.

[73] "The Burmese War," (London) *The Times*, December 4, 1885, p. 5.

[74] No. 750, Sladen to Durand, December 16, 1885 ; in Nos. 748-754.

[75] *Ibid.*

[76] "The Burmese War," (London) *The Times*, December 4, 1885, p. 5.

[77] Enclosure 2 in No. 10, Sladen to Durand, December 16, 1885 ; in C. 4887, pp. 4-8.

[78] *Ibid.* (Thebaw later claimed that he had left many more treasures than were ever recorded in the official records. Thebaw said that Sladen had told him he would keep the treasures for Thebaw until he would want them. A doubtful story. For Thebaw's petitions *see* : Foreign, Secret-E, November 1886, Nos. 279-288 (NAI). *Also* : Foreign, Secret-E, October 1887, Nos. 174-179 (NAI). *Also* : Foreign, General-A, March 1912, Nos. 12-13 (NAI). *Lastly :* Maj. E. C. Brown, *The Coming of the Great Queen*, pp. 177-179).

[79-80] *Ibid.*

[81] Major E. C. Brown, *Coming of the Great Queen*, p. 183.

[82] *Ibid.*

[83] *Ibid*, pp. 184-185.

[84] J. G. Scott and J. P. Hardiman. *Gazetteer of Upper Burma* . . . . , *Vol. 1, Part I*, p. 113.

[85] *Ibid.*

[86] Sir Mortimer Durand, *The Life of Field Marshal Sir George White, Vol. I*, London, 1915, pp. 315-319. Excerpts from White's letters.

[87] *Ibid.*

[88-89] *Ibid.*

[90] J. G. Scott and J. P. Hardiman, *Gazetteer of Upper Burma* . . . . , p. 114. *Also see :* Lt. H. E. Stanton, *The Third Burmese War*, p. 35.

[91] "King Thebaw a Prisoner," (Calcutta) *Englishman*, December 4, 1885, p. 4.

[92] "The Burma Expedition," (Allahabad) *Pioneer Mail*, December 8, 1885, p. 591.

[93] Major E. C. Brown, *Coming of the Great Queen*, p. 187.

[94] *Ibid.*

[95] "The Burma Expedition," (Allahabad) *Pioneer Mail*, December 8, 1885, p. 591.

[96] Sir Mortimer Durand, *Life of* . . . . . . *White*, pp. 315-319.

[97] H. Fielding-Hall, *Thibaw's Queen*, pp. 292-293.

[98] No. 764, Bernard's Secretary to Durand, January 12, 1886 ; in Foreign, Secret-E, January 1886, Nos. 764-767 (NAI).

[99] Denis Sinor, "Foreigner Barbarian Monster," in *East West in Art*, ed. by Theodore Bowie, Bloomington, 1966, pp. 155-159.

[100] H. Fielding-Hall, *Thibaw's Queen*, pp. 253-260.

10

'Dacoity' and Annexation: the Vicious Circle

Introduction

Dufferin had the major responsibility for determining the future of Upper Burma after November 28, 1885. His choice was essentially between a 'protected Prince' with a basically Burmese-administration, or annexation with a basically European-administration.

The London Foreign Office had become concerned over the imperfectly understood Chinese 'decennial tribute' claim against Upper Burma.[1] Such claims, however, had relatively little influence on Dufferin's final decision made on February 13, 1885 in favour of annexation. This decision was made almost six months before the 'decennial tribute' question was finally resolved in the July 25, 1886 agreement signed at Peking.[2]

There were two important factors that did influence Dufferin to make his recommendation in favour of annexation. The first factor was the 'dacoit' problem and the inability of the *Hlutdaw*, the most important remaining feature of Burmese rule, to control them.

The second factor that influenced Dufferin to make his recommendation for annexation was his concept of his relationship with the Secretary of State for India. This was essentially that of a diplomat carrying out the conceptions of the Home Government. Dufferin's willingness to submerge his desires and opinions on

Indian problems, and to accept those of the India Office, was a source of worry to that Office.

For example, on April 16, 1886, A. Mackenzie, the Indian home secretary, wrote to Dufferin from London.   MacKenzie commented on his conversations with India Office officials: "It was hinted by more than one that it would...save difficulty if the Viceroy marked out his own lines decisively and.. .leaving them only the task of approving and accepting. Some...think that we have been almost too ready to refer points for decision *here*."[3]

In short, Dufferin never fully exercised his power to decide the future of Upper Burma.[4]   Dufferin's concept of his position *vis-a-vis* the India Office would never allow him to forget that both Lord Churchill and Lord Kimberley, Churchill's successor at the end of January 1886, were in favour of annexation.

It should also be pointed out that *The Times* was outspoken in its pro-annexation stand;[5] and that both Lord Salisbury and William Gladstone, who succeeded Salisbury as Prime Minister at the end of January 1886, were in favour of annexation.   From what is known of Dufferin's subservient character, it is rather surprising—and admirable—that he resisted the above persons and groups as long as he did.

The sections below will examine (1) the political vacuum in Upper Burma after November 28, 1885, and (2) the consequent growth of 'dacoity'. The succeeding sections will examine Dufferin's intellectual journey, which culminated in his February 13, 1886 recommendation in favour of annexation.

The Political Vacuum After November 28, 1885

Prendergast's victory over the conventional Burmese troops in November 1885 had been so complete that the civilian authorities supposed that the Third Burmese War was over.   They ignored the fact that Prendergast had 10,000 troops stretched in a thin line along the Irrawaddy River from Sinbaungwe in the south to Bhamo in the north.   The British Government further ignored the fact that Prendergast could not possibly occupy the country-side away from the River and restore order with so few troops and only 100 horses.[6]

Instead of acting promptly, the British Government allowed a political vacuum to prevail in Upper Burma from November 28,

1885 to February 1886. In the absence of any decision as to the future form of Government, Col. Sladen attempted to use the *Hlutdaw's* considerable prestige, and the Taingda's reputed influence with the 'decoits', to restore order.[7]

Sladen believed—with considerable logic—that the Taingda and the Kinwun could not get along. Sladen, however, did not seem to realize that both ministers would have to be represented on the *Hlutdaw* if it was to be effective. Sladen thought that the Taingda would be more useful in restoring order and suppressing the 'dacoits', because he had employed a number of such 'dacoits' around Mandalay before the War. With a surprising lack of appreciation for the Kinwun's former services—and his current usefulness—Sladen had him diported to Rangoon on November 30, 1885.[8]

Prendergast and Bernard disagreed with Sladen's decision,[9] but Bernard allowed Sladen to retain the Taingda until December 28, 1885. Then, Bernard had the Taingda deported to Rangoon, and the Kinwun brought back to Mandalay.[10] Sladen and Bernard had *both* made a serious mistake by not retaining both ministers at Mandalay. The Kinwun could have been appointed as 'Regent and President of the *Hlutdaw*'. The Taingda could have been appointed as Justice and Finance Minister and told to restore order and revenue collections in the country-side—or else! At least, Sladen could have used the Kinwun's vast prestige with the Upper Burmese people, and with non-Burmese. Unfortunately, Sladen had allowed the Kinwun's prestige to be separated from his efforts to retain the *Hlutdaw* as the key feature of the new Government.[11]

Sladen's mistake in retaining only the Taingda gave rise to widespread criticism. The *Hlutdaw* was charged with being 'anti-British' and 'pro-dacoit'. The Taingda's removal to Rangoon did not dampen the criticism. Instead, it grew more virulent due in part to the prejudiced reporting of E. K. Moylan, *The Times'* Burma correspondent and also the BBTC's Burma lawyer. According to Moylan, the 'natives' were not to be trusted with a mechanism of self-government, such as the *Hlutdaw*.[12] By late-January 1886, the *Hlutdaw* and the related concept of a 'protected Prince' were virtually doomed.

'Dacoity' : the Vicious Ecological Circle

The 'dacoit' movement after November 28, 1885 was almost inevitable, and should be thought of as essentially a series of almost unconnected local governments. In most areas, the modes of government higher than that of the village had collapsed after the taking-away of the Royal Couple. The 'dacoit' groups developed in all localities where the Indian Government did not have sufficient troops to restore law, order, and the everyday functions of government. In short, the 'dacoits' were a local attempt to *overcome* the anarchy that gripped much of the country-side after November 28, 1885.[13]

A vicious ecological circle had begun. There was hunger and a shortage of money due to the virtual stoppage of trade between the villages. The stoppage of trade had occurred because of the collapse of law, order, and government in the country-side between the villages. In order to eat, and to obtain the other goods they needed, the villagers *i.e.* 'dacoits' began to rob the neighbouring villages. The raiders—in turn—had to guard themselves against reprisals.[14]

The villagers became afraid to harvest the food crops that were available locally, because the food-stocks would only attract 'dacoits' *i.e.* neighbouring villagers. The result was a continuing lack of food and products, which further harmed what little trade remained between the villages. This in turn led to still more hunger, 'dacoities', and anarchy in the country-side.[15]

Grattan Geary gave a dramatic example of how complete was the economic and social breakdown. He wrote that "In ordinary times every Burman house is also a shop, where something or another is always on sale. This petty trade is now [virtually] at an end," because of the anarchy beyond the village. Geary related the story of a Chinese wholesaler, who had not realized this fact. The merchant had landed 250 bags of rice on the river-bank near the Upper Burmese rivertown of Pokokko.[16]

He found to his dismay that there were no 'front-porch' traders and no regular rice-retailers with enough money to buy his rice. The anarchy had virtually severed the trade between the villages, thus reducing the flow of money and goods into the village. There was a demand in the village for rice. But there was almost no money or goods with which to pay for it; and, few persons dared to take in the harvest because it would attract 'dacoits'.

The only alternative had been to raid the neighbouring villages.[17]

The upshot was that the terrified rice-wholesaler was afraid of being robbed by almost everyone within a ten or fifteen mile radius. He had to remain awake all night—with one rusty sword—atop his 250 bags of rice. He had been forced to give up his rifle a short time before to an Indian Army patrol, who were confiscating all weapons in an attempt to halt the 'dacoity' problem in the neighbourhood.[18]

In December 1885, the 'dacoities' had "next to nothing....to do with patriotism, or even with the desire of pillage; it is a fight for food....[and] is in no way directed against the English. It is local in its aims and objects if not in its general causes."[19] The only response that the Indian Army could make was to execute—after a civil trial—those 'dacoits' that fell into its hands. The Indian Army did not have sufficient troops or horses to restore law, order, and government in the country-side. If Prendergast had had sufficient troops, he would still not have been able to establish a government. Viceroy Dufferin had *not* as yet decided upon the form of that government.

The unfortunate result was that "the promiscuous shooting of so-called dacoits was....a great, if....not the sole, cause of the rapid spread of the movement of resistance."[20] By the end of December, the villagers had begun to organize into groups of 500-1,000 men from several villages. The village confederacies carried out raids against other village-groups; ambushed Indian Army patrols; and, harassed the tiny fifty-man garrisons dotting the countryside by firing at the sentries at night.[21]

By early-January 1886, much of Upper Burma away from the Irrawaddy River had been organized around similar confederacies or 'circles'. Their leaders usually assumed the right to a golden umbrella, and set-up their own minature 'Mt. Meru'. Once they had secured food and restored order in their immediate neighbourhood, they resolved to conquer Mandalay and the Palace, the earthly 'Mt. Meru'. In order to do this, they had to fight (1) other confederacies ; (2) remnants of the old Royal Burmese Army that had lapsed into 'dacoity'; and lastly, (3) the Indian Army which currently held 'Mt. Meru'.[22]

By early January, the British authorities were saying that such an outbreak was really not surprising, A similar wave of 'dacoities' had occurred in Lower Burma after the Second Burmese War, and

25,000 to 30,000 troops had been required there for three years to pacify the region.[23]   Geary quoted an exciteable, but highly-placed administrator in Burma, who believed that perhaps 60,000 troops would be needed to pacify Upper Burma.[24]   Geary thought that the estimate was rather exaggerated, but it did reveal the concern that the 'dacoit' problem was causing by mid-January 1886.

By late-January the 'dacoits' were beginning to group them- selves under two Princes, "who have turned up unexpectedly when no one counted upon such an apparition."[25]   The bazaar 'gup' stated that one Prince's army totalled 9,000 men, and the other's from 2,000 to 5,000 men.   The latter Prince was gaining adherents by raids into the harvest fields and villages.   When villagers refused to join his force, the Prince burnt the offending village to the ground.   He boasted that he would soon take Mandalay and 'Mt. Meru' from its alien conquerors.[26]

Meanwhile, Col. Sladen had become most unpopular with many Europeans, and even with many Burmese, because he still supported the Taingda and the *Hlutdaw*.   After the Taingda was deported to Lower Burma on December 28,[27] Sladen told the *Hlutdaw* that they would have performed much better against the 'dacoits' in King Thebaw's time.   If the ministers had not, they would have lost their lives.[28]

The Hlaythin Atwinwun, the former admiral of the warboats, felt the criticism keenly.   He sent several assassins with muskets to Sagaing only eleven miles away where they joined the army of Prince Kyu Nyo, one of the two Princes mentioned above.   Prince Kyu Nyo was a son of the late Heir Designate, who had been assassinated by the Myngun Prince in 1866.   After worming their way into Prince Kyu Nyo's confidence, the assassins shot him dead during an Indian Army attack on his camp on January 23, 1886, and fled back to Mandalay.[29]

A howl of protest went up concerning the 'barbaric uncivilized murder'.   The protests came from many of the same persons, who had somehow managed to overlook the military executions of 'dacoits'.   This according to Grattan Geary was the chief cause of the growth of 'dacoity' since November 1885.[30]

The Hlaythin Atwinwun maintained that nothing had been done that was not in accord with the British usages of war.   He confessed that he was not able to understand why the shooting of 'dacoits' had been acceptable for two months, and yet the shooting

6. *November 17, 1885. The Second Bengal Light Infantry charging the gallant Burmese defenders of Minhla.* (Illustrated London News, January 23, 1886, pp. 84-85).

of the head 'dacoit', namely the Kyu Nyo Prince, was somehow not acceptable. The Hlaythin "professed to be much hurt at the imputation upon his honour and honesty."[31]

By February 3, 1886, the *Hlutdaw* was in considerable danger of being abolished. The popular view among many Burmese and non-Burmese was that the ministers—and Gen. Prendergast—had not been effective in stamping out the 'dacoit' problem. The future of the *Hlutdaw* and of Upper Burma lay in the hands of Lord Dufferin. He and Lady Dufferin were about to descend upon Mandalay in mid-February on an inspection-tour. It was rumoured that Dufferin would then announce his decision concerning the future form of government for Upper Burma. The following sections will examine the process by which Dufferin arrived at his decision.

The Case for the 'Protected Prince'

Dufferin did *not* want to annex Upper Burma, because it would have caused great financial and military strains upon the already over-extended Indian Empire and upon the Indian tax-payers. Many other officials and journalists also shared his reluctance.[32] Gradually, however, Dufferin came to the conclusion that there was no other alternative.

On October 19, 1885, Dufferin had listed six arguments that favoured annexation.[33] Many of these arguments had been provided by Bernard since late-July. On November 9, Dufferin presented the arguments against annexation and for the concept of a 'protected Prince'. These arguments had been supplied to him by Sir C. U. Aitchison, Lt. Gov. of the Punjab and the former Chief Commissioner of Lower Burma who had been most responsible for the withdrawal of the Mandalay Residency on October 6, 1879. The four arguments against annexation follow below.[34]

(1) Upper Burma had a rich potential when developed by a good government, *i.e.* European. However, it would require many years before the Upper Burmese revenues would equal the administrative costs.[35]

(2) The Burmese were personally brave, but they had no sense of military discipline. Indian troops would be required to maintain order for several years until local levies could be trained. However, the Indian Government could not afford to become

involved in a further military 'adventure' on India's east, because of the confrontation with Russia over Herat and the long-range 'Russian Threat' to India's northwest.[36]

(3) Thebaw's northern frontier was ill-defined, and the many wild tribes would be a constant law and order problem. Once the northern and northeastern areas came under Indian rule, the tribal depredations would have to be punished. The 'protected' or independent Burmese state, on the other hand, would be able to ignore most depredations with comparative impunity.[37]

(4) The Chinese ambassador to London, and the Chinese Foreign Office at Peking, had expressed their concern over Upper Burma in late-October. If there was any chance of trouble with the Chinese over the northern frontier of Upper Burma, or if an actual armed-clash occurred, this would wreck the potential British trade with Yunnan and Southern China.[38]

A 'protected state' would, however, tend to ease the tense situation. Dufferin concluded that another Prince, such as the Nyaungoke, might be placed upon the throne. Thebaw should probably be deposed, because of his Government's refusal of the Ultimatum.[39]

Churchill had been making a separate but similar enquiry in London. On November 18, he wrote to Dufferin that Gen. Duncan, the resident at Mandalay from 1875-1878, was against annexation. Duncan, who had lived twenty-three years in Burma, claimed that the Burmese were devoted to the King.[40]

Duncan also stated that the occupation of Mandalay was virtually the occupation of the entire country, which would then involve the Indian Government in constant wars with the Shans, Kachins, Chins, and other hill-tribes. A very large Indian Army garrison would be required for several years. If annexation under a European administration would occur, it would require additional years before the country could return revenues equal to the cost of the administration.[41]

Duncan added that it had taken ten years after each of the two previous annexations of Lower Burma in 1824-1826 and 1852-1853, for the annexed territories to be brought to complete order. Duncan claimed that the two earlier annexations had been comparatively easy. The people of Lower Burma were not true Burmans for the most part. Instead, they were Karens, Mons, Shans, and other ethnic groups, who were living in foreign territory

that had been occupied by the despised Burman overlords.[42]

Also, it had required a decade after each of the two earlier annexations for the Government to show an excess of receipts over expenses. Even at the present time, the Lower Burma finances would have been in a bad way if it were not for the export duty on rice. Upper Burma could not levy a similar duty on rice, because it had to import about 68,000 tons of rice annually from Lower Burma in order to avoid food shortages.[43]

Therefore, Duncan proposed that another Burmese Prince should be enthroned. He could be controlled by a British Resident in the usual way as was done with any other important Indian princely state. Churchill admitted that Duncan's arguments were difficult to refute, but Churchill was bothered by two questions. These were (1) could a suitable Prince be found, and (2) would the Resident have actual control, especially against French and other European 'intrigues'?[44]

Churchill added that if the current opportunity to protect India's eastern frontier was not taken, "events may follow a course analogous to what has taken place [with Russia] in the N. W." The future aggressions against India's eastern frontier could come from France, Germany, Italy, or all three. Churchill concluded his letter by suggesting that the annexation of Upper Burma would prevent further European or other foreign 'intrigues' in the area.[45]

On December 5, Churchill telegraphed in reply to Dufferin's November 9 letter, which had suggested four drawbacks to the annexation of Upper Burma. Churchill stated that Salisbury tended to be against another Prince on the throne, because there would be incessant French and Italian 'intrigues'. They would become serious when the French extended their influence up the Mekong River Valley in the next few years. However, Salisbury was aware of the financial savings possible with a retention of the old Burmese administration, instead of establishing an expensive European administration.[46]

Therefore, Salisbury suggested with Churchill's concurrence that a Lt. Governor or a Chief Commissioner could administer Upper Burma for a few years with a largely Burmese administration. The Indian Government would interfere only in those offices that required reform. Churchill asked for Dufferin's reactions to the proposal.[47]

Dufferin did not reply immediately to Churchill's December 5 telegram. Dufferin had previously sent a telegram to Bernard on December 3 to enquire if a Burmese Raja located at Bhamo would be workable. The Raja could send the 'decennial tribute' that the Chinese claimed had been customarily sent by Mandalay. Bernard was also directed to determine the real views of the Burmese towards annexation.[48]

Churchill's December 5 telegram prompted Dufferin to make a second proposal to Bernard on December 7. Dufferin asked if a six-year-old Prince could be enthroned as 'Prince' instead of as 'King'. While Dufferin did not name the Prince that he had in mind, it was obviously the six-year-old son of the late Nyaungyan Prince. Dufferin suggested that the Prince could be assisted by the *Hlutdaw* and an English financial secretary. The military forts would remain with the Indian Army.[49]

Dufferin thought that a 'protected Prince' would solve the Chinese 'decennial tribute' problem, which Dufferin thought was a very serious diplomatic-issue. The 'decennial tribute' would not be paid directly by the Indian Government, but would be paid in the Prince's name. Dufferin asked Bernard to investigate the idea.[50]

On the same day, December 7, Bernard responded to Dufferin's earlier December 3 telegram enquiring about a Bhamo Raja to pay the 'decennial tribute' to China. Bernard stated that the idea was not practical. A Bhamo Raja would not command the loyalty of the people of the area, which had never been very loyal to Mandalay. The Raja could not resist the incursions of the fierce Kachins and other frontier tribes, who with a Chinese renegade had actually captured Bhamo and held it for two months in early-1885. Such a Raja would require constant Indian Army support. If the Raja belonged to the Alaungpaya dynasty, he would probably be a centre of intrigues against Indian interests.[51]

Finally, Bernard provided some of the first precise information concerning the 'decennial tribute' to China. The tribute had only been an exchange of letters every ten years, and/or an 'embassy' such as that sent by King Mindon in 1874. The Chinese Emperor had always sent the first letter addressed to the Burmese King, along with minor presents. The King of Burma then replied on terms of equality addressing the Emperor as "my Royal Friend," and enclosing a more valuable present.[52] In short, the 'decennial

tribute' was a comparatively unimportant diplomatic-modality, and did not imply any Chinese political control.[53]

On the following day, December 8, Bernard telegraphed in reply to Dufferin's December 7 enquiry about placing a six-year-old Prince upon the throne. Bernard thought that the "scheme for placing...son of late Nyaungyan...on the throne [is] the best solution of question."[54]   However, the precise relationship between the Prince and the Indian Government would have to be worked out, along with the financial responsibilities of the Mandalay Government towards the upkeep of the Indian Army garrison.[55]

The Case Grows Against the 'Protected Prince'

But Bernard was soon to retreat from his December 8 telegram in support of a 'Protected Prince'. On December 21, Bernard telegraphed to Durand, the Indian foreign secretary, that he was not satisfied with the *Hlutdaw*. He was particularly dissatisfied with the Taingda's 'anti-British' clique, whose continued presence in the *Hlutdaw* tended to discredit that body.[56]

In a similar December 24 despatch to Durand, Bernard wrote that the *Hlutdaw* had not "yet done anything much."[57]   Bernard stated that he was deporting the Taingda to Rangoon over Sladen's objections, and was also recalling the Kinwun. This was an effort to infuse some life into the political corpse that was the *Hlutdaw*.[58]

The failure of the *Hlutdaw* to put down the 'dacoits', and to restore order, caused Bernard to reconsider his December 8 stand in favour of a 'protected Prince'. On January 27, 1886, Bernard despatched the results of a poll that had been conducted among Burmese officials and commoners as to whether they preferred a 'protected Prince' or full annexation.[59]   The poll had been conducted in response to Dufferin's request for such a poll in Dufferin's December 3 and December 7, 1885 telegrams.

The Burmese commoners and officials polled expressed a strong sentimental attachment to the idea of monarchy. However, the majority had no real objections to annexation just so long as it would restore order and normal trade as quickly or more quickly than a 'protected Prince'.[60]

Bernard could not concur with Colonel Sladen's contention in the report that "a Burman Prince would immediately pacify the country."[61]   Bernard concluded that the Indian Government would have to assume all the functions of government in Upper Burma, and that order and normal trade could be restored by the end of 1886. The Burmese people would then "acquiesce contentedly in their country having been incorporated with Her Majesty's dominions."[62]

Dufferin, however, had remained *unwilling* to assume the additional financial and military responsibilities that an annexation of Upper Burma would have entailed. For example, on December 22, Dufferin wrote to Churchill that he, Dufferin, was afraid that the Chinese would have large forces in Yunnan to direct against Upper Burma. By way of contrast, it appeared that the French might be abandoning their 'Forward Policy' up the Mekong River Valley towards Yunnan.[63]

In order to avoid a confrontation between the Indian and Chinese Governments over Upper Burma and the frontier areas, Dufferin proposed to "take a child as near as possible to the legitimate line of succession, and to make him Prince...in Upper Burmah."[64] The Government would be conducted in the Prince's name under such an amount of British supervision as might be required.[65]

Indian troops at Mandalay and at Bhamo would secure the young Prince's control. This would be all that would be required to exclude all foreign intrigues from the Upper Irrawaddy Valley for the next fifteen or twenty years. At this point in Dufferin's letter, he once again revealed his conception of himself in relation to his superior, Lord Churchill. Apparently hesitant to go against his superior's preference for annexation, Dufferin did not name the six-year-old Prince that he had in mind.[66]

Instead, Dufferin veered off from his concept by noting that "Of course this is merely an idea praised upon a very shadowy basis."[67] Such was *not* Dufferin's real conviction at all. In the next few sentences he stated that he agreed with Gen. Duncan's comments against annexation as quoted in Churchill's November 18, 1885 letter. In particular, Dufferin concurred with Duncan's contention that Upper Burma would not be a paying province for many years if annexed into the Indian Empire.[68]

The financial problem was in Dufferin's view the "most weighty consideration" against annexation. His implication was obvious that a 'protected Prince' would cost less to 'protect' than an annexed state would cost to directly administer.[69] Unfortunately, in this letter as with so many Dufferin despatches to Churchill, Dufferin once again merely implicated courses of action, instead of firmly advocating what he actually felt.

On December 28, Dufferin wrote to Churchill concerning the impending January 1, 1886 Proclamation that would incorporate Upper Burma into the Queen's domain. Dufferin stated that Bernard had refused to use any terms in the Proclamation that might imply the annexation of Upper Burma. Dufferin emphasized that "My Council too are very adverse to such a step on various grounds. *My* only doubt about it is the effect it might have on China."[70]

Dufferin had never contended in any of his previous despatches that his *only* objection to annexation was its effect upon China. Dufferin began to emphasize the 'decennial tribute' issue at this time, and throughout January 1886, for two reasons. The first reason was that his Foreign Office background had made him extremely conscious of diplomatic modalities, such as the 'decennial tribute'. Secondly, it had become obvious to Dufferin that the India Office, the two political parties, and the British public, had not accepted the argument that the annexation of Upper Burma would cause an undue financial and military strain upon the Indian Government. and upon the Indian tax-payers.

Dufferin, therefore, shifted his tactics to one of emphasizing the tribute issue. This in turn kept alive the concept of the 'protected Prince'. The Indian Government could not pay such a tribute directly to China, which supposedly the Indian Government would have to do if it annexed Upper Burma. However, a 'protected Prince' could pay the tribute without involving the Indian Government in a position of inferiority.

Meanwhile, the Foreign Office in London was mounting a somewhat similar campaign. They had professed to be greatly concerned over the 'decennial tribute' and the Burma-China boundary questions. The Foreign Office was playing up these questions in order to prevent the India Office from intruding into what the Foreign Office considered was its bureaucratic domain.

Dufferin fell in with the Foreign Office line on the tribute question, because he was (1) concerned about the tribute, and (2) the question would give him more time to solve the Indian Government's most pressing problem. By parroting the Foreign Office line on the tribute question, Dufferin was actually seeking the best interests of both India and Upper Burma, namely a 'protected Prince' instead of full annexation.

Dufferin did not have to wait for many days to receive the views of the Foreign Office on the tribute issue. On January 2, 1886, N. E. O'Conor, H. M.'s charge d'affaires at Peking, sent a telegram. He stated that the Chinese Government was willing to "leave us a free hand in internal [Upper Burma] administration and control·of Burmah foreign relations, provided that tribute relationship, founded on prescriptive right, is maintained."[71]

O'Conor stated that the Peking Government desired at least a nominal successor to Thebaw, whom they professed not to admire. The Chinese thought that the abolition of the Upper Burma monarchy would be a blow to Chinese prestige, because of the probable termination of the 'decennial tribute'.[72]

On January 7, O'Conor telegraphed the reaction of the Peking Foreign Office to Dufferin's January 1 Proclamation, which had incorporated Upper Burma into the Queen's domain. The Chinese Grand Secretary and the Foreign Minister had called upon O'Conor to express their uneasiness over the proclamation. The ministers maintained that the proclamation was inconsistent with the assurances given to Marquis Tseng, Chinese ambassador to London, by the London Foreign Office.[73]

When questioned by O'Conor, the ministers stated that China's rights in Burma were limited to the 'decennial tribute', and that Peking would recognize any King set up by the Indian Government. The ministers also agreed that the Indian Government would have control over both the internal and external relations of Upper Burma. Before leaving, the two Chinese ministers had requested a prompt understanding on Upper Burma's future.[74]

On the following day, January 8, O'Conor telegraphed again. He stated that if Upper Burma was annexed, the tribute would still be "required."[75] If on the other hand, a Burmese ruler were set up "ecclesiastical preferable, ruling under British Agent, but.... [called] Prince if possible," the Chinese would accept the 'decennial tribute' from him.[76]

In a further January 11 despatch, O'Conor continued his encouragement of the idea of a Burmese ecclesiastical official, who might appoint the persons to send the tribute to the Peking Emperor.[77] Dufferin made enquiries, and refined the concept. He kept in mind the fact that his superiors Churchill and Salisbury desired full annexation, *i.e.* no King or 'protected Prince'.

At the same time, Dufferin did not forget his primary objection to annexation, namely that the required European administration would cost more than the revenues of the country for several years. It had required *ten* years after each of the two previous annexations of Lower Burma before there had been a surplus of revenues. The end-result of Dufferin's enquiries was telegraphed to Churchill on January 21.

Dufferin stated that there was a *Thathanabaing*, the Buddhist archbishop at Mandalay, who was the head of the Burmese branch of Buddhism. The archbishop had been appointed by the former King, and had in turn appointed the subordinate religious officials. Dufferin then made a fantastic statement. He wrote that no Christian Government could appoint the archbishop. He claimed that this fact caused "great anxiety to the inhabitants of Upper and Lower Burma *[sic]* who fear....great confusion will be introduced into all their ecclesiastical arrangements."[78]

Dufferin's solution was to have the Chinese Emperor, who was a Confucianist ruling over a supposedly 'Buddhist' country, appoint the *Thathanabaing*. This official would in turn undertake the 'decennial tribute'. Dufferin concluded that the concession would be one that would be greatly appreciated by the Chinese Government. The proposal would not in any way require the Indian Government to depart from its long-time policy of non-interference in religious affairs.[79]

Dufferin made his January 21 proposal in order to postpone the prospect of having to declare for full annexation. The proposal would give the Chinese their tribute, and Churchill and Salisbury would be pleased that there would not be a 'protected Prince'. Dufferin was still hopeful that enough Burmese administration could be retained so as to ease the financial strain upon the Indian Government and upon the Indian tax-payers.

Dufferin's proposal met with a cool reception at the India Office. The India Office wanted no further delay in reaching a decision on Upper Burma. Dufferin's proposal would have required further time to analyze. The Chinese were so overwhelmingly in favour of the idea that even the Foreign Office became suspicious. Finally, if Dufferin's January 21 proposal had been adopted, it would mean that the Foreign Office would continue to 'meddle' in Upper Burma affairs that were by 'right' the concern of the Indian

Government and the India Office.[80]

Sir Ashley Eden, former chief commissioner of Lower Burma (1871-1875) and now a member of the India Council, wrote to Dufferin on February 19, and summed-up the general view of the India Office. Eden hoped that Dufferin was not too annoyed with him for having opposed the idea. But, "I could not help feeling that you must have been misinformed."[81] Eden pointed out that Burmese Buddhism and Chinese Buddhism were essentially different religions, and had virtually nothing in common. Therefore, Dufferin's January 21 proposal was not a practical one.[82]

Eden expressed the view of the India Office towards the entire 'decennial tribute' issue. "The Foreign Office have let the Chinese see that they are very squeezable, and I think that [the] Foreign Office has an exaggerated idea of the importance of Chinese support in Burma."[83] Eden conclded that the Chinese could not really hurt the Indian Government in Burma. All that the Chinese could "properly ask is that we should compensate them for any well proved loss to them of position or other consideration by our taking the place of Burma."[84]

After the quick collapse of Dufferin's 'Grand Lama' scheme, he never again expressed any serious concern about the 'decennial' tribute or about Burma's frontier with China. Dufferin had brought these questions to the fore in late-December 1885 and throughout January 1886 in order to keep alive the idea of a 'protected Prince'. If this was not possible, Dufferin *still* hoped that the Indian Government and the Indian tax-payers could avoid the financial strain that a full-annexation of Upper Burma would cause.

It is true that Dufferin was unduly subservient to his superiors, and did not press his objections, in particular the financial and military ones, with sufficient emphasis. His subservience, as was mentioned previously, came from his diplomatic training and his concept of the Viceroy *vis-a-vis* the India Office. Nevertheless, a word in Dufferin's defence is necessary, because it would have taken an extremely brave man to continue to oppose almost every important newspaper and public official in England.

The Times, for example, had declared as early as September 28 and 30, 1885 that it was in favour of the conquest and annexation of Upper Burma. *The Times'* Burma correspondent, E. K. Moylan, had since late-November 1885 despatched a number of articles ridiculing 'native' rule, *i.e.* the *Hlutdaw*. Since mid-January 1886,

Moylan had also despatched a series of lurid reports concerning the alleged 'massacre' of 'dacoits' by Indian Army troops.[85] On January 25, *The Times* published another strongly worded editorial advocating the immediate annexation of Upper Burma.[86]

Even the Liberal Party was in favour of the annexation of Upper Burma. At the end of January, William Gladstone toppled the Salisbury Conservative Government on issues not related to the Burma question, and became Prime Minister for the third time.[87] On January 26, Gladstone arose in the Commons and announced that he would soon introduce a formal resolution approving the despatch of Indian troops outside of India to fight the Third Burmese War. Also, the resolution would annex Upper Burma into the Indian Empire. Gladstone concluded that "I have no doubt whatever as to what the verdict of the House on that issue will be. (Cheers)."[88]

The 'China questions' that Dufferin had advanced in late-December 1885 and throughout January 1886 had been his way of keeping off the above persons and groups, while he examined all the possible alternatives to annexation. It cannot be denied that Dufferin was genuinely concerned about the 'China questions', but they were essentially his way of *reducing* the Indian Government's involvement in Upper Burma to something short of annexation. When the 'China questions' were refused by the India Office, Dufferin's last defence against the concept of annexation had been breached.

Dufferin Recommends the Annexation of Upper Burma

Dufferin undertook his long postponed inspection-tour of Upper Burma where he would finally make his recommendation concerning Burma's future. He and Lady Dufferin arrived at Mandalay at 10 a.m., February 12, and entered into the city in an elaborate reception ceremony.

Almost immediately, he received a telegram from Lord Kimberley, the new Liberal secretary of state for India, requesting more information about Moylan's allegations in *The Times*. Kimberley emphasized that precise information about the allegedly 'brutal' executions of 'dacoits' was required immediately, because Parliament would reassemble on February 18, and questions on the charges would be asked.[89]

After making enquiries, Dufferin telegraphed on February 15 that all persons executed by military firing squads at Mandalay had been tried first by a civil court. "Elsewhere, when troops catch the marauders red-handed, leaders are occasonally shot; in each case all act upon advice of civil officers who accompany columns."[90] Dufferin pointed out that it was "difficult to discriminate between insurgents and dacoits; both classes plunder and kill innocent villagers, and compel peaceable people to join them."[91]   He added that 'dacoity' had long been a problem in Burma.[92]

Dufferin sent a second telegram on the same day, February 15. He stated that he had not found any case where "undue severity" had been meted out to Burmese prisoners. He concluded that "General Prendergast is a calm and humane man, and Mr. Bernard's well-known character is sufficient guarantee against..having countenanced excessive retribution."[93]

It was not an accident that Dufferin recommended the annexation of Upper Burma on February 13. It had been on this day that he had received Kimberley's telegram enquiring about the allegedly 'brutal' executions of 'dacoits'. It was also no accident that the *Hlutdaw* was told on February 18 that they would be abolished and the country annexed. It was on February 18 that Parliament was to reassemble. In short, it appears that Dufferin wished to forestall much of the criticism that would have arisen about the 'dacoit' executions, and indeed of all facets of the Indian Government's presence in Upper Burma, by confronting his critics with a *fait accompli*.

In addition, there were two other events that precipitated Dufferin's decision for full annexation on February 13. The first event was the news that the Myngun Prince had escaped a few days previously from French Pondicherry, and apparently with French assistance. If the Myngun was able to reach the Shan States, most of the Shan leaders and the 'dacoits' around Mandalay would rally to him. He would be a real *threat* to the Indian Army, and would probably overthrow any 'protected Prince' that the Indian Government might establish.[94]

The Myngun, however, was not a 'Burmese Napoleon' escaping from an oriental 'Elba'. On the way to Colombo, the Myngun became sea-sick as he had in his 1884 escape from Chandernagore. Once at Colombo, the Myngun found that he would have to use the harbour-boat in order to reach another steamer bound for

Saigon. The Myngun was afraid that the British would seize him if he used the harbour-boat. The French captain of the *Tibre*, on which Myngun had escaped from Pondicherry, declined to use one of his boats. A dejected Myngun had to return to Pondicherry.[95]

However, it was obvious that the Myngun would escape again and again as long as there was a 'protected Prince' for him to overthrow. A full and complete annexation of Upper Burma appeared to be the only way to forestall the Myngun Prince and the French from further constant 'intrigues'.

The event that *clinched* the case for annexation was the insult that the *Hlutdaw* inflicted upon Dufferin on February 12. Lord and Lady Dufferin were greeted with an elaborate reception ceremony upon their entry into Mandalay. The local officials received them in a temporary building especially constructed for the occasion. The Viceregal Couple were seated on the thrones formerly used on state occasions by Thebaw and Supayalat. According to *The Times'* Moylan, there was a single jarring note in the welcoming ceremony:

> The...Hlootdaw [members] were seated in the building, but took no part in the proceedings. They presented no address and extended no welcome... The action....was......meant to be openly defiant. They first sought to escape attending by demanding that chairs should be provided for all the members and that they should wear their shoes. [All]...The demands of the Hlootdaw were granted. They then attended nearly 100 strong, the usual number of members attending the Hlootdaw being about 20. Petty officers, the subordinates of subordinates, who would not be allowed to remain standing in the presence of a Burmese Woon, attended as members of the Hlootdaw, and attempted to monopolize all the front places and to force the English officers and officials of high rank to remain behind them. This was, however, prevented.[96]

The *Hlutdaw* members' behaviour was foolish, even after one allows for Moylan's obvious bias. The members had heard rumours that they might be dismissed from office, and the *Hlutdaw* dissolved. Their only remaining chance to save their positions, and to effect a restoration of a Burmese King, was to greet Dufferin courteously and responsibly. Instead, their behaviour was exactly the opposite. Dufferin could not help but be unfavourably impressed, when such discourtesy was coupled with Bernard's report of the

Hlutdaw's inefficiency, and Moylan's sensational *Times* articles decrying 'native' rule.

On the next day, February 13, Dufferin telegraphed to Kimberley in London and recommended the full annexation of Upper Burma. Dufferin stated that Thebaw's weak government had contributed to the spread of 'dacoity' in previous years. This problem could not be resolved under a 'protected Prince'. Dufferin conceded that a King would be very popular with many Burmese. However, most of the people were indifferent to the form of government just as long as it protected them from gang robberies.[97]

Dufferin cited Bernard and Sladen, who had stated that a 'protected Prince' could not maintain his throne against his rivals, such as the Myngun, without Indian troops. The Indian Government's responsibilities would, therefore, remain almost as great as those involved with full annexation. However, "our hands would be tied by the intrigues, jealousies, and procrastinations of a Ruler ...who could prove extremely unlikely to listen to reason."[98]

Dufferin said that his recommendation was quite unbiased, because he had been inclined towards a 'protected Prince' "had it been practicable."[99] However, none of the available princes seemed to have the stature that would be required. The Nyaungoke was unpopular with his own countrymen in the *Hlutdaw*, and the Myngun was a French puppet.[100]

The only remaining possibility would have been to place the six-year-old son of the Nyaungyan Prince upon the throne. Dufferin stated that he had finally rejected the idea, because "this would be tying ourselves down for the future without curtailing our obligations, or reaping any present advantage."[101]

Dufferin then made a most optimistic estimate that the cost of the military 'pacification' for the year 1885-1886 would total between thirty and thirty-five lakhs. He cited Bernard, who had claimed that during the year 1886-1887 the cost of 'pacification' and civilian administration would exceed the revenues from Upper Burma by only three lakhs.[102]

Dufferin made the further claim that the revenues from Upper Burma would show a surplus over expenses in the near future. He concluded the telegram by stating that "Until all uncertainty is removed as to our intentions, we can not expect" Burmese officials to render courteous assistance in restoring law and order.[103]

By February 17, it was an open secret in Mandalay that the

country would be annexed. On the same day, Dufferin despatched a long minute describing his mental journey for the previous four months. He wrote that he had first considered making Upper Burma into a 'buffer state'. This would have placed Upper Burma in the same position that it would have held, had the Mandalay Government accepted the October 22, 1885 Ultimatum."[104]

Thebaw, or perhaps a successor chosen by the Indian Government, would have continued in power with the Indian Foreign Dept. supervising his foreign policy. Upper Burma would have become a 'buffer state' against the French on India's eastern frontier. This would have placed the Burmese King in a position analogous to that of Amir Abdur Rahman of Afghanistan, who held a 'buffer' position against the Russians on India's northwest.[105]

However, the 'buffer state' concept had not been feasible. Upper Burma had "neither the elasticity nor the ultimate power of resistance which a 'buffer state' ought to possess, as our recent expedition has clearly shown."[106] A 'buffer state' would also, in Dufferin's view, have hindered trade with Yunnan and Southern China, and would have encouraged interference from Peking.[107]

The so-called 'semi-protected' state was next considered and rejected. The Indian Army would have been required in Upper Burma to police the 'dacoit' disturbances, and to pay the considerable cost in money and men. However, the ostensible control of such military and police forces would have remained with the Burmese King.[108]

A 'semi-protected' King "would always be jealous of our interference, and would probably prove at the most critical moment unreasonable and obstructive, and pehaps disloyal."[109] A 'semi-protected' King could also easily drag India into wars with neighbouring powers, such as China, French Indo-China, or Siam, and the Indian Government would have little say in the matter.[110]

The next alternative, which Dufferin had only *reluctantly* rejected, was the 'fully-protected' state. This was a Burmese state 'with a native dynasty and native officials, but under a British Resident, who should exercise a certain control over the internal administration, as well as over its relations with foreign powers."[111] Upper Burma would have assumed the status of a Kashmir, Nepal, Mysore, or other major princely-state of India.[112]

However, Dufferin had come to the conclusion that there was no reality behind such political analogies. The situations of the princely-states and Upper Burma were vastly different. Besides such differences, there were no Alaungpaya Dynasty princes considered to be trustworthy.   The Myngun Prince was ineligible because he was a French puppet ; and also because he had murdered his uncle, the Heir Designate, in 1866, and had attempted to kill his father, King Mindon.[113]

The Nyaungoke Prince was apparently unpopular with most Burmese at Mandalay, and would have had an even harder time than the Myngun in establishing himself. Dufferin wrote that he had then considered the Nyaungyan's six-year-old son, who would rule with Indian officials until he became of age fifteen years hence.[114]

However, this would have immediately imposed upon the Indian Government all the trouble and cost of full annexation, but without any corresponding advantages.   The Indian Government would have committed itself far into the future "to an arrangement which, in the end, would probably disappoint our expectations."[115]

The rebutal to this argument was that a 'protected Prince' would restore order quicker than annexation and a largely European administration.   A 'protected Prince' would give the Burmese people a symbol of unity to rally around. Dufferin pointed out that there were at least three pretenders to the throne fighting the Indian Army at that very moment. Even when Thebaw was on the throne, the Princes Myngun, Nyaungyan, Nyaungoke, and others had always been able to escape confinement and to raise a rebellion.   Therefore, Royalty was easily as divisive as it might have been unifying.[116]

Dufferin then recounted his 'Grand Lama' scheme involving the Buddhist archbishop of Mandalay.   Dufferin said that he had given up the idea, because it "possessed too experimental a character to have jusified its proposal as a practical solution of the problem."[117]   Therefore, full annexation and direct administration by covenanted European officers was the only alternative. It seemed to offer "the best prospect of securing the peace and prosperity of Upper Burma and our own Imperial and commercial interests."[118]

On the evening of February 17, Dufferin announced the annexation of Upper Burma in a dinner speech. On the following day, Dufferin sent his secretary to read a similar speech before the assembled—and disgruntled—*Hlutdaw*.[119]   The secretary also announced that Charles Bernard would officially dissolve the

Hlutdaw when he returned to Rangoon in about ten days. Meanwhile, in London on February 19 Lord Kimberley wrote to Dufferin, and stated that "We had no doubt......that the only course open to us was to follow your advice and to give up the idea of erecting a....Protected State."[120]

On February 22, Lord Kimberley and Prime Minister Gladstone rushed approval of the despatch of Indian troops to Upper Burma and of the annexation through both houses of Parliament.[121] Upper Burma was incorporated into the Indian Empire as of February 26, 1886. The Kinwun and the Pangyet, among others of the old *Hlutdaw*, were retained as key officials in the new administration.

The last remnant of independent, 'traditional' Burma had ceased to exist. However, Dufferin's troubles in combating the 'dacoit' disturbances and in administering the newest province of the Indian Empire were just beginning. "Such was the price he had to pay for subjecting the Viceroyalty to........the Secretary of State for India" and for annexing Burma—an act which the November 15, 1886 *Hindoo Patriot* concluded was unjustified.[122]

FOOTNOTES

1 "Foreign affairs were abruptly extended as a result of [Indian] contact [north of Bhamo] with Imperial China, while at the same time they became unduly complicated by the Foreign Office, which played up such questionable issues as Burmese tribute and boundaries with China in order to keep the Indian Office from encroaching upon one of its bureaucratic domains." Briton Martin Jnr., *"The Viceroyalty...,"* p. 830.

3 For the broader aspects of the Chinese-Burma 'tributary' question *see :* China-Burmah Negotiations, 1885-1886, Pol. and Secret Dept., India Office, London, 1886 (IOL). *Also:* C. 4861, China No. 5-1886, The Treaty at Peking, July 24, 1886 (NAI, IOL). *Also:* Mrs. Nancy Iu So Yan-Kit, *Anglo-Chinese Diplomacy Regarding Burma 1885-1897*, Ph. D. Thesis, Un. of London, 1960. *Lastly see :* Dorothy Woodman, *The Making of Burma*, pp. 247-274.

3 No. 64, MacKenzie to Dufferin's Secretary, April 16, 1886 ; in Dufferin Papers, Reel 525/36, p. 74.

4 Briton Martin, Jr., *New India 1885*, pp. 255-260, 315.

5 *See :* Appendix K entitled Moylan's Malicious Reporting.

6 Grattan Geary, *Burma After the Conquest*, pp. 36-38.

7 *Ibid*, pp. 39-40.

8 Foreign, Secret-E, April 1886, Nos. 215-220 (NAI). Sladen's defence of his actions and Bernard's rebutal.

⁹ No. 515, Telegram from Bernard to Dufferin, Decmber 4, 1885; in Dufferin Papers, Reel 528/48, p. 384f.

¹⁰ No. 604a, Bernard to Durand, December 24, 1885 ; in Dufferin Papers, Reel 529/49, p. 439. *See also :* Foreign, Secret-E, August 1886, Nos. 553-574 (NAI).

¹¹ Grattan Geary, *Burma After the Conquest,* pp. 39-40, 220-226.

¹² *Ibid.,* (*See* Appendix K entitled Moylan's Malicious Reporting.)

¹³ *Ibid*, pp. 50-54, 74-79. *(See also :* Sir Charles Crosthwaite, *The Pacification of Burma,* London, 1912, pp. 2, 14-18, 103, 112. *Also see :* Maung Tha Aung and Maung Mya Din, (ed. by H. R. Alexander), "The Pacification of Burma: A Vernacular History," (Rangoon) *JBRS.* Vol. XXXI, Part 11, 1941, pp. 80-136. *Also :* Sao Saimong Mangrai, *The Shan States..·,* pp. 112-147. *Also :* H. Fielding-Hall, *A People At School,* pp. 60-65, 82-83, 133-138. *Also:* Ivan P. Meyineff, (trans. by H. Sanyal and others), *Travels and Diaries of India and Burma,* Calcutta, 1958, pp. 114-215. *Also :* [Prendergast], "The Conquest of Burma," (Edinburgh) *The Edinburgh Review,* Vol. CLXL, January-April 1887, pp. 489-511. *Also :* J. A. Farrer, "Why Keep Burma ?," (London) *The Gentleman's Magazine,* Vol. CCLXII, January-June 1887, pp. 117-126. *Also:* Brig. Gen. C. B. Protheroe, "Burma 1885-87," (Simla) *The Journal of the United Service Institution of India,* Vol. XXI, No. 110, 1892, pp. 590-613. *Also :* No. 56, H. T. White's Minute on Bo Shwe, December 6, 1886; in Mss. Eur. E. 254, Sir H. T. White Collection, Box I (IOL). *Lastly:* H. T. White, *A Civil Servant in Burma,* pp. 257-265.

For the disturbances in Lower Burma during 1885-1886 *see :* J. G. Scott and J. P. Hardiman, *Gazetteer..*, *Part I, Vol. II,* pp. 7-8. *Also :* "Editorial Notes," (Calcutta) *Statesman,* Feburary 20, 1886, p. 3. *Lastly :* Col. Plant, *Narrative of the Insurrection in the Tenasserim Division During 1885-1886,* Rangoon, 1886, (BM).)

¹⁴⁻¹⁵ *Ibid.*

¹⁶⁻¹⁷ *Ibid.*

¹⁸ *Ibid.*

¹⁹ *Ibid*, p. 50.

²⁰ *Ibid*, pp. 248-249.

²¹ *Ibid*, pp. 227-229.

²²⁻²⁴ *Ibid*, pp. 53-55, 77.

²⁵ *Ibid*, pp. 268-269.

²⁶ *Ibid.* (*See also*: Prendergast's statement concerning the Burmese soldier at the end of the military section of Chapter IX. Prendergast added that "It seems absurd and unjust to class whole divisions of troops in the field as 'dacoits', and to speak of 10,000 gang-robbers being assembled in a district [;] and to stigmatize patriots fighting in defence of their country, and bands of warriors not more guilty than the foragers in the days of Rob Roy, as 'dacoits'." Gen. Sir H. N. D. Prendergast, "Burman Dacoity and Patriotism and Burman Politics," p. 276.)

²⁷ *Ibid*, pp. 220-226. (At 5 p. m., December 28, 1885, the Taingda was taken

from a *Hlutdaw* meeting. Mr. Forde, the British head of police, took the Taingda past the burial-ground. It contained the more than 300 persons that the Taingda had murdered during the September 21-22, 1884 'Jailbreak' Massacre. Taingda cried out: "This is the place in which you are going to kill me! Alas! Spare my life! Spare my life!" Forde assured the old rascal that he was merely going into exile for a year or two. Taingda later met Lord Dufferin and charmed him completely. Taingda died in 1896 as one of the wealthiest merchants in all of Burma. *See also*: E. C. Brown, *The Coming of the Great Queen*, pp. 229-231. *Also*: Foreign, Secret-E, August 1886, Nos. 553-574 (NAI).)

[28] *Ibid*, pp. 283-284.

[29] *Ibid.* (*See also*: No. 18, Telegram from Bernard's Secretary to Durand, January 27, 1886; in C. 4690, Burmah No. 2 (1886), p. 9 (NAI).)

[30] *Ibid*, pp. 248-249, 256-257, 268-269.

[31] *Ibid*, pp. 283-284.

[32] Geary thought that Prince Htack Tin U Zun, the six-year-old son of the deceased Nyaungyan Prince, should have been placed on the throne. As a 'protected Prince', his Burmese administration would save the expense of establishing an immediate and costly European administration. The Prince would also restore law and order more quickly, because a King would bring respect once again to the Mandalay Government. The claims of China for 'compensation' for her 'decennial tribute' would have been easier to solve with a 'protected Prince'. Lastly, the day when India would have a contiguous frontier with China and with French Indo-China would have been postponed. With it would have been postponed the threat of future Anglo-French wars over the remaining Shan and Lao States. *Ibid*, pp. v-viii.

Geary also thought that there was considerable merit in a Rangoon merchant's suggestion that Supayalat and the Taingda should have been deported, while Thebaw and the Kinwun were left behind in Mandalay. With Col. Sladen or some other capable officer "as guide, philosopher and friend, the present anarchy, threatening the ruin of the country would never have arisen.... Thebaw is said by those who knew him to be by far the best of the Mandalay ruling clique, but his wife and his mother-in-law and his ministers did what they liked with him."

Geary concluded that "dacoity will cease in a few weeks [if the Nyaungyan's son or any Prince became King], for then the people will know they have a government, and will be protected in their villages, and that things will go on as before." *Ibid*, pp. 71-72, 79.

[33] No. 58, Dufferin to Churchill, October 19, 1885; in Dufferin Papers, Reel 517/28, pp. 241-242.

[34] No. 61, Dufferin to Churchill, November 9, 1885; in Dufferin Papers, Reel 517/18, pp. 250-252. *See also*: No. 404, Aitchison to Dufferin's Secretary, October 22, 1885; in Dufferin Papers, Reel 528/48, p. 319. *Also*: No. 440a, Aitchison to Dufferin's Secretary, November 2, 1885; in Dufferin Papers, Reel 528/48, p. 345.

[35-36] *Ibid.*

[37-39] *Ibid.* Bernard, and two former Chief Commissioners of Lower Burma, namely C. Crosthwaite and Rivers Thompson, also advised against annexation at this time. They, like A. C. Lyall, the former Indian foreign secretary, preferred a 'protected Prince'.

[40] No. 79, Churchill to Dufferin, November 18, 1885; in Dufferin Papers, Reel 517/18, pp. 207-209.

[41] *Ibid.*

[42] *Ibid.* (Sir C. U. Aitchison agreed with Gen. Duncan that a 'protected Prince' was preferable to annexation. *See:* No. 460a, Aitchison to Dufferin, November 11, 1885; in Dufferin Papers, Reel 528/48, pp. 356a-356b.)

[43-45] *Ibid.*

[46] No. 436, Telegram from Churchill to Dufferin, December 5, 1885; in Dufferin Papers, Reel 519/25, p. 125.

[47] *Ibid.*

[48] No. 183, Telegram from Dufferin to Bernard, December 3, 1885; in Dufferin Papers, Reel 529/49, p. 103.

[49] No. 201, Telegram from Dufferin to Bernard, December 7, 1885; in Dufferin Papers, Reel 529/49, p. 109.

[50] *Ibid.*

[51] No. 537, Telegram from Bernard to Dufferin, December 7, 1885; in Dufferin Papers, Reel 529/49, p. 403.

[52] *Ibid.*

[53] Additional information on the 'decennial tribute' question reached Dufferin's desk shortly afterwards. *See :* No. 449; in Foreign, Secret-E, August 1886, Nos. 428-520 (NAI). *See also :* Foreign, Secret-E, August 1886, Nos. 575-600 (NAI). *Lastly :* Foreign, Secret-E, August 1886, Nos. 731-765 (NAI).

[54] No. 543, Telegram from Bernard to Dufferin, December 8, 1885; in Dufferin Papers, Reel 529/49, p. 406.

[55] *Ibid.*

[56] No. 594, Telegram from Bernard to Durand, December 21, 1885; in Dufferin Papers, Reel 529/49, p. 434. Bernard was never very happy about the continuance of Taingda at Mandalay, while the Kinwun was sent to Rangoon on November 30. *See :* No. 515, Telegram from Bernard to Dufferin, December 4, 1885; in Dufferin Papers, Reel 528/48, p. 384f. *See also :* Foreign, Secret-E, April 1886, Nos. 215-220 (NAI).

[57] No. 604a, Bernard to Durand, December 24, 1885; in Dufferin Papers, Reel 529/49, p. 439.

[58] *Ibid. See also :* Foreign, Secret-E, August 1886, Nos. 553-574 (NAI).

[59] No. 431, Bernard's Secretary to Durand, January 27, 1886; in Foreign, Secret-E, July 1886, Nos. 431-438 (NAI).

[60-61] *Ibid.*

[62] *Ibid.*

[63] No. 66, Dufferin to Churchill, December 22, 1885; in Dufferin Papers, Reel 517/18, p. 263.

[64-65] *Ibid.*

[66-69] *Ibid.*

[70] No. 67, Dufferin to Churchill, December 28, 1885; in Dufferin Papers, Reel 517/18, p. 267. The January 1, 1886 Proclamation was mainly intended to extinguish any French, German or Italian Treaty claims. It read:

"By command of the Queen-Empress it is hereby notified that the territories formerly governed by King Theebaw will no longer be under his rule, but have become part of Her Majesty's dominions, and will during Her Majesty's pleasure be administered by such Officers as the Viceroy and Governor General of India may from time to time appoint." No. 181 Dufferin's Proclamation, January 1, 1886; in C. 4614, p. 266. For the legal discussion within the Indian Government as to the exact Proclamation *see :* Foreign, Secret-E, January 1886, Nos. 731-748 (NAI).

[71] No. 2, Telegram from O'Conor to Dufferin, January 2, 1886 ; in Dufferin Papers, Reel 525/37, pp. 1-2.

[72] *Ibid.*

[73] No. 6, Telegram from O'Conor to Dufferin; January 7, 1886 ; in Dufferin Papers, Reel 525/37, p. 4.

[74] *Ibid.*

[75] No. 10, Telegram from O'Conor to Dufferin, January 8, 1886 ; in Dufferin Papers, Reel 525/37, p. 8.

[76] *Ibid.*

[77] No. 12, O'Conor to Dufferin, January 11, 1886 ; in Dufferin Papers, Reel 525/37, pp. 9-10.

[78] No. 407, Telegram from Dufferin to Churchill, January 21, 1886, in Dufferin Papers, Reel 519/25, pp. 136-137.

[79] *Ibid.* On February 22, Dufferin telegraphed to Lord Kimberley, and said that the Burmese were hostile to the idea of the Emperor of China appointing the *Thathanabaing.* The Burmese had no objection to the Burmese Government, Buddhist or Christian, appointing the archbishop. (Such had been requested of the Lower Burma Government for many years previously.) Dufferin stated that "we should allow the Chief Ecclesiastic at Mandalay to extend his jurisdiction over Lower Burmah, if his co-religionists are willing....as I imagine they will be."

Dufferin's idea, and the recognition of the Buddhist ecclesiastic common law in all cases where it did not conflict with the Indian Civil Code, would have done considerable to halt the 'dacoity' and social disintegration. However, the Indian Government had the policy of never 'interfering' in religious matters. Dufferin's idea was never accepted, although Bernard, Sladen, and Rev. J. A. Colbeck supported it. *See:* No. 476, Telegram from Dufferin to Kimberley, February 22, 1886 ; in Dufferin Papers, Reel 519/25, p. 162. *Also see :* No. 436, Colbeck to Bernard, January 10, 1886 ;

in Nos. 431-438. *Lastly :* Donald Eugene Smith, *Religions and Politics in Burma,* Princeton, 1965, pp. 43-50, 59, 66.

80 The 'Grand Lama' scheme was squashed in London, mostly because the Chinese reaction was so enthusiastic that it aroused suspicion at the Foreign and India Offices. Marquis Tseng, Chinese ambassador to London, said later that his Government had thought that their rights were being overwhelmingly accepted in Burma with the 'Grand Lama' proposal. When they would have discovered that the offer was not what they thought, the Marquis claimed that he would have been in severe difficulty with the *Yamen,* Peking foreign office, for 'misinforming' them as to the foreigners' real intentions. Marquis Tseng expressed his thanks that the London Government had discovered the misconception on their own account, and that they had withdrawn the offer.

81 No. 26, Eden to Dufferin, February 19, 1886 ; in Dufferin Papers, Reel 525/37, pp. 26a-26b.

82-84 *Ibid.*

85 *See :* Appendix K entitled Moylan's Malicious Reporting.

86 Editorial advocating annexation, (London) *The Times,* January 25, 1886, p. 9.

87 "The Defeat of Lord Salisbury," (London) *The Times,* January 28, 1886, p. 5.

88 "Parliamentary Intelligence," (London) *The Times,* January 26, 1886, p. 6. *See also :* the related story on p. 9 of the same issue.

89 No. 20, Telegram from Kimberley to Dufferin, February 12, 1886 ; in C. 4690, pp. 9-10.

90 No. 21, Telegram from Dufferin to Kimberley, February 15, 1886 ; in C. 4690, p. 10.

91-92 *Ibid.*

93 No. 22, Telegram from Dufferin to Kimberley February 15, 1886 ; in C. 4690, p. 10. Dufferin added in a February 26 letter to Kimberley that Prendergast had won the November 1885 war with a loss of just over twenty men. His "desire to....avoid bloodshed" enabled him to resist his own officers and men who wished him to fire on the Avan Forts. "Had he done so....[it] might have been made to assume the appearance of a victorious battle instead of a useless butchery. But he stood firm, and, as a result, he entered Mandalay unopposed and captured the King." Prendergast's "subsequent military arrangements seem to have been good, and the same moderation and desire to avoid fighting....averted a collision.... between....our troops and a Shan chief. Nevertheless....Everything he does will stink in the nostrils of the *Times* correspondent." No. 8, Dufferin to Kimberley, February 26, 1886; in Dufferin Papers, Reel 517/18, pp. 17-18.

94 "Burmah" (London) *The Times,* February 15, 1886 ; p. 5. *Also see :* "Burmah," (London) *The Times,* February 16, 1886, p. 5. *Also see :* "Burmah," (London) *The Times,* February 22, 1886, p. 5. *Lastly see :* Grattan Geary, *Burma After the Conquest,* pp. 199-200.

[95] *Ibid.*

[96] "Burmah," (London) *The Times*, February 15, 1886, p. 5.

[97] No. 445, Telegram from Dufferin to Kimberley, February 13, 1886 ; in Dufferin Papers, Reel 519/25, pp. 150-151.

[98-99] *Ibid.*

[100] *Ibid.* (Few persons had ever considered the Limbin Prince, the bastard-son of the late Heir Designate who had been assassinated by the Myngun in 1866. The Limbin in 1886 was installed as 'King' by a number of Shan rulers in the short-lived 'Limbin League'. *See :* Sao Saimong Mangrai, *The Shan States....*, pp. 112-147.)

[101-102] *Ibid.*

[103] *Ibid.*

[104] Enclosure in No. 30, Dufferin's Annexation Minute, February 17, 1886 ; in C. 4887, pp. 21-26.

[105] *Ibid.*

[106-110] *Ibid.*

[111-112] *Ibid.*

[113-114] *Ibid.* Dufferin reflected the bias of the Indian Foreign Dept. against the so-called 'French puppet' Prince Myngun. On October 22, 1885, Myngun wrote to Col. Sladen and compared himself to Amir Abdul Rahman of Afghanistan. The Amir had been a Russian protege for over ten years, and yet once he became Amir was a good and loyal friend of the British. The Myngun wrote that "I am well aware of the power of the English.... and if ever I am assisted by them to gain my right, I will do my utmost to advance their interest and make it my chief duty to accede to all their wishes." *See :* Myngun to Sladen, October 22, 1885 ; in Mss. Eur. E. 290, The Sir Edward Sladen Papers, 290/8, p. 3 (IOL.)

[115-118] *Ibid.*

[119] "Speech by the Viceroy," and "The Viceroy and the Hlutdaw," (Calcutta) *Englishman*, February 23, 1886, p. 4.

[120] No. 6, Kimberley to Dufferin, February 19, 1886; in Dufferin Papers, Reel 517/18, pp. 9-10.

[121] *Hansard's Debates, Third Series, Vol. 302*, pp. 607, 849-866, 939-989 (NAI, IOL). *See also:* "Parliamentary Intelligence," (London) *The Times*, February 23, 1886, pp. 5-6.

[122] Briton Martin Jnr., "The Viceroyalty......," p. 830. The November 15, 1886 *Hindoo Patriot* commented upon the first anniversary of the War that Dufferin's arguments against the (1) 'buffer state' and (2) the 'semi-protected state' were ignored in Afghanistan. Amir Abdur Rahman certainly had the power to drag India and England into war with Russia. What about Penjdeh and Herat in 1885, which had brought England and Russia to the very brink of war? In the case of Upper Burma, the presence of a Resident would have prevented such wars and any foreign intrigues— unlike Afghanistan where the Indian Government had no Resident. As concerned Dufferin's argument that Burma lacked the resistance to be a

'buffer state', the 'dacoits' had taken care of that argument.   By November 1886, 40,000 soldiers and mounted police were fighting the 'dacoits' in Upper Burma.

A 'protected state' would have been practical.   Lord Dufferin had recognized the Shumshere Brothers in Nepal, who had murdered their uncle and first cousin.   Surely, Dufferin could have overlooked Myngun's murder of his uncle.   Amir Abdur Rahman of Afghanistan had been a pensioner of Russia for almost twelve years.   Yet, he was not a Russian puppet, but a good friend of India.   Would the Myngun have become a puppet of the French after living in French territory for only three years?

The *Hindoo Patriot* concluded that the presence of the British Resident at Mandalay would have ended all French and other foreign intrigues. The objectives for which the Indian Government had invaded Upper Burma in November 1885 could have been gained by a 'protected state'.   In short, there was no justification for "the incorporation of Thebaw's territory.... and the minute [of February 17, 1886] simply brings that fact out in a pronounced manner."   *See:* "Lord Dufferin's Plea for the Annexation of Burma," (Calcutta) *Hindoo Patriot*, November 15, 1886, pp. 532-533.

Conclusion

Some Relationships Between Ecology and Empires

The Strategic-Political Model Tested in This Study

A short summary of the findings of each chapter follows below. The final section will give the conclusion to this study. It investigated whether British economic interests were more important than British strategic-political interests (which included the 'Russian Threat' to India's northwest frontier and its eastern counterpart the 'French Threat') in determining British India's relations with Mandalay from 1878-1886.

Chapter 1

The withdrawal of the Mandalay Residency on October 6, 1879 was studied in Chapter 1. In 1878, Viceroy Lytton had proposed that Lower Burma should be given back to Upper Burma. However, after the February 15-17, 1879 Mandalay Massacre, he suggested that an ultimatum be sent to Upper Burma in order to resolve the differences between the two countries. Lytton wanted to pacify India's eastern frontier in order that he could concentrate his energies on the northwest, the Second Afghan War, and on the 'Russian Threat'.

The London Government refused the proposed ultimatum. The Conservatives were afraid of becoming involved in a third war right before the 1880 Elections. The Secretary of State for India believed that Lytton's aim of quieting the eastern frontier could be gained by retaining the Resident at Mandalay, and by not sending an ultimatum.

However, Chief Commissioner Aitchison of Lower Burma and Col. Horace Browne, the temporary Resident at Mandalay, had a different view. They preferred either an ultimatum to Mandalay which would settle the differences between the two countries, or a virtual withdrawal of the Residency. The Residency was withdrawn after the Kabul Massacre on September 3, 1879. Lytton and the Conservatives were not willing to run the risk of a similar massacre at Mandalay, which would have resulted in a third major war, and a certain electoral defeat in 1880. Also, there was no other European power 'threatening' British interests in Burma. It was safe and desirable to once again de-emphasize India's eastern-flank and concentrate on the 'threat' from the 'west'.

In the absence of British pressure as represented by the Resident, the 'traditionalists' at the Mandalay Court, such as the Taingda, were able to block most of the Kinwun Mingyi's 'reforms'. Therefore, many grievances between the two countries remained unsettled. These grievances included (1) the 'French Threat' to Upper Burma and to India's eastern frontier; (2) the "Shoe Question" which 'prevented' the Resident from seeing the Burmese King; and, (3) the various Burmese 'violations' of the 1862 and 1867 Commercial Treaties. An eventual Third Burmese War was made almost inevitable by the unnecessary withdrawal of the Residency.

Chapter 2

The failure of the Myaungla Mission of October 1879 to June 1880 was studied in Chapter 2. The Mission was sent primarily to excuse the Mandalay Government from any blame in the withdrawal of the Residency. The Mission had no proposals to make concerning such issues as (1) the "Shoe Question"; (2) a new riverside Residency; or (3) an increased Residency Guard. However, the Secretary of State for India stated that the Mission could have been allowed to meet with Chief Commissioner Aitchison until the negotiations became pointless.

Thebaw, for his part, took good care of British subjects' interests, even though there was no longer a Resident at

Mandalay. The three raids on IFC steamers, and the prompt punishment of the guilty parties, were ample proof of the Burmese Government's determination to protect British subjects' rights.

However, four members of Viceroy Lord Ripon's Council wanted to use the steamer incidents as a justification for a uni-lateral withdrawal from the 1862 and 1867 Treaties. The Secretary of State for India refused three such appeals on the ground that a withdrawal would have wrecked trade, and was not warranted by the minor steamer incidents.

In the comparative absence of Indian Government pressure against Mandalay, the 'traditionalists', such as Yanaung and Taingda, became over-confident. They began a sale of Royal monopolies after July 1881, which did not violate the 1862 and 1867 Burmese-British Treaties. After Bernard had sent two protests to Mandalay, which were refused, Viceroy Ripon advised him to send a third and most emphatic protest.

In the meantime, U Kyi, a secret envoy, had been sent to Rangoon by the Kinwun, who offered to negotiate all outstanding issues between the two countries. Bernard's January 4, 1882 protest strengthened the Kinwun and Queen Supayalat in their struggle to abolish the monopolies, and to overthrow the Yanaung faction which had benefited most from the sales of Royal monopolies.

Chapter 3

The machinations at the Mandalay Court, which led to the overthrow of the Yanaung Mintha on March 16, 1882, and the despatch of the 1882 Burmese Simla Mission on April 2, were studied in Chapter 3. At Simla, the Mission presented a draft treaty that was un-acceptable to the Indian Government. However, in mid-July the Pangyet, the head of the Mission, accepted the concept of two treaties. One treaty was to be a commercial treaty between Upper Burma and India, and the second treaty was to be a direct friendship treaty between King Thebaw and Queen Victoria.

With these two treaties, the Burmese had gained (1) direct relations with Queen Victoria; (2) guarantees that the Indian Government would assist in the collection of duties and would prevent the 'escape' of the exiled princes; and lastly, (3) the impor-tation of arms. In return, the Indian Government had gained the abolition of the notorious "Shoe Question" that had poisoned Burmese-Indian relations for so long. The Pangyet was apparently hesitant about only one clause in the treaties, namely a Residency Guard with no specific limit on the number of men.

Unfortunately, several groups at Mandalay worked to eventually destroy the 1882 treaty. Two of these groups were composed of foreigners. They were the Italian weapons-makers who would have lost money with a free import of arms; and the *kalamas* who would have lost their positions with a restored Resident able to talk directly to Thebaw and Supayalat. The Mandalay Government rejected the treaty, and attempted to get the arms and other concessions that it required from the French Government during 1883 to 1885.

Chapter 4

The 1883-1885 Burmese Treaty Mission to Paris was studied in Chapter 4. The Mission obtained the activation of the 1873 Burmese-French Treaty, but without the clauses providing for an Offensive-Defensive Alliance and French shipments of arms. It was these two provisions that Mons. Deloncle inserted into a letter of instruction from the Kinwun during Deloncle's unauthorized 'negotiations' at Mandalay during May 1884.

The French Government never recognized Deloncle's 'negotiations', and the final January 15, 1885 Burmese-French Treaty was a commercial treaty with no Offensive-Defensive Alliance or arms clause. However, Jules Ferry, the French premier, gave the Burmese ambassadors a 'secret letter' promising at some unspecified future time to allow arms-imports through Tongkin.

The public portion of the January 15, 1885 treaty did not reveal any clauses that would give rise to any immediate French commercial 'threat' in Upper Burma. However, Charles Bernard thought that the future political relations with Upper Burma might become strained with a French Consul at Mandalay, and with the Indian Government not having a Resident.

In the meantime, the Indian Government was negotiating with the Myngun, Nyaungyan, and Nyaungoke Princes to place one of them on the Burmese throne instead of Thebaw. The negotiations were an attempt by the Indian Government to counteract the Burmese-French Treaty. The September 21-22, 1884 'Jailbreak'

Massacre at Mandalay ended the 'treaty negotiations' that were going on between one of Supayalat's *kalamas* and Viceroy Ripon's chaplain.

Chapter 5

The debate concerning the decline of trade to Upper Burma during 1883-1885 was studied in Chapter 5. Many non-Europeans and Europeans at Rangoon and elsewhere claimed that Thebaw's 'misrule' had caused a 'drought' in the southern provinces of Upper Burma during 1883-1885. A failure of the crops, 'dacoity', the near-bankruptcy of the Burmese treasury, and a decline in trade had followed. The annexationists advocated the annexation of Upper Burma, or the replacement of Thebaw with the Nyaun-gyan or another Prince.

Charles Bernard refuted the claim that trade to Upper Burma had declined. However, by February 1885, he conceded that the high trade-figures were misleading. The Upper Burmese had switched their purchases from British-imports to Lower Burma rice and food-stuffs. Viceroy Dufferin rejected the annexationists' claim that Thebaw's 'misrule' had caused the decline in the exports of British-goods to Upper Burma.

Dufferin stated that, in general, the decline of trade was world-wide. The distress of the non-European and European merchants at Rangoon was mainly caused by the collapse of the rice and teak markets in Europe, which would not be improved by a change of government at Mandalay. In the meantime, Lord Kimberley, the secretary of state for India, authorized Dufferin to reinstate the Resident at Mandalay whenever he thought it best.

The 'drought', crop failures, 'dacoity', and decline in the sales of British-goods to Upper Burma, were essentially caused by the extensive Deforestation of the southern provinces of Upper Burma after 1862. Thebaw's 'misrule' was not the main cause if indeed a cause at all. The Deforestation had been caused mostly by Burmese ministers and foreign timber-firms, who together ruined many forests for their own profit. Chapter 7 and Appendix B corroborated this view.

Chapter 6

A number of French commercial negotiations with the

Burmese from 1883-1885 were studied in Chapter 6. These dealings centered about a proposed Toungoo-Mandalay Railroad and a Royal Bank. Other proposed contracts included the Mogok Ruby Mines. The British were most concerned about Article 13 of the proposed Bank Contract, which appeared to give the French Government a major control over the revenues of Upper Burma. The political control of Upper Burma by the French would have inevitably followed.

Mons. Frederic Haas, the new French consul, arrived at Mandalay in May 1885. He refused to doff his shoes before King Thebaw until early July. Haas' advice that the Mandalay Government should request the return of the British Resident was ignored. Haas used Giovanni Andreino, the Italian consul and Indian Government spy, in order to inform the Indian Government that France only wished to establish commercial interests in Upper Burma. The Indian Government's predominant political interests in Upper Burma were not under challenge.

Andreino received copies of the various Burmese treaties and the business contracts from the jilted Mattie Calogreedy Antram. The contracts appeared to be officially sponsored by the French Government. Lord Randolph Churchill, the secretary of state for India, stated in an August 7, 1885 letter to Dufferin that demands for explanations would be made of Paris. Thebaw was to be left strictly alone.

The Paris Government, however, denied that it had officially sponsored the Contracts. The Quai d'Orsay further denied all responsibility for Haas' actions on the grounds that he had 'exceeded' his instructions. As a consequence, the British then demanded explanations from Mandalay concerning the continued spread of the 'French Threat' to British subjects' interests in Upper Burma, and to India's eastern frontier.

Chapter 7

The 1885 BBTC Teak Case was studied in Chapter 7. The Case was an effort by the Taingda group at the Mandalay Court to gain a few more lakhs from the BBTC, which had stolen thousands of logs without paying any duty. The Case was also 'got up' by the Taingda's group in order to crush the Kinwun Mingyi, the other great beneficiary of the BBTC's 'largesse'. The Government's

Judgment against the BBTC for Rs. 23,59,066 neglected to mention that the BBTC could not have stolen timber without the cooperation of Burmese officials. As the Kinwun put it, the Judgment was "aligah," nonsense.

The fine of twenty-three lakhs was set by the Kinwun to embarrass his opponent. The Taingda had wanted a lower fine and suddenly found himself in the unusual position of being the BBTC's *protector*. The Kinwun wanted the Indian Government to protest the fine, which would strengthen his hand at Court against the Taingda's faction.

The two attempts of Haas to 'interfere' in the Case were rejected by the Burmese Government. The Kinwun as Foreign Minister did not even deign to reply to over fifteen of Haas' letters. The fine against the BBTC was merely an effort to gain a few more lakhs from the company. The Taingda and other instigators of the Case made this clear with a number of 'unofficial' offers to the Indian Government to settle the Case.

Unfortunately, the Mandalay Government thought that it would lose 'face' by officially admitting its willingness to accept an arbitrator appointed by Viceroy Dufferin. The rejection gave the Indian Government a "convenient pretext" for addressing an October 22, 1885 Ultimatum to Mandalay that was designed to oust all French influence from Upper Burma.

Chapter 8

The 'French Threat' to India's eastern frontier was studied in Chapter 8. The 'French Threat' must be understood within the larger context of the 'Russian Threat' to India's northwest frontier. In 1885, the Russian and British Governments had come to the brink of war over Herat, the 'Key to India' in western Afghanistan.

The Indian Government simply could *not* afford to become involved—either militarily or financially—on both the northwest and on the east at the same time. In this sense, Viceroy Dufferin's concerns in 1885 were much the same as Viceroy Lytton's in 1879. Both men wanted to avoid involvement on India's eastern frontier in order to concentrate their respective energies on the northwest.

However in 1885, it appeared that a French-dominated Upper Burma would soon run alongside India's eastern frontier. It was this 'threat' more than the hope of new British markets in Yunnan that prompted Dufferin to send the October 22, 1885 Ultimatum to Mandalay. The Ultimatum was designed to end all French influence in Upper Burma, and the possibility that French Indo-China would run contiguously with India's eastern frontier.

The Ultimatum would therefore save the Indian Government from the spectre of having to fight the Russians in the northwest and the French on the east simultaneously. The Indian Government could again largely forget about India's eastern flank, and devote its energies to the northwest and the 'Russian Threat'.

The Tangyet, the Burmese ambassador to Paris, and the Quai d'Orsay made several attempts to stop the approaching invasion of Upper Burma. The Kinwun's November 5, 1885 reply to the Ultimatum did not accept the Ultimatum's first two demands that an envoy be accepted at Mandalay to settle the BBTC Teak Case. Instead, the Kinwun stated that Thebaw would be pleased to receive a BBTC petition for a Royal Review of the Case.

The Kinwun did not accept demand three, which would have ended the "Shoe Question" and reinstated the Resident at Mandalay under European etiquette. Demand four would have placed Burmese foreign affairs under the Indian Foreign Dept., and would have ousted French influence from Upper Burma. The Kinwun suggested that Mandalay could follow the joint decision of all countries with which it had treaties. This proposal was totally unacceptable to the Indian Government, which would have had three European nations 'threatening' India's eastern frontier instead of only the French.

Demand five had stated that the Mandalay Government would assist British subjects in establishing trade with Yunnan and Southern China. The Kinwun replied that his Government was always willing to help increase British and other subjects' trade with Southern China. On November 13, 1885, the Kinwun's reply was rejected, and the Indian Army invaded Upper Burma on the following day.

Chapter 9

The removal of Thebaw from power at the close of the Third Burmese War was studied in Chapter 9. The military reasons for the quick Burmese defeat would include (1) the overwhelming military power of the Indian Army; and (2) the fantastic speed with which the Force advanced up the Irrawaddy. The Mandalay Government did not have time to block the river, and thusly the defences up-river were never properly established.

The political reasons for the defeat would include (1) the 'pseudo-Prince', Maung Ba Than, brought along by the British, which many Burmese thought was their favourite Prince coming to take the throne. Many soldiers did not fight, especially when (2) conflicting orders to surrender and not to surrender were telegraphed by the Kinwun and the Taingda, respectively. Finally, (3) the Kinwun and the Taingda joined forces to deliver the Royal Couple into British hands. It is understandable why there was little military or political resistance to the invasion.

Chapter 10

The intellectual journey that Viceroy Lord Dufferin underwent from November 28, 1885 to February 13, 1886 was studied in Chapter 10. Dufferin had initially favoured a 'protected Prince' in Upper Burma, instead of full annexation. However, two important factors persuaded him to change his mind. These factors were (1) the 'dacoit' problem and the inability of the *Hlutdaw* to control them; and (2) Dufferin's subservient relationship with his superior, the secretary of state for India.

The points in favour of a 'protected Prince' included the following. It would save the expense of establishing a costly European administration. The Prince would be able to restore law and order more quickly than annexation. The Chinese claims for a 'decennial tribute' would be much easier to solve with a 'protected Prince'.

Lastly, the day when India would have had a contiguous frontier with French Indo-China would have been postponed, and with it the spectre of future Anglo-French wars over the Shan and Lao States. Annexation, on the other hand, would have defeated the main purpose of the Third Burmese War, namely to prevent French-controlled territory from running contiguously with and 'threatening' India's eastern frontier.

Dufferin stated in his February 17, 1886 minute that he favoured annexation. Upper Burma did not have the military resilience to become a 'buffer state'. No 'reliable' Prince could be found, and if one had been placed upon the throne, he might have proved to be an 'obstructionist'. There was no proof that a 'protected Prince' would have actually restored law and order more quickly than annexation. The Burmese princes had been a divisive as well as a uniting force.

Lastly, the Indian Government would have had to spend considerable money and men to restore order in Upper Burma—regardless of the form of government. Annexation was the only form of government that would give the Indian Government the political and military control necessary to secure "the peace and prosperity of Upper Burma and our own imperial and commercial interests."

The Consequences of Annexation

The annexation of Upper Burma on February 26, 1886 brought the Indian and French-Tongkin frontiers to within a few hundred kilometres of each other. The intervening *pannas* were also claimed by France. By January 1896, the frontiers ran contiguously together for a long stretch. This propinquity was largely responsible for the continuing tensions between the two countries after 1885, which subsided only with the signing of the Entente Cordiale by Britain and France in 1904.

The tensions would probably have been much reduced had Upper Burma been allowed to continue after 1885 as a 'buffer' between the two powers, and under a 'protected Prince' instead of full annexation. The necessary modernization of Upper Burma could have taken place almost unnoticed behind the reassuring figure of a 'protected Prince', such as King Thebaw, the Myngun Prince, or the young son of the Nyaungyan Prince. Such modernization would probably have caused less social and religious upheaval, and less of a wound to Burmese national pride, than the modernization introduced by the British after 1885 without a King. Such a modernization had occurred in Mysore with its restored 'protected Prince' after 1881. Why not in Burma?

Conclusion

This study has indicated some of the relationships between tropical ecology and empires; in this case the effects of the race to deforest Upper Burma after 1862, which had met with the eager

8. *Thebaw and his family being removed from the Palace to the steamers.* (*London Graphic, January 30, 1886, p. 120*).

cooperation of the Mandalay officials. This ecological process of
Deforestation set-off a number of other ecological disturbances in
Upper Burma, culminating in the partially man-made 'drought' of
1883-1885.

This in turn disrupted much of Upper Burma's social and political life; caused a decline in the volume of trade between Upper
and Lower Burma; prompted a number of mercantile and other
groups to demand the annexation of Upper Burma; and made the
country an even more inviting area for further French expansion
westward from French Indo-China.

This study investigated whether the above British economic-
interests were more important than British strategic-political interests (which included the 'Russian Threat' to India's northwest frontier and its eastern counterpart the 'French Threat') in determining
British India's relations with Mandalay from 1878 to the annexation
of Upper Burma in 1886. The study stated that the British could
not allow the extension of French influence into Upper Burma, because India's eastern frontier would then be directly under 'threat'
from the French; and the potential new British trade in Yunnan
and Southern China would be blocked by the intrusion of France
into Upper Burma.

The 'French Threat' to India's eastern frontier ultimately
resulted in the Third Burmese War in 1885, and in the eventual
annexation of Upper Burma in 1886. In other words, the study
has stated that British strategic-political interests were *more important* than British economic-interests in determining British India's
relations with Mandalay from 1878-1886.

The above findings indicated that the dominant and secondary
recurring 'patterns' in British-Burmese relations from about 1600-
1878 were *continued* with only slight variations between 1878-1886.
These 'patterns' complemented each other, and were created in the
main by *human* preferences and choices, and not primarily by 'impersonal historical forces' or by a 'predetermined historical pattern'.

Finally, this study has suggested some concepts or perhaps
a model or two concerning the relationships between tropical
ecology and empires, which might be applicable to a broader study
of the effects of Deforestation upon the rise-and-fall of human
societies. Indeed, such concepts might well be applicable to the
study of Man's interaction with his environment in any period of
history including our own.

APPENDIX A

THE RAIN-FALL OF BURMA

It is not quite an exercise in futility to draw a map showing the rain-zones of Burma. But, it is better to cite the average yearly-rainfall for different towns on the map. In a 'normal' year, Akyab in Arakan receives about 203.8″ of rainfall. An annual rainfall of 100″ and more extends all along the coastline to Moulmein, which receives 189.6″.

Inland from the coast, the rains diminish rapidly to 98.3″ at Rangoon; to 47″ at Prome; to 37.8″ at Thayetmyo; to 35.3″ at Minbu; and to 20″ to 25″ in the eighty-mile-stretch below the confluence of the Chindwin and the Irrawaddy Rivers. At Mandalay, the rains begin to rise to a total of 33.1″ per annum. North of Shwebo, the rains gradually rise to about 80″ or more at Bhamo, and in many parts of the Shan States.

The 1883-1885 'drought' in Upper Burma's Dry Zone extended from Shwebo (Moutshobo) southwards to Minhla near the frontier between the two Burmas.

APPENDIX B

DEFORESTATION CAUSES THE COLLAPSE
OF TRADE AND ORDER IN UPPER BURMA, 1883-1885

Introduction

The initial section explains the general principles of Deforestation, and the probable role of Deforestation in the collapse of several 'traditional' societies. The succeeding sections apply the points made in the initial section to Upper Burma, a 'traditional' society abruptly faced with 'modern' conditions of Deforestation in the twenty years after 1862.

While reading these sections, the reader should keep in mind the analogy that ecologists often use, namely that timber and other ground-cover bear the same relationship to the earth as does skin to the human-body. The removal of either 'skin' causes a painful and fatal *drying-out* of the 'body' underneath.

'Traditional' Examples of Deforestation

Deforestation has been the major cause or a main cause of the collapse of a number of ancient civilizations. A few of these civilizations would include the Aztecs,[1] the Mayas, other Indian civilizations on the western coast of South America, and the civilizations in the Tarin Basin of Central Asia and in Northwest China.[2] Many civilizations around the Mediterranean suffered from Deforestation, including Mesopotamia, Palmyra, Roman Africa, Phoenicia, Egypt, the apparent kingdom of the Queen of Sheba;[3] and also seventeenth century Spain.[4] But perhaps the Harappan Culture was typical of most civilizations, which have undergone the effects of Deforestation.

Sir Mortimer Wheeler wrote that Deforestation was an important cause of the deterioration of Harappan agricultural conditions. The deterioration was not likely to have been caused by a climatic change, although a small reduction in rain might have occurred at cyclical intervals. Wheeler stated that human interference—or neglect—was the primary factor contributing to the increasing aridity of the land.[5]

Wheeler thought that Deforestation might have caused a reduction in rainfall.[6] Many experts would disagree that Deforestation by itself would cause a reduction, since so many other factors were involved.[7] The controversy would not seriously affect the accuracy of Wheeler's conclusion, namely that Deforestation caused the land to become arid. Even if the rainfall had remained constant, there would no longer be enough tree leaves, branches, trunks, and roots along with other ground-cover to *hold* the rainfall in a 'sponge effect', and to allow it to slowly seep out into the surrounding cropland.[8]

Instead, the uncaught rainfall evaporated at a much higher rate, or rushed off into the streams in a flash-flood. The crops were therefore left without water for those periods when the rains did not fall.[9] In a few years there would be a decline in the quantity and quality of crops. The extremes of 'flood-water' and 'low-water' would hamper navigation, which required an even water-level in order to transport goods or troops to suppress a revolt.

The silt washed into the streams would soon *clog* the irrigation canals and water-storage areas behind dams and tanks.[10] The exhausted masses would no longer be willing to clean such irrigation systems as they would only become fouled again the next year. Hunger would become frequent, revolts would occur, and the collapsing society would become an easy prey to outside enemies—as perhaps were Harappa and Mohenjodaro.

Other deforested cultures, such as the Tarin Basin civilization in Central Asia, abandoned their cities. A few years of wind and dust erosion completed the Deforestation process begun by Man.[11] Such a Man-caused devolution from green to desert required centuries under 'traditional' conditions. A well-known example occurred with the Arabs after the Hegira, when they commenced to deforest many areas about the Mediterranean Sea. It required several centuries before the land was denuded of ground cover, and the desert was allowed to creep to the Mediterranean in some places.

The Deforestation process continues today in West and East Africa, but at a much faster pace. The pasture lands of the Masai and others are rapidly becoming depleted, and the desert gains more than 100,000 hectares (247,000 acres) per year on the average. In some spots, the desert advances up to thirty miles a year.

In summary, under 'modern' conditions of Deforestation, such as in Brazil, it appears that twenty years would be more than sufficient to perform the *complete* cycle from forest or grass-land to Man-made desert. Two other examples of 'modern' Deforestation appear to be the American 'Dust Bowl' during the 1930's,[12] and the Russian 'drought' of 1893.[13] In both cases millions of acres of grass and timber land were turned into desert in only twenty years. A similar process of 'modern' Deforestation appears to have taken place in Upper Burma in the twenty years after 1862.

'Decline' of Rainfall in Upper Burma?

According to the Dry Zone peasants, there had been a noticeable 'decline' in rainfall during the reign of King Mindon (1852-1878), and especially during Thebaw's reign (1878-1885). In almost every Dry Zone village there were rice-paddies, which had not been farmed for decades. The villagers said that the lands would have raised a good crop when there were sufficient rains. Unfortunately, such rains had come only once or twice in their lifetimes.[14]

However, good rains had come in their fathers' and grand-fathers' time. The farmers claimed that their fathers had reaped a crop from the dry lands every second year, and that their grand-fathers had raised a crop every year. It was *not* likely that the peasants' ancestors would have capriciously built rice-paddies beyond any hope of irrigation. Therefore, it appeared that there had been a long-term decline in rainfall.[15]

A modern ecologist would probably agree that there was a decline in the Dry Zone rainfall from 1883-1885, but would doubt that there had been any long-term or permanent decline. By January 1886, the rains had returned to 'normal', and were usually sufficient until the early 1890's. Then a period of declining rainfall occurred, culminating in another 'drought' in 1895 to 1897.[16]

Therefore, one should conclude that there was a cyclical dip in the Dry Zone rainfall from 1883-1885, but *no* long-term or permanent decline. A decline of only five inches a year would mean about a twenty per cent reduction in the annual rainfall of twenty to forty inches. Such a reduction in the Dry Zone, which was a semi-desert in many places, would cause a widespread 'drought' crop failures, hunger, and many of the calamities attributed to Thebaw's 'misrule'. By way of contrast, a decline of five inches in the annual Delta rainfall of 100-200 inches would have little or no effect upon the rice and other crops.

The effects of the *temporary* decline of rainfall in the Dry Zone during 1883-1885 were much exaggerated by the wide-spread Deforestation that had taken place in the southern provinces of Upper Burma in the twenty years after 1862.[17] Before 1862, the region in and around the Dry Zone was probably forested with cutch, teak, padauk, ironwood, and other ground cover sufficient to catch the rainfall, whether 'normal' or 'under-normal'. The leaves, branches, trunks, and roots would have *held* the water in a 'sponge effect', and would have allowed it to slowly seep out into the surrounding croplands.[18]

King Mindon commenced after 1862 to sell leases in the Ningyan, Shweli, Taw, Pakokku, Chindwin, Yaw, Taungdwingyi, Pyaungshu, Malun, and other forests.[19] A considerable portion of these forests and other ground-cover had been removed by 1883, thereby allowing the rains to evaporate at a much higher rate—or to rush off into the streams. The silt washed into the streams *clogged* many of the irrigation-canals and water-storage areas behind dams and tanks near Mandalay and elsewhere, and some of these irrigation systems were being abandoned even before 1883.

It was this process of Deforestation that explains why so many croplands were going out of use during the reigns of Mindon and Thebaw. This was the explanation for the increasing dryness, especially during Thebaw's reign, which the Dry Zone peasants attributed to 'declining rainfall'. When a slight cyclical-dip in the annual rainfall occurred, the result was the 1883-1885 'drought'.

'Low' Water, 'Flood' Water a Sign of Deforestation

The streams in Upper Burma during 1883-1885 were very low. There was so little water in the streams that much of the teak crop could not be floated down into Lower Burma in 1883-1884, but was placed aside on the river banks to await future floods.[20] It is possible that there would have been enough water in the streams had Deforestation not already occurred over wide areas in and around the Dry Zone.

It is interesting to note that the flood-stages of most streams and the Irrawaddy River were usually enormous. They were so enormous that Robert Gorden, head flood control engineer in Lower Burma, suspected that the Irrawaddy had a 'secret tributary' in Tibet. It did not occur to him that the enormous quantities of flood-water discharged by the Irrawaddy, and the minute quantities discharged during the dry months, were *two key symptoms* of Deforestation.

Gordon's theory of a 'secret tributary' to the Irrawaddy was disproven shortly after 1885. However, an article in defence of his theory is most interesting. Gordon claimed that the Irrawaddy discharged every year about 521,794 million cubic yards of water past a measured point.[21] The enormous amount of water had *other* causes, besides the fact that the Delta had a high (100 inches or more) monsoon rainfall. Gordon pointed out that the water discharged by the Irrawaddy was nearly four-fifths of the total discharge of the Mississippi River at its mouth.

But while this discharges pretty evenly on the average all the year round, the Irawadi sends down three-fourths of its total in the three months, July, August, and September, or, in other words, the monthly flood average is more than twice as great as that of the Mississippi [also a monsoon river].[22]

Gordon recorded the extreme flood discharge of the Irrawaddy for one day in 1877 at the rate of nearly 2,000,000 cubic feet per second. The highest flood discharge in one day was fifty per cent *greater* than that of the Mississippi, and double that of any European river. Gordon stated that the Irrawaddy was a greater river in the amount of water discharged yearly :

...than the Danube, or any river of Europe. It is greater than the Yang-tse-kiang above the lake near Hankow. It is probably greater than either the Brahmaputra [monsoon area] or the Ganges [another monsoon river] at their greatest. It is certainly much larger than the St. Lawrence at Montreal ; and it is about equal to the Mississippi at St. Louis, where it has received the Missouri.[23]

Gordon pointed out that *seventy-five* per cent of this Irrawaddy water rushed down in July, August, and September, while the six dry months from December to May ejected only thirteen per cent of the total. The record low discharge was 50,000 cubic feet per second recorded in 1877. This was only one-fortieth of the record high discharge per second of nearly 2,000,000 cubic-feet, also recorded in 1877.[24]   The extremes of low and high water-discharge implied that *considerable* Deforestation had taken place in the Dry Zone and in the adjacent areas in ancient times and since 1862.

The Drop in Cutch Exports Indicates Deforestation

The acacia tree was a valuable wood, which was chipped and boiled in cauldrons until a yellow dye called cutch, tanning agents, and other by-products were obtained.   The cutch tree grew most profusely in the southern part of the Dry Zone below Mandalay where the rainfall was only twenty or thirty inches a year.

In contrast, the teak tree grew in only a few 'wet' spots in the Dry Zone.   The most valuable teak trees grew at the edges of the Dry Zone where the rainfall increased to forty and more inches a year.   These forests included the Ningyan Forest at the southern edge of the Dry Zone, and the Chindwin Forest on the north-western edge.

The virtual *extinction* of the cutch forests during Thebaw's reign is well-documented.   In 1883-1884, the cutch exported to Lower Burma via Allanmyo totaled almost 150,000 maunds.[25]   In 1884-1885, the total declined to 104,000 maunds; in 1885-1886, to 70,000 maunds; and in 1886-1887, the exports totalled only 54,000 maunds.[26]   In four years the cutch exports had declined by almost two-thirds of what they had been in 1883-1884.   The less important cutch exports via Toungoo declined in the same four-year period from 10,000 maunds in 1883-1884 to only *four* maunds in 1886-1887.[27]

The value of cutch exports via Allanmyo had declined from almost eleven lakhs in 1883-1884 to under five lakhs in 1886-1887. The *Indian Forester* attributed the drop to "the reckless and wasteful way in which the supply has been dealt with."[28]   As there was no forest conservation under Thebaw's government, the cutch, teak, and other forests had been leased to the highest bidders—or in many cases to the highest bribers.   Then the leasees were allowed to do what they liked with the forests.[29]

The leasees harvested undersized cutch, teak, and other trees, because if they did not some other leasee would.   The leasees pushed aside the approximately 1,400 'useless' species in order to harvest the commercially valuable trees, such as cutch, teak, iron-wood, and padauk.   The cutch trees were not so difficult to extract, because they usually grew in dry, open country. Teak, on the other hand, usually grew inside forests in clumps of a few hundred yards in length. Such clumps rarely extended for as much as one mile, and often grew on slopes which were easily eroded.[30]

The teak tree occurred in 'general forests' in a ratio of one teak-tree for every 500 other trees. In the so-called 'teak forests', the ratio was one teak-tree for every 300 other trees.[31] In short, the 300-500 other trees were often shoved aside in order to harvest the one valuable teak tree. The partial Deforestation of the teak forests, including the Ningyan Forest, the most lucrative of all the BBTC's forests, was studied in the first sections of Chapter 7. In conclusion, the extensive Deforestation of the teak, cutch, and other forests after 1862 was the main cause of the Dry Zone 'drought' of 1883-1885, and of the consequent deterioration in order and trade.

Deforestation in the Chindwin River Valley

Chapter 7 and the cutch section immediately above have described some of the timber extractions from the southern portion of the Dry Zone. A somewhat similar Deforestation was also occurring in the Chindwin River Valley along the northern edges of the Dry Zone above Mandalay. This area, which contained the Chindwin and Mu Forests, the second most lucrative forests leased by the BBTC, was the scene of a continued denudation of ground cover for decades before—and after—Annexation.[32]

According to the *Lower Chindwin District Gazetteer*, there were four 'symptoms' which indicated that the Deforestation was at a fairly advanced state. These 'symptoms' included : (a) stretches of *abandoned* rice paddies in even the most populated areas. (b) The population was increasing very rapidly, and large new tracts of land were being brought under cultivation. There were, however, very *few* new rice-paddies being embanked ; instead the tendency was to level down the old paddy embankments.[33]

(c) Rice was being phased out in many of these areas in favour of short-lived, dry-crop staples, such as the seventy-five day variety of late sesamum. (d) The old cycle of upland rice cultivation was being abandoned in the hilly western areas in favour of the ordinary dry-crop cycle of millet and sesamum.[34]

The *Gazetteer*, then commented on the four 'symptoms' of

Deforestation as follows :

With regard to (a) a Burman would not—at any rate in the less remote tracts—give up trying to raise a rice crop on a field already embanked for that form of cultivation, unless he felt quite sure that the attempt to secure a crop would be fruitless. The fields once won a rice crop, and it appears certain that they must once have had *more* water than they can now count upon.

With regard to (b), much of the land which was brought under the plough soon after annexation is in the south-west of the district, where the soil is black clay, of excellent quality for the growth of rice, and almost level, so that the minimum of labour would be needed to embank it. In other tracts, again, some of the new land lies in natural depressions, which would lend themselves to the process of embanking. Rice is the favourite food-grain of the Burman, and the cultivator is prepared to undergo toilsome labour, not one year but every year, if he thinks that there is a chance of reaping a rice crop at the end. It is difficult to account for the absence of new rice land except by admitting a *deficiency* in the supply of water available for cultivation.

With regard to (c), the shorter-lived variety of sesamum is rather more expensive to plant, and a little less lucrative than the longer-aged crop [of sesamum or rice which required more water].

With regard to (d), the upland rice-cycle (one or two years rice, one year sesamum, five or six years fallow) calls for a large area of land and pressure of population is contributing to diminish that form of cultivation, but people also adduce decreasing rainfall as a reason.

Taking all the facts into consideration, it is difficult to escape the conclusion that the available water-supply is *less* than it used to be, and that the reason lies in *the denudation of forest growth.*[35]

In summary, the cuttings by timber firms, the forest fires, the fellings for local use, the clearing of hill-sides for regular crops, and in other areas for shifting rice-cultivation resulted in Deforestation. This—in combination with a slight cyclical-dip in the annual rainfall from 1883-1885—was the main cause of the 'drought' of those years.

Greed Causes Deforestation

The greed was mutual with both Mandalay ministers and timber firms involved. The *ultimate* responsibility, however, for the extensive Deforestation of the southern provinces of Upper Burma in the twenty years after 1862 must be laid in the laps of certain ministers, such as Taingda, Kinwun, and others. It was they who sold the cutting rights, and who received considerable bribes from the greedy bidders for teak and other leases.[36] The sad result of such a scramble prompted Charles Bernard to write in 1886 that :

......vague, undefined leases of vast forests cause very great destruction and waste of valuable timber. Experience has shown that leasees of this type, or their agents, destroy forests, put a stop to natural reproduction, prevent conservation or reproduction of forest resources, and denude the country to its great and lasting loss.[37]

An exhaustive survey of Upper Burma timber resources after Annexation showed that the teak forests had suffered greatly from the wasteful manner in which they had been exploited prior to 1885.[38] Corroborating evidence came from John Nisbet, Burma conservator of forests, who stated that forest fires destroyed hundreds of thousands of trees and other ground-cover every year.[39] In addition, Burmese peasants and hill-tribesmen felled hundreds of thousands of trees annually for local use or sale, or to clear the soil for shifting rice-cultivation.[40]

In conclusion, the cuttings by timber firms, the forest fires, the fellings for local use, the clearing of hill-sides for regular crops, and in other areas for shifting rice-cultivation resulted in Deforestation. This—in combination with a slight cyclical-dip in the annual rainfall from 1883-1885—was the main cause of the 'drought' of these years, and of many of the other calamities attributed to Thebaw's 'misrule'.[41]

FOOTNOTES

[1] Lorus and Margery Milne, *Water and Life*, London, 1965, pp. 127-128. *Also see :* Paul B. Sears, *Deserts on the March*, Norman, 1959, pp. 3-59. *Lastly see :* Ted Morello, "Deserts Into Forests," (Athens) *Ekistics*, April 1970, pp. 264-266.

[2] W. C. Loudermilk, "Man Made Deserts," (Honolulu) *Pacific Affairs*, Vol. VIII, No. 4, December 1935, pp. 411-416.

[3] *Ibid.*

[4] Dr. F. Regnault, "Deboisement and Decadence," (Allahabad) *The Indian Forester*, Vol. XXX, No. 8, August 1904, pp. 346-349. *Also see :* Tom Dale and Vernon Gill Carter, *Topsoil and Civilization*, Norman, 1955. When Dale and Carter deal with a small historical area, such as Phoenicia (pp. 68-75), their Deforestation 'model' fits very well indeed. However, when they attempt to apply Deforestation to a vast historical area, such as the Roman Empire, the 'model' does not seem to fit all of the variables. *Also see :* Rhoades Murphy, "The Ruin of Ancient Ceylon," (Ann Arbor) *The Journal of Asian Studies*, Vol. XVI, No. 2, February 1957, pp. 181-200. Ancient Ceylon may also have suffered from some Deforestation.

[5] Sir Mortimer Wheeler, *The Indus Civilization*, Cambridge, 1960, pp. 8-9. *Also see :* B. B. Lal and B. K. Thapar, "Excavations at Kalibangan," (New Delhi) *Cultural Forum*, July 1967, p. 88.

[6] *Ibid. See also :* Reid Bryson and David A. Barreis, "Possibilities of Major Climatic Modification and Their Implications : Northwest India, a Case for Study," (Athens) *Ekistics*, September 1967, pp. 245-249.

[7] Rudolf Geiger, *Climate Near the Ground*, Cambridge, Mass., 1965, pp. 360-368. Geiger stated that the increased rainfall, which usually occurs in re-forested plains and steppes, comes from the fact that the winds are slowed by the trees and drop more of their moisture. Geiger cited a test, which showed that the wind velocity increased almost forty per cent. over a deforested area as compared to the wind velocity over the same area when it was forested. Geiger attributed the drop in rainfall in the deforested area to the increased wind velocity, which blew the rains beyond the deforested area. A similar phenomenon appears to have occurred in the Dry Zone, especially after 1862.

[8] Dietrich Brandis, *Indirect Influence of Forests*, Calcutta, 1882, pp. 2-14 (IOL). *See also :* Berthold Ribbentrop, *Forestry in British India*, Calcutta, 1900, pp. 40-59 (IOL).

[9] Surgeon-General David Balfour, "Influence Exercised by Trees on the Climate and Productiveness of the Peninsula of India," (Calcutta) *The Indian Forester*, Vol. IV, No. 2, October 1878, pp. 113-150. *See also :* "On the Influence of Forests Upon Climate," (Roorkee), *The Indian Forester*, Vol. XII, No. 2, February 1886, pp. 75-79. *Lastly :* L. Parquet, "The Influence of Forests on Water-Supply," (Roorkee) *The Indian Forester*, Vol. XVIII, No. 7, July 1892, pp. 277-280.

[10] W. C. Loudermilk, "Man Made Deserts," pp. 411-416.

[11] *Ibid.*

[12] *Ibid.,* pp. 418-419. The American Great Plains had been covered with sod for millions of years before 1914. Then, wheat and grain prices, which had been high for a decade before WWI, rose sharply. Millions of acres were plowed under. When the rains did not come in the later-1920's, animals were grazed thereby completing the destruction of the ground-cover. In May 1934, exactly twenty years after the first plowings, the dust storms

began. In one year, 5,000,000 acres were turned into desert, with another 60,000,000 acres on the way to becoming desert. The 'Deforestation' process was eventually reversed with 'modern' methods of 'Reforestation'.

13 John Nisbet, "The Climatic and National-Economic Influence of Forests," in *Essays on Sylvicultural Subjects,* London, 1893, pp. 20-21, (IOL). Nisbet pointed out that the 1893 deficit in the Russian budget was due to the great 'drought' caused in turn by Deforestation. Millions of acres of forests in European Russia had been sold-off in the previous twenty years in order to build the railroads. Peasants had not re-planted their forest lots, and the process of Deforestation into desert had occurred over enormous areas.

14 H. Fielding [Hall] "How the Famine Came to Burma," (Edinburgh) *Blackwood's Edinburgh Magazine,* Vol. CLXI, April 1897, pp. 536-537.

15-16 *Ibid.*

17 "There is no doubt that the influence of the forest is the greater the more inhospitable the nature of a territory is to the growth of trees. In the boundaries between arid and humid climates...the beneficial effects of forests may become very great." Likewise, the removal of these forests and other ground-cover will have many harmful effects, such as 'drought', crop-failures, hunger, and revolution. Rudolf Geiger, *Climate Near the Ground,* p. 368.

18 Sir George Scott wrote of the 'Dry Zone' that : "In the absence of any protective cover from forests clothing the ground,...deluges erode and carry away the surface soil. Since the water from these rain-storms runs off in a few hours, cultivation for rice depends on irrigation where flat land can be irrigated." Sir J. George Scott, *Burma,* London, 1911, p. 217.

19 A. C. Pointon, *The Bombay Burmah Trading Corporation...,* pp. 8, 12.

20 P. L. Simonds, "The Teak Forests of India and the East, and our British Imports of Teak," (London) *Journal of the Society of Arts,* Vol. 38, February 27, 1885, pp. 348-349.

21 Robert Gordon, "The Irawadi River," (London) *Proceedings of the Royal Geographical Society,* May 1885, pp. 4, 12.

22 *Ibid.*

23-24 *Ibid See also :* C. G. Bates and A. J. Henry, "Forest and Stream-Flow Experiment at Wagon Wheel Gap, Col.," (Washington) *Monthly Weather Review,* Supplement No. 30, 1928. *Also see :* Raphael Zon, "Forests and Water in the Light of Scientific Investigation," (Washington) *U. S. Forest Service,* (no Vol. no.) 1927.

These two classic studies, and some others like them in more recent years, tend to contradict each other. This was in part due to the fact that the Bates-Henry study was of an area of less than one square mile, while Zon's study was of entire river basins of very large area. The author would be grateful to learn from authorities if similar stream-flow studies conducted in Burma could be projected backwards with any validity or accuracy to the years 1862-1885.

25 A maund is 82-2/7 pounds.

26 T. H. A., "Cutch Exports from Upper Burma," (Roorkee) *The Indian Forester,* Vol. XIV, No. 2, February 1888, pp. 70-71.

[27-29] *Ibid.*

[30] Dr. McClelland, "Report on the Teak Forest of Pegu," 1854 ; as cited in Lt. Gen. Albert Fytche, *Burma Past and Present,* Vol. 1, London, 1878, p. 303.

[31] *Ibid.*

[32] *Lower Chindwin District Gazetteer*, Vol. A, Rangoon, 1912, pp. 145-147.

[33] *Ibid.*

[34-35] *Ibid.* Italics added.

[36] Bernard to Durand, Memorandum on the BBTC's Leases, February 3, 1886; in No. 2, Forest Proceedings of February 1886, pp. 4-5. Bound in Burma Proceedings, Vol. 2663, Burma Forests (Home Dept.) 1886 (IOL).

[37] *Ibid.*

[38] Muir-Mackenzie to Chief Commissioner, October 31, 1891; in Progress Reports on Forest Administration in Upper Burma 1890-1891, p. 1 (BM).

[39] John Nisbet, *Burma Under British Rule*..., Vol. 11, pp. 63-64.

[40] *Ibid*, Vol. 1, p. 368.

[41] A final bit of evidence. The Seabrook Farms (New Jersey, U. S. A.) found that sandy waste-land ("the barrens") could absorb only one inch of waste-water. However, 600 feet away, the same sandy waste-land covered with weeds and low 'junk' trees could absorb five inches of water an hour for ten hours, or thirty-five inches a week, averaging 600 inches a year. In one area of the woods the absorption rate was 1,200 inches a year. In short, trees and other ground-cover absorb water and help to prevent 'droughts'. William L. Thomas Jr., *Man's Role in Changing the Face of the Earth*, Chicago, 1955, pp. 424-425, 580-581.

Appendix C

TREATIES BETWEEN BURMA AND BRITISH INDIA, 1862-1885[42]

The 1862 Treaty, November 10, 1862

(Introduction)

ARTICLE 1

The Burmese and British Rulers have for a long time remained at peace and in friendship; peace shall now be extended to future generations, both parties being careful to observe the conditions of a firm and lasting friendship.

ARTICLE 2

In accordance with the great friendship existing between the two countries, traders and other subjects of the Burmese Government, who may travel and trade in the British territory shall, in conformity with the custom of great countries, be treated and protected in the same manner as if they were subjects of the British Government.

ARTICLE 3

Traders and other subjects of the British Government, who may travel and trade in the Burmese territory, shall, in accordance with the custom of great countries, be treated and protected in the same manner as if they were subjects of the Burmese Government.

ARTICLE 4

When goods are imported into Rangoon from any British or foreign territory and declared to be for export by the Irrawaddy River to the Burmese territory, the English Ruler shall, provided bulk is not broken, and he believes the manifest to be true, charge one per cent. on their value, and if he so desires, shall allow them to be conveyed under the charge of an officer until arrived at Maloon and Menhla. The tariff value of goods shall be forwarded yearly to the Burmese Ruler. If such goods are declared for export to other territories, and not for sale in the Burmese territories, the Burmese Ruler shall, if he believes the manifest to be true, not cause bulk to be broken, and such goods shall be free of duty.

ARTICLE 5

When goods are imported into Burmah by persons residing in the Burmese or any foreign territory, and declared to be for export by the Irrawaddy River to Rangoon, the Burmese Ruler shall, provided bulk is not broken, and he believes the manifest to be true, charge one per cent on their value, and if he so desires, shall allow them to be conveyed under the charge of an officer to Thayet Myo, and the tariff value of such goods shall be forwarded yearly to the British Ruler. If such goods are declared for export to other territories, and not for sale in British territory, such goods shall be free according to the Customs Schedule, but goods liable to sea-board duty will pay the usual rate.

ARTICLE 6

Traders from the Burmese territory who may desire to travel in the British territory, either by land or by water through the whole course of the Irrawaddy River, shall conform to the customs of the British territory, and be allowed to travel in such manner as they please, without hindrance from the British Ruler, and to purchase whatever they may require. Burmese merchants will be allowed to settle and to have land for the erection of houses of business in any part of the British territory.

ARTICLE 7

Traders from the British territory who may desire to travel in the Burmese territory, either by land or by water, through the whole extent of the Irrawaddy River, shall conform to the customs of the Burmese territory, and shall be allowed to travel in such manner as they please, without hindrance by the Burmese Ruler, and to purchase whatever they may require. British merchants will be allowed to settle and to have lands for the erection of houses of business in any part of the Burmese territory.

ARTICLE 8

Should the British Ruler, within one year after the conclusion of this Treaty, abolish the duties now taken at Thayet Myo and Toungoo, the Burmese Ruler, with a regard to the benefit of the people of his country, will, if so inclined, after one, two, three, or four years, abolish the duties now taken at Maloon and Toungoo (in the Burmese territory).

ARTICLE 9

People from whatever country or nation, who may wish to proceed to the British territory, the Burmese Ruler shall allow to pass without hindrance. People from whatever country, who may desire to proceed to the Burmese territory, the British Ruler shall allow to pass without hindrance.[43]

(Signatories)

The 1867 Treaty, October 25, 1867

(Introduction)

ARTICLE 1

Save and except earth-oil, timber, and precious stones, which are hereby reserved as Royal monopolies, all goods and merchandise passing between British and Burmese territory shall be liable, at the Burmese Customs Houses, to the payment of a uniform import and export duty of five per cent *ad valorem* for a period of ten years, commencing from the first day of the Burmese year 1229, corresponding with 15th April 1867. No indirect dues or payments of any kind shall be levied or demanded on such goods over and above the five per cent *ad valorem* duty.

ARTICLE 2

But after the expiration of ten years, during which customs duties will be collected as provided for above in Article 1, it shall be optional with the Burmese Government, whilst estimating the capabilities and requirements of trade, either to increase or decrease the existing five per cent import and export duties, so that the increase shall at no time exceed (10) ten, or the decrease be reduced below a (3) three per cent *ad valorem* rate on any particular article of commerce. Three months' notice shall be given of any intention to increase or decrease the rates of customs duty as above previous to the commencement of the year in which such increase or decrease shall have effect.

ARTICLE 3

The British Government hereby stipulates that it will adhere to the abolition of frontier customs duty as expressed in Article 8 of the Treaty of 1862 during such time as the Burmese Government shall collect five per cent *ad valorem* duties, or a lesser rate, as provided for in Articles 1 and 2 of this Treaty.

ARTICLE 4

Both Governments further stipulate to furnish each other annually with price lists showing the market value of all goods imported and exported under Articles 1 and 2. Such price lists shall be furnished two months before the commencement of the year during which they are to have effect, and may be corrected from time to time as found necessary, by the mutual consent of both Governments through their respective Political Agents.

ARTICLE 5

The British Government is hereby privileged to establish a Resident or Political Agent in Burmese territory, with full and final jurisdiction in all civil suits arising between registered British subjects at the capital. Civil cases between Burmese subjects and registered British subjects shall be heard and finally decided by a mixed Court composed of the British Political Agent and a suitable

Burmese Officer of high rank. The Burmese Government reserves to itself the right of establishing a Resident or Political Agent in British territory whenever it may choose to do so.

ARTICLE 6

The British Government is further allowed the right of appointing British officials to reside at any or each of the stations in Burmese territory at which customs duty may be leviable. Such officials shall watch and enquire into all cases affecting trade and its relation to customs duty, and may purchase land and build suitable dwelling-houses at every town or station where they may be appointed to reside.

ARTICLE 7

In like manner, the Burmese Government is also allowed the right of appointing Burmese officials to reside at any or each of the stations in British Burmah at which customs duties may be leviable. Such officials shall watch and enquire into all cases affecting trade in its relations to customs duty and may purchase land and build suitable dwelling-houses at any town or station where they may be appointed to reside.

ARTICLE 8

In accordance with the great friendship which exists between the two Governments, the subjects of either shall be allowed free trade in the import and export of gold and silver bullion between the two countries, without let or hindrance of any kind, on due declaration being made at the time of import or export. The Burmese Government shall further be allowed permission to purchase arms, ammunition, and war materials generally in British territory, subject only to the consent and approval in each case of the Chief Commissioner of British Burmah and Agent to the Governor-General.

ARTICLE 9

Persons found in British territory, being Burmese subjects, charged with having committed any of the following offences, viz., murder, robbery, dacoity, or theft, in Burmese territory, may be apprehended and delivered up to the Burmese Government for trial, on due demand being made by the Government, provided that the charge on which the demand is made shall have been investigated by the proper Burmese officers in the presence of the British Political Agent; and provided also the British Political Agent shall consider that sufficient cause exists under British Law Procedure to justify the said demand and place the accused persons on their trial. The demand and delivery in each case shall be made through the British Political Agent at the capital.

ARTICLE 10

Persons found in Burmese territory, being British subjects, charged with having committed any of the following offences, viz., murder, robbery, dacoity, or theft, in British territory, may be apprehended and delivered up to the British Government, for trial, on due demand being made by that Government, provided that the charge on which the demand is made shall have been investigated by the proper British officers, in the presence of the Burmese Political Agent; and provided also that the Burmese Political Agent shall be satisfied that sufficient cause exists under Burmese Law Procedure to justify the said demand and put the accused persons on their trial. The demand and delivery in each case shall be made through the Burmese Political Agent in British territory.

ARTICLE 11

Persons found in Burmese territory, being Burmese subjects, charged with having committed any of the following offences, viz., murder, robbery, dacoity or theft, in British territory, shall, on apprehension, be tried and punished in accordance with Burmese Law and custom. A special Officer may be appointed by the British Government to watch the proceeding on the trial of all persons apprehended under this Article.

ARTICLE 12

Persons found in British territory, being British subjects, charged with having committed any of the following offences, viz., murder, robbery, dacoity or theft, in Burmese territory, shall, on apprehension, be tried and punished in accordance with British Law and custom. A special Officer may be appointed by the Burmese Government to watch the proceedings on the trial of all persons apprehended under this Article.

ARTICLE 13

The Treaty which was concluded on the 10th November, 1862 shall remain in full force; the stipulations now made and agreed to in the above Articles being deemed as subsidiary only, and is in no way affecting the several provisions of that Treaty.

(*Signatories*)[44]

(A)

It is laid down in the eighth Article of the subsidiary Treaty concluded this day, being the 25th October 1867, that the Burmese Government shall be allowed the right of purchasing arms, ammunition, and war material generally, subject only to the consent and approval of the Chief Commissioner, British Burmah, in each instance of purchase. This consent and approval will not be withheld so long as the two countries remain on friendly relations with each other.

(signed)   *A. Fytche*, Colonel, Chief Commissioner, British Burmah, and Agent to the Viceroy and Governor General of India.[45]

THE MIXED COURT RULES, JULY 26, 1869

(Introduction)

1. *Suits between registered British subjects*—All civil suits between registered British subjects shall be finally disposed of on trial in the Political Agent's Court.
2. *Mixed suits*—When a registered British subject is plaintiff in any mixed suit which may arise between Burmese and registered British subjects, he must, in the first instance, file his plaint in the

Political Agent's Court. The Political Agent will submit the said plaint to the Burmese Judge appointed to sit with him on the trial of mixed suits; and if they are mutually agreed that a cause of action exists, the Burmese defendant will be summoned to appear at the Political Agent's Court on a day to be appointed by the Burmese Judge. The suit will then be tried and finally disposed of on its merits by the Political Agent in conjunction with the Burmese Judge.

3. *Mixed suits*—When a Burmese subject is plaintiff in any mixed suit which may arise between Burmese and registered British subjects, he shall, in the first instance, make his complaint to the Burmese Judge appointed to sit on the trial of mixed suits with the Political Agent. The Burmese Judge will submit the said plaint to the Political Agent, and if both Judges are mutually agreed that a real cause of action exists, the registered British subject, as defendant, will be summoned to appear at the Political Agent's Court on a day to be appointed by the Political Agent. The suit will then be heard and finally disposed of on its merits by the Political Agent in conjunction with the Burmese Judge.

4. *Mixed suits*—When the Political Agent and the Burmese Judge are unable to come to a final decision in any mixed suit, the parties shall have the right of nominating a single arbitrator, and shall bind themselves to the Court by a written agreement to abide by his award. In cases, however, in which the services of a single arbitrator are not available, either party to the suit, plaintiff or defendant, shall each be allowed to name one arbitrator to the Court, and the Political Agent and Burmese Judge shall mutually agree in the selection of a third. The three arbitrators thus appointed shall proceed to try the case, and the decision of the majority on trial shall be final.

5. *Mixed suits*—The cost to be decreed in any mixed suit shall never exceed 10 per cent on the amount of the original claim.

6. The Burmese Government agrees to attach a bailiff and six peons to the Court of the Political Agent to act in conjunction with the Political Agent's establishment in the service and execution of Court processes and in giving effect to all lawful orders which may be communicated to them by the Political Agent himself, or by the duly authorised officers of his Court.[46]

FOOTNOTES

[42] Some other Burmese treaties not included in Appendices C and D would include: No. 725, Burma-Italy Treaty, March 3, 1871; in Foreign, Political-A, July 1873, Nos. 724-727 (NAI). *Also:* No. 5, Burma-Persia Treaty, June 22, 1877; in Foreign, Political-A, February 1878, Nos. 4-6 (NAI).

[43] Sir C. U. Aitchison, *A Collection of Treaties, Engagements, and Sanads: Relating to India and Neighbouring Countries....*, *Vol. II*, Calcutta, 1909, pp. 40-42.

[44] *Ibid*, pp. 43-46. All text before this footnote-number is the official Indian Government version. Fytche's Annexe was deleted by Aitchison.

[45] House of Commons Parliamentary Paper No. 251, June 8, 1869, pp. 37-38; in *Accounts and Papers, East India, 10 December, 1868-11 August 1869, Vol. XLVI* (BM). Fytche's explanation of the Treaty included a passage on p. 36 that read: "The Burmese Ministers agreed, on their part, to enter in the treaty that the purchase of arms be subjected to the approval of the Chief Commissioner, conditionally that I should give them a letter saying that this approval would not be withheld so long as the two countries remain on friendly terms with each other. I accordingly furnished the Minister with letter to that effect, copy of which is appended."

All concerned Calcutta and London officials appended their approval of the entire Treaty. Their letters appear on pp. 49-52.

[46] Sir C. U. Aitchison, *A Collection of Treaties, Engagements and Sanads....*, *Vol. 11*, pp. 46-47.

APPENDIX D

TREATIES BETWEEN BURMA AND FRANCE 1873-1885

The Treaty with France, January 24, 1873

(Introduction)

ARTICLE I

Burmese subjects residing in France and French subjects residing in Burma shall be allowed to go and come and live and stay and sell and buy as they may wish, and they shall be allowed consistently with the standing laws of the country to purchase land or sell land purchased and owned by them, to construct dwelling-houses, ware-houses, magazines and such other structures as they may wish for the purpose of mining and smelting material existing in their land, or of cultivating gardens, fields, and such other plantations as they may wish. In matters connected with the parents, wives or children of the said subjects, the protection of their property, and the maintenance of their interests, the Burmese and French Governments shall afford the same support and assistance as they may have afforded or hereafter may afford to (the subjects of) the most favoured foreign nation. French missionaries coming to Burma and residing therein shall be given the same support and assistance as missionaries of other nations, coming to Burma and residing therein.

French subjects visiting Burma for the purpose of travelling about therein in the interests of geography, natural history, that is to say geology, botany, ethnology, and zoology, or any other scientific research, will be afforded every assistance for the carrying out of their purposes with facility. Burmese subjects visiting France for the like purposes will be given similar assistance.

ARTICLE II

On goods imported or exported to or from France by Burmese subjects and on goods imported or exported to or from Burma by

French subjects, a duty shall be levied not exceeding that levied on imports or exports belonging to Burmese subjects in Burma and French subjects in France, or that levied on imports or exports belonging to subjects of the most favoured nation.

The imposition of duty on Burmese manufactured articles brought to France for sale and French manufactured articles brought to Burma for sale, the inspection and custody (?) thereof and all other formalities affecting them shall be the same as on articles of the same class or kind manufactured by subjects of the most favoured nation.

The Burmese Government being desirous of affording facilities to private persons depending upon Burma and France for the carrying on of trade hereby makes the following concession, namely, that French manufactured goods in Burma on which duty not exceeding five per cent has once been levied shall be exempt from the payment of every duty or revenue notwithstanding that the same may have been transferred from time to time to any person or place.

ARTICLE III

Both parties may agree and reciprocally appoint a Burmese diplomatic officer for the purpose of negotiating political matters with the French Government, as well as Consuls and Vice (?) Consuls in any suitable place in Burma and France (to watch over) the interests of their countrymen. The said officers shall be allowed to set up in their residences the insignia and flags of their rank and nationality, and with respect to their protection and the due discharge of their functions, both parties shall reciprocally allow them the same privileges which may be granted to officers of the same rank and standing who may be accredited by the present or future most favoured nation.

ARTICLE IV

The Burmese Government desiring that French subjects may come largely and reside and carry on trade in Burma hereby agrees to make the following concession, namely, that civil disputes arising between French subjects shall be transferred for hearing and decision to the French Consul, and civil disputes arising between

Burmese and French subjects shall be heard and decided in Court by a suitable Burmese officer and the French Consul in consultation.

ARTICLE V

Should Burmese subjects die while residing and trading in France, or French subjects die while residing and trading in Burma, the estate of the deceased persons shall be handed to their heirs, and if there are no heirs, shall be handed to the Consul of their respective nation for delivery to such heirs as may be duly entitled thereto by law.

ARTICLE VI

This treaty shall take effect for ever, so long as one Government does not make any amendment of its provisions. Should one party desire to make any amendment or addition to provisions of this treaty, the original provision may be cancelled and the amendment or addition made after one year's previous notice thereof has been given to the other. After ratification and exchange of copies one year or within from the date of its execution the provisions of this treaty shall take effect.[47]

(Signatories)

The Burma-France Supplementary Treaty, January 15, 1885

(Introduction)

ARTICLE I

Burma and France and her possessions shall not enter into enmity or strife or go to war. They shall be friends in the long future. Both parties shall reciprocally afford facilities for the carrying on of trade between the two countries and the ingress and egress of merchant vessels. Persons coming from one country to the other and residing whether temporarily or permanently in any village, town, district or port in Burma or France shall pay such duties and revenues with respect to their trade or business as are now imposed or may hereafter be imposed upon natives of the country. They shall equally receive the same privileges which are accorded or which may hereafter be accorded to natives of the country with respect to carrying on of trades and manufacturers, to the receiving of medals granted to inventors, and of patents for manufactured articles, and to the traffic of merchant vessels not provided for in this treaty.

ARTICLE II

With respect to Burmese and French subjects sending their vessels to the sea or river ports respectively belonging to Burma and France and shipping goods thereat, or visiting such village, town or district as they may desire, constructing offices, factories, warehouses, shops or dwellings and residing therein, or buying or selling dwelling-houses, warehouses or shops great or small, or purchasing all kinds of moveable goods, wares or fabrics, or carrying on various trade processes or callings, and selling in large or small quantities, or importing or exporting by land or by water manufactured stuffs and gold and silver articles, or receiving and holding merchandize of one class or other whether coming from within or without, both parties shall reciprocally accord the same privileges as are accorded to natives of the country and to subjects of the most favoured foreign nation. With respect to the duties and revenues to be paid on the above mentioned purchases, manufactures, importations and exportations, they shall be similar to and shall not exceed the duties and revenues which are now paid or which may hereafter be paid by the natives of the country or by subjects of the most favoured nation.

When special rules hereafter shall have been made in Burma regulating the purchase and sale of land and permission is granted to subjects of the most favoured nation to buy and sell land, to mine and smelt materials existing in their land, and to make gardens, fields, and plantations in their land, French subjects residing in Burma shall receive consistently with the laws of the country the same privileges which may be accorded to subjects of the most favoured nation. When Burmese subjects residing in France and French subjects residing in Burma carry on trade in the various articles of merchandize belonging to them in the two countries, they shall be entitled to determine by agreement the price of the said articles and to import or export or buy or sell the same as they may wish. With respect to the said subjects carrying on trade in the various articles of merchandize belonging to them, or shipping or landing the same, or paying duty or revenue thereon they shall be entitled to conduct their business personally or by agent. When French subjects residing in Burma carry on trade they shall not be subject to the valuations (of their goods) by royal brokers or other middlemen of the like nature at present found or hereafter to be found on the right and left banks of the river Irrawaddy and in other villages, towns and stations where trade exists; they shall be entitled to buy or sell as they may desire.

ARTICLE III

The Burmese Government gives the following permission to French subjects in order that they may not encounter difficulties when residing in or wishing to travel about in Burma. The French official passports usually carried by them shall be produced before the proper Burmese authorities who will enquire and note the place of residence desired or the locality intended to be visited, and after signing the passports so as to make manifest the fact that the persons are French subjects will return the same to the persons producing them, when the latter shall be at liberty to visit or travel about or reside in the village, town or district desired.

The above mentioned production of papers for the purposes of residence or travel shall be as in the case of (subjects) of foreign nations.

ARTICLE IV

With respect to the various revenues or the various military expenses and rates which according to the customary rules are now imposed or which may hereafter be imposed, Burmese subjects residing in France and French subjects residing in Burma shall be subject to the same rules as may be imposed upon subjects of the most favoured foreign nation. Burmese subjects residing in France and French subjects residing in Burma shall not be charged with military, naval, or police service: they shall be exempt therefrom.

ARTICLE V

With the exception of wet tea among those articles of trade which appertain to the people of the country, the remaining articles shall not form directly or indirectly articles of royal trade. They shall form articles of general trade, wet tea alone being made an article of trade by the Burmese Government. The French Government distinctly recognize the fact that precious articles, stones, timber, earth-oil, jade, and other various products of His Majesty the King of Burma's possessions are royal property and perquisites and articles of royal merchandize.

ARTICLE VI

Gold and silver bullion and specie, and articles of personal wear, use or consumption in small quantities not intended for sale, brought into or taken out of Burma shall be exempt from every kind of duty or revenue. On all other articles of merchandize imported or exported shall be levied the same duties and revenues as are now levied or may hereafter be levied upon articles of merchandize belonging to subjects of the most favoured nation. And until the first day of the 1257th year of the Koja Era corresponding with April 1895 of the Christian Era duty shall be levied at a rate not exceeding 30 per cent on opium and bhang, or 5 per cent on all other articles of merchandize. On the expiration of the period fixed the Burmese Government shall be entitled, after taking into consideration the state and circumstances of trade, to levy the duty as usually levied upon opium and bhang, and to amend and enhance the tariff on all other articles of merchandize to a rate not exceeding 10 per cent *ad valorem*, six months previous notice having been given of the proposed amendment of tariff to the French Government.

ARTICLE VII

Those articles of merchandize upon which duty is leviable by both Governments as contained in this treaty, shall have duty levied upon them according to their values which shall consist of the sum total of their original buying price, and the expenses of freight, commission and insurance thereon. The original owners of the articles of merchandize bringing the same shall produce before and for the satisfaction of the Custom-house officers their invoices and other lists and memoranda showing the original prices and expenses. Should the Burmese Customs officers not be satisfied with the original prices submitted by traders, and a dispute should arise, the prices as determined jointly by one or two traders on behalf of the Burmese officers and one or two traders on behalf of the French Consul shall be the prices on which duty shall be levied. Should the Burmese customs officers not be satisfied with the joint determination they shall be entitled to purchase the articles, if so willing, at a value one-fifth above the original buying prices as submitted by the traders. The Burmese Government shall hold themselves responsible that the value of the purchase is fully paid up within 15 days from the date of purchase.

ARTICLE VIII

All articles of merchandise forwarded as samples from one country to the other by French merchants, manufacturers or commercial travellers residing in Burma, or Burmese merchants, manufacturers or commercial travellers residing in France, shall on their arrival at the Customs stations of the two countries be exempt from duty or revenue. Samples of merchandise in order that they may be returned as such to the country from which they were originally forwarded shall be accurately marked and forwarded in conformity with rules to be prescribed in the Customs office, which rules shall be framed by the two Governments in consultation.

ARTICLE IX

In the event of the one friendly Government allowing to another friendly Government any increased privileges connected with reduction of duties or revenues, or in connection with commerce (generally) in Burma or France, the Burmese and French Governments reciprocally engage themselves that each shall allow the other to enjoy (the same) benefits without favour. The two Governments mutually engage that on the buying and selling of various articles of trade or consumption in the two countries, on their collection or removal, on their re-exportation, trans-shipment, or transit through the country, on commercial transactions, and on the in-

gress or egress of merchant vessels, the same imposts shall be levied
and allowances made as are levied and allowed in the case of subjects of the most favoured nation. The rules making dutiable or
contraband articles of merchandise imported or exported into or
in transit through Burma or France shall be the same as those
making dutiable or contraband articles of merchandise belonging
to subjects of the most favoured nation.

ARTICLE X

With respect to the entry clearance and mooring of merchant
vessels belonging to Burmese and French subjects in France and
Burma at the sea or river ports respectively belonging to each, the
same concessions shall be given to the said vessels as may be given
vessels belonging to subjects of the country and to subjects of the
most favoured nation, and the entry clearance and mooring of the
said vessels shall be in conformity with the rules prescribed by the
Government of the territory (concerned).

ARTICLE XI

When vessels of French merchants arrive at the collecting station
on the borders of Burma and they carry weapons of warfare over
and above the few swords, muskets and weapons, &c., usually
carried by the commanders, mates and engineers for their self-
defence, the commanders shall deliver the arms and weapons
carried to the Burmese Custom-house officers. The Customs
Collectorate officers shall unship the arms delivered by the commanders and shall retain them so that they may neither get lost
nor mixed up with others and shall re-ship and restore them to the
commanders to take out (of the country) when the vessels return
to the Collectorate station.

ARTICLE XII

When French merchant vessels arrive at a duty-levying station
in Burma, the Burmese Custom-house officers shall be entitled to
demand the ships' records and papers, and papers proving her
nationality; and the commanders shall within 24 French hours or
60 Burmese hours after arrival produce before the Custom-house

officers detailed and complete lists showing the names of the vessels
and their tonnage, the commander, mates, engineers, crew and passengers, and the description, quality, number, size and weight of her
cargo, within three French hours after the production of which
they shall receive permission to discharge.   After the expiration of
the three hours they shall be entitled to discharge, although they
may not have received permission from the Burmese Custom-house
officers.   Should the provisions herein contained not be observed
and the (commanders) omit or delay to produce (the papers and
records) required to be produced, or discharge cargo before the
expiration of the three French hours prescribed, for each and every
occasion on which they commit the offence, the offending commanders shall pay a penalty of Rs. 200 to the Burmese Government.

ARTICLE XIII

With respect to the shipping and landing of goods, the shippers
or consignees or their agents shall come and make examination at
the spot where the goods are shipped or landed, and the Burmese
Custom-house officers shall exert themselves and make examination
so that the work of shipping or landing may not be interrupted or
delayed.

ARTICLE XIV

If French subjects residing in Burma borrow money, and
through spending the same or suffering losses are unable to repay
their creditors, the agent appointed by the French Government
shall seize and sell the debtors' property and effects, and after making *pro rata* shares of the money realized shall hand over the same
to their respective creditors.

ARTICLE XV

If Burmese subjects borrow money from French subjects residing in Burma, and after spending the same, either refuse or fraudulently evade repayment, the Burmese Government shall exert themselves to assist the creditors so that they may recover their dues.
If French subjects residing in Burma borrow money from Burmese
subjects, and after spending the same, either refuse or fraudulently

10. *December 28, 1885.   The Wun of Bhamo goes to visit General Prendergast after the Indian Army had captured the town.*
(Illustrated London News, February 20, 1886, p. 181.)

11. Mid-February 1886. *Viceroy Lord Dufferin holding a levee in the Grand Throne Room of the Mandalay Palace.* (Illustrated London News, April 3, 1886, p. 350).

evade repayment, the agent appointed by the French Government shall exert himself to assist the creditors so that they may recover their dues.

ARTICLE XVI

Burmese subjects coming to reside in France or her possessions shall receive the same treatment and privileges as are accorded to subjects of the most favoured nation coming to reside therein.

ARTICLE XVII

Until a settlement has been come to between the two Governments with reference to the proposed negotiation about criminal jurisdiction as contained in the memorandum of agreement dated the 24th January 1873 (Burmese date given), when rules shall be specially framed hereafter providing for the trial of foreigners committing criminal offences in Burma and foreigners are treated with special privileges, the Burmese Government shall deal with French subjects committing criminal offences in Burma in the same manner as they deal with subjects of the most favoured nation.

ARTICLE XVIII

Burmese subjects committing in France or her possessions murder, brigandage, arson, robbery or theft and taking shelter in Burma, shall on their arrest be tried by the Burmese Government in conformity with the Burmese laws. French subjects committing in Burma murder, brigandage, arson, robbery or theft and taking shelter in France or her possessions, shall on their arrest be tried by the French authorities in conformity with the French laws.

ARTICLE XIX

Subjects of either nation residing in Burma or France and her possessions committing in the country of their residence offences as contained in Article XVIII, other than political offences against the laws, and fleeing from that country and found taking shelter in the other, shall upon one Government demanding them from the other be delivered by the Burmese officers or French officers as the case may be to the diplomatic Agent or Consul of the Government making the demand.

ARTICLE XX

The two Governments shall be entitled after discussion and upon mutual agreement to make supplementary additions to this treaty where they discover any clauses which are obscure or which it will be productive of real advantage (to add).

ARTICLE XXI

The ratification and exchange of copies of this treaty shall be carried out according to custom one year or within from the date of its execution. From the date of exchange of copies it shall take effect for ever, so long as one Government does not make any amendment. Should one Government desire either to amend or add to the provisions of this treaty or cancel the treaty itself, one year's previous notice thereof shall be given to the other, when the amendment or cancelment shall be effected after discussion and upon mutual agreement.[48]

(*Signatories*)

FERRY'S SECRET LETTER GIVEN TO THE BURMESE AMBASSADOR, JANUARY 15, 1885

Your Excellency,

With reference to Your Excellency's verbal communication that it is the desire of the Burmese Government that the French Government should take care, having regard to the actions and circumstances of certain Burmese subjects who have taken shelter in India, that the latter do not at some future time commit any molestation of Burmese territory (I have the honour to inform Your Excellency) that although those persons who come for shelter to India are received and are allowed a residence, yet the molestation of the territory of a friendly Sovereign by them is an act which is against the French laws. The French Government therefore distinctly undertake that they will take care that certain of the Burmese subjects taking shelter in the French possessions of India shall not use that territory as a basis for collecting arms and men or molesting the territory of the friendly State of Burma.

With respect to the transport through the province of Tonkin to Burma of arms of various kinds, ammunition, and military stores generally, amicable arrangements will be come to with the Burmese Government for the passage of the same, when peace and order prevails in Tonkin and the officers stationed there are satisfied that it is proper and that there is no danger.

With respect to the proposed opening out of a road from Burma to Tonkin in order that facilities may exist for trade and communication between Burma and that French possession to the mutual prosperity of both, the French Government will render what help they may be able when the Burmese Government gives them notice.

(*Signed*) JULES FERRY[49]

FOOTNOTES

[47] No. 43, Burma-France Treaty, January 24, 1873: in Foreign Secret-E, August 1885, Nos. 40-49 (NAI). The small document activating this Treaty was: No. 44, Declaration activating Treaty as of June 1, 1884, April 4, 1884; in Nos. 40-49.

[48] No. 45, The Burma-France Supplementary Treaty, January 15, 1885; in Nos. 40-49.

[49] No. 46, Ferry's Secret Letter, January 15, 1885; in Nos. 40-49.

Appendix E

THE *HLUTDAW'S* JUDGMENT IN THE BBTC TEAK
CASE, AUGUST 12, 1885

In the case respecting timber between the Toungoo residence thitgaungs, Kyaukmaw, Myozaye, Nga Kya Myo; Wannigon Myothugyi's agent, Nga Sa; Ela Myothugyi's agents, Nga Hnin, Nga Taw, Nga Min, and their fellow thitgaungs on the one part, and the English merchants Bombay Burma Company, Bryce, Maxwell, and Agent Andreino on the other.

Nga Po, Nga Shwe Moung, Nga Pok and the other Thitgoungs state that they worked as Thitgoungs in the Thitkyeikkye forests in the Toungoo Yameithein district, and handed over to the Agents of the Bombay-Burma Company, Bryce and Maxwell.

in 1245 B. E. 42,233 logs.
in 1246 B. E. 47,567 ,,
——
Total .. 89,800 logs.
——

The Agents of the Company did not submit complete lists, nor completely settle accounts, but submitted lists and settled accounts for—

18,259 logs in 1245 B. E., and
13,869 ,, in 1246 ,,
——
Total .. 32,128 logs only.
——

The chief and subordinate Thitgoungs state that they are sufferers and submit lists. The Bombay-Burma Company Bryce and Maxwell's Agent Andreino on being questioned states that for the two years 1245 and 1246, the Bombay-Burma Company's Agents settled each year's accounts for the timber mentioned in the *thitshe kun shin* contract (contract for long or full-sized logs of timber under a fluctuating rate of revenue) other than the timber mentioned in the *thitto kun the* contract (contract for short or under-sized logs of timber under a fixed rate of revenue), and that no timber was received or taken out in excess of that submitted to the Revenue Court.

Taking into consideration the likelihood that, if the items submitted by each party were to be gone into and cleared up (in Court in detail), it would occupy a long and protracted period, and that the chief and subordinate Thitgoungs would suffer by having to incur further expenses, and in view of clearly ascertaining facts and deciding the case with justice, the Chief Commissioner of British Burma was asked by letter to allow those who were sent down in conjunction by both parties to take copies of the statements of timber floated down and arriving at the Toungoo Forest Office during the years 1244, 1245 and 1246, *i.e.*, from the year when the Company first worked under contract. Copies of the statements recorded in the Forest Office were taken in English and in Burmese and authenticated with the forest office seal, and these showed that during the three years 1244, 1245, and 1246 there were 2,430 rafts of timber floated down which comprised—

93,791	*du*	logs
20,021	*hlwa*	,,
321	*yat*	,,
Total	114,133	logs

The lists submitted by the Bombay-Burma Company's Agents once a year under which they settled accounts showed—

23,391	logs in 1244
18,423	,, in 1245
14,364	,, in 1246

Total .. 44,008 *du* logs
12,170 *hlwa* logs, or a total of

56,178 logs only

Comparing the two statements, there is a difference shown during the three years of—

49,783 *du*   logs
7,851 *hlwa*   „
321 *yat*   „
———
Total .. 57,955 logs
———

On examining the Agents of the Bombay-Burma Company as to this difference, they state that after the first contract had been entered into in 1243 B. E., a second contract was entered into which provided for the payment of a *kun the* revenue (a fixed rate of revenue) *viz.*, rupees one lakh a year, for *pe* logs (rejected logs) excluded from the first contract, and for *pinyin ngok kyan* logs (under-sized logs) which were under 3 cubits in girth and 12 cubits in length; that the logs taken out under this second contract have been mixed up with the others and have occasioned the difference that, although they are termed *hlwa* logs in the statements of which copies were taken, *thitto* (short) logs of great girth alone are called *hlwa* logs, and that therefore a large number of the logs taken out under the second contract would properly be included under that term (*hlwa*).

On further examining the Thitgoungs, they state that the Forest Office records show only three kinds of timber, *viz.*, *du, hlwa* and *yat* logs; that those records contained no *thitto* logs for this reason, *viz.*, that although provision was made in the second contract for the taking out (by the Co.) of *thitto* logs, yet that no *thitto* timber, or timber under 12 cubits in length had been felled or marked out, and that only logs which would have properly been included in the first contract had been fraudulently taken out as coming under the second contract; that it was in consequence of this that the Forest Office records which showed correctly the number of logs of timber arriving in rafts, showed no statement of *thitto* (short) logs.

On taking into consideration the plaint, reply, and the examination of both parties, the matter is one connected with a concession made by Government (to the public) according to the rules and customs of the State, and it concerns an industry which may be productive of either benefit or loss to the locality and State to Thitgoungs and merchants. It should therefore be decided solely upon the basis of the first, second, and third contracts under which the forests were worked, and upon the statements from the Toungoo Forest Office authenticated by seal. The *du* logs and *hlwa* logs contained in the Forest Office statements should not be connected, included or mixed up with the kind of timber mentioned in the second contract *viz.*, *thitto* logs and *yat* logs; they should be included amongst the logs felled and worked out under the first contract. Accordingly deducting from the 114,133 logs contained in the Forest Office statement, the following, *viz.*, 1,457 logs with John Darwood's name, 321 *yat* logs which should properly be included (amongst the timber worked out) under the second contract, as also 56,178 logs accounted for by the Company's Agent during the three years, or 57,956 logs in all, the remainder, *viz*:—

48,326 *du* logs,
7,851 *hlwa* logs,

——

Total   56,177 logs,

——

is clearly ascertained to be what the Bombay-Burma Company, Bryce and Maxwell's Agents have taken out in excess.

Let the Thitgoungs, therefore, submit statements of accounts of expenses, &c., upon the excess 56,177 logs, and of whatever balance may be due to them: and let the same after examination be fully paid by the Bombay Burma Company, Bryce and Maxwell's Agents. Respecting the working and export of timber by the Bombay-Burma Company Bryce and Maxwell's Agents, the Thitgoung will file a suit against the Company's Agents for money due for expenses, and this will be enquired into and examined and settled. It has been clearly ascertained that in breach of the provisions of the first, second, and third contracts 48,326 *du* logs, 7,851 *hlwa* logs, or 56,177 logs in all were taken out during the years 1244, 1245 and 1246 in excess fraudulently without payment of revenue. Excess logs so taken out whether personal property or *pan* (thit?) logs should according to the rules of the State be confiscated to the King. Accordingly let the 48,326 *du* logs and 7,851 *hlwa* logs, or 56,177 logs in all be calculated, according to the "Royal" logs of good quality as mentioned in the first contract, and by way of penalty for fraudulently taking out the same, let the Bombay-Burma Company, Bryce and Maxwell's Agents, pay in double the amount of revenue thereon.

State [Seal]	Judgment delivered on the 2nd waxing Wagoung 1247 (12th August, 1885) By three Wungyis, five Atwin woons, two Woondouks, and two other Ministers in Council.[50]

[50] No. 86, The *Hlutdaw's* Judgment in the Teak Case, August 12, 1885; in Foreign, Secret-E, September, 1885, Nos. 27-97 (NAI).

Appendix F

AN ASSESSMENT OF THEBAW

Thebaw made a personal defence of his reign that was most illuminating. On the morning of November 29, 1885, Thebaw and Supayalat held an interview in the Palace garden-pavilion with E. K. Moylan, the London *Times* correspondent. The interview, and the comments of several of Thebaw's contemporaries, follow below and in the footnotes.[51]

Thebaw began by stating that he wished to be "kept quiet."[52] He had given everything to the English, and he asked Col. Edward Sladen to govern Upper Burma in the future. At the end of five years when Sladen would have put the country in order, he, Thebaw, would come back and rule by Sladen's advice. Thebaw added that if Sladen had remained as Resident as in Mindon's time, the war would never have occurred. Thebaw said that he had been badly advised and that he had been seized when young, and made a mere puppet :

I have now to suffer for what Tinedah and others forced me to do. [Taingda, the Pangyet, and the Hlaythin] urged me on to war, and when the fighting commenced they were the first to abandon me......I did not hear of the English taking Minhla ; but when I heard of your arrival at Pagan, I said, no more fighting must occur, as the Burmese could not resist.

My ministers told me that only five vessels with 2,000 soldiers were coming to make a treaty. My mother-in-law, [the Dowager Queen] was always very anxious to prevent war. Not one of them has waited on me since the English arrived in Mandalay.[53]

Col. Sladen remarked that the British would not respect such ministers for deserting their King. Thebaw returned to justifying his reign, and commented at length upon the February 15-17, 1879 Royal Massacre :

You English think that I killed all my relatives, but it is not so. I was under a guard myself, and they [relatives] were murdered. The reason that I was not murdered myself was that before the King [Mindon] died he told the [Dowager] Queen I was the quiet son. A horoscope was also drawn by the priests, and my name came out first.

For the first seven months after I became King I was not allowed to interfere. I was not even crowned [until June 1879]. I continued to wear the Phoongyee priest's robes. I ordered that my relatives should not be killed but imprisoned, so that there might not be a disturbance in the country.[54] I was sleeping in bed when the order to kill them was given by the Ministers.

......The English people knew much that I did, but not of what was going on behind me.......I wish the English to know that I am not a drunkard. I am a religious Buddhist.[55]

One would conclude from Thebaw's statements that he was a young man of mild and benign character.[56] However, certain other qualities are also required if one is to be an effective, *i.e.* 'good' ruler. Thebaw lacked the will to translate his kindly sentiments into positive acts. He also lacked the will to support those ministers, such as the Kinwun and the 'reformers', who were willing to make positive changes. The end result was that Thebaw's lack of will seriously injured his reputation or 'face', and caused his country to pass under foreign domination.[57]

FOOTNOTES

[51] "The Burmese War," (London) *The Times*, December 5, 1885, p. 5.

[52] *Ibid.* A very critical assessment of Thebaw's reign was given by the Tangyet Wundauk, Burmese ambassador to Paris, during a December 5, 1885 dinner interview. The Tangyet said he had repeatedly telegraphed his Government that the French would not help them in case of war with Great Britain. "But my advice to the King was concealed." The Tangyet added that he had advised all along not to go to war, but to accept the Indian Government's demands. "I knew very well that our soldiers would not make any stand, for the Ministers were unpopular all over the country and detested by the soldiers who would not fight for them. The King's reply was foolish. It was a needless provocation."

Tangyet said Thebaw was weak, Supayalat was a spendthrift, her mother the Dowager Queen was ambitious, and the ministers were greedy. The Royal Couple wasted thirty lakhs, which disappeared for useless fancies and into the pockets of favorites. "There was misery for everyone except themselves." Slavery had been abolished, but it continued in other forms. The 'reforms' had been sham reforms, "the only result of which was to reproduce under various pretexts, the abuses that were thought to be extirpated."

The hour of reckoning had finally come with the British invasion. The Tangyet deplored the loss of his country's independence, "but I have at least the satisfaction of being able to say freely what I think." "The Burmese Envoy in Paris," (London) *The Times,* December 7, 1885, p. 5.

[53] *Ibid.*

[54] *Ibid.* (*See also*: "Burma," (Calcutta) *Englishman,* December 16, 1878, p. 3. The article stated that "The clemency [Thebaw]......has shown to his imprisoned brothers is remarkable. They are not in such miserable pight as has frequently been rumoured......[;] [Thebaw]......allows Rs. 5 per diem for each one's messing, and......strict orders have been issued by him to see that nothing is attempted in the way of rendering life a burden to them." *Note:* An unskilled labourer in Mandalay received one-fourth rupee per day in 1878.)

[55] *Ibid.* J. A. Bryce, the BBTC official who negotiated the 1880 and 1882 BBTC Teak Contracts at Mandalay, stated that Thebaw had nothing to do with the February 15-17, 1879 Massacre. Bryce contended that Thebaw had taken to drink "in a great measure to drown the remorse which he suffered" when he thought of the Massacre. "......he had been brought up in a monastery, amongst the monks, and anything in the nature of slaughter was extremely repulsive and repugnant to him." H. T. White, "Upper Burma Under British Rule," (London) *Journal of the Society of Arts,* Vol. 41, 1893, p. 165. *Also*: J. A. Bryce to Bernard, May 29, 1882; in Foreign, Secret-E, July 1883, Nos. 125-145 (NAI).

[56] Grattan Geary stated that Thebaw was not considered a tyrant by his people. The February 15-17, 1879 Massacre was popular with most Burmese. Thebaw extracted fewer taxes from his people, "in other words, perhaps, he was more successfully robbed by his subordinates." After the British Resident left on October 6, 1879, Thebaw saw to it that the English Church built by his father was not destroyed by vandals. When the Expedition arrived at Mandalay on November 28, 1885, they found the church virtually intact, except for six little marble legs that had held up the marble font. "A church abandoned to itself for seven years in civilized and Christian London would certainly not be found ready for divine service at the end of the time."

Thebaw also wanted to found a University of Mandalay where Burmese, English, French, German, Italian, Pali, and other languages would be taught. Unfortunately, "Thebaw let his grand project fall through. His name will not go down to posterity as the founder of the University of Mandalay." Grattan Geary, *Burma After the Conquest,* pp. 326-329.

[57] In later years Thebaw had an interesting explanation for his fall. He sent a testimonial letter to Maung Shway Kun, former master of the Royal Cigar Factory at Mandalay and now a cigar manufacturer. A copy of Thebaw's testimonial was carried on every box of Maung Shwag Kun's popular Burmese Esoof Cheroots:

"My late father, the Royal Mindon Min, the golden-footed lord of the white elephant, master of a thousand gold umbrellas, owner of the Royal peacocks, lord of the sea and of the world, whose face was like the sun, always smoked the Esoof cheroot while meditating on his treatment of the bull-faced, earthswallowing English. Had I done the same I should never have lost my throne, but I used the opium-drugged cheroots from Manila and the trash which was sent me from San Francisco, and I fell. (Signed) THEBAW, formerly King." "Why Thebaw Lost Burmah," (London) *The Times*, March 28, 1890, p. 4.

APPENDIX G

THE PROPOSED REFORMS OF THE KINWUN, THE MAGWE, AND DR. CLEMENT WILLIAMS

The proposed reforms of the Kinwun, the Magwe and their friend, Dr. Clement Williams, the former British Political Agent at Mandalay from 1861-1865, included a Constitution that would have reduced the King from the earthly counterpart of Lord Indra, the King of the Gods atop Mt. Meru, to a titular constitutional monarch. The King would no longer own everything in the country, but would be limited to a privy purse or civil list. The amount would be determined by the ministers, who would have the ultimate authority in financial as well as in other matters of government.

Although such reforms appeared to be revolutionary, Robert Shaw, the British Resident at Mandalay in 1878-1879, noted that the idea of a ministerial check upon the King had always been present. Shaw wrote that:

> Every edict of the King's has to be brought first to the [Hlutdaw] ....where it is registered as by a French Parlement under the ancient regime. ....at times....influential Ministers have delayed the promulgation of Royal orders, and have got them quashed. The system which the present Ministers are now trying to establish [is]....no novelty in form.[58]

Further reforms of the ministers included a proposed division of the Government into departments based on a portfolio system, i.e, treasury, foreign affairs, public works, agriculture, etc. This would replace the old 'Merucentric' division of the government, which had alloted positions based on the points of the compass, i.e. wungyis, atwinwuns and wundauks of the North, East, South and West.[59]

To accomplish the above reorganization, the 'reformers' proposed to send Thebaw and Supayalat on a grand tour of England and perhaps Europe. Thebaw was eager to go until Supayalat talked him out of it. Despite this set-back, the Kinwun's cabinet of fourteen ministries was established by November 11, 1878. The Kinwun was war minister; the Yenangyaung was agriculture minister; the Kampat was public works minister; the Magwe was treasury minister; and the atwinwun, U Waik, was religions and education minister. Several wundauks headed the other ministries of industries; justice; foreign affairs and telegraphs; marine; aliens; and interior, which was the ministry in charge of liaison with the Shan rulers and the provincial officials. Two wundauks also served as the *myowuns*, co-ministers, of the city of Mandalay.

The treasury ministry, headed by the Magwe and two assisting atwinwuns, was not allowed to pay out funds to the King and Queen without the Magwe's approval. The Magwe in turn was limited in his financial powers, because no individual minister could meet privately with the King and Queen. Instead, all the ministers had to meet as one body with the Royal Couple to report affairs and to suggest or receive courses of action or instruction.

This new proto-parliament was set up to stop corruption and increase governmental efficiency, and seriously cramped the style of merchants and others accustomed to bribing one of the ministers to gain a Royal ruling favourable to the petitioner's request. Unfortunately, a typically Burmese reaction soon occurred. As described in the first sections of Chapter I, all of the ministers soon had to be bribed under the new system. This was enough in itself to turn 'public opinion' against the proto-parliament after less than four months.

A "New System" was also proposed by the Magwe in November, 1878, and was published as an official pamphlet by the Burmese Government. The proposals included the abolition of all Royal Monopolies. New roads were to be built into the interior of the country. One-half of the nation's soldiers were to be sent to the villages to help with the crops. The other one-half would remain in Mandalay, and were to be dressed in European uniforms and drilled by the Comte de Trevelec, a French cavalry adviser.[60]

P. H. Bonvillain, the French manager of the King's Sagaing and Mandalay iron foundries, was to build fifty small steam-boats to join the Irrawaddy River at all important points. Government employees were to receive a fixed monthly salary, and provincial officials would not be allowed to 'eat' their jurisdictions as they had formerly. Modern accounting methods were to be introduced into the Treasury Department.[61]

The Lower Burma railroad from Rangoon was to be extended north of the frontier to Mandalay; and Dr. Williams was given the contract on January 16, 1879.[62] In addition, the "New System" proposed a systematic and conservation-minded exploitation of the country's natural resourses. Forests and mines were to be developed by *kala* firms for the mutual benefit of all. Unfortunately, much of the "New System" was put aside after the February 15-17, 1879 Massacre, except for the division of the Government into ministries (portfolio system).[63]

Some reforms were put into effect, such as the cutting-off of cheats from the list of 10,000 Mandalay 'monks', who had received daily offerings from the public treasury.[64] Still another reform was the opening of registration offices for legal documents to replace the old trial-by-ordeal in case of legal disagreements.[65]

The July 26, 1880 cabinet reshuffle saw the ministerial portfolios monopolized by the Yanaung's faction. However, the Kinwun was still listed as a largely powerless 'Prime Minister and President of the *Hlutdaw*'. His key function was to sign all letters to the Indian Government. He was also listed as head of the moribund committee to draft a Royal Constitution.

However, the Kinwun regained much of his old power after the overthrow of Yanaung's group on March 16, 1882. In 1883, the Kinwun was able to establish a ten department *Hlutdaw* consisting of himselfas head of the legislation department; the Hlaythin as head of the marine department; and with additional departments of war; finance; *thathameda* taxation; agriculture; industries; foreign affairs, religion and education; civil justice; and criminal justice.

In July 1883, the Kinwun was apparently responsible for persuading King Thebaw to order a census of all pagoda and other slaves in Mandalay, both male and female. All slave-holders were ordered to present their bonds before the *Hlutdaw*. These bonds listed the amount of debt each slave had contracted while free, and how much had been paid towards the liquidation of the debt. The owners, the slaves, and the persons who had sold them, were then examined by Royal judges; and King Thebaw eventually paid about Rs. 40,000 for the emancipation of several thousand slaves. A total of 1,394 ex-slaves became monks, 240 of them as full monks, *ranhas*, and another 1,154 as novices. Thebaw gave all of them presents of money and monks' robes. However, slavery continued in other forms, according to the Tangyet Wundauk, the Burmese ambassador to Paris. (See footnote 52, p. 378).

In 1884, the Kinwun was apparently also responsible for persuading Thebaw to divide the country into ten or more *Kayaings* or divisions, each division to be administered by a *kayaing wun* or roving commissioner. These posts were patterned after the posts that the Kinwun had held in the late-1860's and early-1870's when King Mindon had sent him on trouble-shooting missions to the south of the country. Indeed, the Kinwun's popular title, *kinwun*, had come from an early such commissionership as the man in charge of the frontier-police and duty-collections after the signing of the 1867 treaty with the Indian Government.

The roving commissioners would have greatly improved the local administrations of the divisions under their control, and would have formed the long-missing but sorely needed direct-link between the King-*Hlutdaw* and the provincial Governors. Unfortunately, the Kingdom had only a few more months of independence, and the roving commissioners had no time to become effective.

In February 1885, the Lower Burma and Indian newspapers mentioned that the Kinwun's moribund Constitution committee was once again showing signs of life. Thebaw (and the Kinwun) had also proposed to the French Bishop, Dr. Bourdon, that he become the first Vice-Chancellor of a new University of Mandalay, which would teach Burmese, English, French, German, Italian, Pali and other subjects. Unfortunately, Thebaw was only willing to allot about Rs. 100 per month for the University. Bourdon (who had volunteered to work without salary) had to tell him that a university couldn't be established on such a small amount. So, Thebaw let his idea drop.[66]

In conclusion, many of the Kinwun's proposed reforms never had enough time to grow and develop. Many of them remained still-born due to the lack of support by the King and Queen, and also because of the unnecessary withdrawal of the British Resident on October 6, 1879.

FOOTNOTES

[58] No. 84, Shaw to Lyall, October 13, 1878; in Foreign, Secret, March 1879, Nos. 60-111 (NAI). For some anecdotes of how the ministers checked even so powerful a King as Mindon, *see*: Ma Kyan, "King Mindon's Councillors," pp. 51-58.

[59] Daw Mya Sein, *Administration of Burma: Sir Charles Crosthwaite and the Consolidation of Burma,* Rangoon, 1938, pp. 17-18, 27-31. *Also :* Paul J. Bennett, *Conference......,* pp. 76-80, 84.

[60] Philippe Preschez, "Les Relations....," pp. 344-345. *(See also:* "Occasional Notes," (Allahabad) *Pioneer Mail,* November 2, 1878, pp. 2-3).

[61] *Ibid.*

[62] *Ibid. (See also:* No. 289, MCD, January 24, 1879; in Foreign, Secret, July 1879, Nos. 248-471 (NAI). Dr. Williams signed the contract with the Magwe Mingyi, which was that official's last major act before being sacked on January 20. Williams contracted to build the ninety miles from the iron and coal area of Poppadaung to Mandalay within four years. The railroad would carry iron and coal to the proposed new Sagaing iron-works for which Williams had already provided most of the machinery. Williams fully expected to extend the railroad to Toungoo, but died in Europe later in 1879 while raising funds.)

[63] *Ibid. See also :* No. 144, Foreign, Political-A, September 1880, Nos. 143-149. A list of ministers and ministries as of July 26, 1880.

[64] "Burma," (Calcutta) *Englishman,* October 29, 1878, p. 3.

[65] "Occasional Notes," (Allahabad) *Pioneer Mail,,* December 21, 1878, p. 2.

[66] Aung Than Tun, "The First Burmese Minister to Go West," (Rangoon) *The Guardian,* May 1961, pp. 21-23. *Also :* J. G. Scott and J. P. Hardiman, *Gazetteer....,* pp. 94-95. *Lastly:* Grattan Geary, *Burma After the Conquest,* pp. 326-329.

Appendix H

THE "SHOE QUESTION" AND THE 'MERU-CENTRIC' TRADITION

The "Shoe Question" was at the very heart of the 'Meru-centric' concept. Robert Heine-Geldern stated that the Mandalay Palace grounds were an enclosed square of more than a mile on each side, and aligned with the four points of the compass. The royal Palace in the centre, and more specifically the seven-tiered tower over the great audience hall, was the earthly manifestation of Mt. Meru. Mandalay, itself, was the earthly parallel of the heavenly stars spread out around the celestial mountain in the centre.[67]

As the King was the parallel on earth of Lord Indra only by virtue of his ownership of the Palace — the earthly parallel of Mt. Meru — the idea of seizing the Palace (and the country-universe) was a constant temptation for would-be usurpers. This explains why more than eighty members of the Royal Family were massacred on February 15-17, 1879.[68]

In the case of the "Shoe Question", the Burmese Kings thought that they had to hold to their prerogative. Yet, as was shown at King Mindon's funeral, there was 'give' in the Burmese position *outside* the Palace. In 1881, A. C. Lyall, Indian foreign secretary, suggested that the British Resident might retain his shoes, and meet the Burmese King *outside* the Palace. Such was being done with the Emperor of China. Unfortunately, no formal proposal was ever made to the Mandalay authorities.[69]

The Court ritual held *indoors* was described by Mrs. Ellen Rowett, the wife of a Rangoon merchant. "Now it really is not so bad to go a few yards in one's stockings....one can put on two or more pairs of stockings, and even slip a thick cork sole inside, anything provided no shoes are seen."[70]

Mrs. Rowett wore long, loose skirts. "All that is necessary is to keep one's feet out of sight" by sitting tailor-fashion. However, pants-wearing males "twist themselves into positions that soon become torture in order to keep their feet behind them."[71] For the Burmese court-official with his loose robes, almost like Mrs. Rowett's skirts, such protocol was no serious problem.

The formal *sheiko* position, which consisted of squatting forward on one's elbows and knees, was usually required of all in the Royal presence. However, Burmese and foreigners were usually allowed to relax after a few minutes, and assume the 'tailor' position described above by Mrs. Rowett.[72] For males wearing European attire with tight pants, the formal *sheiko* position of squatting forward on elbows and knees with one's bottom in the air was most *informal* and undignified.

FOOTNOTES

[67] Robert Heine-Geldern, "State and Kingship in Southeast Asia," (New York) *The Far Eastern Quarterly*, Vol. 11, No. 1, November 1942, pp. 19-24.

[68] *Ibid.*

[69] Lyall to Bernard, February 7, 1881 ; in Foreign, Secret, February 1881, Nos. 136-137, p. 3-4, 6 (NAI).

[70] Mrs. Ellen Rowett, "A Visit to the Queen of Burma," (London) *Frazier's Magazine*, Vol. XXV, January-June 1882, pp. 637-640.

[71] *Ibid.*

[72] *Ibid.*

APPENDIX I

MANDALAY ARMS SMUGGLING

The 'Fytche Annexe' attached to the 1867 Treaty was not recognized by the Indian Government. Therefore, the Mandalay Government smuggled arms illegally. For example in 1878, King Mindon smuggled 6,000 rifle-barrels through Rangoon Customs:

The King was seized with a most innocent desire to fence his royal garden with steel railing. . .imported from England. Every one of the 6,000 rails is a gun barrel complete, bored, and ready for the stock. Every one is fitted with lead for bullets, the two ends being screwed, and plugs so nicely fitted that it would have taken a very clever expert to have detected them.[73]

In July 1879, the Pangyet minister set off an enormous bomb in a pond within the Palace grounds. The Pangyet and the other technically-minded officials had planned to use telegraph and electric-light wire as leads to set off bombs. These would be placed in the Irrawaddy to blow up IFC steamers carrying invading Indian troops.

Col. Horace Browne wrote on August 26, 1879 that "The Burmans now....have a good stock of dynamite....they smuggle it up [on the IFC steamers] in soup and biscuit tins."[74] Very large supplies of percussion caps had also been recently received, and concealed in various ingenious ways. Fifty thousand caps were said to have come up in one steamer.[75] In July 1882, the Italian weapons-makers at Mandalay received 500 Martini rifles and revolvers. They had been hidden in an oil shipment carried on an IFC steamer.[76]

A later smuggling incident involved empty Martini cartridges. In June 1885, the Edmund Jones Co. of Rangoon received seven cases of 'macaroni' from the Florio Rubattino Co. of Venice, and filled the order of M. Civote, one of the Italian weapons-makers at Mandalay.[77]

Civote was not informed that his 'macaroni' had arrived at the Mandalay Customs Shed. Finally, a bored customs clerk opened the cases in order to have something to do. The Kinwun had a good laugh before finally allowing Civote to retrieve his 'macaroni'.

Charles Bernard, however, was not amused, and revoked the Jones
Co.'s license to import and sell arms.[78]

In September 1885, the Tangyet Wundauk, Burmese ambassador
to Paris, negotiated with the Mackenzie Brothers, London, to buy
six Whitworth cannons and 600 rounds. The cannons were to be
dis-assembled and shipped in several smaller crates in order to save
freight charges. Such shipments would also have a better chance
of passing undetected through the Rangoon Customs. However,
the Third Burmese War interrupted the negotiations.[79]

In conclusion, the Rangoon Customs checked most goods
consigned to Mandalay. Burmese diplomats returning from
abroad were also searched. In one such search in 1879, the Pangyet
minister who had just returned from Paris was found to be
carrying no weapons, but instead a number of *erotic* French match
boxes.[80]

FOOTNOTES

[73] "Notes of the Week," (Calcutta) *Statesman*, September 28, 1878, p. 850.
[74] No. 2, MCD, August 26, 1879 ; Foreign, Secret, November 1879, Nos. 1-14 (NAI).
[75] *Ibid.*
[76] K. W. No. 5, Two Memos dated August 2 and August 3, 1882, enclosed with Bernard to Grant, August 15, 1882 ; in Foreign, Secret-F, January 1883, Nos. 524-629, p. 3 (NAI).
[77] (5249) Italy-3, Corr. on the Smuggling of Arms to Burma, Foreign Office, March 1886 (PRO).
[78] *Ibid.*
[79] Foreign, Secret-E, June 1886, Nos. 52-57 (NAI). A large gun was once dis-assembled, packed in a large number of wooden crates, shipped as 'ordinary heavy freight', and passed through the Rangoon Customs as a 'pump'. *See* : "Notes of the Week," (Calcutta) *Statesman*, September 28, 1878, p. 850.
[80] K. W. No. 1, Aitchison to Lyall, August 20, 1879 ; in Foreign, Secret, March 1880, Nos. 100-113, p. 1 (NAI).

Appendix J

HAAS AND THE *QUAYMATHA* AFFAIR

In September 1885, Haas received a third rebuff in addition to the Burmese refusals of his offers of August 3 and September 5 to provide, respectively, French teak-firms in place of the BBTC, and to assist in arbitrating the BBTC Teak Case. The third rebuff involved his appeal on behalf of Bentabole, his secretary.

Bentabole had claimed that he was a Royal bugler at Rs. 300 per month, and that he had not been paid for several months. However, the Palace did not regard Bentabole as one of their servants, and "only give him a little present from time to time according to the *noise* he made."[81] Haas believed Bentabole's statements, and wrote to the Taingda and the other ministers requesting a settlement. Haas was informed in cold, formal terms that Mons. Bentabole was *not* a royal employee. Haas was terribly annoyed with Bentabole for having misled him.[82]

Haas tried to turn the embarrasing incident to his advantage. He told Andreino and others that the affair showed how little influence France had at Mandalay.[83] Haas knew that the British Government was extremely concerned over his actions at Mandalay. Haas' Government was also extremely concerned, and had put him under orders as of August 18 to show "the greatest reserve" in any actions at Mandalay that might in any way effect British subjects' commerce and other interests.

The suspicions of both Governments concerning his actions at Mandalay would be reduced if the Bentabole affair became known. Tensions between the two Governments would be lowered, and meanwhile, French interests would continue to work their way into Upper Burma.[84] Haas asked E. M. Pascal, a frequent guest at Haas' residence for the previous two months, to write a letter relating the Bentabole incident to the *Rangoon Gazette*.[85]

Pascal had been King Mindon's agent (Consul) at Calcutta in the 1870's. His main qualification for the position was his ability to steal printed copies of the Mandalay Resident's Diary and other Burma correspondence from the Calcutta Foreign Office.[86] King Mindon at Mandalay had often received his printed copy of the

Diary *before* the Resident received his. Col. Edward Sladen, political agent at Mandalay from 1865-1869, said that he could always tell by Mindon's amused expression if the King had received his copy of Sladen's Diary.[87] In short, Pascal seemed ideal for Haas' purposes. Unfortunately for Haas, Pascal was in the secret employ of Bernard.[88]

Pascal wrote his letter, and left on the steamer for Rangoon. His letter was published in the August 31 edition of the Rangoon *Gazette.* It stated that the Taingda had become so enraged upon receiving Haas' letter requesting a settlement of Bentabole's bugling-wages, that the minister had called Haas a *quaymatha*, son of a bitch.[89] The Taingda said later that he could not recall having said such a thing.

The French colony at Mandalay was humiliated. They had not dreamed that Pascal would so literally follow Haas' instructions to 'minimize' French influence at Mandalay. Andreino wrote that if the incident ever reached French newspapers, or reached the notice of the Quai d'Orsay, it would *not* raise their opinions of Haas' abilities.[90]

FOOTNOTES

[81] No. 137, Andreino to Jones, September 13, 1885 ; in Foreign, Secret-E, October 1885, Nos. 134-159 (NAI).

[82] *Ibid.*

[83] No. 147, Andreino to Jones, September 16, 1885 ; in Nos. 134-159.

[84-85] *Ibid.*

[86] Bernard to C. Grant, February 22, 1882 ; in Foreign, A-Political-E, November 1882, Nos. 1-50, p. 6 (NAI).

[87] Bernard to Durand, August 11, 1885 ; in Mss. Eur. D. 727/3 (Book No. 1), Confidential Demi-Official Letters to H. M. Durand, July 1885 to July 1886 (IOL).

[88] No. 199, Pascal's Report on Foreigners Living in Mandalay, September 18, 1885 ; in Foreign, Secret-E, October 1885, Nos. 198-200 (NAI).

[89] No. 147, Andreino to Jones, September 16, 1885 ; in Nos. 134-159.

[90] *Ibid.* *See also* : No. 56, Jones to Moylan, September 19, 1885 ; in Foreign, Secret-E, November 1885, Nos. 55-56 (NAI). One can understand why the Quai d'Orsay made Haas do six years of penance as a glorified clerk before despatching him to China as a Consul, and allowing him to publish (in 1892) his version of the French defeat in Upper Burma. Haas' defence was published under the name : Philippe Lehault, *La France et l' Angleterre en Asie*, Paris, 1892.

Appendix K

MOYLAN'S MALICIOUS REPORTING

By August 1886, the biased reporting of E. K. Moylan, *The Times*' Burma correspondent and also the BBTC's Burma lawyer, had become famous. On August 24, Dufferin wrote to Lord Kimberley, the secretary of state for India, that "I am convinced... if the Duke of Wellington had had a brute like Moylan at his heels, he would have been recalled from Spain over and over again by an indignant British public."[91]

The trouble with Moylan had begun when Gen. Prendergast took offense at one of Moylan's stories and had him deported to Rangoon in early-December 1885. Moylan had described the minor robberies that had occurred on the night of November 29 after Thebaw and Supayalat had been placed on board the *Thooreah*. Moylan's article had stated that the robberies had caused more loss of life than any battle during the Third Burmese War. This was a totally false statement, and gave the inaccurate implication that Prendergast had been amiss in his provisions for the maintenance of law and order in Mandalay.[92]

In his own defence, Gen. Prendergast stated that Moylan had broken his press contract, and had admitted lying to press officers in order to despatch his story. In Prendergast's view, Moylan had threatened persons with the loss of life, reputation and security by his false report. Moylan's reporting, in general, showed a bias against the official experiment at Mandalay of retaining the *Hlutdaw*, and at least some other features of the old Burmese administration.[93]

Neverthless, Churchill saw to it that Moylan was sent back to Mandalay in late-December 1885. After January 12, 1886, Moylan attacked everything that smacked of 'native' government, and by extension and innuendo, Col. Sladen and Gen. Prendergast. For example, on January 14, Moylan claimed that the *Hlutdaw, i.e.* continued 'native' rule, was gross and corrupt. "It is essential for the peace of the country that the Hlootdaw should be dissolved."[94] Moylan had already stated this theme in a milder form in his January 12 despatch, and he repeated it over and over again in his

January 14, 15, 23, 28, 29; and February 15, 16, and 22 despatches.[95]

On January 21, Moylan commented upon the 'brutal' executions of 'dacoits' that had allegedly taken place at the Palace. Moylan never claimed to have actually witnessed these 'brutal' executions, but instead received his information second-hand.[96] It appears that Moylan exaggerated his accounts in order to strike back at Prendergast and the military for deporting him.

On the following day, Moylan claimed that a 'sadistic' Colonel Hooper, the Provost Marshal, had held up the firing squad between the commands "ready" and "fire". "The Provost-Marshal fixes his camera on the prisoners, who at times are kept waiting for some minutes in that position."[97] The firing-squad officer, according to Moylan, had given the order to "fire" only after Hooper was ready to expose his photographic-plate.

Hooper and his assistant, Lt. Burrows, were also alleged to have threatened 'Wooguet', a Burman, with the firing squad, unless he gave testimony that would link certain *Hlutdaw* ministers with the 'dacoits'. 'Wooguet' testified, but Col. Sladen and Charles Bernard had refused to accept the testimony, because it had been extracted under the threat of death.[98]

Moylan's January 21 and 22 reports shocked Churchill. He telegraphed to Dufferin on January 23 that if Moylan's charges were "in any degree true, gravest and most immediate action must be taken....Question now pending in Parliament. These reports are creating a very unfavourable impression. To save time I have reported this to Bernard direct."[99]

On January 23, Dufferin wired Bernard that the "Effect upon public opinion in England, in Europe, and in India, if such transactions should have taken place, cannot fail to be most disastrous."[100] Dufferin sent an almost identical telegram to Prendergast.[101] On January 26, Dufferin wired Churchill that he, Dufferin, had ordered a halt to all military executions.[102]

On February 3, in London, the India Office issued a statement to *The Times* and other newspapers. This was in response to the continuing uproar over the 'dacoit' executions, which Moylan had encouraged anew by his January 27 and 29 despatches.[103] The India Office statement repeated a February 2 telegram from Dufferin. It stated that the 'dacoits' executed by military authorities at Mandalay had been tried previously and found guilty by a civil court.[104]

As concerned Col. Hooper, the India Office stated that he had taken photographs of the condemned men upon two occasions. But he did not "arrange details of execution so as to suit his camera, as alleged. Condemned men were blindfolded, and were consequently unaware of what was going on, and no delay took place."[105]   However, Lt. Burrows admitted that he had threatened 'Wooguet' and other prisoners with death, unless they gave evidence linking certain *Hlutdaw* members with the 'dacoits'.[106]

Other than this, Moylan's accounts of the executions were false. Moylan conceded that he had not personally witnessed the photographings or shootings. In his January 27 despatch he had cited Melton Prior of the *Illustrated London News* and Mr. Rose of the Rangoon *Gazette* as eyewitnesses. These correspondents later denied Moylan's allegations.[107]   During Col. Hooper's court martial, he was ably defended by Sir Charles Bernard among others. Hooper was reassigned to another post away from Burma.

In summary, Moylan's reports were apparently motivated by a bias against 'native' rule, and an equally virulent bias against the military officials. Moylan's dual employment as (1) *The Times*' Burma correspondent, and (2) the BBTC's Burma lawyer aroused *further* doubts as to his 'objectivity'.

For example, Bernard arrived in Mandalay on December 15, 1885 after Moylan had been deported. Bernard discovered that the Burmese originals of the BBTC's Upper Burma teak-leases had —mysteriously—disappeared from the Palace archives.[108]   It is certain that Moylan in his role as the BBTC's lawyer would not have been allowed to roam freely. However, it is equally certain that Moylan in his role as *The Times*' correspondent could come and go in the Palace as he chose.

Shortly afterwards, Moylan began the legal battle to save the BBTC's Upper Burma leases. This was not an impossible task since the firm now possessed the *only* version of its leases in existence. The firm was eventually able to retain its Upper Burma leases at a rate of payment very close to the old 1885 figures[109]— thanks in large part to Moylan's varied abilities as (1) *Times* correspondent, (2) BBTC lawyer, and (3) *thief.*[110]

FOOTNOTES

[91] No. 36, Dufferin to Kimberley, August 24, 1886; in Dufferin Papers, Reel 517/18, p. 140. *Also :* A. T. Q. Stewart, *The Pagoda War*, London, 1972, pp. 118-176.

[92] "The Burmese War," (London) *The Times*, December, 5, 1885, p. 5. Moylan also stated that a mob of Burmese had beseiged Andreino, the BBTC's Mandalay agent, in his house. This was true, and the reader is aware of why the attack occurred. Moylan, naturally, would not state the reason for the attack, because it involved his other employer, the BBTC. For an accurate report of the robberies *see:* Grattan Geary, *Burma After the Conquest*, pp. 31-37.

[93] Col. Henry M. Vibart, *The Life of General Sir Harry N. D. Prendergast* (*The Happy Warrior*), London, 1914, pp. 278-280.

[94] "Burmah," (London) *The Times*, January 14, 1886, p. 5.

[95] *See* the following Moylan despatches in *The Times*: "Burmah," January 12, 1886, p. 5; "Burmah" January 14, 1886, p. 5; "Burmah," January 15, 1886, p. 5; "Burmah," January 23, 1886, p. 5; "Burmah," January 28, 1886, p. 5; "Burmah," January 29, 1886, p. 5; "Burmah," February 15, 1886, p. 5; "Burmah," February 16, 1886, p. 5; and, finally, "Burmah," February 22, 1886, p. 5. Moylan's February 22, 1886 despatch was sent before the Annexation was announced on February 17 and 18.

[96] "Burmah," (London) *The Times*, January 21, 1886, p. 5.

[97] "Burmah," (London) *The Times*, January 22, 1886, p. 5.

[98] *Ibid.* Moylan got the man's name wrong. According to Geary, the man's name was Nga Neing. *See :* Grattan Geary, *Burma After The Conquest*, pp. 238-241. Geary was not a witness to the scene, and repeats some inaccuracies gained second-hand. However, Geary was a conscientious reporter, who could sift a fair amount of the truth from even the poorest material.

[99] No. 10, Telegram from Churchill to Dufferin, January 22, 1886; in C. 4690, p. 7.

[100] No. 11, Telegram from Dufferin to Bernard, January 23, 1886; in C. 4690, p. 7.

[101] No. 12, Telegram from Dufferin to Prendergast, January 23, 1886; in C. 4690, p. 7.

[102] No. 16, Telegram from Dufferin to Churchill, January 26, 1886; in C. 4690, p. 9.

[103] "Burmah," (London) *The Times*, January 27, 1886, p. 5; and, "Burmah," (London) *The Times*, January 29, 1886, p. 5.

[104] "Burmah," (London) *The Times*, February 3, 1886, p. 5.

[105] No. 19, Telegram from Dufferin to Churchill, February 2, 1886; in C. 4690, p. 9.

[106] *Ibid.*

[107] No. 29, Telegram from Dufferin to Kimberley, March 1, 1886; in C. 4690, pp. 11-12. *See also:* Grattan Geary, *Burma After the Conquest*, pp. 238-243.

[108] Bernard to Durand, Memorandum on the BBTC's Leases, February 3, 1886; in No. 2, Forest Proceedings of February 1886, p. 2. Bound in Burma Proceedings, Vol. 2663, Burma Forests (Home Dept.) 1886 (IOL).

[109] John Nisbet, *Burma Under...*, Vol. 1, pp. 79-81.

[110] One should examine Moylan's background. For example, he had been dismissed from the post of Attorney-General of Grenada, then ousted as a barrister in that colony for "grave misconduct." *See :* No. 40, Kimberley's Secretary to Dufferin's Secretary, March 12, 1886; in Dufferin Papers, Reel 525/36, p. 47.

See also: No. 48, Dufferin to Sec. of State-India, October 18, 1886; in Dufferin Papers, Reel 517/18, pp. 209-210. (1) Moylan had been dismissed for corruption from his Attorney General's post, and then from the bar in Grenada. (2) Moylan was treated most kindly by Gen. Prendergast until Moylan cheated on his own signed contract, and broke security. When Prendergast deported him, Moylan's articles made him "famous and a martyr." (3) Moylan invented most of the Hooper story. (4) Moylan had threatened Bernard that either Bernard *would* approve certain cases for compensations, which Moylan represented, or else Moylan would smear Bernard in his *Times* articles. One such case was, apparently, the eleven lakhs requested on behalf of the BBTC in: No. 692, Moylan to Bernard's Secretary, March 9, 1886; in Foreign, Secret-E, August 1886, Nos. 650-703 (NAI).

"Bernard, of course, treated his threats with contempt, and he further provoked Mr. Moylan's wrath by stating at the [Hooper trial] that he believed Moylan's exaggerations in the Hooper case to have been prompted by personal animosity towards the military. ....from that time forth Moylan has turned upon Bernard, and has never ceased decrying him." When Moylan "fabricates some more monstrous and damaging falsehood than usual, in order to save his own responsibility, he introduces it by 'It is said,' 'It is believed.' "

A TYPICAL YEARLY BUDGET OF THE BURMESE GOVERNMENT, CIRCA 1883-1884.

The following is a translation of an official document which, according to the Wetmasut Wundauk, was a summary of the yearly revenue received by King Thebaw and of the way in which it was spent. It is interesting to note that the government expenses totalled only Rs. 54,74,556, which left Rs. 41,23,626-4-0 in Thebaw's hands as his private fund.

RECEIPTS

	Rs.
Revenue collected from 76 different sources, *e.g.*, sale of licenses for bazaars, customs stations, import stations, ferries; paid in monthly, or every three, four or six months, or yearly.	46,79,802
Thathameda—Collected elsewhere than in the capital and its neighbourhood, the Shan States and Myelat, at an average rate of Rs. 10 per house.	36,53,325

NOTE 1.—The total number of houses was 4,74,230, but 68,305 of these were exempted on account of the old age, infirmity or destitution of the house-holders.

NOTE 2.—*Thathameda* collected from the slaves attached to pagodas and monasteries, amounting to Rs. 29,764 was not paid into the Treasury, but was used by the Council of State to defray the wages of the watchmen of pagodas and monasteries and of the warders in the *Letmahtauk* prison.

Thathameda collected in the Shan States by Shan Chiefs and Feoflees under their own arrangement.	6,00,000
Revenue collected in paddy from King's *kaukkyi*, and *mayin* land in Kyauksé *Kokhayaing* and other places, 8,31,319 baskets converted at Rs. 80 a hundred baskets.	6,65,055-4
Total receipts	95,98,182-4

EXPENDITURE

Salaries

Members of the Royal family, princes of various ranks, commanders, including those who had a place in the order of precedence and those who had not; persons supported from the Privy Purse, 45 in number.	Rs. 29,340
Officials of the Council of State, 99 in number.	1,50,000
Officials of the Privy Council, 60 in number.	1,00,680
Officials of the Police Court, 103 in number.	33,180
Officials of the Women's Court, 24 in number.	16,440
Officials of the Civil Court, 39 in number.	15,840
Governors, Superintendents, Military Officers, Court Officials, Learned Men, 89 in number.	2,02,464
Officials of the Treasury, Tailor's Shop, Repository of Royal Paraphernalia, Record Keepers, Secretaries, 85 in number.	44,100
Lesser Court Officials, Waiters, Butlers, Betel, Umbrella and Sword Attendants, Permanent Attendants, *Yenyun* and *Natshin Yannaung* Guards, Doctors, Masseurs, Snakebite Doctors, Old Family Servants, 1,113 in number.	3,08,160
Former Officials of the Forty Rupee Corps, Servants in charge of the Betel Nut Paraphernalia, Negro Servants, 196 in number.	37,680
3 Shan Chiefs, 38 District Commissioners, 16 Assistant Commissioners, 12 King's Messengers, 67 Town Clerks, 6 Chief Constables, 142 in all.	1,96,764

North Dawé		
South Dawé		
North Tayangasé	Members of the 6 inner	5,65,872
South Tayangasé	units of musketeers,	
North Marabin	4,041 in number.	
Shwepyihmankin		
Natsu Left Wing		
Natsu Right Wing		
Ywe Left Wing	Members of the 6 outer	4,65,876
Ywe Right Wing	units of musketeers,	
Gyaung Left Wing	3,327 in number.	
Gyaung Right Wing		

Marabin		
Shwehlan		
Natshin Ywe		
Naukwingyin	Members of 9 miscellaneous	6,35,472
Linsin Kinda	units of musketeers,	
Thuyè	4,538 in number.	
Tagani		
Bôndawpyit		
Bôndawto		

Members of artillery units, 795 in number.   1,10,220

Kathè		
Ekkabat		
Yebet		
Shwepyiyanaung		
Myinsugyi		
Myanma		
Shan	Members of 14 units of	8,62,440
Zimmè pa	cavalry, 5,118 in number.	
Thwethaukasu		
Nauk daw pa		
Lamaing		
Nanu mingala		
Mingala Yényun		
Sidaw		

East Win		
Left Win		
Right Win		
West Win	Members of 7 units of	2,51,380
So lesédaing	guards, 1,582 in number.	
Kaunghan		
Yun		

Boats
Barges
Ships   Members of 6 units of   6,67,602
Sampans   water-men, 6,238 in
Punts   number.
Boatmakers

[Total number of musketeers, artillery, cavalry, guards, watermen, and *not* including elephantery: 25,639 soldiers at a total cost of Rs. 35,58,862.]

Foreign servants, 26 in number.   1,00,920
Old family elephant riders, drummers, time keepers,   92,100
    printers, elephant grass cutters, carpenters (emp-
    loyed without the Palace), carpenters (employed
    about the royal possessions), persons born on the
    same day as the King, shield bearers, painters in
    colours, painters in gold, elephant guards, car-
    penters in the Treasury, members of miscellaneous
    units, 63 in number.
Cooks for the King and the monks whom he fed,   34,980
    suppliers of clear water, puppet showmen, Bur-
    mese tailors, Shan tailors, Indian tailors, mem-
    bers of miscellaneous units, 229 in number.
Runners, Brahmins in charge of the shrines of the   56,364
    15 great spirits, Indian masons, goldsmiths, men
    attached to the Minister of the Treasury, jewel-
    lers employed in the Palace, makers of library
    books, rulers of lines in books, *Mayaman* ivory
    workers, wood carvers, watchmen of durian
    gardens, members of miscellaneous units, 369 in
    number.
Milkmen, forerunners, attendants, makers of royal   2,02,692
    apparel, *Kaunghan* guards, men employed in the
    Arsenal, men who spread curtains to shade the
    King when he halted on a royal progress, feeders
    of the white elephant, Burmese actors, Siamese
    actors, players in the Palace band, acrobats, men
    actually serving as elephant riders, members of
    miscellaneous units, 1,327 in number.

Brahmins in charge of the clock, braziers, niello   2,59,008
workers, barbers, gong makers from Shweda,
Kanthaya and Halin, watchmen of the Great
Council from Hkinu, Tedaw, Sidoktaya and
Myothit, lamp lighters, carriers of presents,
guards of stations and stairways, bird scarers,
sweepers, messengers of the Women's Court, warders of the Western Prison, workers in gold
thread, button makers, palanquin bearers, watchmen over the white umbrellas, keepers of presents,
watchmen in the Treasury, Tailor's Shop, Record
Office, Repository of the Royal Paraphernalia,
and Charcoal Store, ushers for boors and rustics,
makers of wooden platters, makers of gunpow-
der, planters of worm wood trees, gong makers,
wood polishers, officers and sergeants of elephantery, elephant doctors and attendants, officers of
the moat and of the gardens, watchmen of the
moat and of canoes thereon, grooms and stable-
men, gold lace makers, midwives, coachmen,
masons in the Treasury, Indian painters, watchmen in the Betelnut Court, comb makers, makers
of white folding books, men employed in the gun
factory, shipyard, engineering shops, weaving
factory, dye factory, water works, sugar refinery,
betelnut crushing mill, rice mill and furnace, iron
smelters from Sagaing, blacksmiths, metal refi-
ners, members of 72 miscellaneous units, 1,514
in number. Instead of which [salaries] they got
paddy at the rate of 100 baskets for Rs. 80
amounting to 323,760 baskets of paddy.

Fifty two warders in the *Letmàhtauk* prison, 100   34,980
watchmen of pagodas, 120 watchmen of monas-
teries, members of three units, 272 in number.

Total Salaries   54,74,556

The balance Rs. 41,23,626-4-0 was spent by the King on grants and presents to the queens, princes, princesses and ladies of the Court, and in other ways for his private purposes as well as on the erection of pagodas, monasteries, libraries and the support of *pongyis* and other religious mendicants.[111]

FOOTNOTE

[111] H. F. Searle, *Mandalay District Gazetteer, Vol. A,* Rangoon, 1928, pp. 254-257.

SELECTED BIBLIOGRAPHY

A. PRIMARY SOURCES

1. Private Papers.
   Cranbrook Papers (IpRO).
   Dufferin Papers (NAI).
       516/26, Letters from Queen, 1884-1886.
       516/28, Letters to Queen, 1883-1886.
       517/18, Letters from Sec. of State, 1884-1886.
       517/18, Letters to Sec. of State, 1884-1886.
       519/22, Telegrams from Sec. of State, 1884-1885.
       519/22, Telegrams to Sec. of State, 1884-1885.
       519/25, Telegrams from Sec. of State, 1885-1886.
       519/25, Telegrams to Sec. of State, 1885-1886.
       521/27, Viceroy's Notes and Minutes, 1885-1886.
       525/36, Letters from England, 1884-1885.
       525/36, Letters to England, 1884-1885.
       525/37, Letters from England, 1886.
       525/37, Letters to England, 1886.
       528/47, Letters from Persons in India, 1884-1885.
       528/47, Letters to Persons in India, 1884-1885.
       528/48, Letters from Persons in India, 1885.
       529/49, Letters from Persons in India, 1885.
       529/49, Letters to Persons in India, 1885.
       529/49, Letters from Persons in India, 1886.
       529/49, Letters to Persons in India, 1886.
   Sir H. M. Durand Papers (IOL).
       Demi-Official Letters to Durand, July 1885-July 1886.
   Sir Alfred Comyn Lyall Papers (IOL).
   Lytton Papers (IOL).
       516/3, Letters from Sec. of State, 1878.
       516/4, Letters from Sec. of State, 1879.
       516/5, Letters from Sec. of State, 1880.
       516/6, Lord Dufferin's Letter to Lytton, October 15, 1885.
       517/6, Letters from England, July-December 1878.
       517/7, Letters from England, January-June 1879.
       517/8, Letters from England, July-December 1879.
       517/9, Letters from England, January-June, 1880.
       518/1, Letters Despatched from India, 1876.
       518/3, Letters Despatched from India, 1878.
       518/4, Letters Despatched from India, 1879.
       518/6, Letters Despatched from India, 1880.
       519/9, Corr. in India, September-December 1878.

519/10, Corr. in India, January-April 1879.

519/11, Corr. in India, May-August 1879.

519/12, Corr. in India, September-December 1879.

519/13, Corr. in India, 1880.

520/2, Minutes and Notes, 1878.

520/3, Minutes and Notes, 1879-1880.

522/1, Minutes and Notes, 1879.

522/2, Minutes and Notes, 1880.

Northbrook Papers (IOL).

Corr. Between Northbrook and Ripon, 1880-1884.

Corr. Between Northbrook and Dufferin, 1884-1888.

Corr. Between Northbrook and Persons in India, 1878-1880.

Ripon Papers, Second Series (BM).

Corr. With the Queen, 1880-1884.

Corr. With Kimberley, Sec. of State, 1880-1884.

Corr. With Hartington, Sec. of State, 1880-1884.

Corr. With Earl of Northbrook, 1880-1884.

Official Corr. of Ripon as Viceroy of India, 1880-1884.

Letters from Bernard and Crosthwaite, Chief Commissioners of British Burma, 1880-1884.

Corr. With Sir Alfred Lyall, Sec. of Indian Foreign Dept., 1880-1884.

Corr. With Charles Grant, Sec. of Indian Foreign Dept., 1880-1884.

Ripon Papers, India Misc. Pub. Documents (BM).

I. S. 290/4, Corr. With the Queen, 1880-1884.

I. S. 290/5, Corr. With Sec. of State, 1880-1884.

I. S. 290/6, Telegraphic Corr. With Sec. of State, 1880-1884.

I. S. 290/7, Corr. With Persons in England, 1880-1884.

I. S. 290/8, Corr. With Persons in India, 1880-1884.

Ripon Papers (IOL).

Hartington Telegraphic Corr. With Ripon, April 1880-December 1882.

Sir Edward Sladen Papers (IOL).

Sir George White Collection (IOL).

Lt. J. R. Dyas, Diary and Recollections, 1885-1886.

Gen. White's Private Diary for 1885-January 1886.

Sir Herbert Thirkell White Collection (IOL).

2. Official Records.

Admiralty 127/17, The Burma War 1885-1887 (PRO).

BAR/4 and 5., MS 56/002, Journal of the Naval Brigade in the Burma War (NMM).

Burma Proceedings (IOL).

Vol. 2433, Military and Marine, December 1884-1885.

Vol. 2434, Forests (Home Dept.), December 1884-1885.

Vol. 2435, Foreign and Political, December 1884-1885.

Vol. 2436, Finance and Commerce, December 1884-1885.

Vol. 2662, Military and Foreign, 1886.

Vol. 2663, Finance, Commerce and Forests (Home Dept.), 1886.

Vol. 2664A, Military, Forests, Foreign, Finance, and Commerce Proceedings for Upper Burma, 1886.

Field Operations in Upper Burma, 1885-1886 (Despatches of General H. Prendergast), Simla, May 14, 1886 (BM).

Foreign Office (PRO).

   Conf. Corr. (5162) Respecting the Relations Between France and Burmah, 1878-1885, Foreign Office, December 1885.

   (5249) Italy-3, Corr. on the Smuggling of Arms to Burma, Foreign Office, March 1886.

India Foreign (Political) Proceedings, 1878-1886 (NAI and IOL).

India Foreign (Secret) Proceedings, 1878-1886 (NAI and IOL).

L/P & S/7, Political and Secret Letters and Enclosures (IOL).

   Received from India, Vols. 19 (August-October 1878) to 47 (May-August 1886).

   Despatched to India, Vols. 4 (1878) to 12 (1886).

L/P & S/8, Political and Secret Demi-Official Corr. (IOL).

   Received from India, Vol. 1 (1872-1886).

   Despatched to India, Vol. 2 (August 1873 to December 1886).

L/P & S/18, Political and Secret Memoranda, Vol. 1, 1887 (IOL).

   B 18.   Policy in Upper Burma, Letter from Major A. R. McMahon, 1878.

   B 20.   Burma: The Question of Karennee, A. W. Moore, 1879.

   B 21.   Corr. Relating to the Affairs of Burma: Part I, 1878-1880, A. W. Moore; and Part II, 1880-1885, E. Neel.

   B 26.   Burma: Attitude of King Thebaw, 1884.

   B 31.   Burma, Siam and Indo-China. Report of the "Project de Loi" approving the Supplementary Commercial Convention signed at Paris, January 15, 1885 between France and Burma. M. de Lanessan with a Note by Col. H. Yule, 1885.

   B 32.   Burma: Note by Mr. H. Soltan, Missionary, Bhamo, 1885.

   B 33.   Burma: Opinion of Law Officers as to Annexation and Correspondence Thereof, 1885.

   B 34.   Chinese Claims to Sovereignty over Burma, E. Neel, 1886. Part I, October 1885 to January 1886. Part II, January to March 1886. Part III, April to July 1886.

   B 35.   Relations Between China and Burma. Col. H. Yule, 1885.

   B 36.   Relations Between the Government of India and Upper Burma During the Present King's Reign. Sir O. T. Burne, 1885.

   B 37.   The Shan States. Col. H. Yule and Sir A. Eden, 1886.

   B 38.   Burmah and China. Concessions. Col. H. Yule, 1886.

   B 39.   Burmah. Sir O. T. Burne, 1886.

   B 103. Shan States Tributary to Burma. R. H. Pilcher, 1885.

L/P & S/20, "The Burma Memorandas" (IOL).

   Burmah Memoranda, 1871-1880, India Office, London, 1880.

   D. 180, Burma Embassy File, 1882-1883, India Office, London, 1883.

   Burma Memoranda, 1878-1885, India Office, London, December 1, 1885.

   China-Burma Negotiations, 1885-1886, India Office, London, 1886.

116/73 (Case 219), Operations in Burmah and Proceedings of Naval Brigade (1885-1886), Parts 1-3 (PRO).

Plant, Colonel, Narrative of the Insurrection in the Tennaserim Division During 1885-1886, Rangoon, July 1886 (BM).

Stanton, Lt. H. E., *ed.*, The Third Burmese War, Simla, May 16, 1888 (NAI).

"Trouble at Mandalay" Collection (IOL).

   British Burma: Trouble at Mandalay No. 1, November 1878-June 1879.

   Burma: Trouble in Mandalay No. 2, June 1879-November 1879.

3. Parliamentary Papers.

   H. of C. No. 251, June 8, 1869; in Accounts and Papers, East India, 10 December, 1868-11 August, 1869, Vol. XLVI (BM).

   C. 3501, Burmah (1883), Papers Relating to Recent Negotiations Between the Governments of India and Burmah (NAI).

   C. 4614 (1886), Corr. Relating to Burmah Since the Accession of King Thebaw, October 1878 (NAI).

   C. 4690, Burmah No. 2 (1886), Telegraphic Corr. Relating to Military Executions and Dacoity in Burmah (NAI).

   C. 4887, Burmah No. 3 (1886), Further Corr. Relating to Burmah (NAI).

   C. 4861, China No. 5 (1886), July 24, 1886 Pekin Treaty (NAI).

4. Debates.

   Hansard's Parliamentary Debates, 3rd Series, 1878-1886 (NAI). 1879, Vols. 244, 245; 1880, Vol. 253; 1881, Vol. 258; 1882, Vol. 273; 1883, Vols. 278. 282; 1884-1885, Vols. 295, 298; and 1886, Vol. 302.

5. Gazetteers, and Other Government Publications.

   Aitchison, Sir C. U., A Collection of Treaties, Engagements, and Sanads, Vol. II, Calcutta, 1909 (NAI).

   Annual Report of the Archeological Survey of India, 1902-1903, Calcutta, 1903 (IOL).

   Brandis, Dietrich, Indirect Influence of Forests, Calcutta, 1882 (IOL).

   British Burma Annual Administration Reports, Rangoon, 1878-1886 (IOL, NAI).

   British Burma Annual Inland Trade Reports, Rangoon, 1878-1886 (IOL, NAI).

   The Burma Forest Act 1881 (As amended by Act V of 1890 and Act XII of 1891), Rangoon, 1896 (IOL).

   Duroiselle, Charles, Guide to the Mandalay Palace, Rangoon, 1925 (IOL).

   Forchhammer, Dr. E., Burmese Law: The Jardine Prize Winner, Rangoon, 1885 (IOL).

   Frontier and Overseas Expeditions from India, Vol. V-Burma, Simla, 1907 (NAI).

   Gordon, Robert, Works in the Irrawaddy Circle, Rangoon, 1883 (IOL).

   The Historical Record of No. 4 (Hazara) Mountain Battery, Lahore, 1888 (BM).

   Lower Chindwin District Gazetteer, Vol. A, Rangoon, 1912 (IOL).

   Macneill, Major Douglas, Report and Gazetteer of Burma, Native and British (In Three Parts), Simla, 1883 (IOL).

   ————, Maps and Plans to Accompany Report and Gazetteer of Burma, Native and British (In Three Parts), Simla, 1883 (IOL).

Moral and Material Progress and Condition of India Reports, Calcutta, 1878-1886 (NAI).

Nisbet, John, "The Climatic and National-Economic Influences on Forests," in Essays on Sylvicultural Subjects, London, 1893 (IOL).

Progress Reports on Forest Administration in Lower Burma, Rangoon, 1878-1891 (BM).

Progress Reports on Forest Administration in Upper Burma, Rangoon, 1890-1891 (BM).

I. S. 270/3, Reprint of Geological Papers on Burma, Calcutta, 1882 (BM).

Ribbentrop, Berthold, Forestry in British India, Calcutta, 1900 (BM).

Scott, J. G., and J. P. Hardiman, Gazetteer of Upper Burma and the Shan States, Rangoon, 1900 (NAI).

Searle, H. F., Mandalay District Gazetteer, Vol. A, Rangoon, 1928 (IOL).

Spearman, H. R., British Burma Gazetteer, Rangoon, 1879-1880 (IOL).

Taw Sein Ko, The Mandalay Palace, Calcutta, 1904 (IOL).

————, Burmese Sketches, Rangoon, 1913 (ULTC).

————, Archaeological Notes on Mandalay (With Two Plans) Rangoon, 1917 (IOL).

————, Archaeological Notes on Mandalay, Rangoon, 1924 (IOL).

6. Contemporary Books.

Chailley-Bert, J., La Colonisation de L' Indo-Chine, L' experience Anglaise, Paris, 1893.

Colquhoun, Archibald R., Across Chryse, 2 Vols., London, 1883.

————, Burma and the Burmans, or the Best Unopened Market in the World, London, 1885.

————, and Holt S. Hallett, Report on the Railway Connexion of Burmah and China, London, 1885 and later eds.

Cordier, Henri, Historique Abrege des Relations de la Grande-Bretagne Avec La Birmanie, Paris, 1894.

Crosthwaite, Sir Charles, The Pacification of Burma, London, 1912.

Fielding-Hall, H., Thibaw's Queen, London, 1899.

————, The Soul of a People, London, 1899, 1902.

————, A People at School, London, 1906.

Forbes, Capt. C. J. F. S., British Burma and Its People, London, 1878.

Fytche, Lt. Gen. Albert, Burma Past and Present, London, 1878.

Geary, Grattan, Burma After the Conquest, London, 1886.

Graham, Col. R. B., Photographic Illustrations, With Descriptions of Mandalay and Upper Burma Expeditionary Force, 1886-1887, Birmingham, 1887.

Gray, David M., Mandalay Massacres: Upper Burma During the Reign of King Theebaw, Rangoon, 1884.

Laurie, Col. W. F. B., Our Burmese Wars and Relations With Burma, London, 1880.

————, Ashe Pyee: The Superior Country, London, 1882.

————, Burma, the Foremost Country, London, 1884.

'Lehault, Philippe', (*psued.* of Frederic Haas), La France et l' Angleterre en Asie; Tome 1, Indochine: Les derniers jours de la dynastie des rois d' Ava, Paris, 1892.

MacMahon, Maj.-Gen. A. R., Far Cathay and Farther India, London, 1893.

Marshall, W. H., Four Years in Burma, 2 Vols., London, 1860.

Mason, Rev. F., Burma, Its People and Productions, 2 Vols,, Hertford, 1883.

Nisbet, John, Burma Under British Rule—And Before, 2 Vols., Westminister, 1901.

Phayre, Sir Arthur, History of Burma From the Earliest Time to the End of the First War With British India, London, 1883.

Sangermano, Father, The Burmese Empire (A Hundred Years Ago), With Introduction by John Jardine, Westminister, 1893.

Scott, J. G., France and Tongkin, London, 1885.

————, Burma, As It Was, As It Is, and As It Will Be, London, 1886.

'Shway Yoe' (*psued.* of J. G. Scott), The Burman, His Life and Notions, London, 1896.

Vibart, Col. Henry M., The Life of General Sir Harry N. D. Prendergast (The Happy Warrior), London, 1914.

Yule, Captain Henry, A Narrative of the Mission to the Court of Ava in 1855, London, 1858.

7. Contemporary Newspapers.
    Individual Papers.
Allahabad Pioneer Mail.
Bombay Gazette.
Bombay Times of India.
Calcutta Bengalee.
Calcutta Englishman.
Calcutta Hindoo Patriot.
Calcutta Indian Daily News.
Calcutta Statesman (with several title variations).
London Standard.
London The Times.
Rangoon Gazette.
Rangoon Times.
    Official Extracts of Indian Newspaper Opinion (NAI).
Report on Native Newspapers (Bengal), 1878-1886.
Report on Native Newspapers (Bombay), 1878-1886.
Report on Native Newspapers (Madras), 1878-1886.
Report on Native Newspapers (N. W. P. and Punjab), 1878-1886.
    Periodical of Newspaper Opinion.
The (Bombay) Voice of India, monthly digest of Indian newspaper opinion. Vol. 3, No. 11, November 1885 thru Vol. 4, No. 3, March 1886. November 1885, pp. 553-562; December 1885, pp. 622-634; January 1886, pp. 3-17; February 1886, pp. 89-96; and March 1886, pp. 116-121, 124-125.

8. Contemporary Periodical Articles.
Ardaugh, Maj.-Gen. R. D., "Recent Annexation of Upper Burma," (London) Journal of the East India Association, Vol. XVIII, 1886,

pp. 89-128.

Balfour, Surgeon-General David, "Influence Exercised by Trees on the Climate and Productiveness of the Peninsula of India," (Calcutta) The Indian Forester, Vol. IV., No. 2, October 1878, pp. 113-150.

Bernard, Sir Charles, "Burma: The New British Province." (Edinburgh) The Scottish Geographical Magazine, Vol. IV, No. 2, February 1888, p. 79.

Bryce, J. A., "Burma: Latest Addition to the Empire," (London) Proceedings of the Royal Colonial Institute, Vol. 17, 1885-1886, pp. 180-209.

————, "Burma: The Country and People," (London) Proceedings of the Royal Geographical Society, Vol. VIII, No. 8, August 1886, pp. 481-501.

"Burmah," (London) The Saturday Review, October 3, 1885, p. 435.

"Burmah," (London) The Saturday Review, December 19, 1885, pp. 794-795.

"Burma, Past and Present," (London) The Quarterly Review, Vol. 162, January and April 1886, pp. 210-238.

Colquhoun, Archibald R., "An Anglo-Chinese Commercial Alliance," (London) The National Review, Vol. VI, September 1885 to February 1886, pp. 162-173.

————, "The Crisis in Burma," Parts I and II, (London) The Graphic Weekly Illustrated Newspaper, October 31, 1885 and November 14, 1885, pp. 489-492, and pp. 545-548.

Douglas, R. K., "Burmah and China," Asiatic Quarterly Review, January-April 1886, Vol. I, pp. 141-164.

Farrer, J. A., "The Burmese War," (London) The Gentleman's Magazine, Vol. CCLX, January-June 1886. pp. 62-74.

————, "Why Keep Burma?," (London) The Gentleman's Magazine, Vol. CCLXII, January-June 1887, pp. 117-126.

Fielding-Hall, H., "The Last Days of An Empire," (Edinburgh) Blackwood's Edinburgh Magazine, Vol. 153, May 1893, pp. 658-669.

————, "My Maid of Honour," (Edinburgh) Blackwood's Edinburgh Magazine, Vol. 158, August 1895, pp. 261-271.

————, "How the Famine Came to Burma," (Edinburgh) Blackwood's Edinburgh Magazine, Vol. CLXI, April 1897, pp. 536-537.

"Forest Progress Report for British Burmah, 1881-1882," (Roorkee) The Indian Forester, Vol. 9, No. 4, April 1883, pp. 213-217.

Gordon, Robert, "The Irawadi River," (London) Proceedings of the Royal Geographical Society, May 1885, pp. 4, 12.

————, "On the Ruby Mines Near Mogok, Burma," (London) Proceedings of the Royal Geographical Society, Vol. X, No. 5, May 1888, pp. 261-275.

'Grandis, Tectona', "The Teak Monopoly in Burma," (Roorkee) The Indian Forester, Vol. XII, No. 2, February 1886, pp. 81-83.

Grant, Sir Charles, "The Burmese Question," (London) The Contemporary Review, Vol. XLIX, January-June 1886, pp. 32-43.

Hallet, Holt S. "Burmah, Present and Future," (London) Journal of the

Society of Arts, Vol. 36, December 18, 1885, pp. 96-110.

————, "Exploration Survey for a Railway Connection Between India, Siam, and China," (London) Proceedings of the Royal Geographical Society, Vol. VIII, No. 1, January 1886, pp. 1-20.

Laurie, Col. W. F. B., "British and Upper Burma," (London) Journal of the Society of Arts, Vol. 28, June 11, 1880, pp. 640-644.

MacMahon, Maj.-Gen. A. R., "The Situation In Burma," (London) The National Review, Vol. VI, September 1885 to February 1886, pp. 254-265.

————, "Matters In Burma," (London) Macmillan's Magazine, Vol. LIII, November 1885 to April 1886, pp. 314-320.

————, "Burmese Border Tribes and Trade Routes," (Edinburgh) Blackwood's Edinburgh Magazine, Vol. 140, September 1886, pp. 394-407.

"On the Influence of Forests Upon Climate," (Roorkee) The Indian Forester, Vol. XII, No. 2, February 1886, pp. 75-79.

Parquet, L., "The Influence of Forests on Water Supply," (Roorkee) The Indian Forester, Vol. XVIII, No. 7, July 1892, pp. 277-280.

Phayre, Gen. Sir Arthur, "British Burma," (London) Journal of the Society of Arts, Vol. 29, May 27, 1881, pp. 580-586.

Anonymous (probably Maj.-Gen. H. N. D. Prendergast), "The Conquest of Burma," (Edindurgh) The Edinburgh Review, CLXI, January-April 1887, pp. 489-511.

Prendergast, Gen. Sir H. N. D., "Burman Dacoity and Patriotism and Burman Politics," (Edinburgh) Blackwood's Edinburgh Magazine, New Series-Vol. V., January-April 1893, pp. 271-280.

Protheroe, Brig.-Gen. C. B., "Burma—1885-87," (Simla) The Journal of the United Service Institution of India, Vol. XXI, No. 100, 1892, pp. 599-613.

Redway, Jacques W., "The Influence of Rainfall on Commerical Development: A Study of the Arid Region," (Philadelphia) Proceedings of the Engineer's Club of Philadelphia, Vol. IX, No. 4, Ocober 1892, pp. 1-14.

Regnault, Dr. F., "Deboisement and Decadence," (Allahabad) The Indian Forester, Vol. XXX, No. 8, August 1904, pp. 346-349.

Rowett, Mrs. Ellen, "A Visit to the Queen of Burmah," (London) Frasier's Magazine, Vol. XXV, January-June 1882, pp. 632-642.

Scott, J. George, "Burma: The Eastern Country and the Race of the Brahmas," (London) Journal of the Society of Arts, Vol. 34, January 29, 1886, pp. 177-194.

Simonds, P. L., "The Teak Forests of India and the East, and our British Imports of Teak," (London) Journal of the Society of Arts, Vol. 33, February 27, 1885, pp. 348-349.

T. H. A., "Cutch Exports From Upper Burma," (Roorkee) The Indian Forester, Vol. XIV, No. 2, February 1888, pp. 70-71.

"The Annexation of Burmah," (London) The Saturday Review, January 2, 1886, pp. 10-11.

"The Upper Burma Forests," (Roorkee) The Indian Forester, Vol. XII,

No. 5, May 1886, pp. 232-234.

Thornton, W. T., "Forest Denudation and Famines," (Calcutta) The Indian Forester, Vol. IV., No. 4, April 1879, pp. 354-355.

"Upper Burma Affairs," (Roorkee) The Indian Forester, Vol. XII, No. 2. February 1886, pp. 83-84.

"Upper Burma Forest Leases," (Roorkee) The Indian Forester, Vol. XIV, No. 7, July 1888, pp. 334-337.

W. B. B., "Upper Burma During 1886," (Edinburgh) The Scottish Geographical Magazine, Vol. III, No. 8, August 1887, pp. 410-421.

White, H. Thirkell, "Upper Burma Under British Rule," (London) Journal of the Society of Arts, Vol. 41, 1893, pp. 150-166.

9. Autobiographies, Diaries, and Reminiscences.

Brown, Major E. C., The Coming of the Great Queen, London, 1888.

Browne, Gen. Horace A., Reminiscences of the Court of Mandalay, Woking, 1907.

Colbeck, James Alfred, Letters From Mandalay, Knaresborough, 1892.

Mahe de la Bourdonnais, A., Un Francais en Birmanie, Paris, 1886.

Marks, John Ebenezer, Forty Years in Burma, London, 1917.

Minayeff, Ivan P., (trans. by H. Sanyal and others), Travels and Diaries of India and Burma, Calcutta, 1958.

(Nibs) Nisbet, Hugh, Experiences of a Jungle-Wallah, St. Albans, 1936.

B.   SECONDARY SOURCES

1. Selected Books and Biographies.

Adler, G. J., British India's Northern Frontier, 1865-95, London, 1963.

Banerjee, A. C., The Annexation of Burma, Calcutta, 1944.

Baretto, W. L., Heroes of Burma, Rangoon, 1934.

————, King Mindon, Rangoon, 1935.

Blunt, Wilfred Scawen, India Under Ripon: A Private Diary, London, 1909.

Bodelsen, S. A., Studies in Mid-Victorian Imperialism, Copenhagen, 1924.

Cady, John F., A History of Modern Burma, Ithaca, 1959.

————, Southeast Asia : Its Historical Development, New York, 1964.

Christian, John Leroy, Modern Burma, Los Angeles, 1942.

Churchill, Winston Spencer, Lord Randolph Churchill, 2 Vols., London, 1906.

Clifford, Hugh, Further India-Being the Story of Exploration From the Earliest Times in Burma, Malaya, Siam, and Indo-China, London, 1904.

Coedes, G. (trans. H. M. Wright), The Making of South East Asia, Berkeley and L. A., 1966.

————, (trans. Susan Brown Cowing), The Indianized States of Southeast Asia, Honolulu, 1968.

Collis, Maurice, Sanda Mala, London, 1939.

————, Into Hidden Burma, London, 1953.

Dale, Tom and Vernon Gill Carter, Top-Soil and Civilization, Norman, 1955.

Dautremer, Joseph, (trans. by J. G. Scott), Burma Under British Rule, London, 1912.

Desai, Walter S., The History of the British Residency in Burma, Rangoon, 1939.

————, India and Burma, Calcutta, 1954.

————, A Pageant of Burmese History, Calcutta, 1961.

————, Deposed King Thibaw of Burma in India, 1885-1916, Bombay, 1967.

Durand, Sir Mortimer, The Life of Field-Marshal Sir George White, 2 Vols., Edinburgh and London, 1915.

Enriquez, Major C. M., A Burmese Wonderland, Calcutta and Simla, 1922.

Ferrars, Max and Bertha, Burma, London, 1901.

Fieldhouse, D. K., The Colonial Empires, London, 1966.

Fisher, Charles A., South East Asia, London, 1964.

Foucar, E. C. V., They Reigned At Mandalay, London, 1946.

————, Mandalay the Golden, London, 1963.

Furnivall, J. S., Colonial Policy and Practice, London, 1948.

Geiger, Rudolf, Climate Near the Ground, Cambridge, Mass., 1965.

Ghose, Dilip Kumar, England and Afghanistan, Calcutta, 1960.

Gillard, D. R., "Salisbury and the Indian Defence Problem, 1885-1902;" in K. Bourne and D. C. Watt, Studies in International History, London, 1967.

Greaves, R. L., Persia and the Defence of India, 1884-1892, London, 1959.

Grenville, J. A. S., Lord Salisbury and Foreign Policy, London, 1961.

Hall, D. G. E., The Dalhousie-Phayre Correspondence, 1852-1856, London, 1932.

————, Europe and Burma, Oxford, 1945.

————, Burma, London, 1950.

————, Michael Symes, London, 1955.

————, A History of South-East Asia, New York, 1964.

————, Early English Intercourse With Burma, 1587-1743, London, 1967.

Harmer, Ernest George, The Story of Burma, London, 1902.

Harvey, G. E., History of Burma From the Earliest Times to 10 March 1824, the Beginning of the English Conquest, London, 1925, 1967.

————, British Rule In Burma, 1824-1942, London, 1946.

————, Outline of Burmese History, London and Calcutta, 1947.

Jacks, G. V. and R. O. Whyte, The Rape of the Earth, London, 1939.

James, Robert Rhodes, Lord Randolph Churchill, London, 1959.

Jesse, F. Tennyson, The Lacquer Lady, New York, 1930.

————, The Story of Burma, Toronto and London, 1946.

Kelly, R. Talbot, Burma Painted and Described, London, 1912.

Kessel, Joseph, (trans. Stella Rodway), Mogok: The Valley of Rubies, London, 1960.

Langer, W. L., The Diplomacy of Imperialism, New York, 1951.

Lyall, Sir Alfred, The Life of the Marquis of Dufferin and Ava, 2 Vols., London, 1905.

Martin, Briton Jr., New India 1885, Berkeley, 1969.

Maung Htin Aung, The Stricken Peacock, The Hague, 1965.

————, A History of Burma, New York, 1967.

Maung Maung, Burma in the Family of Nations, Amsterdam, 1957.

Maung Shein, Burma's Transport and Foreign Trade, 1885-1914, Rangoon, 1964.

Milne, Lorus and Margery, Water and Life, London, 1965.

Mya Sein Daw, The Administration of Burma: Sir Charles Crosthwaite and the Consolidation of Burma, Rangoon, 1938.

Nash, Manning, The Golden Road to Modernity (Village Life in Contemporary Burma), New York, 1965.

Norris, J. A., The First Afghan War, 1838-1842, Cambridge, 1967.

O' Connor, V. C. Scott, Mandalay and Other Cities of the Past in Burma, London, 1907.

Pelling, Henry, Social Geography of British Elections, 1885-1910, London, 1967.

Pelzer, Karl J., Pioneer Settlement in the Asiatic Tropics, New York, 1945.

Pointon, A. C., The Bombay Burma Trading Corporation, Limited, 1863-1963, Southampton, 1963.

Powers, Thomas F., Jules Ferry and the Renaissance of French Imperialism, Morningside Heights, 1944.

Pye, Lucian W., Politics, Personality, and Nation Building, New Haven, 1963.

Rastogi, R. S., Indo-Afghan Relations, 1880-1900, Lucknow, 1965.

Sao Saimong Mangrai, The Shan States and the British Annexation, Ithaca, 1965.

Sarkisyanz, E., Buddhist Backgrounds of the Burmese Revolution, The Hague, 1965.

Scott, Sir J. George, Burma, London, 1911.

————, Burma From the Earliest Times to the Present Day, London, 1925.

————, Burma and Beyond, London, 1932.

Sears, Paul B., Deserts on the March, Norman, 1959.

Sein, Kenneth (Maung Khe) and J. A. Withey, The Great Po Sein: A Chronicle of the Burmese Theatre, Bloomington, 1965.

Singhal, D. P., The Annexation of Upper Burma, Singapore, 1960.

Sinor, Denis, "Foreigner-Barbarian-Monster," in East-West In Art, by Theodore Bowie and others, Bloomington, 1966.

Smith, Donald Eugene, Religion and Politics in Burma, Princeton, 1965.

Spiro, Melford E., Burmese Supernaturalism, Englewood Cliffs, 1967.

Stebbing, E. P., The Forests of India, Vols. II and III, London, 1923, 1926.

Stewart, A. T. Q., The Pagoda War. London, 1972.

Stokes, Eric, The English Utilitarians and India, London, 1959.

Stuart, John, Burma Through the Centuries, London, 1910.

Tomahs, William L. Jr., Man's Role in Changing the Face of the Earth,

Chicago, 1955.

Wheeler, Sir Mortimer, The Indus Civilization, Cambridge, 1960.

Woodman, Dorothy, The Making of Burma, London, 1962.

2. Selected Periodical Articles.

Adas, Michael, "Imperialist Rehtoric and Modern Historiography: The Case of Lower Burma Before and After Conquest," (Singapore) Journal of Southeast Asian Studies, Vol. III, No. 2, September 1972, pp. 175-192.

Aung Than Tun, "Hluttaw Under the Burmese Kings," (Rangoon) The Guardian, April 1964, pp. 25-27.

Ba, Vivian, "The Second Embassy From the Kingdom of Burma to France in 1872, Part One," (Rangoon) The Guardian, May 1962, pp. 31-33.

————, "Ivan Pavlovich Minayeff and His Burma Diary, Part 1," (Rangoon) The Guardian, Vol. XII, No. 4, April 1965, pp. 20-25. Also: Part 2, Vol. XII, No. 5, May 1965, pp. 9-17.

————, "The Mandalay Regalia at a Glance," (Rangoon) The Guardian, Vol. XII, No. 9, September 1965, pp. 24-25.

————, "King Mindon and the World Fair of 1867 Held in Paris," (Rangoon) JBRS, Vol. XLVIII, Part 2, December 1965, pp. 17-23.

————, "Court Life and Festival in King Mindon's Palace, Part 1." (Rangoon) The Guardian, Vol. XIV, No. 10, October 1967, pp. 20-24. Also: Part 2, Vol. XIV, No. 11, November 1967, pp. 16-20.

Bates, C. G. and A. J. Henry, "Forest and Stream-Flow Experiment at Wagon Wheel Gap, Col.," (Washington) Monthly Weather Review Supplement No. 30, 1928.

Bryson, Reid, and David A. Barreis, "Possibilities of Major Climatic Modification and Their Implications: Northwest India, a Case for Study," (Athens) Ekistics, September 1967, pp. 245-249.

Caneiro, Robert L., "A Theory of the Origin of the State," (Washington), Science, August 21, 1970, Vol. 169, pp. 733-738.

Chew, Ernest, "The Withdrawal of the Last British Residency from Upper Burma in 1879," (Singapore) Journal of Southeast Asian History, Vol. X, No. 2, September 1969, pp. 253-278.

Christian, John L. "Trans-Burma Trade Routes to China," (New York) Pacific Affairs, Vol. XIII, No. 2, June 1940, pp. 175-185.

————, "Anglo-French Rivalry in Southeast Asia: Its Historical Geography and Diplomatic Climate," (New York) The Geographical Review, Vol. XXXI, 1941, pp. 272-282.

————, "King Thebaw," (New York) The Far Eastern Quarterly, Vol. 3, 1944, pp. 309-312.

Desai, Walter S., "Foreign Relations of Burma's Last King," (New Delhi) International Studies Quarterly, Vol. II, No. 1, July 1960, pp. 2-3.

Frasier, W. G., "Old Rangoon," (Rangoon) JBRS, Vol. X, Part II, August 1920, pp. 1-19.

Furnivall, J. S., "Safety First—A Study in the Economic History of Burma," (Rangoon) JBRS, Vol. XL, Part I, June 1957, pp. 24-38.

Hall, D. G. E., "On the Study of Southeast Asian History," (Honolulu)

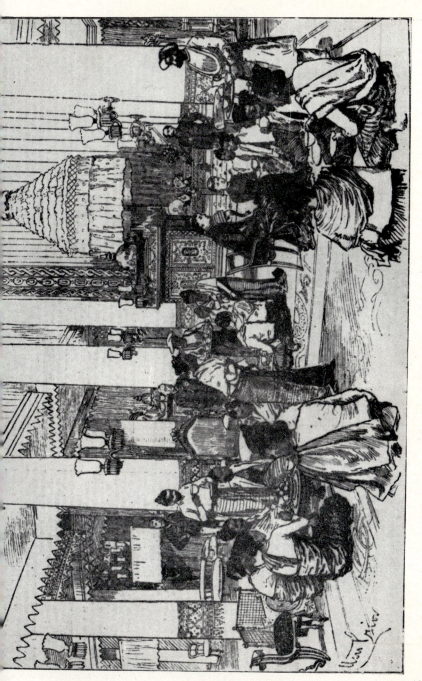

12. *Burmese ladies taking afternoon tea with Lady Dufferin in the Mandalay Palace.* (Illustrated London News, *April 3, 1886, p. 350*).

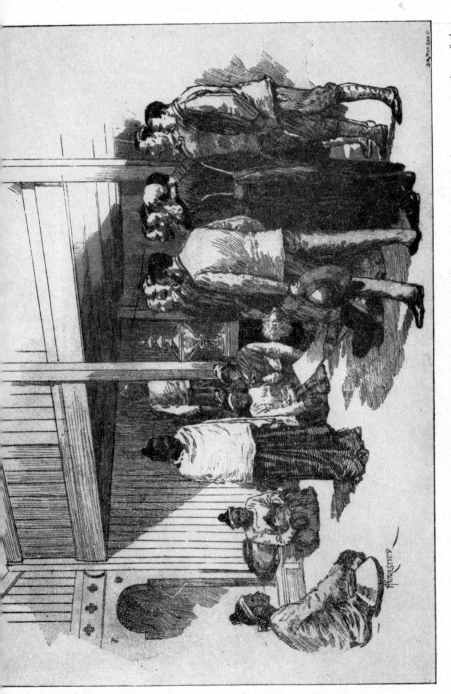

13. *The Kinwun Mingyi, the great Burmese patriot and former prime minister, receiving a letter of thanks from representatives of the [...] The Kinwun had protected their lives and property during the Third Burmese War.*

Pacific Affairs, Vol. XXXIII, No. 3, September 1960, pp. 268-281.

Heine-Geldern, Robert, "State and Kingship in Southeast Asia," (New York) The Far Eastern Quarterly, Vol. II, No. 1, November 1942, pp. 20-24.

James, Robert Rhodes, "Lord Randolph Churchill," (London) History Today, Vol. V., No. 3, March 1955, pp. 145-153.

Lal, B. B., and B. K. Thapar, "Excavation at Kalibangan," (New Delhi) Cultural Forum, July 1967, p. 88.

Langham-Carter, R. R., "The Kinwun Mingyi At Home," (Rangoon) JBRS, Vol. XXV, Part 3, 1935, pp. 121-128.

————, "Burmese Rule on the Toungoo Frontier," (Rangoon) JBRS, Vol. XXVII, Part I, 1937, pp, 21, 24, 26.

————, "The Burmese Army," (Rangoon) JBRS, Vol. XXVII, Part I, 1937, pp. 254-276.

Loudermilk, W. C., "Man Made Deserts," (Honolulu) Pacific Affairs, Vol. VIII, No. 4, December 1935, pp. 411-416, 418-419.

Luce, G. H., "Economic Life of the Early Burman," (Rangoon) JBRS, Vol. XXX, Part I, April 1940, pp. 283-335.

Mackenzie, J. C., "Climate in Burmese History," (Rangoon) JBRS, Vol. 3, Part I, 1913, pp. 40-46.

MacKirdy, K. A., "The Fear of American Intervention as a Factor in British Expansion: Western Australia and Natal," (Berkeley) Pacific Historical Review, Vol. XXXV, No. 2, May 1966, pp. 138-139.

Ma Kyan, "King Mindon's Councillors," (Rangoon) JBRS, Vol. XLIV, June 1961, Part 1, pp. 43-60.

Martin, Briton Jnr., "The Viceroyalty of Lord Dufferin, Part I," (London) History Today, December 1960, pp. 821-830. Also: Part 2, January 1961, pp. 56-64.

Maung Maung Tin and Thomas Owen Morris, "Mindon Min's Development Plan for the Mandalay Area," (Rangoon) JBRS, Vol. XLIX, Part I, 1966, pp. 29-34.

Maung Shein, "State Investment in Burma Railways, 1874-1914," (Rangoon) JBRS, Vol. XLIV, December 1961, Part II, pp. 165-182.

Maung Tha Aung and Maung Mya Din (R. Alexander, ed.), "Pacification of Upper Burma: A Vernacular History," (Rangoon) JBRS, Vol. XXXI, Part II, 1941, pp. 134-136.

Ma Yi, "Burmese Sources for the History of the Konbaung Period, 1752-1885," (Singapore) Journal of Southeast Asian History, March 1965, pp. 64-65.

Morello, Ted, "Deserts Into Forests," (Athens) Ekistics, April 1970, pp. 264-266.

Murphy, Rhoades, "The Ruin of Ancient Ceylon." (Ann Arbor) The Journal of Asian Studies, Vol. XVI, No. 2, February 1957, pp. 181-200.

Nolan, J. J., "Rangoon in the Seventies," (Rangoon) JBRS, Vol. XIV, Part I, 1924, pp. 21-38.

"Notes and Queries (2)," (Rangoon) JBRS, Vol. XXX, Part I, 1940, pp. 345-346.

Taw Sein Ko, 'A Study in Burmese Sociology," (Rangoon) JBRS, Vol.

X, Part II, 1919, pp. 104-106.

Than Tun, "Former Fighting Forces of Burma," (Rangoon) The Guardian, July 1967, pp. 9-10.

Thaung Blackmore, "The Founding of the City of Mandalay by King Mindon," (Hongkong) Journal of Oriental Studies, Vol. V, Nos. 1-2, 1959-1960, pp. 82-97.

————, "Dilemma of the British Representative to the Burmese Court After the Outbreak of a Palace Revolution in 1866," (Singapore) Journal of Southeast Asian History, Vol. X, No. 2, September 1969, pp. 236-251.

Thaung Daw, "Burmese Kingship in Theory and in Practice During the Reign of Mindon," (Rangoon) JBRS, Vol. XLII, December 1959, Part II, pp. 171-185.

'Theophilus' (Major Enrique), "The King and Queen Ate Sausages," (Rangoon) The Guardian, October 1957, pp. 17-18.

Trager, F. N., "Review of Burma in the Family of Nations," (Rangoon) The Guardian, January 1957, pp. 31-32.

————, "Recent Southeast Asian Historiography," (Honolulu) Pacific Affairs, Vol. XXX, No. 4, December 1957, pp. 358-366.

U Aung Than, "Relation Between the Sanghas and State and Laity," (Rangoon) JBRS, XLVIII, Part I, June 1965, pp. 1-7.

U Pu, "Burmese Court Paraphernalia," (Rangoon) The Guardian, Vol. XII, No. 5, May 1965, pp. 42-45.

Yi Yi, "The Thrones of the Burmese Kings," (Rangoon) JBRS, Vol. XLIII, December 1960, Part II, pp. 97-123.

————, "Life at the Burmese Court Under the Konbaung Kings," (Rangoon) JBRS, Vol. XLIV, Part II, 1961, p. 122.

————, "The Judicial System of King Mindon," (Rangoon) JBRS, Vol. XLV, June 1962, Part I, pp. 7-27.

Zon, Raphael, "Forests and Water in the Light of Scientific Investigation," (Washington) U. S. Forest Service, (no Vol. number), 1927.

3. Special Studies.

Bennett, Paul J., Conference Under the Tamarind Tree, New Haven, 1971.

Iu So Yan-kit, Mrs. Nancy, Anglo-Chinese Diplomacy Regarding Burma, 1885-1897, Ph. D. Thesis, Univ. of London, 1960.

Lewis, Brian L., The Attitudes and Policies of Great Britain and China Towards French Expansion in Cochin China, Cambodia, Annam and Tongkin, 1858-1883, Ph. D. Thesis, Univ. of London, 1961.

Ma Thuang, British Interest in Trans-Burma Trade Routes to China, 1826-1876, Ph. D. Thesis, Univ. of London, 1954.

Murti, B. S. N., Anglo-French Relations With Siam, 1876-1904, Ph. D. Thesis, Univ. of London, 1952.

Preschez, Philippe, "Les Relations Franco-Burmese aux XVIII et XIX Siecles," (Paris) France-Asie, Vol. XXI, No. 3 (189-190), 1967, pp. 340-417.

Preston, Adrian William, British Military Policy and the Defense of India ....During the Russian Crisis, 1876-1880, Ph.D. Thesis, Univ. of

London, 1966.

Saw Sick Hwa, The Rice Industry of Burma, 1852-1940, Ph. D. Thesis, Univ. of London, 1963.

Singhal, D. P., Indian External Policy With Special Reference to the Northwest and Eastern Frontiers, 1876-1898, Ph. D. Thesis, Univ. of London, 1955.

4. Interviews.
   a. Personal.

   Prof. Walter S. Desai, Retired Head of the Dept. of History, Univ. of Rangoon, New Delhi. Advice on sources.

   Prof. C. A. Fisher, Head of the Asian Geography Dept., Univ. of London, London. Advice on Deforestation.

   'A. Nonymous', An Executive of the Bombay-Burma Trading Corp., London. The author was not allowed to look at BBTC records of the period 1878-1886 concerning teak-extractions from the Ningyan Forest and other leases. The author is grateful, however, for other valuable information given to him by the above executive.

   b. By Letter.

   Reply from Vivian Ba, c/o The Burmese Embassy, Paris. Advice on sources.

   Reply from Prof. Karl J. Pelzer, Yale Univ., New Haven, Conn. Advice on Deforestation.

   Reply from Lord Ritchie-Calder of Balmashannar, Scotland. Advice on Deforestation.

INDEX

A

ABDUR Rahman (Amir of Afghanistan)   234, 317

Afghan War, Second   28, 31-33, 43-44, 71, 182-83, 327

Afghanistan   17, 31-32, 42-43, 74, 182-83, 233-34, 241

Aitchison, C.U (Chief Commissioner of Lower Burma)   31-34, 37, 40-42, 44-49, 63-67, 69-74, 303, 328

Akyab   6

Alaungpaya, King (1752-1760)   4-5, 306, 318

—Dynasty Princes   306, 318

Allent, G. (Editor of Pioneer)   260

Anawrahta, King of Pagan (1044-1077)   3

Andreino, Giovanni (Italian Consul)   8, 32, 35, 66, 78, 93, 123, 136, 165, 169-75, 178-79, 201, 207-08, 210-11, 213-14, 216-219, 221, 223-24, 238, 245, 250, 254-55, 259-61, 290, 332

Angelo, Tavarozzi   108

Anglo-Afghan Relations   31-32, 42-43, 234, 241

—Afghan War, Second   31-33

——Gandamak Treaty   42-43

Anglo-Burmese Treaties   5, 7-8, 38, 43, 51, 62-67, 74-80, 70-71, 87-88, 96- 112, 129, 145, 154, 177, 179-80, 187, 189, 219, 221, 281, 328-30

—Burmese Treaty Missions

——Kinwun Mission (1872-73)   65

——Myaungla Mission (1879)   62-67, 87, 98, 328

——Pangyet Mission (1882)   96-112, 329-30

Burma, Lower   8, 10, 12, 32, 43, 49, 62, 67-68, 73-77, 129, 137, 144-53, 157, 177, 179, 190, 203, 221-23, 304, 327

—Trade Relations with Burma, Upper   144-47, 149-53

Burma, Upper

—History   1-12

——Annexation by the British   69-70, 144-55, 171, 179-80, 189, 242-43, 253, 324-326, 331, 335-36

—Treaty of 1826 (Yandabo)   5, 24, 64, 97, 99, 104, 281

—Treaty of 1862   38, 43, 51, 70-71, 74, 80, 99, 145, 179, 328-29

—Treaty of 1867   38, 43, 51, 70-71, 74-80, 88, 96-97, 99, 104-05, 145, 179, 199, 219, 328-29

——Fytche Annexe   8, 75, 96-97, 104-05

—Treaty of 1882 (Proposed)   98-112, 329-30

Anglo-Burmese War   5, 11, 19, 191, 233-72, 274-81 283-85, 289-91, 333-35

—First (1824-26)   5, 11, 257, 281

—Second (1852-53)   5-6, 11, 19, 191, 257, 301

—Third (1885)   233-72, 274-78, 280-81, 283-84, 289-91

——Burma (British) Expeditionary Force   243-44, 252-53, 264, 274-81, 284-85, 289-91, 334-35

——Reasons for Burmese Defeat

———Military   275-78, 290, 334-35

———Political   278-80, 290-91, 335

———Ultimatum (British)   199, 233-72, 283, 333-34

———Ultimatum Demands   240-41, 262-63, 334

Anglo-Chinese Relations   153, 237-38, 241, 262-63, 304, 306-13, 317, 334

Anglo-Egyptian War (1882)   107-10

Anglo-French Relations   12, 42, 51, 137, 163-64, 169-91, 219, 233-45, 282, 327-28 332-34, 336

—Entente Cordiale (1904)   336

Anglo-French Treaties   5, 130

—Treaty of 1763   5

—Treaty of 1879   130

Anglo-Russian Relations   11-12, 17, 28, 32, 42, 71, 75, 120, 137, 233-37, 241, 304-05, 317, 327, 333-34, 337

Annam   50, 126, 164, 185, 187, 190

Annexation of Burma *See* under Burma, Upper

Antram, Mattie Calogreedy   10, 89, 95, 101-02, 109, 123, 166, 173-74, 332

Arab (Traders)   2

Arakan   5-6, 9, 257

Arms Question *See* under Anglo-Burmese Treaties and its Sub-Heading 'Fytche Annexe'

Assam   5, 257

Ava   3, 71, 147, 154, 274, 277, 282-85, 291

B

BAC-LE Ambush	126, 163-64
Balkans	235
Banares	31, 110, 130
Barbieri, (Dr.)	261
Bassac (Lao State)	190
Bassein	3
Bayinnaung (1551-1581)	3
Beckman, Captain	69
Beg, Yakub (Turkestan Ruler)	17
Bengal	2, 5, 36
Bentabole	211, 213, 245
Bentinck, William (Governor-General of India)	5
Bernard, Charles (Chief Commissioner of Lower Burma)	67, 71-74, 77-80, 92-93, 102, 168-08, 119, 123, 128-29, 132, 134, 137, 143-49, 151-57, 169, 171, 174-80, 182, 186, 191, 200, 203, 208-11, 218-23, 238-39, 242, 244, 246-49, 255, 260-61, 264, 279, 299, 303, 306-07, 309, 314-16, 318, 329-30
Bhamo	8, 9, 42, 72, 105, 148, 154, 157, 237, 241, 275, 298, 306, 308
Bhamo-Yunnan Trade	263
Binnya Dala, King	4
Birmingham	152, 182-83, 236, 251
Bismarck	163
Bo,	97-98
Bo Hmau-Ken (Atwinwun)	285
Bodawapaya, King (1782-1819)	5
Boers, South African	28
Bombay-Burma Trading Corporation (BBTC)	7, 93, 107, 109, 129, 146, 157, 168, 173-74, 178, 185, 191, 199-224, 239-40, 247-52, 255, 262, 282, 332-34
—BBTC Teak Case	7, 199-224, 239-40, 247-51
——Arbitration Demand	218-24, 239-40, 247-49, 251
——And Hlutdaw	199-200, 210-11, 213-14, 216-18, 221-24, 250, 332-34
—Lump Sum Contract (1884)	204-08
—Shorts Contract (1882)	202-04, 215
—Variable Duty Contract (1880)	201-04
Bonvillan, P.H. (French Engineer)	123-24, 128, 166, 173-74, 219
Bouham, G.	249
Bright, John	38, 21 13,652

Brown, E.C., Major — 276, 284, 289

Browne, Horace A. (British Resident) — 36-37, 40-41, 43-48, 76-77, 328

Bryce, J.A. (BBTC Contract Negotiator) — 102, 165, 178, 185, 201

Buddhism — 2

Buddhist Law — 19

Buddhist Lent — 49

Bulgaria — 235

Burma, Lower — 8, 10, 12, 43, 49, 62, 67-68. 73-77, 129, 137, 144-53, 157, 177, 179, 190, 203, 221-22, 304, 327

—Trade relations with upper Burma — 144-47, 149-53

Burma Expeditionary Force — 243-44, 252-53, 264, 274-81, 284-85, 289-91, 234-35

Burna-Yunan Railroad — 238

Burmans — 1-4

Burmese-Chinese Relations — 65, 75-76, 79-80, 297, 306-07, 307-13, 335

—China Decennial Tribute Claim — 297, 306-07, 309-13, 335

Burmese-French Relations — 8, 11, 65, 133, 153-55, 164-83, 213, 219, 236, 241, 262-63, 305, 331-32

—Forbes Memorandum — 154-55

Burmese-French Treaties — 8, 65, 119-297, 132-33, 150, 154, 166, 175-77, 180-81, 184, 187, 189, 221, 330

—Burmese Treaty Mission to France (Kinwun) (1872-73) — 65

—Burmese Treaty Mission to France, (Myohit) (1883-85) — 119-23, 181, 188

—Ferry's Secret Letter — 127, 176, 184

—French Treaty Mission to Burma (Deloncle) — 8, 123-25, 166, 330

——Offensive-Defensive Alliance — 8, 124-25, 166, 330

—Kinwun's Declaration — 124-25, 166

—Treaty of 1873 — 120-21, 132, 150, 154, 175, 184, 330

—Treaty of January 15, 1885 — 121-29, 132-33, 154, 177, 180. 187, 189, 221

——Supplementary Commercial Treaty — 121-29, 132-33

——British India's Reaction — 128-29

Burmese-German Treaty (1885) — 175

Burmese-Italian Relations — 165, 167

Burmese-Italian Treaty (1871) — 65, 127

—— Burmese-Italian Treaty Mission — 65

Burne, Owen T. (India Office Official) — 96

C

CALCUTTA — 6, 8, 35-37, 43, 47, 63-64, 88, 97-98, 111, 119, 130, 132, 152, 152, 169

Calogreedy, Mrs. — 109
Cambodia — 50, 185
Campbell, James Duncan — 126
Carey, Col. Robert — 274, 276
Cetewayo (Zulu Chief) — 28
Cavagnari, Louis (British Resident in Kabul) — 43-44
Challemel-Lacour (French Foreign Minister) — 120
Chandernagore — 110, 130-31, 314
Chiengmai — 3, 125, 237
China — 1, 18, 65, 76, 79-80, 122, 125-26, 133, 164, 237, 263, 297, 306-13, 317, 335
China, Southern — 72, 75, 153, 191, 235-39, 241, 262-63, 304, 334, 337
Chindwin (Forests) — 109, 201, 204-05
Chinese Emperor — 25, 74, 263, 306, 311
— Shoe Question — 74, 263
Chinese (Traders) — 79, 80
Chinese-French Treaties
— Tientsin Treaty (1884) — 125-26, 133, 164
Chinese-French War — 122, 125-26, 164
Chins — 304
Churchill, Randolph (Secy. of State for India) — 125, 178, 182-85, 187, 190-91, 233-44, 249, 251, 298, 304-06, 308-10, 332
Clemenceau — 125-26, 163
Clive, Robert — 170
Cochin-China — 50
Colbeck, James A. — 22-23, 39
Colombo — 130, 314
Colquhoun, A. R. — 237-38
Comotto (Italian Engineer) — 276-77, 280
Constantinople — 235
Cranbrook, Lord (Secy. of State for India) — 31-33, 36, 42, 44-46, 70
Crosthwaite, C. H. T. — 119

D

DACOITS and Dacoity — 135, 143-51, 157, 257, 284-85, 297, 299-03, 307, 313-14 316-17, 319, 331, 335

Dalhousie, Lord (Governor-General of India) — 6
Danube (River) — 177, 179

Dardanelles	235
Darlington (Rangoon Customs Collector)	71
Darvall, Captain	98
Darwood, John	208, 214
d'Avera, M.	22
Davies, Col. H. D.	62-64
De Facieu, Gen.	219, 246
De Freyinet (French Foreign Minister)	164, 184, 189, 252-53
De la Bourdonnais, Comte A. Mahe	167-68, 188
De Trevelec, Comte (French Cavalry Adviser to Burma)	119-20, 168-69, 181, 187
Deforestation process *See* under Forests and Forestry	
Deloncle Mission *See* under Burmese-French Treaties	
Denigre (French Weaver)	28
Disraeli (British Prime Minister)	33
D'Orsay, Quai	123-25, 130, 166-68, 187-88 211-13, 253, 332, 334
Doyle (IFC Captain)	22
Dufferin, Lord (Governor-General of India)	125, 131, 153, 155, 166, 168-69, 171, 176, 178-79, 181-86, 191, 218, 223, 236-42, 244, 251, 254, 297-98, 301, 303, 306, 308-17, 319, 331-35
Duncan, Col. (British Resident)	9, 96, 304-05, 308
Durand, Mortimer (Indian Foreign Secy.)	72-74, 128-29, 148, 180, 218, 221, 239, 242, 245, 260-61, 264, 307
Dutch East India Company	4
Dutch (Traders)	11

E

East India Company	4, 11, 170
Eden, Ashley (Chief Commissioner of Lower Burma)	36-37, 39, 312
Egypt	2
Egyptian War 1882 *See* Anglo-Egyptian War	
Ekkahabat (Myingwun)	90-91, 95
Elba	314
Entente Cordiale (Great Britain and France), 1904	336
Europe	2, 37, 170, 178

F

FAMINE (1883-85)	131, 143-44, 147, 156-57, 220-21, 331, 337

Farman (London *Standard* Correspondent)   187-89, 247-49, 251
Ferris (British Surgeon)   49
Ferry, Jules (French Prime Minister)   120-22, 125-26, 163-64, 175-76, 184, 330
Fielding-Hall, H.   222, 258
Fitzpatrick, D.   98
Forbes, G. S.   154-55, 191
Forests and Forestry
— Deforestation Process   1, 7, 12, 143-44, 156-57, 331, 336-37

  — Different Forests
— — Chindwin   109, 204-05
— — Karenni   6
— — Malun   204
— — Moo   201
— — Ningyan   7, 171, 173, 175, 185, 200-01, 204-06, 208-09, 214
— — Pyaungshu   201, 204-05
— — Taungdwingyi   205
— — Toungoo   7, 209
— — Yaw   204-05
Forsyth, Douglas   17
French Compaigne Royale des Indes Orientales   4
French Mission to Burma *See* Burmese-French Treaties
Furnivall, J. S.   9
Fytche, Albert (Chief Commissioner of Lower Burma)   96

G

GANDAMAK Treaty *See* under Anglo-Afghan Relations
Geary, Grattan   156, 216, 277, 300, 302
Germany   127, 153, 175, 177, 183, 236, 262, 305
— Burmese-German Treaty (1885)   175
Gladstone, (British Prime Minister)   70, 176, 234, 298, 313, 319
Glasgow   153
Glasgow Chamber of Commerce   152
Goldenberg (BBTC Official)   200
Gordon, Gen.   234
'Grand Lama' Scheme   312, 318
Grant, Charles   98, 102-05, 111, 147
Granville, Earl   120
Gue Gyoun Kamyc   274
Gujerat   2
Gurkhas   5

H

HALLET, H. S. | 238
Hamilton Report (1881) | 145
Hanoi | 187
Hanthawaddy (District) | 145
Hart, Robert | 126
Hartington, Lord | 66, 71, 73-74, 96, 102-03
Haas, Frederic (French Consul) | 169-72, 176-77, 179-185, 187, 189, 191, 207, 211-13, 217, 219-20, 237, 239, 241, 244, 246, 254, 282, 332-33

Hecquard (French National) | 165
Henzada (District) | 5, 145
Herat | 304, 333-36
Hlaythin (Atwinwun) | 30, 95, 218, 257, 259, 274, 277, 281, 302
Hlutdaw (Royal Council) | 18-20, 26-27, 37-38, 51, 78, 87-96, 132, 185, 199-200, 210-11, 213-14, 216-18, 221-24, 248, 250, 254-58, 260, 264, 280, 287, 297, 299, 302-03, 306-07, 312, 314-16, 318-19, 328-29, 332-35
— And BBTC Teak Case, | 199, 200, 210-11, 213-14, 216-18, 221-24, 250, 332-34
— And Dacoits | 149, 297, 299, 302-03, 307, 335
— Kinwun Group or Reform Party | 18-19, 26-27, 37-38, 51, 78 87-89, 217-18, 221-23, 248 256-57, 328, 332-33, 335
— Taingda Group | 217-18, 221-23, 248, 254, 256-57, 260, 328, 332-33, 335
— Yanaung Mintha Group | 78, 87-96
House of Commons (British Parliament) | 70
Hue | 187

I

IBN Arabi (Egyptian General) | 107
Ibrahim, Mulla | 68, 76
India Council | 312, 329
India Office | 96, 121, 312-13
Indignation Meeting *See* Rangoon Indignation Meeting (Oct. 11, 1884)
Indra, Lord | 93-94, 131, 157, 275

Indo-China (French)	18, 124, 126, 153-54, 164, 179, 186, 253, 317, 334, 337
Irrawaddy	8, 21, 38, 64, 66-67, 71-72, 79, 81, 149, 151, 154, 169-70, 174, 177-78, 180-81, 242, 264, 275-76, 279, 290, 298, 301, 308, 335
Irrawaddy Flotilla Co. (IFC)	9, 22, 35-36, 49, 66, 69, 79, 108, 120, 147-48, 151, 170, 173, 254, 261, 264, 275, 281, 329
Isandhlwana (S. Africa)	28
Ismael, Mohammad	68, 78, 169, 261
Italians	28, 106-09, 127, 259, 330
— Weapon-Makers	107-09, 330
Italy	165-66
Izembert, Alexandra	7-8, 62, 65, 127, 165, 167, 262, 305

J

JAILBREAK Massacre *See* Mandalay 'Jailbreak' Massacre	
Javanese	2
Jesse, F, T.	173
Jones, S. G. (BBTC Official)	176, 178, 208, 210-11, 213, 218, 221-22

K

KABUL	43-44, 47-48, 182
Kabul Massacre (September 3, 1879)	44-49, 328
Kachins (Also Spelt Kakhyen)	144, 156, 304, 306
—Revolt (1884)	144
Kampat (Mingyi)	18-19, 89-90, 95
Kanne (Atwinwun)	90, 95
Karenni (Forests)	6
Karens	5, 304
Kashgar	17-18
Kashmir	317
Kaunghan Wun	95
Kengtung	144, 275
Kennedy, F. C.	147-48, 176
Kerr, Rev.	133-34
Khartoum	234
Kimberley, Lord (Secy. of State for India)	152-53, 155, 169, 191, 254, 298, 313-14, 316, 319, 331
King Kueh Yee	148-49

Kinwun (Mingyi) — 8, 18-20, 21-24, 26-28, 30, 32, 34-40, 43-46, 48-51, 62-63, 65, 67, 69, 77-81, 87-89, 91-94, 96, 110-11, 119 123-24, 132, 134, 149, 155, 168-70, 172-73, 176, 179, 200, 207-08, 210, 212-13, 216-18, 220-21, 223-24, 240, 245-46, 248, 250, 254-56, 258, 260-63, 278-82, 286, 290, 299, 307, 319, 328-30, 332-35

Kinwun's Secret Declaration (1884) — 124-25, 133, 166, 175
Ko Law Ko — 69
Ko Set Kyee — 77-78, 94
Kublai Khan — 3
Kyu Nyo, Prince — 302-03
Kyaukse (District) — 1

L

LAMBAY and Geranger — 171
Lambert, Commodore (British Naval Officer in Second Anglo (War) — 6
Lanessan Report (French Senate Committee) — 190-91
Langson — 163
Lao States — 3, 127, 190, 335
Lawrence, Gov. Gen. Sir John (1864-69) — 67
Leeds — 244
Lewis, Brian L. — 123, 187
Lhermitte (Chandernagore Judge) — 130
Li (Chinese Diplomat) — 237
Liverpool — 244
London — 64, 73, 99, 101, 152, 169, 244
Luang Prabang (Lao State) — 190
Luangshe (Mingyi) — 18
Lyall, A. C. (Indian Foreign Secy.) — 18, 31, 34-35, 39-42, 44-47, 63, 67, 69, 73-74
Lyons, Lord (British Envoy to France) — 120-23, 125-27, 164, 247-51, 253
Lytton, Lord (Governor-General of India) — 25, 31-33, 36, 37, 42, 44-48, 62, 66, 71, 182, 327-28, 333

M

MACCLESFIELD — 152
Macclesfield Chamber of Commerce — 152

Mackenzie, (India Home Secy.) — 298
Magwe (Mingyi) — 22, 26-27, 29, 148-49
Malabar — 2
Malacca — 2-3
Manchester — 152, 183, 236, 244
Mandalay Jail-break Massacre — 134-37, 143-45, 147, 153, 330-31
Mandalay Massacre of Princes (February 1879) — 27-32, 48, 327
Mandalay Royal Bank (Proposed) — 165-68, 176, 178, 181, 183, 185, 187-88, 221, 235, 238, 241, 260, 332
Manipur — 3, 5, 97, 257
—Boundary Dispute — 97
Manook, J. S. — 102
Martaban — 2, 4
Marathas — 5
Massacre of Princes *See* Mandalay Massacre of Princes (February 1879)
Maung Ba Than — 279
Maung Paw Tun (Burmese Counsel to Calcutta) — 25, 97
Maung Po Zan — 209-10
Maung Shway Gaung — 222
Maxwell, H. — 201
Mayo, Lord (Governor-General of India) — 31
Mayotha (Wundauk) — 25, 35-36, 38-41, 43, 76-77
Mekhara, Prince — 17, 20-21, 27, 30
Mekong (River) — 122, 124-26, 137, 170, 172, 305, 308
Merv — 234, 301-02
Meru-centric Plowing Ceremony — 131, 157
Meru-centric Tradition — 23, 131, 157
Mi Hkin-gyi — 90-92, 95-96, 101
Mindon, King — 7-10, 17-23, 27, 30-31, 38, 65, 75-76, 88, 92, 97, 102, 105, 120, 143-44, 156, 176, 181, 200, 208, 263, 306, 318
Mines and Metals
—Mogok Ruby Mines — 165-67, 173, 176, 178, 332
Minhla — 8, 245, 259-60, 274, 277, 279, 281
Mimu — 147
Mir Jafar (Nawab of Bengal) — 170
Mixed Court — 32, 35, 38-41, 65, 73, 76, 100, 152-53, 199, 219, 223
Mogok Ruby Mines, — 165-67, 173, 176, 178, 332

Mogaung   157, 275

Molinari (Italian Engineer)   276-77, 280

Mong Nai   8, 144, 275

Mon States   1

Monopolies (Royal)   7, 75-81, 92-95, 99, 107, 111, 128, 145, 180, 329

—Anglo-Burmese Treaty (1867)   75-79, 92-95

Mons   1-5, 304

Moulmein (Port)   6

Moulmein-Yunnan Railroad Project   236-37

Moylan, E. K. (*Times* Burma Correspondent)   299, 312-13, 315-16

Muslims   25

Myaungla Mission *See* Under Anglo-Burmese Treaties

Myingyan   22

Myngun, Prince   17, 30-31, 88, 92, 104, 110-11, 129-30, 131-34, 137, 145, 169-70, 172-73, 175, 180, 245, 252-53, 274, 277, 279, 281, 302, 314-16, 318, 330, 336

Myotha (Wundauk)   36, 38-39, 41

Myothit (Atwinwun)   119, 127, 170, 210

Mysore   317

N

NAGORE (India)   2

Natteik Pass   8

Nazu (Village)   283

Negrais (Island)   4

Nepal   317

Neutral Zone   179, 186

Neutralism   177, 179, 186

New Herbrides (French Colony)   211

Ngwekun Wun   95

Ningyan (Forest)   7, 171, 173, 175, 185, 200-01, 204-06, 208-09, 214-17, 221, 278, 290

Northbrook, Lord (Governor-General of India)   9, 23, 31, 96

North-West Province and Oudh (India)   34

Nyaungbinmaw   259, 274

Nyaungoke, Prince   18, 22, 30-51, 88-89, 111, 129, 131, 279, 304, 316, 318, 330

Nyaungyan, Prince   19-20, 22-23, 30-31, 34, 36-37, 39, 41, 43, 70, 88, 101-02, 104, 129, 131, 133, 146, 150,

172-73, 278, 280, 306-07, 316, 330, 336

O

O'CONOR, N. E. — 310
Orissa (Ussa) — 2

P

PAGAN (Atwinwun) — 90,95, 274
Pagan Empire — 3
Pagan, King — 6-7
Pangyet Kyauk Maung Atwinwun — 12, 65, 97-98, 101, 103, 105-07, 110, 119, 123, 132, 165, 218, 257, 282-83, 285, 319, 330

Pangyet Mission *See* under Anglo-Burmese Treaties
Pannas — 122-26, 133, 154, 164, 336
Panthey War, Yunnan (1855-1873) — 8, 263
Paris — 119, 170, 180
Pasai (Sumatra) — 2
Patterson, Captaia — 108
Pedir (Sumatra) — 2
Pegu (Mon Port) — 2-3, 36, 145, 257
Pegu (Province) — 7-9
Penjdeh — 234
Peking — 63, 297
Penang — 5
Persia — 17, 233
Persian Gulf — 2
Persian (Traders) — 2
Pilcher, R. Hope (Asstt. Commissioner at Thayetmyo) — 97-98, 103, 105, 120, 132, 134, 168
Pindaris (Indian Dacoits) — 5
Pintha — 30, 90-91, 95
Plunkett (British Envoy to France) — 120
Podaung — 5
Pokokko (Town) — 300
Pondicherry — 130-32, 134
Poppert (Pegu Forest Conservator) — 214
Portugal — 62, 65
Portugese East India Company — 4
Pouk Myine (Atwinwun) — 171, 206, 222, 224, 250, 255
Prato, Signor — 167

Prendergast, Harry, Gen. (Third Burmese War Commander-in-Chief) — 244, 264, 276-77, 282-85, 287-88, 291, 298-99, 303, 314

Preschez, Philippe — 212

Prome — 5

Protected Prince Scheme — 17, 69, 137, 145-46, 152-53, 155, 242-43, 253, 278, 282, 299, 303-19, 335-36

—And Decennial Tribute Question — 306-12, 318

Pulicat — 2

Punjab — 34, 303

Pyaungshu (Forest) — 201, 204-05

Pyinmana, Prince — 19

Pyus — 1

Q

QUETTA — 145

R

RANGOON — 5-9, 35-37, 39, 44-45, 47, 64, 66-68, 70-71, 77, 79-80, 88, 91, 106, 111, 127-28, 131, 134, 146, 149-50, 152, 169-71, 180, 190, 208-10, 244, 257, 261, 282, 299, 307, 319, 329, 331

Rangoon Chamber of Commerce — 79

Rangoon Indignation Meeting (October 11, 1884) — 144, 146-47

Rangoon Press — 36, 49

Rawlings (British News-Collector) — 66, 93, 95, 97, 101, 123, 136-37

Red Sea — 2

Residency, British (Mandalay) — 9, 23-24, 40-42, 44-48, 50-51, 62-63, 65-66, 72-73, 97, 99-100, 111, 129, 132, 152, 155, 171-72, 188-89, 191, 240, 248-49, 256, 263, 305, 327-30

—Residency Guard Question — 24, 97, 99, 111, 132, 189, 240, 249, 263, 328-30

—Residency Site Question — 23, 63, 65, 72-73, 240, 263, 329

—Withdrawal — 40-42, 46-48, 50-51, 62, 66, 100, 327-28

Ribbentrop, Berthold — 204, 206, 215

Ripon, Lord (Governor-General of India) 66, 70, 73, 80, 91-93, 102-03, 105-06, 111, 130, 132, 245, 329, 331

Roberts, Lord (Indian Army C-in-C.) 234
Roche (Fort) 163
Roumelia, Eastern 235
Russia 11-12, 17, 28, 32, 42, 71, 75, 120, 137, 182, 233-37, 241, 304-05, 317, 327, 333-34, 337

—Relations with Afghanistan 182
—Relations with British India 11-12, 17, 28, 32, 42, 71, 75, 120, 137, 233-37, 241, 304-05, 317, 327, 333-34, 337

S

SAGAING (District) 8, 149, 274, 302
Saigon 131, 315
Salaymyo (District) 148-49
Salisbury, Lord (British Prime Minister) 182, 184-87, 189, 234-35, 252-54, 298, 305, 310, 313

Bhocel Swun 93
Sedan 163
Shan States 8, 77, 90, 127, 130, 134, 144 149, 157, 170, 275, 314, 335

Shans 150, 157, 304
Shaw, Robert B. (British Resident) 9, 17-18, 22-25, 28-30, 32, 34-36, 38-40, 42-43, 45, 48, 63, 173

Sheffield 236, 244
Shere Ali (Amir of Afghanistan) 182
Shoe Question 3, 9, 23-25, 32, 35, 51, 64-65, 74, 97, 99, 101, 111, 122, 132, 171, 188, 224, 240, 263-64, 286, 328, 330, 334.

Shway Laung Peh-hnin 78, 90
Shwe Myo Steamer Incident 68, 70-71, 73
Shwebo 102
Shwegyin 208, 213, 215
Shwepyi (Yaw Atwinwun) 18-19
Siam *See* Thailand
Simla Treaty Confreence (1882) 96-112, 119, 155, 245, 256 259-60, 274-75, 279, 298
Sinbaungwe 5
Singapore 17, 234-35
Sinkiang 151, 208, 215, 222
Sittang (River)

Simla   37, 63-64, 78-79, 92, 98,
                                                         100-01, 112, 178, 219, 329
Sladen, Edward, Col. (British Political Officer)   282, 284, 286-88, 299, 302,
                                                         307, 316
Sophia, Sister (French Roman Catholic Nun)   109
South East Asia   129
Spain   62, 65
Spanish-American War (1898)   276
Spheres of Interest Proposal (Lord Salisbury)   186, 253-54
St. Barbe, H. L.   42, 44-45, 48-49, 199, 219
Stokes, W.   73
Strachey, John   73
Strover, Maj. G. A.   200
Stuart, J. (Rangoon Chamber of Commerce   146, 149-50
    Secy.)
Suez Canal   9, 127
Sumatra   3
Supayalat, Queen   9-10, 25-28, 49. 78, 81,
                                                         88-95, 108-09, 123, 129, 131,
                                                         134, 157, 166, 173, 254,
                                                         256-58, 264, 274, 280-82,
                                                         286-87, 289-90, 315
Syriam   3-4

T

TABINSHWEHTI, King of Toungoo (1531-   3
    1550)
Taingda (Mingyi)   27-28, 30, 37-38, 40, 50-51,
                                                         78, 87, 89-90, 92, 97, 105,
                                                         110, 123, 132, 134, 136, 149,
                                                         170, 173, 199, 206-08, 211,
                                                         217, 220-23, 240, 250, 254-57,
                                                         259-61, 278-82, 286-87, 290,
                                                         299, 302, 307, 319, 328,
                                                         332-33, 335
Tamilnad   2
Tangyet (Wundauk)   97, 119, 127, 168, 170, 177-
                                                         78, 180-81, 187-89, 248-51,
                                                         334
Taungdwingyi   8
Taungdwingyi (Forests)   204-05
Taungtaman-Lesa   90-91, 95
Taungwin (Mingyi)   132, 134, 136, 207, 218
Tenasserim   5-6, 9, 145, 257
Thalun, King (1629-1648)   3
Thailand   3, 101, 167, 186, 189, 317

Thambyadin Steamer Incident	99, 73
Tharrawaddy	145
Thathanabaing (Buddhist Archbishop)	176, 254, 311
Thaton (Mon Port)	2
Thayetmyo	34, 62, 79, 120, 132, 168, 180, 238, 242, 253, 259, 261, 274, 276, 278-79
Thebaw, King	10, 19, 27, 31-32, 36-37, 39-40, 43, 49,64, 67-68, 70, 73-76, 88-90, 92-96, 101-03, 106-07, 110, 112, 124, 127, 129, 131, 135, 143, 150, 165, 167, 169-70, 172, 176-77, 180, 182-84, 187, 191, 217, 224, 233, 227-38, 240, 242, 247, 249, 252, 254-55, 257-58, 261, 263, 274, 278-80, 282-83, 285-91, 302, 304, 310, 315-18, 328-32, 334, 336
Therese, Sister (French Roman Catholic Nun)	109, 133-34
Thongze, Prince	19-21, 29-30
Tongkin	42, 50, 121-22, 124, 126-27, 133, 154, 163-64, 166, 169-70, 172, 174-76, 184-85, 187, 190, 330
Toungoo	3, 200-08, 213, 215
Toungoo (Forest)	7, 209
Toungoo-Mandalay Railroad Contract (Proposal)	124, 165-68, 175-76, 178-80, 183-85, 187, 221, 235, 238-39, 241, 247, 260, 264, 332
Trade and Commmerce	144-54, 331
—Bernard's views	144-47, 150-51, 153
—Duferin's views	153-54
—Rangoon Indignation Meeting	144
Trade Depression (1885)	183
Tsawbwas	90, 156, 275
Tseng, Marquis (Chinese Envoy to Great Britain)	310
Turkish Rule	235
Tunis	184
Turkestan (Present-day Sinkiang)	17-18, 234-35

U

U. Gaung (Kinwun Mingyi)	200
U Gyi	216
U Keikti	89
U Kyi (Burmese Envoy to Lower Burma)	80, 91, 210, 245, 261, 329

U Mya   97
U Paw Tun   119
United States (U. S.)   5, 153, 193, 236

                          V

VENGEANCE, E.   219
Victoria, Queen   102-03, 283, 329
Vince, Captain   68
Voisson, (French Consul of Rangoon)   126, 165-66, 245

                          W

WADDINGTON   (French   Envoy   to   Great   184, 186
    Britain)
Walker   201-02
Walsham, John   185-87, 249
Wallace, William   200
Waterloo   163, 234
Wetmasut (Wundauk)   97, 282, 285
White, George   288-89
William, Clement   32
Wolseley, Garnet   110

                          Y

YANAUNG (Buddhist Monk)   19
Yanaung Mintha   19, 27, 30, 75-76, 78, 80-81,
                                              88-95, 97-98, 102, 329
Yanmin (Famous Dacoit)   135
Yaw (Forests)   201, 204-05
Yenang Yaung (Mingyi)   18-20, 27, 30
Yule, Henry   191
Yunnan   8, 50, 68, 73, 75, 149, 153,
                                              164, 170, 179, 183, 236-37,
                                              239, 241, 262, 304, 308, 334,
                                              337

                          Z

ZULU War (South Africa)   33